A DETAILED ANALYSIS OF THE LAWS OF COMMUNIST PARTY GOVERNANCE

Compiled by
QU QINGSHAN
Translated by
JAMES TRAPP AND MARTIN WARD

ACA PUBLISHING LTD

Published by ACA Publishing Ltd
London - Beijing
info@alaincharlesasia.com ☎ +44 20 3289 3885
www.alaincharlesasia.com

Published by ACA Publishing Ltd, in arrangement with
People's Publishing House, Beijing, China

Compiled by: Qu Qingshan
Translators: James Trapp, Martin Ward
Editor: Martin Savery

Original Chinese Text © 共产党执政规律研究 *(gong chan dang zhi zheng gui lü yan jiu)* 2020, People's Publishing House, Beijing, China

ALL RIGHTS RESERVED. NO PART OF THIS PUBLICATION MAY BE REPRODUCED IN MATERIAL FORM, BY ANY MEANS, WHETHER GRAPHIC, ELECTRONIC, MECHANICAL OR OTHER, INCLUDING PHOTOCOPYING OR INFORMATION STORAGE, IN WHOLE OR IN PART, AND MAY NOT BE USED TO PREPARE OTHER PUBLICATIONS WITHOUT WRITTEN PERMISSION FROM THE PUBLISHER.

English Translation text © 2023 ACA Publishing Ltd, London, UK. A catalogue record for *A Detailed Analysis of the Laws of Communist Party Governance* is available from the National Bibliographic Service of the British Library.

The greatest care has been taken to ensure accuracy but the publisher can accept no responsibility for errors or omissions, or for any liability occasioned by relying on its content.

Paperback ISBN: 978-1-83890-013-7
eBook ISBN: 978-1-83890-014-4

B & R Book Program

CONTENTS

INTRODUCTION

PART I

Part II

THE FOUNDATION OF THE CPC'S GOVERNANCE AND AN EXPLORATION OF THE PATH IT HAS TAKEN

Part III

THE CREATION AND DEVELOPMENT OF A NEW PATH OF CPC GOVERNANCE

Part IV
A NEW REALM OF UNDERSTANDING OF THE LAWS OF COMMUNIST PARTY GOVERNANCE

CONCLUSION

INTRODUCTION

Xi Jinping observed emphatically that: "Parties that study Marxism must have the scientific spirit and scientific attitude demonstrated by the ability to have a firm grasp of the law. Laws are the essential connections and inevitable trend in the course of the development of affairs. Any political party must act in accordance with objective laws in order to achieve results from its governance. The governance of the Communist Party of China (CPC) is no exception."

On 2 June 1847, the world's first communist party, the Justice League of German Workers Organisation (the Communist League), was formed in London, England; on 24 February 1848, Marx and Engels's 'Communist Manifesto' was published, also in London, and for the first time declared a Marxist political party's fundamental position in the world, the national way forward and the future. This basic programme and its lofty ideals have become important milestones in human political civilisation. For more than 170 years, international communism has developed from theory to practice, from one country to many countries, from triumphant marches to major setbacks, and then to the bright prospects of the world-renowned socialism with Chinese characteristics led by the CPC. Today's CPC has raised aloft in the world the great banner of socialism with Chinese characteristics and has become the mainstay of the world socialist movement. Chinese ways, Chinese wisdom and Chinese solutions have become major topics of worldwide research. The Chinese way provides a new choice for countries and nations that both want to accelerate development and maintain their independence; a choice that lies outside the West. In the face of major changes unseen in a century and in the context of an era of profound changes in the world's political landscape and party-based politics, today, as we once again review and take to heart the major historical events and difficult journeys that have taken place on the communist party's road to power, our understanding of the communist party, of socialism and of the laws of human society has become more profound and timeless. The complete and systematic promotion of in-depth research on these major laws is undoubtedly the solemn and undeniable mission of CPC members and the majority of theoreticians in the new era for Marxism, socialism and the development of human civilisation.

1

THE SIGNIFICANCE OF DEEPENING RESEARCH INTO THE COMMUNIST PARTY'S RULES OF GOVERNANCE

Deepening research into the communist party's rules of governance is a major task of deep political, ideological, academic and practical significance. It is of great historical and practical importance for the CPC in the new era to lead the whole party and the people of all ethnic groups to carry out great struggles, build great projects, advance great undertakings and realise great dreams.

(I) CONCERNING THE NEED TO SUMMARISE AND ABSORB THE LESSONS OF THE WORLD'S POLITICAL PARTIES, ESPECIALLY THE WORLD SOCIALIST MOVEMENT

Political parties are a product of modern world history. The birth of political parties in the modern sense took place in Britain in the 1740s. Discounting more than 20 countries such as Qatar, Kuwait, the United Arab Emirates, Oman, Bahrain, Saudi Arabia, the Maldives and Bhutan, where political parties are either banned or where the unity of church and state makes it difficult for political parties to have a popular base or find room for survival, there are more than 5,000 political parties, large and small, in more than 200 countries and regions around the world. The largest ones have tens of millions of party members and the smallest ones have only a few hundred. In the course of the development of this great plethora of political parties, some have swept to power as soon as they were formed; some held great power for a long period only to suffer a sudden setback and be torn apart; some, through innovation and change, have gained power only to lose it and then regain it, but the vast majority end up drifting to the periphery of power and all have provided society with a colourful and thought-provoking picture of themselves. The communist party is a Marxist party, of which there are a total of 127 in the world, distributed in more than 100 countries; 36 of them have more than 10,000 members; only five are in power and 17 are actively participating in politics. The international communist movement (known as the 'world socialist movement' since 1943) has drawn experience and lessons from its more than 170-year history, all of which are precious. The lessons of the failure of the European Revolution from 1848 to 1849 and the failure of the Paris Commune revolution in 1871 showed that the Communists at that time had not given enough thought to a programme of socialist governance and their political theory was not mature enough. Their failure to resolutely suppress counter-revolution, to attack the reactionary forces at Versailles in time, to seize the assets of the Bank of France, and to get a response from other cities and provinces, all provided valuable experience for the future. After the victory of the October Revolution led by Lenin, the first socialist country governed by the communist party was established. From 1918 to 1919, the Third International used the beneficial interests of the international revolution to forcibly advance the Soviet-model Soviet revolutionary road on the world but ignored the diverse and ever-changing national conditions of different countries. Although it has brought about the climax of proletarian revolutionary struggles and national liberation struggles in colonial and semi-colonial countries, it has also caused some undesirable consequences. After the second world war, the socialist movement led by the communist party spread like wildfire, forming a strong socialist faction and providing opposition to the capitalist counter-faction for more than 40 years. The drastic changes in the Soviet Union and Eastern Europe in the late 1980s and early 1990s shocked the world, and world socialism suffered major setbacks. The Communist Party of the Soviet Union (CPSU) was victorious in the October Revolution when it had 200,000 members and it won the Anti-Fascist War when it had 2 million members but it lost the position of power it had held for 74 years when it had nearly 20 million members. All of these phenomena merit our in-depth consideration and research.

Experience has shown that the nature of a party is not directly related to its grasp of the of the rules of governance. No matter what the nature of a party, it can play a positive role in national development and social progress through a better grasp of the rules of governance, and it can also play a positive role in the development of the country and its social progress because of its influence on the governing law. Equally, it can also lose its position of power due to insufficient understanding, ignorance or even violation of the rules of governance, and by going against the trend and against the will of the people. The reasons for the upheaval in the Soviet Union and Eastern Europe are multifaceted and comprehensive but, in the long term, the roots lie in the closed and rigid road they followed. There was no improvement in the quality of lives of the people over an extended period; indeed it declined over a period of time and this led the party and the countries into crisis. In the end, the party was disbanded and the countries disintegrated.

History has a profound warning for us that throughout the history of hundreds of years spent exploring the socialist road, the universal lessons and mistakes are often not problems concerning specific policy measures; rather they are problems in understanding and grasping the overall direction of the rules of governance: concentrating too closely on communism, underestimating capitalism, allowing socialism to become too rigid, ignoring feudalism, exceeding the pragmatic reality, bypassing necessary stages and violating rules. The more cool-headed Communists are in their attitude to the rules of governance, the deeper is their understanding of them, and the firmer their grasp on the rules of governance, the more scientific its practice of governance, the more successful it will be in governing the country and the stronger its ruling position will be.

(II) CONCERNING THE STRENGTHENING OF THE WHOLE PARTY'S AWARENESS OF GOVERNANCE AND OF HARDSHIP WHERE IT OCCURS, AND AWARENESS OF THE ABSOLUTE NECESSITY OF FORGING AHEAD AND MAINTAINING A FORWARD-LOOKING STATE OF MIND

After more than 40 years of reform and opening up, China has developed into the world's second largest economy, with a gross domestic product (GDP) exceeding 99 trillion yuan in 2019, and for many years in a row, its contribution rate to the world economy has exceeded 30%, surpassing the combined contribution rates of the US, the Eurozone and Japan. However, the more you achieve results, the more you must be as cautious as if walking on thin ice, and the more you must be prepared for danger in times of peace; you must not make strategic and self-destructive mistakes. At the end of the 20th century, the Liberal Democratic Party of Japan, the Mexican Revolutionary Institutional Party, the Indian National Congress and other large, well-established parties that had been in power for a long time, lost their positions of power, in a way that both shocked and fascinated the rest of the world. Fundamentally speaking, the whole problem stemmed from the balance between correctness and error, unanimity and divergence, persistence and hesitancy, and conservatism and progressiveness of the road they followed and their programmes and policies. The fundamental reason why the Mexican Revolutionary Institutional Party, once the pride of Latin America, turned from a deeply established ruling party to an opposition party is that it abandoned the principles and ways of revolutionary nationalism and replaced them with what they called social liberalism but was actually neoliberalism. The overemphasis on economic freedom and the lack of attention and concern for social issues led to a disproportionate concentration of wealth in the hands of a few and increasing social polarisation.

On 5 January 2018, there was a seminar for new members, alternate members and leading cadres at the provincial and ministerial levels to study and implement Xi Jinping's thought on socialism with Chinese characteristics for the new era and the spirit of the 19th Party Congress. There, Xi Jinping enumerated, in one go, eight aspects and sixteen risk points that needed to be given high priority; he called on all party comrades never to show pride in their victories, never to slacken off because of their achievements and never to retreat because of difficulties. He also called on all party comrades to consistently adhere to and develop socialism with Chinese characteristics, to promote the new great project of party building, to enhance the awareness of danger, to prevent risks and challenges, to be consistent and to strive to make socialism with Chinese characteristics a more powerful and persuasive force for truth. As we look at the world, we are facing major changes unseen in the last hundred years. As long as our party always maintains as respectful an attitude as ever, follows and responds to the trends, grasps the overall situation and accelerates development, it will surely be able to unite and lead more than 1.4 billion people to realise the great rejuvenation of the Chinese nation. Conversely, if you become hidebound by convention, remain stuck in the old ways and do nothing except go with the flow, you will inevitably lose the support and love of the people, to the extent that you lose your ruling position and are ruthlessly eliminated by the trend of historical development. As the Fourth Plenary Session of the 16th Central Committee of the party profoundly pointed out, the entire party must keep in mind that neither the party's progressiveness nor the party's ruling position is permanent and immutable. Having been advanced in the past does not mean being advanced now, and being advanced now does not mean being advanced forever; possessing something in the past does not mean possessing it now, and possessing something now does not mean possessing it forever.

(III) CONCERNING THE NEED TO ENHANCE THE PARTY'S ABILITY TO GOVERN, AND TO STRENGTHEN AND IMPROVE ITS SELF-CONSTRUCTION

The proper management of China's affairs lies with the party itself. Persevering with and refining the party's leadership is where the fundamentals of the party and the nation lie, are their lifeblood, and where the interests and happiness of the people of all ethnic groups reside.

In the 70 years since the founding of New China, major changes have taken place in the historical position of our party, the internal and external situations it faces, and the historical tasks it shoulders. The party's political construction, ideological construction, organisational construction, work ethos construction, discipline construction, as well as the systemic construction, the fight against corruption and other constituents and requirements that run through it, have all become more onerous and taxing. Xi Jinping once pointed out with great profundity: "We must prepare for a great struggle with many new historical characteristics." Also: "The concept of 'new historical features' has a profound meaning, and is an important judgment drawn from a comprehensive review and judgment of the overall development of the domestic and international situations." At present, our country is in a period of promising historical opportunity. The fundamental development situation is good and the overall situation is stable. However, the international situation is turbulent, the surrounding environment is complex and sensitive, the tasks of reform, development and stabilisation are arduous and onerous, and the great task of national rejuvenation is in a critical period of negotiating stumbling blocks in its upward path. From an international point of view, the theme of the era of peace and development has not changed. The world's multipolarisation, economic globalisation, social informatisation, and cultural diversification have developed extensively. At the same time, the international financial crisis has continued to have long-term, deep-seated effects, and the retrogressive trend of American supremacy and isolationism is on the rise. China is facing complex changes in geopolitical relations and many international storms are related to the so-called "colour revolutions" initiated by some Western countries, and the external environment is becoming unstable and uncertain. From a domestic perspective, our country has a solid material foundation, abundant human resources, a huge marketplace, enormous development potential and the fundamental long-term economic improvement has not changed. However, at the same time, the downward pressure on the economy is increasing, and problems such as uneven and unsustainable development, and insufficient innovation drivers are still very much in evidence; prominent economic structural reforms still need to be promoted, the construction of the rule of law needs to be strengthened, and the online public opinion environment needs further attention. From the party's point of view, since the 18th National Congress of the CPC, under the strong leadership of the Party Central Committee with Comrade Xi Jinping as the core, it has taken the lead in setting a top-down example and shown its determination to curb chaos with strong medicine and severe laws. The courage to "scrape the poison from the bone" and to "amputate diseased limbs" in the overall administration of the party means that the work of party building has become more innovative, has improved in consolidation and has achieved major historical successes, with the result that the great new project of party building has seen continuous advances. At the same time, the various factors that affect the party's progressive nature and dilute the party's purity are highly dangerous and destructive; the tests faced by the party's governance, by the reform and opening-up process, by the market economy and the external environment will be long term and complex. The dangers faced by the party of mental slackness, lack of competence, being divorced from the masses and passive corruption will be acute and severe.

In such a situation, the questions are: how to make our party the backbone of the people in the historical process of dealing with these various risks and tests at home and abroad, and to be the strong leading core in the historical process of realising the Chinese dream of the great rejuvenation of the Chinese nation? And how to build the party into a Marxist ruling party that is always at the forefront of the times, wholeheartedly supported by the people, courageous in self-revolution, able to withstand all kinds of storms, and full of vigour. The answers are that it is necessary to properly summarise and understand the positive and negative experiences since the founding of the party, especially since the founding of New China; to continuously deepen our understanding and grasp of the rules of governance; to reinforce our grasp of the direction and requirements of development of the party and the state in the new era; to strengthen the foundations; to pioneer and innovate; to continuously enhance the party's capacity for self-purification, self-improvement, self-renewal and self-improvement; to continuously strengthen the party's political leadership, ideological leadership, power of mass organisation and social appeal. All of this will ensure that the party always has vigour, vitality and strong combat effectiveness, and will provide a strong political guarantee for the development of the party and the country.

(IV) CONCERNING THE NEED TO ENRICH AND DEVELOP MARXIST PARTY DOCTRINES UNDER THE NEW HISTORICAL CONDITIONS

Marxism does not end in the truth but opens up the road to truth. Engels once said: "Marx's entire worldview is not a doctrine, but a method. What it provides is not a ready-made dogma but a starting point for further research and a method for such research." Faced with the characteristics and practical requirements of the new era in China, Marxism has always faced the problem of further Sinicisation, modernisation and popularisation. Its theoretical essence is to emancipate the mind, seek truth from facts, advance with the times, pursue the truth and be pragmatic. In 1921, the party's first congress established Marxism-Leninism as the guiding ideology of the party and over the course of nearly 100 years of history, the CPC has insisted on combining the basic principles of Marxism with the concrete reality of China. It has successively established Mao Zedong Thought, Deng Xiaoping Theory, the important concept of the Three Represents, the Scientific Outlook on Development and Xi Jinping Thought on Socialism with Chinese Characteristics for a New Era. In particular, since the 18th Party Congress, the Party Central Committee, with Comrade Xi Jinping at its core, has made unprecedented efforts to comprehensively deepen reform and to comprehensively follow the rule of law. The party has been ruled with unprecedented rigour and, with equally unprecedented energy, has built a moderately prosperous society, safeguarded the core interests of the country, and promoted a new international order of governance. It has deepened our party's understanding of the laws of communist rule, socialist construction and human social development with a series of innovative new ideas and arguments, opening up a whole new realm of Marxism. Therefore, research on party building must keep pace with the party's practical and theoretical innovations, study the experiences of the rise and fall of communist parties in other countries, and further summarise and grasp the rich accumulation of governing experience, the systematic development of theories of governance and the important rules of governance mastered by the CPC in its long-term governing practice. In particular, the comprehensive and groundbreaking historical achievements made, the profound and fundamental changes implemented, and the fruitful new theoretical contributions made by the party since the 18th National Congress should be summarised and firmly grasped, raising them to the level of the law, so as to make a new contribution to the enrichment and development of the treasury of ideas of Marxist political parties.

For nearly 100 years, the CPC has always adhered to the guidance of

Marxism-Leninism and the innovative theoretical results of the Sinicisation of Marxism, leading the people of all ethnic groups across the country to complete the new democratic revolution and to establish a new China; it has carried out socialist transformation and established a fundamental socialist system; the great process of reform and opening up has been carried out and socialism with Chinese characteristics has been created, upheld and developed. It has realised the great leap of the Chinese nation from rising up and becoming prosperous to becoming strong, and has pushed socialism with Chinese characteristics into a new era. Following the continuous development of socialism with Chinese characteristics, that system has become more and more mature, and its superiority will be further manifested. China's way forward will also become wider and wider, and its influence on the world will inevitably become greater. We can say with complete confidence that today the most profound theoretical innovations of scientific socialism are to be found in China, as are the most extensive practical applications and the most remarkable development achievements. We can also confidently state that, in a sense, the study of the CPC and its experience of governance and its rules constitutes a universal overview and understanding of the rules governing communist parties in general. Therefore, it is only natural that the party's theoretical work should also have a different mission and responsibilities from the ordinary.

The deepening of the study of the laws of communist rule is a contribution of the CPC to the world socialist movement and to the enrichment and development of the Marxist theory of political parties. This contribution not only provides a reference for other socialist countries and broadens their horizons but also opens up a wider scope for other types of political parties in the world to explore the means and paths of governance.

2

STATUS QUO AND EVALUATION OF THE RESEARCH ON THE LAWS OF COMMUNIST PARTY GOVERNANCE

Marx, Engels and Lenin, as the founders of the proletarian revolutionary party, and their theories, were created from, at the outset, taking the proletarian revolutionary party as the party in power. Therefore, in a certain sense, their theories on party building during the period of seizure of power by the proletariat are also applicable to the party building practice during the period the proletarian dictatorship is actually in power; and their scientific assumptions about the party's programme and strategy during the period of the proletarian dictatorship are essentially a direct exploration of the rules of governance of the communist party.

Since the founding of the CPC, its members, mainly represented by comrades Mao Zedong, Deng Xiaoping, Jiang Zemin, Hu Jintao, and Xi Jinping, have always attached great importance to the construction of political power, the study and accumulation of the experience of governance, and the summary and exploration of its rules. It can be said that they are the principal explorers of, and contributors to, the philosophical and theoretical successes of the party's rules of governance. In July 1945, the democrat Huang Yanpei asked Mao Zedong how the governance of the CPC could escape the "periodic cycle of history". This prompted comrades throughout the party to think about the rules of governance. In 2001, on the occasion of the 80th anniversary of the founding of the party, Jiang Zemin put forward for the first time the important concept of "the rules of governance of the communist party" and raised the major issue of deepening the understanding of those rules. He highlighted the need to continuously deepen our understanding of them, of the laws of socialist construction and of the laws of human social development. This marked the beginning of the CPC's understanding of the rules of governance of the communist party moving from the summing up of experience to new frontiers in the exploration of those rules, which was enthusiastically received by the whole party. This set off a wave of research in theoretical and academic circles which peaked in 2005. Since then, the results of this research have tended to decline but have continued to a certain degree.

(I) DOMESTIC ACADEMIC RESEARCH ON THE LAWS OF COMMUNIST PARTY GOVERNANCE

Research into communist party rules of governance tends to be academic and theoretical but has never stayed purely at an academic theoretical level; rather, over time, it has always been more or less integrated with real political needs and closely integrated with party building, the party's practice of governance and the practice of socialist construction. Since 2001, there have been more than 500 academic monographs on the subject of communist party rules of governance in theoretical and academic circles, and more than 5,000 research papers have been published. These works and papers have made a relatively comprehensive study of the basic connotation, research significance, research process and profound enlightenment of communist party rules of governance from different perspectives and levels, such as basic theory, applied theory, and political science and administrative management. Looking at the four main research institutions of universities, social science colleges, the party school (school of administration), and the party and government sector, their respective professional and academic backgrounds are different, and the research perspectives, thinking, methods and focus are also different. Therefore, they form their own relatively distinct characteristics in terms of both style and results.

First, colleges and universities. The research style is mainly attributable to factors such as the scholar's personal academic background and interests. Its main characteristics are: first, it has a strong academic and theoretical nature; the research results have strong characteristics of political science, history and other disciplines, and the average quality is relatively high; second, they draw more extensively on some Western academic research methods, and more frequently use the tools of interdisciplinary research; third, the systemic academic viewpoints are very different, and it is difficult to form an overarching academic viewpoint and theoretical system; fourth, there is an overall lack of understanding and research on the existing system and real-life cases, and some of them even produce theoretical studies and criticisms that go beyond the existing basic political system.

Second, social science institutes. Based on the role of government think tanks at all levels, research usually has the direct purpose of informing government. The Chinese Academy of Social Sciences (CASS), as the highest-level academic institution and comprehensive research centre for philosophical and social science research in China, is particularly conspicuous in the character of its research. First, it has a deep knowledge base to draw on and a solid theoretical background; it is familiar with research in related fields both at home and abroad, and the quality of its research results is high. Second, the ideological influence is strong, and the theoretical orientation is more obvious. Third, the research results tend to be consistent with each other and form a self-contained system.

Third, the party school (school of administration). As the party's think-tank and training institution, it is responsible for the interpretation of the party's theoretical innovations and the teaching of party and government leaders, and its research is mainly aimed at informing and educating people. It has the following characteristics: first, as a party department, its research reflects some of the theoretical needs of the party in its governance activities and has a certain degree of practicality and specificity, while at the same time it has some characteristics of a university and is, to a certain degree, theoretical and academic in nature; second, the research methods are lively and diverse, adhering to the Marxist worldview and methodology, but also having a broader international perspective and angle of approach, and widely adopting methods such as system theory, mathematical models and empirical research; third, the research content is *avant-garde* and extensive. Compared with researchers in party and government departments, they are less confined to some theoretical frameworks and concepts, and are often more advanced, daring to offer criticism and suggest countermeasures to real problems; fourth, research on the rules of governance has been a longstanding concern, with many research results and a rich theoretical resource, with the focus on combining research and teaching.

Fourth, the party and government sector. Research is often based on practical needs and has the following characteristics: First, researchers are often familiar with the whole process of party governance, and can understand the operational procedures, work intentions and decision-making information of party organisations at all levels in a timely manner, as well as obtain social and public reactions to the governance process, so research is often forward-looking and purposeful, and research results can often directly influence decision-making and governance processes. Second, the topics are often supported by a large number of sample cases and real-life situations, providing a more solid research foundation, more targeted and operational measures, and a higher conversion rate from research to results. Third, research is mostly aimed at guiding practice and promoting work, and less at theoretical research and innovation, so most of it does not go deep enough in terms of levels of thinking and research, and is more limited to the analysis and solution of specific problems and the improvement and reform of relevant systems.

In terms of the audience for and influence of research results, the total number of research articles published in party newspapers and journals at all levels is relatively small, but the attention they attract is extremely high, and they play a broad role in practical guidance, propaganda and education among party members and cadres. The main function of academic journals and conferences is to provide a platform for academic exchange, and the results are mainly limited in impact to professional researchers but the in-depth research and concentrated discussion of cutting-edge issues in theoretical and academic circles have had a very important impact on the development of the rules and discipline of communist party governance.

(II) OVERSEAS SCHOLARS' STUDIES ON THE CPC'S LAWS OF GOVERNANCE

As early as the 1960s and 1970s, overseas scholars began to pay attention to the development path of the new China, and gradually shifted from in-depth studies of sensitive historical and practical hot issues to multi-disciplinary studies on the details and foundations of governance. The main features and trends are as follows.

First, the number of researchers and research subjects continues to increase, and their influence continues to expand. The rules of governance of the CPC have become a core theme of research in the field of the rules of governance of communist parties in general. At present, most countries and regions in the world have institutions to conduct research on China and the CPC. For example, in the US, there are more than 200 research institutions concentrating on China issues with over 3,000 researchers and many more schools have established centres for China issues, such as the Fairbank Centre for China Studies at Harvard University.

Second, research materials have become richer and more systematic, providing a better academic basis for the study of the rules of governance of the CPC. Many libraries and research institutions in the US, Japan, Russia and other countries have collected and collated a large number of research materials on the CPC. For example, the library of the Institute of Chinese Studies in Japan focuses on the study of modern China and is particularly famous for its collection of research materials on rural China and the building of the CPC.

Third, international academic exchanges have been intensifying, with increasingly frequent cooperation and exchanges between Chinese and foreign scholars, and between research institutions in various countries. For example, on the occasion of the 90th anniversary of the founding of the CPC, many political parties, organisations and research institutes, such as the Communist Party of Russia (CPR), the European Union Headquarters in Brussels, the German Society for Marxist China Studies and the Centre for Strategic Studies of the Bulgarian Socialist Party, all organised relevant seminars.

Fourth, research methods, theories and perspectives have become more diverse, greatly expanding the scope and depth of research on the rules of governance of the CPC. For example, the monograph *Contemporary Chinese Politics: New Resources, Methods and Disciplinary Strategies* by Allen Karlsson, Mary E Gallagher, Li Kanru, Mo Ning and others introduces the latest advances in research methods in various branches of contemporary Chinese studies, starting from the academic discipline of political science. It greatly enriches the methods and approaches to related issues and has received high praise from overseas academics.

Fifth, the theoretical nature of the research results has continued to increase and more attention has been paid to current affairs and real-life issues in China. For example, around the time of the 18th National Congress of the CPC, the international journal *East Asian Policy* of the East Asia Research Institute of the National University of Singapore published the second issue of 2012 as a "Special research edition on the 18th National Congress of the CPC". When the 19th CPC National Congress was held, there was a great deal of coverage, research and commentary from overseas academic, media and political circles, all of which had a huge impact.

First, the research and investigation of the "China Model" from a political perspective. In the research of overseas scholars, the predecessor of the concept of the "China Model" is the "Beijing Consensus". The primary focus of this formulation was to confront the "Washington Consensus", and more and more scholars soon replaced the "Beijing Consensus" with the "China Model". Discussion of the "Chinese model" by overseas scholars has been highly politicised from the very beginning. With the tremendous achievements made in China's economic construction since the reform and opening up, especially since China held out against the global financial crisis in 2008 more effectively than the West, overseas scholars' interest in the "China Model" has further increased, and the perspectives and research methods used have also diversified. Overseas scholars' interpretation of the "China Model" is principally divided into three views: the first is to deny the existence of a specific "China Model" and believes that China's development model is unsustainable and cannot be used for reference; the second is that China has already formed its own unique development model which has had an impact on, and threatens, Western values; the third goes further in believing that the "China Model" is superior to the Western development model. No matter which point of view they hold, scholars have studied the "China Model" from the perspective of the governance of the CPC. A prominent example is Francis Fukuyama, a leading American scholar of Japanese descent, who argues that the CPC is currently establishing a high-quality 'authoritarian government', which is in the Chinese political tradition of a 'responsible authoritative system', a strong centralised power, an independent administrative bureaucracy and a 'people-oriented' government that is more concerned with the legitimacy of its own rights and which derives that legitimacy from its ability to realise the interests of the people, especially economically. Moreover, it is not subject to the rule of law and democratic systems that accompany a market economy and export-led growth model. In his study of the 'China Model', Zheng Yongnian, the current Director of the East Asia Institute at the National University of Singapore, points out that the socio-economic transformation of China and the transformation of the CPC itself are two closely related aspects of the 'China Model'. Since the reform and opening up, the CPC has transformed from a party that governed the country by revolutionary means to a party that governs the country administratively, and it has now begun to transform from a party that governs the country administratively to a party that governs the country politically.

Second, the study of CPC leaders and their method of governance. The study of CPC leaders and their ideology is the prime focus and hot topic of overseas scholars' research on the CPC. In recent years, with the ongoing deepening of China's reform and opening up, and the increasing number of publicly available archival materials, overseas scholars have shown a tendency to deepen their research on CPC leaders and their way of governance. First, research has been shifting from narrative to theoretical; second, the objects and methods of the study of individuals have been continuously expanding. Some scholars have observed that the development of water conservancy and heavy industry during the Mao era, the improvement of people's living and health standards, and the political debates of the Cultural Revolution laid the foundation for China's further development; that Deng Xiaoping's decisive adjustment of the CPC's way of governance has led to China's great economic success, but that it still faces many potential threats. The key to dealing with these problems lies in the ability of CPC leaders to govern. Other scholars have pointed out that Deng Xiaoping, as the chief architect of reform and opening up, reshaped China with state intervention in the market economy. In reality, the CPC is guided by Leninism and adheres to the pragmatic socialism of one-party rule, which is a great initiative of the CPC. Some scholars believe that Jiang Zemin transformed China as it stood on the brink of a cliff. He was a "pragmatic non-dogmatist" with "the blood of economic reform and polit-ical stability flowing in his veins", and his goal of future transformation lay in "development-oriented authoritarianism". Some scholars point out that Hu Jintao's thinking embodied a systematic method of adjusting social structure and promoting national development, that is, a "harmonious society" and "scientific development concept" in domestic affairs, and "peaceful development" in foreign affairs; they believe that the core of Chinese leaders' thinking is found in self-esteem, stability, responsibility and vision. Some scholars have analysed and interpreted a series of theo-ries, ideas and policies of the Party Central Committee, with Comrade Xi Jinping at its core, since the 18th National Congress of the CPC. It may be said that the Chinese dream is that in times of peace, people will live happily, enjoy a good education, do work that they are interested in, have no wars and protect the environment. Specifically, these are the "dream of education", the "dream of employment" and the "dream of environmental protection" for the Chinese people. Scholars have also pointed out that the Chinese Dream is "the result of heightened national emotions" and that it "induces historical memories and evokes a sense of shame among the Chinese people: in this it is a reflection of China's nationalist narrative". Additionally, the strategic plan of the "Four Comprehensives" has also been a hot topic of research for overseas scholars. Some scholars have pointed out that Xi Jinping's strategic plan of coordinating and promoting the "Four Comprehensives" provides strategic guidance for the new stage of China's reform and development, with each "comprehensive" corre-sponding to a current major challenge. According to others, the Four Comprehensives have given a new connotation to China's development, promoting and achieving sustainable and more inclusive growth; yet others have pointed out that "Xi Jinping's philosophy of governance is beneficial to the world" and that each of the Four Comprehensives has its own specific significance, with "building a moderately prosperous society in all aspects" as the goal, "deepening reform in all aspects" as the means, "ruling the country in accordance with the rule of law in all aspects" as the principle, and "building a moderately prosperous society in all aspects" as the goal.

Third, research on major historical issues and major political decisions of the CPC. In this field, the research of overseas scholars shows the following characteristics: first, they have maintained long-term focus and attention on major political movements such as the "Great Leap Forward" and the "Cultural Revolution" that have had a huge impact on China; second, research has increased on current affairs, and research on historical issues often includes important social, economic and political issues of the time. As early as the 1960s and 1970s, the famous American scholar J P Harrison demonstrated in his works the development process of the CPC from its establishment to the acquisition of power, and analysed the reasons why the CPC gradually moved toward power and became the ruling party; the renowned Chinese scholar Bao Dake has studied and analysed the political, economic and ideological difficulties faced by the CPC during its early years in power (1949-1955), the various measures it took and the changes it underwent; to do so he draws on the official publications of the CPC and his own interviews in the field. From these he compiled multiple reports on the establishment and consolidation of power by the CPC, on social control and political organisation, on social propaganda and indoctrination, on mass mobilisation and economic development, with the overall observation that "it was during this period that China established its own regime and certain fundamental policies". In addition, overseas scholars have also come up with a substantial body of research results on the socialist transformation of private capitalist industry and commerce.

Fourth, research on the training of CPC cadres. This is a research theme that overseas scholars often include in studying the rules of governance and the CPC's ability to implement them as they attempt to explore the "adaptive governance" of the CPC and its ability to change. As early as 1952, American historian W E Gourlay's *The Chinese Communist Cadre: Key to Political Control* introduced the framework of the CPC's political organisation and pointed out that for cadres to function correctly, they must be armed with Marxism-Leninism and Mao Zedong Thought. The development of a large number of reliable cadres was very important to the new regime at that time: "Cadres are the key to the CPC's political control." Some scholars have used the cadre education in party schools as the main line of research and starting point for a detailed study and analysis of cadre education across the CPC, and have used this to study the positioning and reform of the party. They highlight the two major trends of the centralisation and marketisation of cadre training in party schools and argue that cadre training in the CPC is aimed at improving professional knowledge and socialist consciousness. They rate very highly the CPC's cadre training policies, and training and administrative reforms.

Fifth, the study of the foundations of the governance of the CPC, challenges to its legitimacy and its responses. This area has also long been a focus of attention for overseas scholars and, particularly after the introduction of "adaptability" into the study of the CPC, the systems, depth and breadth of these studies have been further improved. Some scholars have observed that the CPC has adapted to economic and social changes through self-reinvention, constantly changing the relationship between the military, the law and the executive, and by consolidating its ruling base through rebuilding urban communities, limiting trade union rights and re-establishing rural governance, thereby creating a mix of the 'raw materials' for legitimacy. The development of democracy in the CPC as an 'authoritarian party' must be evaluated with caution, as China is likely to remain a hybrid of 'authoritarian dictatorship' and 'democracy' for a long time. Some scholars have focused on the relationships and changes therein between classes and groups such as private entrepreneurs, farmers, workers and migrant workers, and the government, and have used this to analyse the foundations, methods and strategies of CPC governance. Some scholars argue that the changing power of the rural power elite during the economic transition has transformed some rural cadres from protectors of the countryside into selfish individuals who use state policies and power to deprive the peasants of their interests; other scholars point out that private entrepreneurs have always collaborated with the CPC as the ruling party in the process of promoting economic development and maintaining the political status quo. By promoting the development of the private sector, maintaining a dialogue with it, encouraging its participation in public service and in the decision-making process with the Chinese government, and integrating the private sector into the Chinese political system, the CPC has created a form of 'partnership communism'. The integration of wealth and power is now and will remain, for the foreseeable future, the survival strategy of the CPC. Some scholars argue that modern society in China under the communist party is in the midst of an essential transformation from a dualistic structure to a ternary one composed of central, local and grassroots; state, semi-state and society; urban, semi-urban and rural; workers, migrant workers and peasants.

Sixth, the study of political system reform in China. International scholarship in this area has undergone a transition from denial to gradual recognition. Many scholars in the international academic and policy research community have viewed China's political reforms from the perspective of 'democratisation', arguing that 'China has only economic reforms but no political reforms'; but this view is now increasingly being challenged. Some scholars have pointed out that state institution-building has been at the heart of China's political reforms over the past 30 years, and that without political reforms it is difficult to imagine how China's achievements in economic development could have been achieved, or to explain the vast differences between contemporary Chinese politics and those of pre-reform China. According to some scholars, the success of China's reforms lies in the CPC's balanced political philosophy and style of collective discussion, as well as its gradual, fine-tuned 'crossing the river by feeling the stones' approach to reform; the CPC has the twin advantages of flexibility and authority as the ruling party. Some scholars have analysed China's political system and argue that the CPC's leaders have been trying to integrate local traditions and world civilisations into China's modernisation; that the CPC and the government will continue to maintain control over society but will embrace more freedom and a wider range of political views; that market-oriented reforms will continue to be strengthened; and that the central government will decentralise more power to the provinces, cities and counties. There are some scholars who say that the logic of Western democratisation does not suit China. China's economic development has not led to demands for greater freedom and autonomy from private entrepreneurs, who prefer to enter the system the better to pursue their own development; the emerging classes that have formed as a result of economic development are enthusiastic for political participation but are more interested in their interests being facilitated within the system and them being given the right to be adequately informed and to express their demands effectively, rather than being represented politically. Some scholars have argued that the CPC should maintain its ideological leadership of society through competition within the process of governing, and that the 'statist economic model' of total domination and control in certain key areas and sectors needs to be revised. The primary task of the CPC's political reform is to build a modern state system and to solve the problems of "GDPism" among officials caused by insufficient system supply, the problems of the relationship between the central government and local authorities, and the problem of the lack of openness in the political system.

It is true that study of the CPC's rules of governance has received widespread attention and both inside and outside the party, and at home and abroad; it made considerable achievements at several levels, which have largely advanced the scientific level of the construction of the CPC. However, we can also see clearly that systematic research on this topic has not kept pace with the historical contributions made by the CPC, and does not reflect the historical status it deserves, the theoretical and practical significance it brings to us, nor its overall significance both to China itself and globally, both in breadth and depth. It may be said that research in many areas has at best made a good start.

3

THE PRINCIPAL METHODS OF RESEARCH INTO THE CPC'S LAWS OF GOVERNANCE

Research on this subject is guided by Xi Jinping's thoughts on socialism with Chinese characteristics in the new era involving strengthening the "four consciousnesses" and the "four self-confidences" and achieving the "two safeguards". It adheres to the use of dialectical materialism and historical materialism to summarise the governance practices of the CPC, to clarify the nature of the CPC's governance and to explore the rules of that governance. It also adheres to the integration of theory and practice, focuses on the actual problems of reform and opening up, and socialist modernisation; focuses on what is actually being done; focuses on the application of Marxist theory; focuses on theoretical thinking on practical issues; focuses on new practice and new development; it strives to reflect the characteristics of the times, closely observes the rules, and to be creative; it also strives to keep up with the requirements of the Party Central Committee, to keep up with the progress of the times, and to keep up with the needs of the development of the overall cause.

On 5 January 2013, at a special seminar for new and alternate members of the Central Committee to study and implement the spirit of the 18th Party Congress, Xi Jinping outlined the history of socialism with Chinese characteristics from the emergence and development of utopian socialism, and the creation of a scientific socialist theoretical system by Marx and Engels to the triumph of the October Revolution led by Lenin and the practice of socialism, the gradual formation of the Soviet model, the exploration and practice of socialism by the party after the founding of the new China, and the historical decision of the party to carry out reform and opening up, and to create and develop socialism with Chinese characteristics. These six time periods, including the party's historic decision to reform and open up, and the creation and development of socialism with Chinese characteristics, outline the tortuous history of the development of socialism in the world over the past 500 years, and profoundly reveal the historical inevitability of socialism with Chinese characteristics, providing the underlying foundation and direct guidance for an in-depth study of the history of the communist party's rules of governance. The history of the development of world socialism is actually the history of exploring the proletarian party seizing power and consolidating the rules for wielding that power. Therefore, in researching the subject, we make full use and realise the potential of the advantages provided by the historical research of the Central Party History and Documentation Research Institute of the CPC Central Committee and adhere to the unified use of history and logic, so that we may reveal the rules of governance of Marxist parties from the works of classic writers and revolutionary mentors. The historical process of exploring the laws of communist party rule can be retraced across six time periods and through several major events: Lenin led the October Revolution to victory and to the practice of socialism, the Soviet model was gradually formed, the CPC was established and began to explore new ways to govern, the CPC went on to create and develop new rules of governance, and the rules of governance of the party have been deepened and developed since the 18th National Congress of the CPC with Comrade Xi Jinping at the core. On the basis of this study, the 12 basic issues of the communist party's rules of governance can be summarised and elaborated. These issues are: the leadership, the guiding ideology of governance, the road to governance, the fundamental tasks of governance, the dynamics of governance, the system of governance and leadership, the mode of governance, the basis of governance, the common ideological foundations of governance, the pillars of governance, the external conditions of governance, and the construction of the ruling party itself. Through a comprehensive review and in-depth summary of the history of the governance of the communist party, it is possible to obtain a deep understanding of the difficulty and hard-won nature of the exploration of the rules governance of the communist party, the historic contribution of the CPC to the exploration of that governance, and the important historical position of socialism with Chinese characteristics in the understanding of it.

In the specific research process, the subject takes political science principles as the cornerstone, philosophical categories as the framework, and CPC history as the content, and makes extensive use of documentary and empirical research, as well as econometric statistics, case studies and other research methods, paying particular attention to the following three research dimensions.

(I) THE DIALECTICAL RELATIONSHIP BETWEEN THE GENERAL AND THE SPECIFIC

As the ruling party, the communist party must make the effort consciously to follow the general rules governing political parties in modern society, such as the position of the people and the masses, the control and supervision of power, governing by law and economic development, and so on. If we only emphasise the specificity and individuality of the communist party and ignore the universality and commonality of political parties and the general rules of party governance, we will be limited in our understanding of problems and our approach to solving them, resulting in our economic, political and cultural isolation from the international community, and in our political parties rejecting the valuable experience of human political civilisation, or even deviating from the mainstream of human political civilisation and from fundamental human civilisation itself. At the same time, the specificity of the communist party as a proletarian party is distinct, concrete and fundamental. Without a firm grasp of that specificity, governance is bound to be detached from the national situation, and the result will inevitably be disorderly and ineffective, or even disastrous. In terms of the main differences, first, the means of gaining power are different. In Western countries, political parties gain power mainly through election by simple majority or proportional representation, and the electoral methods and priorities differ depending on the particular political system. Communist parties, on the other hand, mainly seize power through revolutionary means. In countries where there is no parliamentary democracy or a weak democratic system, the only means of gaining power is to overthrow the old regime and establish a new one. Second, the actual status of the ruling party is different. The basic function of political parties in Western countries is to win over voters. After the elections are over, the party's function is weakened, and it is mainly up to the government and parliament to enact leadership of the country. Communist rule is essentially one-party rule, with only participating parties and no opposition parties. The party's own functions are not weakened after it comes to power, and it still has the onerous responsibility of formulating the party's line, programme, guidelines and policies, of formulating the country's economic and social development strategy and of leading all aspects of national and social life. Third, the relationship with state power is different. The function of party organisations in Western countries is to send their leaders or cadres to the institutions of power, which hold state power and are not accountable to political parties for their actions; political parties are not directly involved in state administration. In contrast, the communist party organisation at all levels has a supervisory and guarantor role over the apparatus of state power, and the role of the party organisation is different from that of Western countries. In short, when studying the rules of governance of the communist party, we must not copy the governing experience of Western political parties, and we must not use the rules of governance of Western political parties to guide those of the communist party. At the same time, we need to pay attention to the fact that in the new historical era, the understanding, grasp and practice of the phenomenon of a higher degree of integration between the communist party and state power must be realised at the institutional and legal levels. The party should operate as the ruling force within the state system to lead the life of the state.

(II) THE HISTORICAL POSITION OF THE NEW ERA

The CPC is at a different stage in history, facing a different governing environment and a different governing mission, and the embodiment and role of its rules of governance laws are also different. To study the laws of communist rule today, we must look down on history from the heights of the new era, pinpoint the correct coordinates, observe the stars and explore the way forward.

Since entering the new era, the international situation has shown that the world as a whole is in a period of great development, change and adjustment, with peaceful development remaining the theme of the times. Changes in the system of global governance and international order are accelerating, the interconnectedness and interdependence of countries is deepening, the balance of international power is becoming more settled, and the general trend of peaceful development is irreversible. The international flow of capital, technology, information and people, means that knowledge, culture, values and ideology are moving around the world beyond national borders. At the same time, the world is facing extraordinary instability and uncertainty, insufficient economic growth, growing polarisation between rich and poor, the emergence of regional hotspots, the continued spread of non-traditional security threats involving terrorism, cyber security, major infectious diseases and climate change, and many common challenges facing humankind. Because of all this, the collision, shock, penetration and integration of various cultures are bound to become increasingly intense. In terms of the domestic situation, under the strong influence of the CPC's wave of reform and opening up, the Sixth Congress of the Communist Party of Vietnam proposed a line of "renewal and opening up" in 1986; the Fourth Congress of the Communist Party of Cuba proposed a policy of opening up to the outside world in 1991; the Fourth Congress of the Lao People's Revolutionary Party proposed a series of political and economic reforms to be carried out by the government in 1986; and the first special economic zone, the Raijin-Sonbong Economic Free Trade Zone (later renamed the Rason Special Economic Zone), was established in North Korea in late 1991. In April 2018, the Third Plenary Session of the Seventh Central Committee of the Workers' Party of Korea launched the strategic line of "concentrating all the efforts of the party and the country on socialist economic construction at the present stage when the Democratic People's Republic of Korea is steadily advancing to the status of a world-class political, ideological and military power".

The reform and opening up of these five socialist countries have strengthened the momentum of socialism, developed and consolidated the cause of socialism, and made the trend of socialism irreversible in the world; however, development is also extremely uneven. This imbalance just confirms what Xi Jinping emphasised in the report of the 19th National Congress of the CPC: "Openness brings progress, and closure inevitably leaves us behind." From the perspective of the CPC's self-construction, since the 18th National Congress of the CPC, the Party Central Committee with Comrade Xi Jinping at its core has bravely faced the major risks and challenges faced by the party and the outstanding problems within the party and has used tenacious will and quality to impose discipline, fight corruption and punish wrongdoing. It has eliminated serious hidden dangers within the party and the country, the political life within the party has been updated, the political ecology within the party has improved significantly, the party's creativity, cohesion, and combat effectiveness have been significantly enhanced, the party's unity and cohesion have been consolidated, and the relationship between the party and the masses has been significantly improved. The party has become stronger in the forging of revolution, radiating new and powerful vitality, and providing a strong political guarantee for the development of the party and the country. At the same time, we must also be soberly aware that the ruling environment facing the party is complex, as are the factors affecting the party's advancement and weakening its purity, and that the outstanding problems in the party, such as impurity of ideology, organisation and style, have not yet been fundamentally resolved. The Communist Party of Vietnam, the Lao People's Revolutionary Party, the Communist Party of Cuba and the Workers' Party of Korea have emphasised that the strength of the party originates from its organisation, and they have all made efforts to strengthen that organisation and further develop the role it plays. They have stressed that, by adhering to democratic centralism, the party should realise internal democracy and organically combine a high degree of discipline with internal democracy; they have emphasised that party leaders and cadres should maintain the admirable principle of maintaining close contact with the masses, working hard and accepting no privileges. In this way, party construction has made new and greater progress. At the same time, some communist parties have internal and external problems and rely entirely on the model of strong ideological education and leadership to maintain party unity; the rise of non-socialist and anti-socialist thinking and decentralisation in some communist parties warrants great caution.

Pluralisation, globalisation, informatisation and diversification are the markers of a new historical era and a new perspective of understanding. If any political party or country becomes detached from this specific development context and orientation, it will bring down on itself the inevitable results of that detachment.

(III) THE INTRINSIC LINK BETWEEN THE THREE LAWS OF ORGANIC UNITY

The rules of governance of the communist party, the laws of socialist construction, and the laws of human social development each have different connotations and categories, and are practised at different levels. The rules of governance of the communist party reveal the rules of the party's practice through analysis of the party's special status, role and activities; the laws of socialist construction reveal the specific perspective of the world socialist movement, in particular, the development and practice of socialism with Chinese characteristics. The laws of human social development reveal the universal law of social development from the broad perspective of human development from ancient times to the present and on into the future. Obviously, the three laws are an inseparable organic whole, with an inherent unity of understanding and unity of practice. The rules of governance of the communist party and of socialist construction are special laws of human social development. Only by profoundly knowing and understanding the laws of social development can we properly understand and grasp the rules of governance of communist party rule and of socialist construction. To explore and study the rules of governance, we must take the development of human society as the background and follow the basic laws of human social development. The fundamental aim of communist party governance is to promote the progress and development of human society, so it must also conform to the laws of human social development. For example, it is the most fundamental law of human social development that the relationships of production must be adapted to the conditions of the productive forces and the superstructure must be adapted to the conditions of the economic base. The communist party's decisions over whether or not to change the relationships of production and the superstructure, as well as the path and manner of change, must be in accordance with this basic law. Therefore, in a certain sense, the rules of communist governance are ultimately an objective demonstration of the law of human social development. The communist party and socialism are an inseparable community. It is the sacred duty of the communist party to build a socialist country and to promote its continuous socialist development. Exploring and studying the rules of governance of the communist party and the laws of socialist construction are to a large extent the same process, or two sides of the same coin. Therefore, when we discuss the rules of governance of the communist party, we must summarise the practice of the world socialist movement, especially the historical experience and lessons of the two major socialist countries, China and the Soviet Union. We should focus on the important, basic question of "what is socialism and how to build it". It is on this basis that we can uncover the laws that govern the success and failure of socialism. In short, understanding and discussing the rules of governance of the communist party must not be carried out in isolation from the laws of socialist construction and the laws of human social development. The deep understanding and grasp of the three together has a bearing on the degree to which a Marxist ruling Marxist party can reflect on and recognise the lessons of historical experience and lessons on the maturity of its ideological theory, and on its overall progress from a new historical starting point. Only by correctly recognising and understanding the intrinsic relationship between the three laws can we truly grasp the rules of governance of the communist party.

The study of the laws of governance of the communist party is an area of great concern to the theoretical and academic communities and is also a major issue of great political importance. First, it is important to consider how to make breakthroughs and innovations in the research framework that affect the interpretation of important issues on the basis of existing research results and in the light of the new era. Second, the study involves all aspects of the content of the rules of governance: how to grasp their essential, core content from an academic perspective, how to clarify the relationship between core issues and extended or derivative ones, and how to categorise and present them. The need for adjustment, phasing and allowance for contemporary characteristics are other areas of research on this topic. Third, the communist party's exploration and practice of its rules of governance are still a work in progress, and part of an open and evolving process. How to make the research findings stand up to practical tests and contain a degree of foresight, and how to combine history and reality, theory and practice, and achieve unity between political and academic understanding, are major challenges in terms of research methodology. It is therefore a major test of the researcher's political stance and academic approach as to how to liberate the mind, seek truth from facts, keep abreast of the times and be pragmatic in academic research on specific issues; also, how to find realistic political and strategic worth in academic research on specific issues, so as to achieve organic unity and scientific balance between the academic and political aspects.

PART I

PRELIMINARY EXPLANATIONS OF THE RULES OF GOVERNANCE OF MARXIST PARTIES BY CLASSIC AUTHORS AND REVOLUTIONARY MENTORS

The exploration of the rules of governance of any political party is based on particular theories and practices of governance and has its own theoretical and practical sources. The theoretical concepts and initial practice of Marx and Engels, and the exploration of, and lessons learnt from, the governance of the CPSU, provide theoretical guidance and a historical reference for the CPC's exploration of the rules of governance.

1

THE INITIAL MARXIST REVELATION OF THE LAWS OF PROLETARIAN PARTIES IN POWER

The gradual establishment of the capitalist mode of production not only led to huge changes in human society, with the formation of two classes, the bourgeoisie and the proletariat, but also gave rise to political revolutions, party politics and, as a result of the insurmountable contradictions of capitalism itself, fierce class struggles. In this process, Marx and Engels expended a lot of thought in the exploration of the process of summing up the experience and lessons learnt from the rule of the bourgeois parties and the short-term power of the proletariat; they also formed the earliest theory of the rule of proletarian parties, which first revealed the basic law of governance of such parties. These ideological concepts are the theoretical source of the CPC's own understanding and exploration of their rules of governance and are also an extremely valuable spiritual treasure.

(I) THE EMERGENCE OF POLITICAL PARTIES AND THE SHARP CLASS AND SOCIAL CONTRADICTIONS UNDER WESTERN PARTY POLITICS

Political parties are the product of a certain historical stage in the development of political activity and civilisation in human society. With the gradual establishment of the capitalist mode of production, the bourgeoisie, in its political struggle against the feudal aristocracy, increasingly took an organised form, giving rise to political parties in the modern sense.

Broadly speaking, political parties first originated in 17th century England. A group of members of the English Parliament, represented by

Lord Danby, advocated the extension of royal power, the restriction of the role of Parliament and the suppression of Protestants, representing overall the interests of the declining landed classes. This group was known to their political opponents as the Tories. The Shaftesbury Party represented the interests of the merchants, financiers and freelancers who were skilled in the business of governance and advocated the restriction of royal power, the increase of parliamentary power and religious tolerance. This group was called the Whigs by their political opponents. The Habeas Corpus Act of 1679 was passed by the English Parliament thanks to the efforts of the Whigs. At the time, both Tory (originally an Irish term of abuse meaning "gangster" or "ruffian") and Whig (originally a Scottish term of abuse meaning "thief" or "robber") were pejorative terms, intended as personal attacks.

During the first parliamentary reforms in Britain in 1831-1832, the Tories and Whigs became the Conservative Party and the Liberal Party respectively. "Conservative" as a party name did not mean resistance to reform and social progress but rather showing prudence in decision-making and not being rash or reckless. On the other hand, as a party name, "Liberal" was more about reducing regulation and encouraging free trade and bold reform. In the late 19th and early 20th centuries, when liberal capitalism was replaced by monopoly capitalism, many industrial capitalists turned to the Conservative Party and the Liberal Party went into gradual decline. Later, the rise of the Labour Party saw it replace the Liberals in 1924 and begin to take turns with the Conservatives to hold power.

When the US was founded, many people were opposed to political parties. When Washington left politics, he warned the country against forming political parties, arguing that they were a tool for political speculation by politicians and that a multiplicity of parties would divide the country and give foreigners an opportunity to take advantage of them. In his administration, however, politicians were divided into two groups over what kind of country to build. One group, represented by Hamilton, believed that the central government should remain strong and that it would be in the interests of the country's development; they were known as the Federalists. The Jeffersonians believed that the interests of small farmers, artisans and frontiersmen should be protected, that the states should retain more power and that the central government should have less power; were known as the Anti-Federalists. The Anti-Federalists called themselves Democratic-Republicans. In 1795, the Democratic-Republicans in Congress met in secret and decided to adopt a united attitude towards the bills discussed in Congress, demonstrating that a party caucus had already formed. In the presidential election of 1796, the party lines were already clear, resulting in the election of John Adams, a Federalist. The presidential election of 1800 saw the election of Jefferson, a Democratic-Republican, and the Democratic-Republican Party came to power for 24 years. However, this election led to a split in the Democratic-Republican Party, with some forming the Democratic Party and others forming the National Republican Party. In 1834, the National Republican Party became the Whig Party. Other parties also split and regrouped, culminating in a two-party confrontation between the Democrats and the Whigs. In 1854, the Whig Party merged with the Free Land Party to create the Republican Party. Since then, the successive presidential and congressional elections in the US have been between the Democratic and Republican parties, truly entering the era of the two-party system, and the names of the two parties have not changed since. The creation of political parties and the consequent development and stability of party politics fundamentally stems from the fact that human society has always needed a political organisation that connects the population to the power of the state. Because public power is never exercised by one person or by all, it can only be exercised by a particular group. This need of human society does not depend on the development of productivity and, at the same time, it is not only expressed in times of peace but also in times of revolution. There is a classic quotation from Lenin regarding the latter: "Give us an organisation of revolutionaries and we can turn Russia upside down![1]" He therefore proposed that the first and most urgent practical task of the party at that time was to build a revolutionary organisation that would give strength, stability and continuity to the political struggle. The most advanced form of such a revolutionary organisation, as human society entered the age of industrial civilisation, was the political party.

In addition, political parties were also a more rational form of social and political organisation after the end of the feudal monarchy.

Monarchy and aristocracy both relied on blood ties and the relationship between the ruler and his ministers to maintain control of the state. Party politics, on the other hand, has diluted those ties; they rely mainly on political groups with convergent interests and ideas to achieve control of state power by linking and interacting with the people and public rights, and bridging the conflicts between different social groups. Under a party-political system, democracy replaces autocracy, and the power of the state is transformed from the monarch's monopoly in feudal society to that of a political party or a coalition of several political parties, which form the bridge between state power and the people.

Party politics are conducive to the progressive development of political civilisation. In terms of society as a whole, the political activities of political parties are characterised by openness, mass participation, procedure and the rule of law. From the viewpoint of the ruling group, it must implement an electoral system, a system of tenure, of checks and balances, of supervision and of accountability. This kind of political system is undoubtedly a huge step forward compared to the previous monarchical dictatorship. The autocratic, secretive and impermanent nature of monarchical rule, its lifetime system and the family monopoly on succession are extremely oppressive for the populace and may bring much misfortune on those within the ruling group. Party politics emerged as part of the process of shifting politics towards democracy and were also the basic form of political democratisation.

Party politics facilitates the harmonious integration of social forces. Modern society has a large number of interests to express, which are often contradictory and in conflict with each other. Political parties are the intermediaries between society and the power of the state. "Political parties are the bridge with society at one end and the state at the other. To use a different analogy, political parties are the conduits and sluices that channel and direct the current of thought and discussion in society into the waterwheel of the political establishment."[2]

Political parties bring together the demands of different social groups and distil, filter and synthesise them into policy ideas that are as acceptable as possible to all classes and strata of society. If the demands of some people cannot be met at any given time, a lot of explaining, persuading and convincing has to be done. This is conducive to balancing the interests of all parties, reducing conflicts and contradictions among them, and facilitating the stable development of society.

Political parties are conducive to the development and prosperity of a nation-state. Political parties are made up of the most active, dynamic and aware members of interest groups, and they have become a powerful force in uniting the hearts and minds of society, leading progress and breaking through bottlenecks in national development. Looking at the development of Britain, France, Germany, the US, Russia and Japan moving from weakness to strength in modern times, we can see the important role played by political parties in this process. Britain was the first country in the world to establish party politics. The decline of royal power and the development of parliamentary politics led to the rise of party politics in Britain. Although party politics emerged relatively late in the US, that did not prevent it from becoming an irreplaceable factor in the country's development and growth. The two major parties, the Democrats and the Republicans, not only competed and cooperated to manipulate elections and select bourgeois political spokesmen from them, but also managed to achieve political stability through mutual checks and balances and complementarity between the two parties, so that there were no major deviations or imbalances in the political trajectory and general policies of the US. This has contributed significantly to the economic growth and social development of the US and also effectively shaped and maintained its global dominance. Of course, the emergence of party politics did not solve the acute social contradictions that emerged in the formation and development of capitalist society, nor could it conceal its essential attributes of class oppression and exploitation. The most striking manifestations of this were the periodic economic crises, the continuous popular resistance movements and the way in which the capitalist ruling clique, in order to escape from the crisis and divert the contradictions, resorted to expansion and invasion, and to the subjugation and colonisation of people of other countries. Nor did they baulk at inciting outbreaks of internal chaos and external wars, and even the human catastrophe of world war.

In July 1825, the first cyclical economic crisis of widespread overproduction broke out in Britain. This was followed by a considerable period of economic crises, on average every ten years or so, such as in 1837, 1847, 1857 and 1866. Other capitalist countries have also experienced economic crises to varying degrees. In fact, the overproduction of a capitalist economy is a relative surplus due to its own insurmountable contradictions, except that its production capacity is excessive in relation to the working people's ability to pay. When the crisis occurred, a large quantity of commodities could not be sold on the market, while the general public lost their jobs, the wages of the working population were drastically reduced, people had no money to buy goods, and the whole society was thrown into a state of extreme panic and chaos. However, even in times when there is no large-scale crisis, the problems of capitalist society, such as the division between rich and poor, class antagonism, corruption, environmental pollution, moral degradation and rising crime rates, are still widespread, causing pain, tearing society apart and always brewing a crisis. In Marx's words: "At one pole is the accumulation of wealth while at the other, on the part of the class that produces its own products as capital, is the accumulation of poverty, the torment of labour, servitude, ignorance, coarseness and moral degradation."[3]

The industrial revolution, which could have been used to relieve workers of heavy labour, became more of a tool for extracting the blood and sweat of workers in the early stages of capitalist development. The use of machinery led to a more detailed and specialised division of labour but capitalists often replaced skilled workers with large numbers of unskilled workers, and replaced adult male workers with female and child workers, in order to reduce or suppress inputs and costs, and extract profits swiftly. This highly irrational anomaly is just as Marx pointed out in regard to the UK: "Britannia's industry, like a vampire, can only survive by sucking people's blood, including the blood of children." "The standard of living of the masses of the working class is declining steeply everywhere, at least as much as the classes standing above them are rising up the social ladder. Neither the improvement of machinery, the application of science to production, the improvement of means of transport, the opening up of new colonies, emigration, the expansion of markets, free trade, nor all these together can eliminate the poverty of the working masses; any new development of the productive forces of labour, on the basis of this modern evil, inevitably deepens social contrasts and strengthens social antagonisms."[4] As a result, society was divided into two opposing classes, the bourgeoisie and the proletariat, with increasingly sharp contradictions and conflicts, and the workers' movement surged forward.

Fundamentally, the sharp social contradictions that emerge in capitalist society are determined by the fundamental contradictions of capitalist society: "the real limit to capitalist production is capital itself"[5]. The emergence of party politics has broadened the scope of political participation by members of society and harmonised and integrated the plurality of social interests but it has not changed the fundamental economic and political system of capitalism, and although it is a great improvement over feudal autocracy, its drawbacks and contradictions are obvious.

In capitalist society, any political party in power claims to represent the general interests of society but in reality, they only represent the interests of particular classes and strata. Marx and Engels pointed out that "every new class which seeks to replace the old ruling class is obliged, in order to achieve its aims, to present its interests as the common interests of all members of society, that is to say, this is expressed conceptually by giving a universal form to its ideas and portraying them as the only rational and universal ideas."[6] This reflects the hypocrisy and deceitfulness in the propaganda and claims of the bourgeois parties.

Bourgeois political parties advocate equality in the letter of the law, while in reality upholding inequality. Under capitalist party politics, freedom, democracy and equality are explicitly stipulated, and in superficial legal terms, they are given to the people. But because the means of production are in private hands, democracy in capitalist society becomes the privilege of personalised capital, the democracy of the private possessors of the means of production. Engels said that in capitalist society, "money replaces the sword as the first lever of social power "[7]. No bourgeois party wants to change this incompatibility of freedom and equality in word only, with the truth, because they are all beneficiaries of this institutional arrangement.

Bourgeois parties promoted freedom, equality and human rights at home, but practised the exact opposite towards the people of other countries. Modern China was a semi-colonial, semi-feudal society, which was deeply bullied and oppressed by the imperialist powers. The Chinese people felt the huge contrasts in the internal and external policies of the political parties of the capitalist countries extremely deeply. For a time, China studied the West avidly, regarding them as their teachers, but came to wonder: "it is strange; why are the masters always invading the students?"[8]. In fact, this is the result of the bourgeoisie's two-faced nature in its internal and external policies. In his exposure of British rule in India, Marx observed pointedly: "When we turn our gaze from the homeland of bourgeois civilisation to the colonies, the extreme hypocrisy of bourgeois civilisation and its barbaric nature are laid bare before us; it puts on a facade of decency in its homeland but in the colonies it does not disguise it at all."[9] The inconsistency in internal and external policies also reveals the self-contradiction and incompleteness of the bourgeois party's claims.

(II) THE BIRTH OF MARXISM AND THE CREATION OF A NEW PROLETARIAN PARTY

Any era of great change is the result of great theories and breeds new great theories because the "problems" of each era attract wise minds to find theoretical "solutions" and inspire socially responsible people to forge their way out of difficult situations. Faced with capitalism shattering the old order but not building a new Europe, and faced with the materialism and moral degradation brought about by industrialisation, some conscientious and rational people in Europe were thinking and searching for a new course. One of the salient features of this search was the commitment to a new political and economic ideology or system of thought, and this search has continued to the present day, resonating with the world of today and sharing weal and woe.

Some people emphasised the continuity and inheritance of social development and considered social reform to be conservative in the sense that it could not destroy tradition. This doctrine saw the whole transformation of society as a terrible mistake, hated industrialism and *laissez-faire* individualism, and despised the emerging middle class. Therefore, they advocated the suppression of equality of status and political rights, opposed written constitutions and contractual relations, and believed that only the monarchy could provide political security and stability.

The overall success of the capitalist economic, political and social revolution was a triumph for liberalism, which also sought solutions to the contradictory problems that arose from the establishment of the capitalist mode of production, and which eventually opened the way for the transformation of liberalism from the traditional (classical) to the modern. The wise men of the bourgeoisie began to strengthen the intervention of the state and the authority of government in the political and economic spheres, and to extend bourgeois democracy, thereby extending political rights to all male citizens; the working class also began to have the right to vote. In terms of social policy, the realisation that fair opportunities and equal conditions require certain social services led to the recognition of the responsibility of the state for the welfare of all citizens. Western European countries, led by Germany, adopted social reform programmes, including old-age pensions, minimum wage laws, sickness, accident and unemployment insurance, and regulations on working hours and conditions. Universal compulsory education was introduced, and public education was seen as the main means of instilling a sense of citizenship and of developing serious work habits among the lower classes.

However, liberal adjustments failed to win the support of the emerging working class at the time, not only because of the limited extent of policy adjustments and the lag in institutional reconstruction but also because socialism offered a more cutting-edge and quicker solution.

At that time, workers living in the crowded cities were beginning to demonstrate the first signs of political consciousness in the face of the polarisation of wealth and social conflict brought about by capitalism. They increasingly felt that their interests were not the same as those of their employers and that their situation could only be improved through joint action on their part.

As a result, the workers, or rather the intellectuals who led them, developed a new ideology - socialism. It rejected the liberal order of individual competition, arguing that the bourgeois revolution had put an end to one inequality but created another, even more intolerable than the old one; they also held that that the proletariat was not the innocent victim of a bad economic system but was a new social class and a potential instrument for social renewal. Unlike conservatism, socialism does not advocate a return to the old system but rather a continuous advance to abolish private ownership completely and, through a political, economic and social revolution on all fronts, achieve equality and freedom in the true sense of the word in a new society.

The rise of capitalism in the 16th and 17th centuries saw the emergence of early utopian socialism, represented by the Englishman, Sir Thomas More. At the beginning of the 19th century, as the industrial revolution in Britain progressed and bourgeois rule was established in France, there emerged the idealistic socialism represented by the Frenchmen Henri de Saint-Simon and Charles Fourier and the Englishman Robert Owen. They argued for a dialectical view of history, exposed and criticised the ills of capitalist society, considered competition and anarchy to be the worst of all disasters, and put forward ideas for a future society that would replace the capitalist system. Saint-Simon advocated the planned organisation of production and life, and Fourier proposed the organisation of labour communes. However, "all these idealistic socialists had one basic characteristic in common. They focused their attention on the principles and explicit *modus operandi* of the model societies they devised. However, the question of how these model societies would replace existing societies was never seriously considered. They had vague expectations of receiving help from wealthy or powerful patrons"; "while they had a programme for social change, they did not expect and intend it to be achieved through an uprising of the proletariat. They certainly did not think in terms of revolution or class struggle. In fact, they gave little thought to how their carefully crafted blueprint could be put into practice"[10].

"We must expose the old world once and for all, and actively build the new."[11] Marx and Engels drew on classical German philosophy and classical British political economy in their efforts to rescue socialism from its false starting point in utopia. They critically absorbed the "rational core" of dialectics from Hegel's philosophy and abandoned his idealistic system; they drew on the "basic core" of materialism in Feuerbach's philosophy and abandoned his mechanistic and metaphysical views to create dialectical materialism. Marx and Engels also promoted the use of the principles of dialectical materialism in the study of human social history, creating historical materialism. They also used historical materialism to reveal the relationship between social existence and consciousness, arguing that the history of human social development is the history of changes in the mode of production driven by the development of the productive forces. The development of productive forces and class struggle are the driving forces of social development, and the masses of the people are the masters of history.

They absorbed the reasonable parts of the 'labour theory of value' of the classical British political economists Adam Smith and David Ricardo, criticised their class-biased and erroneous views, carefully studied the production of commodities under the capitalist system, revealed the relationship between people from the relationship between commodities, and advanced the doctrine of surplus value. They pointed out that the wages received by workers were only a small part of the value created by their labour, while the other, larger part was appropriated by the capitalists. This latter was the surplus value, the source of the capitalists' profits, and the real secret of the bourgeoisie's wealth and domination, while the proletariat was exploited and oppressed.

In creating the concept of historical materialism and the doctrine of surplus value, the theories of Marx and Engels revealed the laws of human social development, especially the law of the emergence, development and inevitable demise of capitalist society; they clarified the historical status and great mission of the proletariat as the gravediggers of the capitalist system and the creators of the socialist system; they pointed out that only through the proletarian revolution, the abolition of private ownership and the establishment of proletarian power could the proletariat overthrow the capitalist system and realise the future of socialism. They thereby created the theory of scientific socialism, and the proletarians and other working people of the world began to have a powerful ideological weapon for understanding and transforming the world: Marxism.

As the proletariat grew rapidly, workers began to realise from their struggle that their political and economic powerlessness was the root cause of their poverty, and their struggle against the bourgeoisie was increasingly directed against the capitalist system of exploitation itself. Since the previously scattered and sporadic struggles all ended in failure in the face of the mighty arsenal of capitalist domination, they also gradually realised that if the proletariat was to fight for its rights and interests and even for the victory of the social revolution, the whole proletariat had to unite in a conscious, programmed, targeted and directed unified action. As a result, in the 1930s and 1940s, the proletariat in Britain, France, Germany and other countries launched independent political movements, which were principally manifested in the famous British Charter Movement, the Canut Revolts in Lyon, France, and the Textile Workers' Uprising in Silesia, Germany. In these three major workers' movements, the proletariat advanced its own independent political and economic demands, impacting capitalist institutional arrangements and establishing political organisations such as the National Chartist Association, the Société des Saisons and the League of the Just.

In 1836, some German political exiles in Paris secretly formed the League of the Just. The members were handicraftsmen and utopian socialists, mainly garment-makers. The League was one of the most radical of the German secret societies, simultaneously organising propaganda and carrying out revolutionary conspiracies. They established branches in London, Switzerland and Germany before moving their headquarters to London, where they became an international organisation with nearly 1,000 members by the end of 1847.

In the British Charter Movement, in July 1840, representatives of Chartists from all over Britain met at a convention in Manchester and proclaimed the formation of the National Charter Association. The Association had a programme focused on the struggle for the right of the working class to vote, in other words, for proletarian rule. It had both central and local organisation systems that worked along democratic lines; there were tens of thousands of people who sympathised with the Association's aims and principles, and who paid regular subscriptions; and there were millions of people who were in contact with it in one way or another. It therefore fulfilled the basic conditions for a political party to become "an independent political party" and was, indeed, "the first workers' party of modern times"[12].

After moving to Paris at the end of 1843, Marx began to communicate with French socialists. He attended most of the meetings of most of the French workers' associations and took an active part in the League of the Just. After emigrating to Brussels in Belgium in 1845, he took part in the establishment of the Communist Correspondence Committee, which brought socialists from Germany, France and Britain into contact with each other and worked to spread communism. He made a timely summation of the experience of the workers' movement and the class struggle, and explicitly stated that if the proletariat was to overthrow capitalism and seek complete liberation, it must build a new proletarian party armed with scientific socialist theory. He said: "One cannot eliminate exploitation in the way imagined by utopian socialists, who lead workers away from class struggle. There is only one way out: the overthrow of the bourgeoisie by all the forces of the proletariat, organised under the leadership of a revolutionary party. The working class must build its own state and liberate all mankind forever from exploitation, and this party will itself be the leader of the oppressed masses."[13] Marx also recognised that scientific socialist theory could not arise spontaneously in the workers' movement and that it was the efforts of advanced parties that would bring "the proletariat to support our convictions"[14]. "In practical terms, the communists are the most determined and are always driving some of the workers' parties in every country; in theoretical terms, they are superior to the rest of the proletarian masses in their understanding of the conditions, processes and general results of the proletarian movement."[15] Therefore it is only through an advanced party of the vanguard of the proletariat that scientific socialism can be transformed into an ideological weapon for millions of working people and produce a powerful material force for the transformation of the world.

In the spring of 1847, the League of the Just invited Marx and Engels to join them and to guide their reorganisation.

Marx and Engels readily agreed to try to lead the world communist revolution by establishing an international communist party. Of course, the proletarian party that Marx and Engels were trying to establish at this time was essentially an international political group.

From 2 to 9 June of the same year, the League of the Just held a reorganisation conference in London. Marx was unable to attend but Engels, together with Wilhelm Wolff, directed the reorganisation of the League according to a plan agreed in advance with Marx. The meeting adopted a number of documents, including the Constitution of the Communist League and the Draft Communist Creed, which more fully reflected Marx's and Engels' theoretical ideas about the proletarian party.

At the suggestion of Marx and Engels, the Congress decided to change the name of the League of the Just into the Communist League to make it clear that the use of secret conspiracies was inappropriate. They stipulated that "the aim of the League was: to destroy the old society by all means of propaganda and political struggle; to overthrow the bourgeoisie; to liberate the proletariat spiritually, politically and economically; and to bring about a communist revolution"[16]. It was decided to abolish the League's original slogan "All men are brothers" and replace it with "Working men of all countries, unite!"

The Communist League also abolished some of the stereotypes inherited from its clandestine and sectarian activities. The Constitution of the Communist League stipulates that members "shall not participate in any organisational or local requirements hostile to the aims of the League or obstructive to the achievement of those aims" and "must swear to obey unconditionally the resolutions of the League". The organisational structure of the League consisted of branches, district sections, a central committee and a congress. "The Congress is the legislative body of the League" and holds an annual session, "which hears reports from the Central Committee on all its activities and on the state of the League; the Central Committee attends the Congress without the right to vote. The Congress sets out the principles of the League's policy which must be followed, decides on the question of amending the Statutes and designates the location of the Central Committee for the following year". "The Central Committee is the executive organ of the League" and "may convene extraordinary Congresses in case of emergency"[17].

According to Marx, this rejected "everything that fosters superstitious authority"[18]. According to Engels, the League "is in itself completely democratic, its committees are elected and can be dismissed at any time, and this alone has blocked the way for any conspiratorial fanatics who demand dictatorship"[19]. From then on, Marx and Engels always adhered to this principle and in their struggle against the anarchism of Proudhon and Bakunin, they made it particularly clear that the two most fundamental principles were the broadest possible democracy and centralism.

The Communist League thus became the first organisational form of the international proletariat as a political party. A new type of political party was born, the Communist League, the party of the proletariat.

In late November and early December 1847, the Communist League held its second Congress in London. Marx and Engels attended the meeting together. After more than ten days of heated debate, the Congress approved the constitution and declared: "The aims of the League: to overthrow the bourgeoisie, to establish proletarian rule, to destroy the old bourgeois society based on class antagonism and to build a new society without classes and without private ownership."[20] The Congress adopted the principles proposed by Marx and Engels for drafting the programme of the League and entrusted them with the task of drafting a programme to be published as the party's manifesto. This was to become the Communist Manifesto.

The Communist Manifesto was officially published in London on 24 February 1848. It is the first programmatic document of scientific socialism and marks the birth of Marxism. It profoundly reveals the laws governing the emergence, development and inevitable demise of capitalism; comprehensively discusses the nature, programme and guiding ideology of proletarian political parties; systematically criticises various non-proletarian schools of thought; clarifies the strategic principles of the proletarian party; and embodies Marx and Engels' initial understanding of the communist party's rules of governance.

Regarding the inevitability and necessity of establishing a communist party, Marx and Engels reaffirmed, in the Communist Manifesto, the dialectical materialism and materialistic view of history already established earlier on, and argued that due to the rapid development of capitalism and the irreconcilable contradictions between the proletariat and the bourgeoisie, the proletariat in all civilised countries would inevitably unite and establish a proletarian party. In the end, the demise of the bourgeoisie and the victory of the proletariat were equally inevitable. At the same time, it is not possible for the proletariat's struggle against the bourgeoisie to be a spontaneous, decentralised struggle; it has to be an organised struggle guided by scientific theory, that is, it must be led by the proletarian party, that being the communist party, otherwise it cannot act as a "gravedigger" for capitalism. The establishment of a political party by the proletariat is one of the first conditions for the emancipation of the proletariat.

Regarding the nature and characteristics of the communist party, some bourgeois scholars of the time saw political parties as the ideological union of people which had no connection with their class status, and declared bourgeois parties to be parties that superseded class. Utopian socialists of all kinds looked down on the working class and advocated the creation of their own parties among the educated representatives of the proletariat. Marx and Engels, on the other hand, openly declared that the communist party they wanted to build was a proletarian party and representative of the interests and will of the proletariat.

The Communist Manifesto states that the communist party is international and that it "has no interests different from those of the prole-tariat as a whole". "Communists always represent the interests of the whole movement."[21] The communist party is not opposed to other work-ing-class parties but differs from them principally; first, in its adherence to the principle of proletarian internationalism; second, in its adherence to the subordination of present interests to long-term interests and of local interests to the interests of the whole; third, in its composition consisting of the most advanced members and most determined sections of the prole-tariat; and fourth, in its guidance by the scientific theory of communism.

Regarding the fundamental programme of the communist party, Marx and Engels believed that "one practical step is more important than a dozen programmes", but that "the formulation of a principled programme", "which is to establish a benchmark against which the level of the party movement can be measured"[22], is "a banner which is publicly erected and by which the outside world judges the party"[23]. The Commu-nist Manifesto was their first detailed programme for the communist party, setting out the party's immediate and ultimate aims, and the basic revolu-tionary path to achieve its programme. "The immediate aim of communist party members is the same as that of all other proletarian parties: the formation of the proletariat as a class, the overthrow of the bourgeoisie and the seizure of power by the proletariat." Because "their aim can only be achieved by the violent overthrow of the whole existing social system"[24], the highest programme is the complete elimination of private ownership and the creation of a new communist society free from exploitation, oppression and class.

On the tasks of the communist party once it comes to power, the Communist Manifesto states that "the proletariat will use its political domination step by step to seize the entire capital of the bourgeoisie, to concentrate all the instruments of production in the hands of the state; that is to see the proletariat organised as a ruling class, and to increase the total volume of productive forces as rapidly as possible." This includes the confiscation of property, the imposition of high and progressive taxes, the abolition of inheritance rights, the centralisation of credit, the nationalisation of transport, the introduction of planned production, and the implementation of universal labour obligations and compulsory education. At the same time, a victorious proletariat must revolutionise society not only in the material sphere but also in the spiritual sphere. "The communist revolution is the most radical break with traditional relationships to ownership, so it is not surprising that it has to make the most radical break with traditional ideas in the course of its own development." "In place of the old bourgeois society, with its classes and class antagonisms, there will be a union where the free development of one is the condition for the free development of all."[25]

Regarding the basic strategic and tactical principles of the communist party, in the 1830s and 1840s, before and after the founding of the Communist League, which was guided by scientific socialism, other workers' political factions and parties emerged in Europe and the US, such as the London Workers' Association (later to become the National Chartist Association) in Britain, the Société des Saisons and the Proudhonists in France, the Weitlingists in Germany, and the Antirenter Party in the US (later to become the "National Reformist Association"). On the basis of the need for the proletariat to strengthen its unity, Marx and Engels believed that "Communists are not a special party in opposition to other workers' parties"[26] and that they should ensure they handle correctly the various intricate relations with other workers' parties. On the one hand, it was based on the international solidarity of the proletariat and "does not propose any special principles to shape the proletarian movement"; on the other hand, it adhered to scientific socialism, grasped "the conditions, processes and general results of the proletarian movement" and "always represents the interests of the entire movement"[27]. It led the other workers' parties also to think in terms of the long-term and fundamental interests of the proletariat, and to raise the level of their own theories and struggles. In dealing with non-worker parties, the Communist Manifesto states that "Communists everywhere support all revolutionary movements against existing social and political systems" and that "Communists everywhere strive for unity and coordination among democratic political parties throughout the world". It emphasises the need for both flexibility of strategy and firmness of principle when working with other parties: "In all these movements they emphasise that the question of ownership is the fundamental issue of the movement, whatever the degree of development of this issue"[28]. That is to say, they must never lose sight of their ultimate goal.

It is clear that the Communist Manifesto is the first complete and systematic exposition of the new Communist world view and is a "complete, systematic and still the best exposition" of the "historical world role of the proletariat as the creator of socialist society"[29]. It became the first "detailed theoretical and practical programme" of a proletarian party. According to the Communist Manifesto, the communist party was endowed with a highly distinctive nature and identity, and from its birth it dramatically influenced and changed the political map and vision of world development in unprecedented theory and action, posture and appearance.

(III) SUMMARY OF THE EXPERIENCE OF THE FIRST INTERNATIONAL AND THE PARIS COMMUNE: AN INITIAL REVELATION AND OUTLINE OF THE GENERAL LAWS OF COMMUNIST RULE

Shortly after the publication of the Communist Manifesto, a bourgeois-democratic revolutionary movement of enormous proportions broke out on the European continent. Marx and Engels were actively involved in the practical activities of the revolution, founding the newspaper *Neue Rheinische Zeitung* and writing a series of important theoretical works, including *The Class Struggles in France 1848-1850*, *Address of the Central Committee to the Communist League* and *The Eighteenth Brumaire of Louis Bonaparte*, which enriched and developed the theory of proletarian party politics.

With regard to the indications of the importance of proletarian parties building a strong organisation, the contribution of the Communist League in the bourgeois-democratic revolution in Europe in 1848 was mainly through its theoretical views and the individual role of its members, and it did not play a leading role as a party organisation as a whole. As the German democrats, that is, the petty bourgeois parties, grew in strength and took the lead in the movement in general, the working-class parties found themselves without any strong organisation and in a subordinate position. Marx and Engels tried to change this unfavourable situation in the course of the revolution but failed due to the rapid deterioration of the political situation. Immediately after the defeat of the revolution, they called for an immediate end to the disorganisation of the League and for its restoration and strengthening, proposing that the party should be built into a "strong organisation".

In emphasising the importance of the independence of the proletarian party, after the defeat of the revolution, Marx and Engels repeatedly stressed, when summing up their experience, that the failure of the Communist League to build an independent mass party was one of the major reasons for the defeat of the revolution. "The workers' party must act as organised, as united and as independent as possible". "The workers, and above all, the Communist League, should not lower themselves again to the role of a chorus that echoes the bourgeois democrats but should seek to establish both a secret and an open independent workers' party organisation alongside the formal democrats, and should make each branch the centre and nucleus of a workers' association in which proletarian positions and questions of interest should be able to be discussed independently and without bourgeois influence."[30]

The slogan "permanent revolution" and the concept of the "dictatorship of the proletariat" were introduced. Marx and Engels developed the idea of the violent overthrow of the bourgeoisie and the establishment of their own rule in the Communist Manifesto, proposing that "revolution is the locomotive of history" and that, if the proletariat wanted to liberate itself, it must overthrow the bourgeoisie and establish the dictatorship of the proletariat. "There must be permanent revolution until the rule of all property-owning classes, large and small, is destroyed; until the proletariat seizes state power; until the union of the proletarians develops not only in one country but in all the important countries of the world to the extent that the competition between the proletarians of these countries ceases; or at least to the extent that the decisive productive forces are concentrated in the hands of the proletarians."[31] Only with the dictatorship of the proletariat can the victorious proletariat use revolutionary violence to crush the resistance of the enemy, consolidate its rule and realise the historical mission of the proletariat. "This kind of dictatorship is the necessary transitional stage to achieve the elimination of all class differences, the elimination of all networks of production from which these differences arise, the elimination of all social relations which correspond to these networks of production, and the necessary fundamental ideological change away from these social relations."[32]

Marx also proposed that the communist party, as the party of the proletariat, must maintain close ties with the proletarian masses and strengthen its leadership of the labour movement and workers' organisations; without the alliance of the peasantry, the proletariat's "solo song becomes a swan-song in all the peasant countries"[33] and it will be impossible to achieve victory in the democratic revolution. On the question of the party's strategy, he clarified the communist party's strategy of struggle in the bourgeois democratic revolution and made timely adjustments to the party's strategy following the defeat of the revolution, enriching and developing the strategic planning put forward in the Communist Manifesto.

After the defeat of the 1848 revolution, a period of economic prosperity in countries such as Britain and the US led Marx to revise his earlier optimism that a commercial crisis and revolution would come together, stating that 'in this general prosperity, that is, when the productive forces of bourgeois society are flourishing as fast as they can in the whole range of bourgeois relations, there can be no talk of a real revolution. Such a revolution is only possible when the two elements of modern productive forces and the bourgeois mode of production are in conflict with each other"[34]. In November 1852, the Communist League, faced with internal divisions and external repression, could no longer function properly and was forced to disband. But Marx was convinced that 'a new revolution can only be possible after a new crisis, but the coming of a new revolution is as inevitable as the coming of a new crisis"[35].

This proved to be the case, as the rapid development of capitalism allowed the workforce in Europe to grow, dramatically changing the class structure of European countries. In the 1860s, there were 8.74 million industrial workers and 1.12 million craft workers in Europe. As a result of the increase in the level of machine-powered mass production and the discipline learned from the factory system, the working class in the major industrial countries also became more organised, aware and combative than it had been before the 1850s. Especially after the worldwide economic crisis in 1857, the workers' movement, which had been at a low ebb after the defeat of the revolution, regained momentum. A number of industrial workers' federations were formed in Britain to lead the workers in their fierce struggle against the capitalists. At the same time, the cross-border movement of people and the intensification of competition between countries, fuelled by globalisation, made workers' organisations, which had already achieved initial national unity, realise the need to further strengthen international unity.

In Britain, based on their judgment of the "common victory" of the proletarian revolution, Marx and Engels began to devote themselves to working for the establishment of international working-class organisations similar in nature to political parties to achieve the emancipation of the working class by this means. They actively disseminated education and propaganda among British workers and union activists in order to influence the masses of workers. They also paid special attention to the training of the leaders of the international workers' movement and sought to establish extensive contacts with revolutionaries everywhere, in the hope that they would learn and master revolutionary theory and embrace the new upsurge of revolution.

In 1863, a national uprising broke out in Poland against the rule of Tsarist Russia. Marx and Engels attached great importance to this and mobilised the working class in various European countries to show their solidarity with the revolutionary movement of the Polish people. On 22 July 1863, the London Council of the British General Federation of Trade Unions held a mass meeting to protest against the suppression of the Polish uprising by Tsarist Russia and to show solidarity with the Polish people in their just struggle. A delegation of French workers took part in the congress and exchanged views with the leaders of the British TUC on the question of joint action. On 10 November of the same year, the British Workers' Congress adopted the Appeal of the British Workers to the French Workers, calling on the workers of both countries to strengthen their solidarity and fight together.

On 28 September 1864, the British General Federation of Trade Unions held a mass meeting in the concert hall of St Martin's Church in London to welcome a delegation of French workers who were visiting in response to the Appeal. Also present were workers' representatives from Germany, Italy, Poland and Ireland, as well as a number of bourgeois democrats. At the proposal of the British and French workers' delegates, the congress decided to set up an international workers' association and elected an interim committee of 21 members (called the "Central Committee" from 18 October 1864 and renamed the "General Committee" in the summer of 1866). The International Workers' Association (or First International) was founded. On 5 October 1864, the first meeting of the interim committee was held to elect the members representing the various countries.

Marx did not participate in the planning of this historic event. He was still an exile at the time, so he tended to avoid directly participating in any political activities in the UK. A few hours before the inaugural meeting, he received an invitation from one of the conveners of the meeting, William Cremer, and attended the meeting as a representative of Germany.

At the meeting, Marx didn't say a word, but he was elected to the Interim Committee, the leading body of the International Workers' Association, and later to the nine-member small committee responsible for drafting the declaration and interim constitution. As a result, he drafted the First International's political programme, the *Declaration on the Establishment of the International Workers' Association* and the *Interim Constitution of the International Workers' Association* for the Association. On 1 November, once approved by the Central Committee of the Association, it was announced and implemented as a temporary charter. At the Geneva Congress of 1866, the *Common Constitution of the International Workers' Association* was formally approved.

In his Declaration on the Founding of the International Workers' Association, Marx devoted much space to an analysis of the development of capitalism over the last decade or so and the antagonism it had produced between the landowners and the bourgeoisie on the one hand and the working class on the other. He vividly pointed out the accumulation of wealth on the one hand and poverty, hunger and disease on the other. He went on to stress that "any new development of the productive forces of labour, on the basis of this modern evil, inevitably deepens social contrasts and intensifies social antagonisms." It was then that he made the famous assertion that "the seizure of power has become the great mission of the working class"[36]. The first sentence of the Common Constitution of the International Workers' Association is: "The emancipation of the working class should be fought for by the working class itself; the struggle for the emancipation of the working class is not for class privileges and monopolies but for equal rights and duties, and for the elimination of all class domination."[37] The Constitution emphasised that the proletariat in its struggle against the property-owning classes had to build a party different from all the old parties, in order to act as a class itself and guarantee the victory of the social revolution. Marx also stressed the need for the growing workers' organisations in Europe to work together as brothers and to be closely united in the struggle for social emancipation; the need to resist the foreign policy of the European powers; and the need to make "the simple norms of morality and justice the supreme norms in the relations between peoples."[38]

Objectively speaking, when the First International was founded, it was a massive trade union organisation, which was essentially an international political organisation made up of organisations and individuals of very different natures. Marxism was only a minor school of thought within it and when its dissolution was announced in 1876, there were very few Marxists among its members, at most 20 or 30, and they were scattered all over Europe and the USA. Of the Proudhonists, Bakuninists (anarchists), trade unions, followers of Lassalle and Mazzini, and others who participated, the vast majority did not believe in Marxism. Although they favoured the idea of socialism, they conceived the path and principles for the adoption of the future society according to their own ideas of how to solve the social problems; although they shared the desire for an international union of the proletariat, they tried to use international unity to serve their own sectarian interests or as a means to achieve them.

The General Federation of Trade Unions was the best organised workers' group in the world at that time. As the UK had the highest level of workers' movements in Europe and America, it became a link for workers in other countries and made a major contribution to the preparation for the creation of the First International. However, trade unionism only advocated engaging in trade union movements, not political parties, and only economic struggle, not political struggle.

The General German Workers' Association, followers of Ferdinand Lassalle, refused to join the First International but some individuals did so in a personal capacity. Lassalle believed that the solution to the poverty of the working class under capitalism was to break the "iron rule of wages" by establishing production cooperatives with the help of the state and making workers the owners of enterprises. To do this, it was necessary to fight for universal suffrage and to carry out peaceful and legal propaganda campaigns to lead the workers' movement onto the path of socialism.

Proudhonism was an influential petty-bourgeois socialist and anarchist ideology that was widespread in Western Europe in the 1850s and 1860s. The Paris branch of the International, founded by the Proudhonists, and the French provincial branches, led by other Proudhonists, were powerful pillars of the First International, which was second only to the British General Federation of Trade Unions. This faction led strikes and political struggles in its own country, supported strikes in continental European countries and in Britain, and practised the principles of proletarian internationalism. But Proudhonism believed that both communism and capitalism were flawed and irrational, and that "freedom" or anarchy, transcending private and public ownership, was the best model of society. They advocated the establishment of a "people's bank" based on interest-free loans as the fundamental way to transform the capitalist system and realise a society of "mutual assistance"; they preached class reconciliation and peaceful revolution, and opposed violent revolution and the dictatorship of the proletariat; they advocated absolute freedom of the individual and they rejected any country and government, and opposed all authority. The core of Proudhonism was the establishment of a small craft production system through peaceful reforms and the realisation of petty-bourgeois socialism.

Bakunin was a Russian anarchist; although he himself held Marx in high esteem and described himself as a student of Marx, the Socialist Democratic League he led, under the banner of socialist democracy, believed that action could only be determined by one's own will and advocated the rejection of authority, the elimination of the state and the establishment of an ideal society of freedom and equality. He believed that "any state, even in its freest and most democratic form, is necessarily based on control, domination, violence and, therefore, dictatorship" and that "where there is a state, there is necessarily control and therefore slavery"[39]. Also: "Governments are systematic poisoners of the people, self-serving anaesthetisers"[40]. He advocated workers' autonomy and opposed proletarian revolution and the dictatorship of the proletariat, saying "If the proletariat becomes the ruling class, who will it rule? That is to say, there would have to be another proletariat to submit to this new rule, this new state". Since the majority could not all rule, a minority council would have to be set up, and this minority group would undoubtedly be made up of those with greater knowledge or ability; when they had the power of the state, especially a centralised state that controlled all the means of production, they would degenerate into a new privileged class, the so-called bureaucratic class, due to human nature's natural lust for power and profit. In the end, "they all end up with the saddest result of all: a privileged minority ruling over the vast majority of the masses"[41]. He therefore considered Marx's ideas to be totalitarian and, if Marxism were in power, it would be worse than the ruling class they had opposed.

Obviously, these factions were in agreement with Marx on the revolutionary goals of overthrowing exploitative capitalism and bourgeois ownership and transcending the modern nation-state to achieve socialism, but there were fundamental differences in how to achieve this ultimate goal. The theories and ideas of these schools of thought were fundamentally unable to provide a direction and path for the proletariat's struggle for liberation. However, it should not be overlooked that the emergence of these factions was mostly linked to the political and economic situation in their countries, and to a certain extent reflected the actual level and development of the workers' movement in their countries. Both subjectively and objectively speaking, they played a relatively progressive role in promoting the development of the workers' movement. Despite the growing antagonism between the proletariat and the bourgeoisie at the time, extreme poverty also made the rapid improvement of living conditions of overriding importance to the working class, and made the underlying factors that led to this poverty less important. The low level of education also made it impossible at the time for the working class to understand the fundamental opposition between private ownership and labour, the revolutionary nature of the class to which it belonged and the rationality of the communist movement. Some of the theories and actions of these factions reflected, from different angles, some of the demands of the workers' movement at the time, had a positive effect on the struggle against capitalism and had a relatively progressive effect on the development of the workers' movement at the time.

For this reason, at the beginning of the First International, Marx made some necessary compromises and concessions to the various non-proletarian socialist factions of the time while adhering to his revolutionary principles. When drafting the Declaration on the Establishment of the International Workers' Association and the Common Statutes of the International Workers' Association, he did not explicitly include the programme and demands of communism, but only implicitly presented the ideas of the Communist Manifesto in an attempt to unite the entire fighting working class of Europe and America into one large army in a "moderate" form. In other words, in the early days of the First International, apart from the common point of emphasising the unity of workers from various countries, it did not have a common theoretical programme, but was just a "centre for liaison and cooperation" among workers from various countries[42].

This did not mean that Marx abandoned his ideological principles; he still insisted on the priority of unifying the various socialist doctrines onto the right path. He believed that if the working class was catered for with the promise of increased material wealth and equal social status, it could quickly unite a large number of workers in the socialist movement in the short term, but this was by no means a permanent solution. In the long run, it would weaken the thoroughness of the working class revolution and the workers' movement would eventually fail without the guidance of scientific socialism.

Marx therefore took an intensive part in the discussions of the association and tried to find common ground between the different factions, adopting a strategy of both unity and struggle against the members and leaders of the different schools. The main focus was on unity, treating them realistically and trying to win them over to a change of ideology, while firmly isolating and breaking up with the few who persisted in their misguided positions and betrayed the interests of the proletariat. In this way, the attempt was made to try to turn this "centre of liaison and cooperation" into a central organ of the international activities of the working class in all countries and to turn the First International into a great lever for the proletarian revolution.

As a result of the determined struggle of communists such as Marx, some international leaders and the general membership, who had previously believed in non-scientific socialism, began to turn towards accepting, or at least moving closer to, scientific socialism. On the basis of Marx's report, at the 1868 Brussels Congress, the First International decided to argue for the communal ownership of the means of production and the need for working-class political action. This marked the decline and failure of Proudhonism. At the Hague Congress of 1872, the last general assembly of the Association, Engels made a report on his investigation into the destructive activities of the Bakunin group, pointing out that it was the splitting up of the International Workers' Association was which was contrary to the historical mission of the proletariat, not the destruction of the capitalist system of exploitation. On the basis of Engels' report, the Congress expelled the Bakuninists from the First International.

At the same time, the First International actively supported and led the workers' struggles for class rights, the struggles for liberation of oppressed peoples and the democratic movements in various countries. Although the First International never became a "powerful machine" to lead revolutions in other countries or a "great lever" of proletarian revolution, it spread Marxist revolutionary ideas, sowed the seeds of revolution and gave birth to its "spiritual child" in the Paris Commune.

In the 1860s France was facing a serious political, economic and national crisis. In 1870, after a crushing defeat in the Franco-Prussian War, the people of Paris overthrew the Second Empire and established the Third Republic. However, the newly formed bourgeois government betrayed national interests externally, opposed the proletariat internally and attempted to disarm the workers. In this context, the Parisian proletariat led a heroic uprising on 18 March 1871, and on 28 March founded the Paris Commune, the first proletarian regime in the world.

The Paris Commune did not come into being under the direct leadership of the First International, nor was its creation the fruit of any prior planning. But its revolutionary activities embodied the principles of the First International concerning the seizure of power by the proletariat, and it was the first heroic attempt by the proletariat to destroy the old state apparatus and establish a new democratic regime of its own. In terms of regime building, the old army and police were abolished, as were the bourgeois courts and parliament to be replaced by a national self-defence army, along with the working class's own security, judicial and legislative institutions; it was stipulated that public officials were to be democratically elected and that the people had the right to supervise and dismiss them. In socio-economic terms, the factories of fugitive capitalists were confiscated and handed over to workers' cooperatives to look after railway transport and munitions production; the salaries of public officials were limited to a maximum of 6,000 francs a year, which was the maximum wage for workers. Unfortunately, instead of proposing and establishing a system of public ownership, taking over the Bank of France, marching on Versailles, making contact with revolutionaries in the provinces and mobilising the peasantry, the Commune inappropriately busied itself with elections. This led directly to the dispersal of forces, financial constraints and isolation, and gave the reactionaries a breathing space. As a result, the commune lasted only 72 days and was defeated on 27 May when the last 147 members of the commune died in action in the cemetery of Père Lachaise.

Although the Paris Commune lasted for a short time, it left behind many valuable practical lessons and explorations. Marx made a careful and systematic summary of this and gained a thorough and comprehensive understanding of the problems of the governance issues facing a working-class party. On 30 May 1871, Marx directly adopted the vocabulary of the Communist Manifesto in the open manifesto of the General Committee of the International, *The French Civil War*, and for the first time systematically and openly propounded the principles of scientific communism to the proletariat. He positively acknowledged the great initiative of the Paris Commune in dispossessing the dispossessors and handing over the factories of fugitive entrepreneurs to workers' cooperatives. He spoke highly of the first attempt to establish a new proletarian state after the Commune Revolution; he also made important amendments and additions to the Communist Manifesto in the light of the practical experience of the Paris Commune and proposed the revolutionary principle of "perpetuity". This was that: "the working class cannot simply take over the ready-made state apparatus and use it to achieve its aims."[43] The proletariat must use violent revolution to destroy and smash the old state apparatus and establish proletarian power. At the beginning of the First International, Marx had believed that the development of the workers' movement in various European countries had reached the moment when it was possible to achieve the political goal of uniting the proletariat throughout the world, and that the purpose of the International was therefore "to replace those socialist or semi-socialist sects with a genuine fighting organisation of the working class"[44]. In the 1860s and 1870s, however, industrialisation and globalisation brought about not only the development of the workers' movement but also the flourishing of European nationalism and the widespread establishment and consolidation of nation states. The major countries of Western Europe and North America had largely completed their transformation from ancient to modern states on the basis of reunification, and some of the less industrially developed countries of northern and eastern Europe and other industrially underdeveloped countries had also begun to create modern nation states, with the concept of the fatherland becoming increasingly popular. As a result of this, the workers' movements in each country took a path of independent development, and workers' unions developed from individual or small groups to national participation as a whole. Thus, the proletarian movement entered a new period of building proletarian parties in the different nation states.

In August 1869, the Social Democratic Workers' Party of Germany was founded in Eisenach, the first proletarian party in the world to exist within a nation state. In the Gotha Programme, adopted in May 1875 when it merged with the Lassallle faction, the German party clearly positioned itself as "first and foremost within the modern nation state", leaving "the international brotherhood of nations" as a secondary or future matter.

As originally conceived, and in the light of the actual development of the workers' movement at the time, Marx saw the communist party as a broad international alliance of the many proletarian parties that had joined the First International Workers' Association. This is why he said that the Gotha Programme was permeated by Lassalle's "narrowest of national views" and "said nothing about the international responsibilities of the German working class!"[45] However, it cannot be overlooked that the modern nation-state was beginning to take a central role at the heart of the emerging international order, and that nationhood was beginning to override class in its influence on political activity. Marx revised his thinking in time and proposed the idea of establishing proletarian parties in various countries.

In this way, the struggle between the different schools of thought and factions within the International became increasingly intense and divided, inhibited by nationalism and the repression and siege by governments after the defeat of the Paris Commune. Marx believed that the International was no longer suitable for the developing national workers' movements and had become obsolete. Later, he concluded: "It did once lead the movement. But in recent years socialism has grown so vigorously that the existence of the International is no longer necessary. Newspapers have begun to be published in various countries to exchange views with each other, and this is the only connection between the parties of the different countries ...... The interests of the socialist parties of the different countries are not the same."[46] Engels shared Marx's views on the demise of the First International, but he had a different vision of future action. He believed that the next goal "would be a purely communist International" and still advocated unity of action and policy of the working class in all countries, a common plan, to: "ensure the unity of goals and the overall consistency of the methods adopted to achieve the common goal of the working class's own liberation of itself"[47].

After 1872, Marx and Engels suggested that the General Committee should be relocated to New York and facilitated the dissolution of the First International. In 1876 the First International was formally dissolved in Philadelphia, after which it split into anarchist and social-democratic factions, and the development of the proletarian party entered a period of major strategic and tactical adjustment.

It should be said that the period of the First International and the Paris Commune was the richest and most comprehensive period in which Marx and Engels led and influenced the practical activities of the proletarian parties. It was also a completely new stage in the development of their theory of political parties, especially the theory of the communist party in power. In summary, the main ideological views on the rules of governance of the communist party are as follows.

First, the establishment of an independent proletarian party is the basic condition for the victory of the proletarian revolution. Marx and Engels argued that building the proletariat's own party is the primary issue in the struggle of the working class, and that "only by organising itself as a political party distinct from and opposed to all the old parties founded by the proletariat can it act as a class"[48]. The experience of the Paris Commune shows that without a revolutionary party the working class cannot seize power, and even if it does, it cannot retain it. For this reason, it was necessary to carry out political struggle to prepare and educate workers for the revolutionary seizure of power. This requires political struggle to prepare and educate the workers for the revolution to seize power. "The best way to do this is to establish a proletarian party in each country with its own policy, a policy which is clearly different from that of other parties because it must express the conditions for the liberation of the working class. The details of such a policy can vary according to the particular circumstances of each country."[49] With an independent party, one can counteract the bourgeois parties without being the tail of the bourgeoisie.

Second, the dictatorship of the proletariat is a necessary condition and a necessary stage for the realisation of communism. Summing up the lessons learned from the anarchist controversy with Bakunin and the failure of the Paris Commune, and through a concrete analysis of the history of the emergence, development and evolution of the bourgeois state apparatus, Marx proposed that the proletariat must use revolutionary violence to destroy and smash the old state apparatus and implement the dictatorship of the proletariat. For "between capitalist society and communist society there is a period of revolutionary transformation from the former to the latter. In line with this period, there is also a period of political transition in which the state can only be the revolutionary dictatorship of the proletariat "[50].

Third, the fundamental task of the communist party in power is to turn the state into a semi-state as soon as possible, until the state dies out on its own and enters the first stage of communism. In other words, in communism and its first stage (that is to say the socialist stage, according to Lenin), there will be no state. At that point, the dictatorship of the proletariat under communist rule will begin to be replaced by the "community of free men" and its social administration organisations.

Fourth, there must be a radical break with traditional ownership and traditional attitudes. To break with traditional ownership means to centralise the means of production currently in the hands of the capitalists, in the hands of the state, and to establish a system of public ownership; to break completely with traditional ideas means to eliminate the ideology and cultural ideas of the bourgeois state and to establish a new proletarian culture. During the period of communist rule, the main social contradiction that must be resolved is that between the proletariat and the bourgeoisie, which means eradicating the economic basis on which the bourgeoisie exists and eliminating the bourgeoisie.

Fifth, social productive forces must be vigorously developed. During the period when the communist party is in power, in the process of socialist transformation of the private ownership of the means of production, it was necessary to vigorously develop social productivity and increase the total amount of productive forces as soon as possible, so as to consolidate the state power of the dictatorship of the proletariat. The reason why Marx and Engels came to this major conclusion is inseparable from their historical materialist perspective. According to historical materialism, productive forces determine the relations of productivity and the sum of the relations of productivity constitute the economic base of a society, which in turn determines the superstructure of society. Therefore, social productive forces are the most basic, fundamental and dynamic part of the entire social structure, and any society in which they are stagnant will suffer major losses and disasters.

Sixth, disparity in income must be resolutely eliminated. Marx and Engels appreciated the fact that all public officials from the top to the bottom of the Paris Commune were only "paid the equivalent of a worker's wage" and fully recognised that "all the privileges and official allowances formerly enjoyed by the high and prominent officials of the state disappeared with the disappearance of these people themselves."[51] For Marx and Engels, disparity in income was a fundamental feature of the old society. When the communist party comes to power, it must eliminate this social phenomenon.

Seventh, we must ensure that the people are the masters of their own house and prevent the working-class parties from changing from "social servants" to "social masters". One of the core principles of the theory of governance is who governs for whom. Marx and Engels believed that, after victory in the revolution, the people must be the masters of the country. Ever since mankind entered class society, all the previously created states were essentially controlled by the ruling class, and universal elections would lead to their disintegration. Regarding the heroic attempt of the Paris Commune, Marx and Engels commented: "The commune was composed of municipal councillors elected by universal suffrage in each district of Paris. These members were accountable to the electorate and could be removed at any time. Naturally, most of them were workers or recognised representatives of the working class."[52] The fact that they were universally elected and could be removed at any time shows that the real owners of the commune were the people, while the municipal councillors were only their elected clerks and attendants.

Eighth, a lean and efficient organ of state power must be established. After the proletariat has smashed the old state apparatus, what form of administration should it adopt? Marx summed up the experience of the revolution in the Paris Commune and pointed out that the commune was "essentially the government of the working class, the product of the struggle between the producer class and the possessor class, and a political form that has finally been found to enable the economic emancipation of labour."[53] "The commune is a practical rather than a parliamentary institution and it is both an executive and a legislature at the same time."[54] This shows that Marx opposed the political system of separation of powers and advocated the establishment of a political structure that integrates parliamentary and executive powers. Unity of parliament and executive means that the executive is the executive body of the legislature, accountable to it and supervised by it.

Ninth, one must master one's own weapons. "The first prerequisite for the establishment of the dictatorship of the proletariat is a proletarian army. The working class must win the right to its own emancipation on the battlefield."[55] In *The French Civil War*, Marx pointed out that: "Paris was able to resist only because the siege freed it from the army and replaced it with a national self-defence force composed mainly of workers. This circumstance had then to be made an institution, so the first decree of the commune was to abolish the standing army and replace it with an armed proletariat."[56] An important lesson from the failure of the Paris Commune is that, sadly, it 'wasted precious time' organising democratic elections instead of quickly destroying the Versailles army. According to Engels: "A revolution is when one part of the population uses the barrel of the gun, the bayonet, the cannon, and so uses very powerful and authoritative means to force the other part of the population to accept its will. The party that achieves victory must rely on the fear it has created in the reactionaries with its weapons to maintain its rule if it does not wish to lose the gains it has striven for."[57] Consequently, the fact that the working class is in control of its own arms and that it is only by destroying counter-revolutionary violence with revolutionary violence that it can seize power and consolidate it, should be a universal law of proletarian revolution that the communist party must always bear in mind.

Tenth, the principle of democratic centralism must be applied. During this period, although Marx and Engels did not explicitly advance the concept of democratic centralism, they did put forward its basic ideas and practised specific related institutional mechanisms. In order to safeguard democracy, they advocated the implementation of an electoral system, a congress system, a replacement system, and a system of equality of party members, while at the same time emphasising the role of centralised leadership and authority of the party. In accordance with the constitution of the International, an open congress should be held once a year, that is, an annual meeting of the party congress, but as conditions were not suitable, they initiated a secret congress in time to solve the political and organisational problems faced by the International at that time. They pointed out that a proletarian party must have a unified programme, revolutionary authority and discipline, and a central, regional and branch organisational system; that all members of the party must obey all party resolutions and implement the party's constitution; that "the Paris Commune was destroyed because of the lack of concentration and authority"; also "in order to carry on the struggle, we must pinch together all our forces and concentrate them on the same point of attack."[58] Engels also argued the necessity of "on the one hand, a certain authority, however formed, and on the other, a certain obedience, both of which we have to accept, regardless of the material conditions under which social organisation and the circulation of production and products take place". Those who argued for "the abolition of the authoritative political state in one fell swoop, before the social conditions that gave rise to it have been removed "[59] were either confused or reactionary.

Eleventh, it is necessary to adapt the form of party organisation to historical conditions and the requirements of the task. On the basis of combining scientific socialism with the workers' movement, Marx and Engels were involved in leading the creation of several forms of proletarian party organisations, which greatly contributed to the development of the international communist movement. In the process, they both adhered to the idea that the tasks of the party are determined by historical conditions, and that when historical conditions change, the tasks of the party must change with them, and the form of party organisation must also adapt to those changes. In practice, this also meant that they raised and initially resolved the major question of how to ensure continuous improvement in the party's leadership.

(IV) GUIDING INDEPENDENT PARTY BUILDING IN THE NATION-STATE AND THE UNDERSTANDING AND EXPLORATIONS OF MARX AND ENGELS IN THEIR LATER YEARS

From the 1860s and 1870s, capitalist society entered a new historical period with the rapid development of big industry in Western Europe and the gradual move from free competitive capitalism to organised, monopolistic capitalism. "What followed was an era of unprecedented growth of the workers' movement in all countries of the world, that is, an era of broadening of the workers' movement and the establishment of mass socialist workers' parties based in individual nation states."[60] Following the establishment of the unified Socialist Workers' Party of Germany in 1875, the Socialist Workers' Party (later renamed the Socialist Labour Party) was established in the USA in 1876, the Workers' Party in France in 1879 and the Social Democratic Federation in Britain in 1884. Socialist parties or organisations were established in other countries such as Denmark, the Czech Republic, Spain, Italy, the Netherlands, Belgium, Russia and Sweden. At the same time, the economic and political development of capitalism during this period was of a "peaceful" nature, and in some countries the proletariat fought for universal suffrage, "one of the sharpest weapons of all".

In response to this development, Marx and Engels lent their full enthusiasm, support and active guidance to the building of proletarian parties in France, Germany and other major capitalist countries. Marx believed that the first task was to educate the people and inculcate class consciousness. After Marx's death in March 1883, Engels, who had helped him so much in his life and career, continued their unfinished work. On the one hand, he worked to complete the codification of *Das Kapital* using Marx's manuscripts; on the other, he guided the work of the German Social Democratic Party from afar and directed the establishment of the Second International.

In its early days, the Second International played a positive role in spreading Marxism and promoting the development of the workers' movement in various countries. Historically, however, the Second International revealed its fatal weaknesses from its inception: it had no programme, no constitution, no formal unified top-to-bottom organisation, no unified party literature and a complex membership structure. This led to some rightist tendencies in its early activities. The right-leaning opportunists in the German party openly preached class collaboration and advocated social reform instead of social revolution. In response, Engels published a series of treatises: "Introduction to the French Civil War", "Critique of the Draft Erfurt Programme", "The French-German Peasant Question", "Introduction to the French Class Struggle", and so on, which criticised all the denials of the Marxist programme and Bernsteinism, which advocated a "peaceful transition" and defended Marxism's ideas about the proletarian revolution and the proletariat. Engels died in London in August 1895.

Compared with the previous period, a distinctive feature of the thinking and practice of Marx and Engels during this period is that they focused on a comprehensive examination and in-depth study of the new changes in the capitalist world, made timely adjustments to the strategic and tactical principles of working-class parties, stressed the link between theory and practice, opposed and overcame the tendency of dogmatism, and further developed and perfected the doctrine of the proletarian party.

The theory of the two stages of communism and the transitional period. The *Critique of the Gotha Programme* begins by dividing communist society into two stages of development: the primary stage and the advanced stage. Marx pointed out that after the proletariat had succeeded in seizing power, it was necessarily the primary stage of communism that it entered. At this point society still bears in many ways the traits of the old capitalist society from which it has just emerged. The advanced stage of communist society, on the other hand, is based on the great enrichment of social productive forces. He also pointed out that after the proletariat had risen to the ruling class, there was bound to be a transitional stage in which efforts had to be made to transform society as a whole, and that it was inappropriate to talk about "freedom".

On the ways and means of achieving the party's programme and goals. In the 1860s, Marx and Engels considered universal suffrage in countries like Germany to be an instrument of bourgeois deception and a trap. By the 1870s and 1880s, based on the achievements made by Germany in the use of universal suffrage, they argued that "universal suffrage has given us a remarkable means of action."[61] Engels further argued that "thanks to the German workers' adept use of universal suffrage, introduced in 1866, the amazing growth of the party was revealed to the world in indisputable numbers. ... They gave the comrades of the world a new weapon - the sharpest of weapons... one of the sharpest weapons of all"[62]. He argued that, at that stage, the working-class parties should use the electoral movement to fight the bourgeoisie, and use the democratic rights they had won from the ruling class, to win over the masses, to build up and train revolutionary forces, and to prepare for the decisive battle ahead. At the same time, Engels also argued that the use of universal suffrage by the workers' parties was only a tactic of struggle, not a renunciation of violent revolution and of their own revolutionary rights. He repeatedly exhorted the working-class parties to "understand that the revolutionary right is the only real 'historical right.'"[63] The proletariat had to constantly increase its revolutionary power beyond what the capitalist system could control, and preserve this power carefully within the proletarian movement until the time of the decisive battle with the bourgeoisie. Once the bourgeoisie resorted to violence, the proletariat must use revolutionary violence against counter-revolutionary violence.

On the construction of proletarian power after coming to power. Engels emphasised that "breaking up the old state apparatus" did not mean total "destruction", but that some of the rational elements of bourgeois democracy should be adapted and used. He said: "Apart from England and Switzerland, the Netherlands was the only Western European country in the 16th to 18th centuries that was not a monarchy; it therefore had certain advantages, among them that what remained of local and provincial autonomy did not have the smell of real bureaucracy evident in France or Prussia. This is of great benefit to the development of the national character at the time and in the future; with a few changes, the labour force (the people) can establish here the free autonomy which should be our best weapon in the transformation of the mode of production."[64]

On the construction of the communist party itself. In terms of guiding ideology, Engels stressed the need for the proletarian party to link theory with practice and rejected a dogmatic approach to Marxism. He repeatedly raised criticisms of the dogmatic approach of the "youth wing" of the German party, which treated Marxism as a cure for all ills: "Our theory is a developing theory, not a dogma that must be memorised and repeated mechanically."[65]

He taught the youth to combine theory with practical actions and demanded that revolutionaries should take part in all the genuine universal working-class movements and consider the actual starting points of those movements in a pragmatic way. Marx did not specifically address the question of building the cadre contingent of the communist party, and it was Engels who elaborated on it for the first time. He said: "In our party everyone should start as an ordinary soldier; to hold a responsible position in the party it is not enough to have literary skills or theoretical knowledge, or even both; to hold a leading position, one needs to be familiar with the conditions of the party struggle, to master the methods of that struggle, to have tried and tested loyalty and a strong character, and finally to voluntarily include oneself in the ranks of the warriors."[66] "Anyone in a high position has no right to ask others to adopt a different and docile attitude towards themselves"[67] and "There is no future for a party that would rather tolerate any fool's wanton domineering in running the party than dare openly to refuse to recognise him."[68]

On interparty relations after a proletarian party comes to power. Following the establishment of independent proletarian parties in various countries, the question arose of how to deal properly with inter-party relations. Engels applied the viewpoint of proletarian internationalism to advance, for the first time, clear guidelines for the even-handed treatment of proletarian party relations. He pointed out that the relationship between parties should be autonomous and equal. If problems did arise, they must be resolved by negotiation on the basis of democracy and equality. "Any international action must be preceded by consultation as to its substance and form. "[69] On the question of how proletarian parties should handle foreign relations when they come to power, Engels observed that "the victorious proletariat can force no blessings of any kind upon any foreign nation without undermining its own victory by so doing."[70]

Marx once pointed out that "revolution requires passive elements and material foundations. The extent to which a theory is realised in a country is always determined by the extent to which it meets the needs of that country."[71] Marx and Engels lived in the age of steam power and the telegraph, when the proletariat stepped onto the stage of history as an independent political force and the workers' movement was in full swing; but at this time there was no national proletarian party in power, the working class was not yet clearly differentiated, and the technological revolution, led by electrical technology, was still developing. At the same time, as capitalism was also in the early stages of its growth and development, having flourished for only a little more than a hundred years, the system itself was still imperfect, and various social elements were still in a period of friction, leaving Marx and Engels with immature social material for considering and exploring the future of human society. Consequently, Marx and Engels' understanding of the laws governing proletarian parties was mainly derived from their understanding and criticisms of the laws of human social development and the laws governing capitalist parties; it also came from their experience of the initial political practice of reorganising the Communist League, founding the First International and guiding

66

the establishment of working-class parties in various European countries. Their theories on proletarian parties, especially their understanding of the laws of proletarian parties after they come to power, are naturally mostly theoretical arguments formed by deduction, and general guidance, and are mostly either fragmentary or only roughly formulated. At the same time, there were certain inevitable historical limitations and shortcomings, especially in terms of the comprehensive and in-depth theoretical elaboration of such issues as how to prevent people's representatives from becoming rulers, how to start building productive forces, how to cultivate a new conceptual culture, and how to deal with the relationship between different social systems and civilisational systems. These are issues which the communist party is bound to encounter and must resolve after coming to power.

Of course, Marx also pointed out that although the future might not be very clear, "the merit of the new trend of thought lies precisely in the fact that we do not want to anticipate the future dogmatically, but only to discover the new world by criticising the old one". Therefore, he does not advocate "raising any banner of dogmatism, but rather, the opposite"; "if our task is not to conceive of the future and make it fit for all time, then we can know more clearly what it is we should do now, by which I mean we must be ruthlessly critical of everything that currently exists."[72] Marx and Engels' understanding and expression of the laws of communist rule undoubtedly fully reflected their ideology. Therefore, what they left to posterity was more about how the communist party could lead the people to overthrow capitalism through violent revolution, while the question of how to be a good home for the people and govern them well was a subject that communists had to face later.

In conclusion, the laws of building, developing and governing proletarian parties as understood and revealed by Marx and Engels not only laid the foundations for proletarian parties to explore those laws and provided the basic positions and methods, but also foretold that the further exploration of the rules of governance by the proletariat after the victorious revolution would be a historical project full of difficult challenges as well as infinite possibilities.

2

THE SOVIET COMMUNIST PARTY'S INITIAL EXPLORATION OF THE LAWS OF COMMUNIST GOVERNANCE UNDER LENIN

At the end of the 19th century and the beginning of the 20th century, human society began to enter an era of imperialism and proletarian revolution, and as capitalism expanded to the East, the socialist movement followed it. The Russian Marxists, represented by Lenin, combined scientific socialism with the Russian workers' movement to create a new type of political party, seize state power and carry out socialist revolution and construction. In this, they were turning socialist theory into living reality in a concrete way, which greatly promoted the understanding and exploration of the rules of governance by Marxist political parties.

(I) THE BOLSHEVIKS: THE BIRTH OF A NEW PROLETARIAN PARTY

Before 1917, Russia was ruled by the Romanov dynasty, which had been established in 1613. At the end of its reign, despite rapid industrialisation, Russia lagged far behind the other Western powers, was a predominantly agrarian country and its social relations had not undergone any fundamental change. As a result, the bourgeoisie was weak and the bourgeois political parties came into being even later than the proletarian parties.

Just as it straddled Eurasia and sought to balance East and West, Russia in the 19th century was torn between revolution and reform. Most of the country's progressive intellectuals, as represented by Herzen and Chernyshevsky, were populists. They were committed to exposing the suffering of the peasantry and the evils of the capitalist system, favouring the consolidation of rural communes in which all peasants received equal benefits and burdens; they argued that the horrific capitalist stage could be overtaken in Russia and that social revolution was more important than political change. At the same time, some advanced elements of the populists began to study and introduce scientific socialist theory in their struggle against the Tsarist dictatorship. In August 1883, Plekhanov and others founded the first Russian social-democratic organisation, the Society for the Liberation of Labour, in Geneva. They translated and introduced to Russia works of Marx and Engels such as *Wage Labour and Capital, The Poverty of Philosophy* and *Theses on Feuerbach*, and promoted the establishment of socialist groups and Marxist cells in St Petersburg, Moscow, Kiev, Odessa, Kazan and elsewhere. As a result of this, and the fact that the populist defence of the peasant commune had become hopeless in the face of the unstoppable growth of Russian capitalism, many revolutionary intellectuals, including Lenin, began to turn from populism to Marxism.

The spread of Marxism in Russia coincided with the rapid growth of its urban population and the increasing numbers of industrial workers and workers' strikes. From the 1860s to the late 1890s, the rural population increased by about one and a half times, and the urban population doubled. Cities began to play a dominant role in industrial and commercial life, as well as in the political and cultural life of the country. By the beginning of the 20th century, the Russian working class numbered 22 million people (including families), or about 18% of the Russian population, including about three million workers in large industries, mining and transport.[1] The Russian proletariat was mainly made up of bankrupt peasants and craftsmen, with relatively few skilled workers and almost no workers' aristocracy, and the whole group was cohesive and easily organised. Because of the extreme weight of oppression, the sense of resistance was also strong, which nurtured and accumulated a huge reserve of revolutionary energy. It was on this basis that, in November 1895, on Lenin's advice, more than 20 Marxist groups in St Petersburg united to form a secret social-democratic organisation, the Society for the Struggle for the Liberation of the Working Class.

In March 1898, with the encouragement of exiles abroad, the first congress of Russian social-democratic representatives was held secretly in Minsk. It adopted a resolution on the formation of the Russian Social-Democratic Labour Party, elected a Central Committee consisting of Radchenko, Edelman and Kremel, and approved the party's organ and its foreign representative offices, thereby proclaiming the birth of the Russian proletarian party. However, the congress failed to adopt a clear party programme and constitution, or to form a strong leadership. Soon after the congress ended, most of the delegates and members of the central committee were unfortunately arrested and the unified proletarian party of Russia was not really properly established.

For Marx and Engels, the proletariat was supposed to be the natural leader of the communist revolutionary movement. However, Lenin found in the practice of the Russian revolution that "class political consciousness can only be instilled in the workers from outside."[2] The proletariat and the social masses needed education, guidance and leadership, and the leadership of the revolution must and could only be in the hands of professional revolutionaries who were disciplined and loyal to the party; the proletarian party should become a collection of professional revolutionaries, and its members should emphasise not only their class affiliation but also their political loyalty. In order to change the isolation of local organisations, the party must have unified will and action. He began to vigorously argue that the top priority in Russia was to create a secret, lean, strong revolutionary organisation, that is to say, a highly centralised and unified party, and he actively made ideological and organisational preparations for this. In July-August 1903, the Russian Social Democratic Labour Party held its second congress in Brussels and London. The congresses were attended by political exiles such as Lenin and representatives of the Russian underground, as well as social democrats and members of smaller organisations. The main agenda of the congress was the approval of the party programme, the party statutes and the election of the central leadership of the party. Lenin insisted on the creation of a "new type of party" based on democratic centralism, with extremely strict centralisation, iron discipline and tight organisation, to preserve "the firmness, thoroughness and purity of the party", so that the party as a whole could cope with the complex changes in the revolutionary situation and improve its ability to win in the competition for survival. The faction represented by Plekhanov, Martov and Trotsky maintained that Lenin's intention was to eliminate freedom within the party and eventually lead to a personal dictatorship. There were also heated debates on the question of whether to include the dictatorship of the proletariat in the party programme and on the handling of party membership in the party constitution. The result of the vote was that Lenin's view was adopted on the party programme, which included the dictatorship of the proletariat, and his view was rejected on the membership issue, which provided that members did not have to join the party's organisations but only had to work under the "supervision and leadership of the party organs". When it came to the final election of the party's central leadership, some of the delegates opposed to Lenin withdrew from the congress, leaving the pro-Lenin faction with a majority. The Russian

Social Democratic Labour Party then formed two factions, the majority and the minority: "Bolshevik" literally means "member of the majority" and "Menshevik" literally means "member of the minority".

In 1905, during the Russo-Japanese War, the first bourgeois revolution broke out in Russia and Lenin led the Third Congress of the Russian Social Democratic Labour Party in London, which was attended only by the Bolsheviks. The conference set out the strategic line of the Bolsheviks: the bourgeois democratic revolution in Russia must be led by the proletariat, rely on the alliance of workers and peasants, and isolate the bourgeoisie; they must overthrow the Tsarist government through armed insurrection, establish a provisional revolutionary government and realise the democratic dictatorship of the workers and peasants; they must carry out the bourgeois democratic revolution to the end and make the transition to the socialist revolution without delay. The congress re-examined the party constitution, adopted Lenin's provisions on membership, abolished the system of two central organs of the party (the central committee and the central official newspaper) and established the central committee as the central unified leadership of the party. In November of the same year, Lenin secretly returned to Russia to organise the revolutionary struggle in real terms and to actively fight for the party's leadership of the revolution.

After the failure of the revolution, Lenin left Russia in December 1907 and went into exile in Paris and other places in Western Europe. He continued to study Marxism, published a large number of theoretical works, gradually developing his own ideological and theoretical system. This was mainly reflected in his publications before and during this period, *What is to be Done?*, *One Step Forward, Two Steps Back*, *The State and Revolution*, *Materialist and Empiricist Criticism* and other classic works, as well as a series of articles published in the newspaper *Iskra*. These treatises focused on clarifying the pressing issues in the Russian revolutionary movement and systematically expounded the theory of proletarian party building, which became the guiding ideology and guide to action for the Bolsheviks in building and governing the party. The main point was that it was essential to form a solid ideological unity guided by Marxism, and this Marxist ideological unity was a principle that Lenin always adhered to in party building. He said: "Only the doctrines of scientific socialism and class struggle are now revolutionary theories and can serve as the banner of the revolutionary movement."[3] He saw the great significance of revolutionary theory for the proletarian party in three main ways: first, "only a party guided by advanced theory can realise the role of an advanced fighter"[4] and "espousing organisation without ideas is meaningless; it would in fact turn the workers into the poor servants of the ruling bourgeoisie."[5] Second, only by mastering the theoretical weapons of Marxism can we effectively inculcate socialist ideas into the spontaneous workers' movement and realise the union of socialism with the workers' movement. Third, only by adhering to Marxist theory can we draw a line under all opportunism and achieve consolidated ideological party unity. This means that only by unifying party ideology can revolutionary forces be brought together around revolutionary goals and, at the same time, significantly undermine the political legitimacy of hostile forces. Lenin also pointed out that "we are entirely based on Marx's theory" but "in no way do we regard Marx's theory as something immutable and sacrosanct; on the contrary, we are convinced that it merely lays the foundations of a science which socialists, if they do not wish to lag behind real life, should advance in every respect." "For the Russian socialists in particular it is necessary to explore Marx's theory independently because it offers only general guiding principles, the application of which differs specifically in England from France, in France from Germany and in Germany from Russia."[6]

There must be a political programme that upholds the proletarian revolution and the dictatorship of the proletariat. During the founding of the Russian Social Democratic Labour Party, Lenin put forward three draft programmes in 1895-1896, 1899 and 1902. In the course of writing these, Lenin systematically discussed the question of the party's programme in the light of the conditions of the time and the particular characteristics of Russia. He believed that the party programme was the basis for the consolidation and development of the party. It was necessary to overcome the fragmentation of the social-democratic movement, to consolidate the links between the socialist intelligentsia and the ideologically-aware workers, to dispel misunderstandings in the world of public opinion, to make the people understand what the social-democrats were and what their demands were, and to thereby realise the party's leadership over all democratic elements in Russia; it was also necessary to overcome differences of opinion within the party, to consolidate ideological consensus, and to thereby strengthen the party and develop the proletarian cause. To this end, the party's programme must unequivocally express the ideas of communist revolution, the dictatorship of the proletariat and the proletarian class struggle, and never "present the masses with even a single ambiguous slogan"[7]; it must specify the objectives of the recent struggle in order to avoid petty-bourgeois and anarchist misinterpretations of the tasks of the proletarian struggle; it must follow the principle of unity between the experience of the international workers' movement and the characteristics of the Russian revolution.

The material unity of the organisation must be used to consolidate the unity of thought. Lenin believed that the ideological unity of the proletarian party, formed on Marxist principles, could only be consolidated by the material unity of the organisation, and that only under such conditions could the proletariat become an invincible force. To this end, Lenin repeatedly called for a well organised, strictly disciplined, consolidated and centralised party, capable of leading both preparatory struggles and any sudden outbreaks, and also of leading the final showdown. He also stressed that "the proletariat has no weapon in the struggle for power other than organisation."[8] Lenin followed the theoretical principles of Marx and Engels on the party and comprehensively expounded the organisational principles of the new proletarian party on the basis of a careful summary of past lessons. This included: first, the party is the advanced force of the working class. "The party is the advanced, aware layer of the proletarian class, its vanguard. This vanguard is ten times, a hundred times or more, more powerful than its actual numbers."[9] Therefore, it acts as leader to other workers' organisations, such as the trade unions, which should work under the leadership and supervision of the party. "It is clearly absolutely impossible to confuse the party, which is the advanced unit of the working class, with the class as a whole."[10] Second, the party is an organised force of the working class. Every member of the party must join one of the party's organisations, obey the party's resolutions and observe its discipline. Lenin pointed out that the party should be the sum of its organisations, in a tightly controlled system. Only when all its members are organised as a unified force can the party actually lead the struggle of the working class and direct it towards a general goal. Cosequently, he asserted that the party is the "highest form of organisation" of the working class. Third, the party must be organised on the principles of democratic centralism. According to Lenin: "The Russian Social Democratic Labour Party is democratically organised. This means that all party affairs are conducted by all party members, directly or through representatives, on an equal footing and without exception; and that all responsible persons, all members of the party leadership, and all representative bodies are elected, must report to the members and can be replaced." (1) But the implementation of the "principle of broad democracy" involves two necessary conditions: "First, complete openness; second, all offices are elected. It is ridiculous to speak of democracy without openness, and this openness must not be limited to the members of the organisation." The Russian Federation did not have such conditions, and the complete democratisation of the party was only empty talk, as it required "unanimity of action, and freedom of discussion and criticism."[11] The principle of democratic centralism was applied, which meant that the minority was subordinated to the majority, that the highest organ of the party was the congress, that the central organ of the party was directly elected by the congress, that all party publications had to be absolutely subordinate to the party congress and the corresponding central or local organisations, and that the rights of any minority within the party must be clearly defined.[12]

The leadership of the revolution had to be kept firmly in hand. The Mensheviks believed that the revolution in Russia at that time was a bourgeois revolution, that the bourgeoisie should take the leadership and that the Duma should be used to carry out reforms. In exchange for the legitimate existence of the party, they repeatedly demanded the complete abolition of the secret revolutionary party of the working class. For this reason, they were known as the liquidation faction. Lenin "believed that an independent, uncompromising Marxist party of the revolutionary proletariat was the only guarantee for the victory of socialism, and the broad road to victory. Therefore, at no time, even at the most revolutionary moments, will we give up the complete independence of the Social Democratic Party or the complete uncompromising nature of our ideological system."[13] He stressed that in a country like Russia, the working class was suffering not so much from the development of capitalism as from its lack of development. The Russian proletariat must therefore both actively participate in the bourgeois democratic revolution and, in the process, fight for the leadership of the revolution, combining legitimate forms of struggle with clandestine ones. Otherwise, the revolution would fail because of the two-faced nature of the bourgeoisie. In the light of the relevant ideas of Marx and Engels and the class situation in Russia, he also pointed out that the peasants were capable of thoroughly and wholeheartedly supporting the democratic revolution and were reliable allies of the proletariat; that only by forming an alliance with the peasants could the proletariat win the democratic revolution; and that the alliance of workers and peasants was the basic condition for realising the leadership of the proletariat.

In January 1912, the Sixth National Congress of the Russian Social Democratic Labour Party was held in Prague. It was decided that the Menshevik abolitionists and other opportunist factions would be expelled from the party, ending the coexistence of the Bolsheviks and the Mensheviks in the same party. Thereafter, the Bolsheviks everywhere broke off their relations with the Mensheviks and began to grow into an independent, unified proletarian party called the Russian Social Democratic Labour Party[14], which gradually became the core leadership of the Russian Communist Revolution.

(II) THE VICTORY OF THE OCTOBER REVOLUTION IN RUSSIA: SOCIALISM CHANGES FROM THEORY TO PRACTICE.

In March 1861, the Russian Tsar Alexander II approved the decree and proclamation abolishing serfdom. With that reform in full swing, the Russian monarchy began to evolve into a bourgeois monarchy. Both the bourgeoisie and the Tsarists made economic development a priority and a close economic relationship was forged between the two. This relationship was beneficial to both sides, as the bourgeoisie needed the political power of the autocracy to protect and support its development, and the Tsarists needed the bourgeoisie to develop the economy, increase national power and achieve social stability. This political situation also resulted in the conservatism, weakness and disorganisation of the Russian bourgeoisie, who for a long time did not concern themselves with changing the country's power structure and seizing power. In the end, however, the dictatorial Tsarist regime and the bourgeoisie represented two different eras and two different forces, and it was inevitable that the conflicts between them would eventually intensify.

In 1903, the local self-government bureaus of Russia's 25 provinces submitted petitions to allow them to elect their own representatives to participate in the work of the legislature. These self-government bureaus were institutions that emerged after the serfdom reforms of 1861 as elected bodies to manage local economic, healthcare and some national education matters, and were mainly controlled by the Tsarist government but had some independence. In January 1904, the first national political organisation of the Russian bourgeoisie, the Union of Liberation, was announced, advocating the promulgation of a constitution, the establishment of the principles of civil liberties, the establishment of a legal order and the convening of a constitutional assembly to discuss the form of state administration. Under the agitation of the bourgeoisie to implement democratic constitutionalism, petitions continued in various places, and the tsarist government was at a loss for a suitable response. This resulted in the "Bloody Sunday" incident in which more than a thousand people died on 22 January 1905. The situation forced the Tsar to agree to reforms. On 30 October, he announced the implementation of a constitutional monarchy, convened the State Duma, lifted party bans, and guaranteed citizens' freedom of belief, speech, assembly, and association.

The bourgeoisie cheered the Tsar's announcement. Believing that their time had come, they formed political parties in anticipation of the forthcoming elections to the Constituent Assembly. It was against this background that the more prominent Russian bourgeois parties, such as the

Constitutional Democratic Party and the October Party, emerged. According to Lenin, this marked the "first time in the revolution that the Russian bourgeoisie began to form itself as a class, forming a unified and conscious political force."[15] At the same time, soviets of workers' deputies, soviets of rural deputies and even soviets of soldiers' deputies emerged in Russia. These soviets began as bodies to lead revolutionary strikes and later developed into a rudimentary form of state power.

History has proved countless times that "the ruling class will never cede its power to the oppressed class"[16].

The constitutional monarchy introduced by the Tsarist regime had no substance and did not allow the people any real right to participate in politics. The Tsar's real intention was to return Russia to the authoritarian totalitarian rule of the 17th century. The Fundamental Law of the State, published in May 1906, gave the Tsar and the Duma powers that worked hand in hand. The signing of international treaties and the command of the army and navy remained the prerogative of the Tsar's government, while the Duma's role was limited to turning the Council of State into a second chamber, and draft laws had to be approved by both the Duma and the Council of State before they could be submitted to the Tsar. Obviously, such an institutional arrangement could not meet the needs inherent in the development and progress of Russian society.

In July 1914, the First World War broke out and Europe split into two armed camps. The brutal war not only plunged the people of many countries into misery but also deepened the split in the international workers' movement. In fact, after the death of Engels in 1895, contradictions and differences arose among the social democrats of various countries on such major issues as how to view the new changes in capitalism and determine the goals and path of socialist revolution. Between 1907 and 1910 there were between 2,000 and 2,500 peasant revolts each year, and in 1910 there were over 6,000. The number of strikers was 100,000 in 1911, 1 million in 1912, nearly 1.27 million in 1913 and 1.3 million in the first half of 1914. Moreover, 1.5 million people left Russia in the decade between 1900 and 1910.[17]

The faction represented by Bernstein, Macdonald and Otto Powell began a complete revision of Marxism. They argued that, with the advent of the second industrial revolution, society did not become increasingly divided into two opposing classes, as Marx had analysed, but that the social structure became increasingly complex, with the middle class being maintained and heavily supplemented by a "new middle class" of employees and civil servants, due to the increased tasks of private economic management and public administration. The working class itself showed a tendency towards increasing internal differentiation in terms of education, occupational status and income, but not overall towards increasing impoverishment. The emergence of monopolistic organisations caused the easing of the capitalist economic crisis; socialism became a long-term construction task and, with socialisation no longer an end in itself, democracy became the only viable path to socialism.

The faction represented by Karl Kautsky advanced the theory of 'ultra-imperialism'. They argued that imperialism was a product of highly developed industrial capitalism and a policy of expansion of the bourgeoisie and its governments into agricultural areas; when this imperialist policy, characterised by a form of violent expansion, changed from a means of developing capitalism to a means of impeding it, it could be replaced by a policy of "ultra-imperialism", a policy of joint exploitation of the whole world by the various imperialist powers, and imperialism would enter a new phase, moving from peace into warfare. Therefore, "ultra-imperialism may temporarily also bring about an era of new hopes and expectations within capitalism" and "it is premature to speak of the complete and final bankruptcy of capitalism, even if only morally."[18] As a result of this, in the Reichstag, the French Parliament and the parliaments of other countries, the socialist parties in many of them voted for war in the name of "defending the motherland", and some socialists among the workers joined in the mobilisation for war, as did others. In fact, the war was a profound reflection of the crisis and limitations of the capitalist process.

Lenin began to study the problem of imperialism at the end of the 19th century, and the realities of the international communist movement after the outbreak of the war prompted him to intensify his research, writing such works as *Imperialism is the Highest Stage of Capitalism* and *On the Slogan for a United States of Europe* in order to theoretically condemn world capitalism to death. He argued that monopoly capitalism did not change the essence of capitalism and that monopolies did not eliminate capitalist economic crises; on the contrary, the contradictions of capitalism became increasingly acute and "imperialism is a special historical stage of capitalism. This characteristic is divided into three aspects: (1) imperialism is monopoly capitalism; (2) imperialism is parasitic or decaying capitalism; (3) imperialism is dying capitalism."[19] Based on this judgement, Lenin put forward a new conclusion about the socialist revolution in the overall strategy of the proletarian world revolution: "the imbalance of economic and political development is the absolute law of capitalism."[20] This imbalance will inevitably lead to internecine imperialist war and produce weak points in imperialist domination, giving the opportunity to break through the imperialist front and seize victory in the proletarian revolution. As a result, "socialism cannot be victorious in all countries at the same time. It will triumph first in one country or in a few countries"[21] and Russia was the weak link in the imperialist system. Based on the above judgement, Lenin's central strategic slogan abroad was: "Turn imperialist wars into domestic wars" and "Make the government of this country lose in war". The intention was to link the war with the revolution and to use the ruling class crisis caused by the war to speed up the revolutionary process in the country.

In 1915, after Germany and the Austro-Hungarian Empire had thrown their weight on the battlefield against Russia, the country's economic and technological base, corrupt government, isolated diplomacy and poor weaponry led to repeated defeats, heavy losses and the depletion of its forces. By August, Russia had lost 3.5 million men on the front line and a large part of its economically and strategically important territory.[22] The national economy was also severely damaged, with fuel scares, transport paralysis, barren land and food shortages. By the end of January 1917, Petrograd had only 10 days' worth of flour, and meat had already disappeared from the market. War and famine threatened the livelihoods of millions of people. In order to keep the war going and save the monarchy, the Tsarist government tried to make a separate peace with Germany, establish a military dictatorship in the country and intensify the repression of the revolutionary movement. All this led to a deep resentment of Tsarist rule among all sectors of society, and the soldiers became so war-weary and anti-war that two million Russian troops deserted in early 1917.[23]

In March 1917 there was a huge wave of revolt in Russia, protesting against food shortages and soaring prices, which developed from a general strike into an armed uprising. The crowds gathered with slogans such as "Down with the war", "Down with the Tsarist government" and "Against hunger"; the troops deployed to suppress them refused to fire on the insurgents and some deserted to join the workers. As a result, the workers and soldiers joined forces to organise combat teams to occupy municipal offices. On 12 March, the Mensheviks, Bolsheviks and the Socialist Revolutionary Party, which had the support of the peasants, united to form the Petrograd Soviet of Workers' and Soldiers' Deputies, which formed a 12-member executive committee to carry out the functions of the All-Russian leadership. They gradually received the positive support of more than 500 soviets throughout the country. On the 15th, the Executive Committee of the Soviet reached an agreement with the Council of the Interim State Duma to set up a provisional government headed by Duke Georgy Lvov and, following the example of the European revolutions, called for the election of a constitutional assembly through the universal suffrage of men, to be held at the end of 1917. On the same day, Nicholas II signed his abdication and passed the throne to his younger brother, Grand Duke Mikhail Alexandrovich. On the 16th, Mikhail also announced his abdication, and the Romanov dynasty, which had ruled Russia for over 300 years, retired from the stage of history. According to the traditional Russian calendar, the month was February, hence the name "February Revolution".

Lenin believed that the overthrow of Tsarist rule was the result of a combination of forces. He said: "The first stage of this revolution showed us above all that there were two forces working together against the Tsarist system: on the one hand, the entire Russian bourgeoisie and landowners with all their unthinking followers, plus all their aware leaders, as well as the ambassadors and assorted capitalists of France and the United Kingdom; on the other hand, the Soviets of Workers; Representatives, which had already begun to include both soldiers and peasants."[24] It was also the case that the Provisional Government set up after the revolution was made up of the leading figures of the bourgeois parties, especially the leaders of the Constitutional Revolutionary Party, the Socialist Revolutionary Party and the October Party. They were unable to solve the difficult problems of inflation, the restoration of transport, and the distribution of land to the peasants; they also believed that a free parliamentary system of government could not be established in Russia unless the German Empire was defeated. So, in external affairs, they still insisted on entering the World War and, especially after Kerensky came to power, decided to organise offensive operations.

In April 1917, Lenin ended his exile abroad and returned to Russia via Germany. He believed that: "to defeat a stronger enemy, we must do our utmost, and at the same time we must be extremely careful, extremely attentive, extremely cautious, and extremely clever to exploit all the 'cracks' between the enemies, even the smallest ones; that means to take advantage of all conflicts in the different interests of the bourgeoisie of various countries and between the various groups or categories of the bourgeoisie in each country. On the other hand, it is necessary to use all opportunities, even the smallest ones, to obtain a large number of allies, temporary, shaky, unstable, unreliable and conditional as they may be. Whoever does not understand this, does not understand either Marxism or modern scientific socialism in the slightest."[25] Therefore, immediately after his return to Russia, he delivered the speech that came to be known as the "April Theses", setting out a clear line and concrete plan for the transition from bourgeois democratic revolution to socialist revolution.

He believed that the current situation in Russia characterised the transition from the first to the second stage of the revolution, that the overthrow of the Tsarist system must be followed by a socialist revolution, that power should be transferred to the proletariat and the poor peasants, that the new state should take the form of a soviet republic rather than a parliamentary republic, that all landowners' land should be confiscated and nationalised, that a national bank should be established and that the soviets should supervise finance, social production and distribution. As the two regimes existed side by side, "no support for the Provisional Government" and "full power to the Soviets" were needed to make the Soviets break with the bourgeois provisional government. He also proposed changing the name of the Russian Social Democratic Labour Party to the Communist Party of Russia and creating a new Communist International.

At first his revolutionary line was questioned within the party but it was then approved at the Seventh All-Russian Congress of the Bolshevik Party in Petrograd in May. On the basis of this programme, the Bolshevik Party launched a vigorous organisational and propaganda campaign among the masses, with Lenin frequently attending and speaking at the meetings.

In June of the same year, the First Congress of the All-Russian Soviets of Workers' and Soldiers' Deputies was held in Petrograd. It was attended by 285 Social Revolutionaries, 248 Mensheviks and 105 Bolsheviks, as well as representatives of smaller socialist parties. At the conference, Lenin proposed that "to transfer power to the revolutionary proletariat with the support of the poor peasants is to transfer the revolutionary struggle for peace in the most reliable way with the least suffering in the history of mankind; it is to transfer it so that the revolutionary workers have the guarantee of power and victory not only in Russia but throughout the world."[26] For their part, the Mensheviks defended the coalition government, claiming that no single party in Russia was willing to take power alone and be responsible for the future fate of the country. Lenin countered tersely by saying that the Bolsheviks were "ready to take full power every minute."[27] In the end, the Mensheviks' views prevailed, and the conference adopted a resolution which ostensibly condemned the war but in fact recognised the interim government's right to launch an offensive on the front line in accordance with its strategy.

During the conference, the Russian army's front-line offensive was launched but soon ended in a crushing defeat with the loss of more than 58,000 men. The news triggered huge demonstrations demanding that the Soviet Executive Committee seize power, which were met with bloody repression by the interim government, bringing an end to the co-existence

of the two regimes. However, the interim government's perverse actions
not only led to its internal disintegration but also provoked a wave of mass
protests, changing the political balance of power in Russia and accelerating
the Bolshevisation of the Soviets.

At the beginning of September, Kornilov, the Supreme Commander of
the Russian Army, started a rebellion and marched into Petrograd in an
attempt to go against the tide, dissolve the Soviets and establish a military
dictatorship. The working class saw no reasonable solution to the problems of ownership, political power, free education, the right to labour and
rest, and no respite for the peasants who suffered from landlessness,
hunger and ransom, working for the rich landowners. This included also
the soldiers who had fled from the war front and began to distrust the
existing political and social institutions in favour of the Bolshevik Party.
The establishment of a new political and economic order through revolution, and in particular the creation of stronger and more centralised leadership and administration, was widely seen as an effective way to end all the
hardships and disasters.

In September-October, as the state and the army were falling apart, the
united Bolsheviks successively gained leadership of the Petrograd,
Moscow, Kazan and Kiev soviets and were on the rise throughout the
country, with Trotsky being elected president of the Petrograd Soviet. If the
Bolsheviks had acted differently, hesitating and watching and waiting, the
people would have abandoned them as they had abandoned the interim
government, and the bourgeoisie would have been given a respite. Lenin
immediately concluded that the moment had arrived and that the Soviet of
Workers' and Soldiers' Deputies, led by the Bolsheviks, could and should
take control of the state through an armed uprising.

At this time, differences arose within the Bolshevik Party on the issue
of whether to hold an armed uprising immediately. Lenin insisted that the
Bolsheviks seize power immediately instead of waiting for the Constituent
Assembly; Zinoviev, Kamenev and others opposed Lenin's ideas and
specific plans for an armed uprising in the belief that the conditions for the
revolution were not yet mature and authorisation from the Soviets should
be sought rather than creating a *fait accompli*. At an important turning
point in history, Lenin quickly made accurate judgments and choices. At
an important turning point in history, Lenin quickly made accurate judgments and choices. He pointed out that Marxism is not a dogma but a
guide to action: "The biggest and most fatal mistake that a Marxist can
make is to treat empty talk as fact and treat false appearances as substance
or something important."[28] He believed that the subjective and objective
conditions for Russia's armed seizure of power had by then matured. In

the end, the Bolshevik Party decided to adopt the policy of armed uprising and once again proposed the slogan "All power to the Soviets". Party organisations at all levels also set to work accordingly.

On the evening of 6 November 1917, Lenin wrote to the Central Committee stating that "whatever happens, the members of the government must be arrested this evening or in the course of this night" and that "history will not forgive those revolutionaries who delay."[29] Late at night, Lenin arrived at the Smolny Palace to lead the armed uprising, and the Workers' Red Guards and revolutionary soldiers under the leadership of the Bolshevik Party, began to occupy strategic positions in Petrograd. On the morning of the 7th, the whole city was in the hands of the insurgents. At around 9.40pm, the cruiser *Aurora* was ordered to open fire, giving the signal to attack the Winter Palace. The Bolsheviks entered the Winter Palace with part of their armed force, fought off sporadic resistance and arrested the last members of the interim government, Kerensky having fled from Petrograd in the morning. At the same time, the Second All-Russian Congress of Workers' and Soldiers' Deputies, which opened at 10pm in the Smolny Palace, declared the overthrow of the interim government led by the Mensheviks of the Social Democratic Party and the mainstream Socialist Revolutionary Party. It was decided that "all local power should be transferred to the local Soviets of Workers', Soldiers' and Peasants' Deputies, which should be responsible for ensuring the real revolutionary order."[30] On the 8th, the ongoing Congress unanimously adopted the "Peace Decree" and the "Land Decree" on the basis of Lenin's report. The "Peace Decree" declared that the Soviet regime recommended to the people of all belligerent countries and their governments that they immediately negotiate a just and democratic peace treaty with no concessions and no reparations. The "Land Decree" proclaimed the abolition of private ownership of land, the confiscation of the land of the landlords, royal family, monasteries and churches, and the return of all land to the state for the use of the peasants. The Congress elected a new Central Executive Committee of the Soviets, consisting of 101 members, 62 of whom were Bolsheviks, 29 leftist social revolutionaries and 10 from other parties. The Congress decided to establish the Council of People's Commissars as the governmental organ of the state, with Lenin as its chairman. The world's first dictatorship of the proletariat was thereby proclaimed.

On 7 November, the Moscow Soviet was also proclaimed, and the Kremlin was captured on the 16th of the same month. The proletarian revolution in Russia began to progress smoothly along the path from the big cities to the small and medium-sized towns and into the vast rural areas. By February and March 1918, in just over four months, Soviet power was established throughout Russia. Lenin called it the period of the triumphant march of the Soviet regime.

Since "neither of the two groups of robbers could immediately lunge at the other or unite against" the Bolsheviks, the Russian communist "revolution had a fortunate moment" and "achieved a glorious march of victory in Europe and Russia."[31] Although the revolution fell silent in Russia more than 70 years later, the October Revolution was undoubtedly an epoch-making event in human history, a turning point as significant as the French Revolution of 1789. It turned the Marxist theory of the proletarian revolution into reality and opened up a new era of proletarian revolution and proletarian party rule, fully demonstrating the decisive role that Marxism, the proletariat and the proletarian party play in leading and driving historical progress. As Russia lies halfway between the West and the latecomers to development, the victory of the October Revolution also opened up a brand-new path of modernisation without capitalism or the Western model, and a new model of united action against the imperialist division and domination of the world. Influenced by this, and especially inspired by Lenin's ideas on national liberation in the colonies and semi-colonies, revolutionary movements for national independence and people's liberation broke out in many late-developing countries. Of course, all this also marked the beginning of a completely new historical period in the proletarian parties' exploration and understanding of the rules of governance.

(III) LENIN'S ELUCIDATION OF THE LAWS OF COMMUNIST PARTY GOVERNANCE IN THE PRACTICE OF CONSOLIDATING POLITICAL POWER

"Never before in history has there been a revolution in which victory was followed by everything going well and people enjoying peace and quiet."[32] After the victory of the October Revolution, although the new regime had been established, it was faced with a serious domestic and foreign crisis. The country was on the brink of extinction; the rebellious Russian landlords and bourgeoisie who were unhappy with their defeat, launched a rebellion, and 14 capitalist countries, including Britain, France, the US and Japan, also began armed intervention, threatening to overthrow the new proletarian regime at any moment. In addition, when they came to power, the Bolsheviks did not have a clear blueprint for construction and a clear strategy for governance, and there were questions, debates and even confusion and disappointment both inside and outside the party. How to overcome the difficulties, resolve the crisis and stay in power for a long time became an urgent question that the Bolsheviks had to answer. As the supreme leader of the ruling party of the Russian working class, Lenin, in the process of consolidating the theoretical and practical achievements of the October Revolution, courageously led the party in the practice of socialist revolution and construction, and conducted a painstaking and remarkable exploration of the rules of communist party governance.

1. Establishment and consolidation of a one-party proletarian regime

After the victory of the October Revolution, the rule of the Soviets was, by nature, only a transitional and provisional government. The consensus in Russia at the time was to commit to the election and convening of the Constitutional Assembly and to see it as the real and legitimate organ of power in the country. Lenin also re-emphasised that the reluctance of the bourgeois provisional government to convene a constituent assembly was one of the reasons for its overthrow, and stressed that the forthcoming constituent assembly was the only organ with the power to decide on national issues. At this time, of course, Lenin was thinking more of using the parliamentary system to consolidate the power he already held. Through November and December 1917, under Bolshevik auspices, the election of delegates to the Constituent Assembly was officially held, with some remote areas delayed until January 1918. As a result, of the 715 delegates elected, 175 were Bolsheviks, 40 were leftist Social Revolutionaries, 86 were representatives of popular groups and the rest were rightist Social Revolutionaries and Mensheviks. Events unfolded in a way that Lenin had not expected, and he pointed out that the members of the Constituent Assembly, elected on the basis of the lists of candidates proposed before the October Revolution, did not reflect the true contrast in class forces after the victory of the October Revolution: "To hand over all power to the Constituent Assembly would be to make a compromise with the vicious bourgeoisie."[33] "A democratic republic, a Constituent Assembly, universal suffrage and so on, constitute, in fact, a bourgeois dictatorship; there is no other way to liberate labour from the oppression of capital than to replace this dictatorship with the dictatorship of the proletariat."[34] It was then decided to dissolve the Constituent Assembly, declare martial law in Petrograd, and send the loyalist Bolshevik army into the capital.

On 18 January 1918 the Constituent Assembly was convened, excluding the Constitutional Democrats. At the meeting, the Bolsheviks, in conjunction with the leftist Socialist Revolutionary Party, presented a draft constitution drawn up under Lenin's supervision and proposed that the Constituent Assembly must dissolve itself after handing over its powers to the Soviet government, as the People's Council had demanded. Naturally, this demand was rejected by the majority of the deputies of the Constituent Assembly. The Bolsheviks withdrew from the conference with the delegates of the leftist Socialist Revolutionary Party and the building was immediately surrounded by armed sailors brought in by the Bolsheviks. On the 19th, the All-Russian Central Executive Committee passed a decree dissolving the Constituent Assembly. On the 23rd , the Third All-Russian Congress of Soviets of Workers' Deputies was held in Petrograd, and on the 26th , the Third All-Russian Congress of Soviets of Peasants' Deputies was also held. Under the leadership of the Bolsheviks, the two congresses unanimously agreed to merge. The combined congresses adopted the Declaration on the Rights of the Exploited Working People, the Decree on the Federal System of the Russian Republic and other decrees, declaring Russia a Soviet Republic of Workers', Soldiers' and Peasants' Deputies and that the country should take the form of a federation of Russian national republics.

In this way, the plans of the rightist Social Revolutionary Party, the Mensheviks and the Constitutional Democrats to form a coalition government were completely crushed and the Soviet became the ruling political organisation of the dictatorship of the Russian proletariat. The All-Russian Congress of Soviets was the highest organ of state governance. Its powers were exercised by the All-Russian Central Executive Committee when the Congress was not in session. The People's Council was responsible to the All-Russian Congress of Soviets and the All-Russian Central Executive Committee and had the right to legislate on its own initiative. The All-Russian Congress of Soviets and its Executive Committee had the right to supervise and replace the government. The Soviet became both a legislative and an executive body.

Of course, there were also leftist Socialist Revolutionaries in the People's Committee who had taken part in the joint seizure of power and supported the dissolution of the Constituent Assembly, and who had a wide influence among the peasants. Because of their different political views, they had serious differences with the Bolsheviks over the organisation of power, the Brest Peace Treaty, grain collection and other such matters. In May 1918, Lenin argued that "now that political power has been seized, maintained and consolidated by one party, the proletarian party", "there is no longer, nor can there ever be, the question of the division of power and the abandonment of the dictatorship of the proletarians over the bourgeoisie."[35] In July of the same year, the Fifth All-Russian Congress of Soviets passed a resolution to remove the leftist Social Revolutionaries from the Soviets and the coalition of the two parties in power broke down completely. In March 1922, the Eleventh Congress of the CPR stated that, in order to consolidate the victory of the proletariat and defend the dictatorship of the proletariat, the CPR "should deprive all political groups hostile to Soviet power of their freedom to organise. The CPR is now the only legitimate political party in the country." [36] Consequently, in the end, a single party system was established.

At the same time, in November 1917, the All-Russian Central Executive Committee and People's Council issued a decree abolishing the system of ranks and official titles, getting rid of all grades, statuses and official civil titles in Russia, and referring to all inhabitants as "citizens of the Russian Republic". The old Russian judicial system was abolished and replaced by democratically elected revolutionary courts and people's tribunals. In November 1917, the Soviet government also issued the Declaration of the Rights of the Peoples of All Nationalities in Russia, which proclaimed the elimination of national oppression and the achievement of equality and freedom for all peoples until the national self-determination of nations was achieved. On the instructions of Lenin and the Party Central Committee, the Soviet Government recognised the independence of Finland, Poland and the three Baltic states of Lithuania, Estonia and Latvia. In July 1918, the Fifth All-Russian Congress of Soviets adopted the Constitution of the Russian Soviet Federal Socialist Republic. This was the first constitution of a dictatorship of the proletariat in the world, which fixed in law a series of achievements of the October Revolution, principally including: the dictatorship of the proletariat as the form of Soviet power, the abolition of capitalist and landlord ownership, the principles of the construction of the Soviet state, the guarantee of democratic rights and freedoms for the majority of the population, the denial of the right to vote to exploiters of labour, the equality and fraternity of all peoples and the proletarian internationalism of all nations.

With regard to the military system, on 15 January 1918, the People's Council adopted a decree on the establishment of the Workers' and Peasants' Red Army, deciding to abandon the idea of a universal armed force in favour of a standing army. In early September, the Central Executive Committee of the All-Russian Soviet decided to set up the Revolutionary Military Council of the Republic to lead all military organs and fronts in the country, and to be responsible for implementing the instructions of the Party Central Committee and the Soviet Government on military issues. The posts of Chairman of the Revolutionary Military Council and People's Commissar of the Army and Navy were both held by Trotsky. Outstanding communist party members, workers and peasants joined the Red Army in large numbers and went to the front. By October, the Red Army had reached a strength of more than 800,000 men, and by the end of the following year that had risen to 4.5 million. To reinforce its leadership, the communist party established a system of political work within the army, carried out ideological and political education, developed the party's organisation, and put military commanders and political commissars jointly in charge of the military and political affairs of their units, thereby ensuring the unity of the troops, their courage and tenacity. Throughout the civil war, the Red Army, under the leadership of the CPR, fought for three bloody years to eliminate the White Guard movement throughout Russia and successfully defend the gains of the revolution.

In order to quickly consolidate the new regime, Lenin asked Dzerzhinsky to set up the All-Russian Extraordinary Commission for Combating Counter-Revolution and Sabotage (the Cheka) in December 1917 to fight against the old government officials and counter-revolutionary sabotage and subversion. The following year, anti-counter-revolutionary mechanisms were set up in the transport sector, in the army and in the border areas. The Cheka gradually acquired extensive powers, with a mandate to deal with speculators, other political parties and the reactionary press, and to intervene in the internal affairs of the army and the Soviet organs, with full judicial functions of investigation, arrest, trial, judgment and execution of sentences. In the autumn of 1918, Sapronov, then chairman of the Moscow Provincial Soviet Executive Committee and others were the first to question and challenge the legitimacy of this body. They used a series of resolutions adopted by the Moscow party and government organisations to accuse the local anti-counter-revolutionary committees of being free from any local supervision and of acting lawlessly. They demanded that they be placed under the leadership of the local soviets and opposed the vertical leadership structure of the central authorities. However, in March 1919, the Eighth Congress of the CPR rejected their views, stating that the party was in a situation where the strictest centralisation and discipline were absolutely necessary, that all resolutions of the higher organs must be carried out absolutely by the lower organs, and that, at the current stage, the party must exercise direct military discipline.[37]

In October 1922, the People's Revolutionary Army defeated the Japanese incursionists and the White Guards, and troops marched into Vladivostok, taking full control of the Primorsky Krai (maritime region) and bringing the Russian Civil War to an end. On 30 December, the Union of Soviet Socialist Republics (USSR), a union of Russia, Ukraine, Belarus and the South Caucasus Federation, was formed and Lenin was elected Chairman of the People's Committee of the Soviet Union. The new union was a form of national and international state power made up of legally sovereign constituent republics. Lenin saw this form of state structure as the nucleus of the Soviet Republic that would continue to unite the peoples of neighbouring nations. On 31 January 1924, the Second Congress of the Soviet Union adopted the Constitution of the Union of Soviet Socialists which confirmed the USSR as a unified union of Soviet socialist states. By the end of 1925, six republics, 15 autonomous republics and 16 autonomous regions had joined the USSR and the dictatorship of the proletariat had been consolidated.

2. From wartime communism to a new economic policy

After Russia's involvement in the first world war, the long-term conflict brought the country's economy to the brink of collapse and nightmarish famine tormented the ordinary people. After the October Revolution, the Soviet government put forward the principle of "everything for the front, everything to defeat the enemy" in order to concentrate its limited financial and material resources on repelling the combined attacks of domestic and foreign hostile forces. It introduced a series of extraordinary measures adapted to the needs of the war effort, that practically turned the Republic into a giant military camp and effectively tried to make a direct transition to communism. As these measures were of a military communist nature, they became known as "wartime communist" policies. Their main elements included the nationalisation of all industry and the dispossession of the ownership class; the collection of surplus grain; the prohibition of grain trading; the sanctioning and weakening of rich peasants; the nationalisation of the commercial supply system; the restriction of markets and private trade; the implementation and strict adherence to the principle of "no food without labour"; the introduction of compulsory adult labour; the introduction of a standardised communist distribution system and so on.

This "wartime communism" was an emergency measure adopted under the difficult circumstances of the war and the extreme scarcity of materials, and it provided the necessary guarantees for a short-term victory in the war and the defence and consolidation of Soviet power. However, such a policy was not only contrary to the promises made to the population during the revolutionary period, it was also clearly temporary and transitional in nature; at the same time, the lack of foreign capital and technology made it difficult for Russia itself to initiate the recovery and development of the national economy. It is estimated that in 1921 the country's mines and factories produced only 20% of their pre-first world war levels, its arable land was at only 62% of the pre-war average and its harvests only 37% of normal levels. The Russian rouble plummeted from 2 roubles to the dollar in 1914 to 1,200 roubles to the dollar in 1920.[38] Moreover, these negative effects eventually affected social security and stability, leading to serious political and economic crises.

In 1918, 245 peasant revolts broke out. In 1919, whole regions and even some provinces were controlled by peasant bands totalling tens of thousands. In 1920, workers' strikes and peasant uprisings continued on a large scale. In February-March 1921, 27,000 sailors and Red Army soldiers in Kronstadt, who had been an important military force in the October Revolution, launched a revolt. They made clear their demands for the establishment of freely elected soviets, an end to one-party dictatorship, guaranteed freedom of speech, press, assembly and association, a constitutional assembly, an end to the compulsory collection of surplus grain and an end to state control of the economy. The reduction in arable land, coupled with severe drought and transport paralysis, also led to a famine in which millions of people starved to death. All this forced the communist party to reflect deeply on its policy of "wartime communism". Lenin frankly admitted: "The reality of life shows that we were wrong"[39] and that "we have gone too far in our economic offensive. ...... The direct transition to a purely socialist form and pure socialist distribution is beyond our means."[40]

In order to change this critical situation, Lenin pointed out that since a direct transition from small production to socialism could not be achieved, capitalism, as a spontaneous product of small production, was to a certain extent inevitable and that state capitalism should be used as an intermediate link. In other words, the development of productive forces through state capitalism was the way to lay a solid material foundation for the transition to socialism. In March 1921, the 10th Congress of the CPR formally decided to move from wartime communism to the implementation of a new economic policy.

The basic elements of the new economic policy were that the state would take control of the economy and continue to maintain state ownership of production enterprises, while allowing the existence of a commercial economy and private trade. The new economic policy was to replace the system of surplus grain collection with a system of grain taxation, whereby peasants were required to pay only a portion of their harvest to the state as a tax, while the rest of the grain went to the individual, with the individual enjoying full rights of disposal; to allow free private trade and to restore a commodity-currency relationship and to allow the existence of commercial capitalists; to allow the development of small private industrial enterprises and to return some of the small industrial enterprises that had been nationalised to private ownership. In order to enable them to resume production as soon as possible they reinstated forms of state capitalism such as: leasing and renting; the cooperative system, and buying and selling on behalf of the state; leasing large state-owned industrial enterprises that were temporarily unable to resume production to foreign capitalists; using capitalist funds and technology; reform of the industrial management system; the introduction of economic accounting in state-owned enterprises (SOEs); calculation of costs and profits, and the evaluation of enterprises on the basis of profitability; the introduction of material rewards for workers; the introduction of more pay for more work; the abolition of the compulsory labour system; the introduction of the eight-hour working day; changing the egalitarian distribution system; strengthening economic contacts and cooperation with capitalist countries and the learning of foreign experience and technology, and so on.

The implementation of this new economic policy soon produced tangible results in economic life, the CPSU emerged from its crisis of power and the serious damage caused by the war and the revolution was repaired. Between 1925 and 1927 the Soviet Union found itself in its best position since the October Revolution and the task of large-scale economic construction was realistically on the agenda. Of course, the transition from a small peasant economy to a large-scale socialist economy, the industrialisation of socialism and the transformation of an agrarian country into a powerful socialist industrial state were not only unprecedented and difficult processes but there were also serious differences of opinion within the party.

3. Taking control of ideological and cultural construction

When the Bolsheviks came to power, apart from the serious economic crisis, they were also faced with serious social contradictions. At that time, the Russian people were culturally backward, mentally lax and small peasant consciousness was prevalent, with over 80% of the population illiterate. Workers, peasants and soldiers alike were fiercely unhappy with the longstanding difficulties in production and in life. In response, Lenin argued that old and decadent ideas, and the low level of literacy of the people were impeding the construction and development of Soviet Russia as a whole, and that while political and economic construction was important, ideological and cultural construction also had to be strengthened: "You cannot build a communist society in an illiterate country."[41] At the same time,"the first task of any political party that represents the future is to convince the majority of the people that its programme and strategy are correct."[42] In order to establish and consolidate socialism, it is necessary to strengthen its commitment to ideology, and cultural and artistic undertakings: "use your own brave spirit in the revolutionary struggle against capital to attract all the exploited and working people, attract them, organise them, and lead them to overthrow the bourgeoisie and completely suppress all bourgeois resistance"[43], "It is not just a question of military and political resistance; the deepest and most intense resistance is intellectual and ideological."[44]

In the first months of the Soviet regime, Lenin proposed to "transform the press from an instrument of daily political news to an important tool for the economic education of the masses."[45] This led to the establishment of an extremely strict system of censorship of books and newspapers. In January 1918, the People's Committee issued a decree on the separation of the church from the state and of schools from the church, which forbade the teaching of religious doctrine and the performance of religious rituals in schools, and prevented the church from interfering in school affairs. The government also issued a decree on literacy, requiring all countrymen from the age of 8 to 50 to learn to read and write. The works of Marx, Engels, Lenin and others were published in large numbers to help carry out education in the theory of communism. In 1919, Bukharin and others wrote *The ABC of Communism* (originally entitled *Introduction to Communism*), which was reprinted nearly 20 times by the early 1930s and translated into more than 20 foreign languages. In March 1923, the First Congress of Proletarian Writers was held in Moscow, and the All-Union Association of Proletarian Writers (known as VAPP) was founded, calling for proletarian literature to "organise the psyche and consciousness of the working class and the masses of workers, and adapt them to the ultimate task of the proletariat as the transformer of the world and builder of communist society." In January 1925, proletarian literature was launched with the title *Mop*, which called for "organising the psychology and consciousness of the working class and the masses of workers, adapting them to the ultimate task of the proletariat as transformers of the world and builders of communist society."[46] In January 1925, the first All-Soviet Conference of Proletarian Writers was held, with VAPP centre stage, and the Russian Association of Proletarian Writers (RAPP) was founded, beginning the search for a form of literary realism. The ideas and tenets of collectivism, comradeship, the glory of labour and the equality of all peoples began to be widely proclaimed throughout society and became real socialist values.

4. Unifying the proletariat and oppressed peoples of the world in a world revolution

Faced with the extremely dangerous situation at home and abroad in the early years of his rule, Lenin believed that the Soviet power could not exist alone under siege from the imperialist countries, that the Russian revolution was only a domestic stage of the world revolution, and that the summoning of a world revolution should be an important part of foreign policy strategy. At the Seventh Congress of the CPR in March 1918, he said: "From the perspective of world history, if there is no revolutionary movement in other countries, then there is no doubt that there is no hope for the final victory of our own revolution. ...... I repeat, what will save us from all these difficulties is an all-European revolution."[47]

However, the delay in the arrival of socialist revolutions in Europe and the rapid failure of the communist revolutions in Germany and Hungary forced Lenin to change his international strategy and adopt a more sober and realistic attitude, taking the initiative to engage with the capitalist governments and making greater concessions and sacrifices to establish normal contacts. He pointedly noted: "The international revolution is developing while the economic crisis in Europe is intensifying. But in any case, it would be madness for us to conclude on this basis that Europe will come to our aid in the short term with a solid proletarian revolution."[48] On the basis of this understanding and judgment, the Soviet regime, after signing the Treaty of Brest-Litovsk with Germany, restored economic ties with a large number of capitalist countries and established diplomatic relations in order to gain a moment of peaceful respite to save the Soviet Union. At the same time, in order to continue to promote the world communist movement and to coordinate and guide the revolutionary struggle in various countries, a conference of delegates to the Communist International was held in March 1919, attended by 52 delegates from 35 political parties and groups from 21 countries in Europe, Asia and America. The Congress issued the Declaration of the Communist International to the Proletarians of the World, proclaiming the formation of the Third International and calling on them to fight for the defence of Soviet Russia and for the victory of the Soviets in all countries of the world.

At this time, the continued growth of democratic movements among the peoples of the East prompted Lenin to turn his attention from the West to the countries of the East in an attempt to find a political force with which he could unite, so that the international proletariat and the oppressed peoples could prevent the Allies from attacking Soviet Russia from both the imperialist frontlines and their rear, and defend their own political power. In June 1920, on the eve of the Second Congress of the Comintern, he published his *Preliminary Draft Outline of the Issue of Nations and Colonies*, stating that, since the world had been divided into the oppressed and the oppressor in the age of imperialism, the whole policy of the Comintern on the national and colonial question was to unite the proletarians and oppressed peoples of the world in a revolutionary struggle against the landlords and the bourgeoisie. Only this union could guarantee victory over capitalism; otherwise, there could be no talk of eliminating national oppression. He also emphasised the need for national liberation movements to support and forge the closest alliance with Soviet

Russia, based on the judgement that the centre of the world's political struggle at the time was in the opposition to and defence of the Soviet Union. In September of the same year, a congress of the peoples of the East was held in Baku, attended by representatives of more than 30 countries, including China, India and Iran. It was decided to set up a "Committee of Propaganda and Action for the Peoples of the East" and the Comintern raised the slogan "United proletarians and oppressed peoples of the world!" The Communist International also adopted the slogan "Proletarians and Oppressed Peoples of the World Unite!" As a result of this, the original national liberation struggles in China, Korea, India, Turkey and some countries in Africa moved into full swing.

5. Building a truly proletarian ruling party

After the victory of the October Revolution, the Bolsheviks became the ruling party of the first socialist country in the world, and the number of party members increased sharply but with uneven quality, lax discipline, and lawlessness occurring from time to time. It was a major challenge for the proletarian party to strengthen itself after it had assumed state power, the better to fulfil its historic mission.

Lenin argued that: "our party is the ruling party and therefore naturally the open party, the party that offers the possibility of power to people who join it and during this period we have to fight to prevent bad elements, the dregs of old capitalism, from getting into and mixing with the ruling party."[49] "The ruling party, which relies on a healthy and powerful advanced class, should be good at cleansing its own ranks"[50]; it should "pay attention not to the quantity of party members but to the improvement of their quality and to the cleansing of those who have "infiltrated" the party. "We do not want members in name only, however freely they lend that name."[51] In March 1919, the Eighth Congress of the CPR decided to carry out a general re-registration of all party members, after which the party had to pay particular attention to its social composition. At the same time, the CPR also used the conditions of war to test the party spirit of the membership, removing those who did not want to go to the frontlines; it used the "Communist Voluntary Saturday Labour" to purge the party, stipulating that "all members of the party who joined after 25 October 1917 and who have no special work skills or merit need to be examined in this way to prove that they are absolutely reliable and capable of being a communist."[52] This was followed by the 13th Congress of the CPR in January 1924, which proposed that every effort should be made to increase the number of the proletarian core in the party and its weight in the party's overall policy making, and that at least 100,000 industrial workers from the proletarian base should be admitted to the party within the next year.

In response to the differences of opinion and factional activities within the CPR, Lenin argued that "we must remember that the internal danger is in a sense greater than that of Denikin and Yudenich, and therefore we need not only a formal unity but a very real and solid unity."[53] The 10th Congress of the CPR, held in March 1921, adopted the Resolution on Party Unity, drafted by Lenin, which ordered the dissolution of all factions and groups, and authorised the Central Committee to take extreme measures, up to and including expulsion, against members of the Central Committee who engaged in factional activities; at the same time, it enjoined the party organisations at all levels to take care that any factional activity was prohibited. Lenin believed that "any factional activity is harmful and inadmissible because even if the representatives of individual groups are full of the desire to maintain the unity of the party, factional activity is in fact bound to weaken the unity of effort and to intensify the activities of those enemies who have infiltrated the ruling party in order to deepen the divisions in the party and use them for counter-revolutionary purposes."[54]

Furthermore, Lenin believed that "the possibility of pride and arrogance in some political parties is often a prelude to failure and decline" and that "our party may now be in very great danger of becoming arrogant. This is very stupid, shameful and ridiculous."[55] He proposed that after the proletariat had seized power, it must make practicality and realism its main slogans: "talk less with pretty words and do more ordinary, everyday work", "sing fewer political high notes and pay more attention to the very ordinary but vivid things that come from life, are tested by life and are relevant to the construction of communism"[56]; he insisted that they should not hide the weaknesses of the movement but "learn from mistakes" and "learn to do things through self-criticism."[57]

It was in the course of solving the serious crisis of governance faced by the party that Lenin and other leaders of the CPR developed a more systematic theory of governance, which initially revealed the rules of communist governance. This mainly included the need to oppose dogmatism in ideology: "The doctrine of Marx and Engels is not a dogma that we memorise by rote. It should be taken as a guide for action."[58] Lenin continued to emphasise this point after the October Revolution. He stated unequivocally: "For Russia too, the time for arguing about the socialist programme on the basis of books has passed; I am convinced that it is gone. Today one can only speak of socialism on the basis of experience."[59] Because "everything now lies in practice, and we have reached a point in history where theory is being turned into practice, where theory is given life by practice, is revised by practice and is tested by practice."[60] Clearly, for the CPR, the grain monopoly, the army grain requisition, the committees of the poor peasants, the declaration of war on the rich peasants, the creation of a standing army, the signing of the Brest Peace Treaty, doing business with the capitalist countries, and so on, were the experience and reality of socialism. Lenin proposed that the basic principles of communism must be "correctly adapted in certain details to the differences of nations and nation states, and correctly applied to those differences". He asserted that "the essence of Marxism, the living soul of Marxism is the concrete analysis of specific situations."[61]

The party must take a leading role in all the work of the state. The victory of the October Revolution proved the great role of the working-class party. In solving the most important political, economic and military tasks facing the new regime, it has also been proved that the leadership and pioneering role of the party were decisive issues for winning the hearts and minds of the people, consolidating power and starting the construction of a new society. Lenin concluded: "It was only because the party was on the alert, because it was disciplined and because its prestige unified all organs and departments, that dozens, hundreds, thousands and even millions of people acted in unison in accordance with the slogans put forward by the centre; and only because we endured unprecedented sacrifices, that the miracle we have today has come about."[62] "The dictatorship was achieved by the proletariat organised in the soviets, and the proletariat is led by the Bolshevik Communist Party."[63] Consequently "the party is the direct ruling vanguard of the proletariat and its leader" and "all the political and economic work of the state power is led by the communist party, the vanguard of the consciousness of the working class."[64] The prerequisite for the other parties to share power is that they must unconditionally guarantee the implementation of the programme leading to socialism. Thereby, within a few years of the October Revolution, Russia was transformed into a one party state. The Bolsheviks not only banned the other parties but also headed the state legislature and the executive, were the leaders of all organisations, organised all political and economic movements in the country, and "the decisions adopted by the party congresses were obligatory for the whole republic "[65]; and "no state organ may decide on any major political or organisational issue without instructions from the Party Central Committee "[66].

The dictatorship of the proletariat must constantly consolidate the alliance of workers and peasants. Although the majority of the Russian population were peasants, for a long time the progressive elements in Russia had belittled the role of the peasantry and advocated working in the cities and among the intelligentsia. The Bolsheviks shared this tendency in the early days and only later realised that the Russian proletariat could not even begin a revolution on its own, let alone consolidate its gains. After the triumph of the revolution, faced with the vast, poor and backward rural areas, Lenin came to the sober realisation that in Russia "the most essential and fundamental question of the whole revolution and of all future socialist revolutions (namely, the worldwide socialist revolution)", "is the relationship between the working class and the peasantry."[67] "As labourers, the peasants are the friends of the proletarian state and the most faithful allies of the workers in the struggle against the landlord-capitalists."[68] "The socialist revolution cannot be accomplished without the working class; nor can it be accomplished if the working class does not accumulate sufficient strength to lead the millions of peasants oppressed, tortured, kept illiterate and scattered by the capitalists."[69] "Only by consolidating the alliance of workers and peasants can mankind generally escape from scourges like the great imperialist struggle of the recent past, and from the strange contradictions we now see in the capitalist world, where a very few of the richest and most powerful nations are choking on their wealth, while the masses of the earth's inhabitants are impoverished and unable to enjoy existing civilisation and to make use of the rich resources that have no outlet because of inadequate distribution."[70]

Attention must be turned to building the economy. In April 1918, in his article "The Current Tasks of Soviet Power", Lenin proposed that the fundamental task of the transition period was to increase the productivity of labour and develop productive forces. He said that the historical task of the Russian proletariat had changed from the "seizure of Russia" to the "management of Russia". When the proletariat had "largely and essentially solved the task of dispossessing the property-owning class and suppressing their resistance, the fundamental task of creating a social structure superior to that of capitalism must be brought to the fore, and this fundamental task involves the raising of labour productivity."[71] Lenin had previously repeatedly stressed the need to shift the focus of party and state work to economic construction but this had been prevented by the outbreak of civil war. In 1920, immediately after the end of the civil war, Lenin raised the issue again. He said: "The economic front and economic tasks are once again brought before us as the principal, fundamental things we must address"[72] It is necessary to "turn all our attention to this economic construction." He also issued a call for "everyone to do economic work", asking communists to learn economic work skills. Following Lenin's advice, the Eighth All-Russian Congress of Soviets, held in December 1920, made the decision to make this major strategic shift and adopted the first ambitious plan for the electrification of the country. Lenin extolled this and even used the formula "Communism is Soviet power plus national electrification"[73] to illustrate the importance of national electrification. His intention was also to highlight the vital importance of economic development for the consolidation of power.

A proletarian army must be created and led. In the struggle for the armed defence of the new regime, Lenin advanced many new theoretical ideas on the building of the Workers' and Peasants' Red Army and the strengthening of national defence. He believed that, in order to protect the workers' and peasants' regime from invasion, a victorious proletarian state must have a strong Red Army, which must not only always remain armed but must also maintain its guard at all times, and must care for and protect the defence capabilities of the army and the state as much as one cares for and protects one's own eyes. The whole country and all its people must take defence seriously, estimate the contrast of forces accurately, develop the country's economy and continually strengthen its defence forces. "The abolition of armed forces is the ideal of socialism. In a socialist society there will be no war and therefore the abolition of armed forces will be achieved. But whoever expects to achieve socialism without a social revolution and the dictatorship of the proletariat is not a socialist. "[74] "As long as the ruling class, that is, the proletariat, is willing to rule and continue to rule, it should also use its own military organisation to prove this."[75] In order to grow the army as quickly as possible, he also stressed in particular that "the Red Army is more important than anything else. Every organisation in Soviet Russia has to put the question of the army first."[76]

Socialism must be built using the fruits of capitalist civilisation and develop through them, as Marx and Engels always advocated. In the early days of leading Soviet Russia's economic construction, Lenin was also deeply aware that to make up for the inherent deficiencies of building socialism there, it was necessary to actively study the technology and management experience of Western capitalist countries. He opposed the abstract dichotomy between capitalism and socialism, and repeatedly stressed that socialist civilisation could not be a separate state of civilisation isolated from the rest of the world but, on the contrary, it must be a new state of civilisation incorporating the best achievements of all of human civilisation. "The destruction of capitalism alone will not fill the stomach. It is necessary to acquire the entire culture left behind by capitalism and use it to build socialism. All science, technology, knowledge and art must be acquired."[77] "Socialism can only be built by using the materials that capitalism has created to oppose us; we should use all this to build socialism and consolidate it."[78] "We can only build communism if we use bourgeois science and technology to make it something more acceptable to the masses. It will not do to try to build a communist society by another method."[79] To this end he also proposed a famous formula, "Soviet power + Prussian railway order + American technology and trust organisations + American national education etc. etc. + + = sum total = socialism."[80]

(IV) LENIN'S IN-DEPTH THINKING ON THE LAWS OF COMMUNIST RULE IN HIS LATER YEARS

By the end of 1919, under Lenin's leadership, Soviet Russia had won a decisive victory in its struggle to crush foreign armed intervention and quell counter-revolutionary rebellions in the country. With the end of the civil war, socialist construction became a priority for the CPR and a historical challenge to turn its theoretical vision into a realistic one. At the same time, the advent of peace, the complexity of the tasks of government and the diversity of the paths of construction also put the party, which had survived and flourished in a revolutionary state, to the severe test of continuing to maintain ideological unity and discipline. "Whether a party is a genuine workers' party depends not only on whether it is composed of workers but also on who leads it and what its actions and political tactics are. Only on the basis of the latter can it be determined whether the party is a genuine party of the proletariat."[81] From the spring of 1921 onwards, Lenin's basic understanding and views on the question of what socialism is and how to build it underwent a major transformation, and he conducted a series of trials and explorations. Many new ideological views on the laws of communist party governance were formed at this time.

The party's ideology and theory had to respond positively to the concerns of the times and society. After the victory of the October Revolution, faced with the difficulties of the post-reign period and the huge gap between theory and reality, all fingers were pointed at the October Revolution itself, both in Russia and abroad, and also within the CPR itself. They believed that the conditions for a socialist revolution did not exist in an economically and culturally backward country and it did not conform to the general Marxist law of the historical process of human social development.

Without being able to explain the rationality and inevitability of the October Revolution in Russia, it would be impossible to unify social understanding, unite people and begin the construction of socialism. To this end, Lenin concentrated his thoughts and explanations on the path of development and the future destiny of Russian society. He used Marxist methods to examine the reality of Russia in depth and concluded that an economically and culturally backward country did not have to follow in the footsteps of the West, and that Russia could take a different path to socialism than the West. In response to Kautsky, Sukhanov and others who argued that Russia did not have the objective economic prerequisites for socialism, Lenin criticised them for seeing only the fixed path of capitalist development in Western Europe, without understanding the particularities of the Russian situation. He pointed out that the general law of the development of world history not only did not in any way exclude the specificity of individual stages in terms of the form or sequence of development but was, in fact, premised on it. This particularity did not change the general line of development of world history: Russia was perfectly capable of first obtaining the political prerequisites for socialism by revolutionary means and then creating the level of productivity and culture needed to build socialism on the basis of workers' and peasants' power and the Soviet system. He admonished people both to learn from foreign countries and to follow their own path and absolutely never lose their independence. He told Stalin: "We must keep a firm hand on the rudder and follow our own path, and never fall for the flattery or blackmail of others."[82] At the same time, he made it clear that the path of socialism for backward countries was complex and that the choice of the path of development would be made "not from abstract principles but from the concrete realities of life in all its forms"[83] and from their own national conditions. He predicted that "in the countries of the East, with their huge populations and their hugely complex social situations, future revolutions will undoubtedly be even more particular and idiosyncratic than the Russian revolution."[84]

The party and the state must change the focus of their work from revolution to construction. It was Lenin's consistent view that if this shift was not successfully made, the consolidation of the new system would lack a firm foundation and the restoration of the old one would be inevitable. In January 1923 he concluded: "We have to admit that our whole view of socialism has fundamentally changed. This fundamental change is reflected in the fact that whereas before we had focused and should have focused on political struggle, revolution, the seizure of power and so on, now the focus has shifted to the work of peaceful 'cultural' organisation."[85] The culture we are talking about here is culture in the broad sense of the word, falling into the category of civilisation, which includes not only spiritual culture but also political and material culture.

Socialism must create higher labour productivity than capitalism. It was a fundamental view of Marx and Engels that the proletariat must increase the total productive forces as soon as possible after seizing power. As mentioned earlier, immediately after the victory of the October Revolution, Lenin also made it clear that "labour productivity, in the final analysis, is the primary and most important thing that will bring about the triumph of the new social system"[86] and this idea became one of the central points in his final letters and articles. He wanted to base the consolidation of communist party rule on the rapid development of productive forces, repeatedly emphasising the development of large-scale mechanised industry, and likening this development to "changing horses", that is, "from the horse of the peasant, of the farmer, of the poor, from the horse of the peasant state, which relies on the economy of the broken peasant state, to the horse of the proletariat that cannot help but seek new pastures, to the horse of large-scale mechanised industry, of electrification, of the Volkhov Hydroelectric Project, and so on."[87]

The transition period must make use of the commodity-finance relationship. Marx and Engels envisaged that there would be no commodity-finance relationship in a socialist society, an assumption that was premised on a capitalist society with a highly developed market economy and highly developed social productivity. On the basis of the lessons learnt from practical experience after the victory of the October Revolution, Lenin gave profound thought to the issue of the commodity-finance relationship during the transitional period, believing that the development of state capitalism was inevitable for a small peasant country like Soviet Russia; the small peasant economy was constantly producing capitalist elements all the time but it was also progressive in comparison to the old scattered and isolated small peasant mode of production. He proposed: "Commodity exchange should be given primacy as the main lever of the new economic policy. Without a systematic exchange of commodities or products between industry and agriculture, it will be impossible to establish normal relations between the proletariat and the peasantry and to build a solid economic alliance during the transition from capitalism to socialism."[88] He asked party members to pay attention to and familiarize themselves with commercial work and "to combine revolutionary spirit and revolutionary enthusiasm, which we have fully demonstrated and which has been fully successful, with (and here I rather have to say it) the ability to be an informed and calculating businessman (these skills being what is needed to make an outstanding cooperative worker). "[89]

Backward countries must guide their peasants towards socialism through cooperatives. Russia was a traditionally agrarian country with a large proportion of peasants in its population, and their participation was indispensable in both revolution and construction. The new economic policy adopted by Lenin took into account the interests of the peasants and corrected the deviation of the "wartime communist" policy which ignored the interests of the peasants. He said: "We should not expect to adopt the transitional methods of communism directly. It must be based on integration with the individual interests of the peasants."[90] He then proposed the idea of developing agricultural cooperatives, linking socialist large-scale industry with the small peasant economy to bring about the socialist transformation of agriculture. In his view, cooperativisation was the fundamental way to attract the peasants to participate in socialist construction, to consolidate the workers' and peasants' alliance, and to build the foundation of the socialist economy, and it was also a way to make the peasants feel free and comfortable in accepting the change. To this end, the will of the peasants had to be given full consideration, policies had to be simple and easy to implement, the state had to provide policy-oriented and financial support, and the relationship between industry and cooperatives must be managed well. He even concluded that: "Under the conditions of public ownership of the means of production, and under the conditions of class victory of the proletariat over the bourgeoisie, the system of civilised cooperative workers is the system of socialism."[91]

It is necessary to constantly improve the way the party leads and governs. After the proletarian party came to power, the question that was a matter of constant concern to Lenin in his final years was how to ensure the leadership of the party in all the work of the state by improving the state organs, improving the system of leadership, defining the boundaries of power, improving the style and methods of work, and so on. The resolution adopted by the Eighth Congress of the CPR in March 1919 stipulated that: "the functions of the party organisation and those of the state organs, that is the Soviets, should not in any way become confused. Such confusion has extremely dangerous consequences, especially in the military sphere. The party should carry out its decisions through the Soviet organs and within the limits of the Soviet Constitution. The party endeavours to lead the work of the Soviets but not to replace them."[92] But these provisions were not put into practice, and in response Lenin corresponded frequently with those concerned, repeatedly negotiating and formulating measures. He proposed that "the responsibilities of the party (and its Central Committee) and of the power of the Soviets must be very clearly delineated; that the responsibility and independence of the Soviets' organs and personnel must be increased, and that the party's task must be to exercise general leadership over the work of all state organs but not to intervene too frequently, extraordinarily and often trivially, as they do at present."[93] He demanded that the Politburo and the Central Committee "should put an end to the practice of turning to the Central Committee for every trivial matter and should enhance the prestige of the People's

Committees" and "make the People's Commissars responsible for their own work, instead of referring problems first to the People's Committees and then to the Politburo."[94] He pointed out that the real task of the communist party in management was not to do "everything" "by hand", but "to check the work of tens and hundreds of assistants, to organise bottom-up inspections of their work, that is to say, real checks carried out by ordinary people; on the one hand to direct the work, and on the other, to learn from those with the relevant knowledge (experts) and those with experience in organising large enterprises (capitalists)."[95]

Socialist democracy must be developed and perfected. After the victory of the October Revolution, the serious challenges to the seizure and consolidation of power naturally led the CPR to transform the party's organisational principles and mechanisms of power into the basic principles of state and social construction, and to directly manage and intervene in all trivial matters. However, this highly centralised and unified organisational principle and system not only left little space and few channels for the expression and defence of people's rights but also provided the institutional ground for the conflation of party and government functions and the growth of bureaucracy. "Victorious socialism without full democracy cannot maintain the victories it has achieved and will lead the population to the demise of the state."[96] In his later years, Lenin always considered the construction of the political system for the Bolsheviks and the Soviet state as a major theoretical issue, and the problems of lack of discipline, bureaucratism and excessive concentration of power became one of his major concerns. He regarded bureaucratism as the worst enemy within the Soviet Union and repeatedly warned the party that if communists became overly bureaucratic, it would destroy both the country and the cause. He also proposed some theoretical principles and policy measures such as building a democratic system, reforming the cadre system, improving the system of supervision and streamlining institutions. Among these, he also particularly emphasised the need to develop socialist democracy, to attract the majority of the people to participate in the administration of the state and to strengthen the state apparatus – these were the fundamental prerequisites for building socialism. For this reason, he suggested that the restructuring of the Workers' and Peasants' Procuratorate should be the breakthrough point, so that it could exercise effective supervision and control over the various state organs, enterprises and institutions, and realise the supervision and control of power through power. Of course, he also made it clear that, due to various constraints, it was impossible immediately to achieve direct participation by everyone in the democratic management of the state, and that democracy-building required a process that should be promoted gradually.

Great importance must be attached to ideological and cultural construction. In his *Diary Extracts*, Lenin proposed a cultural revolution. He believed that cultural revolution should not only carry out an educational and national revolution, especially by strengthening basic education and literacy of the peasants, so that the masses of people would have a certain cultural basis, but also by actually making the working people the creators of culture. Most importantly, he believed it was possible, through ideological and cultural reforms, to break down the remnants of the old Russian feudal and capitalist ideology, inculcate Marxism in the masses, change the ideology, construct a socialist moral code and maintain the rule of the regime. At the same time, he stressed that the cultural revolution and cultural construction in the Soviet Union had its own particularities and complexities, and that attention must be paid to comprehensiveness and permanence, as well as to the need to critically absorb and to draw on cultural heritage and learn from the advanced cultural achievements of capitalism. He constantly reiterated that: "Proletarian culture does not fall from the sky, nor is it invented by those who pretend to be experts in it ... Proletarian culture should be the natural development of all the knowledge created by man under the oppression of capitalists, landlords and bureaucratic societies."[97]

A foreign policy of peaceful coexistence must be implemented. Since the socialist revolution could not be victorious in all countries at the same time, in order to build socialism successfully, Lenin believed that the Soviet state should pursue a policy of peaceful coexistence with other non-socialist countries, establishing relations with them in their affairs, but also constantly strengthening its defence and armed forces. He proposed to strive for the peaceful coexistence of the two systems by opposing the imperialist policy of war and aggression, and supporting the just struggles of all peoples on the one hand, and by trying to maintain peaceful diplomatic relations with capitalist countries and develop international trade exchanges on the other. "Our only aim is to create the conditions for the survival of the socialist republic by exploiting the greed for profit of the capitalists and the hostility between commercial trusts in the context of the encirclement of capitalism. A socialist republic cannot survive without ties to the world, and in the present circumstances should link its own survival to its relationship with capitalism."[98] At the same time, the world's first socialist state should also raise the banner of proletarian internationalism, give full support to the revolutionary movements of the peoples of all countries, and "forge an alliance with revolutionaries in advanced countries and with the oppressed nations, to oppose all imperialists."[99] Lenin pointed out that: "We have always understood and will never forget that our cause is an international one, so that before the revolution in all countries (including the richest and most civilised) is complete, we have achieved only half our victory, and perhaps less than half."[100] "In the decisive battle of the future world revolution, the movement of the majority of the world's population, acting originally for national liberation, will inevitably oppose capitalism and imperialism. It may play a much more revolutionary role than we expect." "The working masses of the colonial countries, the peasants, though still backward, will certainly play a huge revolutionary role in the later stages of the world revolution."[101]

All measures must be taken to consolidate and build the ruling party. "All the revolutionary parties that have perished, have done so because they were proud and arrogant, could not see where their strengths lay and were afraid to speak out about their weaknesses." "We are not afraid to speak of our weaknesses and can learn to overcome them."[102] In the period after the October Revolution, in response to the pressing domestic and international situation, the Bolshevik Party placed great emphasis on the concentration of power. The party conference at the time decided to introduce "extreme centralisation" and a "combat order system" within the party during the militarised period; "these combat orders were issued by the leading organs of the party to be carried out by ordinary party members absolutely and unconditionally, without discussion."[103] But Lenin was also very conscious of the urgency and importance of the transformation of intra-party relations, believing that "as the objective conditions of revolutionary development change, any form of organisation and corresponding methods of work may turn from being part of the development of the party organisation into an obstacle to such development." He determined to replace "extreme centralism" with "workers' democracy" and to change the emphasis from obedience to the stimulation of internal party activity. To this end, he carried out creative explorations and advanced many important ideas, such as the need to implement democratic centralism and uphold the principle of collective leadership of the party while, at the same time, implementing a system of individual division of labour and responsibility. He pointed out that it was necessary to strengthen the ideological construction of the party, pay attention to the quality of its members and the purity of its ranks; to strive to "create a group of experienced party leaders with high prestige";[104] to maintain strong ties between the party and the majority of workers and peasants, stressing that "among the people, we are after all a drop in the ocean"[105], and that disconnection from the masses is "one of the most serious and terrible dangers"; to recognise the need to exercise strict supervision over party organisations and party cadres at all levels and to improve the party's supervision system; and also the need to strictly prohibit factional activities within the party and to ensure party unity.

In December 1922, after suffering his second stroke, Lenin began to feel that there was no greater danger to the country than a split in the party, and that this split was likely to be caused by conflicts between the party leaders. He raised the question of maintaining the stability of the party, arguing that the fundamental condition for strengthening party unity was to ensure the unity of the Central Committee, to enhance its prestige and to implement the principle of collective leadership at all times; he suggested that the ability to ensure party unity and to prevent a split in the party depended to a large extent on the relations between some prominent members of the Central Committee and on correctly employing them. To this end, he suggested reforming the internal system of the party, enlarging the size of the Central Committee, electing some workers and peasants to the Central Committee and developing a system of internal inspection within the party, so as to actively promote the renewal and improvement of the work of party organs; he hoped that senior party leaders would always use the power given to them by the people with the utmost care, adhere to democratic principles, improve their ideological training and unite their comrades, so that the party leadership would not be confused by his death or riven by internal differences and conflicts. Lenin believed that the Central Committee must always apply the principles of democratic centralism and collective leadership in all circumstances, as that was of decisive significance in ensuring the party unity and the correctness of its policies.

"At the meeting point of rapid historical change, often even advanced political parties fail to adapt to the new situation for a long period of time and continue to repeat old slogans. Such slogans, which were correct yesterday, have lost any meaning today."[106] It was on the basis of this sober understanding and judgement that Lenin adhered to the theoretical principles and scientific methods of Marxism and, with the keen insight and extraordinary courage of a proletarian revolutionary, made a scientific theoretical summary of the experience of socialist construction in Soviet Russia at that time. At the same time, he also made profound reflections on, and a preliminary summary of, the rules of governance of proletarian parties. This represented a great step forward in the understanding of the rules of communist governance based on concrete practice and experience.

Of course, Lenin's understanding and explorations were still tentative in many respects, and due to the speed of the revolution and his early death, they were short-lived and fragmentary, failing to produce properly systematic and settled theoretical results. He died amidst many intellectual perplexities and worries, but he left behind many valuable theoretical legacies and practical achievements that not only enriched and developed Marxism but also provided a solid foundation for the communists to continue their explorations.

3

THE SOVIET COMMUNIST PARTY'S INITIAL SUMMARY OF THE LAWS OF COMMUNIST GOVERNANCE UNDER STALIN

The period between the mid-1920s and the early 1950s was an important period of social construction in the history of the Soviet Union. In the absence of any ready-made models or experiences to draw on, the CPSU, under Stalin's leadership, carried out an extensive and in-depth creative exploration of consolidating and building the world's first socialist state, achieving brilliant results, but also leaving behind extremely painful lessons and deeply hidden problems. In the process, the CPSU continued in many ways to develop and deepen its Marxist understanding of the rules of governance for communist parties.

(I) THE EXPLORATION AND PRACTICE OF CONSOLIDATING AND DEVELOPING THE SOCIALIST SYSTEM

On 21 January 1924, Lenin died in Moscow after a long illness. Where was the world's first socialist state headed? Doubts abounded.

At that time, the Soviet Union was faced with a very difficult and complex situation at home and abroad, as it found itself an isolated socialist island surrounded by capitalism. In order to prevent the Soviet revolution from having an impact on the rest of the world, the imperialist countries were intensifying their economic blockade and military siege of the Soviet Union and were planning a new armed intervention. At the same time, these capitalist countries were experiencing serious economic crises and, in order to solve them, they were trying to shift them abroad. In 1933, the fascist forces of Germany came to power and Japan intensified its aggressive policy in the Far East. In 1936, Germany and Japan concluded the so-called "International Anti-Communist Pact", which was openly directed against the Commintern and the Soviet Union, and which Italy and Spain were later to join. However, Britain, France and other major Western countries adopted a policy of "appeasement" towards the fascists and tried to "divert the trouble to the east" and use the power of fascism to bring down the Soviet Union.

Domestically, the world's first socialist country, established after the October Revolution, was still very backward in terms of economic development compared to the advanced capitalist countries, with a weak industrial base and agriculture dominated by a small-peasant economy. Although the New Economic Policy enabled the Soviet economy to recover and develop rapidly, it also constrained the country's industrialisation and provoked opposition and resistance to socialist transformation and future development goals from the urban petty bourgeoisie and wealthy rural peasants. Doubts over whether the revolution might prove "regressive" developed in the minds of the people. Although Lenin proposed and successfully put into practice the theory that a socialist revolution could first be won in one country, he never gave a clear and positive answer to the question of whether a socialist system could be successfully built in that country, even though he had discussed this in some of his later writings. There were heated debates at the top of the CPSU about whether socialism could be built in the Soviet Union, what kind of socialism to build, and what path to choose for its construction.

The "left-wing" opposition, led by Trotsky, believed that socialism in one country was impossible without the assistance of world revolution and advocated a non-stop march towards the goals of the proletariat on all fronts around the world through the strong leadership of the party and the state. In response to the bureaucratic tendencies within the party, he advocated greater freedom of expression and wider participation by party members, suggesting that a new mass movement should be launched to energise the party. He called for more vigorous development of the collectivisation of industry and agriculture, and for the immediate adoption of a comprehensive programme of centralised control and management of the entire economic life of the country. Zinoviev and Kamenev also argued that the New Economic Policy was only a stop-gap measure to overcome economic difficulties and that it could not be celebrated as real socialism. Rather it was a series of harsh policies that had to be adopted to combat the forces of private capitalism and to get rid of the rich peasants.

Stalin, on the other hand, argued that socialism could be built in the Soviet Union alone. He argued in his works such as *On the Foundations of*

Leninism, On Some Problems of Leninism and *On the Social-Democratic Tendency in Our Party* that the Soviet regime had created the conditions for overcoming all the internal difficulties. The establishment of the dictatorship of the proletariat laid the political foundations for building socialism. The problem lay in the integration of agriculture and socialist industry into an overall economy, thereby establishing a socialist economic foundation. As the proletariat held the power and economic lifeline of the state, it led and attracted the great mass of the peasants to participate in socialist construction, thereby creating the important internal conditions and guarantees in a country for the successful building of socialism. After the first world war, although the capitalist world was relatively stable and the proletarian revolutionary movement was temporarily at a low ebb, the capitalist countries were still full of contradictions and the imperialist countries were unable to relaunch armed intervention against the Soviet Union. This gave the soviet state the opportunity to build peace and take advantage of international conditions for the country to establish socialism. As for the New Economic Policy, it was just a "stop-gap" measure in the post-war period of economic recovery. The Soviet Union was under siege from capitalism and had to concentrate its resources and strength to the maximum extent possible to speed up the industrialisation of the country and the collectivisation of agriculture; it could not rely on taking slow steps towards socialism.

In order to promote his ideas and gain the support of the whole communist party, Stalin criticised Trotsky's theories as Menshevist and pulled together forces to oppose him. In December 1927, the 15th Congress of the CPSU adopted resolutions on the full-scale collectivisation of agriculture and on the transformation of agriculture into socialist mass production based on new technologies. It also approved the decision of the Central Committee and the Central Supervisory Commission to expel Trotsky and Zinoviev from the party, and also to expel the key elements of the so-called "Trotsky-Zinoviev Alliance", Kamenev, Pyatakov, Radek and 75 others. The Congress also called on all levels of the party to work to purify its ranks of "all incorrigible Trotskyist opposition elements".

The 15th Congress of the CPSU marked the end of the New Economic Policy and the beginning of the construction of socialism in the Soviet Union. However, this did not receive the support of the peasants. Despite a good harvest in 1928, the state acquired only 300 million pounds of grain, far less than the 430 million pounds in 1927. This led to a serious disagreement between Stalin's faction on the one hand and Bukharin's on the other over the question of how to carry out socialist industrialisation and the socialist transformation of the countryside. The essence of the disagreement lay in whether to continue following Lenin's ideas on the New Economic Policy in his later years and whether to adhere to and develop the principles and measures of the New Economic Policy. Bukharin, Likov and others argued that Lenin's New Economic Policy was a long-term policy that should be continued and that the development of the commodity economy should be continued, the market should be activated and the market economy should be "normalised". Bukharin believed that in a country that was economically and culturally backward and where capitalism was not fully developed, a "backward socialism" should be built and socialism should be built at "tortoise speed"; the development of the national economy must be integrated and balanced, respecting objective economic laws in regard to industry and agriculture, heavy and light industry, accumulation and consumption. He also believed that the proletarian state should enter socialism peacefully during the transitional period, that is, the proletarian state should not resort to depriving the non-socialist economy but should use economic struggle to gradually transform it into a socialist economy. Therefore, he opposed the wholesale collectivisation campaign of the CPSU Central Committee, headed by Stalin, and also the use of coercion to "drive the peasants into communes", arguing that collective farms could not save everything; instead, he advocated the development of cooperatives in accordance with Lenin's ideas in his later years and guiding peasants towards socialism through cooperatives in accordance with economic laws. Stalin, on the other hand, used the idea of the peasants paying a "tribute tax" and the working class building an industrialised country to convince the party, and adopted a brutal and repressive approach to the struggle, criticising Bukharin and others as right-leaning capitulators, and gradually expelling them from the party leadership.

After the theoretical debate and the choice of the path had been settled, Stalin led the Soviet Union to accelerate industrialisation and the collectivisation of agriculture, and to vigorously advance socialist construction. This was how the Soviet model of socialist construction was developed.

1. The rapid industrialisation and collectivisation of agriculture

In December 1925, the 14th CPSU Congress adopted a resolution proposing a socialist approach to industrialisation by giving priority to the development of heavy industry, and decided not to follow the path of the Western capitalist countries, which began with the development of light industry and ended with industrialisation after a long period of primitive capital accumulation. In 1928, after a series of preparations, the Soviet Union began its first five-year plan, which aimed at rapid industrialisation and the collectivisation of agriculture. The following year, Stalin publicly announced the abandonment of the New Economic Policy. In his speech "On Some Problems of Soviet Agrarian Policy" he stated: "We adopted the New Economic Policy because it served the socialist cause. When it ceased to serve the socialist cause, we discarded it. Lenin said that the New Economic Policy would be implemented in a serious and long-term manner but he never said that it was to be carried out permanently."[1]

Industrialisation in the Soviet Union was characterised by two distinctive features: the high speed and the priority given to the development of heavy industry, including mechanical manufacturing. Since the Soviet Union had to maintain its own independent and autonomous development in the face of a hostile capitalist encirclement, both Lenin and Stalin believed that "without heavy industry the independence of the state cannot be maintained; without it the Soviet system will perish."[2] Stalin also believed that "To slow down is to lag behind and the laggards will be beaten."[3] He called on the Soviet Union to close the gap of 50 to 100 years with the advanced capitalist countries in a maximum of 10 years.

In order to enable the smooth development and realisation of socialist industrialisation, Stalin proposed the theory of a single socialist ownership structure. He believed that in a socialist society, only socialist ownership should exist, and other forms of non-socialist ownership or mixed ownership should be completely excluded. Moreover, there were only two forms of socialist ownership, namely state ownership and collective farm ownership. The former is a "high-level form" and the latter is a "low-level form". Individual citizens could only own household sideline businesses and personal property, and could not own the means of production. In terms of managing the national economy, Stalin advocated that it should be run according to the principles of centralised planning, and the planned economy should be regarded as one of the fundamental characteristics of socialism.

Stalin's idea of a planned economy was partly derived from the doctrine of socialism as expounded by Engels, partly from the experience of the first world war and the civil war, and even more from the irresistible pressure to cope with the continuous and long-term problems of raising the country's level of production[4]. Through the vigorous development of a planned economy, the Soviet Union not only built up a large number of new industrial sectors and a vast system of planned economic management but also created a strong socialist material base which rapidly transformed the Soviet Union from a backward agricultural country into a powerful industrial state. During the three five-year plans before the second world war, 9,000 new industrial enterprises were launched in the Soviet Union and industrial output increased elevenfold compared to 1913, ranking first in Europe and second in the world. In addition, in the early 1930s, Stalin also proposed to accelerate the development of the central and eastern regions, which had a very weak industrial base, in order to establish a strong and stable strategic rearguard as part of the overall development strategy. Consequently, the Soviet Union's industrialisation programme modernised the Volga Valley, the Urals, Siberia and parts of the Far East, where new industrial cities and industrial defence bases emerged. This was a crucial factor in saving the Soviet Union from destruction during the war after the German occupation and destruction of the old industrial areas of the Don Valley.

By the end of the second world war and into the early 1950s, the Soviet Union had completed its fourth five-year plan, industrial output had surpassed pre-war levels and, as a result of its victory in the war against fascism, the country had become the most powerful in Eurasia and was beginning to compete with the US. Of course, Soviet industrialisation was still inferior to that of the West in terms of quality and efficiency and, although in March 1939 the aim had been to catch up with and surpass the major capitalist countries in terms of per capita output within 10-15 years, this vision was never realised. In addition, in order to sustain industrial development, the Soviet Union had to lower the standard of living of the population and reduce the production and supply of consumer goods that were closely related to people's quality of life. In a sense, the industrialisation of the Soviet Union came at a huge cost to the population, and even in peacetime the whole country was essentially in a state of paramilitary mobilisation.

A closed, agrarian country without foreign loans can only industrialise by relying on its own accumulation of funds, and drawing them mainly from agriculture. Stalin was always conscious of this and suggested that the scattered, backward small-peasant economy must be united and transformed into a socialist collective economy; that accelerating the collectivisation of agriculture and controlling the peasants' labour and production was an important and effective solution to the problems of financing industrialisation, food and other agricultural products; that the use of collective farming was the only correct path for working peasants, and that there was no third path. Accordingly, the Soviet Union pursued a vigorous course of collectivisation of all agriculture. By 1932, the area sown on collective farms and state farms had reached 80% of the total cultivated area; by the end of 1937, 243,700 collective farms had been established throughout the country, uniting 18.5 million peasant households and accounting for 93% of all peasant households; in this way, 99.1% of the country's arable land had been collectivised[5] and the collectivisation process was basically complete.

Between 1926 and 1939, some 20 million peasants also moved from the countryside to the cities[6] to work in new enterprises, providing the necessary labour for industrial production and also contributing to the urbanisation of social life as a whole. All this marked the formation of an economic system conducive to industrialisation and the completion of a profound transformation of traditional agriculture in the Soviet Union.

Just as the process of industrialisation was a mixture of achievements and failures, so too did the collectivisation of agriculture in the Soviet Union have huge flaws. Although the CPSU, including Stalin himself, criticised and corrected the problems of compulsory orders, excessive haste, the violation of the principle of voluntary peasant participation and the laws of agricultural development, and even the "elimination of the rich peasants", it still adopted a coercive approach to collectivisation. As a result, while the agricultural results exceeded the plan, the process also had extremely serious consequences. Between 1932 and 1933 there was a great famine in southeastern Russia and the Ukraine[7]. At the same time, by the beginning of the summer of 1930, the collective farms had acquired a total of four billion roubles by dispossessing rich peasants of the means of production and other property; between the beginning of 1930 and the autumn of 1932, 600,000 rich peasant families were dispossessed as "the worst enemies of socialism" and 240,000 were forcibly relocated. The number of rich peasants across the country dropped from about one million before collectivisation to about 150,000[8]. In addition, the peasants' enthusiasm for production was greatly dampened, and some were ill-disciplined and negligent, concerned only with their own land. The CPSU did not recognise the problems of agricultural collectivisation, nor did it carry out effective reforms, and it was also critical of the limited attempts at adjustment that had once been made, such as contracting to organised groups.

So, under the guidance of Stalin's economic theory, the Soviet Union gradually developed a highly centralised and unified system of state planning and management, and a policy of giving priority to the development of heavy and military industry, which was fixed as the long-term, fundamental economic line and as the only correct model of socialist construction. Under this economic model, the state, as the representative of universal ownership, not only held the main economic lifelines of the country but also managed enterprises directly, mainly by administrative means through various central departments. All macroeconomic and microeconomic decision-making power was concentrated in central government, and the entire national economy was directed and arranged at every level by mandatory plans issued by the state. All human, material, and financial resources were uniformly allocated, arranged and distributed by the central government. The result was an extremely inefficient bureaucratic administration and a system of onerous bureaucracy, which kept the entire national economic system in a rigid state of inactivity for a long time. To solve this problem on the front line of production, the Soviet government mainly used political agitation to stimulate labour enthusiasm, principally through socialist competition campaigns. However, the question of how to increase the relatively low productivity of labour and how to achieve sustainable socioeconomic development remained a historical issue that the CPSU was not able to resolve.

2. The establishment of a highly centralised and unified political system

With the advancing industrialisation of the country and the collectivisation of agriculture, the Soviet Union made great achievements in all aspects of construction. In order to put the achievements of socialist construction into legal form, the Eighth Extraordinary Congress of the All-Russian Soviet Union was held in November and December 1936 and a new constitution was adopted. This constitution clearly stipulated that the Soviet Union was a socialist state of workers and peasants, that its economic basis was socialist public ownership of the means of production; that the principle of the distribution of labour according to the capabilities of each individual should be applied; and that the soviets of working people's deputies at all levels, which had grown and consolidated after the overthrow of the landlord-capitalist regime and the establishment of the dictatorship of the proletariat, were its political basis. In accordance with the new constitution, the South Caucasus Federation was abolished, and the Republics of Armenia, Azerbaijan and Georgia joined the USSR directly as Member Republics; the two autonomous republics of Kazakhstan and Kyrgyzstan were also transformed into Member Republics. The number of Union Republics increased from 7 to 11. The new constitution strengthened central power, limited and reduced the powers of the republics and local governments, and concentrated administrative, legislative and economic powers in the whole Union thereby, in essence, transforming the USSR into a centralised unitary state.

This constitution established the CPSU as the core of all social groups and state organs of the working masses. On the one hand, the party organs, either alone or jointly with the government, made resolutions and issued orders on economic and operational matters; on the other hand, operational departments were set up in the party organs at all levels, as opposed to the functional branches of government, to direct and replace the administrative functions of the various branches of government. In fact, from 1934 onwards, departments specialising in the leadership of the national economy and production were set up in the central and local party committees of the CPSU: "each production operations department should take the Ministry of Agriculture of the Central Committee as an example centrally to lead all party work in the department, lead party organisation, cadre assignment and training, mass agitation and production propaganda; they should also supervise relevant soviets, government agencies, economic agencies, and party organisations in the implementation of party resolutions."[9]

The constitution stipulated that the people had the right to govern the country but did not provide the necessary institutions to ensure effective oversight by the people of the state organs and leaders at all levels, and it was impossible to establish a democratic mechanism that effectively balanced the various interest groups in society. As a result, the party apparatus took over the right to elect and supervise public officials on behalf of the people and all party members. Although party organisations at all levels had supervisory committees, their powers of supervision were increasingly reduced, and the KGB, as a state security organ, continued to be vested with omnipresent powers.

After the CPR seized power, in response to the treacherous circumstances of civil war, a top-down system of cadre assignment was introduced but Lenin did not see it as the fixed cadre system of a socialist state. After Lenin's death, Trotsky and Bukharin opposed this system and called for democratic elections. Stalin criticised such views as "anti-party rhetoric" and imposed the appointment system. Due to the emphasis on the concentration of power, by the 1930s elections to the soviet and party organs were largely a formality, with the party organs exercising the right to appoint all types of cadres, whether elected or not, and with no provision for the length of their terms of office. This created a *de facto* life-time system for cadres and a mechanism whereby "a few people are chosen from a minority". The CPSU gradually formed a relatively stable group of bureaucratic privileges and vested interests.

In this way, the Soviet Union had a highly centralised and unified political system. "Before the second world war, Stalin had raised the issue of differential elections within the party and the freedom of social organisations to nominate candidates, but he had no time or energy to change the Soviet political system in the face of the strong traditionalist forces within the party. During the war, the CPSU also took a number of practical steps to unite the people in the fight against fascism, such as relaxing restrictions on religious activities and promising reforms in political and social relations but the wartime conditions did not lead to many substantial adjustments or changes in the system.

3. Strengthening socialist ideology and culture

In order to begin the task of socialist construction, the Soviet government continued to attach great importance to the ideological and cultural education of the country. In the autumn of 1928, the Central Committee of the Communist Youth League of the Soviet Union responded to the party's call and initiated a campaign against illiteracy and alcoholism in the march towards culture and education, which met with a wide response from all sections of the population, especially the young people. In 1930, at the 16th Congress of the CPSU, it was proposed that universal compulsory primary education and the eradication of illiteracy should be implemented as the main tasks of the party in the near future. By the end of the first five-year plan, 45 million people had been educated and the proportion of literate people had risen to 80%.[10] In August 1930, the Central Executive Committee of the Soviet Union and the People's Committee for Education announced a resolution on the implementation of universal compulsory education throughout the country. As of the 1940-1941 school year, the Soviet Union had more than 35 million students studying in ordinary schools and more than 800,000 students (including correspondence students) in higher education institutions. [11]

In 1938, the Central Committee of the CPSU adopted a resolution to "consolidate the party's propaganda and agitation work in one department by merging the various propaganda and press departments into a unified Central Propaganda and Agitation Bureau of the CPSU, with corresponding propaganda and agitation departments in the party organisations of each republic, krai (a large administrative division typically in remote border areas of the USSR) and oblast."[12] This was designed to centralise the ideological work of the region, including the supervision and leadership of the press, radio, publishing and all mass political agitation. In order to unify the thinking of the party and society as a whole, and to stimulate the political enthusiasm and participation of the people, the CPSU continued to organise the compilation of works by classic writers and the preparation of various textbooks in the social sciences, emphasising that books were combat-oriented and politically relevant, and were the most powerful tool for educating, mobilising and organising the masses around economic and cultural construction. In 1938, the *Concise History of the CPSU* (hereinafter referred to as the *History*), which Stalin edited and reviewed himself, was published. The Central Committee of the CPSU adopted a resolution stating that the *History* was an encyclopaedia of basic knowledge of Marxism-Leninism and a scientific summary of the great experience of the communist party. It was ordered that the use of other textbook versions of party history be stopped immediately throughout the country, and that all official interpretations of party history and the basic theories of Marxism-Leninism must be based on the formulas of the *History*, and that the phenomenon of arbitrary interpretations be eliminated. It should be made compulsory reading for every university student, and systematic study should be organised among the cadres at all three levels: senior, intermediate and junior. In March 1937, at the initiative and under the leadership of the Central Committee of the CPSU, economists in the Soviet Union also began to write a new textbook on political economy in order to summarise the theory of the experience of socialist economic construction.

However, with the publication of Stalin's *On Some Problems of Soviet Agrarian Policy* at the end of 1929 and his critique of the Deborin school of philosophy in 1930, the construction of Soviet ideology and culture began to suffer serious deviations and major mistakes. This was particularly marked by the politicisation and dogmatisation of ideology and culture, and a series of ideological and cultural 'great critiques' in which the party drew its final conclusions on the issues under debate. After the mid-1930s, the CPSU began to prohibit free discussion of theory and science in all fields, leaving it to the party and its leaders to provide answers to all social problems; the academic world had only an interpretive function and was reduced to being a "mouthpiece" and a "scribe" for the party leaders to implement policy guidelines. At the same time, a strict press ban and system of news censorship were imposed, normal academic exchanges between Soviet scientists and the Western scientific community were prohibited, and all capitalist ideas and culture were rejected and criticised without consideration. The above measures were intended to unify the ideology and will of the whole party and the whole country, and to prevent and cut off the invasion of capitalist ideology and culture; but they also suppressed and stifled freedom of thought, blocked exchanges between Soviet culture and capitalist culture, and caused Soviet ideology and culture to become increasingly dogmatic, rigid and regressive. Moreover, this series of critical ideological campaigns did not change after the second world war but rather intensified, with far-reaching and irreversible consequences for the long-term development of the country and the long-term governance of the CPSU.

In the early years of Stalin's rule, he attached great importance to the intellectuals and advanced the slogans "technology decides everything" and "cadres decide everything". In 1939, in his concluding report to the 18th Congress of the CPSU, Stalin specifically addressed the issue of the intellectuals. He criticised the prevailing hostility, contempt and disdain for intellectuals in the party, and the erroneous view of them as a dissident or even hostile force. He pointed out that "the intellectuals have undergone fundamental changes in the period of Soviet development, both in terms of composition and status, and they are not only close to the people but also cooperate sincerely with them. This is the principle difference between them and the old bourgeois intellectuals." Therefore, the old doctrine of distrusting and fighting against the old intellectuals was completely out of date, and "a new doctrine must be adopted for the new intellectuals; one that states that they must be treated with friendship, care, respect and cooperation for the benefit of the working class and the peasantry."[13] In general, however, Stalin's policy on intellectuals was complex and controversial, and as the regime became more entrenched, it gradually moved further and further down the wrong path. It began with the so-called "counter-revolutionary sabotage" case of the Shakhty coal mine's technical engineers in 1928, and with the "Great Criticism", "Great Struggle" and "Great Purge" campaigns. "As a result, a large number of Soviet experts, scholars and professors were suppressed, criticised or sent to prison.

4. The development of a strong and consolidated defence and army

Stalin, like Lenin, attached great importance to the role of the army in the fierce struggle to seize and consolidate power. He noted that in the history of old Russia, "The Mongol Khans have fought us for it; the Turkish nobles have fought us for it; the feudal lords of Sweden have fought us for it; the landowners of Poland and Lithuania have fought us for it. The capitalists of Britain and France have fought us for it. The aristocrats of Japan have fought us for it". The primary reason for this was "our military backwardness".[14] Consequently, in 1924 Stalin solemnly vowed at Lenin's memorial service: "We will spare no effort to strengthen our Red Army and our Red Navy!"[15]

In 1938, the *Resolution on the Admission of Soldiers of the Red Army to the Party* was adopted in order to expand the party's membership and increase the number of party members in the army. In the late 1930s, Stalin changed the 'hybrid system' of the combination of the regular army and the local militia to a single standing army system, in order to concentrate on building a modernised and regularised Red Army to meet the needs of the coming war. In order to accelerate the development of the national defence industry and defence science and technology, the second five-year plan of the Soviet Union (1933-1937) paid particular attention to the development of the basic industrial sectors of technical equipment and weapons production, with the metallurgical industry outpacing the development of industry as a whole; the total output of the machine-building and metal-processing industries increased nineteenfold over the 1913 level[16] and, in 1939, the output of the industry as a whole rose by 16% and that of the defence industry by 46.5%. In 1940, the output of the military industry increased by more than 33 3%.[17] During the third five-year plan, investment in the creation of new defence industrial bases in the Volga Valley, the Urals, Siberia and parts of the Far East at one time accounted for more than a quarter of all industrial investment.[18]

It was these strong political efforts, a strong strategic rear base and adequate strategic material reserves that served as the backbone of the front line after the outbreak of the Great Patriotic War, and laid the material and technical foundations for the final victory over German Fascism, with countless Soviet soldiers demonstrating their lofty heroism and indestructible will. Of course, in the second half of the 1930s and the early 1940s, Stalin's misjudgment of the overall strategic military situation and the military strength of the enemy prevented the Soviet army from preparing for a modern, mobile war with the enemy, resulting in catastrophic losses in the early stages of the German invasion. After victory in the second world war, the Soviet Union, faced with American nuclear blackmail, concentrated its enormous scientific and technological power and material production resources on the development of the atomic bomb, and soon broke the American nuclear monopoly to become an international leader in strategic nuclear power.

5. Building a "strong party with unity and iron discipline".[19]

Stalin continued Lenin's exploration of how to build the proletarian party under the conditions of governance and put forward clear ideas and initiatives for the building of the CPSU itself. These were: to strengthen the political education of the party and to set up a system of training and transferring party cadres through various schools and training courses; to strengthen the review and cleansing of the party's organisation and of those whose revolutionary will had declined; to give full play to the role of party members in the socialist transformation and construction of the party; to strive to absorb thousands of workers, farm labourers, poor peasants and mid-income peasant activists into the ranks of the party; and to "promptly and boldly promote young cadres to leadership positions"[20] to weaken and replace the dissident and bureaucratic conservative forces within the party; to continue to emphasise the promotion of democracy and to sternly condemn formalistic and indifferent bureaucratic attitudes towards the socialist cause and the fate of party members, in order to increase the enthusiasm and initiative of party members and improve the party's internal work as a whole. As a result of its efforts, the CPSU grew enormously. In 1925, at the 14th National Congress, there were 643,000 members and 445,000 reservists; by the end of the first five-year plan, there was one communist party member for every six workers in the Soviet Union; by the autumn of 1932, almost all communists and Komsomol (the All-Union Leninist Young Communist League) members in large Soviet enterprises had taken part in the socialist struggle. By the eve of the Patriotic War, the CPSU was already a large party with four million members. During the Patriotic War, more than five million people became reserve members of the party and 3.5 million became full members. By the time of the 19th Congress in October 1952, membership had grown to 6,882,145, and Komsomol membership had grown from eight million in 1939 to 16 million.[21]

However, the construction of the CPSU during the Stalin era had both the unity of theory and practice as well as the disjointed and divergent aspects of that time. In general, it overemphasized concentration and discipline while neglecting or even trampling on democracy. Too much emphasis was placed on achieving unification and unity through life-and-death struggle. The national party congress was an important institutional organisation for the realisation of democracy within the party, and the holding of regular party congresses was a fundamental sign of the soundness of democratic life within the party. In July 1903, Lenin proposed in his draft party constitution submitted to the Second Congress of the Russian Social Democratic Labour Party that party congresses should be held at least once every two years, if possible. From 1905 onwards, Lenin also advocated the introduction of annual party congresses in the hope of developing internal party democracy and avoiding excessive centralisation of power. After the victory of the October Revolution in 1917, the annual congresses of the CPR were held without interruption, even under the extreme circumstances of armed invasion by 14 imperialist countries and serious internal rebellions. From 1918 to 1923, six party congresses were held as the 7th to 12th Congresses of the CPR. However, from the 1930s onwards, the holding of party congresses and central plenaries became more arbitrary. The interval between the 14th and 15th Communist Party Congresses was two years, between the 15th and 16th congresses three years, between the 16th and 17th congresses four years, between the 17th and 18th congresses five years, and between the 18th and 19th congresses 13 years. The system of annual party congresses was effectively abolished, with the Politburo and the Secretariat overriding both the party congresses and the Central Committee.

Stalin once said: "It is impossible to lead the party outside the collective. After the death of Ilyich, it would be foolish for anyone to imagine doing so"; "collective work, collective leadership, keeping the party united under the condition of the majority, keeping unity in the organs of the centre - this is what we need now."[22] But from the time he became General Secretary of the CPR in 1922, he moved, step by step, to the pinnacle of his personal power. After 1941, he became Chairman of the People's Committee, Chairman of the Defence Committee, People's Commissar for Defence and Supreme Commander of the Soviet Armed Forces, combining party, political and military power. However, unlike Lenin, who relied mainly on his personality, ability and achievements to exercise leadership and influence, Stalin relied mainly on the Russian people's reverence for authority and anarchist traditions to decide party and state policies, and to give direct instructions to the People's Commissariat. He also inappropriately resorted to ideological control, power dictatorship and political intrigue, and used extreme methods such as brutal repression and even physical elimination of dissidents and political opponents. A large number of party, government and military leaders, including Zinoviev, Kamenev, Bukharin, Likov and Tukhachevsky, were dismissed from their posts, expelled from the party and sentenced to prison to await execution. At the 17th Congress in 1934, there were 18,774,488 official members and 935,298 reserve members in the CPSU; by the 18th Congress in 1939, the number of official members had fallen to 1,588,852 and 888,814 reserve members.[23]

Along with this arbitrariness came the cult and fetishisation of the individual. The cult of the individual in the Soviet Union began to take hold in the late 1920s. Stalin's 50th birthday was celebrated on 21 December 1929. One after another, the Soviet press described him as Lenin's sole assistant, the sole successor to Lenin's cause and the living Lenin. Thereafter, a large number of books and propaganda material began to highlight his achievements in all periods of the party's history. In 1948, the first official biography of Stalin was published in Moscow by the Moscow State Political Book Publishing House. It was compiled by the Marx, Engels and Lenin Institute attached to the Central Committee of the CPSU, reviewed by Stalin himself and written by Aleksandrov and Galaktionov. The book describes Stalin as a saint who could do no wrong: "Stalin is the gifted leader and mentor of our party, a great strategist of socialism, the leader and wise commander of the Soviet state", "his mind is as bright as crystal", "Stalin is the leader of the Soviet state today", "Stalin is the Lenin of today".[24] For Stalin's 70th birthday in December 1949, the Soviet Union organised an extremely lavish celebration in his honour, and a huge birthday campaign was launched by communist organisations and communist-ruled countries all over the world.

However, this phenomenon came to an abrupt end when Stalin died of a stroke on 5 March 1953. How to evaluate his life's merits and demerits has become the historical subject of constant disputes in the international communist movement.

6. Advancing world revolution through the Third International

After Lenin's death, Stalin made a new assessment of the present state of the capitalist world and the prospects for world revolution. He believed that the imperialists were preparing for a new war and that the CPSU must take full account of, and exploit the contradictions between, the imperialist countries, postpone the war and take all possible measures to maintain peaceful relations with them. At the beginning of the 1930s, the Soviet Union put forward the slogan "World Peace is Indivisible", actively advocated the idea of the collective defence of world peace by all the countries of the world, and proposed the idea of the concrete implementation of collective security and the establishment of a regional system of collective security in Europe and Asia. To this end, he actively promoted the establishment of diplomatic relations with countries willing to maintain peace, stood by the peoples of the world in major international crises and local wars, and strove to win over Britain and France to oppose the aggressive military expansion of the Fascist countries. In November 1933, the Soviet Union and the US formally established diplomatic relations, ending the 'dysfunctional relations' between the two powers. In September 1934, the Soviet Union accepted the invitation to join the League of Nations and became a permanent member of the Council. "After the outbreak of the second world war, the Soviet Union used various methods to push its borders westwards, building a defensive belt from the Baltic Sea to the Black Sea, the so-called "Eastern Front", in order to prevent the war from spreading eastwards and to strengthen the security of its western borders. By the end of 1941, the Soviet Union had formed an anti-Fascist alliance with Britain and the US, which led to a complete victory in the anti-Fascist war.

Stalin also believed that the expansion of imperialist armies and preparations for war would inevitably intensify the exploitation, oppression and control of the working people and colonial peoples of those countries; that this brutal oppression would inevitably provoke a revolt by those same working classes and colonial people; and that "the revolutionary awakening of the colonies and dependent countries heralds the end of world imperialism" 1. He proposed that the Russian proletarian party should have the international task of "developing, assisting and stimulating revolutions in all countries of the world", as Lenin had demanded. 2. On the premise of maintaining normal relations with the capitalist countries, it should actively support the revolutionary struggles in all countries of the world and integrate the revolutionary struggles of the world's people into the defence of the Soviet Union. The communist parties of other countries should learn from the experience of the Russian Bolsheviks and "Bolshevise" their communist parties as a necessary condition for their seizure of power and the establishment of the dictatorship of the proletariat.

As a result, the CPSU played an important role in spreading Marxism-Leninism, opposing all kinds of opportunism and "left" and right-leaning tendencies, helping to build and strengthen new proletarian parties in the East and West, and supporting the revolutionary struggles of the proletariat in capitalist countries and the national liberation movements of colonial and semi-colonial peoples. However, it cannot be denied that with the increasing consolidation of the ruling position of the CPSU, the Bolshevisation campaign promoted by the Comintern also developed a bias towards big-partyism and national egoism. Through the intermediary of the Third International, the CPSU placed the national interests of the Soviet Union as their top priority and demanded that the communist parties of all countries must follow the "flag bearer" of the Soviet Union and resolutely defend the leadership and core interests of the CPSU. They even went so far as to state: "If you do not defend the Soviet Union, you cannot defend and advance the world revolutionary movement". To a large extent, the Comintern was gradually transformed from the leading centre of the "organisation of the world revolution" into an instrument of Soviet foreign policy.

After the dissolution of the Comintern in 1943, the CPSU maintained its position as the leader of the world revolution and continued to exert control over the communist parties of other countries; this dysfunctional relationship was replicated in the relations between socialist countries. "After the end of the second world war, more than 10 countries in Europe and Asia embarked on the road to socialism and established socialist states. However, under the influence of the Soviet Communists, these countries followed the example of the Soviet Union and established a highly centralised political and economic system, promoting industrialisation and the collectivisation of agriculture. The Communist Party of Yugoslavia and the CPC, for reasons of their revolutionary history and their national conditions, have shown greater independence and autonomy, and have thereby actively explored the rules of governance that suit their national conditions, and have begun to show a new path to power for the communist party.

In March 1946, accompanied by then-US-President Harry Truman, former British Prime Minister Winston Churchill gave a speech at Fulton in the US, highlighting the dangers of communist expansion to the Western capitalist world. Truman then called on Congress to allocate funds for military and economic aid to Greece and Turkey in order to implement the so-called "Truman Doctrine". This was followed by the Marshall Plan to help the European countries devastated by war to rebuild their economies, and the establishment of the North Atlantic Treaty Organisation (NATO) and its armed forces. To break the capitalist blockade, the Communist Intelligence Bureau was set up in September 1947 under the leadership of the CPSU, to replace the defunct Comintern and to coordinate cooperation between European communist parties.

(II) THE INTERPRETATION AND SUMMARY OF THE LAWS OF COMMUNIST RULE BY THE CPSU DURING THE STALINIST PERIOD

Unlike Lenin, who used Marxist principles to create the first socialist state in Russia, Stalin inherited Lenin's cause, built socialism in one country, supported world revolution, promoted the Soviet model, and conducted a comprehensive and in-depth exploration of the laws of communist party governance. His exploration not only adhered to the basic principles of Marxism-Leninism but also bore the distinctive marks of Russian history and culture, the development of the times and his own personal characteristics. It contained many reasonable and useful elements.

The party must be armed with revolutionary theory and unified in its will. Stalin believed that only by mastering revolutionary theory could the proletarian party "give confidence to the movement, give it the ability to determine its course, enable it to understand the internal links of the events around it" and "enable practice to understand not only how and where the classes are marching at present but also how and where they will march in the near future". It is for this reason that the party "should arm itself with revolutionary theory, with knowledge of the laws of movement, and with knowledge of the laws of revolution."[25]

By revolutionary theory, Stalin meant Marxism-Leninism. He believed that Marxism-Leninism, which was scientific, revolutionary and practical, was not a dogma but a guide to action: "The classic Marxist writers of 45 to 55 years ago could not be expected to foresee all the historical twists and turns that would take place in every individual country in the distant future."[26] Therefore, "to master Marxist-Leninist theory does not in any way mean to read all its formulas and conclusions, and to hold on to every word of them. To master Marxist-Leninist theory means to understand its essence and to learn to apply it to the practical problems of the revolutionary movement under the various conditions of the proletarian class struggle. .... to be adept at enriching this theory with new experiences of the revolutionary movement, at enriching it with new principles and conclusions, and at developing and advancing it."[27]

At the same time, "although capitalism has been eliminated from the economy, remnants of the bourgeois outlook still exist and will continue to exist in the future", and adherence to Marxism-Leninism must also be "constantly on guard" as "the forces of capitalist encirclement seek to revive and support these remnants."[28] We must "centralise the party's propaganda and agitation work, expand the propaganda of Marxist-Leninist ideas, raise the theoretical level of our cadres and strengthen their political training."[29] We must continue to oppose the opportunist "left" and right deviations in the party to achieve ideological unity; we must overcome the most obvious and dangerous tendencies of paralysis, panic and retreat in the long and arduous struggle against capitalism, and maintain the spirit of fearlessness and heroism that Lenin displayed in all circumstances.

The dictatorship of the proletariat must be strengthened. According to Marx, Engels and Lenin, during the transitional period from capitalism to socialism after the proletariat has seized power, there are still classes and class struggles, and the state must exercise the dictatorship of the proletariat during this period. In the socialist period, there are no classes or class differences, and there is no class struggle; the country is "an apolitical state". However, this is far from being the case in the circumstances of socialist revolution and construction. Based on the socialist practice of the Soviet Union, Stalin believed that although socialist society had eliminated the exploiting classes and there was no longer any class confrontation, the remnants of those classes still existed and the outside world was still subject to siege, blockade, sabotage and even armed aggression and subversion by imperialism; class and class struggle still remained there, so the dictatorship of the proletariat must be perpetuated. He believed that the fundamental question of Leninism, the starting point of Leninism, the root of Leninism, was the question of the dictatorship of the proletariat.

So what is the dictatorship of the proletariat? According to Stalin, the dictatorship of the proletariat was an instrument of the proletarian revolution, not a democracy for all, but the rule of the proletariat over the bourgeoisie. The Soviet power established after the seizure of power was a form of state dictatorship of the proletariat, which differed in principle from the old bourgeois-democratic and parliamentary forms of state organisation. He also argued that: "The dictatorship of the proletariat is not simple violence but it is the leadership of the non-proletarian working masses and the construction of a socialist economy of a higher type than the capitalist economy, with higher labour productivity. The dictatorship of the proletariat is: (1) the use of unrestricted violence against capitalists and landlords; (2) the leadership of the proletariat over the peasantry; and (3) the socialist construction of society as a whole." "Only by combining all these three aspects can we obtain a complete concept of the dictatorship of the proletariat."[30]

In order to consolidate the dictatorship of the proletariat, Stalin believed that the leadership of the party in state power must be maintained. For: "The communist party is the basic instrument of the dictatorship of the proletariat; the leadership of the party (which does not and cannot share this leadership with other parties) is the basic condition for the dictatorship of the proletariat, without which there can be not even the slightest consolidation and development of the dictatorship of the proletariat."[31] We must "seek to channel through the Soviets and Soviet congresses our own candidates, our own outstanding staff, who are faithful to the proletarian cause and who are willing to serve it wholeheartedly, into the important state jobs in our country". "When any organ of power formulates work plans for industry and agriculture or for commerce and cultural construction, the party must give them general guidelines to determine the nature and direction of their work during the implementation of those plans."[32] At the same time, timely supervision and inspection must be carried out to correct the inevitable mistakes and shortcomings, to help them implement their resolutions effectively and to ensure that they have the support of the masses. Of course, the party must focus on the role of the Soviets, trade unions, production cooperatives and the Communist Youth League, as "levers and transmission mechanisms". "It is the party that realises the dictatorship of the proletariat; however, it does not do so directly but through the trade unions, through the Soviets and their branches."[33]

In order to consolidate the dictatorship of the proletariat, it was also necessary to remove factionalism from the party, not to allow the existence of factions, to resolutely crush the local forces that were digging their heels in and seeking independence, and to combat mercilessly all attempts to shake and undermine the iron discipline and unity of the party. Stalin believed that the interests of the party and the state would always take precedence over those of sectarian groups and localism, and that "the existence of various organised factions within the party would split the unified party into parallel organisations, and would lead to the formation of one or several new party sprouts and cells within the country, that is to say, to the disintegration of the dictatorship of the proletariat."[34]

. . .

The laws of political economy must be followed. In the late 1930s, the Soviet Union declared itself a socialist society with a unified, planned command economy. The change in the system of economic management and operation required of the party a new understanding and exploration of the laws of economic and social development, and to this end, Soviet economists proposed the task of creating a socialist political economy. In 1940, at the initiative and under the leadership of the Central Committee of the CPSU, work began on a new textbook on political economy. In January 1941, the Central Committee and the economists concerned discussed the yet-to-be-finalised draft of the book, affirming that commodities, money, value, profit, land rent and economic accounting still existed in the Soviet Union and proposing that the law of value still played a role in the socialist system. From February to September 1952, Stalin discussed economic construction in a socialist society in his book *On the Socialist Economy of the Soviet Union*, covering issues such as planned economy, the law of value and commodity production.

This book not only represents Stalin's understanding of the subject, but is also a major achievement of the CPSU's efforts after more than 30 years of socialist construction. Stalin began his book by affirming the objectivity of the laws of economics under the socialist system. He pointed out that the laws of political economy, whether in the capitalist or socialist period, are the same objective laws which reflect the process of economic development that does not depend on people's will. One can discover these laws, recognise them, learn to apply them with perfect knowledge and use them for the benefit of society but one cannot transform them, create them or destroy them. He believed that the main characteristic and requirement of the fundamental economic laws of socialism is: "to ensure the maximum satisfaction of the constantly growing material and cultural needs of society as a whole by means of the constant growth and perfection of socialist production on a highly technical basis."[35] In the book, Stalin also recognised that, to a certain extent, commodity production and the law of value were still at work in a socialist society; he suggested that there were still contradictions between the productive forces and the production relationships in Soviet socialist society but that the latter could be adapted to the development of the productive forces through timely adjustment. Although, for both historical and contemporary reasons, Stalin's understanding still had great limitations, such as denying that the means of production were commodities, that there was a commodity exchange relationship within universal ownership, and that the law of value also played a regulatory role in the sphere of production. Even so, the recognition of the existence and functioning of commodity production and the law of value under the socialist social system was undoubtedly a great creative advance for socialist political economy and scientific socialist theory. It also constituted a historic advance in the expansion and deepening of the understanding of the rules of communist governance.

The development of socialism must be constantly improved. In 1938, Stalin proposed the theory of "complete adaptation" to the question of productive forces and production relationships. He said that the tremendous development of industry and agriculture in the Soviet Union over several five-year plans showed that the new production relationships, which had replaced the old ones, were "perfectly adapted to the nature of the productive forces" and that "the communal ownership of the means of production here is perfectly suited to the social nature of the production process". Not only did it not hinder the development of productive forces but it was, in fact, the main and decisive force for their further development: "Consequently, in the USSR there was no economic crisis and no destruction of the productive forces."[36] What is commendable is that Stalin later corrected this misconception. In the 1950s, he argued that the expression "complete adaptation" should not be understood in an absolute sense. Under socialism, the relations of production lag behind the productive forces, and there is and will be a contradiction between them. Under socialism, economic development does not take the form of change but of gradual change, where the old is not simply abolished but changes its nature to fit the new, retaining only its form; and where the new does not simply destroy the old but permeates it, changing its nature and functions, using its form to develop the new. As for the new, it does not simply destroy the old but permeates it, changing its nature and function, not destroying its form but using it to develop the new."[37] Despite their flaws and shortcomings, and the fact that they are not analysed at the level of the question of the comprehensiveness of socialism, these views have their progressive significance and originality.

It is necessary to maintain and strengthen the ties with the millions of workers and peasants. Stalin used the relationship between the hero Antaeus and his mother in ancient Greek mythology to illustrate the importance of maintaining close ties between the party and the masses. He pointed out that the people were the creators of history, the real heroes, and that the time had passed when the leaders were considered the only creators of history without regard for the workers and peasants; the communist party was strong and invincible because it was good at maintaining and strengthening its ties with the millions of workers and peasants in its leadership of the movement. He believed that the interests of the party are the interests of the people, and that the party's cause is the cause of the people. Therefore, when formulating policies, the party must first take into account the interests of the people and make its line and policies correct and aligned with the interests of the working class; they must also be understood, grasped and put into practice by the people. This is what is meant by: "being good at guiding the masses to a revolutionary standpoint in order to convince them, based on personal experience, that the party's slogans are correct. This is the most important condition for winning over millions of workers to the party."[38] For this reason, one should not be detached from the masses but in close contact with them; one should not place oneself above them but go ahead of them and lead them forward; one should stay away from them but mingle with them, and win their trust and support.

In addition, he stressed that bureaucracy was the party's worst enemy and that "as soon as the Bolsheviks were detached from the masses and lost contact with them, as soon as they were infected with bureaucracy, they would lose any strength and become like empty shelves."[39] He proposed that we should rely on the masses from below and on the Central Supervisory Commission and the Workers' and Peasants' Procuratorate from above, and mobilise the masses to expose and criticise bureaucratism in order to enhance the prestige of the party and the government among the people.

The party must be built into an advanced force of the working class. Stalin believed that the proletarian party must be made up of the advanced elements of the working class and must "have its own programme (the immediate and final aims of the movement), its own tactics (the method of struggle) and its own organisational principles (the form of union). The unanimity of programmatic, tactical and organisational views is the basis on which our party is built. Only the consistency of these views can bind party members into a centralised party."[40] He pointed out that "the strength and role of political parties, especially the communist party, depends not so much on the number of its members as on their quality, on their steadfastness and loyalty to the proletarian cause."[41]

To this end, it is necessary to exercise unified proletarian discipline, to implement the principle of subordination of the minority to the majority and of subordinates to superiors, to implement the principles of collective leadership and internal party elections, to resolutely remove opportunist, corrupt and degenerate elements from the party, to increase trust in the party and its prestige, and to attract more of the urban and rural proletarian masses and the peasants to the party. Moreover, the existence of democracy within the party "is not intended to weaken and undermine proletarian discipline within the party but to consolidate and strengthen it."[42]

It is necessary to create a unified and disciplined team of cadres, because "after the correct political line is proposed, the organisational work determines everything, including the fate of the political line itself, namely, its realisation or its failure."[43] We must "attach importance to cadres", "understand them", "cultivate them with care", "promote young and bold new cadres in a bold and timely manner", and "arrange for staff to be trained in a timely manner". "We must "organise our staff in such a way as to ensure that each member of staff has their place, that each member of staff is able to make the most of their talents for our common cause, and that the general orientation of the staffing process is fully adapted to the requirements of the political line to which it belongs."[44] It is necessary to rely on self-criticism to grow stronger and "oppose the vulgarisation of the slogan of self-criticism".[45] He believed that the communist party "needs self-criticism as much as it needs air and water" and that "without self-criticism our party cannot move forward, cannot cut open our abscesses, and cannot eliminate our shortcomings."[46] To this end, criticism and self-criticism should become a regular mass exercise but care should be taken to distinguish strictly between "anti-Bolshevik 'self-criticism', which runs counter to us and is destructive, and our Bolshevik self-criticism; the purpose of our self-criticism is to strengthen the party, consolidate Soviet power, improve our construction work, reinforce our economic cadres and arm the working class". "What we need is not just any self-criticism; what we need is self-criticism that will raise the cultural level of the working class, develop their fighting spirit, consolidate their confidence in victory, strengthen them and help them to become the real masters of the country."[47]

4

THE MAJOR HISTORICAL CONTRIBUTION OF THE SOVIET UNION'S COMMUNIST RULE

OPENING UP A NEW ERA OF HUMAN SOCIAL DEVELOPMENT

Marx once pointed out that "philosophers only interpret the world in different ways but the real challenge is to change it." (6) Just as the CPSU occupies a special place in the history of human social development, its exploration and practice of the rules of communist governance are also pioneering and very special. The success of the revolution it led and its rise to power opened up a new era in the development of human history; its theory and practice of governance have also had an extremely drastic and far-reaching impact on the development of human society. In terms of its pioneering achievements, they are mainly manifested in the following aspects.

First, a historic breakthrough was made in exploring the communist party rules of governance. This is reflected in the extensive literature of Lenin, Stalin and the CPSU, which is only briefly outlined in the book from a historical perspective but can also be summarised in the Declaration of the Conference of Representatives of the Communist and Workers' Parties of the Socialist Countries held in Moscow in November 1957. This declaration outlined some of the main rules governing the process of socialist revolution and socialist construction in the various countries that had embarked on the road to socialism, and argued that these laws were still at work generally, although the characteristics and traditions that had developed in the history of the various peoples were very different and must be given due attention." These common laws are: the working class, with the Marxist-Leninist party at its core, leading the working masses in one form or another of proletarian revolution and establishing the dictatorship of the proletariat in one form or another; the establishment of an alliance of the working class with the masses of the peasantry and other working classes; the elimination of capitalist ownership of the basic means of production and the establishment of its public ownership; the gradual socialist transformation of agriculture; the planned development of the national economy in order to build socialism and communism, and to raise the living standards of the working people; carrying out the socialist revolution in fields of ideology and culture, resulting in the loyalty of the working people; the socialist transformation of agriculture; the systematic development of the national economy with a view to building socialism and communism, and raising the living standards of the working people; carrying out a socialist revolution in the ideological and cultural fields and creating a strong body of intellectuals loyal to the working class, the working people and the socialist cause; the elimination of national oppression and the establishment of equality and fraternity among all nationalities; and the defence of the fruits of socialism from enemies at home and abroad; the implementation of proletarian internationalism and unity with the working class of all countries." Furthermore, the manifesto stressed that "the fundamental principles of communism must be correctly adapted to the particular situation of nationalities and nation states", that "revisionism and dogmatism must be resolutely overcome in the ranks of the communist and workers' parties" and that "the Marxist-Leninist unity of one's own ranks must be upheld, and factions and groups that undermine this unity must not be allowed to exist."[1] It should be said that these statements basically cover the rules of communist governance, and are a summary of the laws of Soviet rule. They also bring advanced revolutionary theory and revolutionary experience to the working class, the working masses, the oppressed people and all political parties struggling against imperialism and for the construction of a new society of justice and equality.

Second, it led the whole country to achieve leapfrog development. The explorations of the CPSU not only transformed socialism from a theory and a movement into a real system, opening up the way to overcome the domination of private ownership and eliminate the system of human exploitation in human history; they also greatly liberated and developed productive forces, enabling the Soviet Union to develop from a large agricultural country with a relatively backward economy and culture into the world's second largest industrial country and a socialist power. In less than 20 years, the Soviet Union had closed a 50-100-year gap with the developed countries of the West. In 1940, the Soviet Union's gross national product (GNP) had increased 7 or 8 times compared to 1917, doubling and redoubling nearly three times. In the 12 years from 1928 to 1940, the Soviet Union was the only country in the world whose economy grew at an average annual double-digit rate. It was thanks to the establishment of a centralised and unified political and economic system with public ownership of the means of production, and to the central role of the communist party, that such a rapid pace and scale of development was achieved, and that the Soviet Union was able to defeat the frenzied German offensive in the Patriotic War and make an outstanding contribution to the decisive victory in the world war against fascism. At the same time, the people of the Soviet Union made historic strides towards freedom from ignorance and poverty while greatly improving the enjoyment of civil rights and the level of civilisation of the whole of Soviet society.

Third, it has transformed socialism from a beautiful ideal that has existed for centuries into a living, objective reality on a global scale. On the one hand, the CPSU explored and established the world's first socialist economic and political system, changing the situation of capitalist domination. "One world, two systems" became a reality, which was an important contribution to the development of human civilisation and social progress. On the other hand, with the support and impetus of the CPSU, the cause of socialism in the world has developed rapidly. This is not only reflected in the theoretical understanding of some things of universal significance which were also drawn upon by the socialist countries established later, many of which are difficult to deny in principle to this day, but also in the concrete practical aspects which also have permanent global significance. In the first half of the 20th century, following the path of the Soviet Union and striving for a socialist future became the goal pursued and fought for by progressive people around the world. In addition, the Western bourgeoisie, forced by its own development dilemmas and concerns about the global revolutionary process, also began to adjust its policies and institutional reforms, drawing extensively on the beneficial practices of the proletarian parties in power to rejuvenate the country and enrich the people.

Of course, although the CPSU illuminated and dominated the world for a time, it also carries sad memories in Russian history. We can see that it did indeed make certain achievements in its exploration of the rules of communist governance during this period, and for a time created epic glories but, on the whole, there were both experiences and lessons, twists and turns, and obvious historical limitations.

First, it failed to achieve continuous innovation in ideology and theory. The specific conclusions of any theory have historical and epochal limitations. The theories of Marx and Engels are no exception and the question is whether they can overcome such limitations through self-reflection and self-criticism. In their early years, Marx and Engels underestimated the life span of capitalism and overestimated the approach of the general crisis it was headed for. Later history proved that some of their ideas were "wrong", "only an illusion", "mistaken" and "impossible".[2] But their value lies not only in their courage to ruthlessly criticise the dark realities and erroneous theories, but also in their courage for self-examination and self-criticism, to constantly overcome their limitations, to keep abreast of the times, to open up new horizons for their theories and to bring them to new heights and levels.

It should be said that the CPSU was full of innovation at the beginning and tried hard to move the revolutionary cause forward through active exploration at a time when the material basis for the survival of the new production relationships was not yet mature. However, it gradually "lagged behind" the developing situation and became "trapped" in the glory it had achieved, so that it eventually fell into a state of blind optimism, rigidity and self-imposed isolation, just as Deng Xiaoping described: "The Soviet Union has been working on it for many years but it still has not completely figured it out."[3] The one-sided and mechanical understanding of Marx's and Engels' specific ideas about socialist revolution and construction was, in many ways, just a continuation and resurrection of Russia's historical and cultural traditions in a new guise. The fetishisation of the Bolsheviks' iron will and invulnerability led to the substitution of the political party for state power and social organisation in the form of an apparently omnipotent and all-encompassing ruling machine and spiritual source. As a result, the essence and true meaning of communism and socialism were lost and swallowed up in slogans and catchphrases, and the power of Marxism to illuminate the future and transform reality was greatly diminished. While making extraordinary achievements in political, economic and cultural construction, this was done at the expense of the fairness, justice and material interests that the Soviet people should have enjoyed at a higher level than the people of capitalist countries. The party, while acquiring and wielding all-embracing state and social power, also became assimilated into the state apparatus and became a class of aristocrats detached from the people; the rotation and renewal of the party leadership became a process of brutal purges and extermination; and the indiscriminate denunciation of different voices within the party as "anti-Marxist" deprived the party of an invaluable source of motivation for ideological and theoretical renewal and progress.

All of this clearly diverges from the direction of the development of the association of free people who, while enjoying certain democratic rights and gradually improving their material living conditions, do not feel that they have become the real masters of history and the country. In the end, this kind of socialist exploration, which ignores historical and environmental conditions and applies or deviates from certain specific ideas and assertions of Marx and Engels, is not only an extremely serious form of dogmatism and fundamentalism, but also runs counter to the laws of human social development and the rules of communist governance that it has revealed.

Second, there has been a failure to develop an effective national system of governance and the capacity to govern. Looking at the great revolutions of modern times, all of them have had a period of extreme emergency. After the end of this extraordinary period, whether to normalise, institutionalise and sanctify the concepts and patterns of the state of emergency, or to modernise the national governance system and its capacity to respond to the development of the situation and tasks it faces, is a major question that any successful revolutionary must answer and resolve. After the CPSU seized power, although it gradually abandoned its efforts to forcefully promote world revolution and embarked on full-scale socialist construction in its own country, it failed to adapt to the times and build a stable and orderly system of state governance to support social development through adjustments in political philosophy, institutional initiatives, development models and self-modernisation. The government has been constantly reinforcing a highly centralised economic and political system, inappropriately promoting the monopoly of power, the cult of the individual and personal patronage, consciously entrenching social structures and hierarchical privileges, and even resorting to large-scale irrational methods to eliminate the forces of class dissent, including the contradictions and divisions within its own camp.

The greatest merit and achievement of this particular governing logic and all-powerful ruling model was its strong organisational mobilisation and aggregation of resources, which ensured that the country's limited resources were swiftly pooled to sustain its rule and create a historical miracle of rapid "leapfrog" development. For a long time, the Soviet Union was a 'socialist island' in a sea of capitalism that could be swallowed up at any time by the turbulent waves of international monopoly capitalism and imperialism. It therefore adapted to the needs of the new regime's survival and development and, in a sense, to certain historical and cultural traditions of the Russian people, in particular the expectation that the empire would grow and multiply endlessly. However, when material and cultural production is still underdeveloped, prolonged attachment and obsession with this model can easily lead to an overemphasis on the class domination and oppressive attributes of the state, to the detriment of the rule of law and civilisation in political construction and economic and social management. This especially applies to the subjective position of the people in the governance of the state, with an overemphasis on the speed of development and catching up with the developed countries of the West as soon as possible, and a desire to get there in one step or shake off the historical burden in one go. At the same time, it is also very easy to open up the road of nation-building and governance in a radical manner, relying on a tumultuous mass movement to govern the country, or even to bring feudal authoritarianism into socialism. This involves not the elimination of, but the continual provision of, the circumstances for the survival and development of groups such as those who uphold personal authority, and those marked by refined egoism, "people wearing masks", "two-faced people" and those with vested interests within the party.

Stalin believed that the elimination of class was not achieved by extinguishing the class struggle, but by strengthening it; that the demise of the state was not achieved by weakening state power, but by strengthening it to the maximum; that the more socialism progressed, the sharper the class struggle became and the more vicious the defeated remnants of the exploiting classes would become. Therefore, what is needed now is not the old method of debate, but a new method of uprooting and crushing them. The deeper the class struggle goes, the more communists are called upon to continuously purge their own ranks, and it is by purging them of opportunist elements that the party is strengthened.[4] These new theories of class struggle have diluted people-centred values and objectives, which has not only led to increasingly closed and rigid political, economic, social, ideological and cultural systems, but also created a vicious circle in which the more emphasis is placed on class struggle, the more class struggle appears to be intensifying. A large number of innocent victims were purged and suffered, large numbers of opportunists poured into the party, large numbers of corrupt officials lept into high places, and the people lived in a state where it was difficult to rationally predict the future. This seriously damaged the reputation of the dictatorship of the proletariat and eroded the foundations of the party's long-term rule.

Lenin pointed out that "the greatest danger, perhaps even the only danger, for a true revolutionary is to exaggerate the role of revolution and to forget the limits and conditions for the proper and effective application of revolutionary methods."[5] After the end of the second world war, the CPSU should have taken advantage of the relatively peaceful post-war situation and conditions and, on the basis of the lessons learnt from the earlier period of construction and exploration, vigorously promoted the modernisation of the system of state governance and its capacity to govern in accordance with the vicissitudes of the times. However, under the influence of the glow of victory and the atmosphere of the Cold War, it did not give the party and the people a chance to take a break to reflect and plan calmly. Instead it continued to lose itself in the usual fervour and extremism, and glide heedlessly along the traditional path.

Third, it has failed to achieve a comprehensive transcendence over capitalism. Since its birth, capitalism has experienced numerous crises that have caused prolonged social suffering, but it has also had no shortage of successful practices and experiences. In the 20th century in particular, the technological revolution gave it a boost and led to an unprecedented increase in the socialisation of production; self-adjustment, increased state regulation and intervention in economic activities, and institutional preferential treatment of socially disadvantaged groups eased social contradictions and mitigated the impact of economic depression on society; the liberalisation and opening up of the world economy and the substantial increase in international investment and trade led to a significant increase in the strength of capitalism and a second 'golden age' of development for the capitalist world emerged. This shows that the bourgeoisie is extremely flexible and adaptable, that it has accumulated a wealth of experience in ruling, and that there is still wide scope for the development of capitalist production relationships, and that the end of bourgeois rule and the demise of capitalism will be a long, tortuous process full of contradictions and struggles. In the face of the historical transformation of capitalism in the post-war period, Western social democratic parties regrouped their forces and changed the situation that they had been in before the second world war; they gained legitimacy in their respective countries, gradually transforming from representing a "class party" in the early 20th century into a "parliamentary party" and a "national people's party", and became a left-wing political counterweight to conservatism in Europe. Clearly, it is unrealistic and blindly optimistic to view the historical trend towards the inevitable demise of capitalism as a "swift end", and the world map presents a new picture of long-term competition and replacement between socialism and capitalism.

In the 1920s, in the face of capitalist encirclement and blockade, the Soviet Union was determined to establish trade and cooperative relations with capitalist countries. Between 1927 and 1928, the Soviet Union imported 86.6 billion roubles worth of machinery and equipment from Germany and 165 billion roubles worth of goods from Britain.[6] However, in general, the CPSU, apart from always believing that capitalism was in a "general sociopolitical and economic crisis" and constantly exporting revolutions abroad, over-emphasised the belief that a country had all the conditions to build socialism. In doing so, it ignored the fact that socialism must be based on highly developed socialised mass production and that, especially when established in underdeveloped countries, it must fully learn from and absorb all the advances and civilised achievements created by developed capitalism.

"During and after the second world war, Stalin tried to rebuild Russia's European image but, due to the US encirclement through the Marshall Plan, NATO and the influence of Russia's chauvinist and expansionist traditions, the CPSU and the socialist countries under its influence have long adopted all-out confrontation with the Western capitalist countries. The CPSU believed that the emergence of the socialist camp had dismantled the unified world market and, as long as there was a unified market within the socialist camp, the socialist economy would be able to catch up with the capitalist economy and socialism would prevail. However, as the result of a closed and rigid attitude, many socialist countries, including the Soviet Union, experienced a period of rapid growth and then fell into a predicament of development in which production was sluggish and people's living standards could barely be raised. This, coupled with the reliance on power and violence to consolidate the socialist camp, led to an increasing lack of vitality and dynamism, with the entire camp falling apart and failing to present a compelling picture of the socialist system to the people of the world. This not only affected the reputation of socialism and damaged the image of the communist party, but also caused the people of this country and the world at large to waver and turn their backs on their belief in socialism.

In short, the CPSU's understanding of the rules of communist party governance was both a pioneering exploration of the history of the international communist movement and in relation to the specific historical conditions in Russia. Although it mostly represented the understanding and practice of how to govern in a relatively economically and culturally backward country in the process of moving towards socialism, and despite the fact that it started gloriously and then ended in failure, it was, in the end, the pioneering attempt in human society to put into practice the model of socialist revolution and construction. Whether it succeeded or failed, it provided a profound historical lesson for future generations to continue to explore the rules of human social development, socialist construction and communist party governance.

PART II
THE FOUNDATION OF THE CPC'S GOVERNANCE AND AN EXPLORATION OF THE PATH IT HAS TAKEN

The CPC is a new type of proletarian political party established in accordance with the principles of Marxism. Since its establishment, the party has set the realisation of communism as its highest ideal and ultimate goal, and its original intention and mission is to work for the happiness of the people and the rejuvenation of the Chinese nation. It insists on combining the basic principles of Marxism with the concrete reality of the Chinese revolution and unity. It has led the people through 28 years of bloody struggle, completed the new democratic revolution, established the People's Republic of China (PRC) and cemented its ruling position in the country. This is the inevitable result of the development of modern Chinese society and the people's revolutionary struggle, and it is the choice of history and of the people.

After the founding of new China, the CPC united and led the people to quickly heal the wounds of war, restore and develop the national economy, consolidate the new people's power, complete the socialist revolution and establish the basic socialist system. On this basis, the party drew on the lessons of the Soviet Union and, taking into account China's national conditions, united and led the people of all ethnic nationalities to carry out large-scale socialist construction; it began to explore China's own road to socialism, starting the process of exploring the rules of governance under the historical conditions of socialism. In the course of its exploration, the CPC achieved original theoretical results and great successes, and accumulated valuable experience in governing but it also made serious mistakes and left behind painful lessons. All this has provided valuable experience, theoretical preparation and a material basis for the creation of socialism with Chinese characteristics in the new period of reform and opening up.

1

CPC RULE IS THE CHOICE OF HISTORY AND THE PEOPLE

According to Marxism, a political party is a product of the development of class struggle to a certain stage, and is the most centralised, complex and highest form of class organisation. Being a new type of proletarian party, the founding of the CPC was the inevitable result of the violent movement of social contradictions and the development of the Chinese revolutionary struggle in modern times, and the inevitable outcome of the combination of Marxism-Leninism and the Chinese workers' movement. The achievement of the ruling position of the party was the choice of history and of the people. It was not through peaceful and democratic means but through a long armed struggle under the leadership of the CPC, at great cost and with bloody sacrifice, and through a new path for the Chinese revolution in which the countryside encircled the cities and power was seized by armed force.

(I) THE BANKRUPTCY OF WESTERN POLITICAL AND PARTY SYSTEMS IN PRACTICE IN CHINA

Over thousands of years of history, the Chinese nation created a long and splendid Chinese civilisation, made remarkable contributions to humanity and became one of the great nations of the world. However, after the Opium War in 1840, with the invasion of Western capitalist-imperialism and the decadence and decline of rule, China was gradually reduced to a semi-colonial and semi-feudal society, and plunged into a miserable situation of internal and external strife. To achieve national independence and the liberation of the people, to achieve national prosperity and people's happiness, and to realise the great rejuvenation of the Chinese nation have become the two major historical tasks and great dreams of the Chinese nation in modern times.

In order to accomplish these two historical tasks and realise their great dream, the Chinese people have fought tirelessly, and countless men and women have painstakingly explored the road to national salvation. For a long period of time, learning from Western political and party systems, and following the path of capitalist development was the goal pursued by these Chinese pioneers. To this end, various political forces and their representatives appeared on the scene, and bourgeois political programmes such as constitutional monarchy, the parliamentary system, the multiparty system and the presidential system were enacted in turn but all ended in failure.

Attempts to change China's political system can be traced back to the Hundred Days Reform in 1898. For the first time, the bourgeois reformists, represented by Kang Youwei and Liang Qichao, explicitly advocated that China should follow the West in introducing political reforms and put forward the political programme of "promoting people's rights, establishing a parliament and creating a constitution", hoping that China would follow the path of constitutional monarchy. In June 1898, the Guangxu Emperor accepted the proposal of the reformists and initiated changes in the law. However, these changes were met with strong hostility and opposition as they undermined the interests of the conservative forces led by Empress Dowager Cixi, and the reform failed after only 103 days. After the Boxer Rebellion and the invasion of China by the Eight-Power Allied Forces, and especially after Japan, a small constitutional monarchy, defeated Russia in the Russo-Japanese War of 1905, the Qing government was forced to implement the New Deal and prepare a constitution. The aim of the Qing government's constitutional preparations was to befriend the Western powers externally and suppress the revolution internally, in order to strengthen imperial power and ultimately maintain feudal autocracy. Therefore, after examination of the constitutions of more than a dozen countries, the centralised German and Japanese models proved the most attractive; a constitution was formulated but it was still considered desirable to use it to put a veneer of legality on the autocratic imperial and monarchical power; consequently, a cabinet system was formed but it was a "royal cabinet". This was contrary to the essence of the modern political system of constitutional monarchy, which is intended to limit, restrict and regulate the power of the monarch. This being the case, the only solution was to replace the constitutional monarchy with a democratic and republican constitution by revolutionary means that would overthrow the monarch completely. The Xinhai Revolution, which broke out in October 1911, was the first historic change in China in the 20th century. It overthrew the autocratic rule of the Qing dynasty, put an end to the monarchy that had ruled China for more than 2,000 years and established the Republic of China. Since then, "the nation will come together to strike down anyone who dares to establish an imperial system for their own benefit."[1]

At the end of the 19th century, when the bourgeoisie was launching the Reform Movement, the bourgeois revolutionaries, represented by Sun Yat-sen, began to engage in revolutionary struggles with the aim of overthrowing the Qing dynasty's autocratic rule. In 1894, Sun Yat-sen shouted the slogan "Revive China" for the first time. In 1905, he founded the Tongmenghui, a bourgeois revolutionary party, and for the first time proposed the revolutionary goal of replacing the feudal Qing dynasty with a bourgeois democratic republic. The Xinhai Revolution, which broke out in 1911, was an anti-imperialist and anti-feudal bourgeois democratic revolution in the fullest sense of the term, establishing the Nanjing Provisional Government, the first bourgeois republican government in Chinese history. The Provisional Government of Nanjing adopted the ideology of a democratic republic and the principle of the separation of powers, and formulated the *Provisional Constitution of the Republic of China (ROC)*, the first bourgeois republican constitution in Chinese history. But after three months of the existence of the Nanjing Provisional Government headed by Sun Yat-sen, under strong pressure from imperialist and feudal forces, the fruits of the Xinhai Revolution then fell into the hands of the Beiyang warlords led by Yuan Shikai. Although the Xinhai Revolution failed, it opened the floodgates of social progress in China and contributed to the awakening of the Chinese nation and the emancipation of its people's minds. After the Xinhai Revolution, various "isms" began to circulate in society, and representatives of various classes and social strata appeared on the stage, and a number of different political parties sprang up. Statistical records show that, "after the outbreak of the Wuchang Revolution, by the end of 1913, there were 682 new open party committees, with 312 that may be considered political parties."[2] The majority of these groups were short-lived but among these groups, the 30 main ones that had some political influence and appeal included the Kuomintang (KMT), the Republican Party, the Democratic Party and the Progressive Party. From December 1912 to February 1913, the first election of bourgeois significance in modern China, for the First National Assembly of the Republic of China, was held nationwide, with the KMT winning a resounding victory. As the *Provisional*

Constitution of the ROC changed the presidential system under the Nanjing Provisional Government to a cabinet system, the KMT's victory meant the restriction and even the hollowing out of the power of Yuan Shikai, and Sun Yat-sen and others once again saw the hope of a democratic republic. However, in March 1913, Song Jiaoren was assassinated, the Assembly was forced to suspend its proceedings in November, and in January 1914, some of its remaining members were sent back home by Yuan Shikai, frustrating the goal of a bourgeois republic. During the Beiyang period, China was divided between warlords, with different factions and constant attacks, the proclaimed "Constitution" was revised and changed, the choice of a presidential system or a cabinet system was argued over, and presidents and premiers were changed one to another. Basically, under the guise of the "ROC" and of a "democratic republic", there was, in fact, an authoritarian dictatorship in power. Even Yuan Shikai and Zhang Xun abandoned any pretence and twice staged farcical attempts to restore the imperial system. The revolutionaries, represented by Dr Sun Yat-sen, fought tirelessly to uphold the democratic republic, but the Second Revolution, the National Defence Movement and the Constitutional Defence Movement were all unsuccessful. Harsh reality prompted people to begin to doubt the bourgeois republican programme and to ponder the feasibility of the previous revolutionary paths and methods. Influenced by the October Revolution in Russia, some old members of the Tongmenghui, such as Dong Biwu, Lin Boqu and Wu Yuzhang, put their faith in Marxism and became early Chinese communists. They realised that "the old revolutionary methods had to be changed" and that "from the lessons of the October Revolution and the May Fourth Movement, we learned we had to rely on the lower classes and follow the path of the Russians". The idea that "through the October Revolution and the May Fourth Movement, we must rely on the lower classes and follow the path of the Russians" was "becoming stronger and clearer."[3] Sun Yat-sen also declared that "the Chinese revolution could not be accomplished unless Russia was taken as a teacher" and put forward three major policies, namely, alliance with Russia, alliance with the CPC and the support of peasants and workers, developing the old "Three Principles of the People" into the new "Three Principles of the People". In 1924, as actively promoted by Sun Yat-sen, the KMT (nationalist) and the CPC (communist) parties collaborated and the National Revolution emerged. With the victory of the Northern Expedition, the rule of the Beiyang warlords was completely overthrown. However, the idea and associated activities of establishing a bourgeois republic and taking the capitalist road in China did not disappear, and the relevant political forces and representatives were very active for a time. During the Nationalist

Government in Nanjing, the nation's bourgeoisie had high hopes of Chiang Kai-shek. It was claimed that China could follow "the path of Kemal Attatürk", that is, a bourgeois republic led by the bourgeoisie, as Attatürk had done in Turkey, and that Chiang Kai-shek was "China's Attatürk". However, Chiang Kai-shek soon betrayed Sun Yat-sen's revolutionary ideals and moved towards a one-party dictatorship, with the Nanjing National Government becoming the representative of the interests of the large landowners and the bourgeoisie. Although the 1931 Constitution of the Government of the ROC, the 1936 Draft Constitution of the ROC and the 1947 Constitution of the ROC were all bourgeois democratic in form and expression, claiming to represent "a democratic republic of the people, by the people and for the people", they were merely superficial. Their essential aim was to maintain the one-party dictatorship of the KMT and to legitimise the personal dictatorship of Chiang Kai-shek. The establishment of a bourgeois republic was, of course, only an illusion.

During the period before and after the victory of the War of Resistance Against Japanese Aggression, "centrist parties" such as the China Democratic League and China National Democratic Construction Association, as well as middlemen such as Shi Fuliang, Zhang Dongsun, and Zhang Lan, enthusiastically advocated the "middle line" or "third way." They argued that China's political system should be modelled on the British and American democratic systems, with a parliamentary cabinet and parliamentary systems, local autonomy and an independent judiciary, while at the same time "using the economic democracy of the Soviet Union to enrich the political democracy of Britain and America". Shi Fuliang was the most explicit advocate of this. He said that the political line of the centrists "must be politically democratic in the Anglo-American sense but must not be manipulated by a few privileged classes (in today's China there are bureaucratic capitalists, comprador capitalists and large landowners); economically it must develop national capitalism and reward the expanded production of the necessities of life but must not allow comprador bureaucratic capital to develop uncontrolled."[4] The essence of this proposition was still to establish a bourgeois democratic system in China. In October 1945, the League of Democrats also held a provisional national congress in Chongqing, which adopted a programme for the realisation of its bourgeois republic. In January 1946, the Political Consultative Conference was held in Chongqing, which adopted resolutions that were most favourable to the "middle parties", such as the reorganisation of the government into a multiparty coalition, the peaceful establishment of the state, the introduction of a constitutional government and nationalisation of the army. But the situation was soon reversed and in June 1946, the ruling clique of the KMT tore up the CPPCC resolution and openly launched an all-out civil war. At the same time, it began the large-scale persecution of the progressive forces of democracy, causing the murderous attacks on Li Gongpu and Wen Yiduo, and convened the "False National Congress". In October 1947, the KMT issued a decree banning the "centrist party", and the "middle line" was again declared politically bankrupt.

History and practice have amply proved that adopting the Western political and party systems and following the path of bourgeois development will not work in China, which is a semi-colonial and semi-feudal society.

On this issue, Mao Zedong once observed perceptively that: "The history of imperialist aggression against China, opposition to Chinese independence and opposition to the development of capitalism in China is the history of modern China."[5] Imperialist powers "became even more dependent on their colonies and semi-colonies for their livelihood and would never allow any of those to establish any capitalist society under the dictatorship of the bourgeoisie."[6] The aim of capitalism and imperialism was to turn China into their semi-colonies and colonies, to develop their own capitalism, to occupy an extremely large market for dumped commodities, to establish an ideal market for capital exports and a supply of cheap raw materials and labour. If China became an independent capitalist state, not only would their colonial interests be lost, but they would also face a strong competitor in the international market. Capitalism and imperialism did everything possible in order to achieve control over China, especially by cultivating a large number of agents within the country, including the comprador class, the feudal landowning class and the bureaucratic bourgeoisie. These reactionary classes were politically represented initially by the Qing government, then by the Beiyang warlords, and finally by the KMT regime. Such reactionary forces, both at home and abroad, became the root cause of the obstacles to the development and progress of modern China, and were the greatest enemies of the Chinese revolution.

It was because of the strength and ferocity of the reactionary forces that the national bourgeoisie in China had to be very powerful, resolute in its struggle and thoroughgoing in its revolution if it was to set China on the path of capitalist development. But the Chinese national bourgeoisie did not have such strength and awareness, once again because of the path along which modern Chinese history had developed. From its birth, Chinese national capitalism was ill-fated, struggling to survive in the gaps between domestic and foreign capital, and developed inadequately, showing obvious characteristics of a semi-colonial, semi-feudal society. Its inextricable links with imperialist capital and feudal land ownership pre-determined the weakness and compromised status of the national bourgeoisie. The fundamental reason for the failure of the Hundred Days Reform was that it dared not repudiate the feudal monarchy. It was this failure that led many reformers to abandon reform and move towards revolution. Although the Xinhai Revolution overthrew the feudal dictatorship, it was unable to formulate a thorough anti-imperialist and anti-feudal revolutionary programme and was detached from the masses, inevitably leading to compromise; all of this simply serves to illustrate the limitations of the national bourgeoisie. Studies by scholars such as Zhou Xirui and Yuzo Mizoguchi show that the decisive force behind the victory of the Xinhai Revolution was not the revolutionary party itself, but the independence of the provinces and reliance on local secessionist forces, later known as warlords.[7] Before Sun Yat-sen put forward the new "Three Principles of the People", which consisted of the three major policies of uniting with Russia, uniting with the communists, and supporting peasants and workers, the old "Three People's Principles" were unable to treat warlords, bureaucrats and landlords as the targets of the revolution, and were unable to tackle the feudal land ownership system head-on because Sun Yat-sen had always relied on one faction of warlords to defeat another. In this regard, Dong Biwu once recalled: "When it comes to the revolution in our country, we used to work with Sun Yat-sen but Sun's way was not right and he always relied on the warlords. As the revolution developed, Sun was unable to control it and, as a result, someone else did. So we began to study the Russian way."[8]

The historical mission of achieving the great rejuvenation of the Chinese nation has therefore historically fallen to a new social force: the Chinese proletariat and its political party. The CPC is fundamentally different from other bourgeois parties in that it is "a disciplined party, armed with Marxist-Leninist theory, adopting a self-critical approach and in touch with the masses."[9] Since its establishment, it has been guided by scientific theory and has taken up the historic mission of achieving the great rejuvenation of the Chinese nation with a revolutionary spirit and historical commitment. "The kind of bourgeois republic which foreign countries have had, China cannot have, because China is a country oppressed by imperialism. The only way is through the people's republic led by the working class" and " to reach socialism and communism through the people's republic."[10] This is the programme of the CPC.

After a long period of struggle, the programme of the CPC not only gained the support of the people but the majority of those who had sincerely fought for the bourgeois republican programme, the "middle line" or the "third way", had likewise changed their position. In January 1948, the China Democratic League declared in Hong Kong: "We in the Democratic League are determined not to have a neutral attitude between right and wrong. As for the middle course of independence, it is even more difficult to make it work in light of the present reality in China". For this reason, the National Democratic League "stands firmly on the side of people's democracy" and "joins hands with the CPC" to "completely destroy the reactionary dictatorship in Nanjing and fight to the end for the complete realisation of a democratic, independent and united new China."[11] After the CPC Central Committee issued the "May Day slogan", the path of the people's democratic dictatorship became the common aim of the people, all democratic parties and individual democrats. As Mao Zedong pointed out: "It was in this way, the civilisation of the Western bourgeoisie, the bourgeois democracy and the programme of a bourgeois republic all broke down in the minds of the Chinese people. Bourgeois democracy gave way to the people's democracy led by the working class, and the bourgeois republic gave way to the people's republic."[12] This is a profound summary of the historical experience of the Chinese revolution over a hundred years, representing the inevitable result of the choice of history and the choice of the people.

(II) EARTH-SHATTERING EVENTS: THE CPC AS CHINA'S NEW LEADING FORCE TAKES TO THE POLITICAL STAGE

In 1921, amidst the violent movements of Chinese society in the modern era, the fierce struggle of the Chinese people against feudal rule and foreign invasion, and the integration of Marxism-Leninism with the Chinese workers' movement, the CPC emerged to take to the political stage as the new leading force in China.

At the time of its founding, the CPC was a small party with just over 50 members, operating in secrecy. In terms of historical significance, its creation was a "ground-breaking event". The history of the Chinese people's fierce struggle against feudal rule and foreign aggression in modern times has fully proved that in a large semi-colonial and semi-feudal oriental country, and in the face of the extraordinarily powerful combined forces of imperialism and feudalism, the two major historical tasks facing the Chinese nation and the great rejuvenation of the Chinese nation could never be achieved without a party comprising members with lofty revolutionary ideals, a high degree of awareness, discipline and self-sacrifice, truly representing and uniting the people. It is the people who have always opened up the way forward in the midst of social contradictions. The facts fully demonstrate that the birth of the CPC was an objective requirement chosen by history and the people, and was the natural outcome of the development of Chinese society in modern times.

The founding of the CPC was a "groundbreaking event" because the party had distinctive characteristics that no other political party in China had ever had before. These characteristics enabled the party to establish its roots in China and to distinguish itself from the other political parties of modern China, becoming the core leadership of the revolutionary struggle of the Chinese people. The Chinese revolution has taken the correct direction, the Chinese working class has had a fighting headquarters, the toiling masses of China have had a leader to liberate them, the Chinese revolution has had a new look, and the destiny of the Chinese people and the Chinese nation has had a bright future.

First, as soon as the CPC was founded, it clearly established Marxism as the fundamental guiding ideology of the party.

What kind of doctrine a country adopts and what kind of road it takes depends on whether that doctrine or road can solve the historical problems facing the country. Anti-imperialism and anti-feudalism were the twin demands of modern China and the litmus paper for the Chinese people to test all "isms" with. From the Heavenly Kingdom Movement of the Taiping to the Xinhai Revolution, the history of failure after failure has fully demonstrated that the old stubborn feudalism and the various capitalist doctrines and trends learnt from the old imperialists could not solve the problem of China's future and destiny. Marxism, as a scientific theory of proletarian and human liberation, not only opposed feudalism but also exposed the exploitative nature of capitalism and called for the establishment of a new social system superior to capitalist society, thereby satisfying the dual demands of the Chinese people against imperialism and feudalism. The Chinese people consequently found the goal and direction for the revolutionary struggle and a powerful ideological weapon to guide it from victory to victory. As Mao Zedong observed: "Ever since the Chinese learned Marxism-Leninism, the Chinese people have moved in spirit from passivity to initiative."[13] The CPC has had Marxism written on its banner from the day it was founded. The *Programme of the CPC*, adopted at the party's first congress, explicitly states that the party is named the "CPC", which clearly answers the question of "Who am I?" and equally clearly declares the original intention and mission of the CPC. Since then, faith in Marxism and belief in socialism and communism have become the "root" and "foundation" of the CPC, and have become the spiritual pillars that have enabled the CPC to withstand any test and remain strong. The reason why the CPC has been able to accomplish the difficult tasks that have been impossible for other political forces in recent times is that it has always taken the scientific theory of Marxism as its guide to action, and insisted on constantly enriching and developing Marxism in practice.

Second, as soon as the CPC was founded, it established the struggle for communism as its platform, indicating both the goal and the correct path of the Chinese revolution.

During the 80 years of arduous exploration after the Opium Wars, no class or political party had been able to show the Chinese people the goal of the revolutionary struggle and find a correct path to lead the Chinese nation to rejuvenation. In response to this long unresolved question, the CPC, from the day it was founded, applied the basic principles of Marxism to observe and analyse the Chinese problem, and came to the conclusion and gave the clear answer that "we should follow the path of the Russians". The *Programme of the CPC*, adopted at the party's first congress, proposed the overthrow of the bourgeoisie by a revolutionary proletarian army and the adoption of the dictatorship of the proletariat in order to achieve the goal of class struggle - the elimination of classes and the abolition of private ownership. The Second Party Congress further revealed the semi-colonial and semi-feudal nature of Chinese society and proposed, for the first time, an anti-imperialist and anti-feudal democratic revolutionary programme, which pointed out the goal of struggle and the correct path for the Chinese people, and also provided a preliminary answer to the questions of "where to go" and "what to do". This was a great and valuable achievement for the CPC, which had only been founded a year earlier. For the first time in the history of the party, the Second Party Congress loudly proclaimed the slogan "Long live the CPC", demonstrating the historical commitment and resolute self-confidence of Chinese communists to work for the happiness of the Chinese people and the rejuvenation of the Chinese nation.

Third, since its establishment, the CPC has always maintained flesh-and-blood ties with the people, and this has won it the deepest and most powerful source of strength for ultimate victory.

Both the Hundred Days' Reform and the Xinhai Revolution launched by the bourgeois reformists represented the special interests of a small number of people, and they could not escape the historical limitations of pursuing their own special interests. They were completely divorced from the masses and ultimately could not escape the fate of failure. The CPC was fundamentally different in that it was the party of the most advanced class, that is the working class, and represented not only their interests but also the interests of the broadest spectrum of people and the Chinese nation as a whole. It had no special interests of its own other than those. This enabled the party to break away from the limitations of all previous political forces in pursuing their own special interests, and to lead and promote the Chinese revolution with a materialist, dialectical scientific spirit, a selfless and generous heart, a flesh-and-blood relationship with the people and a spirit of unrelenting struggle. Immediately after its founding, the CPC went to work among the labouring masses, who make up the majority of China's population, and actively devoted itself to revolutionary activities, organising and developing workers', peasants', women's and youth movements. The Second Party Congress clearly advanced the concept and principle of a "party of the masses", stressing that "since we are a party fighting for the proletarian masses, we must 'go to the masses' and form a big 'party of the masses', emphasising that 'all movements of the party must reach out to the masses.'"[14] The questions of "for whom" and "relying on whom" were the first to be answered. Since its inception, the party has been firmly rooted in the people, sharing the same fate as the people and always maintaining a flesh-and-blood relationship with them. This is what has provided the fundamental guarantee that the party will overcome all difficulties and risks.

Fourth, as soon as the CPC was established, it built up a tight organisation and established strict discipline, so that the party was united like steel in a strong fighting force.

In stark contrast to China's previous political parties, which were complex and loosely organised, and could hardly form a strong force, the CPC is a Marxist party founded on the principle of democratic centralism, with a tight organisation, strict discipline and unity of the whole party. The programme of the First Party Congress provided for the development of party membership, the establishment of central and local bodies, and other organisational systems, and the enforcement of strict discipline. The Second Party Congress emphasised: "When a revolutionary party lacks strict centralised and disciplined organisation and training, it will not have the strength to carry out a revolutionary movement if all it has is the desire to do so."[15] The first party constitution adopted at the Second Party Congress set out provisions on party membership, organisation, meetings, discipline and party fees, establishing the party's organisational structure and the basic norms of conduct for party organisations at all levels and for all party members, establishing a tight organisational system from the bottom up, and stipulating systematic and strict disciplinary rules. The creative application and development of the principle of democratic centralism has enabled the CPC to become a fighting team with a unified will, unified action and unity of purpose, providing a strong organisational guarantee for the party to lead the people of China to victory in both revolution and construction.

The founding of the CPC was an "earth-shattering event" that created the great "Red Boat Spirit". The "Red Boat Spirit", which carries the spirit of pioneering and daring, the spirit of steadfast ideals and indomitable struggle, and the spirit of dedication to the party and the people, has witnessed that "earth-shattering event" in Chinese history, and has become the symbol of the origin of the Chinese revolution. It has become the spiritual source, the fundamental driving force and the "red gene" of the Chinese communists, passed on from generation to generation. Inspired by the "Red Boat Spirit", the CPC has led the revolutionary ship, cut through the waves and created a great historical event that opened up the world.

(III) THE CPC'S GREAT CREATION OF A NEW PATH OF REVOLUTION AND LOCAL GOVERNANCE

In April and July 1927, Chiang Kai-shek's group and Wang Jingwei's group staged counter-revolutionary coups, which led to a complete breakdown of the communist party's cooperation and the failure of the revolution. The Chinese revolution had reached a low ebb but, although the Great Revolution failed, it had a profound and significant impact on the ongoing Chinese revolution. The anti-imperialist and anti-feudal ideas advanced by the CPC became the common voice of the people, and its political influence among the masses expanded rapidly. In particular, through the repeated victories and defeats of the revolution, the party underwent profound training and severe tests. All this prepared the ground for the party to lead the people to open up a new road and a new stage of revolution.

Faced with the awful White Terror in China, the August 7th Conference of 1927 summed up the lessons learned from the failure of the revolution, decided on a policy of agrarian revolution and armed uprising, and laid out the task of "reorganising ourselves and reorganising our own ranks, correcting the serious mistakes of the past, and finding a new path", thereby starting the difficult journey of exploring a new path for the revolution. On 1 August 1927, Zhou Enlai and others led the Nanchang Uprising, firing the first shot of armed resistance against the KMT reactionaries, which kick-started the CPC's independent leadership of the Chinese revolution, the creation of a people's army and the armed seizure of political power. By the beginning of 1928, the party had led more than a hundred armed uprisings, including the Autumn Harvest Uprising and the Guangzhou Uprising, but all of them were aimed at attacking the cities and soon failed. The brutal facts proved that after the failure of the Great Revolution, with the cities tightly controlled by the KMT reactionaries, the workers' movement was suppressed, the environment for struggle was extremely harsh, and the route of attacking the cities was not viable. After being thwarted, some of the forces of the uprising gradually moved to remote rural areas where the KMT was weak and where they mobilised relying on the peasant masses, waged guerrilla warfare, pursued agrarian revolution, struggled to establish workers' and peasants' power, established revolutionary bases, and independently opened up a new road of the Chinese revolution in which the countryside surrounded the cities and seized power by force of arms. The reason why this represented a new path of the Chinese revolution was that, as Mao Zedong pointed out: "Within a country, a small area, or a number of small areas, of red power survived for a long time surrounded by white regimes on all sides. This is something that has never been done before in any country in the world."[16]

This new path was completely different from the bourgeois revolutions of the 17th and 18th centuries in Britain, France and North America, which took place mainly in the cities, including the French bourgeois revolution, which started with an uprising in the capital city of Paris. It was also completely different from previous revolutions led by the proletariat, which focused on the cities, such as the armed uprising of the Paris Commune in 1871 and the October Revolution in Russia in 1917. It was also completely different from the Xinhai Revolution of 1911 and the previous bourgeois armed uprisings, as represented by Sun Yat-sen, which broke out in the big cities like Wuhan. All these previous armed uprisings were also aimed at attacking the cities and were not organised by the workers and peasants, so defeat was practically inevitable. In summing up the experience of the Chinese revolution, Zhou Enlai also pointed out that: "It is unprecedented for the party not to use its main strength to link up with the urban proletariat, but to direct its main strength into the countryside. All the literature of the Communist International, when it comes to the leadership of the proletarian party, is linked to the workers' movement"... "so that no precedent for the encirclement of the cities by the countryside can be found anywhere in history, either in China or abroad."[17]

The opening up of the new path of the Chinese revolution reflected the special laws of development of the Chinese revolution, and was the result of the sacrifice of the lives and blood of the communists and the revolutionary masses after the defeat of the revolution. Among them, it was Mao Zedong who made the most remarkable contribution.

On the eve of the defeat of the revolution, as a result of in-depth investigation and research, Mao Zedong published *the Report on the Investigation of the Peasant Movement in Hunan*, which fully recognised the great role of the peasants in the Chinese revolution, refuted all the fallacies within and outside the party that doubted and accused the peasant revolution, and highlighted the necessity of establishing revolutionary power and peasant armies in the countryside. At the August 7th Conference, he elaborated on the idea that the party must rely on the peasants and master the barrel of the gun, making the famous assertion that: "Political power grows from the barrel of a gun". After the setback in leading the Autumn Harvest Uprising, he decisively abandoned his plan to attack Changsha and retreated to the rural mountain areas in southern Hunan where the enemy's power was weak, to find a place to settle. "Not only did he first put the armed struggle into practice in the countryside, lead the creation of the Jinggangshan base area, and creatively address a series of fundamental problems that had to be resolved in order to maintain and develop his base area in the countryside, but he also gave a preliminary theoretical explanation of the path of the Chinese revolution."[18]

In the resolution on *Political Issues and Tasks of the Border Party* drafted by Mao Zedong for the Second Party Congress on the Xiang-Gan Border in October 1928, and in the report he wrote to the Party Central Committee in November 1928 on behalf of the CPC Fourth Red Army Front Committee, he summed up the lessons learned from the experience of establishing small red regimes in the Jinggangshan base area and other places, analysed the reasons and conditions for the emergence and existence of red regimes in China, clarified the nature and tasks of the Chinese revolution and the essence of red regimes in China, and proposed the idea of "armed secession by the workers and peasants." In his article *A Single Spark Can Start a Prairie Fire* in January 1930, Mao Zedong criticised the urban-centred ideology prevailing in the party, which advocated mobile guerrilla attacks and neglected the establishment of consolidated base areas. He proposed that: "The establishment and development of the Red Army, the guerrillas and the red zones is the highest form of peasant struggle in semi-colonial China under the leadership of the proletariat and the inevitable result of the development of the struggle of the semi-colonial peasantry; this is undoubtedly the most important factor in promoting the upsurge of the National Revolution."[19] He emphasised that it was necessary "to adopt a policy of well-founded, planned political construction, deep agrarian revolution, expansion of the people's armed forces through the village Red Guards, district Red Guard brigades, county Red Guard brigades, the local Red Army and the regular Red Army, and the expansion of power in regular waves."[20] Only in this way was it possible to bring about the climax of the revolution. These statements clarified the importance of the party-led armed struggle, the agrarian revolution, the establishment of revolutionary bases and the significance of the seizure of national power, and advanced the idea of shifting the base of the Chinese revolution from the cities to the countryside, establishing bases in the countryside, encircling the cities from the countryside and seizing power with arms. This marked the basic formation of the theory and path of encircling the cities from the countryside.

After the failure of the fifth anti-encirclement and suppression campaign and the arrival of the Red Army in Shaanxi after the Long March, with the aim of winning the war against Japan, Mao Zedong profoundly summed up the lessons learned during the Agrarian Revolutionary War and the new experiences after the outbreak of the War of Resistance Against Japanese Aggression, and successively published a series of works such as *The Strategic Problems of the Chinese Revolutionary War, War and Strategic Problems* and *The Chinese Revolution and the CPC*. These criticised the dogmatism of copying foreign experience on the road to the Chinese revolution and formed a complete theory of the path of encircling the cities from the countryside and seizing power by force of arms. The main contents of these works are:

- An in-depth analysis of the nature of Chinese society and a clarification of the inevitability of the Chinese revolution taking a new path. Mao Zedong fully affirmed the universal significance of the Marxist-Leninist revolutionary principle that "the central task and highest form of revolution is the armed seizure of power" but, at the same time, stressed that "under the same principle, the manifestation of the proletarian party's implementation of this principle under various conditions varies according to those conditions."[21] China's characteristics are: "It is not an independent democratic state but a semi-colonial and semi-feudal state; without an internal democratic system, it is oppressed by the feudal system; without national independence externally, it is oppressed by imperialism."[22] The particular national situation dictated that China had no parliament to use, no legal right to organise workers' strikes and that, in the Chinese revolution, "the main form of struggle was war, while the main form of organisation was the army". "The communist party's fundamental task was not to enter into uprisings and wars after a long legal struggle, nor to take over the cities before the countryside but to follow the opposite path."[23] This "opposite path" was to focus efforts on the countryside, mobilise peasants, establish rural revolutionary bases, and follow the correct path of encircling the cities from the countryside and seizing power by force.

- Mao Zedong analysed in depth the basic situation facing the Chinese revolution and clarified the importance and possibility of establishing a consolidated peasant revolutionary base. Mao Zedong pointed out that in a semi-colonial and semi-feudal China, the enemies of the Chinese revolution "are not only the powerful imperialists but also the powerful feudal forces and, for a certain period of time, the bourgeois reactionaries who collude with the imperialists and feudal forces as enemies of the people". It was because of such enemies that: "the longevity and cruelty of the Chinese revolution occurred", and "the question of the revolution's base area arose". Mao stressed that since the powerful imperialists and their reactionary allies in China had occupied China's central cities for so long, "it was necessary to make the backward countryside an advanced and consolidated base, a great revolutionary stronghold militarily, politically, economically and culturally, so as to oppose the vicious enemies who were using the cities to attack the rural areas, and so as to gradually win over the whole revolution in a long battle". In this way, we can oppose the vicious enemies who use the cities to attack the rural areas, and gradually strive for total revolutionary victory in the course of the long struggle."[24] Mao Zedong also observed that because of the uneven economic development of China (which was not a unified capitalist economy), its vast land mass (where the revolutionary forces had room to manoeuvre), the disunity and various contradictions within the Chinese counter-revolutionary camps, and the fact that the Chinese revolution was led by the CPC, it was decided that "the Chinese revolution's first chance of victory lay in the rural areas".

- It clarified the major strategies to be grasped with care in following the new path of the Chinese revolution. One was the long-term and arduous nature of seizing national victory due to the unevenness of the revolution, and the long-term revolutionary struggle in the revolutionary base areas, which was "mainly a peasant guerrilla war under the leadership of the CPC." Mao Zedong demanded that "the whole party should focus on war, study military affairs and prepare to fight."[25] The second was that the focus on carrying out armed struggle "does not mean that other forms of struggle can be abandoned; on the contrary, armed struggle cannot be victorious without the cooperation of all other forms of struggle."[26] The third was to focus on work in the rural base areas, "not that urban work and other work in the wider countryside still under enemy rule could be abandoned; on the contrary, without urban work and other rural work, the rural base areas would be isolated and the revolution would fail."[27] Fourth, urban work "must not adopt an impetuous adventurist approach but must adopt the approach of using covert specialist forces, building up strength and waiting for the right moment."[28]

Around the outbreak of the National War of Resistance, Mao Zedong focused on his ideological line, profoundly summed up historical experience, thoroughly criticised the longstanding "leftist" dogmatism in the party, exposed the serious harm it brought to the cause of the Chinese revolution, and systematically expounded the characteristics and special laws of the Chinese revolution, thereby marking the maturity of the theory of the new path of the Chinese revolution.

During the War of Resistance Against Japanese Aggression, the party consciously took the road of encircling the cities from the countryside; carried out guerrilla warfare; carried out extensive mobilisation of the masses; carried out an in-depth agrarian revolution; established and consolidated anti-Japanese base areas behind enemy lines; and rapidly developed and expanded the revolutionary forces under the leadership of the party. All of this played a pivotal role in the war against Japan and became the key to the victory of the Chinese people in that war. The Seventh Party Congress formulated the political line of "going all out to mobilise the masses, strengthening the people's power, defeating the Japanese invaders under the leadership of the party, liberating the whole country and building a new democratic China", laying a solid foundation for the final victory of the anti-Japanese war and the new democratic revolution, and completing the task of anti-imperialism and anti-feudalism.

By the time the second plenary session of the Seventh Party Congress was held in March 1949, the three major battles of Liaoshen, Huaihai and Pingjin had essentially annihilated the main forces of the KMT, and the Chinese revolution was on the verge of national victory. At that second plenary session, Mao Zedong said: "From 1927 to the present, we have focused our efforts on the countryside, gathered strength in the countryside, surrounded the cities from the countryside, and then gained the cities. The period of adopting such a way of working has now come to an end. From now on, the period of moving from the countryside to the cities and leading the countryside from the cities has begun. The focus of the party's work has shifted from the countryside to the cities."[29] This shift of focus marked a decisive victory for the Chinese revolution achieved along the road of encircling the cities from the countryside and seizing power by force of arms.

The CPC accumulated valuable historical experience during its arduous journey to open up a new path for the Chinese revolution:

- It must adhere to the ideological line of seeking truth from facts, start everything from the practical, link theory with reality, and combine the universal principles of Marxism-Leninism with the concrete practice of the Chinese revolution. The new path of the Chinese revolution was blazed amidst the dogmatism that prevailed within the party. In the late 1920s and early 1930s, the international Communist movement and the CPC were characterised by a tendency to dogmatise Marxism and to sanctify the resolutions of the Comintern and the experience of the October Revolution in Russia. These three "leftist" errors led in turn to serious mistakes on the revolutionary road, which was the core issue of the Chinese revolution as they all held the line of conducting city-centred national riots or concentrating the Red Army's forces on attacking the big cities, thereby causing great losses to the party and to the revolutionary cause. On the one hand, this was the result of copying the urban centralism of the Russian October Revolution. After the failure of the Great Revolution, the CPC Central Committee remained in Shanghai, showing that the focus of the party's work was still on the main cities. At the same time, both the guidance of the Comintern and the judgement of the CPC Central Committee on the revolutionary situation consistently underestimated the disparity in power between them and the enemy, and the long-term nature of the revolutionary downturn; they believed that the climax of the revolution had already arrived or would soon arrive. In particular, the "leftist" dogmatism represented by Wang Ming did not correctly understand the special significance of the struggle in the countryside to the Chinese revolution, but criticised the road opened up by Mao Zedong and others to encircle the cities from the countryside. Indeed, they "brutally fought and ruthlessly attacked" Mao and other comrades who adhered to the correct views. It was in the course of fighting this error of "leftist" dogma within the party that the Chinese communists, mainly represented by Comrade Mao Zedong, put forward the slogan "No investigation, no right to speak", expounded the great truth that "the victory of the Chinese revolutionary struggle depends on the Chinese comrades' understanding of the Chinese situation", and creatively solved a series of major problems in integrating the basic principles of Marxism-Leninism with the practice of the Chinese revolution, profoundly analysed the social and class conditions in China, clarified the nature, objectives, tasks and driving force of the Chinese revolution, and opened up a new path for it.

- The party must be built on ideology and always maintain the advanced and pure nature of a Marxist party. As Mao Zedong put it: "An essential condition for the long-term existence and development of the revolutionary base is the strength of the communist party organisation and the absence of mistakes in its policies."[30] Given the predominantly peasant composition of the party, the essence of the strength of the communist organisation and of the formulation and implementation of correct policies was the question of how to maintain the advanced purity of the Marxist party. This was not only an unprecedented problem in the international communist movement but also the core issue of whether the new path of the Chinese revolution could be opened up and sustained. The creative formulation of the principle of ideological party building was a decisive factor in our party's ability to open up and adhere to the new path of the Chinese revolution. In the process of establishing the Jinggangshan revolutionary base, Mao Zedong realised that: "The question of the ideological leadership of the proletariat is a very important issue. The arty in the border counties was almost entirely peasant in composition, and if it was not given the ideological leadership of the proletariat, its tendency would be to make mistakes."[31] In response to the extreme democratisation, the emphasis on the military over politics, the lack of importance attached to the establishment of a consolidated base, the ideology of banditry and warlordism, and other non-proletarian ideas that were growing within the Red Army at that time, the Ninth Congress of the Red Army, held in December 1929, adopted a number of resolutions. The most important of these was a resolution drafted by Mao Zedong on the correction of wrong ideas within the party. It stipulated that the Red Army was an armed group carrying out the political tasks of the revolution, that it must be absolutely subordinate to party leadership, and that it must undertake the "trinity" of fighting, raising funds and working with the masses. Summing up the lessons learned since the creation of the Red Army and the rural base areas, the conference established the principle of focusing on building the party ideologically and the army politically, and called for this to be done with proletarian ideology. This principle creatively solved the major problem of how to build a Marxist party when the party membership was predominantly peasant in composition; it enriched and developed the Marxist doctrine of party building and provided a strong ideological guarantee for adhering to the new path of the Chinese revolution.

- It was essential to persist in "building up the party branches within the army companies", in the absolute leadership of the party over the People's Army, and on strengthening the party's organisational base. The main form of the Chinese revolution can only be a long-term armed struggle, a war to solve problems, and it is necessary to adhere to the absolute leadership of the party over the army and to the long-term armed struggle. This was the correct judgement and conclusion reached by the Chinese communists, principally represented by Comrade Mao Zedong, who combined the universal principles of Marxism-Leninism with the practice of the Chinese revolution, and was the basis and foundation for successfully opening up a new path for the Chinese revolution. After the failure of the Great Revolution, the party was able to pioneer and adhere to the new path of the Chinese revolution. The key lay in "building up party branches within the army divisions", gaining control of the grassroots through party branches, establishing the absolute leadership of the party over the army, and bringing into play the great power of the party's organisation and the People's Army. As early as 1926, the Party Central Committee proposed that "all work should go to the party branches". However, at the time of the Nanchang and Autumn Harvest Uprisings on the Hunan-Jiangxi border, the party was organised in branches imposed on the army regiments, which failed to take root at the grassroots level and failed to fully engage the troops, making it difficult to form an efficient fighting force. In order to change this situation, Mao Zedong reorganised the remaining troops of the Autumn Harvest Uprising in the village of Sanwan in Yongxin, Jiangxi Province, in September and October 1927, and creatively proposed the principle of "building branches on the companies"; he implemented the new system of establishing party branches in companies and party groups in squads and platoons which stipulated that all major issues of the army had to be discussed and decided collectively by the party organisation, effectively solving the problem of party leadership of the army. After that, the army took on a new look, and their cohesion and combat power showed unprecedented improvement. Later, when summing up the experience of the Jinggangshan struggle, Mao Zedong observed: "The Red Army fought hard and did not disintegrate, and the 'branch built on the company' was an important reason for this."[32] Starting from the Sanwan Reformation and further clarified at the Gutian Conference, "branches built on companies" and branches built at the grassroots level became the basic principle and system for building the party and the army, reinforcing the party's already strong organisational foundation. This principle has been upheld to this day and has become a treasured heritage of the party.

The fundamental issue of the revolution is that of political power. In the process of opening up a new path for the Chinese revolution and establishing revolutionary base areas in the countryside, the party began the great practice of ruling locally from the base areas. This was a great creation of the party in the extremely complex war environment, and was an important supporting component of the path of encircling the cities from the countryside and seizing power by force of arms. Due to the circumstances of war, the party's localised rule was characterised by the fragmented and localised nature of its administrative areas and the incomplete nature of its governing system. However, it was through that localised rule that a solid foundation was laid and valuable experience accumulated for the party's long-term rule nationwide.

- It was necessary to establish a state system that was in line with

China's national conditions. The state system refers to the question of the status of the various social classes within the regime. The history of the CPC's local governance fully proves that the question of the understanding and handling of the status and role of the various social classes in power is in line with the national conditions is of the utmost importance to the consolidation of the party's ruling position. During the Russian Agrarian Revolution, the Soviet regime implemented the "democratic dictatorship of the workers and peasants", stressing that the Chinese Soviet Republic was "a democratic dictatorship of the workers and peasants" and that "the entire Soviet regime belongs to the workers, peasants, soldiers of the Red Army and all the toiling people." It insisted on the principle of proletarian leadership in the construction of the regime, stressing that the Soviet regime "must firmly support the leadership of the proletarian political party, that is the communist party". The implementation of the "democratic dictatorship of the workers and peasants" was in line with the basic requirements of the New Democratic Revolution and was a practical attempt by the proletariat to build power. However, the Soviet regime stressed that the nature of the regime was "a dictatorship of workers' and peasants' rights under the leadership of the proletariat" and excluded the national bourgeoisie and the petty bourgeoisie from the composition of the political regime. While this was certainly related to the temporary disengagement of the national bourgeoisie and the upper petty bourgeoisie from the revolutionary camp after the failure of the Great Revolution, the fundamental reason was that it ignored the characteristics of the Chinese Revolution and dogmatically copied the policies of the Soviet Union under socialist conditions in its dealings with the bourgeoisie and its political parties. This seriously affected regime building and had a negative impact on the development of the revolution. This was particularly the case after the September 18th Incident when the political attitudes of the petty bourgeoisie and the national bourgeoisie in China had obviously changed and showed a stronger demand for a national democratic revolution, while the Soviet regime continued to adhere to the "democratic dictatorship of the workers and peasants". This not only failed to assume responsibility for leading the national resistance against Japan but would also seriously weaken the social base of the Soviet regime and the revolutionary forces. The Wayaobao Conference held in December 1935 corrected the long-standing "leftist" error in regime building by changing the title of the "Soviet Workers' and Peasants' Republic" to the "Soviet People's Republic". It also gave the rich peasants and the national capitalist class the political and economic rights they deserved as part of the class composition of the regime, and no longer regarded them as alien forces. On this basis, the regime of the democratic dictatorship of the workers and peasants was further transformed into a democratic regime of anti-Japanese resistance based on the united dictatorship of several revolutionary classes against the Japanese invaders and traitorous reactionaries. The anti-Japanese democratic regime established during the War of Resistance Against Japanese Aggression adopted the "three-three system" as the party's principle and yardstick for building a national united front regime to oppose the Japanese, in which one-third of the members were communists, one-third were non-party leftist progressives and one-third were centrists who were neither left nor right. In this way, the anti-Japanese democratic regime included workers, peasants and other petty bourgeoisie, as well as the middle bourgeoisie and enlightened gentry; it included members of the communist party as well as members of the KMT and other democratic parties, and was a regime for all those who were in favour of resistance and democracy: a democratic dictatorship of the various revolutionary classes united against the Japanese invaders, traitors and reactionaries. In the anti-Japanese democratic regime, the communists strengthened their leadership by improving the democratic system and reinforcing democratic cooperation with people outside the party. In September 1942, the Politburo of the CPC Central Committee adopted the *Decision of the CPC Central Committee on the Unification of the Party Leadership in the Anti-Japanese Base Areas and the Adjustment of Relations between Organisations*, which further strengthened party leadership in the base areas. The "three-three" democratic regime was an innovation of the CPC in the construction of power in the base areas during the anti-Japanese war. It contrasted sharply with the one-party dictatorship of the KMT at the time and played a major role in regulating the interests of the various anti-Japanese classes and consolidating the anti-Japanese national united front.

During the War of Liberation, the Representative Congress of People from All Walks of Life was attended by representatives of all ethnic nationalities and classes, including the working class, the peasant class, the petty bourgeoisie and the national bourgeoisie, who were anti-imperialist, anti-feudal and anti-bureaucratic capitalist, and a united government of all classes was formed. This laid a solid foundation for the establishment of a people's democratic dictatorship led by the working class and based on the alliance of workers and peasants, uniting all democratic classes and all ethnic nationalities in the country.

- It was necessary to establish a form of government that was appropriate to China's national conditions. The form of political organisation, or polity, refers to the principles and means by which the ruling class of a given society organises itself against its enemies, protects itself and governs society. During the Agrarian Revolutionary War, the Soviet regime adopted the system of the Workers', Peasants' and Soldiers' (Soviet) Congress, which was not only established and put into practice for the first time in Chinese history but also, as Zhou Enlai pointed out in his article, *A Study of the Sixth Party Congress*: "With regard to the Soviets, whether the term is appropriate or not, the Soviets are the most important organ of government. Soviets are meetings of workers' and peasants' representatives, and they are different in principle from the bourgeois parliamentary system."[33] It adheres to the organisational principle of democratic centralism and, on the basis of the exercise of full democracy, makes the soviets at all levels organs that truly represent the will and interests of the people; it is also a unity of parliamentary and executive power, with the soviets at all levels having a highly centralised power to exercise legislative and executive authority in a unified manner. These basic principles and norms of regime building embodied the fundamental interests and demands of the masses, and were not only accepted by the Chinese communists but also supported by the masses. Due to the influence of leftist dogmatism, the Soviet regime, especially the Chinese Soviet Republic, copied to a certain extent the model of the Soviet regime in Russia in terms of the system of state power, the establishment and division of functions of the central government, and the activities of the entire regime. The names of some institutions were also copied directly from Russian, and the people and even some party members were confused as to what they meant. The "three-three" system of government during the War of Resistance Against Japanese Aggression took the form of a parliamentary senate which was the same, in terms of name and organisation, as that of the KMT; the parliamentary senate was organised along the "three-three" system in terms of composition, as well as having a bourgeois parliamentary system of nomination and election. All this made the anti-Japanese democratic regime widely representative and it strongly mobilised all sectors of society to unite in the war of resistance. In his 1945 essay, *On United Government*, Mao Zedong proposed that: "The new democratic government organisation should adopt democratic centralism, with people's congresses at all levels deciding on the general policy and electing the government."[34] This important statement represented the inheritance and summation of the experience of implementing the principle of democratic centralism after the Soviet regime, profoundly revealed the connotations and essence of the people's congress system, and pointed the way for the proper establishment of such a system. During the War of Liberation, in the liberated areas and major cities, the party established people's governments by convening people's congresses from all walks of life, thereby laying a good foundation for the establishment of a new Chinese system of government based on these congresses. For the first time, in 1949, the *Common Programme* stipulated the people's congress system as the organisational form of governance in the new China, establishing a completely new political system. The history of the Soviet regime, from a localised and scattered regime to a full-scale democratic dictatorship, has fully proved that it is impossible to successfully copy the political systems of other countries and suddenly bring in a "magic flying mountain" of a political system. It is necessary to combine the Marxist doctrine of the state with the concrete practice of the Chinese revolution and follow a path of regime building that is appropriate to China's national conditions.

- The party must start from the ground up and focus on representing and realising the fundamental interests of the people. In the course of its localised rule at different times, the party paid attention to strengthening investigation and research, listening to the views of the masses, formulating and adopting policies, strategies and measures that were adapted to the actual situation, strengthening the management of various affairs, creatively developing production, strengthening economic construction, developing education and culture, spreading scientific knowledge, practising gender equality, eradicating feudal practices and superstitious activities, and advocating the change of customs. It also contributed to the construction of the revolutionary base areas by promoting gender equality, eradicating feudal customs and superstitious practices, and changing customs. At the same time, the party's new style of governance was demonstrated by strengthening the integrity of the regime and the work style of its cadres. The most prominent and far-reaching impact of this was seen in the various strategic measures taken by the party to represent and realise the fundamental interests of the people.

First, the agrarian revolution was carried out in depth and the peasants' land issue was resolved. Peasants make up the majority of China's population and are the main force of the Chinese revolution. The feudal land system that had existed in China for more than two thousand years was the root cause of the exploitation of the peasants, and the land issue involved the fundamental interests of the peasants and was their most important concern. The resolution of the land issue of the poor peasants was the key to gaining their support and was an important cornerstone of the party's success in local governance. During the Agrarian Revolutionary War, the party formulated the *Jinggangshan Land Law*, the *Xingguo County Land Law* and the *Resolution on the Land Question in the Jinggangshan Base Area and the Gannan and Minxi Base Areas*, and formulated a set of practical agrarian revolutionary policies and methods. Other base areas also carried out vigorous agrarian revolutionary movements and formed a correct agrarian revolutionary line. During the War of Resistance Against Japanese Aggression, the party implemented a land policy of reducing rents and interest rates in rural areas. On the one hand, the landlords had to reduce rent and interest to improve the livelihood of the peasants while, on the other hand, the peasants still had to pay rent and interest to look after the interests of the landlords and rich peasants. During the War of Liberation, the party issued the *May Fourth Directive* and *China's Outline Land Law*, proposing the general line of land reform of "relying on the poor peasants, uniting with the middle rank of peasants, eliminating the feudal exploitation system in a systematic and separate manner, and developing agricultural life". This general line launched a land system reform movement in the various liberated areas, and solved the land issue in the old and semi-old liberated areas, once and for all. The communist party's adoption of a thorough land policy in the liberated areas won the heartfelt support of the peasant masses.

Second, it was necessary to vigorously restore and develop production, and resolve the production and livelihood difficulties of the people. The party's local rule at different times was conducted in a brutal war environment, facing both military encirclement, blockade by the enemy and economic blockade. The active implementation of economic construction in the base areas and the vigorous restoration and development of production was not only an urgent necessity in order to solve the practical difficulties of the people, in terms of productivity and livelihood, but also for the party and its leading People's Army to be able to gain a foothold, develop and grow in the base areas. This was a task of fundamental importance for the party's local governance. During the Agrarian Revolutionary War, the Provisional Soviet Central Government set up a Ministry of National Economy to mobilise and organise the masses to carry out mutual aid and cooperation movements, and to develop the agricultural economy and manual production. In addition, it also launched foreign trade in the base areas and strengthened their finance, banking, post and telecommunications, and transport systems. During the anti-Japanese war, the base areas developed agricultural production, and at the same time as paying attention to that, also concentrated on internal and external trade, as well as establishing banks and issuing currency. In 1941, in order to overcome their serious economic difficulties, the anti-Japanese base areas launched a large-scale production campaign. On the advice of the enlightened member of the scholar-gentry, Li Dingming, a policy of "streamlining and simplifying" was implemented, streamlining the party, government and military agencies and organs in the anti-Japanese base areas, and enriching the companies and the grassroots to reduce the people's burden and increase production. Building on his experience, Mao Zedong systematically outlined the economic construction policy for the base areas: "Developing the economy and safeguarding supplies is the general policy for our economic and financial work."[35] He stressed the necessity of being able to undertake not just political, military and cultural work, but economic work as well. Competent in everything but the economy, would make them a group of useless people who would be defeated by the enemy and fall into ruin. In the course of its local rule the party did indeed always pay attention to strengthening and developing production and economic construction, and this strongly supported the war effort, improved people's lives and consolidated the democratic regime.

Third, it was necessary to vigorously strengthen the integrity of the organs of power and the style of the cadres, so as to maintain the flesh-and-blood ties between the party and the people. The CPC is a Marxist party whose aim is to serve the people wholeheartedly. In the course of its local rule, the party developed a fine style of cadres during the Soviet period and the relevant Yan'an style during the Yan'an period. This demonstrated the excellent attitude of hard work, simplicity, honesty, integrity and diligence towards the people of the CPC, which was in stark contrast to the widespread corruption of the ruling clique of the KMT. This was an important factor in winning the trust and support of the people, and an important lesson for the party's local rule. However, the influence of feudalism meant that the party faced erosion by negative influences from within the regime at the outset of its local rule, such as corruption, waste, bureaucratism and the use of power for personal gain. The party fought resolutely against these negative pheneomena. In November 1931, when the Provisional Central Government of the Chinese Soviet Republic was in place, the Central Workers' and Peasants' Procuratorial Department was set up; at the end of 1933, the anti-corruption decree *On Punishing Corrupt and Wasteful Practices* was issued, and a number of corrupt elements such as Xie Buxiang and Zuo Xiangyun were executed. During the anti-Japanese war, the party made "promoting hard work, practising clean politics and purging corruption" the goal of governance in the anti-Japanese base areas, and the party and the anti-Japanese bases formulated a number of laws and regulations to combat corruption and decadence. For example, the government of the Shaanxi-Ganjiang-Ningxia (Shaan-Gan-Ning) Border Region formulated the *Interim Regulations on Punishing Corruption*, *Regulations on Punishing Corruption*, and the *Convention for Government Officials in the Shaanxi-Ganjiang-Ningxia Border Region*, which set out clear requirements for government staff to practice honesty and purity, and severely punished those who were purged for corruption. At one point, Mao Zedong concluded that the Shaan-Gan-Ning border area was the most progressive place in the country. There were no corrupt officials, no landed gentry, no gambling, no prostitutes, no mistresses, no beggars, no gangsters, no sluggards, no spongers, and no profiteers from national misery. In 1940, after comparing the corruption of the KMT officialdom with the virtues of the communist-led anti-Japanese democratic base, the patriotic overseas Chinese leader Tan Kah Kee concluded that the hope of China lay in Yan'an,. As predicted by Mao Zedong, the CPC led the people of China to adopt the "Yan'an style" to defeat the "Xi'an faction" and achieve the ultimate victory of the new democratic revolution and the establishment of a new China.

(IV) ADVANCING TO VICTORY UNDER THE BANNER OF MAO ZEDONG

On the eve of the final victory in the Chinese People's War of Resistance Against Japanese Aggression, marching victoriously under the banner of Mao Zedong, the Seventh National Congress of the CPC was held in Yan'an from 23 April to 11 June 1945. This congress was held at a crucial moment when the Chinese people were about to win their final victory in the war against Japan and the Chinese nation was about to reach a historical turning point in its great rejuvenation. The Seventh Party Congress is therefore of special significance in the history of the party's development. One of the particularly significant aspects was that the motto of the congress venue reads: "We march forward in victory under the banner of Mao Zedong."

This slogan contains at least three profound connotations and is of great significance: first, it establishes Mao Zedong as the core of the party leadership; second, the Chinese communists, with Comrade Mao Zedong as the main representative, had combined the general principles of Marxism-Leninism with the concrete practice of the Chinese revolution and founded Mao Zedong Thought, so that the Chinese revolution had its own original theory; third, the victory of the Chinese Revolution had to be achieved under the leadership of the Party Central Committee with Comrade Mao Zedong at its core, holding high the great banner of Mao Zedong Thought and following the road guided by Mao Zedong Thought. That is, the new road of the Chinese Revolution of encircling the cities from the countryside and seizing power through force of arms. This was one of the most valuable experiences that the CPC has drawn after 24 years of arduous struggle, reflecting the party's high degree of political consciousness and the common will and voice of the party as a whole. It signified that the party had become a mature Marxist party and had reached a new and unprecedented level of understanding and application of the laws of the Chinese revolution.

The core of leadership in a country or a political party is of paramount importance and has a bearing on the success or failure of that country or party. Outstanding leaders have always been a valuable asset to a political party and the class it represents. The establishment of Mao Zedong as the core of the party was its greatest achievement in the period from its foundation to the Seventh Party Congress. However, Mao Zedong's core leadership did not arise spontaneously but through a long struggle and through correct leadership. It was the inevitable result of the long struggle of the Chinese communists, principally represented by Comrade Mao Zedong, against the "leftist" and "rightist" errors in the party, and of the profound lessons learnt in this regard. It was also the inevitable result of Mao Zedong's support for the party as a great Marxist, a great proletarian revolutionary, strategist and theoretician, and a great pioneer in the Sinicisation of Marxism. From the founding of the party to the Zunyi Conference, the party experienced two major setbacks: the failure of the revolution and the failure of the fifth anti-encirclement campaign. One of the key reasons for this was that "the party had never formed a mature Party Central Committee" or "a capable Central Committee".[36] This was the case with Chen Duxiu, Qu Qubai, Xiang Zhongfa, Li Lisan and Wang Ming. The Zunyi Conference, held in January 1935, put an end to the "leftist" dogmatism of the Central Committee and established Mao Zedong as the leader of the party and the Red Army. The Sixth Plenary Session of the Sixth Party Central Committee, held from September to November 1938, summed up the lessons learned since the war, approved the political line represented by Mao Zedong, fundamentally corrected Wang Ming's right-leaning mistakes, and further established Mao Zedong's party leadership position. During the Yan'an Rectification Campaign, Mao's central leadership position was further consolidated in the organisation. In March 1943, the CPC Central Committee Politburo adopted the *Decision of the Central Committee of the CPC on the Adjustment and Streamlining of the Central Organisations*, which stipulated that between plenary sessions of the Central Committee, the Central Committee Politburo assumed the responsibility of leading the work of the entire party and had the power to decide all major issues. The Politburo acknowledged Mao Zedong as its chairman, and all major ideological, political, military, policy and organisational issues had to be discussed and adopted at Politburo meetings. The Secretariat was the office that dealt with day-to-day work in accordance with the guidelines decided by the Politburo. It was organisationally subordinate to the Politburo but had the power to deal with, and decide on, all issues of a day-to-day nature following the guidelines of the Politburo. The Secretariat consists of Mao Zedong, Liu Shaoqi and Ren Bishi, with Mao Zedong as chairman. The chairman had the final say on the issues discussed at the meetings of the Secretariat. This was a major personnel adjustment, marking the establishment of Mao's central leadership position in the organisation.

The party's theory was closely linked to the core of the party leadership. In the historical process of exploring the development path of the Chinese revolution, the Chinese communists, principally represented by Comrade Mao Zedong, insisted on combining the basic principles of Marxism-Leninism with the concrete practice of the Chinese revolution. They resoundingly proclaimed the slogan of "Sinicising Marxism" and, in the course of long-term revolutionary practice, systematically explored a new revolutionary path suited to Chinese conditions and a series of strategies and original experiences suited to the characteristics of the Chinese revolution. In doing so, they made the first historic leap in combining Marxism with Chinese practice, and forming Mao Zedong Thought, a rich and complete theoretical achievement of the Sinicisation of Marxism.

Since its inception, our party has had Marxism written on its banner but this does not necessarily mean that we can apply the basic principles of Marxism to solve the problems of the Chinese revolution. The key and core is to solve the problem of "integration" and to form our own theory with Chinese characteristics. The practice of the Chinese revolution has fully proved that ignoring the Chinese situation and revolutionary reality, relying on reciting the general principles of Marxism and copying from a book only lead to serious setbacks or even failure. The erroneous tendency of dogmatising Marxism and sanctifying the resolutions of the Comintern and the Soviet experience, which prevailed in the international communist movement and within our party in the late 1920s and early 1930s, almost brought the Chinese revolution to its knees. The root causes of the "leftist" dogmatic errors were manifold but, as far as our party's own construction was concerned, there was a "great weakness" in terms of insufficient theoretical preparation in its early days. In July 1941, Liu Shaoqi clearly pointed out in his letter *Answer to Comrade Song Liang*: "The Chinese party has a great weakness, and this weakness is that its ideological preparation and theoretical cultivation are inadequate and rather naive. Therefore, the repeated failures of the Chinese party in the past were all failures in guidance, failures of the whole party or important parts of it caused by naivety and mistakes in guidance, and not failures in work."[37] This pinpoints the importance of the party's ideological and theoretical construction. The creation of Mao Zedong Thought marked the first time that the party had its own theory combining the basic principles of Marxism-Leninism with the concrete reality of the Chinese revolution, and marked the theoretical maturing of the party.

Mao Zedong Thought was gradually formed and developed in the process of fighting against the erroneous tendencies of dogmatism and profoundly summarised historical experience in this regard. It reached maturity during the late Agrarian Revolutionary War and the anti-Japanese war, when many aspects of it were systematically concentrated and developed. Mao Zedong Thought underwent a process of recognition and acceptance by the whole party. The Yan'an Rectification Campaign, which began in 1942, greatly promoted the spread of Marxist-Leninist theory throughout the party, forcefully criticised and eliminated the influence of mistaken "leftist" and "rightist" ideas in the party and made Mao Zedong Thought generally accepted and widely shared within the party. At that time, the party was already conscious that in order to achieve victory in the Chinese revolution, it was necessary to be guided by the sinicised theory of Marxism - Mao Zedong Thought. It was under such historical conditions that many leaders and theoreticians of our party came to think about how to name the theoretical achievements of the Sinecisation of Marxism after Mao Zedong. On 6 July 1943, Liu Shaoqi published *Eliminating Menshevist Ideology in the Party*, which explicitly advanced the suggestions of *Comrade Mao Zedong's Ideology* and *Comrade Mao Zedong's Ideological System*. On 5 July 1943, Wang Jiaxiang wrote *The Chinese Communist Party and the Road to National Liberation in China*, in which he first introduced the scientific concept of "Mao Zedong Thought". After that, the concept of "Mao Zedong Thought" was soon accepted and endorsed by all party comrades.

As the culmination and conclusion of the Rectification Movement, the *Resolution on Certain Historical Issues* adopted at the Seventh Plenary Session of the Sixth CPC Central Committee drew correct conclusions on a number of major historical issues within the party, concentrating on the important theoretical achievements of the Rectification Movement. It fully affirmed the historical status of Mao Zedong and Mao Zedong Thought. The resolution stated: "In the course of its struggle, the party produced its own leader, Comrade Mao Zedong, and formed a Sinicised Marxist line of thought, the System of Mao Zedong Thought."[38] The resolution stressed that: "The party finally established Comrade Mao Zedong as the leader of the Central Committee and the whole party during the final period of the Agrarian Revolutionary War. This was the greatest achievement of the

CPC during that period and the greatest guarantee that the Chinese people would be liberated."[39] "Today, the whole party has reached an unprecedented consensus recognising the correctness of Mao Zedong Thought and has consciously united under its banner in a way never seen before. A deeper and broader understanding of cadres, party members and the people through Mao Zedong Thought will certainly bring great progress and invincible power to the party and to the Chinese revolution." "Under the correct leadership of Mao Zedong Thought and the Central Committee headed by Comrade Mao Zedong, the Chinese revolution will certainly achieve complete victory."[40] This signified that Mao Zedong and Mao Zedong Thought had been accepted by the whole party, that Mao Zedong had become the core leader of the party, and that Mao Zedong Thought had become the guiding ideology. In this regard, Hu Qiaomu observed: "Without rectification of the historical trend, the whole party's understanding of how to independently solve the problems of the Chinese revolution based on China's reality could not be resolved. Through rectification, the status of Mao Zedong Thought in the party was established. The 'Historical Resolution' reflected the demand of the whole party to formally advance Mao Zedong Thought. It can be imagined that, without it being brought up, it would have been difficult to create ideological unity in the whole party."[41]

In order to establish Mao Zedong's leadership and the guiding position of Mao Zedong Thought, the resolution not only exposed and analysed in detail the development process, main manifestations and dangers of the three "leftist" errors, but also devoted a lot of space to the comparison of the correct line and the wrong line from four different aspects: political, military, organisational and ideological. Consequently, it was clear at a glance where and why the correct line was correct and where and why the wrong line was wrong. Not only was the wrong line forcefully criticised but the main point of view of the Chinese communists, principally represented by Comrade Mao Zedong, on the basic issues of the Chinese revolution were also expounded and discussed in relation to each other, outlining the basic outline and content of Mao Zedong Thought. In this way, the ideological understanding of the party was strengthened, as was party unity. This greatly unified the ideological understanding of the whole party, strengthened it overall, and fully prepared the party ideologically for the triumphant convening of the Seventh Party Congress. To present a contrasting argument, Deng Liqun pointed out: "The dangers of dogmatism need to be thoroughly exposed and systematically understood. Both history and existing conditions demand the use of criticism of such an error, the better to establish the status of Comrade Mao Zedong and the status of Mao Zedong Thought, to unite the party around the Party Central Committee headed by Comrade Mao Zedong, and to unify the party's thinking on Mao Zedong Thought, which combines the universal truths of Marxism-Leninism with the concrete practice of the Chinese revolution. In the main, the 1945 Resolution has indeed fulfilled its historical task and has played a great role in the development of Chinese history."[42]

It was because of the unanimous consensus of the whole party on the leading role of Mao Zedong and the guiding role of Mao Zedong Thought that the striking slogan "Marching forward to victory under the banner of Mao Zedong" was hung in the venue of the Seventh Party Congress, reflecting the common will of the whole party to firmly uphold the leading role of Mao Zedong and to adopt Mao Zedong Thought as the guiding principle of action. The Seventh Party Congress solemnly reaffirmed the common will of the party to uphold the central position of Mao Zedong as its leader and Mao Zedong Thought as the guide for action.

The Seventh Party Congress solemnly wrote Mao Zedong Thought on its own banner. The general outline of the Party Constitution of the Seventh Party Congress stipulated that: "The CPC will take Mao Zedong Thought, which represents the unification of the theory of Marxism-Leninism and the practice of the Chinese revolution, as the guideline for all its work, and will oppose any dogmatic or empiricist bias."[43]

Liu Shaoqi made a report on the revision of the party constitution at the meeting and further elaborated on the historical status of Mao Zedong and the guiding position of Mao Zedong Thought. He observed: "It is a very important thing, that ours is a party with its own great leader. That leader is Comrade Mao Zedong, the organiser and leader of our party and of the modern Chinese revolution. Comrade Mao Zedong is an outstanding representative of our heroic proletariat and of the great tradition of excellence of our great nation. He is a creative Marxist of great genius who, by combining the universal truths of Marxism, the supreme ideology of mankind, with the concrete practice of the Chinese revolution, has raised the ideological level of our nation to a height never reached before and pointed out that the only correct road to complete liberation for the Chinese nation and the Chinese people is Mao Zedong's road." "Because Comrade Mao Zedong is a figure who emerged from the revolutionary struggle of the people and has been tested by history for more than 30 years in the great Chinese revolutionary struggle, he has become familiar to the whole party and to the people of China. His ascent to leadership of our party, of the Chinese nation and of the Chinese people is absolutely the result of the careful choice made by our party and the broad masses of people throughout the country." Liu Shaoqi stressed: "With such a great leader and a large number of such cadres in our party and our nation, we are invincible and will overcome all enemies of the nation and the people."[44] These statements are filled with love and protection, pride and confidence in his leader, Mao Zedong. In this report, Liu Shaoqi gave, for the first time, a very thoroughgoing and systematic overview of the scientific connotations of Mao Zedong Thought. He pointed out that: "Mao Zedong Thought represents the unification of the theory of Marxism-Leninism and the practice of the Chinese revolution. It is Chinese communism and Chinese Marxism." He also said: "Mao Zedong Thought, from his world view to his style of work, is a developed and perfected form of Chinese Marxism, a complete theory of revolutionary nation-building for the Chinese people. These theories are expressed in the various writings of Comrade Mao Zedong and in many of the party's documents."[45] Here, Liu Shaoqi explicitly explained that, on the one hand, the fundamental characteristic of Mao Zedong Thought is "the unity of Marxist-Leninist theory and the practice of the Chinese revolution" or the "combination" of the two; on the other hand, he also highlighted the great importance of Mao Zedong Thought, as "Chinese Marxism", in guiding the Chinese revolution and the central position of Mao himself in the founding of Mao Zedong Thought. Liu Shaoqi summarised the main content of Mao Zedong Thought into nine aspects, namely "the analysis of the current world situation and China's national conditions; the theory and policy on new democracy; the theory and policy on the liberation of the peasants; the theory and policy on the united revolutionary front; the theory and policy on revolutionary war; the theory and policy on revolutionary bases; the theory and policy on building a new democratic republic; the theory and policy on party building; and the theory and policy on culture". This overview gave a comprehensive and systematic answer to a series of fundamental questions about the new democratic revolution in China led by the party, and provided a new framework for understanding and grasping the scientific system of Mao Zedong Thought.

The Seventh National Congress of the CPC established Mao Zedong Thought as the guiding ideology of the party, bringing the party to unprecedented unity and solidarity on the basis of Marxism-Leninism and Mao Zedong Thought, and laying the theoretical foundation for the victory of the Chinese revolution and the great rejuvenation of the Chinese nation.

The Seventh National Congress of the CPC established Mao Zedong as the core of the party leadership and elected a central leadership group with Mao Zedong as the centre; this gave the whole party, the whole army and the whole country a stronger leadership core, and the party achieved unprecedented organisational unity and solidarity, which provided a reliable guarantee for the final victory of the War Against Japanese Aggression and the victory of the New Democratic Revolution in the whole country.

The Seventh National Congress of the CPC summed up the historical experience of the CPC in leading the Chinese Revolution, especially the experience of the eight-year war of resistance, and formulated the correct line, programme and strategy for defeating the Japanese invaders and establishing a new China, showing the way to victory for the whole party and the whole nation.

After the Seventh National Congress of the CPC, the whole party and the people of China firmly "marched victoriously under the banner of Mao Zedong" and totally defeated the Japanese invaders, thereby achieving China's first complete victory against foreign invasion in modern times and marking a turning point in the history of the Chinese nation towards its great rejuvenation; liberating the whole of China and achieving the victory of the New Democratic Revolution across the whole country; establishing the New China and realising its coveted national liberation and national independence; and beginning a new era of Chinese history, and switching on the light of the bright future of the great rejuvenation of the Chinese nation.

(V) THE CPC'S BASIC EXPERIENCE OF SEIZING THE LEADERSHIP POSITION OF THE WHOLE COUNTRY

The road taken by the CPC to lead the Chinese people in the revolution and to seize the position of national leadership was extremely difficult and tortuous, and the party and the people paid a huge price for victory in the revolution and for social progress. In this process, however, the party accumulated a wealth of experience. In summing up the historical experience of the New Democratic Revolution, Mao Zedong observed: "There were three things which were our main weapons in defeating the enemy: a disciplined party, armed with Marxist-Leninist theory, which adopted a self-critical approach and was in touch with the masses; an army led by such a party; and a united front of all revolutionary classes and factions led by such a party." "Relying on these three elements led us to a fundamental victory."[46]

First, we must persist in revolutionary armed struggle and build a People's Army under the absolute leadership of the party.

The principal characteristic and merit of the new democratic revolution under the leadership of the CPC is that armed revolution opposes armed counter-revolution. This is because in semi-colonial and semi-feudal China, there was no democratic system and the reactionary ruling forces always resorted to violent force to exert dictatorial terror over the people. Such conditions dictated that the Chinese revolution could only employ long-term armed struggle as its principal form. "In China, without armed struggle, there is no place for the proletariat, no place for the people, no place for the communist party, and no victory for the revolution."[47] At the same time, China was a large country with a predominantly agrarian economy and unbalanced political and economic development. The rivalry and competition between imperialist forces caused division and conflict between the reactionary ruling groups in China. This characteristic enabled the revolutionary forces to accumulate and develop their strength in the rural areas, where reactionary rule was weak, and to gradually expand their lines of battle. It was therefore decided that the revolutionary armed struggle in China could only take the form of a revolutionary war led by the proletariat with the peasants as the mainstay; the fundamental form of the Chinese revolution was, first and foremost, to lead the peasants in an agrarian revolution. The Chinese communists had to go deep into the countryside, mobilise and arm the peasants, establish revolutionary bases in the countryside, and surround the cities from the countryside in order to gradually win victory in the revolution.

In order to uphold and develop the Chinese revolution, it was necessary to build a new type of People's Army under the absolute leadership of the working class political party. Without a People's Army, there was nothing for the people. On 1 August 1927, the CPC led the Nanchang Uprising, which fired the first shots of armed resistance against the KMT reactionaries and thenceforth ushered in a new era of independent leadership of the revolutionary armed struggle by the CPC. From the time when the party began to lead the Chinese Revolutionary War alone, it started to open up revolutionary bases in the countryside through armed struggle, implementing a three-pronged combination of agrarian revolution, armed struggle and base area construction, and forming a situation of armed secession by workers and peasants in which a number of small pockets of red power existed and developed in the midst of the surrounding white regime. The party gradually corrected the "leftist" error of focusing on urban struggle and seeking a quick victory, shifted its focus to the countryside and carried out long-term armed struggle based on its rural roots. The party succeeded in solving the problem of building a new type of People's Army with a high degree of political awareness and strict discipline, and in close contact with the masses, based on the idea of building a proletarian army with the peasants as the main component. This made the

People's Army both fundamentally different from all the armies of the reactionary ruling forces that brutalised the people, and far superior politically, militarily and organisationally to the old-style historical peasant rebel armies.

The People's Army under party leadership adopted a series of strategies and tactics for people's war. In a situation where the enemy was strong and the party was weak, the strategic thinking of "all reactionaries are paper tigers" was established and the policy that "strategically we should defy all enemies and tactically we should attach importance to all enemies" was implemented. When the People's Army fought, it was "one against ten" in strategy, but "ten against one" in tactics, concentrating its superior forces to destroy the enemy piecemeal. This was one of the fundamental rules of the party in leading the People's Army to overcome the enemy and win victory. In the course of repeated battles against the enemy's "encirclement and suppression" and "rooting out", the People's Army grew from weak to strong and from small to large as it progressed from guerrilla warfare to mobile and strategic warfare, and organised large-scale battles. As the circumstances of the war developed, the party used the people's war to transform the backward countryside step by step into a politically, economically and culturally advanced revolutionary position, and relied on and developed this position to take the new road of the Chinese revolution by encircling the cities from the countryside and seizing power by force of arms. After 22 years of arduous armed struggle, they finally defeated the fierce and better equipped domestic and foreign enemies, and won the great victory in seizing power throughout the country.

Second, it was necessary to build a broad united front and unite all the forces that could be united.

As the Chinese people were severely oppressed by imperialism, feudalism and bureaucratic capitalism, the mass base for building a revolutionary united front in China was very broad. The establishment of a broad united front was the political foundation for persevering with and developing the revolution. China's historical conditions made it both necessary and possible for the Chinese revolution to build the broadest possible revolutionary united front. Chinese society was a "small at both ends and big in the middle" society. The proletariat and the landed bourgeoisie constituted only a minority of the population. The broadest grouping of people consisted of the peasants, the petty bourgeoisie and the national bourgeoisie. But the landlords and the bureaucratic bourgeoisie, in collusion with the imperialist forces, were particularly powerful in their counter-revolutionary efforts. If the proletariat did not fight for and unite with the majority of the population, consolidate the alliance of workers and peasants, and establish and develop the broadest possible united revolutionary front including all ethnic nationalities, classes and strata of the people, apart from the reactionary landlords and bureaucratic bourgeoisie, the Chinese revolution could not have been won. The Chinese revolution had to be under the leadership of the proletariat and its party. However, "if you rely solely on the strength of your own class, you cannot win. And to win, you have to bring together all possible revolutionary classes and strata in a variety of situations and organise a united revolutionary front."[48] There were two alliances in the united front during the New Democratic Revolution: one was between the labouring classes, mainly workers, peasants and the urban petty bourgeoisie; and one was between labourers and non-labourers, mainly workers and the national bourgeoisie, sometimes including temporary alliances with sections of the greater bourgeoisie. The former alliance was fundamental and of primary importance; the latter was subsidiary but still important. It was necessary to rely firmly on the first alliance and to strive to build and expand the second. The national democratic revolution in China was in the interests of the broadest possible range of people and was embraced by them. The party had always insisted on its leadership of the peasantry and relied closely on and united the masses of peasants, which provided a fundamental guarantee for upholding the leadership of the proletariat in the united front. In the process of building that united front, the question of how to handle the relationship with the bourgeoisie was a very important one. Working from a profound analysis of the national situation, the party divided the Chinese bourgeoisie into two parts: the reactionary bureaucratic bourgeoisie, which was dependent on imperialism, and the national bourgeoisie, which was revolutionary and but also hesitant. "Oppose the error of ignoring the possibility of the bourgeoisie taking part in the revolutionary struggle to a certain extent for a certain period of time."[49] When the national bourgeoisie or even a certain section of the bureaucratic bourgeoisie had the possibility of coming over to the revolutionary side for a certain period of time and to a certain extent, the party strove to win them over to the united front and took care to maintain the independence of the proletariat. It applied to them the revolutionary policy of unity and struggle, that is, seeking unity through struggle. When forced to split with the bourgeoisie, mainly the bureaucratic bourgeoisie, it also dared to wage a resolute struggle against them, including a resolute armed struggle, while continuing to win the sympathy, support or, at least, neutrality of the national bourgeoisie.

The party linked the united front to the issue of proletarian leadership and stressed that the proletariat must achieve leadership of the united front through its own party. This was the core of Mao Zedong's united front ideology and the key to the success of the Chinese revolution. Based on the different characteristics of the various social forces in the united front and their different conditions at a certain stage of revolutionary development, the party prescribed and implemented policies to develop progressive forces, win over the middle forces, and isolate the recalcitrant forces. In this way, the party was able to isolate and combat the main enemies to the greatest extent possible, and unite all possible allies to ensure the historic victory of the revolution on a national scale and the passage of Chinese society from new democracy to socialism.

Third, it is necessary to be brave and adept at self-revolution and to vigorously strengthen the party's self-construction.

Since its inception, the CPC had been on the stage of history as the representative of China's advanced productive forces. If the CPC was to play the advanced role of a proletarian party and lead the people to victory in the Chinese revolution, it had to focus firmly on the party's political line, strengthen its own construction, and constantly enhance the party's creativity, cohesion and fighting power. The CPC was a product of the combination of Marxism-Leninism and the Chinese workers' movement, and the growth and development of the working class was a fundamental condition for building the party. However, in China's social conditions, although the vast majority of party members came from the peasantry and other workers, there were also many from the intelligentsia, as well as revolutionary elements from the non-working class. At the same time, the party had been located in the environment of a rural revolutionary base for an extended period. It was an extremely difficult task to build a party that was in the vanguard of the working class in a China where the working class was small in number, even if strong in combat, and where the peasants and other petty bourgeoisie made up the majority of the population. As late as 1940, when Zhou Enlai reported to the Comintern, the Comintern leadership was concerned that the CPC was too far removed from the working class. Zhou Enlai explained: "We have been tempered by long struggles in the countryside and with the leadership of Comrade Mao Zedong, we can be completely proletarianised." However, "some comrades of the Communist International heard this and made a great uproar, remaining unconvinced."[50]

The salient features of the Chinese communists, principally represented by Comrade Mao Zedong, in strengthening the party's self-construction were: first, they insisted that the party's construction was closely linked to the party's political line and ensured the realisation of the party's political line and tasks. The party's political line was the political goal and common code of action of the entire party over a certain period of time. The party's work and party building had to be adapted to the social environment in which the party found itself and to the requirements of its political tasks, so as to ensure the implementation of the party's political line. Second, it focused on building the party ideologically, putting ideological education and ideological leadership at the forefront of party building. The old semi-colonial and semi-feudal China was a large agricultural country where peasants accounted for more than 80% of the country's total population. It is simply impossible to build a broad mass working-class party in China by refusing to allow peasants and other revolutionary elements to join the party. However, a large number of peasants and elements of other classes coming into the party did not pay attention to Marxist ideological education. In order to ensure the workers of the CPC remained compliant with Mao Zedong's Party building doctrine, in the course of the prolonged struggle, the party had to transform itself into a party that was disciplined, founded on Marxist-Leninist theory, self-critical, and that united the masses of the people. In that way it could become a party of heroic fighters who mastered the two weapons of the united front and the armed struggle to charge and entrap the enemy, and the core leadership supported by the people of all ethnic nationalities across the country. During the period of the new democratic revolution, the party grew and expanded from only 50 members to a nationwide Marxist-Leninist party with more than 4.48 million members by September 1949. "Comrade Mao Zedong creatively solved a series of major problems in building a Marxist party under the special socio-historical conditions that prevailed in China, and built the party into a Marxist party armed with scientific theory and revolutionary spirit, was in flesh-and-blood contact with the people, and was fully consolidated ideologically, politically and organisationally."[51] The party was the most advanced and powerful vanguard that guaranteed the victory of the Chinese revolution.

"The people are the rivers and mountains, and the rivers and mountains are the people." Placing the people in the highest position and always adhering to the aim of serving the people wholeheartedly brought the party the deepest and most powerful source of strength for seizing power throughout the country and achieving victory in the new democratic revolution. The party's aims were the fundamental starting point for all actions of the party and an important feature that distinguished it from the other political parties of the exploiting classes. Marx and Engels pointed out in the *Communist Manifesto*: "All movements of the past were movements of the minority or for the benefit of the minority. The movement of the proletariat is an independent movement of the vast majority of people and for the benefit of the vast majority of people."[52] As the party of the most advanced class in China, the CPC represented not only the interests of the working class, but also the interests of the Chinese people and the Chinese nation. Throughout the period of the new democratic revolution, all the struggles carried out by the party were ultimately for the fundamental interests of the broadest possible spectrum of people.

At the Seventh Party Congress in 1945, the aim of "serving the people" was written into the party's constitution, clearly stipulating that "Chinese communists must have the spirit of wholeheartedly serving the people", and that this aim should be carried through and reflected in all the party's work. Mao Zedong observed: "To serve the people wholeheartedly, not to be detached from the masses for a moment; to act in the interests of the people, not in the interests of individuals or small groups; to be accountable to the people and to the leading organs of the party: these are our starting points."[53] The interests of the party are fully consistent with the fundamental interests of the broad masses of the people, and the relationship between party members and the masses of the working people is one of shared joy and hardship, and of common destiny; the CPC serves the people actively, consciously, without any conditions, sincerely and wholeheartedly. The party insists doing everything for the people and relying on them, and also excels at leading them forward. No political party from the exploitative classes can consistently work for the interests of the general public, nor can it have such a deep class foundation and base within the masses as the CPC. Therefore, the party's purpose of wholeheartedly serving the people is a significant difference between it and other parties from the exploitative classes.

Marxism holds that the love and support of the masses of the people on the broadest scale is the basis for the emergence and existence of proletarian parties, and also the source of their development and growth. The fact that history and the people have chosen the party shows that the party has always regarded it as its due responsibility and sacred mission to serve the people wholeheartedly, in line with the wishes of the broad masses of the people. Back at the time of the revolutionary struggle in Jinggangshan, Mao Zedong explained the relationship between the party's cause and the people in the most straightforward language: the masses are like our backstage support, and if that support is unstable, our plays cannot be performed. We do not look to the masses for the sake of the revolution but for the sake of the masses. The "mass line" is a great creation of our party. In his political report to the Seventh Party Congress in 1945, Mao Zedong took close contact with the masses as one of the three major styles of the party, stressing that it was a distinctive mark of our party that distinguished it from any other political party. In his report on the revision of the party constitution at the Seventh Party Congress, Liu Shaoqi proposed that the mass line was the fundamental political line and the fundamental organisational line of the party. Adhering to the fundamental purpose of serving the people wholeheartedly and maintaining a flesh-and-blood relationship with the people at all times were the fundamental prerequisites for the CPC to overcome all kinds of difficulties and hardships, and to achieve victory in the new democratic revolution. In the struggle for national independence and the liberation of the people, the party has always relied closely on the people and sincerely worked for their interests. In all its activities, the party drew breath with the people and shared their destiny, always took the reflection of the will and interests of the people as both the starting point and destination of all its work, drew inexhaustible strength from the wisdom and power of the people to advance the revolutionary cause, and gradually formed a complete set of principles based on "trusting the masses, relying on the masses, coming from the masses and going to the masses." By applying this leadership and working method of the mass line, the party was able to formulate and implement its lines, programmes, guidelines and policies in such a way that they could conform to the demands of the masses to the greatest extent possible and gain their support. In this way, the revolutionary enthusiasm and creativity of the masses could be constantly brought into play and improved. This was the fundamental guarantee of continuous victory for the party.

2

LAYING THE FOUNDATIONS OF THE CPC'S RULES OF NATIONAL GOVERNANCE

The victory of the new democratic revolution and the founding of New China marked the victory of the CPC in leading and organising the new democratic revolution in China, and it became the party of national governance. Practice has amply demonstrated that it was not easy for the CPC to lead the people to seize national power but that it is even more difficult to govern well, especially in the long term. In the face of difficult, complex and arduous historical tasks, the CPC planned and implemented a blueprint for nationwide rule, successfully completed the historical tasks left over from the democratic revolution, consolidated the new people's power on all fronts, strengthened the foundation of the party's nationwide governance, and laid a solid foundation for the party's long-term rule.

(I) THE FOUNDING OF NEW CHINA: DRAWING UP AND IMPLEMENTING THE CPC'S PLAN FOR NATIONAL GOVERNANCE

The founding of the PRC on 1 October 1949 marked the beginning of a new era in the history of the great rejuvenation of the Chinese nation and a new chapter in the history of the CPC. The CPC, which led and organised the victorious new democratic revolution, became the party in power at national level and, in the light of its historic task of achieving national independence and the liberation of the people, took on the important work of leading the people of all ethnic nationalities to achieve national prosperity and the happiness of the people.

In order to draw up a blueprint for the party's national governance, the Party Central Committee, at the same time as leading the nation to final victory in the new democratic revolution from the autumn of 1947 onwards, made thorough preparations for the major policy guidelines for the establishment of the new China. With the victory of the People's Liberation Army (PLA) in the strategic battle with the Nationalist Army and the imminent national victory of the revolution, the Second Plenary Session of the Seventh CPC Central Committee, held in March 1949, formulated the guidelines for promoting that victory, laid down the basic policies of the party in politics, the economy and foreign affairs after victory, and planned the blueprint of the new China. On 30 June 1949, Mao Zedong published an article entitled *On the People's Democratic Dictatorship*. This article and Mao's report to the Second Plenary Session of the Seventh Central Committee laid the theoretical and policy foundation for the founding of the new China. The First Plenary Session of the Chinese People's Political Consultative Conference (CPPCC), held in September 1949, took over the functions of the National People's Congress (NPC) and adopted *the Common Programme of the CPPCC*, completing the most important and fundamental work for the establishment of the new China. The *Common Programme* took the form of a provisional constitution, and set out the state system, political system, party political system and state structure of the new China, stipulated its basic policies, and the fundamental rights and duties of its citizens, clarified a series of important issues such as what kind of new country was to be built and how to build it, established a complete action plan for founding the new China, and drew up a grand blueprint for the CPC to govern the country. As Liu Shaoqi observed, it was: "a revolutionary programme for the people's founding of the nation, created by summing up the experience of the Chinese people in their revolutionary struggle against imperialism, feudalism and bureaucratic capitalism over the past hundred years, and particularly the last twenty years."[1]

First, establishing the leadership and ruling position of the CPC in the country.

The nature of the state, that is, the state system, refers to the position of the various classes of society in the state. The nature of the ruling class determines the nature of the state. *The Common Programme* stipulated that "the PRC is a new democracy, that is, a people's democracy, under the democratic dictatorship of the people, led by the working class, based on the alliance of workers and peasants, and uniting all democratic classes and all ethnic nationalities in the country."[2] This clarified, in the form of a provisional constitution, the position of the various classes in the structure of state power, thereby establishing the leadership of the working class and its representative, the CPC, and the ruling position of the CPC in the country.

The regime established after the victory of the new democratic revolution could only be a people's democratic dictatorship led by the working class and based on the alliance between workers and peasants. The implementation of the people's democratic dictatorship was determined by the class situation in China. The proletariat was the most advanced and revolutionary class in China, and only under its leadership could the Chinese revolution achieve ultimate victory. It was also determined by the nature of China's modern semi-colonial and semi-feudal society. The enemies of the Chinese revolution were so powerful that the Chinese proletariat had to unite with the other revolutionary classes and establish a broad revolutionary united front to accomplish the historic anti-imperialist and anti-feudalist mission through the new democratic revolution.

During the Great Revolution, Chen Duxiu and others severed the link between the democratic revolution and the socialist revolution, believing that the democratic revolution was a matter for the bourgeoisie and that the proletariat only played a supporting role. In this they made the mistake of right-leaning opportunism, thereby giving up the revolutionary leadership of the proletariat and causing a serious setback to the revolutionary cause. However, as it says in the *Analects*, "too far is as bad as not enough" and during the Agrarian Revolutionary War, "left-leaning" dogmatism confused and blurred the boundary between the democratic revolution and the socialist revolution, overemphasised the proletariat's sole leadership of the revolution, and denied the possibility of, and need to, either unite or neutralise various intermediate forces in the democratic revolution. Not only was the leadership unwilling to unite the various petty bourgeois and national bourgeois factions but they also made these "middle classes" their main target, "with the result that they also abandoned the leadership of the proletariat, leaving it to fight alone and making it impossible for the revolution to be won."[3] It was precisely because it excluded the national bourgeoisie and the upper class of the petty bourgeoisie from the composition of the political power class, that the Soviet system during the Agrarian Revolution seriously constrained the construction of the regime and adversely affected the development of the revolution.

During the War of Resistance against Japanese Aggression, the Chinese Communists, represented principally by Comrade Mao Zedong, advanced the theory of new democracy and found the correct theory and means to uphold both the united front and the leadership of the proletariat. In accordance with the principle of the "three-three system", the regime established in the anti-Japanese base areas was in essence a regime of the anti-Japanese national united front and a regime in which several revolutionary classes led by the CPC united to exercise democratic dictatorship over traitors and reactionaries. This regime was adapted to the "small at both ends and big in the middle" nature of the class composition of Chinese society, and fully mobilised the enthusiasm of the various anti-Japanese classes and social strata. But for the CPC to achieve leadership of the whole country, the contrast between class forces still had to be taken into account. Therefore, at first, Mao Zedong was cautious in saying he wished to establish a new democratic republic "led by, or with the participation of, the proletariat" and a "united dictatorship of all revolutionary classes."[4] Around the end of the war, at the Seventh Party Congress, Mao Zedong also proposed the establishment of a coalition government including the KMT.

During the War of Liberation, as the revolutionary situation developed and the power of the CPC and the KMT alternately waxed and waned, in the second half of 1947 the CPC proposed the slogan "Down with Chiang Kai-shek, liberate the whole of China."[5] This completely excluded the KMT from the leadership of the future state power, and added opposition to bureaucratic capitalism to the previously established opposition to imperialism and feudalism. The communist party's leading role in the country was thereby brought to the fore. In *On the People's Democratic Dictatorship*, Mao Zedong went further and stated clearly: "To sum up our experience, it all boils down to one thing: a people's democratic dictatorship based on a workers' and peasants' alliance led by the working class (through the communist party)" and "regarding the democracy of the people and the dictatorship of the reactionary factions, it is in their coming together that people's democratic dictatorship lies." "The people's democratic dictatorship is based on the alliance of the working class, the peasant class and the urban petty bourgeoisie but mainly on the alliance of the workers and the peasants"; "the national bourgeoisie is of great importance at the present stage", " but the national bourgeoisie cannot be the leaders of the revolution and should not occupy a major position in state power."[6] The *Common Programme* fully embodied and implemented Mao Zedong's theory of the people's democratic dictatorship. In this way, the people's democratic dictatorship was established as the state system of the new China in terms of the status of the various classes within the state and their mutual relations, and the leadership and ruling position of the CPC in the country was established.

Second, establishing a fundamental political system in which the people are the masters of the country.

Since its inception, the CPC has taken it as its mission to make the sovereignty of the people a reality. In the course of uniting and leading the people in the revolutionary process, it has fought tirelessly for national independence, the liberation of the people and the realisation of the sovereignty of the people. After the party led the Chinese people to victory in the revolution, how did it organise a state system in which the people were the masters? How could it place close reliance on the people to govern the country? These were fundamental questions concerning the future of the country and the fate of the people. After practical exploration and theoretical reflection, the chinese communists found the answer in the system of People's Congresses.

In the course of leading the Chinese people in their revolution and establishing revolutionary power, the CPC created the system of workers' congresses and peasants' associations during the Great Revolution, the system of workers', peasants' and soldiers' soviet congresses during the Agrarian Revolutionary War, the system of senatorial assemblies during the War of Resistance Against Japanese Aggression, and the system of People's Congresses from all walks of life during the later years of the War of Liberation and the early years of the founding of new China. All these systems were explored and created by the CPC in order to realise the people's right to be the masters of their own house, and they accumulated a rich store of experience for the establishment of the system of People's Congresses. As early as January 1940, Mao Zedong proposed in his *On New Democracy* that the form of political organisation in China should be the People's Congress system, and that "without an appropriate form of government organisation, the state cannot be properly represented. China can now adopt the system of the National People's Congresses, Provincial People's Congresses, County People's Congresses and District People's Congresses right down to Township People's Congresses, and have the government elected by these congresses at all levels."[7] In April 1945, Mao Zedong gave a clear and complete exposition of the system of People's Congresses in *On United Government*: "The organisation of power in the new democracy should adopt a democratic centralist system, with People's Congresses at all levels deciding on general policy and electing the government. This system is both democratic and centralised; that is to say, centralised on the basis of democracy and democratic under centralised guidance. Only such a system is capable of expressing both broad democracy, which gives a high degree of power to the People's Congresses at all levels, and centralisation of state affairs, which enables the governments at all levels to deal centrally with all matters entrusted to them by those People's Congresses and to safeguard all necessary democratic activities of the people."[8] The adoption of the system of People's Congresses as the fundamental political system was proposed by the Chinese communists in accordance with the general Marxist-Leninist theory of regime building "after studying the experience of the bourgeois parliamentary system and the Soviet system."[9] In this regard, Mao Zedong specifically said at a meeting of the Politburo of the Central Committee in September 1948: "On the question of establishing a democratic centralist system of People's Congresses at all levels, should we adopt a parliamentary system or a democratic centralist system for our regime? ...... We have adopted a democratic centralist system instead of a bourgeois parliamentary system. ...... we propose to hold People's Congresses ...... I believe that we can decide on this without having to engage in the bourgeois parliamentary system, the tripartite division of power, and so on."[10]

In accordance with this concept, the *Common Programme* specifies the form of government, that is, the organization of state power, in the New China as follows: "State power in the PRC belongs to the people. The organs through which the people exercise state power are the People's Congresses at all levels and the People's Governments at all levels. The People's Congresses shall be elected by the people through universal suffrage."[11] This established the system of People's Congresses as the fundamental political system of the new China in the form of the interim constitution.

Third, establishing the basic political system of the CPC to govern the country.

While establishing the People's Congress system, the fundamental political system of the new China, the CPC summed up its historical experience and adapted to the new situation by establishing such basic political systems as the multiparty cooperation and political consultation system, and the system of regional national autonomy under the leadership of the CPC. This laid a solid institutional foundation for the party's governance throughout the country and for the development of the new China.

The united front was a "magic wand" for the CPC in leading the new democratic revolution to victory. On the verge of gaining the ruling position in the country, should the party still adhere to the united front or should it have democratic parties? The Chinese communists made a solemn choice. On the eve of the founding of new China, Mao Zedong repeatedly emphasised the need to unite all parties, revolutionary classes and strata to form a democratic coalition government, and made this "the most fundamental political programme of the CPC."[12] On 30 April 1948, the CPC Central Committee issued the "May Day Slogan", calling for the convening of a political consultative conference and the establishment of a democratic coalition government. This was enthusiastically responded to by democratic parties and non-party democratic figures, marking the open and conscious acceptance of the leadership of the CPC by the democratic parties and people without party affiliation, and the opening of the prologue to the consultation between the CPC and people from all parties, organisations and ethnic nationalities on the establishment of the state, and laying the foundation for the multiparty cooperation and political consultation system under the leadership of the CPC. The *Common Programme* clearly stipulated that the People's Democratic Dictatorship was a regime of the people's democratic united front and that "the CPPCC, composed of representatives of the CPC, democratic parties, people's organisations, the regions, the PLA, the ethnic minorities, overseas Chinese and other patriotic democratic elements, is the organisational form of the People's Democratic United Front."[13] So, after the system of people's congresses had been widely established, was there still a need for the CPPCC after the transition to socialism? Was there still a need for democratic parties? This was a common concern among people outside the party during the drafting of the *Common Programme*. In this regard, Zhou Enlai repeatedly stressed that: "It is inappropriate to say that other parties will soon be wiped out"[14]; that the CPPCC "since it is such an organisation, should not end after one meeting but should continue in existence for a long time" and "it is a permanent organisation".[15] The *Common Programme* clearly stated that "after the convening of the universally elected NPC, the CPPCC may put forward proposals to the NPC or the Central People's Government on major, fundamental plans and other important measures related to national construction."[16] This laid the foundation for the long-term existence and continuous development of the multiparty cooperation and political consultation system under the leadership of the CPC.

After the founding of new China, the question of whether the country should adopt a unitary system or a federal system was a major issue of national development. The party's programme and the documents of its conferences during the democratic revolution basically advocated the establishment of a "federation". But this idea was only aimed at solving the current question of ethnic nationalities, as can be seen from the fact that in almost all the literature the word "national" is used in relation to "federation". This was of course related to the ideas of Marx and Lenin on national self-determination, to the trend of "national self-determination" after the First World War, and to the Soviet model of "federation". The question of whether the new China should be a unitary or a federal system was therefore a major issue to be resolved in the drafting of the *Common Programme*. Mao Zedong raised this issue and sought advice from the party. After summing up the practical experience of the revolution and making repeated comparisons, the party determined that the new China would practise a system of regional autonomy for ethnic nationalities within a unified (unitary) state, rather than a federal system. The Common Programme clearly states that: "Regional autonomy for ethnic nationalities shall be practised in areas inhabited by various ethnic minorities."[17] The establishment of the system of regional ethnic autonomy was a great creation of the CPC in applying the Marxist-Leninist theory of ethnicity to solve the ethnic question in China, and has played a significant role in safeguarding national unity and territorial integrity, strengthening ethnic equality and unity, promoting the development of ethnic regions, and enhancing the cohesion of the Chinese nation.

Fourth, clarifying the basic guidelines and policies for the CPC's governance of the country.

As the blueprint was drawn up, the task confronting the CPC became even more daunting. On the one hand, it had to "demolish" and get on with the tasks of the democratic revolution; on the other hand, it had to "build" and create a new world on a China that had been in a state of war and economic decay for more than a century. How to accomplish these tasks required careful design and detailed planning. As a scholar once said about his experience of studying the *Common Programme*: "The *Common Programme* does not just set out the tasks, it also prescribes the specific ways to accomplish them in accordance with the laws of social development."[18]

In terms of political construction, as it was not possible to convene People's Congresses at all levels immediately, and it was still "a difficult question whether this can really be done in three years' time"[19], the *Common Programme* laid down the principle of gradual, step-by-step progress. In general, the democratic establishment of local governments at all levels went through the following steps: in places that were liberated, military rule was imposed at first, the reactionary organs of the KMT regime were abolished, military control committees and local people's governments were formed to lead the people in establishing revolutionary order and suppressing counter-revolutionary activities; when conditions permitted, "People's Congresses from all walks of life" were convened and gradually took over the full functions of those bodies; when conditions were ripe, universal suffrage was introduced and full local People's Congresses were convened.[20] The initial "People's Congresses from all walks of life" were an important transition stage. The difference between

the two forms lay in the fact that the former was elected through consultation, while the latter was elected by universal suffrage.[21]

With regard to the People's Army and military system, the *Common
Programme* stipulates: "The PRC shall establish a unified army", "implement unified command, a unified system, a unified organisation and
unified discipline"; "the political work system should be established on the
basis of the principle of unity among officers and soldiers, and unity
among the people and the military"; "a modern army should be strengthened, and an air force and navy should be built to consolidate national
defence"; "a militia system should be implemented to defend local order."[22]

In terms of economic construction, Mao Zedong pointed out at the
Second Plenary Session of the Seventh Party Congress that after the
national victory, the restoration and development of production was the
central task of the party. To this end, the *Common Programme* clearly set out
the fundamental policy of economic construction in the new China,
namely, "to achieve the goal of developing production and economic prosperity through a policy that strikes a balance between public and private
sectors, and is of mutual benefit between labour and capital, offers mutual
assistance between urban and rural areas, and promotes internal and
external exchanges."[23] The *Common Programme* also clarified the nature,
status and role of the five economic components in the new Chinese state-
run economy: the state economy, the cooperative economy, the individual
economy of peasants and craftsmen, the private capitalist economy and
the state capitalist economy. It stressed that "the various social economic
components should be brought under the leadership of the state economy,
with a division of labour and cooperation, so that each can play its part in
promoting the development of the social economy as a whole."[24] In addition, the *Common Programme* also made clear provisions for the development of agriculture, forestry, fishery and animal husbandry, industry,
transport, cooperatives, banking, finance and taxation.

In terms of ethnic policy, the *Common Programme* stipulated that: "All
nationalities within the PRC are equal and shall practice unity and mutual
assistance, oppose imperialism and the people's enemies within each
nationality, and make the PRC a family of fraternity and cooperation
among all nationalities." "Regional autonomy for nationalities shall be
exercised in areas where those various national minorities live in concentrated communities."[25]

· · ·

In terms of foreign policy, the CPC established an independent diplomatic policy based on the principles of "starting with a new stove", "cleaning up the house before inviting guests" and "turning the other cheek". By "starting with a new stove", it meant not recognising the old diplomatic relations established between the KMT government and other countries, and establishing new diplomatic relations with them on a new basis; by "cleaning up the house before inviting guests", it meant completely abolishing all the privileges of imperialism in China before considering the establishment of diplomatic relations with other countries and seeking their recognition. There was no contradiction between insisting on independence and a "one-sided" foreign policy. In the international situation at that time, if the new people's republic wanted to safeguard its national security and interests, and achieve economic recovery and development as soon as possible, "sitting on the fence was not an option, there was no third way"[26] and "the idea of taking the middle way was very unwise".[27] The Chinese revolution was originally "part of the proletarian socialist world revolution" and an "ally of the world socialist revolutionary front"[28], so naturally, it could only fall on the side of the Soviet Union. All these foreign policy principles were clearly reflected in the *Common Programme*, especially the importance of the "one-sided" foreign policy, which was placed in the General Principles.

In terms of cultural and educational policies, Mao Zedong pointed out as early on as in his *On New Democracy* that: "The national, scientific and popular culture of the people is the culture of the people's opposition to imperialism and feudalism, the culture of new democracy, the new culture of the Chinese nation."[29] The *Common Programme*, with the development of new democratic culture and education as its main task, made specific provisions for the promotion of national ethics, the development of natural science, the study of social science from a "scientific and historical point of view", the "promotion of literature and art in the service of the people", and the development of education, sports, health, the press and publishing. The main issues were what kind of culture to oppose, what kind of culture to promote, what kind of education to develop and how to develop it, and ultimately what kind of people to train and how to train them, "in order to meet the broad needs of revolutionary and national construction work."[30]

Fifth, clarify the direction of travel from an agricultural country to an industrial country and from new democracy to socialism.

The realisation of socialism in China has been the goal of the CPC since its founding and has been the inevitable choice for the development of Chinese society in modern times. The *Common Programme* contained the tasks of the CPC in that stage of realising the new democratic revolution and construction, while at the same time linking it to the future socialist programme in terms of general policies. Liu Shaoqi said in his speech at a meeting of the CPPCC: "There is no doubt that the future of China is to take the direction of socialism and communism. If China's industrialisation does not lead China to socialism, it will turn China into an imperialist country which not just the Chinese people, but even the people of the world, cannot allow."[31]

Despite the fact that, due to China's national conditions and the objective situation of the Chinese revolution, for a long time, the CPC had to operate in the most backward and remote rural areas where modern industry was almost non-existent, the CPC, which was born against the background of modern Chinese history, armed with Marxist theory and as the vanguard of the Chinese working class, always had strong hopes for the development of modern industry in China. During the War of Resistance Against Japanese Aggression, the party attached great importance to industrial development in the base areas and Mao Zedong repeatedly stressed the significance of industrialisation for national independence, national strength and social development.[32] On 31 August 1944, in a letter to Bo Gu, Mao Zedong specifically pointed out: "The foundation of a new democratic society is in factories (social production, public and private) and cooperatives (including the changeover teams) and not a decentralised individual economy. The decentralised individual economy, that is, family agriculture and cottage industry, is the basis of a feudal society, not a democratic society (which includes old democracy, new democracy and socialism), and this is what distinguishes Marxism from populism." "The present rural areas are a temporary base and are not, and cannot be, the main foundation of the entire democratic society of China. To move from an agricultural base to an industrial base is precisely the task of our revolution."[33] In April 1945, in *On United Government*, Mao Zedong also observed that: "The task of the Chinese working class is not only to struggle for the establishment of a new democratic state, but also to struggle for the industrialisation and modernisation of China's agriculture" and demanded that "after the political conditions of the new democracy have been established, the Chinese people and their government must take practical steps to establish a new democratic state in China. After the political conditions for new democracy are met, the Chinese people and their government must take practical steps to gradually build up heavy and light industries over a period of time, so that China can be transformed from an agricultural to an industrial country."[34] Thereafter, Mao reiterated this issue in his New Year's message "Following the Revolution to its End", in his report to the Second Plenary Session of the Seventh Central Committee, and in *On the People's Democratic Dictatorship*. Article 3 of the General Outline of the *Common Programme* states that: "The PRC must abolish all the privileges of the imperialist countries in China, confiscate bureaucratic capital and bring it under the ownership of the people's state, systematically change the feudal and semi-feudal land ownership system to peasant land ownership, protect the public property of the state and the property of the cooperatives, protect the economic interests of the workers, peasants, petty bourgeoisie and national bourgeoisie and their private property, develop a new democratic people's economy, and steadily change the agrarian state into an industrial state."[35] This was the general principle and guideline for economic construction, and it was based on the need to industrialise. As for the specific path of industrialisation, it was "to focus on the systematic rehabilitation and development of heavy industry ...... in order to create the basis for national industrialisation. At the same time, the production of textiles and other light industries that are beneficial to the people's livelihood should be restored and increased in order to meet the needs of the people's daily consumption."[36]

The theory of new democracy clearly stated that the Chinese revolution under the leadership of the CPC should be carried out in two steps, with the first step being the new democratic revolution and the second step being the socialist revolution. The significance of adhering to the theory of stages of revolutionary development was that it clearly distinguished between the revolutionary tasks of the two stages of the democratic revolution and the socialist revolution, in order to prevent the revolution succumbing to "acute disease". It also adhered to the theory of continuous revolution which closely linked the two revolutions and used all means to prepare the conditions for the future socialist revolution during the first stage of the democratic revolution.[37] The *Common Programme* did not explicitly state the future course of socialism, but it embodied the spirit of the above theory. On the eve of the founding of new China, the CPC was already in a position of absolute political leadership; economically, it had also established a policy of confiscating bureaucratic capital and establishing a state-run economy, which was set to take control of the country's economic lifeline and play a decisive role. It could be said that the transition to socialism was on the horizon. However, the sail was in sight but the ship was not yet at the dock.[38] At that time, it was envisaged that after the national victory of the new democratic revolution, it would take another ten or twenty years of building before the transition to socialism would take place, which was "quite a long time in the future"[39] or "very far in the future."[40]

Liu Shaoqi, Zhou Enlai and others have explained this issue: on the one hand, they confirmed the neo-democratic nature of the *Common Programme*, arguing that "if this goal was written into the *Common Programme*, it would be easy for it to confuse the practical steps we have to take today"[41]; they stressed that the future of socialism "is certain and beyond doubt" and that "not to write it out now is not to deny it but to treat it more seriously", and that "the economic part of the programme already provides a practical guarantee of moving towards this future."[42] This was indeed in line with the historical trend and it actually happened sooner than initially expected. By the end of 1952, in the light of the changing circumstances, the party duly proposed a general line for the transitional period, creatively opening up a path of socialist transformation suited to Chinese characteristics and establishing a basic socialist system in China.

The *Common Programme* embodies the blueprint of the CPC for ruling the country. It was a scientific summary of historical experience and a concentrated expression of the will and interests of the people of China, and a programme of action that was truly based on China's reality and that met the needs of the people. This blueprint, after being fully discussed at the First Plenary Session of the CPPCC, which represented the will of the people, was elevated from being CPC ideology to the national will of the new China, becoming the founding programme and blueprint for the construction of the new China, and a common guideline for measuring and regulating the behaviour and activities of all parties, groups and individuals throughout the period of the construction of the new democracy. At 2pm on 1 October 1949, before the founding ceremony of the PRC, the Central People's Government Committee held its first meeting and unanimously resolved: to proclaim the establishment of the Central People's Government of the PRC, to accept the *Common Programme* as the policy of the Central People's Government, to declare to all governments that the Central People's Government of the PRC was the sole lawful government of China, and that it was willing to establish diplomatic relations with any foreign government that abided by the principles of equality, mutual benefit and mutual respect for territorial sovereignty.

At the First Plenary Session of the CPPCC, Liu Shaoqi solemnly declared on behalf of the CPC that it fully complied with all the provisions of the *Common Programme* and called on the people of the country to strive for its complete realisation. After the founding of the new China, the party led the people of all ethnic nationalities to implement the provisions of the *Common Programme* in a comprehensive and serious manner, basically completing the reform of the land system and other national reforms, winning the war against the US and Korea, rapidly restoring the national economy, consolidating the new people's power, and preparing the conditions for the transition to socialism and thereby to industrialisation. In 1953 the party proposed a general line for the transitional period and began to implement the first five-year plan for large-scale economic construction. At the first session of the First NPC held in September 1954, the Constitution of the PRC was considered and adopted. In the form of a fundamental law, the 1954 constitution summed up the historical experience of the working class in opposing imperialism, feudalism and bureaucratic capitalism; confirmed the great achievements of the socialist revolution and in construction over the five years since the founding of new China; and made clear provisions for the direction and path of the socialist revolution and construction in the light of China's national conditions. The birth of the 1954 constitution ended the historical mission of the *Common Programme* as a provisional constitution.

By 1956, the basic system of socialism was established in China with the completion of the socialist transformation of private ownership of the means of production. Since then, China has embarked on a historical journey to achieve the great rejuvenation of the Chinese nation on the road to socialism, and has made painstaking efforts to explore the path of socialist construction that suits China's conditions, making great achievements and gaining valuable experience in socialist construction.

(II) CONSOLIDATION OF THE NEWLY BORN PEOPLE'S POWER

Mao Zedong imaginatively called the new mission undertaken by the CPC to govern the country as a whole "going to Beijing to sit the examination". "We will never be Li Zicheng[43]," he said, "but we all hope to do well in the examination." Immediately after the founding of new China, the question of whether they could safeguard the gains of the people's victory, quickly and effectively consolidate the new people's power, and complete the historic transition from leading the revolutionary war to whole-heartedly building peace, became the new historical "great examination" confronting the Chinese communists.

The enormity, complexity and severity of this "great examination" were unprecedented for the CPC.

First, it faced the daunting task of continuing to complete the democratic revolution. At the time of the founding of the new China, the People's Liberation War had been largely won but the KMT still had millions of troops in southwest China, southern China and the coastal islands. In the newly liberated areas, the KMT had left behind significant remnants of its forces, who were colluding with local hegemonic forces and bandits, and were seriously endangering the new people's power and social order by means of bandit wars. In addition, the newly liberated areas, which had a population of over 300 million, had not yet achieved land reform, and the feudal and semi-feudal land ownership system was still a serious constraint on the development of productive forces. If this situation was not completely changed, the new people's power would not be consolidated and the social productive forces would not be liberated.

Second, after the founding of new China, "the serious task of economic construction confronted us": how to build new homes on the ruins of war; how to heal the wounds of war; how to stop the prolonged vicious inflation and price rises under KMT rule; how to stabilise the economic situation which had reached the brink of collapse; how to clean up a mess that was riddled with holes; how to restore and develop production; and how to establish itself on a firm footing economically and then politically. This was the daunting task and severe test to ensure the consolidation of the new people's power.

Third, in terms of the international environment, the establishment of the new China was recognised and supported by the Soviet Union and the people's democracies of Eastern Europe and Asia, as well as some capitalist countries in Western Europe, and diplomatic relations were established on the basis of equality, mutual benefit and mutual respect for territorial sovereignty and integrity. At the same time, movements for national liberation and national independence were emerging in many countries in Asia and Africa. These were external conditions favourable to the consolidation of the new people's power and the building of a new China. However, the US refused recognition and did its utmost to prevent other countries from recognising the new China, obstructed the restoration of the legal seat of the PRC in the UN and pursued a policy of political isolation, economic blockade and military encirclement of the new China. How to safeguard national dignity and sovereignty through diplomatic struggle and achieve victory in the struggle against imperialism was another difficult task and a severe test for the consolidation of the new people's power.

Fourth, from the perspective of the party itself, as the focus of work shifted from the countryside to the cities, the party changed from ruling locally in the revolutionary bases and liberated areas to ruling nationwide; from the rural environment with which it was familiar in the past to the urban environment; from the military and political struggles with which it was familiar in the past to the economic construction and other areas with which it was not yet familiar; and from the military struggle, in which it excelled in the past, to "the political, economic and cultural struggle against the imperialists, the KMT and the bourgeoisie in the cities, and the diplomatic struggle against the imperialists. We must learn to fight them openly as well as covertly". In this regard, Mao Zedong stressed at the Second Plenary Session of the Seventh Party Congress: "If we do not pay attention to these problems and learn to fight these people and win in these struggles, we will not be able to maintain power, we will be untenable, and we will fail."[44] At the same time, the party was faced with the complacency that threatened as a result of the revolutionary victory and the collapse of corrupt ideas such as hedonism and decadence. How to continuously strengthen the party's own construction and give full play to its central leadership role was also a daunting task and a severe test.

All this shows that it was not easy for the party to lead the people to seize power throughout the country; it was even more difficult to lead them to strengthen internal affairs, foreign affairs and defence, to consolidate the new people's power, and to hold firmly on to power, especially over the long term. As Mao Zedong pointed out at the Second Plenary Session of the Seventh Party Congress, "The Chinese revolution was a great thing but the journey after the revolution is longer and the work is greater and more arduous."[45]

In the face of this arduous, complex and taxing historic task, the CPC, with the *Common Programme* as its basic guideline and the fundamental aim of wholeheartedly serving the people, took a series of revolutionary and effective strategic measures in line with the national, world and party conditions. By means of strict discipline, skill and hard work, they led the people of all nationalities, over three years and more, to successfully complete the task of opposing imperialism, feudalism and bureaucratic capitalism left behind by the democratic revolution, consolidating the new people's power on all fronts and demonstrating its own excellent leadership and skills in government.

The consolidation of the new people's power had an unprecedented breadth and depth of impact on the party, the people, the country and the nation, providing a fundamental guarantee, laying a solid foundation and accumulating valuable experience for socialist revolution and construction, and for the party to govern throughout the country and to remain in power for a long time.

— The fundamental prerequisite and basis for achieving national unity and the great unity of the people of all ethnic nationalities throughout the country. Achieving national unity and the great unity of the people of all nationalities is the fundamental prerequisite and foundation for consolidating the new people's power. After the founding of the new China, the PLA continued to advance into South China, Southwest China and Northwest China in accordance with the deployment of the Central Military Commission, purging the remnants of the KMT army with a thunderous momentum using the strategies of wide detour, penetration and encirclement. By October 1950, after a year of hard fighting, a total of 1.28 million regular KMT troops had been annihilated and more than 1.7 million officers who had mutinied and surrendered to the KMT had been rehabilitated, completing the liberation of all Chinese territory except for Tibet, Taiwan and a few islands. In May 1951, the Central People's Government and the local Tibetan government reached an agreement on the peaceful liberation of Tibet. In October, the PLA marched into Lhasa and Tibet was peacefully liberated. With the PLA's victorious march and the complete destruction of the KMT's reactionary ruling apparatus, the newly liberated areas adopted a graded and democratic approach of establishing military control committees, convening meetings of people's representatives from all walks of life when conditions permitted, and democratically electing local people's governments. Consequently, the people's power at all levels was quickly established, and it effectively performed such functions as suppressing counter-revolutionary sabotage, taking over all public organs of the KMT, maintaining social order and organising the restoration of production. At the same time, the old grassroots regimes in urban and rural areas throughout the country were thoroughly transformed, enabling the organisation of state power to reach out effectively to the grassroots society in urban and rural areas. In this way, an organisational system of people's governments was formed, extending from the central government, major administrative regions, provinces, prefectures (municipalities), counties and districts to the grassroots level of society. This formed a coherent, centralised and efficient state administrative system with a high degree of organisational and mobilising capacity, brought about a fundamental change in China's social and political structure, and laid a substantial organisational foundation for the party's rule throughout the country. The new China implemented the system of equality among all nationalities and regional ethnic autonomy in the country, took vigorous measures to gradually remove the historical barriers between the various nationalities in the country during KMT rule, eased the class confrontations and contradictions within the ethnic minorities, opposed Han Chinese chauvinism and narrow nationalism that hindered national unity, and opposed the ethnic separatist forces that undermined the unity of the motherland. This created a new situation in which all ethnic groups were equal and amicable, united in cooperation, equality and mutual assistance, and working together to build the great motherland.

The overall victory in the revolutionary war, the establishment of a unified people's power and the realisation of the great unity of the people of all ethnic nationalities throughout the country completely ended the situation of a fragmented country and a scattered people in modern China, and provided the fundamental premise and solid foundation for the consolidation of the new people's power, which had far-reaching significance for the party's long-term rule throughout the country.

— Always adhering to the development of production as the central task. Always insisting on the development of production is the central task of consolidating the new people's power. Mao Zedong pointed out at the Second Plenary Session of the Seventh Party Congress that the restoration and development of production after the national victory was the central task of the party. After the founding of new China, it became the central task and highest expression of the CPC to devote all its energy to building peace and to upholding and developing social productive forces.

After the founding of new China, the party led the whole country in taking vigorous measures to restore and develop production and to build homes on the ruins of the war. The main measures were to confiscate bureaucratic capital while carrying out the task of taking over the cities, to rapidly establish a state economy owned by the entire population, to carry out democratic reforms and production reforms, to rely on the working class to restore production, and to provide a powerful material means and foundation for the state to take control of the lifeline of the national economy and organise the restoration of production. Using the necessary administrative and economic measures, the state took the initiative to stabilise the market through the "Silver Dollar War" and the "Rice and Cotton War", which dealt a heavy blow to speculative capital. At the same time, the unification of national revenue, distribution of supplies and cash management was achieved, resulting in the unified management and leadership of the country's financial and economic work and a significant victory on the financial and economic front. After March 1950, fiscal revenue and expenditure were close to being in balance, inflation was halted and prices became increasingly stable, putting an end to the inflation and price hikes that had occurred since the War of Resistance Against Japanese Aggression under the KMT and the fiscal imbalance that had existed for decades in the old China. This created favourable conditions for stabilising people's livelihoods, restoring and developing industrial and agricultural production, and consolidating the new people's power. On this basis, the party fully implemented the fundamental policy of economic construction of "striking a balance between public and private sectors, compensating both labour and capital, mutual assistance between urban and rural areas, and internal and external exchange", and promptly rationalised urban industry and commerce, and expanded urban-rural exchanges. In June 1950, the Third Plenary Session of the Seventh Central Committee of the party made comprehensive plans for the party's work in restoring the national economy and set out the strategic policy of "not attacking on all sides". After the start of the War to Resist US Aggression and Aid Korea, the Party Central Committee decided to adopt the financial and economic policy of "fighting, stabilising and building at the same time", making the stabilisation of the domestic market a central part of its work, fighting the economic blockade and embargo on strategic materials imposed on China by the imperialist countries led by the US, exploiting production potential and expanding internal demand. The Chinese nation quickly changed its dependence on imperialism and accelerated the process of gaining full economic independence. From the winter of 1950 to the spring of 1953, the peasants in the newly liberated areas, which account for more than half of the country's population, were led to complete the largest reform of the land system in China's history, with more than 300 million landless peasants (including those in the old liberated areas) receiving some 700 million *mu* of land and a large amount of production materials without paying compensation to the original owners, completely eradicating the feudal system that had lasted for thousands of years in China. This extensively liberated rural productivity and promoted the development of the rural economy.

After three years of hard work, by the end of 1952, the wounds of the war were healed. The national economy, which was severely damaged before the founding of the PRC, was fully restored and began to develop. The income of workers and farmers increased and their lives improved. This provided a solid economic foundation and material strength for the consolidation of the new people's power.

— Safeguarding national independence, sovereignty and territorial security with determination. National security was the prerequisite for the survival and development of the country and the basis for the happiness and well-being of the people. Resolutely defending national independence, sovereignty and territorial security was a vital task and a guarantee for the consolidation of the new people's power. After the founding of the new China, in accordance with the diplomatic policy of "starting with a new stove", "cleaning up the house before inviting guests" and "turning the other cheek", and on the basis of equality, mutual benefit and mutual respect for territorial sovereignty and integrity, the new China established diplomatic relations with the Soviet Union, people's democratic states such as Bulgaria, Romania, Hungary, the Democratic People's Republic of Korea, Czechoslovakia, Poland, Mongolia, the German Democratic Republic, Albania and the Democratic Republic of Vietnam, independent Asian states such as India, Indonesia, Myanmar and Pakistan, and European capitalist states such as Sweden, Denmark, Switzerland and Finland. To a certain extent, this served to break the isolation and blockade imposed by the US and other Western countries on the new China. In February 1950, the new China and the Soviet Union signed the *Sino-Soviet Friendship, Alliance and Mutual Assistance Treaty* and related agreements, establishing a new type of Sino-Soviet alliance based on equality and mutual assistance. This "fixed the friendship between the two countries in legal form and gave us a reliable ally, thereby facilitating our freedom to carry out domestic construction work, jointly deal with possible imperialist aggression and strive for world peace."[46] The new China abolished the agreements signed by the old China. The new China abolished the unequal treaties signed by the old China, withdrew the imperialists' rights of customs control, military garrisoning, river navigation and all their other old privileges. They cleared the foreign cultural, educational, health, religious and foreign enterprises out of China, purged the imperialists' power and influence in China, resolutely safeguarded the country's independence, sovereignty and economic interests, and completely ended the century-old history of China's sovereignty being trampled on by foreign countries since the Opium Wars. In 1950, when the US invasion forces sent the Seventh Fleet to invade the Taiwan Strait and brought the Korean War to the Yalu River, the Central Committee of the CPC and the Chinese Government, at the invitation of the Government of the Democratic People's Republic of Korea, made the important decision to "resist the US, aid Korea and defend their homes and their country". After two years and nine months of military and political battles, the people and armies of China and North Korea forced the US representatives to sign the Armistice Agreement. The War to Resist US Aggression and Aid Korea was a serious challenge that the new China had to face at the beginning of its existence. It was a comprehensive military, political, economic and diplomatic battle between new China and the US as the main opponents, and was a continuation, under the historical conditions of the founding of the new China, of the long struggle of the Chinese people against imperialism. Victory in that war shattered the myth of the invincibility of US imperialism and taught the US a serious lesson, proving eloquently that: "The time when Western aggressors could dominate a country for centuries by simply setting up a few cannons on a coast in the East is gone forever."[47] The victory in the War to Resist US Aggression and Aid Korea increased the prestige of the CPC in the hearts of the Chinese people, boosted the self-confidence and national pride of the Chinese people, enhanced the international prestige of the new China, and won a comparatively stable and peaceful environment for the consolidation and development of the new China. In consolidating the new people's power, the people's army was strengthened and enhanced, developing from a single army into a composite army including the navy, air force and other technical services, so that it could act as a strong pillar for the people's democratic dictatorship in defending and participating in the construction of the new people's power.

— Achieving social stability and promoting social progress as a fundamental task. Whether or not social stability could be expeditiously achieved and social progress promoted on this basis was a major test facing the new regime, and a fundamental task and a yardstick to measure whether or not the regime had the capacity for social management and governance. After the founding of the new China, with the support of the masses, the PLA carried out large-scale anti-bandit operations in the newly liberated areas . By the first half of 1951, the bandits left over from the history of the old China and abhorred by the masses had been eradicated. From December 1950 onwards, a nationwide campaign to suppress counter-revolutionary activities was launched with a great fanfare. In accordance with Mao Zedong's "steady, accurate and ruthless" approach to suppressing counter-revolutionary activities, bandits, subversive agents, bullies, reactionary sect leaders and cadres of reactionary party groups were firmly suppressed and severely sanctioned. Powerful measures were taken to eradicate the counter-revolutionary remnants left behind on the mainland by the KMT. The stabilisation of social order ensured the consolidation of the new regime, the resumption of production and the smooth implementation of democratic reforms, and provided strong support for land reform and the War to Resist US Aggression and Aid Korea.

With land reform as the centrepiece, the party also led a series of democratic reforms, including social transformation. Through the democratic reform of state-owned industrial and mining enterprises and the rectification of labour organisations, a new type of democratic unity and cooperation relationship and a democratic management system were gradually established in industrial and mining enterprises. This mobilised the enthusiasm of the broad masses of workers to be the masters of their own country and fully exert themselves to increase production. The promulgation of the Marriage Law of the PRC in May 1950 abolished the feudal marriage system, introduced freedom of marriage between men and women, monogamy, equal rights for men and women, and protection of the legitimate interests of women and their children. This brought about a great change in the social and family life of China dating back over thousands of years and promoted the emancipation of women in China; it also resolutely outlawed various ugly phenomena left over from the old society, such as prostitution, drug trafficking and drug addiction, and mass gambling. This served to cleanse the muddy waters of the old society, greatly improved the social atmosphere, purified the social environment, promoted social progress and consolidated the people's power.

— Taking Marxism as the common ideological foundation. The victory of the Chinese revolution and the founding of the new China were achieved under the leadership of the CPC and under the guidance of Marxism-Leninism and Mao Zedong Thought. After the founding of new China, the party attached great importance to the leadership of ideological work, vigorously strengthened ideological and cultural construction, established and consolidated the guiding position of Marxism-Leninism and Mao Zedong Thought in the party and in the country as a whole, laid a solid common ideological foundation for enhancing the unity of the party and the people of all nationalities, and consolidating the new people's power. This provided a strong spiritual force and a powerful ideological guarantee. The first step was to master the tools of ideological propaganda and public opinion. On the one hand, the party's propaganda agencies at all levels were swiftly established and perfected: the *People's Daily* was officially rebranded as the party's central news organ and publicly distributed nationwide, the Central People's Broadcasting Station was established, and the Xinhua News Agency was reorganised into a national news agency, so as to strengthen the party's propaganda and education work. On the other hand, in the process of taking over the cities, a different policy was adopted for the old newspapers, journals, radio stations, news agencies, schools and other means of public opinion propaganda and mass communication, bringing them under the unified leadership of the party and the state. The second step was the setting off of an enthusiastic upsurge in studying and disseminating Marxism-Leninism and Mao Zedong Thought. After the founding of the new China, the Party Central Committee issued a call to the whole country to study and promote Marxism-Leninism and Mao Zedong Thought, demanding that: "Marxism-Leninism be truly disseminated throughout the country and on a large scale, that the people be educated in Marxism-Leninism, that the class consciousness and ideological level of the people be raised, and that the ideological foundation be laid for building socialism and realising communism in our country."[48] To this end, the first volume of *Selected Works of Mao Zedong* was published in October 1950, his *On Practice* was republished in the same year, the second and third volumes of his *Selected Works* were published in April 1952 and April 1953, and Marxism-related courses were offered in higher education institutions, promoting a fervour for the study of Mao's works and the history of the CPC in all sectors of society. The third step was the ideological reform of intellectuals' thinking. In September 1951, Zhou Enlai gave a lecture on *Issues on the Transformation of Intellectuals* to more than 3,000 teachers in the study groups of universities in Beijing and Tianjin. In October, Mao Zedong observed at the Third Session of the National Committee of the CPPCC that: "Ideological reform, first and foremost the ideological reform of intellectuals of all kinds, is one of the important conditions for the complete realisation of all aspects of democratic reform and the gradual industrialisation of our country."[49] From the summer and autumn of 1951 to the winter of 1952, the CPC Central Committee of launched a large-scale ideological reform campaign among intellectuals nationwide, purging them of imperialist cultural influences, criticising feudalist ideology and feudal patriarchal consciousness, and removing the remnants of various reactionary ideas through mobilisation and study, criticism and self-criticism, and purges. In the early years of the founding of the new China, there were criticisms of the film Wu Xun Zhuan, criticism of Liang Shuming's philosophy, criticism of the bourgeois idealism of the Hu Shi school, criticism of Hu Feng's thinking, and so on. Despite the obvious shortcomings of some specific practices, the wrong tendencies in the ideological sphere were corrected, enabling the vast number of intellectuals who had come from the old society to "overcome the old ideas, receive new ideas, and establish an attitude of serving the people", thereby gaining "the direction and strength to move forward". The fourth step was to launch a national campaign to select and honour model workers. In September and October 1950, the National Conference of Model Workers, Peasants and Soldiers was held to honour combat heroes among the troops, workers, peasants and model workers among the soldiers, and to propagate and promote the spirit of model workers in society as a whole. This activity greatly stimulated the nation's sense of ownership and love for the CPC and the new China, and the defence of the fruits of the revolutionary victory and contruction of a new nation became values generally shared and pursued by society as a whole, and the spirit of the people across the whole country took on a new look.

(III) BUILDING A COMPETENT WORKING-CLASS RULING PARTY

After the founding of new China, the CPC changed from being a party that led the people in their struggle to seize national power to a party that led the people to take control of national power and to govern in the long term. This fundamental change brought a series of new issues to the business of party building. In the early years of the founding of the new China, in accordance with the new requirements of the situation and outstanding tasks, and the new changes in the party's situation, the CPC promptly took a series of important measures to strengthen its theoretical armament, safeguard party unity, strengthen its style of work, restructure its organisation, improve its internal and external supervision, and adjust its leadership system, so as not only to build the party into a qualified ruling party of the working class but also to make it a strong leading core of the socialist revolution and construction. It also accumulated rich experience for the party's long-term rule of the country.

First, it was necessary to strengthen the theoretical armament and enhance the ideological construction of the party.

The emphasis on building the party ideologically is an important principle of the Marxist doctrine of party building, and was a distinctive feature and political advantage of the CPC in strengthening its own construction. In the early years of the founding of the new China, the party closely combined the basic principles of Marxism-Leninism with China's concrete reality, and on the basis of restoring the national economy and consolidating the new people's power, it duly proposed the general line of the transitional period, completed the socialist transformation and established the basic socialist system. In April 1956, Mao Zedong stressed in his *Ten Major Relationships* that: "We have to learn what it is that belongs to the universal truth, and that learning must then be integrated with Chinese reality. If we believe that every sentence of Marx's words must be copied, that is unviable. Our theory is a combination of the universal truths of Marxism-Leninism with the concrete practice of the Chinese revolution."[50] This marked the beginning of the CPC's more systematic exploration of China's own path to building socialism. The consolidation of the new people's power, the carrying out and completion of the socialist revolution, and the exploration of China's own road to building socialism, on the one hand, advanced new tasks and requirements for strengthening the party's ideological construction; on the other hand, the series of major decisions and plans made around these great practices further enriched and developed Mao Zedong Thought, indicated the direction for strengthening the theoretical armament of the party, and provided firm ideological and theoretical guidance, and strong spiritual impetus.

In the early days of the founding of new China, the party fully recognised the importance and urgency of strengthening theoretical education for party members and cadres as "a fundamental method for improving cadres and their work."[51] In March 1951, the CPC Central Committee issued the notice on the *Decision to Strengthen Theoretical Education*, criticising the state of theoretical education within the party and stressing that, with the Chinese revolution already victorious and the party facing the complex task of building the new China, systematic theoretical study by the party as a whole "had more favourable conditions and was more urgently needed than at any time in the past". The document raised theoretical study and education to an elevated position: "The lack of development in theoretical learning and the existence of empiricist tendencies are precisely the reasons why some cadres in the party currently know what the party's policies are but do not know why they are there, lack firmness and foresight in their work, lack sensitivity to new things, and have bureaucratic, commandist, and transactionalist tendencies; it is also even the root cause of glory-hunting and degenerate thinking."[52] In 1956, the Eighth Party Congress further pointed out that: "Whether all our tasks can be completed successfully is, in the final analysis, determined by the correctness of the party's leadership. In other words, it depends on whether the party leadership can seek truth from facts and whether it can closely combine the universal truths of Marxism-Leninism with the practice of the Chinese revolution."[53] To this end, the Eighth Party Congress proposed that the basic task of party building was to raise the level of Marxism-Leninism in the party, to adhere to the principle of linking theory with reality and seeking truth from facts, to closely combine the universal truths of Marxism-Leninism with the concrete practice of the Chinese revolution, and to oppose subjectivism, bureaucratism and sectarianism. The Eighth Party Congress highlighted the fact that the whole party, especially senior cadres, should systematically study Marxism-Leninism, improve the ideological level of Marxism-Leninism, improve the ability to use Marxism-Leninism's positions, views and methods to solve problems, judge directions and distinguish right from wrong, and improve the ability to use Marxism-Leninism's search for truth from facts to guide their work.

From 1951 to 1956, the Central Committee issued a series of instructions, circulars, decisions and regulations to strengthen theoretical education for the party as a whole, such as: *Instructions on the Theoretical Education of Cadres for the Period 1953-1954* and its supplementary circulars *Regulations on the Method of Self-Study of Marxism and Leninism for Senior*

Party Cadres; Circular on the Study of Five Documents including 'Transforming Our Learning', and others. These documents made clear provisions and thematic arrangements for the content, system, methods, time and form of theoretical study, and focused on the issue of theoretical study and education for senior cadres. In addition, various safeguards were adopted, such as the re-publication of Mao Zedong's *On Practice* and *On Contradiction* in the *People's Daily* on 29 December 1950 and 1 April 1952 respectively; the successive publication of the first, second and third volumes of Mao Zedong's *Selected Works* from 1951 to 1953; and the publication of Chinese translations of important books such as the complete works of Marx, Engels, Lenin, Stalin and others. At the same time, the role of party schools was given full play. By 1956, 375,000 students had studied in party schools at all levels, where "the graduates had systematically studied the foundations of Marxism-Leninism, the theory of dialectical and historical materialism, political economy, the history of the CPC, and theoretical works on socialist construction."[54] In the early years of the founding of the new China, the CPC always put ideological development at the forefront of its party building, constantly exploring and innovating ways and means of ideological development in the light of new situations and problems, strengthening theoretical learning and education for the whole party, ensuring and promoting organisational development, development of form, institutional development and upright government through ideological development. In this way, it wrote a new chapter in party building, providing a fundamental guarantee for turning the party into a ruling party of the working class.

Second, it is necessary to strengthen party unity and resolutely safeguard its centralised and unified leadership.

The unity and solidarity of the party is the life of the party and the basic guarantee that the party's cause will always remain invincible. It is a fine tradition of the party to safeguard that unity and solidarity. During the democratic revolution, it was thanks to the unified leadership of the Party Central Committee with Comrade Mao Zedong at its core and the unity of the party that the whole nation was led to victory which led to the establishment of new China.

In the early years of the founding of new China, the Party Central Committee and Mao Zedong consistently stressed the centralised and unified leadership of the party and the strengthening of party unity. In particular, before and after the Gao Rao incident was exposed, the Party Central Committee led the party in a resolute struggle against such acts that endangered party unity. In November 1953, at the Second National Conference on Discipline Inspection, Zhu De proposed four tasks for the party's disciplinary work during the transitional period, one of which was to "ensure the centralised and unified leadership of the party" and he also observed that "while ensuring the centralised and unified leadership of the party, the unity of the party should be further strengthened on the basis of promoting democracy, carrying out criticism and self-criticism, especially bottom-up criticism, strengthening collective party leadership and strengthening the links between the party and the people".[55] In December, the study and propaganda outline of the *General Line for the Transition Period*, which was issued by the Propaganda Department of the Central Committee with the approval of the CPC Central Committee, stated: "To realise the party's *General Line for the Transition Period*, it is necessary to promote internal party democracy, to consolidate party discipline and to strengthen party unity. The essence of intra-party democracy is to promote the initiative and enthusiasm of party members, to increase their sense of responsibility for the party's cause, and in this way to consolidate party discipline and party unity. To promote democracy within the party, we must improve the party committee system, give full play to the collective leadership role of party committees at all levels, and overcome fragmentation in the party's leadership work."[56]

The Fourth Plenary Session of the Seventh Party Central Committee, held in February 1954, exposed the conspiratorial activities of Gao Gang and Rao Shushi. The conference unanimously adopted the *Resolution On Enhancing Party Unity*, stating clearly that the party unity was the life of the party and the basic guarantee of victory in the revolution; the unity of senior cadres was the key to the unity of the party as a whole. The resolution stipulated that the interests of party unity were paramount, and therefore the maintenance and consolidation of party unity should be the criteria guiding both words and actions; the only focus of party unity was the Party Central Committee, and any words or actions that impede the unified leadership of the Central Committee and undermine the unity and prestige of the Central Committee must be opposed; one of the important guarantees of party unity is strict adherence to the principles of democratic centralism and collective leadership, and treating the regions and departments under party leadership as independent kingdoms, placing individuals above the organisation, undue and excessive emphasis on the role of individuals, and pride and the personality cult of the individual, must all be opposed; the important political activities and opinions of senior party cadres should be reported and described to the party organisation to which they belong on a regular basis, and in cases of particular importance, directly to the Politburo, the Secretariat or the Chairman of the Central Committee. The resolution also stressed that, in order to strengthen party unity, it was necessary to ensure the full development of internal democracy, criticism and self-criticism, and the conduct of correct internal struggle within the party. The above provisions were, in fact, an important exploration of the party's efforts to improve the democratic centralist system, to tighten political discipline and to treat the internal political life of the party seriously.

After the Fourth Plenary Session of the Seventh Central Committee of the CPC, party organisations at all levels successively studied and implemented the spirit of the session; criticised phenomena that undermined party unity and violated collective leadership, including individualistic ideas and undemocratic practices such as complacency and personal arbitrariness, as well as the phenomenon of fragmented decentralism; carried forward the fine style of criticism and self-criticism; and took concrete measures to correct shortcomings and mistakes. Party unity and collective leadership were significantly strengthened by this. In March 1955, Mao Zedong summed up the Gao Rao incident at the National Congress of the party and pointed out: "In view of all the lessons of history and the fact that individual wisdom must be combined with collective wisdom in order to play a better role and make fewer mistakes in our work, the Central Committee and party committees at all levels must adhere to the principle of collective leadership and continue to oppose both individual dictatorship and decentralism. We must continue to oppose the two erroneous tendencies of individual dictatorship and decentralism."[57] In September 1956, the Party Constitution adopted at the Eighth Party Congress made the maintenance of party unity and centralised leadership an important consideration, stressing that the party: "must endeavour to play its correct leading and central role in all aspects of national life and oppose any decentralising tendency that reduces the party's role and weakens its unity"; and emphasising that: "The unity and solidarity of the party is the life of the party and the source of its strength. ...... the party will not allow any violation of the political line and organisational principles within the party, nor will it allow any splitting of the party, petty organisational activities, disruptively advocating independence, or putting the individual above the party collective."[58] Accordingly, the party constitution also made it a new obligation of party members to safeguard the unity and solidarity of the party.

•   •   •

Third, maintaining close contact with the masses and strengthening the party's work style.

The party's greatest political advantage is its close contact with the masses, and the greatest danger to the party after coming to power is its disengagement from the masses. Since the founding of new China, the party has always stressed the need to unite the masses and rely on them in a series of efforts such as land reform, democratic governance and the restoration and development of the national economy. In the process of building up the party, it adhered to the fundamental aim of serving the people wholeheartedly, implemented the mass line, adopted a series of measures, including opposing bureaucratism, promoting a close relationship between the party and the people, all of which served to further strengthen the party's work style.

In May 1950, after victory in the revolution, some party members and cadres began to show feelings of arrogance, of having "brought the revolution to an end" and of covetous hedonism, some of which had even developed into serious bureaucratic and commandist practices. In response to this, the CPC Central Committee issued instructions to carry out a rectification campaign throughout the party and the army, proposing "to rigorously rectify the style of work of the whole party, first and foremost that of the cadres."[59] Mao Zedong attached great importance to this rectification, stressing that: "A partywide rectification campaign is coming, and this matter has become the central link in the advancement of all current work. If this link is not completed, no work will be able to move forward smoothly."[60] In accordance with the Central Committee's plan, in the second half of 1950, all the central bureaus and local party organisations formulated plans for rectification, had the main comrades in charge make reports on rectification, targeted serious cases of bureaucratism and commandism as study materials, and launched a large-scale rectification campaign.

The first step in the party rectification campaign was a general education of party members on the standards (conditions) for communist party membership. Liu Shaoqi proposed eight conditions for party members, one of which was: "Party members are the people's 'servants', not the people's 'overlords'. All party members must serve the people wholeheartedly, listen humbly to the demands and opinions of the people, report them to the party in a timely manner, and explain the party's policies to the people, so that the party can maintain close contact with the people and lead them forward."[61] In the "three anti's" campaign, Mao Zedong observed that "the development and deepening of the struggle against corruption and waste will inevitably bring us into contact with the various degrees of bureaucratic and liberal work styles that exist in all areas. This style of work is the fundamental cause of the existence and development of corruption and waste."[62] After the end of the "three antis" campaign, the central government still stressed that: "Opposing bureaucratism is a long-term, regular struggle, and cannot be a short-term assault, as was the case with the "three anti's" campaign."[63]

In January 1953, the "new three anti's" campaign was launched, with opposition to bureaucratism being an important strand. Mao Zedong clearly stated: "At present, there are serious instances of commandism and lawlessness among many grassroots organisations and cadres, and the occurrence and growth of such phenomena are inseparable from the bureaucratism of the leading organs and cadres. ...... If we are to carry out large-scale national construction, we must overcome bureaucratism and keep close contact with the people ...... "[64] The Central Committee also specifically called for a focused struggle against bureaucratism in the central-level agencies and stressed: "In this case, bureaucratism mainly refers to certain leading cadres who, because they do not understand the situation, do not check their work, do not study policies, and lack ideological and political leadership, fail to grasp the essential and key issues in their work, fall into the mire of bureaucratism and transactionalism, and are detached from reality and the masses, thereby causing great losses to the state and the people."[65]

In the process of exploring China's own road to building socialism, it became more urgent and important to implement the mass line and overcome bureaucratism. In his political report to the Eighth Party Congress, Liu Shaoqi stressed that: "In many of our state organs, there exists a bureaucratic attitude of superiority, ignoring the opinions of subordinates and the masses, suppressing their opinions, and being indifferent to their lives. This kind of bureaucratism, which is detached from the masses and from reality, seriously hampers the development of democratic life in the country, and hinders the enthusiasm of the masses and the advancement of the socialist cause."[66] The Party Constitution adopted at the Eighth Party Congress included the concept of the "mass line" for the first time, elaborated on the party's view of the masses and the party's mass line, and advanced the important task of opposing bureaucratism. The Constitution of the Eighth Party Congress clearly stated that since the CPC was already the ruling party, it should pay special attention to modesty and prudence, refrain from arrogance, and make great efforts to fight bureaucratism in every party organisation, every state organ and economic organisation which is detached from the masses and from real life. In his *Report on the Revision of the Party Constitution*, Deng Xiaoping first of all highlighted the issue of the party's mass line, enumerated the various manifestations and dangers of bureaucratism, and proposed various measures to overcome it.

Fourth, rectifying the party's grassroots organisations and purging the ranks of party cadres.

It is the party's organisational advantage and also an admirable tradition to attach importance to the building of grassroots organisations. Before and after the founding of the new China, in order to solve the problem of uneven distribution of party organisations, the CPC implemented the policy of "building the arty openly" and continuously expanded the party's organisation and membership. At the same time, the rapid growth of the party's organisation also led to a certain degree of impurity in the party's organisation and membership. Therefore, soon after the founding of new China, the party carried out the largest party rectification campaign since its founding.

In February 1951, the CPC Central Committee convened an enlarged meeting of the Politburo, which called for a three-year project to reorganise the party, improve conditions for party members, and carefully carry out party building work in cities and new districts, so as to better complete the party's various tasks. In accordance with the spirit of the conference, the first national conference on the organisation of the CPC was held in March and April, the theme of which was "the question of revising the party's original organisation and developing new members". The conference adopted the *Resolution on Rectifying the Party's Grassroots Organisations* and the *Resolution on Developing New Party Members*, which made specific arrangements for the rectification of the party and set out the eight basic conditions for communist party membership. Following the Central Committee's plan, the Party Rectification Campaign began in the summer of 1951 and was carried out in a systematic manner throughout the party, and was essentially completed by the spring of 1954.

The first step in the party's reorganisation was to educate the majority of party members on the party's programme, the party's constitution and how to be a party member, so that they would all have a clear understanding of the eight basic criteria for communist party membership. This was followed by the registration of party members, who were then examined and reviewed by the party organisation and dealt with according to their different circumstances. According to the prevailing situation of the party organisation, members were divided into four groups: (1) those who had all the qualifications for membership; (2) those who did not fully meet the conditions of membership; or those who had serious faults that had to be corrected and improved; (3) negative and backward elements who did not meet the conditions of membership; and (4) class dissidents, defectors, opportunists and degenerates who had infiltrated the party. When the party was reorganised, the fourth group of people was the first to be purged in order to purify the party organisation. The second and third groups of people needed to be differentiated, and those who did not fully meet the requirements for party membership, or those who had serious problems, needed to be educated and raised to meet the requirements for party membership; those who, after education, still did not meet the requirements for party membership were to be advised to resign from the party or have their membership revoked.

The combination of the party rectification work and the "three anti's" reform campaign played a mutually reinforcing role.

In February and May 1952, the CPC Central Committee issued the *Instruction on the Combination of the 'Three-Anti's' Campaign and the Party Rectification Campaign* and the *Instruction on Party Rectification and Party Building on the Basis of the 'Three-Anti's' Campaign*, stressing that the "three anti's" campaign was a realistic, profound and powerful campaign to reorganise the party, a rigorous test for communist party members, and a practical and effective clean-up of the party organisation. The combination of the party rectification and the "three anti's" campaign actually marked a change from "rectifying the party behind closed doors" to "rectifying the party through open doors". Through this exposure to the general public, a number of party members and cadres were found to be corrupt, wasteful and too bureaucratic, along with a number of other corrupt and degenerate elements. This constituted a mass review of the party members and the party organisation, and contributed significantly to the further development of the party rectification campaign.

During the period of party consolidation, new party members were actively but carefully recruited in all localities in accordance with the requirements of the Central Committee. By the end of June 1953, 82,000 new party branches had been established throughout the country, and the number of grassroots branches had grown from 246,000 in 1951 to 328,000. In general, party organisations were found in factories, mines and enterprises with more than 50 employees, and in universities and colleges. A total of 328,000 people left the party after it was reorganised. During the three-year period of party consolidation, a total of 1.07 million new members were admitted to the party nationwide, offsetting the number of those who had left the party and increasing the total number of communist party members from 5.8 million to 6.369 million.[67] As a result of the reorganisation and development of the party, there was a marked improvement in the party's organisational composition and the quality of its members, which further unified its ideology, purified the organisation, strengthened discipline and work style, and enabled the party to maintain its progress and purity.

Fifth, resolutely punishing corruption and strengthening the party's fight against corruption and advocacy of integrity.

A clear-cut opposition to corruption has a direct bearing on the hearts and minds of the people and the consolidation of the party's ruling position. In the early years of the founding of new China, the party always had a clear understanding of the dangers of corruption, emphasised the ideological education of party members and cadres, relied on the party's own and mass movements to fight corruption and promote integrity and, at the same time, explored the construction of relevant institutions, thereby achieving remarkable results.

In the early years of the founding of the new China, through the rectification campaign, ideological education and organisational means were used to strengthen the education of all party members and cadres on the ideals, beliefs and purposes of the party, and also to purge from the party some of those who did not meet the requirements for party membership. In December 1951, in response to the many problems revealed during the nationwide campaign to increase production and implement economies, the CPC Central Committee issued the *Decision on Implementing Streamlined Forces and Streamlining Administration, Increasing Production and Saving, Opposing Corruption and Waste, and Opposing Bureaucratism,* which called for the establishment of inspection committees at all levels to increase production and economise under the leadership of the three systems of the party, the government and the army. The leadership was to take on responsibility in a hands-on manner and adopt a combination of top-down and bottom-up methods to carry out this struggle with great ostentation and resoluteness. A large-scale, mass "three anti's" campaign soon took hold throughout the country. By the end of the campaign in October 1952, there were found to be 1.08 million embezzlers of over 1,000 yuan in party and government organs above the county level, of whom the vast majority were small and medium-sized embezzlers, and 3.64% were major embezzlers who had been dealt with by the courts for embezzlement of over 10,000 yuan. The Party Central Committee and Mao Zedong never condoned and severely punished anyone who was exposed during the "three anti's" campaign, no matter who was involved, and they demonstrated their firm determination to control the party and rule it strictly, in particular when they decisively approved the death sentences for Liu Qingshan and Zhang Zishan.

During the "three anti's" movement, the CPC Central Committee, the Central Commission for Discipline Inspection and other bodies successively promulgated a series of regulations and systems, such as the *Decision on the Expulsion of Party Members for Serious Corruption Crimes* and *Opinions on the Handling of Certain Issues in the "Three Anti's" Movement, Several Provisions on the Handling of Corruption and Waste, Several Provisions on the Handling of Corruption, Waste and Overcoming Bureaucratic Errors, Regulations on the Handling of Corruption, Waste and Bureaucratism Committed by Party Members in the "Three Anti's" Campaign, Regulations on the Establishment of People's Courts in the "Three Evils" Movement, Regulations on the Approval Authority for Disciplinary Party Members,* and so on. In April 1952, the *Regulations of the PRC on the Punishment of Corruption* were promulgated and implemented, clearly stipulating the guidelines, methods, procedures and approval powers for handling corruption issues, and bringing the relevant handling process into the court system. At the same time, in order to prevent and curb corruption, waste and embezzlement at source, the CPC Central Committee also strengthened systems in key areas such as finance and infrastructure. The Constitution of the PRC, promulgated in September 1954, stipulated that all members of state organs must be "subject to the supervision of the masses" and gave citizens the right to lodge written or oral complaints against any staff member of state organs who had violated the law or failed in their duties.

The party's important initiatives in fighting corruption and promoting integrity also included strict management of party and government organs and leading cadres, and opposition to privileges. After the founding of the new China, the CPC Central Committee and the State Council successively issued the *Instructions on the Prohibition of Commercial Operations by Institutional Forces,* the *Instructions on Stopping the Mobilisation of the Public to Write Tribute Letters, Send Congratulatory Telegrams and Send Gifts to the Central Government,* the *Decision on Reducing the Salary Grades of Party Cadres Above the Third Level in State Organs,* the *Decision on Uniformly Handling State Organ Production,* the *Regulations on the Prohibition of Offering Transport, Banquets and Gifts by Local Officials During Inspections, Visits, Rest and Recuperation, and Travel to Party, Government and Military Officials,* and so on. In this regard, Mao Zedong and other leading comrades of the Central Committee played an exemplary role. In May 1950, the Shenyang People's Congress wanted to build a memorial pagoda for the founding of the new China and "cast a bronze statue of Chairman Mao" for it. Mao Zedong gave his response in a letter, saying, "Casting a bronze statue is not a good influence, so it should not be done." He also wrote next to "building the memorial pagoda" that "this is possible"; and next to "casting a bronze statue of Chairman Mao" that "it was only to be taken ironically ". In April 1954, he wrote a letter to the party branch of Shicheng Township in Xiangtan, asking the grassroots organisations to cut their relatives loose, saying that "anyone from the Wen family should obey the leadership of the party and the government, just like everyone else in the township, and that they should be diligent and law-abiding and should not be treated as special."[68]

Sixth, strengthening supervision within the party and improving supervision outside the party.

Strengthening and improving internal and external supervision is an inherent requirement of the party's construction. In the early years of the founding of new China, internal party supervision was concentrated on strengthening disciplinary and inspection work; the emphasis of supervision outside the party was concentrated on news, public opinion and the masses, and on exploiting the supervisory role of non-party members.

In the early years of the founding of new China, the party's disciplinary and inspection work was continuously reinforced. On 9 November 1949, the Politburo of the Central Committee decided to set up disciplinary inspection committees both centrally and at all other levels, with Zhu De as the secretary of the Central Disciplinary Inspection Committee. Party committees at all levels also successively set up disciplinary inspection committees as special supervisory bodies to investigate, accept and examine disciplinary offences committed by party organisations, party cadres and party members at all levels. In February 1950, the Central Committee further clarified the leadership structure of the Discipline Inspection Commissions: on the one hand, they were, at all levels, a working department of the party committees, directly under the leadership of the various levels of party committees at every level; on the other hand, the higher-level Discipline Inspection Commissions had a "guiding relationship" with the lower-level Discipline Inspection Commissions in terms of their work and operations.[69] After their establishment, the commissions continued to improve their institutional mechanisms, strengthen their organisations and enrich their teams; they played an important role in the central work of the party and the state, closely integrated with the major tasks of party building such as the rectification of party style, in continuously increasing supervision and the enforcement of discipline. In March 1955, the Party's National Congress decided to set up central and local supervisory committees to replace the original party disciplinary committees at the central and local levels, and clearly defined the method of formation, leadership system, main tasks, responsibilities and powers, and institutional framework of the supervisory committees at all levels. This major reform further improved the leadership system and working mechanism of the party's discipline inspection bodies, elevated the status of the supervisory

216

organs, expanded their powers and strengthened the party's internal supervision.

At the same time, the party attached great importance to the role of mass supervision and supervision of public opinion. In April 1950, the CPC Central Committee issued the *Decision on Criticism and Self-Criticism in Newspapers and Periodicals*, which proposed that "criticism and self-criticism of all mistakes and shortcomings in our work should be carried out on all public occasions, among the people and especially in newspapers and periodicals. It stipulated that: "If the person being criticised refuses to explain his attitude or attacks his critics, he shall be dealt with by the party's Discipline Inspection Committee. If the above-mentioned matters violate administrative discipline and the law, they shall be dealt with by the state supervisory organs and judicial organs."[70] On 30 November, the CPC Central Committee forwarded the *Report of the Secretary's Office of the General Office of the Central Committee on the Handling of Letters from the Masses*, requesting all regions to "set up agencies or designate special people to handle letters and establish the necessary systems for registration, research, referral, inspection and retention of cases", so that letters from the masses were handled seriously and responsibly. On 16 May 1951, Mao Zedong again issued instructions on letters from the masses. The "three anti's" campaign created a powerful force for mass supervision by mobilising the masses to expose corruption, waste and bureaucratism. In the "new three anti's" campaign, the Party Central Committee and Mao Zedong demanded that the starting point should be in examining and dealing with letters from the masses, uncovering and exposing cases of bureaucratism, commandism and lawlessness, and publicising typical examples in the newspapers. In this regard, the *People's Daily* pointed out that "Mass criticism from the bottom up is an important key to opposing bureaucratism and newspapers are the key to unlocking that key."[71]

In terms of supervision outside the party, the role of the democratic parties was also highly valued and given full play.

In the early years of the founding of new China, Mao Zedong and other leading comrades of the Central Committee on various occasions severely criticised and corrected the party's "closed-door tendency on the issue of the united front", and not only arranged for an appropriate place for non-party members in the regime, but also encouraged them to take an active part and play a supervisory role in the process of land reform, democratic political construction, economic construction and even party building. The Constitution of the PRC, adopted at the first session of the First NPC, further clarified the importance of the united front and the status and role of the democratic parties in the form of a fundamental law. In April 1956,

Mao Zedong advanced the "Two Long Lives Slogan": "Long live the communist party and long live the democratic parties", saying: "Long live the communist party and long live the democratic parties. That they can look to us is also a kind of democracy. The communist party has two things to be afraid of: one is the people and the other is the democrats."[72] The Eighth National Congress of the CPC established "long-term co-existence and mutual supervision" as the basic policy for relations between the communist party and the democratic parties. Deng Xiaoping observed in this regard: "These democrats outside the party can provide a kind of supervision to the party that is not easily provided by party members alone, can discover mistakes and shortcomings in our work that we have not discovered, and can provide useful help to our work."[73]

Seventh, adjusting the party's leadership system and work system, and improving the party's leadership style.

The party's leadership system and working system, and the means by which it leads and governs, have a bearing on the success and failure of the party's cause and on the consolidation of the party's ruling position. During the period of the democratic revolution, the party established and developed an organisational leadership system, trained a group of leaders and managers in political and financial management, and formed a system to lead the construction of revolutionary base areas, which provided an important organisational foundation for the party to govern throughout the country and accumulate valuable leadership experience. At the beginning of the founding of the new China, the institutions of power at all levels were still in their infancy, while the party's leading organs and organisations at all levels were relatively strict and sound, and the party's integrated leadership style developed during the anti-Japanese war was thereby continued.

The basic feature of the party's integrated leadership was that the Central Bureau and the local party committees were the supreme leadership organs in their respective regions, unifying the leadership of the work of the party, the government, the military and the people in their respective localities; the decisions and instructions of the Central Bureau and the party committees at all levels had to be implemented unconditionally by the party caucuses (later party groups) of the government at the same level, the military and political committees of the army, and the party caucuses and members of the people's organisations. In November 1949, the CPC Central Committee issued the *Decision on the Establishment of the CPC Committee within the Central People's Government* and *the Decision on the Establishment of the CPC Group within the Central People's Government*. The above decisions were to be implemented at all levels of government at both central and local levels. The function of the party committees of government organs at all levels was mainly to ensure the completion of the administrative tasks of government departments in accordance with the policy resolutions of the Central People's Government. At the same time, in all committees, ministries, commissions, councils, courts, departments and branches under the Central People's Government, party groups were formed by members of the communist party who were responsible for their work, and the party groups had to ensure that all decisions and instructions of the Central Committee of the party relating to the work of the government were carried out and not violated. The system of party groups was extended from the central state organs to local government departments at all levels, including the CPPCC and people's organisations at all levels, and has been maintained ever since. In addition, the principle of party control of cadres was applied to the personnel system, which meant that all cadres in the state were managed in a uniform manner in accordance with the relevant guidelines, policies and principles of the party.

The leadership of the CPC does not amount to "taking control of everything". The party had a clear understanding of this during the War of Resistance Against Japanese Aggression and further explored it after the founding of the new China. On 30 October 1949, at the request of the Party Central Committee, the Central Propaganda Department and the Xinhua News Agency issued the *Instruction on Precautions to be Taken in Propaganda Work after the Establishment of the Central People's Government*, stating clearly that: "After the establishment of the Central People's Government, all matters falling within the purview of the government should be discussed and decided by the Central People's Government, and promulgated and implemented by explicit government decree. Those which affect the whole country should be promulgated by the central government, and those which fall within the scope of the local government should be promulgated by the local government. Decisions, resolutions or circulars of an administrative nature should not be issued to the people in the name of the CPC, as was sometimes done in the past."[74] Zhou Enlai, Dong Biwu and other party and state leaders repeatedly pointed out that there are both connections and differences between the party and the government. The party cannot take over the work of the organs of power just because it leads them, nor can it abolish the functions of the party's own organisation just because it leads the organs of power. Dong Biwu stressed that the correct relationship between the party and the organs of state power could be summarised in the following three points: first, the giving of definite instructions on the nature and direction of the work of the organs of power; second, the implementation of the party's policies through the organs of power and their work departments and the supervision of their activities; and third, the selection and promotion of loyal and competent cadres (party and non-party) to work in the organs of power.

It is permissible to have orders that are not successful and prohibitions that do not work but it is never permissible to have policies at the top that are countermanded at the bottom; at the same time, what must at all costs be avoided are the phenomena of excessive centralisation of power, arbitrariness, paternalism and one voice overriding all others. Deng Xiaoping made the profound observation that: "The phenomenon of excessive concentration of power is that under the slogan of strengthening the integrated leadership of the party, all power is inappropriately and unquestioningly concentrated in the party committee, and the power of the party committee is often concentrated in a few secretaries, especially in the First Secretary, who has to take charge and make the decision on everything. The party's integrated leadership often turned into personal leadership as a result."[75] Historically, from the Zunyi Conference to the period of socialist transformation, the Party Central Committee and Mao Zedong had always paid more attention to collective leadership and democratic centralisation, and political life within the party was relatively normal. After 1957, the democratic life of the party and the state gradually departed from the normal, and phenomena such as personal decision-making on major issues, the cult of the individual and the supremacy of the individual over the organisation continued to grow. This was an important cause of many "leftist" mistakes, including even the Cultural Revolution, which caused serious damage to the party and the state and taught a very profound lesson.

3

ESTABLISHMENT OF THE BASIC SOCIALIST SYSTEM AND THE EXPLORATION OF NEW WAYS OF GOVERNING

The establishment of a socialist system in China was an inevitable part of China's historical development in modern times. On the basis of the restoration of the national economy and the consolidation of the new people's power, the CPC lost no time in proposing the general line of the transition period, creatively carrying out socialist transformation and establishing the basic socialist system, thereby bringing about the greatest and most profound social transformation in China's history. On the basis of this fundamental political premise and system, the CPC advanced the important idea of a "second marriage" between Marxism and Chinese reality and, learning from the Soviet Union, started the arduous process of exploring China's own path of socialist construction and a new path of governance suited to China's national conditions through self-reliance and hard work. As Deng Xiaoping later concluded, "The formulation of a country's course and policies can only be based on its own reality, and the experience of other countries can only be used as a reference. You have to walk the road you make for yourself, and the road you make for yourself is the most reliable road."[1]

(I) THE GREATEST AND MOST PROFOUND SOCIAL CHANGE IN CHINA: THE ESTABLISHMENT OF THE BASIC SOCIALIST SYSTEM

The history of modern times has amply demonstrated that attempts to follow the path of capitalism in China do not work, and that all struggles to do so, whether by means of improvements or revolution, have failed. This gave rise to the historical necessity of finding a new goal to strive for and a new path. The fact that the CPC, at its founding, explicitly promoted the struggle for socialism and communism was a manifestation of this historical necessity.

However, in a large Eastern country with a semi-colonial and semi-feudal society, China could not achieve socialism directly but had to proceed in two steps. The first step was to carry out a new democratic revolution in order to establish a new democracy. The second step was to carry out a socialist revolution in order to establish socialism. In other words, the road led through new democracy towards socialism.

How, then, would China move towards socialism after the victory of the new democratic revolution? To answer this question, the Second Plenary Session of the Seventh Party Central Committee in 1949 made a preliminary plan, stating that after the victory of the revolution in the country, one of the fundamental tasks of the party was to steadily promote two transformations: first, from an agricultural country to an industrial country and, second, from a new democratic society to a socialist society. As to when and in what way this transformation should be achieved, the Party Central Committee and Mao Zedong advanced some ideas at the beginning of the founding of the new China. Later, as the objective situation changed, new ideas were put forward.

By 1952, after three years of strenuous efforts to revive the national economy, as the situation developed and new experience was accumulated, and as a new understanding of the steps of socialist transformation emerged, the Party Central Committee's original vision of a period of new-democratic construction followed by practical socialist steps to move smoothly into socialism changed. This was because, first, China already had a rapidly developing and relatively strong state economy, which became the material basis for the transition to socialism. Second, the private industrial and commercial sector had been restructured and a considerable part of it had been integrated into the state capitalist course through processing orders, distribution and public-private partnerships. This, in fact, became the first step in the socialist transformation of the capitalist industrial and commercial sector. Once again, the agricultural cooperative movement was widely implemented in the countryside, initially demonstrating the superiority of organising individual farmers to increase agricultural production. Finally, in terms of the international environment, the Western capitalist countries threatened China with military aggression and imposed a tight economic blockade. Only the Soviet Union and the socialist countries of Eastern Europe provided assistance to China, and the acceleration of the transition to socialism was conducive to the strengthening of mutual assistance and cooperation between China and these various socialist countries. In addition, after the end of the second world war, the capitalist countries were in economic recession while the socialist countries were full of vigour and vitality, demonstrating the superiority of socialism over capitalism. In particular, the Soviet Union played a major role in the war against German fascism, and the Soviet model and construction experience had a strong appeal to China. These were also important factors that influenced the proposal to start the transition to socialism.

During this period, some new contradictions also emerged and accumulated in China's social economy. With the beginning of planned economic construction, the small peasant economy, based on private ownership of the means of production, was unable to meet the growing demand for food and raw materials for large-scale industrialisation. There were negative aspects of private capitalism that were not conducive to the livelihood of the nation, which led to contradictions and conflicts with the state-run economy. As a result, the task of socialist transformation of the entire national economy was put on the agenda. Therefore, the party duly formulated the general line of the transition period, clearly setting out the task of a gradual transition to socialism, that is, to carry out socialist transformation of individual agriculture, handicrafts and capitalist industry and commerce, and to integrate them into a planned socialist economy, at the same time as building socialist industrialisation. The party's general line for the transitional period was in line with the reality and laws of social development in the new China and reflected the inevitability of history.

The establishment of China's socialist economic system was achieved through the socialist transformation of the private ownership of the means of production. In 1953, the party led the nation to begin the socialist transformation of individual agriculture, handicrafts and capitalist industry and commerce. By 1956, the socialist transformation had achieved a decisive victory. The individual ownership of farmers and craftspeople was basically transformed into collective ownership by the working masses, and farmers and other individual workers became socialist collective workers. The private ownership of capitalism was basically transformed into state ownership, that is to say, universal ownership. Together with the tremendous development of the state economy in the course of planned economic construction, the two forms of socialist public ownership, namely, universal ownership and collective ownership by the working masses, became absolutely dominant in our national economy. In 1956, compared with 1952, the state economy rose from 19.1% to 32.2%, the cooperative economy from 1.5% to 53.4%, the public-private partnership economy from 0.7% per cent to 7.3%, the individual economy from 71.8% to 7.1% and the capitalist economy from 6.9% to 0%. The socialist state economy, the cooperative economy and the largely socialist public-private partnership economy together accounted for 92.9% of national income. In the countryside, public ownership of land was largely achieved, with 96.3% of the country's farmers joining agricultural production cooperatives. In addition, 91.7% of craftspeople joined handicraft production cooperatives. At the same time, a distribution system based on the distribution of labour was gradually established. The changes in production relations further liberated social productive forces and promoted their development. In 1956, while the socialist transformation was basically completed, the planned economic construction also made great achievements. At constant prices in 1952, the total industrial output value was Rmb70.36 billion, accounting for 51.3% of the total industrial and agricultural output value, within which the growth in the proportion of modern industry laid an important material foundation for the establishment of the socialist economic system. By 1956, with the socialist transformation of the private ownership of the means of production essentially completed, the socialist economic system was established in China.

Along with the establishment of the economic base of socialism, the socialist political system, education, science and cultural system were also basically formed, and all aspects of the political life of the country and the work of the state were developed and improved to suit and serve the establishment of the socialist economic base. Politically, the CPC became the core of the leadership of the socialist cause. The leading position of the working class was strengthened and the alliance between workers and peasants, and between the working class and other working people, was further consolidated on a socialist basis. The promulgation and implementation of the Constitution of the PRC, the formal establishment of the system of people's congresses, the continued development of the multi-party cooperation and political consultation system under the leadership of the CPC, and the gradual establishment of the system of regional national autonomy reflected the fruitful achievements made in the construction of the country's political system over the preceding few years, and the construction of a basic socialist political system. In terms of ideology and culture, the guiding position of Marxism-Leninism and Mao Zedong Thought in the field of ideology was further strengthened. While criticising the corrupt ideas of feudalism and capitalism, the party also absorbed and carried forward the national essence of traditional Chinese culture and absorbed all the beneficial cultural achievements of foreign countries in an effort to build a socialist national, scientific and popular culture. The masses gradually built up a sense of socialism and espoused patriotic and collectivist values. A new type of social relations, with a fine social ethos and moral social codes took shape.

The leadership of the CPC, the state power of the people's democratic dictatorship and the guiding position of Marxism-Leninism and Mao Zedong Thought in the ideological sphere were originally powerful political factors in the superstructure that ensured the transition to a socialist society in China. With the socialist economic base established, they took on the task of consolidating and developing it. Based on this objective process, in September 1956 the Eighth National Party Congress formally declared that: "The socialist social system has essentially been established in our country."[2]

According to the tasks set out in the party's general line for the transitional period, the completion of socialist industrialisation and socialist transformation took more than three five-year plans. The result, in practice, was that the socialist transformation of private ownership of the means of production was basically completed by 1956. In this respect, the task of transition to socialism was achieved. However, in terms of the development of the social productive forces, the transformation of our country from a backward agricultural country into an advanced industrial country, the establishment of an independent and relatively complete industrial system and the basic completion of the task of socialist industrialisation required at least two more five-year plans to lay a preliminary foundation. Therefore, the party did not explicitly declare the end of the transition period to socialism. This was based on the fact that although China had entered a socialist society, the material basis for socialism that had just been established was still very inadequate. After the completion of the socialist transformation, there was still a long way to go in developing the productive forces; the new relations of production established by the socialist transformation needed to be constantly adjusted to the requirements of the development of the productive forces; and the parts of the political and legal superstructure that were not adapted to the economic base also needed to be adjusted and reformed. Therefore, the socialism established in China in the mid-1950s was, in fact, socialism in its primary stage. These were the basic national conditions of China. Until now, these conditions had remained unchanged, until now, when our party has embarked on the path of exploring its own way of building socialism from the basic national conditions and has made brilliant achievements.

China's fundamental foundational political systems have brought great advantages into play since their establishment. The system of people's congresses has enabled deputies from all walks of life to fully express their aspirations and realise real mastery of the work over their own affairs, thereby greatly stimulating the enthusiasm, initiative and creativity of the whole nation in building socialism. The system of multi-party cooperation and political consultation under the leadership of the CPC has provided stability and continuity in Chinese politics, avoiding the political strife that is unavoidable in Western multi-party systems, and enabling consultative democracy to better unite the consensus of society as a whole. The system of regional ethnic autonomy has enabled the ethnic minorities to experience the equality and love of all ethnic nationalities and the warmth of the motherland's big family, and established a stable and united political situation for our party to lead the people across the country in building socialism.

The establishment of China's basic economic system has contributed to the development of the social productive forces and the improvement of people's living conditions. "During the first five-year plan, the total output value of industry and agriculture increased by 10.9% per year. Among them, the total industrial output value grew by an average of 18% per year, higher than the 14.7% stipulated in the first five-year plan; the total agricultural output value grew by an average of 4.5% per year, slightly higher than the 4.3% stipulated in the plan. On the whole, the planned industrial construction progressed smoothly and the economy developed relatively quickly. The market prospered and the people's livelihoods improved significantly. In 1956, the national consumption level rose by 21.3% compared to 1952. The completion of agricultural cooperatives transformed the private ownership of land, which had existed for thousands of years in China's history, into collective ownership, and rural land was transformed from being owned by individual farmers to being owned collectively. This was undoubtedly a great and profound change.

All of the above is ample proof that the establishment of the basic socialist system was an extensive and profound social transformation in Chinese history, laying the fundamental political premise and institutional foundation for all development and progress in contemporary China, laying a solid foundation for achieving national prosperity and people's happiness. The Chinese nation has achieved a great leap forward from continuous decline to a fundamental reversal of its fate and sustained progress towards prosperity and strength.

In the historical evolution of human society, generally speaking, rapid changes in the relations of production have often caused social unrest and different degrees of damage to social productivity. However, the elimination of all systems of exploitation and the relatively smooth achievement of such a complex, challenging and profound change in the social system of China, a country with a population of several hundred million, not only did not cause social unrest but also promoted the development of the social productivity and the unity of all ethnic nationalities. This is a matter of great historical significance.

This shows that socialism was an inevitable choice for China's historical development. At the same time, in leading this social change, the CPC has accumulated a store of original experience and created a series of transitional forms from the primary to the advanced level that suited China's particular characteristics, thereby avoiding social upheaval and damage to the productive forces.

For individual agriculture, the CPC created a transitional form that moved from mutual aid groups to primary agricultural production cooperatives to advanced agricultural production cooperatives, gradually transforming the peasants' individual private ownership into socialist collective ownership. The development of agricultural cooperatives involved changing the traditional production methods and lifestyle of Chinese peasants that had existed for thousands of years. This naturally led to certain contradictions. However, the party demonstrated to the peasants that cooperatives could benefit anyone who had difficulties with production conditions, and thereby gained the support of the majority of the rural population for cooperatives.

With regard to the transformation of capitalist industry and commerce, Marx had envisaged the possibility of the socialist revolution imposing a peaceful economic buy-out, or redemption, of the bourgeoisie. Lenin had proposed just such a policy and programme of peaceful redemption after the October revolution. However, for various reasons, Lenin's programme could not be implemented. The CPC built an alliance with the national bourgeoisie during the new democratic revolution and continued to maintain this alliance during the socialist transformation, which enabled the CPC to effectively carry out a peaceful redemption of the bourgeoisie for the first time in the history of socialism. For the purpose of this redemption, the CPC created a way of not paying a large one-off "ransom" to the capitalists through the state but allowing them to continue to receive a portion of the profits and dividends from the enterprises for a considerable period of time, and also created a series of forms of state capitalism, from the primary to the advanced, to guide the gradual transition from capitalist industry and commerce to socialism. This not only reduced the resistance of the capitalists to the change from private ownership but also continued to make use of the positive role of private capitalism in expanding production, increasing tax revenue, improving technology and enterprise management, and training skilled workers and technicians. Although many capitalists were reluctant to enter into industrywide public-private partnerships, under the ideological education of the communist party, they gradually realised that the path of socialism was the general trend of the times and the right choice for the development and progress of the Chinese nation. In addition, the communist party adopted a correct policy towards the capitalists, and apart from continuing to pay fixed interest, it also arranged for them to work, so that they could continue to enjoy the appropriate political rights and retain their representative status in state institutions, thereby enabling the capitalists to cross the "hurdle" of socialism. In this regard, in June 1956, Chen Yun commented: "The change from private to socialist ownership of enterprises is not a new phenomenon in this world but the adoption of such a peaceful method to make the country's business community accept this change with such enthusiasm is unprecedented."[3]

In the case of individual crafts, the transition from supply and marketing cooperative groups to supply and marketing production cooperatives, and then to craft production cooperatives, transformed the individual private ownership of craftspeople into a socialist collective ownership system.

Thanks to these innovations, China's socialist transformation, although still modelled on that of the Soviet Union, took on Chinese characteristics in its specific path, thereby enriching and developing the Marxist theory of scientific socialism with new experiences and ideas.

All in all, the CPC made the transition from new democracy to socialism and adopted a concrete policy of gradually transforming the private ownership of the means of production in accordance with the political and material conditions created after the victory of the new democratic revolution. In doing so, it achieved stable growth in the national economy and widespread popular support in such a complex, challenging and profound social transformation in a country as economically backward as China and the goal of socialism was achieved relatively smoothly. This basic fact shows how successful the leadership of the CPC was in the process of socialist transformation.

However, due to lack of experience on how to establish and build socialism, the party developed a number of fixed ideas on the interpretation of socialism that were not suited to reality. With regard to the economic basis for building a socialist society, the party's understanding of the socialist economy at the time was that there was a single socialist public ownership system. In September 1953, Zhou Enlai observed: "What does socialism mean? The most basic thing about socialism is the completion of socialist transformation, that is, the abolition of private capitalist ownership of the means of production and their return to state ownership; it is also the collectivisation of agriculture and handicrafts."[4] In December 1953, the *Struggle to Mobilise All Forces to Build China into a Great Socialist Country - Outline for Study and Propaganda on the Party's General Line in the Transition Period*, approved by the CPC Central Committee, stressed that "the essence of the party's general line in the transition period is to make socialist ownership of the means of production the only economic basis of our state and society." In November 1955, Liu Shaoqi pointed out at a conference on the transformation of capitalist industry and commerce that: "To build a socialist society, we must change the capitalist ownership system and individual ownership system, and establish universal ownership and collective ownership. As long as we grasp this point and do not waver on it, then we are basically not contradicting Marxism-Leninism and will not make major mistakes."[5] The result of this understanding and judgment was that the change in the relationships of production was detached from the development progress of productivity, and there was a blind search for perfection, proposing to make capitalism and small production extinct, ignoring or even simply not recognising the positive role of preserving the development of the private and individual economy in the development of the socialist economy over a certain period and under certain conditions, and basically establishing a single socialist system of ownership. There is no doubt that socialist public ownership is the economic foundation of a socialist society. However, socialism does not mean that only a single public ownership system can be practised, without allowing the existence of individual and private economies which are beneficial to the livelihood of the nation.

In addition, the party's understanding of the socialist economy emphasised that "the implementation of a planned economy is the fundamental characteristic of socialism". The hallmark of a planned economy is that the state sets mandatory targets and the commodity economy is considered incompatible with a socialist economy. As a result of this understanding and judgment, after the completion of the socialist transformation, the production and operation of agriculture, handicrafts and capitalist industry and commerce were brought under state planning, and a highly centralised, all-encompassing planned economic system was established. However, the development of the planned economy became more and more restrictive and even cancelled out the benefits of the commodity economy and market regulation.

In terms of the management of the rural collective economy, copying the experience of the Soviet collective farms, with the blind pursuit of centralisation and unified management, ignoring the separation of ownership from management, and giving full play to the enthusiasm of individual peasants and families in running their own businesses, all highlighted the problems of overcentralisation and egalitarianism, which hindered the development of rural productivity.

At the time, it was not surprising that our party had such a simple understanding of socialist economy, as that is what the Marxist books said. Marx and Engels had envisaged a socialist economy linked to a single communal, planned economy. In the 1930s, the Soviet Union established a highly centralised, planned economy and it was on the basis of this system that the Soviet Union was able to overcome the German fascist invasion in the second world war, demonstrating the vitality and unparalleled superiority of socialism. "After the end of the second world war, the basic system of Soviet socialism and its model were regarded as the only correct choice within the socialist camp. It was therefore logical and inevitable that China was heavily influenced by the Soviet Union's highly centralised economic model in the process of its socialist transformation.

The Soviet model, after all, was formed under specific historical conditions and had its historical rationale as well as its historical limitations. In the course of its creation, the Soviet model suffered from a dogmatic understanding and even misinterpretation of scientific socialist theory. For example, restrictions on the development of the commodity economy and the absolutism of its planned economy were all related to a standard and unimaginative understanding of certain theoretical perspectives of scientific socialism. Therefore, for the Chinese communists, it was necessary to treat the basic principles of Marxism historically and scientifically, to proceed from the actual situation, and to consciously liberate their ideological awareness from those anachronistic concepts, practices and institutions, and from the mistaken and dogmatic understanding of Marxism. As China's large-scale economic construction began and the problems of the ruling CPSU were exposed, Mao Zedong advanced the important idea of a "second marriage" between Marxism and Chinese reality and, taking the Soviet Union as a reference, began to explore China's own path of socialist construction.

(II) THE BASIC FORMATION OF THE CPC'S GOVERNANCE SYSTEM AND MECHANISM

The governance of any political party needs to be backed by a set of well-established and effective systems and mechanisms. This is the objective law of modern party governance and an inevitable requirement for a political party to fulfill its governance objectives and achieve its governance goals and missions. For the CPC, which completely broke down the old state apparatus and established a new China, whether it could establish a set of governance systems and mechanisms that continuously improved and matured was a fundamental and overriding issue that concerned whether the party could continuously consolidate its ruling position, achieve long-term governance and ensure the country's prosperity.

When drawing up the blueprint for national governance, the Party Central Committee made careful plans, designs and arrangements for the party's governing system and mechanisms. After the founding of the new China, especially with the completion of the socialist transformation and the establishment of the basic socialist system, the CPC built up a system for leading the people of all nationalities to manage all aspects of national and social affairs, including the party's leadership system, the national political system, the economic system and the systems of science, technology, education, culture and society. They formed a set of closely interlinked and coordinated systems and mechanisms of governance. The party creatively solved the problems of system design and institutional arrangements for the CPC to govern throughout the country and to govern in the long term. In this, it initially answered a series of questions about for whom they governed, who they relied on to govern and how they governed.

This system and mechanism of governance of the CPC is effectively organised in accordance with the principle of democratic centralism. Democratic centralism is not only the party's fundamental organisational and leadership system, which is the greatest institutional advantage of the CPC, but also the principle of the organisation and operation of state institutions with the people's congresses at their core, which is the greatest feature and advantage of the socialist system with Chinese characteristics. The party's governing system and mechanism, formed and established in accordance with the principle of democratic centralism, has played a great role in regulating political relations, consolidating the political order, promoting national development and maintaining social stability. It has laid a solid institutional foundation and accumulated valuable experience for the party to come to power nationwide and remain in power for a long time, as well as to successfully create, uphold and develop socialism with Chinese characteristics.

First, the adjustment and fundamental finalisation of the party's leadership system and mechanism.

Before the founding of new China, the party had, in the course of its long revolutionary practice, established a set of effective, scientific and rigorous organisational and party systems from the party's central, local and grassroots organisations in accordance with the principle of democratic centralism, and applied it to the process of localised rule in the revolutionary base areas. After the founding of the new China, the party applied this set of organisational systems and leadership systems and mechanisms to the practice of national governance, and the integrated leadership style developed during the War of Resistance

Against Japanese Aggression was continued. In order to adapt to the complex and arduous administrative tasks, the need to lead large-scale economic construction and to further strengthen and improve the party's leadership, the party made new adjustments to its organisational and leadership systems in light of the new realities.

From the perspective of the adjustment of the party's central organisations and working organs, and the strengthening of the party's centralised and unified leadership, the party's centralised and unified leadership is, first and foremost, the centralised and unified leadership of the Party Central Committee. The Eighth Party Congress highlighted the vital importance of the party's leading role under the conditions of governance, stating that "efforts must be made for it to play its correct leading and central role in all aspects of national life and to oppose any decentralist tendency to reduce the party's role and weaken its unity." From 1954 to the Eighth Party Congress, the Party Central Committee implemented the principle of democratic centralism, strengthened its centralised and unified leadership over party and state affairs from an institutional perspective, and consolidated the central role of the party in national life. The following seven measures were taken.

- Regulating the term of office of the Party's National Congress. The Party's National Congress is the highest organ of power, the highest organ of leadership and the highest organ of party inspection and supervision. It is one of the basic requirements of the party's democratic centralism to hold the Party's National Congress regularly and to give full play to its role. From 1921 to 1928, the party held six national congresses in accordance with the practice of annual meetings. Later, due to the long and brutal war conditions, there was a gap of 17 years between the Sixth and Seventh National Congresses, and 11 years between the Seventh and Eighth National Congresses. In order to give full play to the role of the Party's National Congresses under the circumstances and conditions of peaceful construction, the Party's Constitution from the Eighth Party Congress stipulated that the term of office of the Party's National Congresses should be five years. After that, because of the Cultural Revolution, there was a gap of 13 years between the 8th and 9th National

Congresses. This provision was inherited and maintained in the new era of reform and opening up, and has been continued to this day. The Eighth Party Congress also abolished the system of meetings of delegates at all levels, which had been stipulated at the Seventh Congress, and itself stipulated for the first time that the party congresses should be permanent. However, this was not adhered to and, as far as the whole party was concerned, the Eighth Party Congress only met twice.

- Making adjustments to the party's central organisation. The Constitution of the Seventh Party Congress stipulated that the Central Committee should elect the Central Politburo and the Central Secretariat at its plenary sessions, and that the Central Secretariat should handle the day-to-day work of the Central Committee under the leadership of the Central Politburo, with functions equivalent to those of the previous and later Standing Committee of the Central Politburo. In 1954, a regular Secretary General's Conference was established under the Central Secretariat to set up a system and working mechanism for the Secretary General's Conference to meet and deliberate regularly, and to assist the Politburo and the Central Secretariat in studying and dealing with the day-to-day affairs of the party and the masses, as well as other matters referred to it by the Politburo and the Central Secretariat. The Party's Eighth Congress made changes to the organisation of the Party's Central Committee by re-establishing the Standing Committee of the Central Politburo to replace the Central Secretariat established at the Seventh Congress; a new Central Secretariat was established to replace the functions of the former Secretary General's Working Conference and to handle the day-to-day work of the Central Committee under the leadership of the Central Politburo and its Standing Committee.

- Streamlining the organisational hierarchy of the party and government institutions. From the late stages of the war of liberation onwards, the people's governments of the major administrative regions (military and political committees) were established in various regions as first-level power-wielding organisations with a full range of party, government and military structures. After 1952, they were transformed into administrative committees, which served as representative bodies of the Central People's Government. This system of large regions played a positive role in the unified implementation of the central government's decrees, the establishment and consolidation of local power, and the promotion of democratic reform and economic recovery. In order to streamline the party's organisational hierarchy and the hierarchy of power, and to strengthen the unity and centralised leadership of the party and state, the enlarged meeting of the Politburo of the CPC Central Committee in April 1954 decided to abolish the party and government bodies at the regional level, and the Central Bureaux and Central Sub-Bureaux, which were the representative organs of the CPC Central Committee, were also abolished with immediate effect.[6]

- Upholding the absolute leadership of the party over the people's army. The 1954 Constitution stipulated that the Revolutionary Military Commission of the Central People's Government would be abolished, and that the National Defence Commission and the Ministry of National Defence would be established within the state apparatus; the State President would be in charge of the national armed forces and would be the Chairman of the National Defence Commission. However, the 1954 Constitution did not stipulate the nature, status and powers of the National Defence Commission or its relationship with other state institutions. Judging from the composition of the National Defence Commission established at the first session of the NPC, it did not have the functions of national military jurisdiction but was an organisation that was part of the united front. Of the 79 members of the National Defence Commission, 29 were from outside the party, with former KMT generals Cheng Qian, Zhang Zhizhong, Fu Zuoyi and Long Yun appointed as Vice-Chairmen of the National Defence Commission. Consequently, after the conclusion of the first session of the NPC, the Politburo decided in September 1954 to set up a Central Military Commission under the Politburo and the Central Secretariat to assume leadership of the entire military. This system embodies the principle of absolute leadership of the party over the people's army from its foundation.

- Strengthening party discipline and internal supervision. The National Party Congress held in March 1955 drew a profound lesson from the struggle against the separatist activities of Gao Gang and Rao Shushi, and stressed the need for strict, regular, systematic, top-down and bottom-up supervision to help party members discover and rectify their mistakes in a timely manner. The conference decided to establish central and local supervisory committees to replace the party's disciplinary inspection committees established at the beginning of the founding of the new China. Since then, local supervisory committees at all levels of the party were successively established. In terms of scope of responsibility, powers, organisation and staffing, the party's supervisory committees were greatly strengthened compared to the previous disciplinary committees, and the party entered a new stage of discipline building and internal supervision.

- Further improving the party's central agencies. The work of the Central Organisation Department, the Central Propaganda Department and the Central United Front Work Department, which had been in existence before the founding of the new China, was generally reinforced. In accordance with work needs, the Central External Liaison Department, the Central Department of Rural Work and some temporary working bodies were established; the Central Workers Committee, the Youth Work Committee and the Women's Work Committee were abolished.

- Establishing party groups in organisations outside the party. As early as November 1949, at the beginning of the founding of the new China, the CPC Central Committee made the *Decision on the Organisation of the CPC Committee within the Central People's Government* and the *Decision on the Establishment of the CPC Group within the Central People's Government*, establishing the party committee system and party group system within the Central People's Government. The Party Constitution of the Eighth Party Congress clearly stipulated that in the leading organs of state agencies and people's organisations, where there were more than three party members in charge of the work, a party group should be set up. Their task was to implement the party's policies and resolutions, strengthen unity with non-party cadres, maintain close ties with the masses, consolidate party and state discipline, and combat bureaucratism.

From the perspective of strengthening the party's local organisation, the main purpose was to put forward new arrangements and requirements for the building of grassroots organisations. To meet the needs of the party's nationwide administration and national construction, and in order to give full play to the role of the provincial and municipal committees, the Central Committee made the *Decision on the Establishment of the Secretariats of Provincial and Municipal Committees* in June 1955, which clarified the establishment, status and duties of the secretariats of provincial and municipal committees, and made adjustments to the organisational form and working system of local governing bodies. In order to give better play to the role of the party's grassroots organisations as bastions of the struggle, the Constitution of the Eighth Party Congress proposed four new tasks building on the Constitution of the Seventh Party Congress. The main tasks were: to lead the masses to participate actively in the political life of the country; to lead the masses to be active and creative; to consolidate labour discipline and to ensure the completion of production and work plans; to carry out criticism and self-criticism; to expose and eliminate shortcomings and mistakes in the workplace; to fight against all examples of lawlessness, corruption, waste and bureaucratism; to provide education on vigilance and to always concentrate on combating the sabotage activities of class enemies.

From the perspective of the cadre and personnel system, the main thing was to continue to adhere to the principle of party management of cadres.

After the political line was determined, cadres were the decisive factor. After the founding of the new China, the practice of the revolutionary war period was continued, and with the exception of military cadres, all cadres of state organs were managed by the central government and the organisational departments of the party committees at all levels in accordance with the party's relevant guidelines and principles. Government personnel departments were a form of organisation for party management of cadres and were under the guidance of the organisational departments of the party committees at the same level. The principle of the party's management of cadres was an important manifestation of party leadership of the work of cadres and personnel, and provided an important guarantee for the consolidation of the party's ruling position and the fulfilment of its governing mission.

Second, the formal establishment of the system of people's congresses and the basic shape of the new Chinese political system.

With the convening of the First Session of the First NPC in September 1954 and the promulgation of the 1954 Constitution, the first constitution of the new China, a new political system in the form of the people's congress system was established in China, a country with a history of more than 5,000 years of civilisation and a population of several hundred million. This was a landmark large-scale reconstruction of the national political system led by the party after it came to power nationwide, laying the foundations of China's socialist political system.

As the fundamental political system of the new China, the core and essence of the people's congress system is to realise that the people are the masters of their own house, to ensure that all powers of the state belong to the people, and that the people participate in the management of state affairs through the organisational form of the people's congresses. This fundamental political system is rich in its connotations. First, all powers of the state belong to the people. The organs through which the people exercise state power are the NPC and the local people's congresses at all levels. Second, the NPC, local people's congresses at all levels and other state organs all practise democratic centralism. Third, the NPC and local people's congresses at all levels are democratically elected, accountable to the people and subject to their supervision. Fourth, the state administrative organs, the judiciary and the procuratorial organs are all elected by the people's congress, accountable to it and subject to its supervision. Fifth, the division of powers and functions between the central and local state organs follows the principle of giving full play to local initiatives and enthusiasm under the unified leadership of the central government. Sixth, the system of regional ethnic autonomy is practised in areas inhabited by ethnic minorities, and all ethnic areas are an inseparable part of the PRC.

It is clear from the basic connotations of the people's congress system that it is not only the fundamental system that regulates the nature, status and powers of the people's congresses but is also a series of systems that regulate the relationship between the people's congresses and the executive and judicial organs, and between the central and local levels. It is a complete system of organisation of state power founded on the basic principle of democratic centralism with the people's congresses at its core. It is a direct manifestation of the whole-state nature of the people's democratic dictatorship, the highest and most important form of realisation of the Chinese people's mastery of their own affairs, an institutional guarantee for the maintenance of national unity and national solidarity, and the coordinated and efficient operation of state organs, and the best way for the party to give full play to democracy in state power, and to strengthen and improve its leadership of state affairs. In this, it has great vitality and significant advantages.

After the founding of the new China, the CPC further strengthened its unity and cooperation with the democratic parties and people without party affiliation, and continued to consolidate and develop the multi-party cooperation and political consultation system under its leadership. First, after the establishment of the people's congress system, the CPPCC continued to function as an organisation of the People's Democratic United Front. After the convening of the First Session of the NPC, there were different views and understandings on whether the CPPCC should continue to exist and what its nature and tasks should be. In December 1954, the Second National Committee of the CPPCC held its first meeting and adopted the statutes of the CPPCC, which stipulated that the nature of the conference was "a democratic united front organisation of the people uniting all nationalities, democratic classes, democratic parties, people's organisations, overseas Chinese and other patriotic people". This further clarified that the CPPCC was a party-affiliated united front organisation and a consultative organ of all parties. The continued existence of the CPPCC was in line with the provision in the 1954 Constitution that "China's People's Democratic United Front will continue to play its role" and was a further development of the multi-party cooperation and political consultation system under the leadership of the CPC. Second, it established the basic policy of "long-term co-existence and mutual supervision" between the CPC and other democratic parties. After the completion of the socialist transformation and the elimination of the exploiting class, people had different views and perceptions about the continued existence of democratic parties. In this regard, in April 1954, Mao Zedong specifically elaborated on the "relationship between the party and the non-party" in his report *On the Ten Relations*, stating: "Is it better to have one party or several? Now, I have to admit that several parties are better. Not only was this true in the past but it can also be true in the future; that is to say, they should co-exist for a long time and supervise each other."[7]

After the founding of the new China, the system of regional ethnic autonomy entered the implementation stage. In August 1952, the Central People's Government promulgated and implemented the *Outline for the Implementation of Regional Ethnic Autonomy in the PRC*, based on the in-depth implementation of the ethnic policy stipulated in the *Common Programme*. The *Implementation Programme* stipulated that autonomous regions inhabited by various ethnic minorities should be established in accordance with local ethnic relations, economic development conditions and historical circumstances, and that the organ of self-government of each autonomous region should be a local authority under the leadership of the Central People's Government and subject to the leadership of the people's government at the highest level. After the promulgation of the *Implementation Programme*, the work of regional ethnic autonomy began to be fully implemented, and by March 1953, 47 autonomous ethnic areas equivalent to and above county level had been established throughout the country. The 1954 Constitution clarified the legal status of regional ethnic autonomy, stipulating that the PRC was a unified multi-ethnic state in which all ethnic nationalities were equal, that regional autonomy was to be exercised in the areas inhabited by ethnic minorities, and that all autonomous ethnic areas were an inseparable part of the PRC. The constitution also contained clear provisions for the organs of self-government of ethnic autonomous areas. After the adoption and promulgation of the 1954 Constitution, the pace of establishing ethnic autonomous areas further accelerated. By 1958, the Xinjiang Uyghur Autonomous Region, the Ningxia Hui Autonomous Region and the Guangxi Zhuang Autonomous Region were successively established. After the establishment of the Tibet Autonomous Region in 1965, together with the Inner Mongolia Autonomous Region, which had already been established before the founding of the new China, China had established a total of five provincial-level ethnic autonomous regions.

Third, the establishment of the socialist economic system and the planned economic system.

After the founding of the new China, by depriving the imperialists of their privileges, confiscating bureaucratic capital and abolishing the feudal land ownership system, an ownership structure was formed in which the state economy was the mainstay, the individual private economy was the main body, and a variety of ownership systems co-existed. On the basis of the restoration of the national economy, from 1953 onwards the party led the nation to embark on large-scale economic reconstruction. Based on Mao Zedong's proposals, the Party Central Committee lost no time in proposing the party's general line for the transitional period, which was to gradually industrialise the country and realise the state's socialist transformation of agriculture, handicrafts, and capitalist industry and commerce. Following this general line, the party successfully blazed a trail of socialist transformation suited to China's national conditions. Under the condition of ensuring the basic stable development of the national economy and gaining widespread support from the people, the party basically completed the socialist transfer of private ownership of the means of production by 1956. The individual ownership of the peasants and craftsmen was essentially transformed into a public system of collective ownership by the workers, and the capitalist system of private ownership was essentially transformed into a public system of ownership by the state, that is to say, by the whole nation. Consequently, together with the development of the state economy, the two forms of public ownership, namely, universal ownership and collective ownership, occupied a position of total dominance. At the same time, a distribution system based on the distribution of labour was gradually established. This marked the creation of a genuine socialist economic system in China.

Soon after the founding of the new China, the central government established a planned economic management agency. In the process of restoring the national economy, the central government unified national fiscal revenue, unified national distribution of materials and unified cash management, and established a unified management and leadership system for national financial and economic work. In order to meet the needs of large-scale economic construction and the formulation and implementation of the first five-year plan, the central government decided, in November 1952, to establish a State Planning Commission under the Central People's Government, responsible for formulating and organising the implementation of national economic planning. "The preparation and implementation of the first five-year plan marked the beginning of comprehensive planning and management of all aspects of the national economy under the centralised and unified leadership of the state, through the drawing up and implementation of mandatory economic development plans. In October 1953, the Party Central Committee decided to implement the planned purchase and supply of grain (referred to as "the state monopoly of purchase and marketing"). This was followed by the introduction of the unified purchase of oil and the unified sale of cooking oil, the unified purchase of cotton and the unified sale of cotton cloth. These major decisions not only promoted the socialist transformation of agriculture and private industry and commerce but also brought agricultural production into the field of the planned economy. Article 15 of the 1954 Constitution clearly stipulated that the state should use economic planning to guide the development and transformation of the national economy, so as to continuously increase productivity in order to improve the material and cultural life of the people and consolidate the independence and security of the country. This confirmed the legal status of the planned economic system within the constitution. By 1956, with the completion of the socialist transformation and the establishment of the socialist economic system, the planned economic system had basically taken shape and a set of highly centralised economic operation systems had been established with the national economic planning and management system at its core. This included a financial system, a financial management system, a circulation system, a foreign trade management system, a material supply system and a labour and wage system.

Fourth, the basic establishment and adjustment of the state administrative and judicial systems.

After the founding of the new China, in accordance with the provisions of the *Common Programme* and the Organic Law of the Central People's Government, the Central People's Government was the summation of the entire central power organisation, consisting of the Central People's Government Commission and the State Council under its authority, the People's Revolutionary Military Commission, the Supreme People's Court and the Supreme People's Procuratorate. In terms of the administrative system, there was the two-tier system of the Central People's Government Committee and the State Council under its leadership, with the State Council being organised by the Central People's Government Committee. In terms of the judicial system, the Supreme People's Court and the Supreme People's Procuratorate were organised by the Central People's Government Committee and were subordinate to it.

The 1954 Constitution and the *Law of the PRC on the Organisation of the State Council*, the *Law of the People's Congresses at Local Levels and Local People's Committees at Local Levels*, the *Law of the People's Courts of the PRC on the Organisation of the Procuratorates of the PRC*, adopted at the First Session of the NPC, made significant adjustments to the state administrative and judicial systems. In terms of the administrative system, first, the State Council, the Central People's Government, was established as the first level of government. The State Council, as the executive organ of the highest organ of state power and the highest organ of state administration, unified and directed the work of local state administrative organs at all levels throughout the country. Under the unified leadership of the State Council, local people's governments at all levels were the executive organs of the local people's congresses at all levels and were the local organs of state administration at all levels, responsible for reporting to the people's congresses at their own level and to the organs of state administration at the next level up. Second, an administrative leadership system combining vertical leadership and dual leadership was established. The working departments of local people's governments at all levels were under the unified leadership of the people's governments at that level, and also under the leadership of the relevant departments of higher-level governments up to the relevant departments of the State Council. Overall, this administrative system was conducive to strengthening the centralised and unified leadership of state administration and improving administrative efficiency. However, in practice, it gave rise to the drawbacks of fragmentation, which had a negative impact on economic and social development. In terms of the judicial system, first, it was made explicit that the Supreme People's Court and the Supreme People's Procuratorate, as judicial organs, exercised judicial and procuratorial powers independently and were accountable to the NPC and the Standing Committee of the NPC. Second, the principles and responsibilities of judicial work and the nature, status, composition, powers and operational norms of the judicial organs were clarified. Third, in order to ensure the accurate and effective implementation of the law, in criminal cases, the judiciary, the procuratorial organs and the public security organs applied the principles of division of responsibility, mutual cooperation and mutual restraint. These provisions and principles were a profound summary of the experience gained from the construction of the judicial system and the practice of judicial work since the founding of the new China, and they marked the formal establishment of its judicial system.

Fifth, adjusting and giving basic shape to the system for the development of scientific, educational, cultural and social undertakings.

After the implementation of the general line of the transition period, science, education, culture and social projects began to shift comprehensively to serve large-scale economic construction. Under the leadership of the party and in response to the actual economic and social development, the relevant institutions underwent profound changes. First, marked by the inaugural meeting of the faculty of the Chinese Academy of Sciences (CAS) in June 1955, a national scientific research system gradually took shape centred on the CAS but including higher education institutions, local research institutes, industrial sector research institutes and defence research institutes. This laid the foundation for the comprehensive development of scientific affairs and the formulation of long-term plans. Second, in line with the needs of national construction, especially industrial construction, higher education was further developed to open doors to industry and agriculture, and large-scale adjustments were made to the structure of institutions, the establishment of faculties and departments, and the enrolment of students. Third, in the area of cultural and artistic work, the party's leadership was strengthened and the guiding position of Marxism in the field of ideology was reinforced by implementing Mao Zedong's policy of "letting a hundred flowers bloom and bringing forth new ideas". In May 1956, Mao Zedong formally announced at the Supreme State Council that letting "a hundred flowers bloom and a hundred schools of thought contend" would be the party's guiding principle for the development of science and the flourishing of literature and art. This became a fundamental and longstanding policy in the field of socialist cultural construction in China. Fourth, in the area of grassroots self-government, in order to regulate and strengthen the construction of residents' committees organised in the cities after the founding of the new China, the *Regulations on the Organisation of Urban Residents' Committees* were promulgated at the Fourth Session of the Standing Committee of the First NPC in December 1954, specifying for the first time in law that they were self-governing mass organisations of residents which, under the guidance of the grassroots authorities or the organs appointed to them, would strengthen the organisation and work of the residents in the streets of the cities and promote the public welfare of the residents. The promulgation and implementation of this regulation gave a strong impetus to the self-governance of the urban masses at the grassroots level.

Sixth, the characteristics, advantages and drawbacks of the CPC's governance system, mechanism of governance and its specific systems.

The party's system and mechanism of governance was guided by the Marxist theory of the state, drawing fully on the party's historical experience in leading the democratic revolution and the period of partial governance during its course, and learning from the system and mechanism of governance of the CPSU. The latter was constantly adjusted, improved and fundamentally reshaped in the light of China's specific historical and practical conditions. It was deeply rooted in the soil of Chinese society, had deep historical roots and a broad practical foundation; it suited China's basic national conditions, met the requirements of economic and social development, and reflected the party's scientific understanding and accurate grasp of the laws of social development in modern China. Therefore, whether compared with the governance system of the CPSU, Eastern

Europe and other socialist countries, or with that of bourgeois parties in the West, the governance system and mechanism of the CPC had distinctive features and unparalleled advantages.

The characteristics of this system and mechanism of governance are as follows: first, it embodied and upheld the leadership of the party, ensuring that the party played a central role in all aspects of national life; second, it embodied and upheld socialism, which was a major achievement of the party's leadership in building a socialist system for the whole nation, ensuring that the party and the state continued to explore and advance along the path of socialism; third, it embodied and upheld people's democracy, ensuring that all power belonged to the people and that the people managed state affairs through a variety of forms and channels; fourth, it embodied and upheld the principle of democratic centralism, ensuring that party organisations and state organs at all levels exercised their powers and performed their duties in accordance with legal authority and procedures under the unified leadership of the party and the state; it also ensured that party organisations at all levels organised and carried out various undertakings in a unified and efficient manner in concert with state agencies to guarantee that the party's line, policies, and decision-making arrangements were fully and effectively implemented in national work; fifth, it embodied and adhered to the principles of hierarchy and classification, ensuring that the party's system of governance was a coordinated and complete system that was vertically and horizontally interlocking, interconnected and mutually supportive and restrictive.

This governing system and mechanism were superior in several aspects: first, it had the unique advantage of being a national system. It was able to concentrate human and material resources, fully mobilise all positive factors, and give full play to the initiative and creativity of the people, ensuring that the socialist system could concentrate its efforts on major issues. Second, it had the advantage of efficient decision-making and implementation. Through the centralised and unified leadership of the party and the state, it ensured that the whole country worked as one, and that government orders flowed smoothly and operated efficiently. Third, it had the advantage of powerful mobilisation and organisational forces. It had a top-down and extensive party organisational system, a top-down and centralised organisational structure and a powerful ideological and propaganda armoury, ensuring that it could effectively mobilise and organise the people of all ethnic nationalities around the Party Central Committee and work towards the achievement of common goals. Fourth, it had the advantages of democracy and consultation. It had both electoral and consultative democracy, and through the mutual complementarity of these two forms, it ensured that the interests of all parties could be taken into account and that the powerful force of a strong consensus could be brought to bear. Fifth, it had the advantage of a planning system. It facilitated the party's formulation and implementation of annual, medium and long-term plans and special plans in some key areas, ensuring that the party's governing mission was steadily realised in the comprehensive development of the country and society. Sixth, it had the advantage of cultivating a team of high-quality cadres. It implemented the principle of party management of cadres, ensuring the orderly selection of talent and the training, management and use of cadres to provide a strong organisational guarantee for consolidating the party's ruling position and promoting the development of the party and the state.

Practice is a process of constant development and change. It was a daunting and long-term task to improve the party's governing system and mechanism, and to make it more mature and firmly established. Due to a lack of experience, and the serious and complex international situation, at one point the party made a "leftist" mistake in its guidelines, and later on there were serious mistakes of an extensive and long-term nature, such as the Cultural Revolution, which gave rise to certain specific systems of the party and the state. The shortcomings and failures of these have not only not been effectively resolved but have gradually emerged, hindering or even seriously impeding the expression of the superiority of socialism. In terms of the leadership and cadre systems of the party and the state, the main problems are bureaucratism, excessive concentration of power, patriarchy, the lifelong system of cadre leadership and other forms of privilege. As Deng Xiaoping observed in 1980: "The various mistakes we made in the past were certainly related to the thinking and style of certain leaders but problems in the organisational and working systems were even more important." He also pointed out that: "Even a great figure like Comrade Mao Zedong was seriously affected by some bad systems, to the extent that it caused great misfortune to the party, to the country and to him personally."[8] In terms of the economic system, the main problem was the one-sided pursuit of the "large in size and collective in nature" form of public ownership, which resulted in an overly homogeneous ownership structure that was out of step with the state of the nation's productive forces. As far as the planned economic system was concerned, within a certain period of time it was essentially adapted to the development of the country's productive forces and played an important role in concentrating the country's limited human and material resources, promoting rapid economic development, establishing an independent and relatively complete industrial system and national economic system. This played an important role in realising the country's economic independence. However, as practice developed, the system became more and more centralised, and its drawbacks became more and more obvious, seriously hampering the development of productivity. The main disadvantages were: the fragmentation of the national economy and the imbalance between supply and demand, which hindered the rational flow of social resources; the government's over-regulation of enterprises, the lack of autonomy of enterprises, the lack of mechanisms governing competition and responsibility, and the lack of momentum in economic development. Additionally, the system of egalitarian distribution and the "big rice pot" significantly affected the people's enthusiasm for production. After the 3rd Plenary Session of the 11th Central Committee of the CPC, in response to these ills and the specific systems, institutions and mechanisms that prevented the superiority of the socialist system from being brought into play, the party, on the basis of adhering to the four basic principles and with the goal of upholding and strengthening the leadership of the party and developing and perfecting the socialist system, steadily pushed forward the reform Chinese characteristics, further developing and perfecting the institutional systems and mechanisms for party governance.

(III) EXPOSURE OF THE CPSU'S GOVERNANCE PROBLEMS AND THE CPC'S TASK TO EXPLORE NEW GOVERNANCE METHODS

After the completion of the socialist transformation and the establishment of the basic socialist system, the party led the people of the whole country into comprehensive and large-scale socialist construction. How to build socialism in China was a completely new subject for which the party could not prepare adequately in advance, neither in terms of time nor of theory and ideology. At the beginning of the construction process, the party called for "learning from the Soviet Union". This was a historical necessity and had some positive effects. But just as the road to revolution cannot be copied from foreign countries, so the road to construction cannot be copied either. In one respect, the successful experience of the Soviet Union did not always suit China's situation; in another, the problems revealed in the CPSU's governance also fully demonstrated that the Soviet experience was not always successful. We can only sum up our own experience, draw on foreign experience and explore it in practice, based on the principle of combining the fundamental principles of Marxism-Leninism with Chinese reality. For this reason, the CPC set out the historical task of exploring new ways of governing and began the process of learning new laws of governing under the conditions of socialist construction, taking the Soviet Union as its reference.

After Lenin's death, Stalin succeeded him and led the Soviet people to establish a basic socialist system, creating the world's first socialist model with a highly centralised political and economic system, focused on the development of heavy industry. Under the leadership of the CPSU, this model ensured the rapid development of heavy industry in the Soviet Union in the 1930s, laying a solid foundation for victory in the Patriotic War Against German Fascist Aggression and making a significant contribution to the complete victory in the world's struggle against fascism. In the face of the heavy losses inflicted on the Soviet Union by the second world war, this model played a huge role in the post-war recovery and reconstruction of Soviet socialism, with industrial production reaching pre-war levels in just two years. This demonstrated the superiority of socialism over capitalism and set an example that provided valuable experience for the socialist construction of other socialist countries. However, while this model adhered to and developed scientific socialism, there were also serious deviations and mistakes caused by special historical conditions as well as institutional and ideological limitations. After the end of the second world war, these serious deviations and mistakes continued to develop, and the shortcomings and rigidities of the Soviet model gradually became apparent.

Stalin was a great Marxist who, in leading the process of socialist construction in the Soviet Union, always insisted on defending Leninism, upholding the leadership of the CPSU and practising socialist public ownership. All these constituted the guiding principles of the basic system of socialism in the Soviet Union. However, Stalin was another Marxist who made serious mistakes without realising that he was wrong. His mistakes were highlighted by the serious flaws and rigidity of the Soviet model.

In economic terms, the Soviet Union had a single form of public ownership and did not allow for a private economy; the basic forms of public ownership were state ownership and collective ownership. At the heart of the Soviet economic system was a system of planned management. This planned economic system was characterised by a high degree of centralisation and strict directives. The state directly managed the enterprises, which themselves lacked autonomy. In terms of economic structure, the emphasis was placed on the development of heavy industry to the neglect of agriculture and light industry, resulting in a serious imbalance in the national economy over a long period of time and a failure to raise people's living standards accordingly.

On the political front, the party's leadership of state power was transformed into a lack of separation between the party and the government, with power being highly concentrated in the central executive body, especially in Stalin himself. The party and the state put a one-sided emphasis on class struggle, exaggerating its seriousness, emphasising the use of violent repression as a means of solving problems, and expanding the scope of purges of counter-revolutionaries. The building of a socialist democratic legal system was neglected, the democratic life of the party and the state was extremely unsound, there was no effective mechanism of supervision and control, and the legal system was imperfect and often undermined.

In terms of ideology and culture, this was characterised by strict control of ideology and culture, and a serious cult of the individual.

While emphasis was placed on the development of education, science, culture and health, normal academic discussion and debate was lacking. Differences in ideological views and arguments between different schools of thought in academia were often labelled as political and elevated to political struggle, and the issue of academic differences was dealt with by means of political struggle.

If these aspects of the Soviet model, which did not meet the essential requirements of socialism, were not reformed in a timely manner but allowed to develop, they would hinder the development of the social productive forces. "After the end of the second world war, historical conditions had changed dramatically but Stalin's rigid ideology fixed the imperfect socialist model of the early years, did not recognise the different paths of the various socialist countries and did not allow reform of the socialist model; he did not attach importance to the building of socialist democracy and the legal system, and unilaterally exaggerated the role of class struggle in the ideological field. This led to a gradual diminishing of the positive aspect of this model and a rise in its negative effects. This led to the concentrated problems that had accumulated over the course of the CPSU's rule being exposed after his death.

In February 1956, the 20th Congress of the CPSU was held. The day before the congress closed, Khrushchev gave a secret report on *The Cult of the Individual and its Consequences*, sharply exposing Stalin's serious mistakes in leading the construction of socialism in the Soviet Union and the serious consequences of his cult of the individual, and touching on some inescapable problems in the political life of the Soviet party and state at that time. This caused a great shock both within the Soviet Union and internationally, and the imperialists took the opportunity to launch a worldwide wave of anti-communism and anti-socialism, causing varying degrees of confusion in the minds of the people and creating great difficulties for the international communist movement.

With the commencement of China's large-scale economic construction and the exposure of the problems of the CPSU's rule, on either side of the 20th National Congress, the CPC took stock and reflected deeply on the mistakes and problems of the CPSU's rule.

- The problems of the Soviet Union's industrialisation and collectivisation of agriculture and its economic management system.

First, the Soviet Union's failure to deal with the relationships between agriculture, and light and heavy industry. On 25 April 1956, at a meeting of the enlarged Politburo of the Central Committee, Mao Zedong criticised the Soviet Union for its "one-sided focus on heavy industry and neglect of agriculture and light industry, resulting in insufficient goods on the market and an unstable currency."[9] He argued that "the Soviet Union has made a serious mistake on this issue."[10] Second, the Soviet Union had tipped the peasants into misery through its handling of the relationship between the state, the collective and the individual. Mao observed: "The Soviet approach pushed the peasants into a very bitter corner. They took too much of what the peasants produced and paid them a very low price by adopting such methods as the so-called compulsory sale system. By accumulating money in this way, they greatly damaged the peasants' incentive to produce."[11] This directly affected agricultural production in the Soviet Union. In this regard, Mao pointed out that it was said that up to the time of the 19th Congress, Soviet grain production had not yet reached the highest level achieved under the Tsarist regime. If this was the case, it was a big problem. Third, the Soviet Union failed in its handling of the relationship between the central and local levels of government. The Soviet economic system was characterised by a high degree of centralisation, with the state issuing orders and resolutions to enterprises through administrative channels and directly controlling their production and business activities. The central economic administration had direct control over people, money and materials, as well as production, supply and marketing, and even "every thousand bricks, every pair of shoes or every piece of underwear had to be allocated by the central government."[12] In response to this, Mao Zedong pointed out at the enlarged meeting of the Central Committee Politburo on 25 April that the Soviet Union had "concentrated everything in the centre and shoved the localities into a tight corner, without any power at all to manoeuvre."[13] Mao's criticism certainly hit the nail on the head in regard to the Soviet industrial management system. In his concluding speech at the conference, Mao added that the question of industrial centralisation, how much overall autonomy the factories should have and how much local autonomy, had not yet been properly studied 40 years after the success of the Soviet revolution. At the 8th Party Congress, Li Fuchun also highlighted problems with the Soviet management system, saying that it had the problem of "excessive and rigid control", which had "to a great extent, restrained the enthusiasm and creativity of various departments, localities and grassroots enterprises."[14]

- The question of the Soviet political system. At the beginning of 1956, Mao Zedong listened to reports from 34 ministries. When it came to the question of the relationship between the party and non-party elements, Mao pointed out that in this respect China was different from the Soviet Union. They were knocking down everything and leaving the other parties naked and exposed, with only the communist party left standing, and it was rare to hear dissenting views. At the enlarged meeting of the Politburo of the CPC Central Committee on 25 April, Mao Zedong raised the question of whether it was better to have one party or several parties. It must be said that it has become evident that it is better to have several parties. In addition, the CPC pointed out sharply the problem of Stalin's personal dictatorship and his undermining of democracy and the rule of law. On 5 April 1956 the *People's Daily* published an editorial *On the Historical Experience of the Dictatorship of the Proletariat*, which was discussed and approved by the enlarged meeting of the Politburo of the CPC Central Committee. The article analysed the mistakes of Stalin in his later years, stating: "In order to defeat a powerful enemy, the dictatorship of the proletariat requires a high degree of centralisation of power. This high degree of centralised power must be combined with a high degree of democracy. When centralisation is too one-sided, many mistakes are made."[15] The Soviet model was a product of the war environment, which required a high degree of centralisation, and it was this condition that Stalin exploited to achieve personal dictatorship and to push centralisation to the extreme. As a result, democracy and the rule of law were undermined and many mistakes were made. In this regard, the article pointed out that, later in his life, Stalin "violated the democratic centralism of the party and the system of combining collective leadership and individual responsibility", he put "individual power in opposition to collective leadership" and "personal power above the party and the masses" with the result that: "certain of his actions were in opposition to some of the basic Marxist-Leninist ideas that he had originally promoted". Stalin's "individual arbitrariness" led to the "expansion of the purges of counter-revolutionaries."[16] In September 1956, Deng Xiaoping also criticised the dangers of personal dictatorship in his *Report on the Revision of the Party Constitution* at the 8th Party Congress. He pointed out that personal decisions on major issues were contrary to the principles on which the communist party was founded, and that mistakes were bound to be made.

The fundamental reason for Stalin's mistakes lay in the lack of certain institutional safeguards, notably the inadequacy and dismantling of the democratic legal system. Mao Zedong was keenly aware of this, saying that "Stalin seriously undermined the socialist legal system" and that "such a thing could not have happened in Western countries such as Britain, France and the US."[17] In November 1956, when Mao Zedong presided over the revision of the *Historical Experience of the Dictatorship of the Proletariat*, he also pointed out that: "Stalin overemphasised dictatorship and destroyed part of the legal system" and that "democracy was not enough" and "there was too much bureaucratism".[18] On 29 December, based on the discussion at the enlarged meeting of the Politburo of the CPC Central Committee, the *People's Daily* published an editorial article entitled *On the Historical Experience of the Dictatorship of the Proletariat*. The article pointed out that "Stalin's personal and arbitrary working methods had to some extent undermined the principle of democratic centralism in the life of the Soviet party and in the state system, and destroyed part of the socialist legal system."[19]

- The problem of the Soviet ideological and cultural system. As mentioned earlier, the fundamental features of the Soviet ideological and cultural system were strict control over ideology and culture; a serious cult of the individual; a one-sided emphasis on cultural hierarchy and the antagonistic nature of culture; neglect of its humanity and inheritance; and a tendency towards absolutism. Among the mistakes of Stalin's later years, one of the more prominent ones was the cult of the individual. The article *The Historical Experience of the Dictatorship of the Proletariat* concentrates more on this aspect of Stalin's problems. It points out that Stalin mistakenly exaggerated his role to an inappropriate extent and "accepted and encouraged the cult of the individual". Especially in the latter part of his life, he "fell deeper and deeper into admiration of the cult of the individual". As a result the following major mistakes were made: "expansion of purges; lack of the necessary vigilance on the eve of the anti-fascist war; lack of due attention to the further development of agriculture and the material well-being of the peasantry; some wrong ideas in the international communist movement, especially mistaken decisions on Yugoslavia." The article also analyses the causes of the cult of the individual, which it believes is simply force of habit for millions of people and which, when it exists in society, can influence state workers: "even leading figures like Stalin were influenced by it". The cult of the individual is a reflection of social phenomena in people's minds, and "when leading figures of the party and the state, like Stalin, are also influenced by such backward thinking, its effects can be felt by society, causing a loss of dedicated impetus and harming the initiative and creativity of the masses."[20] The article *Revisiting the Historical Experience of the Dictatorship of the Proletariat* further pointed out that "Stalin was so overwhelmed by a series of victories and glorifications in his later period that his ideological approach partially but seriously left dialectical materialism and fell into subjectivism. He began to believe in his own wisdom and authority, refused to investigate and study the complexities of the actual situation, to listen carefully to the opinions of his comrades and the voices of the masses, so that the policies and measures he decided on were often contrary to the objective reality of the situation. Moreover, he often stubbornly insisted on implementing these mistakes over a long period, without being able to correct his mistakes on a timely basis."[21]

Mao Zedong revealed many different aspects of the problems of the Soviet ideological and cultural system: first, the deification of individuals; on 24 September 1956, during a meeting with the Yugoslav delegation, Mao said that Stalin advocated dialectical materialism, which sometimes lacked materialism and tended towards the metaphysical; he wrote about historical materialism but often practised historical idealism. "Some of his practices went to extremes of personal deification, of discomfiting others and so on, which departed from materialism."[22] Second, the one-sided emphasis on struggle and the neglect of unity. On 27 January 1957, Mao Zedong observed at a meeting of party secretaries of provincial, municipal and autonomous regions: "In philosophy, materialism and idealism are opposites and part of a unity; these two things struggle against each other. Two other things, known as dialectics and metaphysics are also the unity of opposites and in combat with each other. When we talk about philosophy, these two pairs are indispensable. The Soviet Union now does not work in pairs but only in 'independent households', saying that it only grows fragrant flowers not poisonous weeds and does not recognise the existence of idealism and metaphysics in socialist countries. The fact is that in any country there is materialism, there is metaphysics, and there are poisonous weeds. Many of the poisonous weeds there in the Soviet Union came using the names of fragrant flowers, and many of the perverse arguments there wore the hat of materialism or socialist realism."[23] Mao criticised Stalin for denying opposites and describing German classical idealist philosophy as a reaction of the German aristocracy against the French revolution. He concluded that "he dismissed the whole philosophy of German classical idealism. He dismissed German military science, saying that the Germans had lost the war, that military science could no longer be used, and that Clausewitz's books should no longer be read."[24] According to Mao, Stalin used a lot of metaphysics and taught many people to engage in metaphysics; he spoke only of the struggle of opposites and not of the unity of opposites. In Stalin's view, things are fundamentally opposed and have no unity, they are only mutually exclusive and cannot be transformed. On the question of unity, the *Concise Philosophy Course of Philosophy*, compiled in the Soviet Union, reflected Stalin's view. Mao Zedong also said that the *Concise Course on the History of the CPSU*, in its discussion of the contradictions of things, also speaks only of struggle, not unity. Therefore, Mao said, "This struggle and unity of opposites was something with which Stalin could not connect. The thinking of some people in the Soviet Union was metaphysical, and so hardened that it came down solely to either this or that, without recognising the unity of opposites. As a result, mistakes were made in politics."[25]

In addition, Mao Zedong also exposed the errors of the Soviet Union in engaging in authoritarianism and suppressing dissent in the cultural field. On 8 March 1957, he pointed out in a conversation with representatives of literary and artistic circles that: "After the October revolution in the Soviet Union, dogmatism prevailed, and the literary association RAPP at that time adopted an attitude of commandism towards writers, forcing others to write what they wanted them to. But I have heard that there was some freedom of expression in that period and there were 'fellow travellers', and those 'fellow travellers' had access to publications." However, "from then on, only good things about the party and the government were allowed, no bad things, no criticism and no individualism."[26]

The CPC does not approve of the total denial of the history of the CPSU and the struggle of the people for socialism under Stalin's leadership but rather it believes that lifting the lid on Stalin is of great significance for Marxist political parties in all countries, including itself, in order to break the superstitious belief in the governance of Stalin and the CPSU, to release the shackles of dogmatism and to strive to find a path of revolution and construction that suits the national conditions of our country. By summing up and reflecting on the problems of the rule of the CPSU and learning from it, the CPC was able to formulate the important idea of a "second marriage" between Marxism and the reality of China, and propose the task of exploring new ways to govern.

The important concept of "the second integration" between Marxism and Chinese reality genuinely advanced the task of exploring new ways to govern.

At the end of 1955, Mao Zedong had already raised the issue of "using the Soviet Union as a mirror." At that time, Mao Zedong, Liu Shaoqi and others were engaged in investigation and research and were listening to work reports from relevant ministries and commissions. After learning about the criticism of Stalin at the 20th Congress of the CPSU, the CPC Central Committee convened a Politburo meeting for a special discussion. Some ministries and commissions also had issues related to Stalin and the experience of the Soviet Union when reporting their work so the overall thinking on the matter became clearer. By this time, the CPC had accumulated some experience of its own in economic construction and was finding that some of the experience of the Soviet Union was not relevant to the Chinese reality. Thus, whether or not to start from China's national conditions and learn from the experience of the Soviet Union in exploring a new way of governing that suited those conditions became a major issue affecting the smooth progress of China's socialist construction.

On 24 March 1956, at a meeting of the Politburo of the Central Committee, Mao Zedong endorsed Khrushchev's criticism of Stalin, saying that it had the advantage of dispelling superstition and helping us to think through problems. Socialist construction did not necessarily have to follow the Soviet formula but could be based on the specific conditions of the country, with guidelines and policies appropriate to the country's current situation. At a meeting of the Politburo of the CPC Central Committee on 4 April, Mao Zedong once again elaborated his views. He pointed out that the 20th Congress of the CPSU had opposed Stalin and that we ourselves had to learn a lesson from it. He believed that the most important lesson was to be independent, to investigate and study, to ascertain the situation of our country, to combine Marxism-Leninism with the concrete reality of the Chinese revolution and social construction, and to formulate China's own line, formula and policy. He further said that there were two ways to learn from the Soviet experience, one being the dogmatic approach of accepting it wholesale without analysis or reflection. The other is the Marxist approach, which should involve continuous analysis and should be linked to the reality of the country. Therefore, he advised people to use their brains and think more about the practical problems of building socialism, not to be bound by what the Soviet Union had already done and not to be as superstitious as they had been in the past. Now it was all the more important to try to find a concrete path for building socialism in China. Mao Zedong further set out the task of exploring a new way of governing in his speech *On the Ten Major Relations*. He said: "Recently the Soviet side has exposed some of their shortcomings and mistakes in the process of building socialism. Do you still want to follow the detours they have taken? In the past we took fewer of those detours in the light of the lessons we learned from them, and it is certainly all the more important to continue to learn from them now."

At the same time, other leaders within the party were also thinking about this issue. On 27 June and 2 July 1956, Liu Shaoqi spoke twice about how the "socialist aspect of political economy" was taught in the Central High Party School. He said that China had new experiences concerning some of the problems of socialism, and that it should emphasise the importance of summing up its own experience and solving its own problems by using that experience, not by copying others. Anyone who could think independently would not fail, and anyone who copied others would make mistakes. Even so, many of the Soviet Union's experiences were still worth studying.[27] On 13 July, Liu Shaoqi observed at a meeting with the Romanian Ambassador to China, Nicolae Cioroiu, that any foreign experience should only be used as a reference, and that decisions must be made in the light of the specific circumstances of the country. Any foreign experience, including that of the Soviet Union, could be adapted but not simply copied.[28] On 29 December, the article *Revisiting the Historical Experience of the Dictatorship of the Proletariat* was published in the *People's Daily* and discussed at an enlarged meeting of the Politburo of the CPC Central Committee, pointed out that: "All the experience of the Soviet Union, including the basic experience, should be combined with particular national characteristics and should not simply be copied in its original form by other countries." The article argued that there were mistakes and failures in the Soviet experience and that both successes and failures "are invaluable to those who are good learners because they can help us to make fewer mistakes and suffer fewer losses. On the other hand, if the experience that was successful in the Soviet Union were to be copied without analysis, it could also lead to failure in other countries."[29] In response to the problems that arose in the Soviet Union, the article clearly stated that: "In a socialist country, the task of the party and the state lies in relying on the masses and on collective power to make timely adjustments in all aspects of the economic and political systems, and to detect and correct errors in their work in a timely manner."[30]

The exposure of the problems of the CPSU's rule was an exposure of the shortcomings of the Soviet model. In view of the problems that emerged in the governance of the CPSU, the CPC proposed the task of exploring its own new way of governing and achieved significant initial theoretical and practical results. However, due to the party's lack of experience in how to build socialism and the fact that it had developed a number of fixed ideas in its understanding of socialism that did not suit the actual situation, the problem of a highly centralised and unified economic system not only remained unsolved for a long time but also developed to an increasingly serious degree. As a result, the party again made mistakes in the process of exploring new ways of governing. It was only by carefully summing up historical experience, combining the basic principles of Marxism with China's reality, treating the country's experience correctly, further liberating the mind and following its own path that a new path of governance could be successfully explored.

(IV) THE DEVELOPMENT OF MAO ZEDONG THOUGHT: THE INITIAL RESULTS OF EXPLORING A NEW METHOD OF GOVERNANCE

With the historical task of exploring a new method of governance, the Chinese communists, represented mainly by Comrade Mao Zedong, began to combine the basic principles of Marxism-Leninism with China's concrete reality and, drawing on the experience of the Soviet Union, actively explored the CPC's own method of governance. In doing so, they developed many original theories on the construction of Chinese socialism, covering various aspects such as the economy, politics, culture, national defence and foreign affairs. Mao Zedong Thought was the central embodiment of these theoretical perspectives and they represented a major development of Mao Zedong Thought in the period of socialist revolution and construction.

- Theories on the contradictions of socialist society. In the 1930s, Stalin treated a large number of contradictions within the party and among the people as being caused by his enemies and made the mistake of widening his purges. The 20th Congress of the CPSU exposed Stalin's mistakes and sent shockwaves around the world. In June and October 1956, there were serious incidents in Poland and Hungary. In the autumn and winter of that year, there was also some instability in China. Stalin's mistakes, the Polish and Hungarian incidents, and the situation in China showed that contradictions still existed under the socialist system. It was therefore particularly important to correctly understand and deal with the contradictions in socialist society, especially the increasingly prominent internal contradictions of the people under communist party rule. Therefore, drawing on Stalin's mistakes and the lessons of the Polish and Hungarian incidents, facing the realities of China, summing up its own experience, and correctly understanding and dealing with the various contradictions in Chinese socialist society, became a major issue for the CPC to consider at that time.

After long consideration and deliberation, in February 1957 Mao Zedong delivered a speech at the expanded Supreme State Council on the correct handling of the internal contradictions of the people, systematically expounding his theory on the contradictions in socialist society. Mao Zedong said that the law of unity of opposites was a fundamental universal law. Contradictions are universal, and contradictory opposites both unite and contend, thereby acting as drivers of change. The basic contradictions in socialist society are still the contradictions between productive forces and production relations, between the economic base and the superstructure. However, these contradictions in a socialist society are of a fundamentally different nature and situation from those of old societies, such as capitalist society. Mao Zedong pointed out that in China, "socialist production relations have been established and are compatible with the development of the productive forces; however, they are still far from perfect and these imperfections are in contradiction with the development of productive forces. In addition to the unity and contradiction between production relations and the development of productive forces, there is also the unity and contradiction between the economic superstructure and the economic base."[31] According to Mao, productive forces and production relations in socialist society are basically compatible, so this contradiction can be adjusted and resolved by the socialist system itself. Mao's assertion of the basic contradictions of socialist society broke through the metaphysical viewpoint of the international communist movement, which denied the existence of contradictions in socialist society, and at the same time distinguished between the contradictions in socialist society and those of the old society, revealing for the first time the dynamics of socialist social development in a scientific manner. This effectively opened the way for subsequent socialist reforms.

Mao also raised the issue of two different types of contradiction, saying: "There are two types of social contradictions confronting us: the contradictions between ourselves and the enemy, and contradictions among the people. These are of a completely different nature to each other." In order to strictly distinguish between these two types, Mao Zedong clarified the boundary between the people and the enemy, and listed the various forms of internal contradictions among the people. He also proposed ways to correctly deal with the two different types of contradictions, pointing out that contradictions of different natures could only be solved by different methods. Mao Zedong summed up the method of resolving internal contradictions in the formula: "unity-criticism-unity". That is to say, starting from the desire for unity and moving through criticism or struggle, the contradictions could be resolved to achieve a new unity on a new basis. He also proposed various guidelines and policies for the correct handling of internal conflicts within the people, based on the experience of the CPC since it came to power. Mao Zedong believed that it was essential at this time to raise the issue of drawing a line between the two types of contradictions, and also the issue of the correct handling of internal contradictions among the people, so as to unite the people of all ethnic nationalities, develop China's economy and culture, consolidate its new system and build the new country. This was how the correct handling of internal contradictions among the people became the main theme of national political life.

A scientific analysis and judgment of the main domestic contradictions was a prerequisite for the party to formulate its main tasks and a basis for the formulation and implementation of a correct political line. In September 1956, the Eighth Party Congress correctly analysed the class situation in the country and pointed out that the main contradiction in the country was between the people's demand for an advanced industrial nation and the reality of a backward agricultural country, and between the people's need for rapid economic and cultural development, and the current situation in which the economy and culture could not meet those needs. "The main task of the party and the whole country is to concentrate on solving this contradiction and transforming our country from a backward agricultural country to an advanced industrial nation as soon as possible."

Drawing on the experience of the Soviet Union, Mao Zedong proposed and systematically expounded the doctrine of socialist social contradictions on the basis of a summary of the new problems that had arisen after the completion of China's basic socialist transformation. In doing so, he enriched and developed the Marxist theory of scientific socialism, laying the theoretical foundation for the party's correct understanding of China's national conditions and providing long-term theoretical guidance for the party and the cause of socialist construction.

- Ideas and guidelines on the path of industrialisation in China. In the process of industrialisation, the question of how to deal with the relationship between the development of industry and agriculture, and between the development of heavy industry and light industry, is related to the question of what kind of path to take towards industrialisation. The Soviet Union took the path of one-sided emphasis on the development of heavy industry at the expense of agriculture and light industry, with serious consequences. On the basis of the lessons learnt from the Soviet Union, Mao Zedong conducted an in-depth investigation and study of China's economic construction and propounded his ideas on the road to industrialisation in China.

The issue of the path to industrialisation actually refers to the relationship between heavy industry, light industry and agriculture. After the 20th Congress of the CPSU, Mao Zedong discussed the question of China's path to industrialisation in terms of the relationship between heavy industry, light industry and agriculture, taking into account the actual situation in China. In April 1956, he elaborated on the relationship between the three in his speech *On the Ten Major Relations*. Mao said that heavy industry was the focus of China's construction and priority must be given to creating the means of production. This decision had already been taken but the production of the necessities of life, especially food, should not be neglected as a result. If the nation did not have enough food and other necessities, it could not even feed its workforce in the first place, so how could there be any talk about developing heavy industry? Therefore, "the relationship between heavy industry, light industry and agriculture must be dealt with properly."[32] Mao Zedong believed that the nation needed to be more focused on agriculture and light industry. The current problem was that the ratio of investment in heavy industry to that in agriculture and light industry had to be properly adjusted, with more development of agriculture and light industry. In the current state of affairs, heavy industry still dominated and was the focus of investment. The proportion of investment in agriculture and light industry needed to be increased. In this way, first, the needs of the people's daily lives could be better supplied, and second, the rate of capital accumulation could be increased more quickly, thereby allowing more and better development of heavy industry. Mao Zedong also proposed two approaches to the development of heavy industry: one was to develop less agriculture and light industry, and the other was to develop more agriculture and light industry. From a long-term perspective, the former approach would lead to less and slower development of heavy industry, or at least a less solid foundation, which would not prove to be worthwhile when the total accounts were settled in decades to come. The latter approach would lead to more and faster development of heavy industry, and it would provide a more solid basis for its development as it ensured the needs of the people's livelihood. The question of China's path to industrialisation was clearly set out in Mao Zedong's speech on the correct handling of internal contradictions among the people. He observed: "The question of the path of industrialisation mentioned here principally refers to the relationship between the development of heavy industry, light industry and agriculture. Our economic construction is centred on heavy industry. This must be affirmed. But at the same time, due attention must be paid to the development of agriculture and light industry." China was an agricultural country, with its rural population accounting for more than 80% of the total, therefore, "the development of industry must go hand in hand with the development of agriculture before industry can have the necessary raw materials and markets, and before it can accumulate more funds for the establishment of a strong heavy industry sector."[33]

In 1958, Mao Zedong also proposed the policy of "walking on two legs", including the parallel development of industry and agriculture, heavy industry and light industry, and coastal industry and mainland industry. In 1959, in view of the serious imbalance in the national economy caused by the unilateral development of the iron and steel industry during the "Great Leap Forward" campaign, Mao proposed the idea that the national economy should be arranged in the order of agriculture, light industry and heavy industry. He pointed out: "In the past, the arrangement was heavy industry, light industry and agriculture, but this order should be reversed. We need to study the relationship between agriculture, light industry and heavy industry. In the past, there were ten major relation-ships, that embodied the policy of "walking on two legs", which provided both speed and efficiency of effort but now it must be said that that policy is not being implemented or, at least, is not being implemented very well. In the past, it was about heavy industry, light industry, agriculture, commerce and trade, but now the emphasis is on getting agriculture right, and the order has been changed to agriculture, light industry, heavy indus-try, trade and commerce. It is not contrary to Marxism to give priority to the development of means of production."[34] Between late 1959 and early 1960, Mao Zedong further elaborated on the question of China's path to industrialisation as he read the Soviet *Textbook of Political Economy*. He pointed out that Stalin's shortcoming was that he had overemphasised prioritising the growth of heavy industry, with the result that agriculture was neglected in his planning. "We have crystallised this principle as follows: in giving priority to the development of heavy industry, industry and agriculture are pursued simultaneously. Of the several simultaneous initiatives we have implemented, the simultaneous development of industry and agriculture is the most important."[35] In view of the mistakes made by the Soviet Union in the past, Mao believed that industry should, of course, develop faster than agriculture. However, the formula should be appropriate to the situation, and industry should not be promoted to an inappropriate degree, otherwise problems were bound to occur. He stressed: "Our proposal is to develop industry and agriculture simultane-ously, with the proviso that priority is given to heavy industry. By adopting parallel development, we do not deny that heavy industry has priority over agriculture, nor do we deny that industry is developing faster than agriculture; at the same time, nor does parallel development mean the equal input of impetus."[36] On entering this period of national economic adjustment, Mao Zedong advanced the general policy of developing the national economy based on agriculture and led by industry, further enriching and developing the concept behind China's path to industrialisation.

- Ideas on the development of commodity production and commodity exchange under socialist conditions.

In Stalin's later years, although he affirmed the necessity of preserving commodity production and circulation under the two systems of public ownership and believed that the law of value also held good under the socialist system, he did not recognise the existence of commodity production and exchange within the system of universal ownership, nor did he recognise that the means of production were commodities and that the law of value played a regulating role in the sphere of production. "During the Great Leap Forward and the People's Commune Movement, there were problems such as the denial of commodity production and exchange, and the "communist style". In the autumn and winter of 1958, Mao Zedong began to pay attention to the problem of commodity production under socialist conditions in the course of correcting "leftist tendencies". In the following year or so, Mao Zedong read relevant economic works, studied the issues of commodity production, commodity exchange and the law of value, and advanced a series of important ideas.

In November 1958, at the Zhengzhou Conference, Mao Zedong elaborated more systematically on the issue of commodity production and commodity exchange in socialist society. He argued that China was a very underdeveloped country in terms of commodities and that "there needs to be a stage of developing commodity production" and therefore "it is necessary to affirm that commodity production and commodity exchange in socialism still have a positive role to play."[37] Mao criticised the idea of abolishing commodity production, arguing that it failed to distinguish between socialist and capitalist commodity production and did not understand the importance of utilising the role of commodity production under socialist conditions. Mao Zedong clearly stated: "In the socialist period, commodity production should be used to unite hundreds of millions of peasants. I think that with the people's communes, commodity production and commodity exchange should be developed even more, and socialist commodity production should be developed in a systematic and significant way."[38] What is remarkable is that Mao Zedong did not believe that commodity production under socialist conditions would lead to capitalism. "Commodity production must not be confused with capitalism," he said. "Why are you afraid of commodity production? It is nothing other than the fear of capitalism." "Commodity production depends on the economic system it is linked with: it is capitalist commodity production if it is linked to the capitalist system, and socialist commodity production if it is linked to the socialist system." The situation in China was that the socialist transformation of the capitalist component of the economy had been completed and the capitalists had come to socialism empty-handed. It was the state and the people's communes that dominated in the field of commodity production and commodity circulation, so that "it will not lead to capitalism because there is no longer an economic basis for capitalism."[39] Regarding the reasons for the existence of commodity production and commodity exchange, Mao Zedong observed that "as long as two systems of ownership exist, commodity production and commodity exchange are both highly necessary and useful."[40] It was only after the product was fully developed that the circulation of goods could begin to disappear. It was only when the state had control of all products that the commodity economy could be rendered unnecessary and disappear. It was unrealistic to rush to do without commodities only nine years after the foundation of the new China. In response to Stalin's view that the Soviet Union did not recognise the means of production as commodities, Mao pointed out clearly that: "In our country it is different: the means of production are both commodities and not commodities, in that only some of the means of production are commodities"; and that "only part of the products transferred, as most of them are exchanged for commodities through sale and purchase."[41]

In order to properly recognise the necessity of commodity production and exchange, it is necessary to correct the understanding of the role of the law of value under socialist conditions. Therefore, in the process of correcting "leftist tendencies", Mao Zedong repeatedly criticised the mistake of the "communist wind" (meaning unpaid use of material and human resources) in the people's communes and explicitly affirmed the role of the law of value. Mao Zedong pointed out that in China it was necessary not only to develop commodity production and exchange but also to use the law of value as a tool to serve socialism. In February 1959, at the Second Zhengzhou Conference, Mao Zedong criticised the mistake of transferring the property of production teams without compensation, arguing that this error denied the law of value and exchange of equivalents, and emphasised the need for exchange of equivalents between communities and teams, and between teams. In March of that year, Mao Zedong noted in an endorsement of a report by Tao Lujia, the first secretary of the Shanxi Provincial Party Committee, that: "It is only by settling accounts that the objective law of value can be applied. This law is a great educator, and only by using it can we teach our millions of cadres and many millions of people, and build our socialist and communist society. Otherwise nothing will be possible."[42]

Mao Zedong's ideas on commodity production and exchange under socialist conditions played an important guiding role in the construction of socialism at the time, and were also significant in the history of the development of socialist theory.

- The idea of economic system reform. After the 20th Congress of the CPSU, Mao Zedong drew on the problems revealed by the highly centralised economic system of the Soviet Union to explore the problems of the socialist economic system and initially advanced the idea of reforming the overly centralised and unified economic management system.

On the question of the relationship between the central and regional levels of government, Mao Zedong pointed out in his speech *On the Ten Major Relations* that in order to build a strong socialist state, there must be strong and unified leadership from the central government, and there must be a unified plan and discipline for the whole country. It was not permissible to undermine this necessary unity. At the same time, it was necessary to give full play to local initiatives and each region must be allowed its own special characteristics suited to local conditions. China could not be like the Soviet Union where everything was concentrated in the centre and the regions were stuck in a corner, with no power of manoeuvre at all. Therefore: "What we should pay attention to now is expanding the power of the regions a little bit, giving them more independence and letting them do more things, on the premise of consolidating the unified leadership of the central government. This is in our interest to build a strong socialist state. Our country is so big, our population so large and our situation so complex that it is much better to have two levels of activity, central and regional, rather than just one."[43]

Mao also raised the issue of enterprise "independence". He said: "I am afraid it is not right to concentrate everything in the central government or the provinces and municipalities, without giving the factories a little power, a little room for manoeuvre and a little profit. We do not have much experience in this area and we still have to study the question of what the rights and interests of the central government, the provinces and municipalities and the factories should be. In principle, unity and independence are the unity of opposites and there must be unity as well as independence."[44] Mao Zedong further pointed out when reading the Soviet *Textbook of Political Economy* that: "Enterprises under the control of central departments and those under the control of local government have a certain degree of autonomy under unified leadership and unified planning. Whether or not there is this kind of autonomy has a great bearing on promoting or hindering the development of production. "[45]

Mao Zedong also discussed the issue of the management system of state-owned enterprises (SOEs). In January 1958, he presided over the formulation of the *Sixty Articles on Working Methods (Draft)*, which proposed that cadres should appear as ordinary workers, establish equal relations with workers, and reform the unreasonable rules and regulations that fettered the enthusiasm of the masses. At the Second Session of the Eighth Party Congress, Mao Zedong put forward the demand that cadres should participate in labour and workers participate in management. When he read the Soviet *Textbook on Political Economy*, he raised the issue of "two participations, one reform and three combinations", pointing out that: "The management of enterprises should combine centralised leadership and mass movements; the workers, leading cadres and technicians should work in combination, so that the cadres should participate in labour and the workers in management, and unreasonable rules and regulations should be constantly reformed."[46] In March 1960, Mao Zedong re-emphasised this issue in his instructions to republish a report from the Anshan Municipal Party Committee, calling it the "Ansteel Constitution", which became an important management system for Chinese enterprises for a significant period of time.

- Reflections on the construction of democratic politics. In view of the profound lessons of Stalin's destruction of the democratic rule of law and his personal arbitrariness, especially after the Polish-Hungarian affair, some people in China expressed inappropriate views on the issue of democracy and freedom at home. In response, Mao Zedong systematically elaborated on the relationship between democracy and centralism, discipline and freedom.

Regarding the importance and necessity of practising democratic centralism. First, it facilitates mobilisation of the people's enthusiasm. Mao Zedong believed that the people were divided into different classes, strata and social groups with different demands and interests, and a variety of contradictions. Therefore, only by implementing the principle of democratic centralism, giving full play to democracy and allowing the masses of people to reflect their views and demands could the enthusiasm of the people be stimulated. Second, criticism and self-criticism are the methods of resolving internal contradictions among the people, and "without a fully democratic life and the genuine practice of democratic centralism, it is impossible to practise criticism and self-criticism."[47] Moreover, the implementation of democratic centralism is also necessary for the consolidation of the people's democratic dictatorship. In January 1962, Mao Zedong observed at the enlarged Central Work Conference that "without broad-based people's democracy, the dictatorship of the proletariat cannot be consolidated and the regime will be unstable. Without democracy, without mobilising the masses and without mass supervision, it will be impossible to exercise effective dictatorship over reactionaries and bad elements, or to reform them effectively, and they will continue to make trouble."[48]

Concerning the dialectic of democratic centralism. Mao Zedong pointed out that: "Having civil rights, in political terms, means having the right to freedom and democracy." However, "this freedom is freedom with leadership, and this democracy is democracy under the guidance of centralisation, not anarchy." This means that: "Among the people, democracy comes from centralisation and freedom comes from discipline. These are two contradictory sides of the same unity, contradictory and unified, and we should not one-sidedly emphasise one side to the exclusion of the other. The people cannot be without freedom nor without discipline; they cannot be without democracy nor without centralisation. This unity of democracy and concentration, of freedom and discipline, is our democratic centralism."[49] Mao went on to say that the goal was to "create a political situation in which there is both centralisation and democracy, discipline and freedom, unified will, a mood of individual comfort and liveliness." On the relationship between democracy and centralisation, Mao emphasised centralisation on the basis of democracy. He pointed out: "In our country, if we do not fully develop people's democracy and intra-party democracy, and if we do not fully implement proletarian democracy, there can be no genuine proletarian centralism. Without a high degree of democracy, there cannot be a high degree of centralisation, and without a high degree of centralisation, it is impossible to build a socialist economy."[50]

To implement democratic centralism, Mao Zedong stressed the need for collective leadership and the rejection of individual dictatorship. He said that our centralised system was a centralised system based on democracy. The centralisation of the proletariat was centralisation on a broad democratic base. "Party committees at all levels are the organs that carry out centralised leadership. However, the leadership of the party committees is collective leadership, not the arbitrariness of the First Secretary. Only democratic centralism should be practised within the party committee. The relationship between the First Secretary and the other secretaries and members is one of minority subordination to the majority." "As long as it's a major issue, it has to be discussed collectively and different opinions have to be carefully listened to." "If this is not the case, then one person is acting as a hegemon. Such a First Secretary should be called a hegemon, not a 'class leader' of democratic centralism."[51]

- Concerning policy on cultural construction and intellectuals. In the practice of leading China's socialist cultural construction, the Chinese communists, principally represented by Comrade Mao Zedong, attached great importance to socialist cultural construction and put forward a series of policies on cultural construction and intellectual issues.

In the years following the founding of the new China, the field of science and culture was influenced by the crude style of Soviet academic criticism and dogmatism, and the phenomenon of promoting one school of thought and suppressing another, as well as indiscriminate political labelling, was evident in some academic fields. In response to this situation, Mao Zedong spoke specifically about the *Double Hundred Approach* at an enlarged meeting of the Politburo of the CPC Central Committee in April 1956. He proposed that: "The blooming of a hundred flowers on artistic issues and the contending of a hundred schools of thought on academic issues should, I believe, become our policy."[52] In response to Stalin's usual tendency to elevate the question of right and wrong in literature and science to a political issue, and his one-sided emphasis on the combative nature of the cultural world at the expense of unity, Mao Zedong clearly pointed out that: "When it comes to academics, one can speak of this kind of scholarship and that kind of scholarship, and one should not allow one to overwhelm everything else."[53] In February 1957, Mao Zedong formally proposed the policy of "letting a hundred flowers bloom and a hundred schools of thought contend". He observed that: "The policy of letting a hundred flowers bloom and a hundred schools of thought contend is a policy to promote the development of art and the progress of science, and a policy to promote the prosperity of socialist culture in our country. Different forms and styles in the arts are free to develop, and different schools of thought in science are free to argue. To use administrative power to enforce one style and one school of thought and to ban another style and another school of thought would, in our view, be detrimental to the development of art and science. Questions of right and wrong in art and science should be resolved through free discussion in the artistic and scientific communities, through the practice of art and science, and not through simple methods."[54] In order to prevent a situation similar to the Soviet suppression of reasonable opinions, Mao Zedong stressed that with regard to questions of right and wrong in science and art, "a cautious attitude should be maintained, free discussion should be advocated, and no rash conclusions should be drawn." Adopting such an attitude "can help science and art to develop more smoothly."[55] With regard to ideological problems among the people and the treatment of the spiritual world, Mao believed that simple methods could not be used: not only would they not be effective, they would actually be very harmful. "Only by adopting the method of discussion, the method of criticism, the method of reasoning, can we really develop correct opinions and overcome wrong ones, and genuinely solve problems."[56] In order to accurately judge the rights and wrongs of people's words and actions, Mao proposed six criteria, the central idea of which was to maintain unity, not to damage it, and that all scientific and artistic activities that met these criteria were beneficial.

Mao Zedong also raised the issue of "letting go" and "closing down". He said that there were two different methods, or two different approaches, that could be adopted in leading our country, and these were "letting go" and "closing down". "Letting go" meant to let people speak their minds, so that they dare to speak, to criticise and to argue. "Closing down" meant to forbid people to voice different opinions or to express wrong opinions. With regard to these two very different approaches, Mao Zedong believed that the approach of "letting go" should be adopted because it was the approach conducive to the consolidation and cultural development of the nation. Therefore, Mao Zedong said: "The policy of letting a hundred flowers bloom and a hundred schools of thought contend is not only a good way to make science and art develop, but by extension, it is also a good way to carry out all our work."[57]

Intellectual policy is a major issue closely related to the building of socialist culture. In this regard, in January 1956, Mao Zedong proposed at a conference on intellectual issues that a technological and cultural revolution should be carried out; science should be pursued, and the life of ignorance should be reversed. To carry out such a revolution, it would not be possible to rely solely on the masses without intellectuals. He demanded the development of a large number of senior intellectuals in a relatively short period of time, as well as more ordinary intellectuals. In February 1957, Mao Zedong again pointed out at the enlarged Supreme State Council: "The arduous cause of socialist construction in our country needs as many intellectuals as possible to serve it. We should place our trust in all intellectuals who are genuinely willing to serve the socialist cause, fundamentally improve our relations with them, help them solve the various problems that must be solved, and enable them to give active play to their talents."[58] In December 1958, Mao Zedong stressed in an instruction that it was necessary to correct the current trend and enlist all possible professors, lecturers, teaching assistants and researchers to serve the educational, cultural and scientific undertakings of the proletariat.

The above-mentioned original theoretical achievements were made by the Chinese communists, principally represented by Comrade Mao

Zedong, in their efforts to explore China's own path of socialist construction, drawing on the experience of the Soviet Union.

Although there were twists and turns, and even serious mistakes in this exploration, they prompted people to free themselves further from the shackles of Soviet dogmatism and fully mobilise all positive factors in the service of socialism. This had a significant impact on the CPC's exploration of a new type of governance.

The history of the 10-year search for a new way of governance is the history of the mutual promotion and influence of ideology, theory and practical construction. The further development of Mao Zedong Thought guided socialist modernisation to achievements admired by the rest of the world. In economic construction, in 1966, compared to 1956, the country's industrial fixed assets increased threefold, calculated in terms of original prices. The output of major industrial products such as cotton yarn, raw coal, power generation, crude oil, steel, machinery and equipment all saw huge increases. By the end of 1965, China's petroleum industry had made outstanding advances, achieving full self-sufficiency in crude oil and petroleum products for domestic consumption. The electrical power industry developed considerably, the coal industry gradually advanced towards modernisation, the machine industry developed more than 10 basic sectors such as metallurgy, mining, petrochemical and other industrial equipment manufacturing, as well as aircraft, automobile and engineering machinery manufacturing, and new industries such as electronics, atomic energy and aerospace also gradually developed. An industrial system of considerable scale and with a significant level of technology was fundamentally established. Capital construction and technological transformation were carried out on a large scale in agriculture and gradually yielded results. The number of tractors and the amount of fertilisers used in agriculture increased more than sixfold, and the amount of electricity used in rural areas increased seventyfold. From 1958 to 1965, more than 7,900km of railways were added to the country's network, the volume of freight transported by railways increased by 50.67% and the volume of passenger transport by 31.93% compared with 1957. The quality of education improved significantly, with 4.9 times more graduates from higher education institutions than in the previous seven years. Scientific and technological work also saw outstanding results, with the most notable advances being in defence science and technology. On 16 October 1964, China successfully exploded its first atomic bomb, thereby raising its international standing. Breakthroughs were made in the development of missiles, hydrogen bombs and artificial satellites. In 1965, China developed the world's first synthetic crystalline bovine insulin. The achievements of a decade of construction laid an important material and technological foundation for socialist construction in the new era of reform and opening up, and a number of the basic infrastructure projects and large and medium-sized enterprises of that period are still playing a role in the national economy and social life today.

The 10-year exploration of new ways of governance trained up a considerable supportive core of forces and professionals for socialist modernisation, both in terms of specialists for the construction business and also within the party and the government cadres. After 1956, the CPC Central Committee pushed the need to train experts in all aspects, fields and disciplines. During the next decade, thousands of specialists of all kinds grew up and were put to the test by practice in various fields of socialist construction. Most of these became the backbone of party committees and government departments at all levels, as well as in the economy, education, science and technology, literature and art, health care and sports in the new era of reform and opening up. At the same time, the party ranks and the party cadres were further developed and expanded. The number of party members increased from 10.73 million in 1956 to 18.95 million in 1965. Particularly in the 1960s, the Party Central Committee and Mao Zedong recognised the importance of vigorously training and promoting new forces, and took practical measures to train and cultivate successors to the revolutionary cause. Initial results were achieved, and the succession of the party's cadres was secured. The success of the cause was handed on, and the organisational foundation of the party's governance was consolidated.

The decade-long exploration of new ways of governance left a valuable spiritual legacy for the party and the country. Over the decade, these achievements were made in the face of severe economic difficulties at home and under enormous pressure and the threat of war at the international level. The party and the people were united; they insisted on independence and self-reliance, withstood the pressure, struggled hard and overcame difficulties, and displayed unparalleled heroism and an indomitable spirit. During those 10 years, such exemplary figures as Jiao Yulu, the Party Secretary of Lankao County in Henan Province, Wang Jinxi, an oil worker in Daqing, and Lei Feng, a soldier in the PLA, came to the fore along with outstanding examples of advanced intellectuals such as the scientists Qian Xuesen, Li Siguang, Qian Sanqiang and Mao Yisheng. Many cadres, workers, scientific and technical personnel and PLA officers responded to the party's call to go where the motherland needed them most and made significant contributions to the cutting-edge science and technology of national defence, geological exploration, oil exploration and

Third Front construction. There were also a large number of outstanding models and advanced personnel on various fronts who bequeathed the nation valuable spiritual treasures such as the Daqing Spirit, Red Flag Canal Spirit, the spirit of the "two bombs and one satellite" and the spirit of Lei Feng, which have inspired generations of Chinese children to strive tirelessly for the great rejuvenation of the nation.

It is in the nature of an exploration, that there will inevitably be twists and turns. The cause of socialist construction is a difficult and complex one, and the party's exploration was never going to be smooth sailing. As the party had not been in power for long, it lacked sufficient ideological understanding and experience on how to govern the country and carry out large-scale socialist construction, and its analysis of the situation and understanding of the national conditions were subjectively biased. This resulted in "leftist" mistakes that caused serious setbacks in the construction of Chinese socialism and taught a profound lesson. This proves that socialism with Chinese characteristics did not fall from the sky but was a fundamental achievement made by the party and the people through countless hardships and at great cost. Summing up the exploration process over 10 years, the CPC has not only made many original theoretical achievements in socialist construction but also, as pointed out in the *Resolution on Certain Historical Issues of the Party since the Founding of the PRC*: "A large part of the material and technical foundation on which we are now building our modernisation was built during this period; the backbone of the nation's economic and cultural construction, and their working experience were also cultivated and accumulated during this period. This was the dominant aspect of the party's work." Therefore, full recognition must be given to this period of history and it must be firmly placed in the context of the long history of the CPC since it came to power throughout the country, along with a profound understanding of the valuable experience, theoretical preparation, material foundation and accumulation of talent it has provided for the creation of socialism with Chinese characteristics in the new historical period.

(V) SERIOUS SETBACKS AND LESSONS LEARNED IN THE PROCESS OF EXPLORING NEW WAYS OF GOVERNANCE

After 10 years of hard struggle from the basic completion of the socialist transformation to the start of the Cultural Revolution in 1966, the party made significant achievements in socialist construction and accumulated valuable experience in governance. At the same time, there were serious mistakes in the guidelines of the party's work during this decade, such as the Great Leap Forward and the Cultural Revolution; the process of socialist modernisation and the party's search for the rules of governance went through a tortuous development process, leaving behind painful lessons.

1. Serious setbacks in exploration

Xi Jinping once profoundly observed that: "One of the fundamental reasons for the serious mistakes of our party in the 30 years before reform and opening up was that we still 'took class struggle as the key' after the socialist transformation was basically completed and, for a long time, pushed the task of developing productive forces into a secondary position."[59] This important assertion has profoundly revealed the main root causes of the serious mistakes made by our party in the course of carrying out socialist modernisation and exploring the rules of governance. To sum up, it is principally due to a major mistake in understanding and grasping two major issues: one is the issue of class struggle under socialist conditions and the other is the issue of scale and speed in socialist construction.

From a political point of view, the main problem was the widening of the class struggle and the comprehensive error of expanding the anti-rightist struggle into the Cultural Revolution.

The Eighth National Congress of the CPC correctly gauged class struggle under socialist conditions but the expansion of the anti-rightist struggle in 1957 changed the Congress's scientific assertion on the social contradictions in China and wrongly considered that the struggle between the proletariat and the bourgeoisie was still the main contradiction in the country. This became the theoretical root of the subsequent expansion of class struggle. The Cultural Revolution mistakenly launched in 1966 was the result of the "leftist" error that developed into "taking class struggle as the key".

In terms of cognitive judgment, this kind of expansion of the class struggle is reflected in the guiding ideology of expansion and absolutisation of that struggle that existed for a certain time during the socialist period. From an objective point of view, it was believed that "exploiting classes" still existed during the socialist period, as Mao Zedong expressed in his statement at the Wuchang Conference about the two working classes and the two exploiting classes, and his assertion during the Cultural Revolution about the "bureaucratic class" and the "bourgeoisie within the party". In these the differences in income and labour of different classes were actually treated as class differences. In terms of the duration of the class struggle, it was believed that it would continue until the establishment of socialism, and even then, "the struggle would not cease until the classes were completely eliminated";[60] In terms of the status and role of class struggle, it is believed that the contradiction between the proletariat and the bourgeoisie and the contradiction between the socialist road and the capitalist road are the main contradictions in our society at present" and that "class struggle is the key and the rest is the goal".[61] In terms of the method of class struggle, it is believed that we should continue to use the tempest of mass movement, "openly, comprehensively and from the bottom up mobilise the masses to expose the dark side of the life of the party and the state", to seize power and to carry out the "revolution of one class overthrowing another" by means of "loud voices, loud debate and big-character posters". From the point of view of the development trend of class struggle, it is believed that class struggle always appears periodically in high and low-level bursts, and that it will come again in a few years; it is regarded as an objective law that: "Who wins and who loses in the revolution will only be resolved over a long historical period, and if it is not carried out properly, the restoration of capitalism will remain possible at any time". "Do not think that if there are one or two or three or four Cultural Revolutions, then there will be no more trouble. Whatever happens it is vital to remain eternally vigilant."[62]

In terms of economic construction, the main factor is that it has repeatedly transcended its historical stage and concentrated on the pursuit of speed of development.

The guidelines for national economic construction laid down at the Eighth Party Congress were correct, and the main aim was to break away from the Soviet model of socialist economic construction and create a Chinese-style road to socialist modernisation. However, the general line of socialist construction and its basic points put forward at the Second Session of the Eighth Congress were correct in that they reflected the general desire of the masses to change the backwardness of our economy and culture but were flawed in that they ignored the objective laws of economics. Guided by this general line, the Great Leap Forward and the People's Commune Movement were launched in 1958, leading to the proliferation of "leftist" mistakes, mainly marked by high targets, blind leadership, grandiosity and the "communist wind". In 1959, the "left-leaning" error was further exaggerated when the different opinions within the party were wrongly criticised as "right-leaning". The Great Leap Forward and the struggle against rightist tendencies caused an imbalance in the make-up of the national economy and seriously dampened the peasants' enthusiasm for production. This was the subjective cause of the serious difficulties in the Chinese national economy from 1959 to 1961. Later on, there was criticism of "bourgeois legal rights" (distribution according to labour, the eight-tier wage system, commodities and currency) and there was a pursuit of large, public, politically pure and high-level production relations, which severely restricted the development of productive forces. Mao Zedong acknowledged China's economic and cultural backwardness but he was not willing to accept it and strove to transform it. He summed up the country's situation using the expression "first poor and second blank", meaning it was both financially and culturally impoverished. He said that apart from China's vast territory, large population, long history and the fact that it had great literature such as *Dream of the Red Chamber*, China was inferior to other countries in many respects and could not be proud of itself. At the same time, Mao Zedong did not regard the situation of being "first poor and second blank" as a burden but rather considered that "when one is poor, one wants to change". A blank piece of paper, free of burdens, is good for writing the most modern and finest words, and for drawing the most modern and most beautiful pictures. However, he failed to recognise the extraordinary difficulties of building socialism from the starting point of "poverty and blankness" and the objective conditions for moving from poverty to wealth, and from blankness to beauty. Because of this, he made the mistake of trying to rush success.

There were other mistakes in the process of carrying out socialist modernisation and exploring the rules of governance. First, with regard to the economic basis of governance, while pursuing the "one big, two public" policy, the country continued to adhere to the rigid planned economy system with no distinction between government and enterprise, and too much insistence on conformity. This resulted in a lack of enterprise autonomy and a lack of economic vitality. The market economy was long equated with capitalism and the planned economy with socialism, and the two were absolutely opposed to each other, without giving full play to the role of the market mechanism and the law of value in accordance with national conditions. Second, in terms of the forces on which the government depended, the intellectuals were regarded as "hairs" growing on the "skin" of the bourgeoisie and as dissidents, and they were the first to be targeted in political movements. The misconceptions and erroneous policies towards intellectuals seriously affected the development of science and technology, and the flourishing of literature and art in China. During the Cultural Revolution in particular, scientific, cultural and educational undertakings were very severely affected, widening the gap between the scientific and technological level of China and that of the world's advanced countries, and greatly damaging historical and cultural heritage. Third, with regard to the external governance environment, there was a lack of comprehensive and objective analysis and understanding of the development and characteristics of contemporary capitalism, a failure to absorb the useful scientific and technological knowledge and management experience of capitalist countries to supplement and develop socialism, and the adoption of the mistaken policy of closing the country to the outside world. Fourth, in the institutionalisation of the ruling party, the important role of the legal system was neglected, and its construction almost came to a halt for a period of time. Consequently, the legal system was significantly left behind, with serious long-term adverse effects on the people's understanding of its importance. Fifth, in terms of the construction of the ruling party itself, the fine traditions and high-minded customs of the party and the people were seriously damaged; erroneous metaphysical thinking was rampant during the Cultural Revolution, materialism prevailed, anarchism, extreme individualism and factionalism exerted serious negative influence, and the bad ethos within the party grew.

2. Reasons for the appearance of serious setbacks

The serious mistakes made by the party in its exploration of the laws of socialist modernisation and governance greatly hindered the development of productive forces, harmed the relationship between the party and the people, and seriously undermined the superiority of the socialist system. So, what led to these mistakes, errors, and twists and turns? There is a direct relationship between the party's failure to correctly judge and deal with some of the major problems it faced after entering socialism.

The first question was how to correctly evaluate the external environment and its impact on China after the new regime took power. As soon as new China was founded, it found itself in a Cold War environment with the two camps led by the US and the Soviet Union facing each other, and it was under enormous pressure from outside. In 1956, the 20th Congress of the CPSU, the Polish Incident and the Hungarian Incident occurred, and the imperialists took advantage of the opportunity to launch an anti-communist counter-current, further complicating the international situation. Domestically, a few rightists, some with murderous intent, used the Rectification Movement to launch an attack on the CPC and the socialist system. The divisions, quarrels and Sino-Soviet debates within the world socialist movement at this time led the CPC to raise the banner of "opposition to modern revisionism", which made "China feel as if the whole world was intent on besieging and strangling the only remaining revolutionary shrine."[63] Mao Zedong also lamented that "most of the 100 or more parties in the world no longer believe in Marxism-Leninism"[64] and believed that imperialism, revisionism and the reactionary factions of various countries would collude with domestic class enemies to subvert the leadership of the communist party and the socialist system, and that China was in real danger of the party becoming revisionist and the country changing colour.

The combined attacks and ridicule of the "imperialists and revisionists" on China's domestic policy aroused the national pride of the Chinese people, and this was the basis for Mao's call to oppose "revisionism" and to "prevent the restoration of capitalism". In addition, the party was overly optimistic about the possibility of a world revolution as national liberation movements in Asia, Africa and Latin America flourished, and waves of protest within capitalist societies continued to rise. As a bastion of world revolution, China had to be highly revolutionised domestically and to take up various internationalist revolutionary tasks in order to promote "world revolution" and welcome its climax. This was not only one of the reasons why the party's domestic policy went further and further down the wrong path of "leftism" but also explains, to a certain extent, why the party and the Chinese people were able to endure the enormous difficulties brought about by the long-term "leftist" policy.

Second, there was the question of how to correctly understand the long-term, complex and arduous issues of building socialism.

Under the leadership of the party, the situation in the period before and after the founding of new China developed more favourably and more rapidly than originally expected. The War of Liberation, which was expected to take a long time, was won ahead of schedule; the socialist transformation, which was expected to be very complicated and arduous, was completed within a short time. This series of events gave the superficial impression that there was nothing that could not be done by the Chinese people. The overestimation of our own strength and the incorrect judgment of the level of development led directly to such errors as the Great Leap Forward, which was out of touch with reality, against the rules of governance and exceeded current capabilities.

Third was how to correctly deal with the historical inertia brought about by the wealth of experience accumulated during the war years. In the course of the party's leadership in seeking independence, liberation and prosperity, many historical traditions were established, some of which have proved to be of permanent significance, such as the "three important styles of work", while others were only applicable at a specific stage in history, such as the rich experience of class struggle accumulated during the revolutionary war and the life experience of the war years. A tradition of inertia ensured that, in observing and dealing with the many new problems and difficulties of socialist construction, familiar experiences of the past were relied on, and problems that were not truly part of the class struggle were regarded as such. The method of handling large-scale mass class struggles, the kind of nearly communist life experience that had been effective in the revolutionary army in the war years, was also used as the basis for planning an ideal society. The rapid spread across the country of the Great Leap Forward and the People's Commune Movement was the result of using the mass movement approach.

Fourth, in a country with a long tradition of feudal authoritarianism, there was the question of how to improve the leadership system of the party and the state. Deng Xiaoping once profoundly observed that: "Old China has left us with many feudal authoritarian traditions and very few democratic legal traditions."[65] The negative influence of feudalism cannot be underestimated. For example, the feudalist patriarchal ethic of "the supremacy of the monarch" had considerable influence within the party, even among the old generation of revolutionaries who had been part of the struggle against feudalism since their youth. For example, at the Lushan Conference, some people criticised Peng Dehuai for having "the rebelliousness of Wei Yan", while others used the principle of "being loyal unto death" to persuade Huang Kecheng and others.[66] The fact that this application of feudal ruler-subordinate relations to the party was seen as normal in the party hierarchy, and that most people were comfortable with it, is an indication of the negative influence of traditional culture

Originally, the system of democratic centralism and collective leadership was a fine system and tradition that Mao Zedong had nurtured and practised with his own hands. However, at a time when the CPC was facing the new task of shifting its focus to socialist construction and therefore needed to be particularly cautious, Mao gradually became detached both from reality and from the masses, and his subjectivism and personal autocratic style became increasingly pronounced, overriding the Party Central Committee. Some of the serious deviations in the history of the international communist movement, which were due to failure to properly resolve the issue of the relationship between the leader and the party, also had a negative impact on the CPC. Under the conditions of governance, it became a very difficult task for the party to institutionalise and legalise democracy both within the party and in the political life of the country, and to give the institutions and laws enacted the authority they deserved. When Mao Zedong's prestige within the party and at home and abroad reached its peak, it was inevitable that his "subjectivism and personal arbitrariness became increasingly pronounced", as pointed out in the *Second Party Resolution on History*, and that the party's democratic centralism and the democratic principles of national political life would be difficult to uphold. This also made it difficult for the party and the state to prevent and halt the occurrence and development of such serious global mistakes as the Great Leap Forward and the Cultural Revolution.

3. Lessons accumulated in the course of exploration

The serious setbacks and mistakes made by the party during the historical process of carrying out socialist modernisation and exploring the laws of governance have built up important historical lessons for us.

- After coming to power, it is necessary to take economic construction as the primary task and insist on vigorously developing social productive forces. After the proletariat seized power and established the socialist system, it was essential to "increase the total amount of productivity as quickly as possible."[67] After the completing socialist transformation of the private ownership of the means of production in China, the main social contradiction was no longer the struggle between two classes and two roads but the contradiction between the people's growing material and cultural needs, and backward social production. The party and the state had to concentrate their efforts on developing social productive forces, gradually improving the people's standard of living, and establishing a strong material foundation for consolidation of the socialist system. "Labour productivity, in the final analysis, is the most important thing for the victory of the new social system."[68] The development of social productive forces is not only an economic task but also a political task, a basic element of the political line after the establishment of the socialist system, and the central task of all the tasks of the party and the state. Unless there is a large-scale invasion by foreign enemies, this core must not be shaken by lesser disturbances. Summing up the lessons of this period of history, Deng Xiaoping pointed out: "For many years we have suffered a great loss; the socialist transformation has basically been completed but we still 'take class struggle as the programme' and neglect the development of productive forces."[69] Poverty is not socialism; the fundamental task of socialism is to develop productive forces; this is an important conclusion drawn from the lessons learned from the construction of socialism in China.

- It is necessary to fully understand the national conditions and correctly judge and engage with the historical stage of social development. A scientific judgment of China's national conditions was the prerequisite for the CPC to accurately determine its own line and programme. This was true during the revolutionary period and it is was equally true during the construction period. However, it was a long time before the fundamental questions of how to make an accurate analysis and judgment of China's basic national conditions in terms of the stages of social development, whether socialist society still needed to be divided into different stages of development, and at what stage of development China entered a socialist society, were clearly formulated and correctly resolved. When the Great Leap Forward and the People's Commune Movement were launched in 1958, it was thought that the realisation of communism in China was no longer something in the distant future and so a "communist wind" was whipped up, first in the countryside, to help speed the transition. Later on, these biases were corrected to some extent and Mao Zedong proposed to draw two lines. One was the line between communism and socialism. After reading the Soviet *Textbook of Political Economy*, speaking theoretically, he opined: "The stage of socialism can be further divided into two stages, proto-socialism and developed socialism."[70] This was a very meaningful theoretical exploration. However, at that time, this idea was not discussed, and the idea of the "proto-socialist stage" was not adopted in a way that would have allowed serious and thorough policy adjustments. From an overall general perspective, the idea of transcending the early stage still dominated the party's thinking. As Deng Xiaoping later pointed out when summing up the lessons of this period: "From the second half of 1957 onwards, we made 'leftist' mistakes. In a nutshell, it was that we were closed to the outside world, took the class struggle as the platform internally, neglected the development of productive forces and formulated policies that went beyond the primary stage of socialism."[71] History has proved that the primary stage of socialism is the basic national condition of China; all work must proceed from the reality of the primary stage, and all policies must be formulated on the basis of the national condition of the primary stage. We must fully understand the great achievements and successful experiences of our socialist construction and, at the same time, fully appreciate its long-term, complex and arduous nature, and oppose both negative sentiments and impatient tendencies.

- It is necessary to accurately grasp the basis of the socioeconomic system and to correctly understand and deal with the issue of socialist production relations. For a significant period of time, we thought that the "first large, second collective and third pure" system of ownership of the means of production was in line with the requirements of socialism, as it was detached from the actual level of development of production, emphasising, rather, an understanding of socialism in terms of production relations (principally ownership). The "three red flags" of 1959, especially Mao's vision of the people's communes, may be said to have been somewhat idealistic in nature. Mao's 1966 *May 7th Directive* was a systematic expression of his vision of the socialist model: he wanted to build a form of closed socialism that was "based on class struggle", restricted and criticised the rights of the bourgeoisie, was "first large, second collective", catered for industry, peasant, civilians and military alike, restricted the development of commodities, and was generally evenly distributed. Although the party recognised that contradictions did exist in a socialist society, and that the basic contradiction was still between production relations and productive forces, and between the superstructure and the economic base, it believed that these contradictions were mainly manifested in the fact that the degree of public ownership of the means of production was not yet high enough. Therefore, the party focused its efforts on increasing the level of public ownership, even to the extent of "transition in the spirit of poverty" and "amputating the tail of capitalism", independently of the level of development of productive forces. History has proved that the pursuit of greater public ownership of the means of production and the attempt to promote the development productive forces "on the basis of class struggle" will inevitably suffer setbacks.

- It is necessary to correctly judge the party's historical orientation and to deal with the issue of class struggle under socialist conditions. After the socialist transformation of private ownership of the means of production was essentially completed, "class struggle will persist to a certain extent and may intensify under certain conditions."[72] It was also necessary to understand and deal with class struggle "within a certain range", and to exercise dictatorship over all anti-socialist elements, without which the development of socialist construction could be guaranteed. Deng Xiaoping observed: "To use the power of the people's democratic dictatorship to consolidate the people's power is a matter of justice, and there is room for mistakes."[73] At the same time, it was essential to understand that class struggle was no longer the main contradiction in our society. Under socialist conditions, there was no more necessity to make class struggle the theme of political life, still less to carry out the so-called "continuous revolution under the dictatorship of the proletariat" in which "one class overthrows another". The social contradictions that did not fall within the scope of class struggle needed to be resolved in a correct manner by different means from those used in class struggle; those that fall within the scope of class struggle should also be resolved by legal procedures; when the nature of the problem was unclear, it had first to be dealt with as an internal contradiction among the people, and not be arbitrarily escalated or pushed to extremes. Only in this way could the smooth progress of socialist construction be ensured.

- It is necessary to focus on the rule of law and the standardisation of governance, to strengthen the socialist legal system and to develop socialist democratic politics. In 1954 China formulated and promulgated the constitution but the legal system and its institutions were not yet complete and were still in their infancy. Many party comrades were still accustomed to the practice of substituting policies, mass movements and struggles for laws during the war years. History tells us that we must develop socialist democracy and institutionalise and legalise it, so that the system and its laws do not change with a change in leadership, or with a change in the views and level of attention of the leaders. It was necessary to strengthen the construction of state organs at all levels in accordance with the principle of democratic centralism, to gradually expand democracy in organisations at all levels, and to guarantee the people's basic rights in political and social life. It was also necessary to improve the country's constitution and laws, to make them an inviolable force that everyone must strictly abide by, and to make socialist law a powerful weapon for safeguarding people's rights.

- It is essential to give due importance to the ideological and cultural foundations of governance and to vigorously promote the building of socialist ideology, morality, science and culture. The mistakes made by the party in its explorations were closely linked to mistakes in theoretical and ideological guidance, and the Cultural Revolution was guided by the theory of continuous revolution under the dictatorship of the proletariat. In order to avoid repeating past mistakes, it is necessary to strengthen the ideological and theoretical construction of the party, to train genuine theoreticians and a large number of comrades who have learnt Marxism-Leninism "systematically rather than piecemeal and practically in a hollow manner"[74], to resolutely eradicate disregard for the construction of education, science and culture, and to correctly carry out struggle in the field of ideology. Attention should be focused tightly on construction, on uniting the people and giving full play to their socialist initiative and creative spirit, on meeting their cultural and spiritual needs, and on strengthening the building of morality and education, science and culture. Knowledge and talent must be recognised, and the status and role of education, science and culture in modernisation must be raised. Ideological and political work must be strengthened, and a correct world view, outlook on life and values in society as a whole must be promoted.

- It is necessary to pay great attention to the domestic environment of governance and to maintaining a stable and united political situation. China's socialist modernisation required a stable and united political situation. Deng Xiaoping pointed out: "The overriding problem in China is the need for stability. Without a stable environment, nothing can be done". "China's highest interest is stability. Whatever is conducive to China's stability is a good thing". "Anything that hinders stability must be dealt with making no concessions and no accommodations."[75] Therefore, it is necessary to pay great attention to the various unstable factors in society, guide and deal with them properly, and always pay attention to maintaining a stable political environment and social order, so that reforms can proceed smoothly and all undertakings can move forward. The attempt during the Cultural Revolution to "bring a great deal of chaos to the world in order to bring great peace in the world" did not "disrupt the enemy and train the masses", but rather "disrupted itself". In other words, it disrupted the party, the country, the nation and the people, and brought about a profound disaster to the party and the country. Thus the Cultural Revolution became an internal turmoil. Deng Xiaoping's emphasis that "China must not mess itself up"[76] is a summary of the experience that hits the nail on the head.

- We must correctly understand the external environment in which we govern and deal with the relationship between self-reliance and opening up to the outside world. China's affairs must be run according to China's circumstances and rely on the strength of the Chinese themselves. Independence and self-reliance have been, are and will continue to be the starting point of our work. However, independence and self-reliance are not contradictory to opening up to the outside world. For a period of time after the founding of new China, China mainly developed its relations with the Soviet Union and Eastern European countries, and opened up to socialist and third world countries. Due to the international blockade by hostile forces and our own lack of awareness, especially the ultra-leftist practices of the Gang of Four, we were unable to establish normal economic ties with the developed capitalist countries. Generally speaking, we have largely been isolated or semi-isolated from the outside world. The third technological revolution contributed greatly to the development of the world economy and the improvement of people's living standards, and we missed a historical opportunity to narrow the gap with developed countries. The lessons of history have proved that socialism, as a new stage in the development of human civilisation, cannot leave the main road of the development of human civilisation as a whole. Deng Xiaoping summed up the lessons of history and profoundly pointed out that: "Experience has proved that it is not possible to succeed in building behind closed doors."[77] "If socialism is to win an advantage over capitalism, it must boldly absorb and draw on all the achievements of civilisation created by human society and all the advanced business methods and management methods of countries in the world today which reflect the laws of modern socialised production, including the developed capitalist countries."[78]

- The ruling party must strengthen its own construction and enhance and improve its leadership. We must always adhere to the guiding position of Marxism, treat Marxism in a scientific manner and follow the correct ideological line. The building of democracy within the party must be strengthened and the development of people's democracy must be actively promoted through the development of democracy within the party. Democratic centralism must be upheld, and arbitrariness and weakness opposed. The democratic system within the party must be improved, the principle of collective leadership implemented, and both decentralisation, anarchy and individual arbitrariness opposed. Party organisations at all levels and all party members and cadres must reach out to the masses and the real world, make proper use of the tools of criticism and self-criticism, and resolutely overcome bureaucratism. Party organisations at all levels, like other social organisations, must operate within the confines of the constitution and the law.

The CPC is a Marxist party that always upholds the truth and corrects mistakes. History has shown that when mistakes or even serious errors in exploration occur, the nature and purpose of the party remains unchanged and the party remains the faithful representative of the fundamental interests of the people. The party has constantly corrected mistakes in its explorations and, by summing up the lessons learned, has made them the precursors of correctness. The major setbacks in the process of comprehensively building socialism provided valuable lessons for the party to gradually grasp the laws of socialist construction, accumulated important experience for the later opening up of the road to socialism with Chinese characteristics, and provided an important source of ideas for the formation of the theoretical system of socialism with Chinese characteristics. Deng Xiaoping once said: "Past successes are our wealth, and past mistakes are also our wealth. We absolutely decry the Cultural Revolution but we should also say that the Cultural Revolution' has 'merit' in that it provided a negative lesson. Without the lessons of the Cultural Revolution, it would not have been possible to formulate the ideological, political and organisational lines and the series of policies since the 3rd Plenary Session of the 11th Central Committee."[79]

In January 2013, Xi Jinping observed in his speech at a seminar for new and alternate members of the Central Committee the need to study and implement the spirit of the 18th CPC National Congress that there were two historical periods before and after the reform and opening up of the country, which were interrelated and significantly different, but both were essentially practical explorations of the socialist construction led by the party. Although these two historical periods differ greatly in terms of ideological guidance, policies and practical work of socialist construction, they are in no way separate from each other, let alone fundamentally opposed to each other. The historical period after the reform and opening-up cannot be used to negate the historical period that preceded it, nor vice versa. "Had it not been for the establishment of new China in 1949 and the socialist revolution and construction, which built up important ideological, material and institutional conditions and experience in both positive and negative aspects, it would have been difficult for reform and opening up to advance smoothly."[80] This important statement profoundly clarifies the connection and difference between the two historical periods before and after the reform and opening up, and fully reflects the scientific attitude towards history of a Marxist party.

4

THE FIRST MIRACLE CREATED BY THE CPC'S LEADERSHIP OF THE REVOLUTION AND ESTABLISHMENT OF GOVERNANCE

ACHIEVING THE GREAT LEAP OF THE CHINESE NATION FROM THE 'SICK MAN OF EAST ASIA' TO STANDING PROUD ON ITS OWN TWO FEET

If ever they fall behind, they suffer hardship and humiliation. This is an unforgettable pain in the hearts of the Chinese people and the Chinese nation in modern times. Starting with the Opium Wars, the Western powers waged vicious wars against China time and time again, forcing the corrupt and incompetent Qing government to sign more and more demanding and unequal treaties. China gradually became a semi-colonial and semi-feudal society, and the Chinese people suffered the dual oppressions of feudalism and imperialism. The country was broken and the people in dire straits; the Chinese nation fell into a tragic situation of poverty, weakness and slaughter, and suffered unprecedented suffering and the humiliation of being humiliated as the "sick man of East Asia."

After its foundation, the CPC persisted in combining Marxism with China's specific reality and characteristics of the times, bravely shouldered the historical task of national rejuvenation, and united and led the Chinese people to create successive human miracles. Achieving the great leap of the Chinese nation from "the sick man of East Asia" to standing up on its own two feet, and building the poor and weak semi-colonial and semi-feudal old China into a new socialist China profoundly has changed the direction and development process of the Chinese nation in modern times. This has profoundly changed the future and destiny of the Chinese people and the Chinese nation, and it has profoundly affected the world political landscape. This is the first miracle created by the CPC in its leadership of the revolution and establishment of governance.

(I) THREE MAJOR HISTORICAL ACHIEVEMENTS MARK THE
FIRST MIRACLE CREATED BY THE CPC IN LEADING THE
REVOLUTION AND GOVERNANCE

The first major historical achievement: pioneering a new path for the
Chinese revolution, overthrowing the "three great mountains", establishing
the new China, and leading the Chinese people and the Chinese nation to
achieve political independence.

After 28 years of arduous exploration, the CPC found the correct revolutionary path of encircling the cities from the countryside and seizing
power by force of arms, uniting and leading the people to defeat Japanese
imperialism, defeating the reactionary rule of the KMT and overthrowing
the "three mountains" of imperialism, feudalism and bureaucratic capitalism that were oppressing the Chinese people. The new democratic revolution was completed, and the PRC was established. The founding of new
China completely abolished the unequal treaties imposed on China by the
Western powers and all the privileges of the imperialists in China. It
fundamentally ended the historical phase of the Chinese nation during
which it had been subjected to imperialist aggression and oppression for
more than 100 years and made China a truly independent and sovereign
country. This was a fundamental change in the nature of Chinese society.
China is an ancient civilisation with a history of over 5,000 years but it was
only after the founding of new China and the coming to power of the party
that the people became the masters of their country, their society and their
own destiny, and made the great leap from thousands of years of feudal
autocracy to people's democracy. This was a fundamental change in the
social and political status of the Chinese people. The founding of new
China fundamentally put an end to the history of warlordism and warfare
in the old China, creating a new situation of unity and social stability
among all ethnic groups and strata in the country, and achieving a great
leap from the fragmentation of the old China to a high degree of national
unity and unprecedented solidarity among all ethnic groups. This was a
fundamental change in the prestige of the Chinese people, the prestige of
China and the prestige of the Chinese nation. The founding of new China
profoundly influenced the course of world history in the 20th century,
enabling us, a large country with nearly a quarter of the world's population, to stand up and be counted in the world. It fundamentally changed
the international political landscape after the second world war and had a
broad and far-reaching impact on world development, marking a fundamental change in China's position in world history.

The second major historical achievement was pioneering a new path of socialist revolution, eliminating the systems of exploitation, establishing the basic system of socialism and leading the Chinese people and the Chinese nation onto the path of socialism.

After the founding of new China, the CPC led the Chinese people to carry out socialist transformation of the private ownership of the means of production, establish the economic basis of socialism, and set up a socialist economic system in which public ownership of the means of production and distribution of labour were the principal manifestations. In the course of the socialist revolution, the system of people's congresses was established nationwide as the fundamental political form of China, and the basic political systems, such as multiparty cooperation and political consultation, and the regional national autonomy under the leadership of the CPC, were continuously developed and improved. The party's leadership of ideological work was upheld, the guiding position of Marxism-Leninism and Mao Zedong Thought in the life of the country and society was established and consolidated, socialist consciousness and socialist moral norms were gradually established among the people, and education, science and technology, and culture flourished. All this marked the establishment of the basic socialist system in China and the party's leadership of the Chinese people into a socialist society. This laid the fundamental political premise and institutional foundation for all development and progress in contemporary China and laid a solid foundation for the development and strengthening of the country and the prosperity and happiness of the people. In particular, the most extensive and profound social transformation ever undertaken by the Chinese nation, the eradication of private ownership and the system of exploitation, was accomplished with the widespread support of the people, the essentially stable development of the national economy and the general stability of the social and political situation.

The third major historical achievement was exploring China's own path of socialist construction, carrying out that construction on a large scale, establishing an independent and relatively complete industrial system and national economic system, and leading the Chinese people and the Chinese nation to gain economic independence.

In parallel with the socialist transformation, the party led the formulation and implementation of the first five-year plan for national economic development, initiating planned, large-scale socialist construction. China's socialist construction was carried out in the face of poverty and under poverty-stricken conditions, and it faced international threats and blockade from Western countries. There are two impressive quotations from Mao Zedong. In 1954, he said: "What can we make now? We can make tables and chairs, and we can make tea bowls and teapots; we can grow grain and grind it into flour, we can make paper but we cannot make a car, an aeroplane, a tank or a tractor." On another occasion, when he launched the Great Leap Forward, he said: "China's economic backwardness and weak material base have left us in a state of passivity; we still feel mentally shackled and we have not yet been liberated in this respect. These two quotations are very clear about the level and state of China's economic development at that time and the general aspiration of the Chinese people, long bullied by the imperialist powers, to become rich and strong now they had stood up for themselves. It was the strong desire and urgent demand of the party and the masses to change China's economic and cultural backwardness as soon as possible, to win economic independence after gaining political independence, to seek strength and prosperity after standing up, to build a strong socialist country and to take its rightful place in the world. At the preparatory meeting of the 8th Party Congress, Mao Zedong's statement that failure to carry out construction would lead to expulsion from its "global citizenship" was a concentrated expression of this aspiration. In the process of exploring China's own road to socialism, the party and the people united and withstood all the pressure, and with unparalleled heroism and vigour, independently, with self-reliance and mighty struggle, built up a relatively complete, independent industrial and national economic system, greatly improved the level of agricultural production, and developed education, science, culture, health and sports. Not only did the Chinese nation gain economic independence after achieving political independence but it also provided theoretical preparation and accumulated valuable experience and a material and technical basis for further modernisation.

The history of the CPC's leadership of the revolution and creation of the first miracle after it came to power is ample proof that without the communist party there would be no new China, that only the communist party can save China, and that only socialism can develop China.

(II) THE CPC'S LEADERSHIP OF THE REVOLUTION AND GOVERNANCE CREATED THE FIRST MIRACLE, WHICH HAS HAD A LONG-TERM IMPACT ON THE PARTY'S GOVERNANCE INSPIRATION

The inspiration for the party's long-term rule from the first miracle of the CPC's leadership of the revolution and its rule: "Just as jade needs to be polished, one needs to go through trials and tribulations to be strong." This is the logic of the triumph of all righteous causes and a true reflection of the CPC's leadership of the Chinese people in creating miracles on the planet earth. This historical achievement of the CPC's revolution and rule fully demonstrates the theoretical, political, organisational, institutional and unique advantages of the CPC in terms of its close contact with the masses. These qualities and strengths are the fundamental factors that have led the CPC in the right direction and determined the course of social development in China in modern times. They are the fundamental assets of the CPC in leading the Chinese people to create a miracle on earth.

- The party's theoretical characteristics and unique advantages must be maintained and deployed. During the arduous revolutionary struggle, the Chinese communists, principally represented by Comrade Mao Zedong, insisted on combining the basic principles of Marxism with the concrete reality of the Chinese revolution, followed their own path, vigorously promoted the Sinicisation of Marxism, and founded Mao Zedong Thought, which formed a uniquely Chinese innovative theory and systematically answered and solved a series of basic questions posed by the Chinese revolution. As Liu Shaoqi pointed out at the Seventh Party Congress: "Our party and many of its members once suffered a lot from lack of direction and fumbling in their work because of insufficient theoretical preparation, and took many unnecessary detours. But now, thanks to the painstaking work and genius of Comrade Mao Zedong, the party and the Chinese people have been fully prepared theoretically. This will greatly strengthen the confidence and fighting power of the party and the Chinese people, and greatly speed up the process of victory of the Chinese revolution. "After the founding of the new China, Mao Zedong Thought was enriched and developed in many ways and played a guiding role in exploring China's own path to building socialism. This characteristic and unique advantage of the party has ensured that it has been able to break away from the limitations of all previous political forces in pursuing their own special interests, and has always been able to overcome powerful enemies and survive various risks and challenges with a materialistic and dialectical scientific spirit and a selfless and broad-minded approach. This served constantly to open up the right path for the Chinese people to save and build the country, and to lead them to create a miracle on earth.

- The party's political qualities and unique advantages must be maintained and brought into play. The party's strengths in politics are manifold. Among them, always making the realisation of communism the party's highest ideal and ultimate goal, and maintaining firm faith in Marxism and firm belief in socialism and communism are a powerful source of strength for the Chinese communists to overcome all kinds of hardships and dangers, and a great political advantage for the party. This unique advantage of the party has ensured that it unites the highest and lowest programmes, always stands at the forefront of the times and leads Chinese society in the right direction. It has given rise to an indomitable revolutionary will and revolutionary spirit. From the spirit of the Red Boat, the spirit of Jinggangshan, the spirit of the Long March, the spirit of Yan'an and the spirit of Xibaipo, to the spirit of "two bombs and one satellite", the spirit of Lei Feng, the spirit of Jiao Yulu and the Iron Man Spirit, the great revolutionary spirit formed by the Chinese communists through revolution and construction has been a powerful spiritual force and precious treasure for the party in overcoming all kinds of difficulties and risks on the way forward and in constantly winning new victories in revolution and construction.

- The party's organisational qualities and unique strengths must be maintained and brought into play. The strength of the party comes from its organisation. The CPC was established in accordance with the Marxist principles of party building, and from its inception it has attached great importance to party organisation, forming a tight, scientific organisational system that includes the central, local and grassroots elements of the party. This characteristic and unique advantage has ensured that the party has been able to bring together the advanced elements of the Chinese working class, the Chinese people and the Chinese nation, as well as the best and brightest talent in all fields throughout the country; it has ensured that the party is a unified whole from an organisational point of view, and that the party is unified in its will, actions and pace, thereby creating a powerful advantage and strength that no other political party in the world has. This has provided a strong organisational guarantee for the party to lead the people of China to victory in revolution and construction.

- The party's institutional traits and unique advantages must be maintained and brought into play. Democratic centralism is the fundamental organisational and leadership system of the CPC. It insists on a combination of centralisation on the basis of democracy, and democracy under the guidance of centralisation, giving full play to democracy and giving full play to the enthusiasm and creativity of party organisations and party members at all levels, while resolutely maintaining the unity and centralisation of the party. This is the party's greatest institutional advantage. After the founding of the new China, the party applied the principle of democratic centralism to the organisation and activities of state organs and established the state system of people's democratic dictatorship, the greatest institutional advantage of new China. This characteristic and unique advantage of the party has ensured that the party adheres to the principle of democratic centralism and establishes a strict organisational system, establishes iron-clad discipline, and forms a unity based on both democracy and centralisation. This ensures that the system reflects the interests and aspirations of the whole party and the people, and ensures the correct formulation and effective implementation of the party's policies, forming a strong, cohesive fighting force along with great creativity.

- The party's characteristic and unique advantage of being in close contact with the masses must be maintained and brought into play. The people are the creators of history and the fundamental driving force behind progress and advancement. Since its establishment, the CPC has been firmly rooted in the people, always adhering to the fundamental purpose of wholeheartedly serving the people, implementing the party's mass line, growing, developing and expanding while maintaining its flesh-and-blood ties with the people, through which it is constantly creating miracles on earth. This close contact with the masses and the party's unique advantages have ensured that the party has always taken its fundamental stance from the people, and has always maintained its spirit of unrelenting struggle, its revolutionary spirit of self-revolution and its fine traditional style of work; these have ensured that the party has always put the people in the highest position in its heart, adhered to the principle of doing everything for the people and relying on the people, and has been at one with the people through thick and thin, living and dying together, constantly pushing forward the cause of benefiting the people and the nation. It has also ensured that the party has always kept the people at the forefront of its mind and has always relied on them.

These traits and unique advantages of the party, which have been developed during the its long-term struggle and exploration, are the hereditary genes of the party, the concentrated embodiment of the party's nature and purposes, and the traits and unique advantages that distinguish the party from other political parties. They are the "genetic code" for the party to grow from small to large, from weak to strong, to maintain its advancement and purity, and to keep moving towards victory. The practice of the party in leading the revolution and creating the first miracle in power has fully proved that these qualities and unique advantages are decisive factors for the prosperity of the party and are of decisive significance for it to continuously consolidate its position in power and achieve long-term rule. They must always be adhered to and employed. This is also the valuable inspiration left to us by the CPC, which led the revolution and created the first miracle of its rule.

PART III
THE CREATION AND DEVELOPMENT OF A NEW PATH OF CPC GOVERNANCE

In 1978 The 3rd Plenary Session of the 11th CPC Central Committee achieved a great turning point of profound significance in the history of the party since the founding of new China, opened up a great journey of reform and opening up, and socialist modernisation, and brought about a new situation in the governance of the CPC.

During the new period of reform and opening up, and socialist construction, the party's second generation of central leadership with Comrade Deng Xiaoping as the core, the third generation of central leadership with Comrade Jiang Zemin as the core, and the Party Central Committee with Comrade Hu Jintao as the general secretary, always successfully navigated the demands of the times, national development and the expectations of the people, actively promoted theoretical, practical, and institutional innovation with strong determination and firm will, established, developed and refined socialism with Chinese characteristics, and explored, pioneered and developed a new path of CPC governance, enabling China to make great strides in catching up with the times, thereby achieving the great leap of the Chinese nation from standing up to becoming rich.

1

PIONEERING A NEW PATH OF GOVERNANCE IN THE MIDST OF BRINGING ORDER OUT OF CHAOS, AND REFORM AND OPENING UP

After the 3rd Plenary Session of the 11th CPC Central Committee, the party's second generation of central leadership with Comrade Deng Xiaoping as the core faced the critical situation caused by the Cultural Revolution and, with great political and theoretical courage, united and led the whole party and the people of all of China's ethnic groups to profoundly summarise the positive and negative experiences of China's socialist construction, draw on the historical experience of socialism throughout the world, emancipate the mind and seek truth from facts, and make the historic decision to shift the work focus of the party and state onto economic construction and the implementation of reform and opening up. They clearly proposed that China should follow its own path and the construction of socialism with Chinese characteristics, formulated the development strategy of basically realising socialist modernisation in three steps by the middle of the 21st century, established the basic line of the primary stage of socialism, profoundly revealed the essence of socialism, and established Deng Xiaoping Theory, which scientifically answered a series of basic questions regarding building socialism with Chinese characteristics, succeeded in pioneering socialism with Chinese characteristics and opened up a new path of governance in the course of bringing order out of chaos, and reforming and opening up, and led and drove forward the constant advancement of the cause of socialist modernisation in China.

(I) THE PRELIMINARY RESTORATION OF THE RULING ORDER

The Cultural Revolution that broke out from 1966 to 1976 constituted a case of internal disorder that was mistakenly started by the leaders and exploited by counter-revolutionary groups, bringing serious disaster to the party, the country and the people of all of China's ethnic groups[1]. On 6 October 1976, Hua Guofeng, Ye Jianying and others, on behalf of the Politburo, carried out the will of the party and the people, and imposed an isolation review on Jiang Qing, Zhang Chunqiao, Wang Hongwen, Yao Wenyuan and the backbone of their gang in Beijing, resolutely smashing Jiang Qing's counter-revolutionary clique, ending the Cultural Revolution and saving China's socialist cause from crisis. This created the preconditions for the party and the country to enter a new historical period and for the party to create a new situation in its governance. After the smashing of the "Gang of Four", the party and the government implemented various measures to preliminarily restore the ruling order, and political life gradually normalised.

During the Cultural Revolution, Lin Biao, the Gang of Four and their gang system conspired to seize the supreme leadership of the party and the state, framing and persecuting a large number of leading party, government and military cadres, leaders of democratic parties, prominent figures from all walks of life and the masses. Party and government organs at all levels, and people's congresses and CPPCC organisations at all levels were in a state of paralysis and abnormality for a long time. Dictatorial organs such as those for public security, and procuratorial and judicial organs were disrupted. The fine traditions and working style of the party were destroyed, and political life and the national order were in a state of extreme disorder. After the end of the Cultural Revolution, it became the primary task before the party and the state to remove the gang forces of the Gang of Four, carry out a campaign to expose and criticise the Gang of Four, stabilise the situation and maintain social stability.

In December 1976, the CPC Central Committee released Evidence of the Crimes of the *Anti-Party Clique of Wang Hongwen, Zhang Chunqiao, Jiang Qing and Yao Wenyuan (Documents Part 1)* to expose the Gang of Four's crimes of ganging up and forming a clique, attempting to usurp the party and seize power, and endangering the people. In March and September 1977, more evidence against the Gang of Four, namely *Documents Part 2*, being *The Counter-Revolutionary Face of the Gang of Four and its Criminal History* and *Documents Part 3*, being *The Reactionary Fallacies Spread by the*

Gang of Four in Various Fields, were also issued to further promote the campaign to expose and criticise the Gang of Four. In the course of the campaign to expose and criticise the Gang of Four, the exposing and criticising of the crimes of the Gang of Four was combined with the investigation of their gang system and the reorganisation of leadership at all levels, as well as with the restoration of the national economy and the promotion of stability and unity. In the midst of conducting investigations and exposing and criticising [various parties], the Party Central Committee successively reorganised the leadership in provinces, regions and municipalities deeply affected by the Gang of Four and made the necessary adjustments and strengthening of some important leading departments of the party, government and military. At the same time, the issue of smashing and looting during the Cultural Revolution was investigated. By 1978, the nationwide investigation was basically complete, and the campaign to expose and criticise the Gang of Four had won a decisive victory.

The campaign to expose and criticise the Gang of Four is inevitably linked to the unjust and false charges brought by the 10 years of internal disorder, and rehabilitating persecuted cadres and the masses, especially clarifying the quarrel surrounding the "Criticise Deng [Xiaoping] and Counter Rightist Deviationism" campaign, led to the reintroduction of Deng Xiaoping to work and the redressing of the 1976 Tiananmen Incident. In January 1977, the people held a memorial service to commemorate the first anniversary of Zhou Enlai's death and, while denouncing the Gang of Four, they strongly demanded the redressing of the Tiananmen Incident and expressed their urgent desire for Deng Xiaoping to return to work. At that time, the Party Central Committee headed by Hua Guofeng, although in handling some specific issues were already preparing for the return of Deng Xiaoping, actually maintained a public approach of exposing and criticising the Gang of Four and also criticising Deng. On 7 February 1977, the *People's Daily*, the *PLA Daily* and *Red Flag Magazine*, in an editorial entitled *Study Party Documents to Grasp the Guiding Principles*, openly proposed that, "we will resolutely uphold whatever policy decisions Chairman Mao made, and unswervingly follow whatever instructions Chairman Mao gave" (later known as the "Two Whatevers"), causing the demands of the masses of cadres to remain unfulfilled and the work of bringing order out of chaos to encounter obstacles.

In April 1977, soon after the Two Whatevers policy was proposed, Deng Xiaoping, who had not yet resumed leadership, wrote to Hua Guofeng and Ye Jianying, and also forwarded a copy to the Party Central

Committee, proposing, "We must throughout all generations use accurate and complete Mao Zedong Thought to guide our whole party, whole army and whole nation, and triumphantly advance the cause of the party and socialism and the cause of the international communist movement'[2]. After this, he criticised the Two Whatevers policy on many occasions in various places. Chen Yun, Ye Jianying, Nie Rongzhen, Xu Xiangqian and a number of other veteran comrades repeatedly stressed the fine tradition of seeking truth from facts. All these resisted, to varying degrees, the error of the Two Whatevers. In July 1977, on the basis of the gradual stabilisation of the national situation and at the demand of the whole party, the 3rd Plenary Session of the 10th CPC Central Committee adopted the *Resolution on the Rehabilitation of Comrade Deng Xiaoping*, reinstating all of Deng's posts that had been revoked in 1976. This prepared the ground for Deng Xiaoping to become the core of the second generation of the party's central leadership.

In August 1977, the 11th CPC National Congress declared that the decade-long Cultural Revolution had come to an end and proposed to mobilise all positive elements within and outside the party, in China and overseas, and to unite all the forces that could possibly be united in the struggle to build China into a great modern socialist power in the 20th century. On the basis of the analysis of the domestic and international situation, the congress clarified the eight main tasks of the party in that period and the subsequent one for grasping the guiding principles for national governance, stating "we must carry out the great struggle to expose and criticise the Gang of Four to the very end; we must carry out the rectification of the party and strengthen the construction of the party; we must succeed in improving and building the party; we must rectify and build up the party's leadership at all levels; we must grasp the revolution, promote production and lift up the national economy; we must succeed in implementing revolution in the fields of culture and education, and vigorously develop the cause of socialist culture and education; we must strengthen the people's state apparatus; we must promote democracy and improve democratic centralism; we must implement an approach of integrated and comprehensive arrangement, and mobilise all positive forces in order to build socialism". In his closing speech to the 11th CPC National Congress, Deng Xiaoping called on the party to restore and carry forward the fine traditions and working style of the mass line, seeking truth from facts, criticism and self-criticism, modesty and prudence, guarding against pride, arduous struggle and democratic centralism established by Mao Zedong for the whole party, so that the whole party, army and nation would strive to create a political climate which is both centralised and democratic, both disciplined and free, characterised by freedom, having both a unified will and a calm yet lively mood.

Although the 11th CPC National Congress, as a result of the limitations caused by the historical limitations of the times, was not able to undertake the task of correcting the mistakes of the Cultural Revolution and formulating correct lines and policies for the realisation of a historical turn-around, it played a positive role in exposing and criticising the Gang of Four and mobilising the whole party to build a strong modern socialist country, and played an important role in restoring and stabilising the ruling order. After the 11th CPC National Congress, provinces, regions and municipalities successively held new local party congresses and elected new party committees in accordance with the new party constitution. Organs directly under the central government, central state organs and people's organisations also successively re-established party committees or groups. The newly created party committees or party groups employed a large number of tried and tested veteran cadres who had been attacked during the Cultural Revolution, with the result that the leadership of the party in various regions and departments was enriched and strengthened.

After the 11th CPC National Congress, the NPC and the CPPCC, which had ceased their activities during the Cultural Revolution, gradually resumed their normal activities, and the First Session of the Fifth NPC was convened ahead of time from February to March 1978.

The congress adopted a resolution on the government work report, regarded building China into a modern socialist power within the 20th century as the new long march in the new period, adopted the revised the *Constitution of the People's Republic of China*, adopted the national anthem of the PRC, deliberated and approved the *Outline of the 10-Year Plan for the Development of the National Economy from 1976 to 1985 (Draft)*, and elected leaders of the party and the state, leading to the return of a group of highly respected veteran cadres to leadership positions. At the same time as this, the First Session of the Fifth National Committee of the CPPCC was also held in Beijing and elected Deng Xiaoping as its chairman. Starting from the Fifth NPC and the Fifth National Committee of the CPPCC, the timing, procedures and main content of discussions of the two meetings were basically determined.

After this, women's federations, trade unions, the Communist Youth League of China and other mass organisations also successively resumed their normal activities. In September 1978, the Fourth National Congress of the All-China Women's Federation was held in Beijing. That October, the Ninth National Congress of the All-China Federation of Trade Unions was also held, as was, in the same month, the 10th National Congress of the Communist Youth League. During the preparation for the 10th Congress of the Communist Youth League, the CPC Central Committee also approved the abolition of the Red Guards organisation in schools, and the 1st Plenary Session of the 10th Central Committee of the Communist Youth League also decided to abolish the organisation of the Little Red Guards and restore the Young Pioneers, which had ceased its activities for 11 years.

After the smashing of the Gang of Four, in order to put an end to the chaotic situation of the Cultural Revolution, the CPC carried out a comprehensive campaign to expose and criticise the Gang of Four, rehabilitated persecuted veteran cadres, proposed the main task of grasping guiding principles for national governance, restored and stabilised the ruling order, strove for and safeguarded a united and stable political situation, and created the preconditions for bringing order out of chaos, achieving a great historical turnaround, implementing reform and opening up, and pioneering a new path of governance.

(II) THE REALISATION OF A GREAT HISTORICAL TURNAROUND

The 3rd Plenary Session of the 11th CPC Central Committee, held from 18 to 22 December 1978, at a critical historical juncture when the party and the state were faced with the question of which direction to take from that point, made the historic decision to shift the work focus of the party and the state to economic construction, and implementing reform and opening up, thereby achieving a great turning point of profound significance in the history of the party since the founding of new China. This is a sign that China's socialist construction had embarked on a new path and pioneered a new period of reform and opening up, and it was also the beginning of the CPC's opening up of a new path and new context for governance.

The party's great historical turnaround was premised on criticism of the Two Whatevers and the emancipation of the mind. After the smashing of the Gang of Four, the masses of cadres, faced with the ideological obstructions caused by the Two Whatevers, began to realise that in order to completely clarify the ideological confusion caused by Lin Biao and the Gang of Four, it was vital to first solve these problems and determine the appropriate attitude for dealing with Mao's instructions. After all, what is the standard for determining right and wrong in historical events? Under the strong demand of the masses of cadres to bring order out of chaos, a group of cadres and theoretical workers began to break free from the shackles of the Two Whatevers, discussing the issue of the criterion of

298

truth in various settings, and mulling over and composing related articles.

On 10 May 1978, the internal publication of the Central Party School, *Theoretical Trends*, published the article *Practice is the Only Criterion for Testing Truth*, which was approved by Hu Yaobang, Vice President of the Central Party School. On 11 May, the *Guangming Daily* published this article in the name of a commissioned commentator. This article distinctly proposed that social practice is not only a criterion for testing truth, but also the *only criterion* for this. The theoretical treasury of Marxism is not a pile of rigid and unchanging creeds, therefore it was necessary to touch upon areas where the Gang of Four sought to confine people's thinking and determine right and wrong[3]. Although this article was only a positive exposition of common knowledge about Marxism, it actually criticised the Two Whatevers and immediately led to a heated debate about the two concepts of the Two Whatevers and seeking truth from facts.

At the critical moment, Deng Xiaoping gave timely and strong support to the great discussion on the criterion of truth. In June 1978, he delivered a speech at the All-Army Political Work Conference, focusing on elaborating Mao Zedong's views on seeking truth from facts, criticising the erroneous attitudes of the Two Whatevers in the handling of Mao Zedong and Mao Zedong Thought, and issuing the call that, 'we must purge the poison of Lin Biao and the Gang of Four, bring order out of chaos, and break off spiritual shackles, so that we can achieve the great emancipation of our minds'[4]. Thereafter, the *PLA Daily*, *People's Daily*, *Guangming Daily* and other newspapers successively published articles, and many veteran comrades also supported or participated in the discussion in different ways. With the support of the older generation of revolutionaries, the heads of various departments of the central government, localities and the military all in turn delivered speeches or published articles to show their support, and the theoretical, academic and journalistic circles stood at the forefront of the discussion and participated enthusiastically. Practice has fully demonstrated that the issue of the criterion of truth is not an issue pertaining to theoretical points of view but also a major political issue related to the future prospects of the party and the state. The great discussion on the criterion of truth has provided the ideological precedent for the party and the state to re-establish the ideological line of seeking truth from facts and achieve a great historical turnaround.

The great historical turnaround the party achieved started when the party and state shifted the focus of their work. From the founding of new China up to the Cultural Revolution, the CPC implemented difficult explorations to shift the focus of work. Due to the expansion of class struggle, the party's work gradually deviated from a focus on economic construction, and economic construction failed to achieve anticipated success. After the end of the Cultural Revolution, the Party Central Committee, in the process of leading the campaign to expose and criticise the Gang of Four, raised the issue of shifting the work focus of the party and the state.

From July to September 1978, the State Council held a retreat to focus on studying the issue of how to accelerate China's modernisation. On the basis of summarising lessons learned, many participants put forward proposals to reform the rigid economic management system and introduce advanced foreign technology and capital. Li Xiannian concluded the meeting by pointing out that accomplishing the four modernisations constituted a great revolution which would fundamentally change China's economic and technological backwardness, that this revolution would therefore significantly change China's then backward state of productivity and would inevitably change socioeconomic relations and the superstructure in many ways. He also said that it was vital to have the courage and ability to use foreign advanced technology, equipment, capital and organisational experience to accelerate construction, and not miss the very rare opportunity China was faced with at the time.

In late September that year, the State Council held a national planning meeting and proposed that three changes must be implemented in economic work. First, attention must be turned to the struggle for production and technological revolution. Second, management systems and methods which handle affairs in accordance with economic laws, and a robust combination of democracy and centralisation must be transferred to the path of scientific management and, third, there must be a move to an open policy of switching from a closed or semi-closed state to actively introducing advanced foreign technology, using foreign capital, and boldly entering the international market.

In September 1978, when calls for reform and opening up were getting stronger throughout the party, Deng Xiaoping visited northeast China and other places. He repeatedly stressed that the most urgent task facing China at that time was to develop productivity. China was too poor and too backward, he said, and he honestly felt that the people had been let down. He said that with China as a socialist country, the fundamental manifestation of the superiority of the socialist system was that it allows social productivity to develop rapidly at a rate not seen in China's former society, meaning that it was possible for the growing material and cultural needs of the people to be met. According to historical materialism, the fruits of correct political leadership are ultimately demonstrated by the development of social productivity and the improvement in people's material and cultural life. He went on to say that it was now necessary to accelerate the development of productivity and improve the material and cultural life of the people[5]. As a result of this, Deng Xiaoping proposed to end the mass movement to expose and criticise the Gang of Four in due course and shift the work focus of the party and the state to socialist modernisation. These ideas of Deng Xiaoping laid a solid foundation for achieving a great historical turnaround and for pioneering a new path for governance.

In October 1978, Deng Xiaoping further elaborated on the idea of shifting the focus of work in his message to the Ninth National Congress of the All-China Federation of Trade Unions. He said that the struggle to expose and criticise the Gang of Four had "achieved a decisive victory on a broad scale throughout the country, and we have been able to start a new battle on the basis of this victory", namely carrying out "a great revolution that will fundamentally change the economic and technological backwardness of our country and further consolidate the dictatorship of the proletariat" and accelerate the pace of socialist modernisation[6]. Deng Xiaoping's views on shifting the work focus of the party and the state were strongly endorsed by the Politburo and were included as important topics in the Central Work Conference and the 3rd Plenary Session of the 11th CPC Central Committee which were about to be convened.

From 10 November to 15 December 1978, the CPC Central Committee held its Central Work Conference. The conference was originally supposed to discuss economic work and the established agenda of the conference did not mention the great debate over the issue of the criterion of truth that had already been launched or the issues of correcting the party's ideological line and redressing unjust and false charges that were of general concern both within and outside the party. In response to this, many comrades who wished first to resolve the question of the rights and wrongs of the ideological line and major historical rights and wrongs were very dissatisfied. Chen Yun took the lead in proposing a systematic solution to the historical legacy, drawing strong reactions from most participants, which resulted in a change to the agenda of the meeting. On 25 November, at the strong request of the comrades present, the Politburo made the decision to redress the Tiananmen Incident and the case of "Bo Yibo and the Group of 61 Other Traitors" and other miscarriages of justice, thereby solving a number of major historical legacies. The meeting discussed the differences of opinion on the issue of the criterion of truth. After the exchange of ideas, the meeting called more strongly for the establishment of the ideological line of seeking truth from facts.

On 13 December, at the closing session of the Central Work Conference, Deng Xiaoping gave a speech entitled *Emancipating the Mind, Seeking Truth from Facts, Uniting as One and Looking to the Future*. He pointed out that it is first necessary to emancipate the mind and only when the mind has been emancipated is it possible to properly solve the problems left over from the past and solve a series of newly emerged problems with Marxism-Leninism and Mao Zedong Thought as the guide. He said that for a party, a state and a people, if everything starts from books, then ideology becomes rigid and superstition prevails, such that they cannot move forward and their vitality will cease, and the party and state will perish. He also proposed the task of reforming the economic system and sternly admonished the whole party, saying, "If we do not implement reform now, then modernisation and socialism will be buried"[7]. At a major historical juncture when China was facing the question of the appropriate direction to take, this speech constituted a manifesto for bringing about a new period of reform and opening up and pioneering a new path of governance and, in fact, became the thematic report of the subsequent 3rd Plenary Session of the 11th CPC Central Committee.

From 18 to 22 December, the 3rd Plenary Session of the 11th CPC Central Committee was convened. The plenary session held that the mass movement to expose and criticise Lin Biao and the Gang of Four should be concluded, and the focus of the work of the party and the state should be shifted to socialist modernisation in a timely and decisive manner. The plenary session completely rejected the policy of the Two Whatevers and re-established the guiding ideology of emancipating the mind and seeking truth from facts, thereby accomplishing the reordering of the ideological line, and also ceased using the slogan "taking class struggle as the central task" and made the decision to shift the work focus of the party and the state, thereby successfully bringing order out of chaos along political lines. The plenary session formed the second generation of the party's central leadership with Comrade Deng Xiaoping as the core, thereby achieving the most important result of bringing order out of chaos along organisational lines. It revived the party's fine tradition of democratic centralism and proposed the important task of institutionalising and legalising democracy, and reviewed and resolved a number of major issues left over from history and the merits and demerits of some important leaders, and began to bring order out of chaos by systematically clearing up major historical rights and wrongs. The plenary session also proposed that the historical status of Mao Zedong and the scientific system of Mao Zedong Thought should be treated correctly, pointing out the direction for correcting Mao's mistakes in his later years and for upholding and developing Mao Zedong Thought.

The new decision to implement reform and opening up made at this plenary session began the historic transformation of China from taking class struggle as the central task to a focus on economic construction, from rigidity and semi-rigidity to comprehensive reform, and from a closed or semi-closed state to opening up to the outside world, and laid a solid foundation for the party to explore a new path of socialist construction and pioneer a new situation for governance under the guidance of correct ideology. Marked by the 3rd Plenary Session of the 11th CPC Central Committee, 'China has since entered a new period in the development of the socialist cause'[8].

The 3rd Plenary Session of the 11th CPC Central Committee, at a critical historical juncture when the party and the country were faced with the question of which direction to take from that point, guided by the re-established ideological line of emancipating the mind and seeking truth from facts, broke through the confines of the Two Whatevers and achieved the historic transformation from taking class struggle as the central task to a focus on economic construction, from rigidity and semi-rigidity to comprehensive reform, and from a closed or semi-closed state to opening up to the outside world. The CPC has since opened up a new way to build socialism, pioneered a new path of governance, and opened up the only path to accomplish the transformation for the Chinese nation from standing up to becoming rich and strong.

(III) DETERMINING NEW GOVERNANCE OBJECTIVES AND TASKS

After the 3rd Plenary Session of the 11th CPC Central Committee, the second generation of the party's central leadership with Comrade Deng Xiaoping at its core proposed the idea of Chinese-style modernisation starting with China's actual situation, based on the party's goal since the founding of new China of building China into a strong socialist country with modern agriculture, industry, defence, and science and technology in the 20th century beginning from China's actual situation, and made constructing a moderately prosperous society the phased governance objective of the CPC. The introduction of this new governance objective summarised the lessons learned from China's socialist construction and played an important role in mobilising and motivating the whole party and all the people of China to devote themselves to socialist modernisation.

After the founding of new China, the CPC put forward the phased governance objective of achieving the Four Modernisations in order to build socialism. In December 1964, on the advice of Chairman Mao Zedong, Premier Zhou Enlai solemnly declared to the people of China in his *Government Work Report* at the First Session of the Third NPC, "The main task of developing the national economy henceforth is, in general, to build China into a socialist power with modern agriculture, modern industry, modern defence, and modern science and technology within a relatively short historical period, and to catch up with and surpass the advanced levels of the world." He also specifically stated, "In order to accomplish this great historical task, starting from the third five-year plan, the development of China's national economy can be considered in two steps: the first step is to establish an independent and relatively complete industrial system and national economy, and the second step is to fully modernise agriculture, industry, defence, and science and technology, so that our economy will be at the forefront globally"[9]. In January 1975, Premier Zhou Enlai reiterated at the Fourth NPC the governance objective of achieving the Four Modernisations, that is, starting from the third five-year plan, that the development of China's national economy could be envisioned in two steps: the first step being to build an independent and relatively complete industrial system and national economy in 15 years, namely, by 1980, and the second step being to fully modernise agriculture, industry, defence, and science and technology in the 20th century, so that China's national economy would be at the forefront globally.

Although the governance objective of the Four Modernisations was not achieved by the end of the 20th century and was gradually replaced by the goal of moderate prosperity of affluent people through Chinese-style modernisation, it played a motivating role in the CPC's phased governance objective to gradually establish an independent and relatively complete industrial system and national economy, and to lay an important material and technical foundation for China's socialist modernisation.

One important reason why the governance objective of the Four Modernisations was not achieved was the serious impact of the Cultural Revolution. During the Cultural Revolution, due to the prevalence of ultra-leftist thinking and anarchy, and the intentional disruption and sabotaging of economic work by the Gang of Four, China's main economic proportionality was out of balance for a long time, the economic management system became increasingly rigid, and the entire national economy was on the verge of collapse. During the 10 years of the Cultural Revolution, the loss of national income amounted to Rmb500 billion, according to the projection of accrued benefits of 100 yuan of investment in a normal year. People's living standards were basically not improved and the gap between China and the developed countries widened further. Just as Deng

Xiaoping pointed out, "there was a gap between China and the world in the early 1960s but it was not too wide. In the 11 to 12 years from the late 1960s to the 1970s, the gap between China and the world grew too wide"[10]. It is for this reason that in October 1976, after smashing the Gang of Four and ending the Cultural Revolution, the whole country had an acute sense of the precious time lost and the great losses suffered during the Cultural Revolution, and was therefore anxious to make up for the lost time and losses suffered, and so accelerated the development of China's socialist modernisation.

In the late 1970s, in order to achieve the Four Modernisations and accelerate the development of China's national economy, the party and the government put forward the goal of making a leap forward in economic construction and took the introduction of foreign advanced technology and equipment as the way to achieve it. In February 1978, the *Government Work Report* adopted at the First Session of the Fifth NPC proposed [as follows]: in the next eight years the country plans to build or continue building 120 large-scale projects, including 10 major iron and steel bases, 9 major non-ferrous metal bases, 8 major coal bases, 10 major oil and gas fields, 30 major power stations, 6 new railroad trunk lines and 5 major ports. In September 1978, the State Council, based on the opinions of the Standing Committee of the Politburo retreat, proposed to "organise a new great leap forward", "to achieve modernisation at a faster pace than originally envisioned, and to achieve a higher degree of modernisation by the end of the century". Under the guidance of this ideology, China swiftly signed many import contracts with foreign countries in 1978 without adequate evidence and overall equilibrium. According to statistics, the contracts signed that year for the introduction of new technologies and complete sets of equipment totalled US$7.8 billion involving more than 50 projects, about half of which were signed in a short 10-day period from 20 December to the end of the year, creating great potential pitfalls. Objectively speaking, the original intention of China's large-scale economic construction at that time was good, and the direction of vigorously introducing and using foreign technology, equipment and capital was also correct, but because the scale spread too far too fast, it exceeded the comprehensive national power and China's actual conditions, and so the national economy had to be adjusted.

In March 1979, Li Xiannian and Chen Yun sent a joint letter to the CPC Central Committee on financial and economic work, proposing that the steps forward should be steady, not erratic again, and that it was vital to avoid repetition and becoming derailed on the way to achieving new successes. Additionally, they said that in borrowing foreign debt it was necessary to give full consideration to parties' ability to repay capital and interest payments, consider domestic investment capacity, and generally achieve gradual progress. They said, "There is no overall equilibrium in the national economy now. The disproportionality is quite serious" and, "It will take a period of two or three years of adjustment before the disproportionality in all areas can be generally adjusted upwards"[11]. Deng Xiaoping was very supportive of the idea of adjustment and said that the central task was a three-year adjustment. He said that this was the general orientation and a major policy, and that after the adjustment, new production capacity would be formed more quickly. For this adjustment, it was first of all necessary to have determination; trying to run here and there to attend to every single detail would not work, and only with great determination could a great job be done. In April 1979, the Central Work Conference decided to implement the new so-called eight-character policy of "adjustment, reform, consolidation and improvement" for the national economy and to spend three years on adjusting the national economy.

In the process of adjusting the national economy, Deng Xiaoping repeatedly thought about starting with China's existing problems, summarised the lessons learned from China's socialist construction, proposed the goal of Chinese-style modernisation, adjusted and improved the governance objective of the Four Modernisations, and proposed the concept of a "moderately prosperous society".

In March 1979, when Deng Xiaoping met with a delegation of the Executive Committee of the Anglo-Chinese Cultural Council, he clearly proposed the concept of the "Chinese-style Four Modernisations". He said, "The goal we set is to achieve the Four Modernisations by the end of this century. Our concept is different from that in the West, and I shall tentatively use a new term, the Chinese-style Four Modernisations.' Why was it necessary to redefine the Four Modernisations? Deng Xiaoping made it very clear that in light of conditions in China that was the only governance objective that could be achieved." He said, "Now we are still at the level of technology you had in the West in the 1950s. If we can reach the level you had in the 1970s by the end of this century, it will be very impressive. Even to reach this level, we still have to work very hard. Due to our lack of experience, achieving the Four Modernisations may be a little more difficult than we imagine"[12].

In October 1979, Deng Xiaoping pointed out in his speech at a symposium of the first secretaries of provinces, cities and autonomous regions convened by the CPC Central Committee to discuss the adjustment of the national economy, "What we call politics is the Four Modernisations. We have set a grand goal to achieve the Four Modernisations by the end of this century. Later, we changed the name and called it Chinese-style modernisation, which means lowering the standard a bit. In particular, the GNP, on a per capita basis, will not be very high.' In response to some people who felt that lower development goals and growth targets would 'pour cold water' on modernisation, Deng Xiaoping pointed out, "I agree that the strength should be drummed up and not allowed to leak away. But I want to emphasise one point, which is that we need to drum up real strength, not drum up false strength"[13].

In May 1980, when meeting with former British Prime Minister and Labour Party leader James Callaghan, Deng Xiaoping said, "There is a gap between what we initially envisaged and the actual situation we encountered in our fumbling around", "Our ambition is to achieve the Four Modernisations and to do so by the end of this century. The difference between our Four Modernisations and the modernisation of developed countries, including your country, the UK, is that the population of China is too large, such that if we wanted to achieve a modernisation like yours, with an annual per capita income of US$5,000 to US$7,000, it wouldn't be possible. So, the modernisation we propose is a Chinese-style modernisation"[14].

From the perspective of Deng Xiaoping's discourse, the governance objective of Chinese-style Modernisation was proposed mainly because the Four Modernisations were disturbed by the Cultural Revolution and it was difficult to achieve them according to the original plan. So, it was necessary to propose a more realistic, pragmatic and effective governance objective based on a sober understanding of the arduousness of China's development. In this way, with the adjustment of the national economy and the deepening of the understanding of China's actual national conditions, Deng Xiaoping became clearer and more specific regarding the governance objective of Chinese-style Modernisation and advanced the governance objective of achieving a moderately prosperous society, gradually setting the standard of a moderately prosperous family as meaning an annual per capita income of US$800.

In December 1979, in response to Japanese Prime Minister Ohira Masayoshi's question about what China would be like in the future and how the blueprint for modernisation was conceived, Deng Xiaoping introduced the governance objective of Chinese-style Modernisation and defined it as achieving moderate prosperity. Deng Xiaoping said, "The Four Modernisations we want to achieve are a distinctly Chinese four modernisations. Our conceptualisation of the Four Modernisations is not like your conceptualisation of modernisation but, rather, of a moderately prosperous family. By the end of this century, even if China's Four

Modernisations reach a certain goal, our GDP per capita level will still be very low. It will take a lot of effort to reach the level of the richer countries in the Third World with, for example, a GDP of US$1000 per capita. Even if we reach that level, compared with the West we will still be lagging behind. Therefore, I can only say that China at that time will still only be in a state of moderate prosperity"[15]. Deng Xiaoping explicitly referred to Chinese-style Modernisation as a moderately prosperous family, and the standard he stated was a GDP of US$1000 per capita.

In April 1981, Deng Xiaoping pointed out in a meeting with the Japan-China Friendship Parliamentarians' Union delegation during their visit to China that China was steadfastly "hurrying towards the distinctly Chinese Four Modernisations and suggested that China would not only fail to reach the level of Japan, Europe, the US and some developed countries in the Third World by the end of the 20th century but also the previously envisaged doubling of GDP in 10 years and quadrupling in 20 years. Through this period of fumbling around, he said they had also discovered that even increasing per capita GDP to US$1,000 was not easy and that, "for example with US$800 or US$900, even US$800 is also considered a moderately prosperous standard of living"[16].

In April 1982, when meeting with the head of state of Guinea-Bissau, Deng Xiaoping pointed out that, "the modernisation we are engaged in is not Western modernisation but Chinese-style Modernisation, that is, modernisation to reach a moderately prosperous society. It will take at least 30 to 50 years to accomplish. Now we are trying to achieve the 20-year goal of the first stage, which is to reach a per capita GDP of US$800 by the end of this century"[17].

In August 1982, when Deng Xiaoping and Deng Yingchao met with Chinese American scientists, they emphasised, "We propose to bring about change in 20 years; this is not an unrealistic utopian fantasy or big, empty talk but only a change to achieve a moderately prosperous society, and it is assured. Moderate prosperity means that the GNP reaches US$1trillion, and US$800 per capita'[18].

According to Deng Xiaoping's treatise, what he referred to as 'moderate prosperity' is not simply an economic indicator. In the spring of 1983, when Deng Xiaoping visited Jiangsu, Zhejiang and Shanghai for work inspections, he asked the leaders of Jiangsu Province what the prospects for social development would be if that province reached the level of the total industrial and agricultural output value of Suzhou City of close to US$800 per capita. He was not only concerned with people's livelihoods in terms of food, clothing and housing, the construction of small towns, employment, population mobility and labour transfer but also with future social issues such as education, culture, sports and other public welfare undertakings, as well as changes in spiritual outlook. It can be seen that the moderately prosperous society Deng Xiaoping envisaged refers to Chinese-style Modernisation, which is at a relatively low level with Chinese characteristics, and constitutes the primary stage of socialism.

In September 1982, the 12th CPC National Congress, based on Deng Xiaoping's idea of moderate prosperity and a moderately prosperous society, set the general goal of China's economic construction in the 20th century, namely, "On the premise of continuously improving economic efficiency, we will strive to quadruple the annual gross output value of the country's industry and agriculture, that is, from Rmb710 billion in 1980 to about Rmb2.8 trillion in 2000. When this goal is achieved, China's total national income and the output of major industrial and agricultural products will rank among the top in the world, the modernisation of the entire national economy will have made significant progress, the income of urban and rural people will have increased exponentially, and the material and cultural life of the people will be able to reach the level of moderate prosperity"[19]. From then on, the moderately prosperous society was taken up by the whole party and has become the new governance objective of the CPC.

The moderately prosperous society proposed by Deng Xiaoping originated from the party's realistic thinking about the governance objective of realising the Four Modernisations and was born from the governing ideology of Chinese-style Modernisation and linked to the economic development strategy of 'quadrupling GDP'. This new governance objective of achieving a moderately prosperous society fitted well with traditional Chinese culture and social psychology, reflected the aspirations and pursuit of the Chinese people for a better social life, embodied the people's common enjoyment of a higher level of material and spiritual civilisation, and reflected the CPC's aim of striving for the happiness of the people. At the same time, it was in line with the realities of China's economic and social development, and focused on the unity of long-term and short-term goals, helping to prevent impatience and repeating the mistakes of history. It lay the foundation for the formulation of China's 'three-step' strategy for economic and social development and took solid steps for the CPC to unite and lead the whole party and people to achieve the great rejuvenation of the Chinese nation.

(IV) REFORM OF THE PARTY AND STATE LEADERSHIP SYSTEM

After the 3rd Plenary Session of the 11th CPC Central Committee, the party began to reflect on the causes of the Cultural Revolution, summarised in depth the lessons learned from the party's leadership and governance style since the founding of new China and, in accordance with the objectives and tasks of promoting socialist democracy and improving the socialist legal system proposed at the 3rd Plenary Session of the 11th Central Committee, took reforming the party and state leadership system as an important issue in exploring the governance style and reform of the political system, strengthened and improved the leadership of the party, and consolidated the socialist system, promoting socialist democracy and mobilising the initiative of party members, cadres and the people.

At the outset of reform and opening up in 1978, the CPC raised the issue of how the party should govern in response to the governance lessons learned from the Cultural Revolution and set in motion reform of the party and state leadership system. In December 1978, in his speech *Emancipating the Mind, Seeking Truth from Facts, and Looking Forward with Unity* delivered at the closing session of the Central Work Conference, on the basis of offering the sharp criticism that, "strengthening the leadership of the party has turned into the party running everything and intervening in everything; practicing monolithic leadership has turned into a lack of separation between the party and the government, and substituting the party for the government", Deng Xiaoping clearly pointed out, "In order to guarantee the people's democracy, the legal system must be strengthened. Democracy must be institutionalised and legalised so that such institutions and laws do not change with the change of leaders, or with the change of their views and the amount of attention they pay"[20]. The 3rd Plenary Session of the 11th CPC Central Committee emphasised in this regard that in order to guarantee the people's democracy, it would be necessary to strengthen the socialist legal system, and to institutionalise and legalise democracy, so that these institutions and laws would have stability, continuity and great authority, so that there would be a legal foundation, compliance with the law, strict law enforcement and investigations of violations. From that time on, the plenary session insisted, legislative work should be placed on the important agendas of the NPC and its standing committee, the procuratorial and judicial organs should maintain their due independence and be faithful to the law and institutions, to the interests of the people and to the truth, and ensure that there be equality for all in view of the law and not allow anyone to have privileges above the law[21].

In July 1979, in view of the various painful lessons learned through the lawlessness of the Cultural Revolution, the Second Session of the Fifth NPC adopted seven laws, namely: the *Organic Law of the People's Congresses of the PRC at Local Levels and Local People's Governments at All Levels*; the *Law of the PRC on the Election of the NPC and Local People's Congresses at All Levels*; the *Organic Law of the People's Courts of the PRC*; the *Organic Law of the People's Procuratorate of the PRC*; the *Criminal Law of the PRC*; the *Criminal Procedure Law of the PRC*; and the *Law of the PRC on Chinese-Foreign Equity Joint Ventures*; in order to strengthen the construction of the socialist democratic legal system, which constituted an important step in promoting the legalisation of the socialist democratic legal system. Peng Zhen, who was elected vice chairman of the NPC Standing Committee at the meeting, explained the seven draft laws. He said, "To develop socialist democracy, we must gradually improve the socialist legal system so that the nine hundred million people have rules to follow and when law-breakers commit crimes there are restraints and sanctions. As a result, the people all long to have a sound legal system"[22].

According to the new laws adopted at the Second Session of the Fifth NPC, local people's congresses at all levels above the county level set up party committees consisting of a director and deputy director, and a few members, and local revolutionary committees at all levels were transformed into people's governments, with the titles of provincial governors, municipal mayors, autonomous region chairmen, state governors and county governors being accordingly restored. The new laws also stipulated that the people's congresses of provinces, autonomous regions and municipalities directly under the central government and their standing committees may, in accordance with the specific conditions and practical needs of their administrative regions, formulate and promulgate local laws and regulations, provided that they do not contradict the constitution, laws, policies, ordinances and decrees of the state.

This provision expanded local power and greatly mobilised local motivation and initiative to implement construction of the legal system. The new provisions also included changing the election of deputies to the NPC at all levels from majority to competitive elections, expanding the scope of direct election of deputies to the NPC to the county level, and not subjecting deputies to arrest or trial at local levels above the county level, except with the consent of the people's congress standing committee at that level.

In response to the reality of the common and wanton violations of human rights that occurred during the Cultural Revolution, the newly adopted Criminal Law clearly stipulated that one of the important tasks of the Criminal Law was to protect the legitimate property of private citizens, to protect the personal, democratic and other rights of citizens, and to strictly prohibit the use of torture to extract confessions, the gathering of crowds to vandalise and steal property, illegal detention or other means of illegally depriving people of their personal freedom, and false accusations. The formulation and adoption of these basic laws marked China's entry onto the track of expanding socialist democracy and improving the socialist legal system, and also marked the beginning of a change in the party's governing method.

In the 1980s, in accordance with the requirements of reform, governance and refining the socialist system, and in the face of the exceptionally difficult and onerous task of reform, opening up and socialist modernisation, the CPC Central Committee adopted a series of major measures to accelerate promotion of the reform of the party and state leadership system on the basis of a profound analysis of the various shortcomings in said system.

From 18 to 23 August 1980, the Politburo convened an enlarged meeting to discuss reform of the party and state leadership system and some related issues. There Deng Xiaoping delivered a speech on *Reform of the Party and State Leadership System* in which he discussed in depth the importance and necessity of reforming said system as well as the purpose, requirements and steps of implementation of the reform.

Deng Xiaoping pointed out that the reason why it was necessary to implement reforms in the party and state leadership system was that there were still many shortcomings in the system and in some specific existing systems in China, which were hindering or even seriously impeding exercise of the superiorities of socialism and affecting governance efficiency. These shortcomings, in terms of the party and state leadership system and the cadre system, were mainly bureaucratic phenomena, and phenomena surrounding excessive concentration of power, patriarchy, cadres being in leadership positions for life, and all sorts of privileges. He said that if the shortcomings of the current system were not resolutely reformed, some of the serious problems which had appeared in the past may reappear again in the future.

Deng Xiaoping emphasised that the various mistakes the party had made in the past were certainly related to the ideology and working style of certain leaders but the problems in the organisational system and work system were more important. This aspect of the system effectively prevented bad people from running amok at will but if the system were not good then it would hinder good people from doing good things and even make them do bad things. Issues pertaining to the leadership and organisational systems were of an even more fundamental, all-encompassing, stable and long-term nature. He said the whole party must pay great attention to this type of systemic problem, which is related to whether the party and the country should change colour [political identity], and that only with a planned, systematic, yet resolute and thorough reform of these shortcomings would the people believe in the leadership of the CPC, trust the party and socialism, and imbue the party's cause with unlimited hope.

Deng Xiaoping pointed out that the Central Committee was considering implementing a gradual major reform of the party and state leadership system. First, the Central Committee would advance a proposal to the Third Session of the Fifth NPC to amend the constitution. He said the constitution should be made to effectively guarantee that the people would truly enjoy the right to manage the organisation of the state at all levels and all enterprises and undertakings, and enjoy full civil rights, that each ethnic group would truly exercise ethnic regional autonomy, and that the system of people's congresses at all levels should be improved. The issue of not allowing excessive concentration of power was also to be reflected in the constitution. Second, the Central Committee had already established a committee for discipline inspection and was considering setting up another advisory committee which, together with the Central Committee, was to be elected by the party's national general congress and would have their respective tasks and powers clearly defined. Third, a robust working system from the State Council to local governments at all levels from top to bottom should be truly established. In the future, the State Council and local governments at all levels would discuss, decide and issue documents on all work within the government's remit, and no longer would the Party Central Committee and local party committees at all levels issue instructions and make decisions. Fourth, there are preparations and steps to change the system of factory directors and managers under the leadership of the party committee, and after piloting, gradually promote and separately implement a system of factory directors and managers under the leadership and supervision of factory management committees, company boards of directors and joint committees of economic consortia. Fifth, all enterprises and institutions would universally set up staff congresses or staff representative meetings. Sixth, party committees at all levels should truly implement an integrated system of collective leadership and individual division of labour, and major issues must be discussed and decided by the collective. When making decisions it was vital to strictly implement a system of majority rule with one person one vote, with secretaries only having the right to one vote, and where the final say would not rest with the first secretary[23].

Deng Xiaoping emphasised that reforming the party and state leadership system was not in order to weaken party leadership or make party discipline lax but rather precisely in order to uphold and strengthen the leadership of the party and party discipline. The central point was that the party must be good at leading, and only by constantly improving its leadership would it be able to strengthen it. Reforming and refining the various party and state institutions constitutes a difficult and long-term task, and reforming and refining the party and state leadership system was the key to accomplishing this task.

In summary, this speech of Deng Xiaoping put forward the basic idea of reforming the party and state leadership system and indicated the direction for the reform of China's political system. The constitution is the general charter for governing China and must reflect the historical progress of the cause of the party and the people and be constantly refined and developed in step with the development of the practice of building socialism. In September 1980, the Third Session of the Fifth NPC decided to implement a comprehensive revision of the 1978 Constitution based on the proposal of the CPC Central Committee.

On 4 December 1982, after extensive consultation and many studies and discussions by the Party Central Committee, the Fifth Session of the Fifth NPC deliberated and approved the newly revised 'Constitution of the People's Republic of China'. The new constitution, in the form of a fundamental law, made provisions for major aspects including China's fundamental and basic political institutions, the basic economic system, the fundamental tasks of the state, the basic rights and duties of citizens, the establishment and duties of state institutions, and what constituted the foundation of the CPC's rule in the new period of reform and opening up.

The new constitution clearly stated that the state institutions of the PRC shall apply the principle of democratic centralism. In accordance with this principle, the new constitution made many important new provisions on the establishment of state institutions, the main ones being outlined below. First, the system of people's congresses was to be strengthened and refined by transferring some of the powers and functions previously belonging to the NPC to its Standing Committee, by expanding the powers and functions of the NPC Standing Committee and strengthening its organisation so that the NPC and its Standing Committee may exercise the legislative power of the state, meaning that, except for basic laws, which are formulated by the NPC, other laws were to be formulated by the NPC Standing Committee. The positions of state president and vice president were restored, and the state president was to represent the PRC. Next, the leadership system of the State Council was improved, putting the premier in charge, and the Standing Committee of the State Council was to be comprised of the premier, vice premier, state councillors and the secretary general, with the premier convening and presiding over the Standing Committee and the plenary sessions of the State Council. Also, the Central Military Commission (CMC) was established to lead the national armed forces, with the CMC being under the responsibility of the chairman and accountable to the NPC and its Standing Committee. Under the unified leadership of the central government, the building of local power was strengthened in the following ways: standing committees were established in local people's congresses at all levels above the county level, provincial and municipal people's congresses and their standing committees were empowered to enact and promulgate local laws and regulations; local people's governments at all levels were to be responsible for the system of provincial governors, mayors, county governors, district governors, village chiefs and township governors, and the system of the unity of government and society in rural people's communes was changed, with village (township) authorities being established. The positions of state president, vice president, chairman and vice chairman of the NPC Standing Committee, premier and vice premier of the State Council and state councillors, president of the Supreme People's Court and attorney general of the Supreme People's Procuratorate were established, and state leaders were prohibited from serving more than two consecutive terms.

These new provisions of the new constitution were suited to the new requirements of reform and opening up, and modernisation, summarised the initial experience of the reform of the party and state leadership system, and were of great significance in strengthening the socialist legal system and promoting modernisation of the national system of governance and governability. Peng Zhen, who was in charge of the revision of this new constitution, said in his report on behalf of the Constitutional Revision Committee, "The direction of the new constitution and the requirements embodied in these provisions aim, first, to enable the people as a whole to better exercise state power, second, to enable state organs to more effectively lead and organise the cause of socialist construction and, third, to enable the various state organs to better divide their work and cooperate with each other'[24].

For the CPC to achieve its governance objectives, it must play a role in strengthening and improving the party's leadership role. The purpose of reforming the party and state leadership system, promoting socialist democracy and developing the socialist legal system, is to improve the party's governing method, raise the party's level of governance and lay the institutional cornerstone for the party's long-term rule.

Just as Deng Xiaoping pointed out, "If the shortcomings in the present system are not resolutely reformed, some of the serious problems that have arisen in the past are likely to reappear in the future. Only by carrying out a planned, systematic, yet resolute and thorough reform of these shortcomings will the people trust our leadership, the party and socialism, and will our cause have unlimited hope"[25]. In the process of promoting socialist modernisation, reforming the party and state leadership system, and refining governance methods constitutes a long-term task of great significance.

(V) THE BASIC COMPLETION OF THE TASK OF BRINGING ORDER OUT OF CHAOS AND THE PRELIMINARY SUMMARY OF THE GOVERNING EXPERIENCE

After the 3rd Plenary Session of the 11th CPC Central Committee, the second generation of the party's central leadership with Comrade Deng Xiaoping at its core led the party to comprehensively and effectively bring order out of chaos in the ideological, political, and organisational fields, and began the historic transformation of China, from "taking class struggle as the central task" to a focus on economic construction, from rigidity and semi-rigidity to comprehensive reform, and from a closed or semi-closed state to opening up to the outside world. The adoption of the *Resolution on Several Historical Issues of the Party Since the Founding of the PRC* by the 6th Plenary Session of the 11th CPC Central Committee marked the triumphant completion of the task of bringing order out of chaos with regard to the party's guiding ideology. The plenary session summarised the correct path of socialist modernisation suitable for China's conditions that had been gradually established since the 3rd Plenary Session of the 11th CPC Central Committee, and actually constituted a preliminary summary of the party's experience in governing and clarified the direction for advancing China's socialist modernisation.

The redressing of a large number of unjust and false charges brought about by the Cultural Revolution, the systematic and proper handling of the historical legacy since the founding of new China, and the adjustment of social relations in all aspects, constituted important elements of bringing order out of chaos, as well as important prerequisites and conditions for the party to implement reform and opening up, and modernisation, and open up a new path of governance.

After the 3rd Plenary Session of the 11th CPC Central Committee, the pace of redressing unjust and false charges was accelerated from the central to local levels in accordance with the principle of seeking truth from facts and rectifying mistakes. Consequently, persecuted party, government and military leaders, such as Peng Dehuai and Tao Zhu, as well as a number of persecuted democratic figures, long-suffering intellectuals, and some party members and civilians persecuted during the Cultural Revolution were rehabilitated one after another. At the same time, some major cases from before the Cultural Revolution were also cleaned up and corrected. In February 1979, the CPC Organisation Department and the United Front Work Department jointly convened a national work exchange meeting to re-examine and correct the classification of rightists, which was followed by the screening and correction of rightists classified in the serious expansion of the anti-rightist struggle by various departments in various regions. By June 1980, a total of more than 540,000 cases of people who had been wrongly classified as rightists had been corrected, they had their political reputations restored, and new arrangements were made for their lives and work.

In the work of redressing unjust and false charges, the act with the greatest impact was the rehabilitation of Liu Shaoqi by the 5th Plenary Session of the 11th CPC Central Committee in February 1980. The review of the miscarriage of justice towards Liu Shaoqi, jointly carried out by the Central Committee for Discipline Inspection and the CPC Organisation Department took one year and, in accordance with the facts, completely overturned the various accusations levelled at Liu Shaoqi and restored his reputation as a great Marxist and proletarian revolutionary, and one of the main leaders of the party and the state.

The redressing of Liu Shaoqi's wrongful conviction made it possible for nearly 30,000 people implicated in this unjust and false charge to be cleared of any wrongdoing. The redressing of this, the largest injustice from the Cultural Revolution, stimulated the process of redressing unjust and false cases. After a lot of painstaking and meticulous work, the wide-scale redressing of unjust and false charges nationwide was basically completed by the end of 1982, with more than three million cadres rehabilitated while more than 470,000 communist party members had their party membership restored. These happily returned to work or assumed new positions. The party also dealt with some historical issues by seeking truth from facts, corrected the "leftist" mistakes in work pertaining to ethnic groups and religion, and implemented party policy.

The redressing of unjust and false charges, and the adjustment of social relations and the correct handling of a series of contradictions within the party and amongst the population effectively mobilised the initiative of the entire party and people from all social strata, and played a very important role in consolidating the party's governing position, promoting social stability and unity, consolidating and developing the patriotic united front, and promoting the cause of reform and opening up, and modernisation. In bringing order out of chaos, the most important thing was to do this in terms of guiding ideology. Around the time of the 3rd Plenary Session of the 11th CPC Central Committee the party carried out the work of bringing order out of chaos in terms of guiding ideology and on various fronts, rejected the Cultural Revolution, and re-evaluated some historical issues from the 17 years since the founding of new China. For this reason, some comrades within and outside the party began to have some doubts about socialism and the CPC, and a number of notable phenomena emerged.

On the one hand, some comrades were still influenced by "leftist" mistakes and showed some kind of incomprehension and even resistance to the party's line and policies since the 3rd Plenary Session of the 11th CPC Central Committee. On the other hand, a very small number of people in society took advantage of the opportunity to correct the "leftist" mistakes and, under the banner of "democracy and freedom" and the "emancipation of the mind", spread views sceptical and rejective of CPC leadership and opposing the socialist system and Mao Zedong Thought, and advocated the path of capitalism. There were also a very small number of people in the party who were shaken in their ideology and not only did not recognise the danger of this trend of bourgeois liberalisation but even directly or indirectly supported it to some extent. If these two tendencies were allowed to develop, they would certainly cause ideological chaos and affect the newly formed stability and unity.

On 30 March 1979, Deng Xiaoping, on behalf of the Party Central Committee, delivered a speech entitled the *Four Cardinal Principles* at a theoretical work retreat, clearly stating, "In order to realise the Four Modernisations in China, we must adhere to the four basic principles in ideology and politics. This is the fundamental prerequisite for the realisation of the Four Modernisations. These four principles are. first, upholding the socialist path, second, upholding the dictatorship of the proletariat, third, upholding the leadership of the CPC, and fourth, upholding Marxism-Leninism and Mao Zedong Thought"[26]. He emphasised that, on the one hand, it was necessary to continue to purge the poison of ultra-leftist thinking spread by the Gang of Four and, on the other hand, to resolutely fight against the *zeitgeist* that doubts or opposes the Four Cardinal Principles. From the overall situation and strategic height of China's socialist modernisation, this speech profoundly revealed the intrinsic connection and interaction between a focus on economic construction, upholding the Four Cardinal Principles, and reform and opening up, showing that the reform and opening up the CPC carried out had a clear socialist direction from the very beginning, and laid a solid ideological and political foundation for pioneering and developing socialism with Chinese characteristics. The Four Cardinal Principles, together with the focus on economic construction, and reform and opening up, constituted the basic elements of the political line of the party's 3rd Plenary Session of the 11th CPC Central Committee.

After the 3rd Plenary Session of the 11th CPC Central Committee, with the deepening of bringing order out of chaos, how to regard the history of the CPC since the founding of new China, how to evaluate the Cultural Revolution, how to evaluate the merits and demerits of Mao Zedong, and how to evaluate Mao Zedong Thought, became important issues in the political life of China at that time.

The scientific evaluation of the main leaders of the party and the state, and the scientific treatment of the party's governance history have a bearing on the foundation and reputation of the party's governance, as well as on the future prospects of the party and the state. In order to fundamentally correct the erroneous tendencies of the "left" and "right", align the ideology of the party and the whole nation with socialist modernisation, and further consolidate the foundation of the party's governance, in September 1979 the 4th Plenary Session of 11th CPC Central Committee discussed and adopted Ye Jianying's speech on behalf of the CPC Central Committee, the NPC Standing Committee and the State Council in celebration of the 30th anniversary of the founding of the PRC. The plenary session affirmed the achievements of new China in the previous 30 years, made a preliminary analysis of the Cultural Revolution and "leftist" mistakes from before the Cultural Revolution, and summarised the main lessons of the Cultural Revolution. Ye Jianying's speech called the Cultural Revolution a "decade-long counter-revolutionary havoc" that "caused a great disaster to our people and the most serious setback to our socialist cause since the founding of the country". It was "an appalling catastrophe for the people of all ethnic groups in China". Regarding the Cultural Revolution, he said that "at an appropriate time it should be formally summarised at a special meeting"[27].

In November 1979, the Party Central Committee decided to start work on drafting the *Resolution on Several Historical Issues of the Party since the Founding of the PRC* (hereafter referred to as the *Resolution*). The drafting group was chaired by Deng Xiaoping and Hu Yaobang with Hu Qiaomu in overall charge. From March 1980 to the 6th Plenary Session of the 11th CPC Central Committee, during the drafting process of the *Resolution*, Deng Xiaoping repeatedly articulated his views on the drafting and revision of the draft *Resolution*. These views became the "general principles and the general guiding ideology" for the drafting of the *Resolution*. There were three main principles, the first being to establish the historical status of Comrade Mao Zedong and to uphold and develop Mao Zedong Thought. This was the most central article. The second principle was to conduct an analysis, in accordance with the practice of seeking truth from facts, to determine which of the major events in the 30 years since the founding of the PRC were right and which should not have happened, including the merits and demerits of some responsible comrades, and to make an impartial assessment. The third principle, through the adoption of this resolution, provided a basic, rough summary of the past. The purpose of taking stock of the past was to lead one and all to look forward in unity. It was hoped that, after the adoption of the *Resolution*, clarity would be achieved for correct ideology, and unity of understanding would be achieved within the party and among the people, and that the debate on the major historical issues would basically end there[28].

From 27 to 29 June 1981, the 6th Plenary Session of the 11th CPC Central Committee deliberated and adopted the *Resolution on Several Historical Issues of the Party since the Founding of the PRC*. The *Resolution* was divided into eight parts, namely, a review of the 28 years of history preceding the founding of the PRC, a basic appraisal of the 32 years of history preceding the founding of the PRC, the seven years since the basic completion of the socialist transformation, the 10 years since the beginning of the comprehensive construction of socialism, the 10 years of the Cultural Revolution, the great historical turning point, the historical status of Comrade Mao Zedong and Mao Zedong Thought, and uniting to build a modern socialist power[29].

The *Resolution* correctly summarised the major historical events of the party in the preceding 32 years since the founding of the PRC from the Marxist dialectical and historical materialistic viewpoint, especially with regard to the Cultural Revolution, and scientifically analysed the correct decisions and errors of the party's guiding ideology in these events, as well as the subjective factors and social causes of these errors. The history of the party after the founding of new China is, in general, the history of the party's great achievements in leading the people of all ethnic groups to carry out socialist revolution and construction under the guidance of Marxism-Leninism and Mao Zedong Thought.

Due to having little experience, the party had subjective bias in its analysis of situations and understanding of China's national conditions, and made mistakes such as expanding class struggle and being impatient and impulsive in economic construction, including such serious mistakes as the Cultural Revolution, which was comprehensive in nature and lasted for a long time. This prevented the party from achieving the greater gains it should have achieved.

The *Resolution* evaluated the historical status of Mao Zedong by seeking truth from facts and amply discussed the great significance of Mao Zedong Thought as the guiding ideology of the party. It pointed out that Mao Zedong was a great Marxist, and a great proletarian revolutionary, strategist and theorist. In terms of his life, his contribution to the Chinese revolution far outweighed his faults. His contribution is of primary importance, his mistakes secondary.

The *Resolution* distinguishes between the mistakes of Mao Zedong in his later years and his correct ideas, stating that Mao Zedong Thought is the concrete application and development of Marxism-Leninism in China, the correct theoretical principles and summaries of the experience of the Chinese revolution that have been proven by practice, and the crystallisation of the collective wisdom of the CPC. The *Resolution* emphasises that Mao Zedong Thought is a valuable spiritual asset of the party and will guide its actions for a long time. The party must continue to uphold Mao Zedong Thought and enrich and develop it with new principles and conclusions that conform with reality.

The *Resolution* affirmed the correct path for building a modern and strong socialist country, which has been gradually established since the 3rd Plenary Session of the 11th CPC Central Committee and is suitable for China's situation, provided a preliminary overview of the political line, guidelines and policies since the plenary session, further indicated the direction in which China's socialist cause and the work of the party should continue to move forward, and was of great significance in unifying the ideological understanding of the party as a whole and consolidating the party's governing position.

The adoption of the *Resolution* marked the triumphant completion of the party's process of bringing order out of chaos with regard to its guiding ideology. As it says in the *Records of the Three Kingdoms*, "A mirror illuminates form, and knowledge of ancient events enables understanding of the present". Likewise, the purpose of reviewing history is to sum up historical experience, grasp the laws of history, and bolster the courage and strength needed to forge ahead. The National Day speech of Ye Jianying in September 1979 and the *Resolution* adopted in June 1981 not only drew historical conclusions regarding the major historical events of the party since the founding of new China, especially the Cultural Revolution, and scientifically evaluated the historical status of Mao Zedong and the scientific system of Mao Zedong Thought, but also scientifically summed up the

lessons of history in the light of new realities and developmental requirements, established the correct path for China's socialist modernisation, and
clarified the direction for the party to govern even better.

In his speech, Ye Jianying summarised the "extremely profound
lessons" that the Cultural Revolution had taught the party and the people
of China, and outlined the experience that the party had accumulated in
the process of governance after the Cultural Revolution. The main points
were as follows. For socialism to replace capitalism, it was necessary to
liberate productivity, constantly raise labour productivity and satisfy the
material and cultural needs of the people. It was also necessary to make a
scientific analysis of the state of the class situation and class struggle in
China after the establishment of the socialist system that is in line with
objective reality and to adopt the correct approach and methods. It was
necessary to correctly understand the relationships between the masses,
classes, political parties and leaders, and also to further improve party
discipline and the socialist legal system, to effectively safeguard the democratic rights of all party members and citizens, and to institutionalise and
legalise intraparty democracy and socialist democracy[30].

In June 1981, the *Resolution* adopted at the 6th Plenary Session of the
11th CPC Central Committee on the basis of Ye Jianying's National Day
speech, summed up the positive and negative experiences since the
founding of new China, the fresh experiences of reform and opening up,
and socialist modernisation, especially the mistakes made by the CPC in
governance and lessons learned, and outlined the main points of the path
of socialist modernisation suited to China's national conditions that had
been gradually established by the party since the 3rd Plenary Session of
the 11th CPC Central Committee. These points are as follows:

- After the socialist transformation was basically completed, the main
contradiction to be resolved in China was between the constantly growing
material and cultural needs of the people and backward social production.
The focal point of the work of the party and the state must be shifted to
socialist modernisation with a focus on economic construction, and social
productivity must be greatly developed, and on this basis the material and
cultural life of the people must be gradually improved. The mistakes the
party made in the past constituted, in the final analysis, a failure to determine this strategic shift.

- Socialist economic construction must be carried out in light of China's
national conditions, within the limits of national capabilities and through
active struggle to achieve the goal of modernisation in a methodical and

phased manner. It was vital to be aware of the basic fact that China was still economically and culturally backward, but at the same time to be aware of the achievements and experience already gained in China's economic construction and the favourable conditions at home and abroad, such as the expansion of international economic and technological exchanges, and to make full use of these favourable conditions. This meant opposing both haste and negativity.

- The transformation and refining of socialist relations of production must be adapted to the state of productivity and be conducive to the development of production. There is no fixed set of models for the development of socialist relations of production, and so it is necessary, in accordance with the requirements of the development of China's productivity, to create specific forms of production relations at each stage that are compatible with China's productivity and facilitate their continuation.

- After eliminating the exploiting class as a class, class struggle is no longer the main contradiction. It is necessary to correctly understand the various social contradictions that exist in large numbers within Chinese society that do not fall within the scope of class struggle, and to adopt a method different from class struggle to correctly resolve them. It is vital to unswervingly unite all the forces that can be united and to consolidate and expand the patriotic united front.

- The gradual construction of a highly democratic socialist political system is one of the fundamental tasks of the socialist revolution. State organs at all levels must be strengthened in accordance with the principle of democratic centralism. The people's democratic dictatorship must be consolidated, and the country's constitution and laws must be improved and made inviolable for all to strictly abide by. Chaotic situations similar to the Cultural Revolution must not be allowed to occur again on any scale.

- Socialism must possess a high degree of spiritual civilisation. It Is necessary to strengthen and improve ideological and political work, educate the people and youth with a Marxist world view and communist morality, and adhere to an integrated educational policy of comprehensively developing morals, being both loyal to communism and upholding excellence, integrating the intelligentsia, workers and farmers, and both mental and physical labour. It is also necessary to resist the influence of corrupt bourgeois ideas and remnants of feudalism, overcome the influence of petty bourgeois ideas, and develop the patriotic spirit of putting the interests of the motherland above all else and the spirit of hard work and entrepreneurship to contribute to modernisation.

- It is vital to improve and develop socialist ethnic relations and strengthen ethnic unity. We must uphold the implementation of ethnic regional autonomy and strengthen the construction of legislation surrounding this, effectively help ethnic minority regions to develop their economy and culture, make efforts to train and promote cadres from ethnic minorities, and resolutely oppose all remarks and acts that undermine ethnic unity and equality.

- In an international environment where the danger of war still exists, it is necessary to accelerate the modernisation of national defence, and national defence construction must be in line with the country's economic construction. The fine tradition of close solidarity within the army, between the military and the government, and between the military and the people, must be restored and developed.

- In foreign relations, it is necessary to continue to persist in opposing imperialism, hegemony, colonialism and racism, and safeguard world peace. Also, on the basis of the five principles of peaceful coexistence, we must actively develop relations and economic and cultural exchanges with all countries in the world.

- In light of the lessons of the Cultural Revolution and the current situation of the party, it is necessary to build the party into one with a sound system of democratic centralism. The Marxist view that the party must be led collectively by leaders who have both integrity and talent who arise from the struggles of the masses must be established, and any form of personality cult must be banned.

A high degree of centralisation is to be practised on the basis of a high degree of democracy, which upholds majority rule, individual obedience to the organisation, subordination to superiors and there is partywide submission to central leadership.

The issue of party work style in the ruling party is a matter of life and death for the party. It is necessary to reorganise the party, purify its ranks and remove corrupt and degenerate elements that oppress the people. Party organisations at all levels, like other social organisations, must operate within the confines of the constitution and the law[31].

These 10 summaries summed up the positive and negative experiences since the founding of new China, especially the governance lessons learned from the Cultural Revolution, and in essence preliminarily put forward the questions of what kind of socialism should be constructed in China and how to build it, thereby laying the foundation for the 12th CPC National Congress to propose the idea of building socialism with Chinese characteristics and pioneering a new phase of governance.

The party's adeptness at drawing wisdom and strength from its history and drawing lessons from its practice of governance is an important reason why it has continued to move from one victory to another. Since the 3rd Plenary Session of the 11th CPC Central Committee, the party has drawn profound lessons from the Cultural Revolution, scientifically distinguished between Mao Zedong Thought and Mao Zedong's mistakes in his later years, initially summarised the party's practical experience since the 3rd Plenary Session of the 11th CPC Central Committee, formed a basic framework for the construction of socialism with Chinese characteristics by integrating theory and practice, and guided the party and the country to embark on the great journey of building socialism with Chinese characteristics full of hope and vigour.

(VI) PROPOSING THE THEME OF 'BUILDING SOCIALISM WITH CHINESE CHARACTERISTICS'

In September 1982, the 12th CPC National Congress formulated an ambitious programme to comprehensively pioneer a new phase in socialist modernisation and set out on a new journey to build socialism with Chinese characteristics. In his opening speech to the congress, Deng Xiaoping profoundly summed up historical governance lessons and, based on the party's practice of governance since the 3rd Plenary Session of the 11th CPC Central Committee, put forward the scientific proposition of "building socialism with Chinese characteristics", which pointed the way for the unified struggle of the whole party and nation, and became the glorious banner leading the development and progress of contemporary China.

After smashing the Gang of Four and the end of the Cultural Revolution, China was faced with the difficult test of discerning the right path to pursue from then on. At that time, there were three paths from which the party and people could choose, namely the old path of closure and rigidity, the evil path of abandoning communism altogether, and the new path of opening up anew and exploration. At this critical juncture in history, the second generation of the party's central leadership with Comrade Deng Xiaoping at its core courageously faced reality, summarised its experience up to that point, corrected its mistakes, led the party to rise once more from amidst difficulties, and successfully pioneered socialism with Chinese characteristics, thereby opening up a new path of governance for the CPC.

After the end of the Cultural Revolution, the severe domestic situation and the pressure of international competition forced the people to reflect deeply on, and take stock of, what the 'essence of socialism' is and how to manifest and bring into play the superiority of socialist governance. In December 1977, shortly after his return to political life, in a meeting with the chairman of the Australian Communist Party (Marxist-Leninist) Ted Hill and his wife Joyce, Deng Xiaoping pointedly asked, "How can we manifest the superiority of socialism that Lenin talked about, and what do we mean by superiority? Can it be referred to as superiority if people don't work or study? Can it be called superiority if people's living standards are not improving but regressing? If this is what is referred to as the superiority of socialism, then this type of socialism we too can do without"[32]. In February 1978, when attending the first group meeting of the PLA delegation at the First Session of the Fifth NPC, Deng Xiaoping stated, "Is not socialism superior to capitalism? How could it be called socialism unless it is superior? The Gang of Four do not talk about production. Can the transition to communism be possible without talking about production? What is communism? It is each doing their utmost and distribution according to need. In order to distribute according to need there must be great material abundance. Therefore, the Four Modernisations must be realised and only then will the superiority of socialism be better manifested; otherwise we will always be in a position of being beaten up. Just chanting slogans is useless"[33]. In March 1978, Deng Xiaoping said at the First Plenary Session of the State Council, "What is socialism? ...And in what ways is it better than capitalism? Can it be called the superiority of socialism when each person has an average of about 600 pounds of grain and many people do not have enough food to eat, and only 23 million tons of steel have been made in 28 years? In order to implement socialism, there must be concrete manifestations; production must genuinely be developed, and the living standards of the whole country will then be able to gradually improve accordingly. Only then can the superiority of the socialist system be displayed"[34]. In September 1978, during an inspection tour of the three northeastern provinces of Liaoning, Jilin and Heilongjiang, Deng Xiaoping again said, "We have to think about how much we have really done for the people". "We are too poor, too backward and, frankly, we have let the people down". "Socialism has to demonstrate its superiority ... If we are still this poor after more than 20 years of pursuing it, then what do we need socialism for?"[35] Deng Xiaoping's series of "question marks" actually sent out a strong signal regarding the need to rethink and explore "what the essence of socialism is and how to construct it" in China. In the course of such thinking and exploration, the important task of China following its own path of socialist construction gradually came to the fore.

In March 1979, at a retreat on theoretical work, Deng Xiaoping introduced the term "Chinese-style Modernisation" to represent the concept of "the path of Chinese-style Modernisation" on the basis of a sober understanding of China's actual national conditions. He said that, "socialist modernisation is our greatest political task at present" and that "whether or not we are able to achieve the Four Modernisations will determine the fate of our country and of the peoples of China". In order for China to achieve the Four Modernisations, it is necessary, in line with China's national conditions, to be fully conscious of China's two most distinctive features, namely, first, a poor economic foundation and, second, a large population with little arable land, and from there "walk along a path of Chinese-style Modernisation"[36]. In September 1979, in his National Day speech delivered on behalf of the Party Central Committee, Ye Jianying announced that it was necessary to start from China's actual situation, carefully study the laws of economics and nature, and strive to come up with a path to modernisation suited to China's situation and characteristics. He said it was vital to effectively integrate the acceleration of economic development with the gradual improvement of the living standards of hundreds of millions of people, and effectively integrate fully capitalising on the role of China's existing enterprises with the active introduction of advanced technology from abroad. Under the guidance of a unified national plan, each region was to strive to create specific forms, steps and methods suited to local characteristics in order to achieve the overall goal of the Four Modernisations[37]. Deng Xiaoping's proposal to "walk along a path of Chinese-style Modernisation" and Ye Jianying's proposal to "diligently walk along the path of modernisation suited to China's situation and characteristics" actually provided the direction for the proposal at the 12th CPC National Congress to "build socialism with Chinese characteristics".

In June 1981, the 6th Plenary Session of the 11th CPC Central Committee adopted the *Resolution on Several Historical Issues of the Party Since the Founding of the PRC*, which outlined for the first time the main points of the road to socialist modernisation that had been gradually established since the 3rd Plenary Session of the 11th CPC Central Committee suited to China's national conditions, and preliminarily raised the question of the kind of socialism which should be constructed and how to construct socialism in China. It was in the process of answering this question, that the party continuously deepened its understanding of the laws of socialist construction and the communist party's governance law.

The 12th CPC National Congress was held in Beijing from 1 to 11 September 1982. The purpose of the congress was to systematically sum up the experience of governance gained in the six years since the end of the Cultural Revolution, to further purge the negative consequences of the

Cultural Revolution, to determine the strategic objectives, steps, and priorities and specific corresponding policies to be adopted in order to continue to move forward, and to create a new context for socialist modernisation.

In his opening speech, Deng Xiaoping profoundly summarised the lessons learned from China's socialist construction since the founding of new China and clearly advanced the important proposition of "walking along our own path and building socialism with Chinese characteristics", emphasising that "China's modernisation must be based on China's actual situation. Whether it be revolution or construction, we must pay attention to learning and drawing on the experience of other countries. However, copying and imitating the experience and models of other countries has never been a successful approach. We have had many lessons in this regard. Integrating the universal truths of Marxism with China's concrete reality, taking our own path and building socialism with Chinese characteristics is the basic conclusion we have drawn from summing up our long historical experience"[38]. "Socialism with Chinese characteristics" became the fundamental guiding ideology for reform and opening up, and modernisation in the new period, and the theme for all the party's theory and practice in promoting the development of the various causes of the party and the state.

Guided by the ideology of building socialism with Chinese characteristics, the 12th CPC National Congress, with a focus on the party's governance mission and practice, proposed the party's general task for the new historical period, namely, to unite the people of all ethnicities in China to be self-reliant and struggle hard to gradually modernise industry, agriculture, national defence, and science and technology, and build China into a highly civilised and democratic socialist country. Based on Deng Xiaoping's vision, the congress proposed that the overall goal of China's economic construction in the 20 years from 1981 to the end of the 20th century would be, on the premise of continuously improving economic efficiency, to strive to quadruple the annual gross output value of China's industry and agriculture, that is, from Rmb710 billion in 1980 to about 2.8 trillion yuan in 2000, and to enable the material and cultural life of the people to reach the level of moderate prosperity. In order to achieve this economic development goal, it was most important to solve the problems of agriculture, energy and transport, and education and science. In terms of strategic arrangements, a two-step approach was needed: the first 10 years were mainly focussed on laying a good foundation, building up strength and creating the right conditions, and the second 10 years were about entering a new period of economic revitalisation.

In order to promote a comprehensive social and economic upsurge, the congress proposed that in economic work care should be taken to address the need to concentrate funds on key construction, continue to improve people's lives according to the principle of "subsistence first and development second", uphold the dominant position of the state economy and developing various forms of economy, implement the principle of having the planned economy as the mainstay and market regulation as the supplement, and upholding major principles, such as self-reliance and expanding economic and technological exchanges with other countries. These were all pressing issues in the social and economic development of the time.

A distinctive feature of the 12th CPC National Congress was that, along with the goal of economic construction, it proposed to strive for a high degree of socialist spiritual civilisation and a high degree of socialist democracy. The congress pointed out that socialist spiritual civilisation is an important feature of socialism and an important manifestation of the superiority of the socialist system. The construction of socialist spiritual civilisation can be broadly divided into the two aspects of cultural and ideological construction. Ideological construction determines the socialist nature of the spiritual civilisation, the most important elements of which are revolutionary ideals, morality and discipline. The revolutionary ideology and spirit should be used to invigorate the great enthusiasm of the masses in building socialism, so that more and more members of society will become people with ideals who are moral, literate and disciplined workers. This is a strategic approach to building socialism. Whether or not such a policy is adhered to has a bearing on the success or failure of socialism. The congress also pointed out that the building of a socialist material and spiritual civilisation should be guaranteed and supported by the continued development of socialist democracy. The construction of a high level of socialist democracy is one of the party's fundamental goals and tasks. The construction of socialist democracy must be closely integrated with the building of the socialist legal system, so as to institutionalise and legalise socialist democracy[39].

The 12th CPC National Congress formulated and adopted the *Constitution of the CPC*. The new party constitution removed the "leftist" errors in the party constitution of the 11th CPC National Congress and inherited and developed the merits of the Seventh and Eighth Congress Party Constitutions. In its general outline, the new party constitution contains Marxist provisions on the nature of the party and its guiding ideology, the main contradictions of Chinese society at that stage and the general tasks of the party, and on how the party should properly exercise its leadership role in national life. The new party constitution imposed stricter ideological, political and organisational requirements on party members and party cadres than those set out in each of the previous party constitutions. The new party constitution also emphasised that the principles of democratic centralism and collective leadership must be strictly observed from the party's central leadership to all levels of the organisation, and clearly stipulated that "any form of personality cult is prohibited".

The new party constitution further stipulates that the Party Central Committee shall have no chairman but only a general secretary, that advisory committees shall be set up at the central and provincial levels in order to capitalise on the role of many veteran comrades with rich political experience as advisers to the party's cause, that committees for discipline inspection at all levels of the party shall be elected by the party congresses at those levels, and that organisations at all levels of the party must ascribe importance to the construction of the party and frequently discuss and examine the party's work.

The new party constitution of the 12th CPC National Congress systematically summarised the party's experience in party building and made systematic provisions on the party's nature, objectives, tasks, leadership role, organisational principles, and various systems and basic requirements for party members and organisations, marking a new level of understanding of the communist party's governance law.

The 12th CPC National Congress profoundly summed up the lessons learned from socialist construction since the founding of new China, especially on the basis of the party's practice of modernisation and governance since the 3rd Plenary Session of the 11th CPC Central Committee. The congress put forward the scientific proposition of "building socialism with Chinese characteristics", which correctly reflected the objective laws of socialist construction and focussed on embodying the will, aspirations and demands of the Chinese people of all ethnicities, and gradually explored and opened up the great path of building socialism with Chinese characteristics, becoming the great banner that united the people of China in implementing reform and opening up, and modernisation.

Under the guidance of the ideology and path of socialism with Chinese characteristics, China made great achievements in reform and opening up, and modernisation. The 12th CPC National Congress opened up a new chapter in the governance of the CPC by comprehensively creating a new context in socialist modernisation.

(VII) BUILDING THE PARTY'S CORE STRENGTH TO LEAD THE CAUSE OF SOCIALIST MODERNISATION

As the ruling party, the construction of the CPC itself must be compatible with the party-led reform and opening up, and socialist modernisation. In other words, the party has the great responsibility of leading socialist modernisation and must strengthen its construction to provide a fundamental guarantee for this process. To this end, the 12th CPC National Congress summed up the party's experience of construction since the 3rd Plenary Session of the 11th CPC Central Committee and proposed the major goal of "building the party into a strong core to lead the cause of socialist modernisation"[40], integrating party building with the building of socialism with Chinese characteristics and achieving a fundamental change in the party's thinking on construction. With this goal in mind, the party adopted a series of major initiatives to address salient problems in the areas of ideology, working style and organisation, further deepening its understanding of the communist party's governance law and promoting the continuous achievement of new results in party building.

After the 3rd Plenary Session of the 11th CPC Central Committee, in order to adapt to the shift in the focus of the party's work, and the new situation and new requirements of reform and opening up, the Party Central Committee effectively strengthened party building, and reinforced and refined the leadership of the party in the process of comprehensive efforts to bring order out of chaos. In January 1979, in order to solve prominent problems within the party pertaining to ideology, organisation, discipline and work style, the Central Committee for Discipline Inspection held its first plenary session since its re-establishment to study concrete measures to strengthen party disciplinary education and to improve the party's work style. In his speech, Chen Yun pointed out that adhering to party rules and laws, rectifying the party's work style and forming a lively and active political climate were the most crucial matters for the whole party to focus on, and that only by doing this could the stability and unity of the whole party and the nation, and the four modernisations be achieved. This plenary session proposed that the basic tasks of the party's disciplinary inspection work were to adhere to party rules and laws, protect the rights of party members, muster the revolutionary enthusiasm and zeal for work of party members, combat undesirable tendencies that violate party discipline and undermine the party's fine traditions, and effectively improve the party's work style. Based on summing up the party's historical experience, the plenary session discussed and drew up a draft of the document *Some Guidelines on the Internal Political Life of the*

Party. In March 1979, the CPC Central Committee announced to the whole party the draft of *Some Guidelines on the Internal Political Life of the Party*, requiring this document to be studied and discussed partywide and requesting amendment proposals. In November of the same year, the CPC Central Committee and the State Council issued the document *Some Provisions Concerning the Material Benefits for Senior Cadres*, reaffirming some of the rules and regulations that had been in force before the Cultural Revolution and requiring senior cadres to take the lead in carrying forward the party's fine traditions.

In February 1980, after extensive consultation and repeated revisions, the 5th Plenary Session of the 11th CPC Central Committee formally adopted the document *Certain Guidelines on Political Life Within the Party*. The 12 articles of the *Guidelines* emphasise upholding the party's political and ideological line, upholding collective leadership and opposition to individual arbitrariness, safeguarding the centralised unity of the party and strict adherence to party discipline, upholding the party spirit and the eradication of factionalism, honest speech and consistency in word and deed, promoting internal party democracy and treating different opinions correctly, safeguarding the inviolability of the rights of party members, fully reflecting the will of electors in elections, fighting against misguided tendencies and malefactors, treating erring comrades correctly, accepting supervision by the party and the masses, and not permitting anyone to have special privileges, and studying hard to be both faithful red communists and expert. In the process of implementing the *Guidelines* the plenary session called for ideological and political education on upholding the party's political and ideological line, strengthening its unity and solidarity, and enhancing its democratic centralism and organisational discipline. Accordingly, organisations at all levels of the party and every individual party member were to carefully examine their own work and work style in light of the provisions of the *Guidelines*, and build on their achievements and overcome their shortcomings. Anything contrary to the provisions of the *Guidelines* was to be rectified in a timely and practical manner, and the phenomena of disorganisation and indiscipline of individual party organisations and certain party members, and continual factionalism and disunity of direction were to be completely changed. The plenary session reaffirmed that by upholding the principles of the obedience of individual party members to the party organisation, majority rule, submission to superiors and the whole party submitting to the party's central leadership, the whole party would be able to unify its thoughts and actions under the leadership of the Central Committee and ensure the smooth implementation of socialist modernisation[41]. The *Guidelines* concretised, standardised and systematised the relevant provisions of the party constitution, the fine traditions and practices of the party, the major boundaries between right and wrong in the political life of the party, and the important principles for handling intraparty relations. They play an important role in improving the democratic life of the party, safeguarding the party's centralisation and unity, and strengthening institutional construction centred on democratic centralism.

After the 5th Plenary Session of the 11th CPC Central Committee adopted *Some Guidelines on the Internal Political Life of the Party,* much work was done in many places and departments to correct unjust practices. However, on the whole, compared with the early days after the founding of new China, the party's work style did not as yet fundamentally improve, and in many areas and departments the unjust practices of some party members and cadres were quite serious. There were still some comrades who did not adequately comprehend the major significance of improving the party's work style, and even claimed that the party's work style was in opposition to stability and unity, modernisation and construction, and let unhealthy practices go unchecked or even condoned and gave safe haven to them. In November 1980, Chen Yun proposed at the Third Symposium on the Implementation of *Some Guidelines on the Internal Political Life of the Party* held by the Central Commission for Discipline Inspection that, "the question of the party's style of party governance pertains to the survival of the party itself"[42]. According to Chen Yun, the state of the party's work style is related to the hearts and minds of the people and determines the fate of the party. If the party culture is good, then the party will be able to gain the sincere support and endorsement of the people and will thereby possess a source of strength and the foundation for victory. But if the party culture is bad, then the party will be abandoned by the people, and will become a party without supporters, and such a party cannot exist. Therefore, the issue of party style must be urgently and permanently addressed. This important assertion by Chen Yun, from the strategic height of the survival and development of the ruling party and the rise and fall of the government, scientifically summed up the CPC's experience of governance and the historical lessons of world socialism. It also profoundly revealed the extreme importance, urgency and long-term nature of strengthening the construction of party culture in the new era, which is of great significance in constructing and enhancing the party's governability.

In June 1981, the *Resolution on Several Historical Issues of the Party Since the Founding of the PRC* adopted at the 6th Plenary Session of the 11th CPC Central Committee proposed, in light of the lessons of the Cultural Revolution and the state of the party at that time, that the CPC must be built into a party with a sound system of democratic centralism. In September 1982, the 12th CPC National Congress adopted the *Constitution of the CPC*. The new party constitution summarised both positive and negative experiences and made six provisions on the basic principles of democratic centralism, which became the basic guidelines for the political life of the party and the handling of intraparty relations and were of great significance in further developing intraparty democracy and ensuring the centralised unity of the party on the basis of democracy. The new party constitution proposed that at that time four issues must be addressed, namely, first, improving the party's system of democratic centralism and further normalising the internal political life of the party, second, reforming the leadership and cadre system to achieve the revolutionisation, rejuvenation, intellectualisation and professionalisation of the ranks of cadres, third, strengthening the party's work among workers, farmers and intelligentsia, and creating closer ties between the party and the masses, and fourth, implementing the rectification of the party in a planned and systematic manner so as to bring about a fundamental improvement in party culture. In order to bring about this fundamental change, the Central Committee decided to carry out a comprehensive overhaul of the party's work style and organisation.

In October 1983, in order to solve salient problems within the party, the 2nd Plenary Session of the 12th CPC Central Committee issued the *Decision of the CPC Central Committee on the Rectification of the Party*, determining that a comprehensive rectification of the party's work style and organisation would be carried out from the top down, step by step and group by group, starting from the winter of 1983.

The overall aim and requirement of this party rectification was to, under the guidance of Marxism-Leninism and Mao Zedong Thought, rely on the revolutionary consciousness of all party comrades and make proper use of the incisive weapon of criticism and self-criticism to enforce party discipline, expose and solve the problems of serious impurity in the party's ideology, work style and organisation, achieve a fundamental change in party culture, raise the ideological and work level of the party as a whole, bring the party and the people closer together, and strive to build the party into a strong core to lead the cause of socialist modernisation. The basic task of this party rectification was to unify ideology, rectify work style, strengthen discipline and purify organisation. The procedure for rectifying the party was to implement it starting from the party's central leadership then to the grassroots level, from top to bottom, step by step and group by group. The rectification of the party in each unit was also to be carried out from top to bottom, starting with leadership teams and leading cadres, followed by the masses of party members. The basic method of party rectification was to carry out criticism and self-criticism on the basis of careful study of party documents and improved ideological understanding, so as to distinguish between right and wrong, redress errors and purify the organisation. Throughout the whole process of party rectification, ideological education was to be strengthened with a view to raising the ideological awareness of the majority of party members[43]. In order to safeguard the day-to-day leadership of the work of party rectification, the plenary session elected the Central Steering Committee for Party Rectification Work after extensive exploratory discussions. Under the leadership of the party Central Committee and the Central Steering Committee for Party Rectification Work, the rectification of the party was basically completed by May 1987. This party rectification constituted a major step taken by the CPC in the new era to win a great new victory and a fundamental guarantee for building China into a modernised, highly civilised and highly democratic socialist country.

Through the rectification of the party, the majority of party members, especially party cadres, deepened their understanding of the party's line and policies since the 3rd Plenary Session of the 11th CPC Central Committee and became more conscious of the importance of keeping in line with the party Central Committee in ideology, politics and action. In addition, a number of cases of serious violations of law and discipline by party members and cadres in various places were investigated and dealt with, and the "three kinds of people", namely, instigators of rebellion, supporters of the Gang of Four and "beaters, smashers and looters", from the time of the Cultural Revolution were resolutely purged, thereby further purifying the party's organisation. There were also some deficiencies in this party rectification, such as uneven implementation of work, with some units not fully completing the task of party rectification, and some even simply went superficially through the motions. However, on the whole, this rectification of the party changed the situation of impure ideology, work style, and organisation and lax discipline within the party, and strengthened and improved the construction of the party, ensuring that the party would always be the strong leadership core of reform and opening up, and socialist modernisation.

The self-construction of the ruling party has a bearing on whether the CPC can maintain its advanced nature, improve its governability, consolidate its ruling position and fulfil its governance mission. Only when the ruling party is well established can its governance strategy be put into practice, can long-term rule be guaranteed and can its governance mission be achieved. After the 12th CPC National Congress, the party strengthened and improved the construction of its ideology, organisation and work style through a series of initiatives such as party rectification, ensuring that the party would always be the strong core leading the cause of reform and opening up, and socialist modernisation, and establishing a strong governance safeguard for pioneering the governance of the party by charting a new course for the party to govern and invigorate the nation.

(VIII) IMPLEMENTING REFORM AND OPENING UP: NEW OPPORTUNITIES AND TESTS FOR CPC GOVERNANCE

After the 3rd Plenary Session of the 11th CPC Central Committee, the party led the whole nation to vigorously promote reform and opening up, undergoing a truly momentous historical process from rural to urban reform, from economic reform to various kinds of systemic reforms, and from internal revitalisation to opening up to the outside world, greatly mobilising the zeal of hundreds of millions of people. This historically unprecedented reform and opening up presented both opportunities and advantages, as well as risks and tests, for party governance.

The party's historic decision to implement reform and opening up in the late 1970s was based on a profound grasp of the future prospects of the party and the country, a profound stocktaking of the practice of socialist revolution and construction, profound insight into the trends of the times, and profound understanding of people's expectations and needs. At that time, the global economy was developing rapidly and technology was relentlessly advancing while the internal disorder of the Cultural Revolution had brought China's economy to the verge of collapse, the people were finding it difficult to have sufficient food and clothing, and national construction was still as yet not being implemented. There were strong calls both within and outside the party to redress the mistakes of the Cultural Revolution so that the party and the country could rise once again from amidst crisis. The 3rd Plenary Session of the 11th CPC Central Committee broke through the grave shackles of longstanding "leftist" mistakes and decisively put an end to the approach of "taking class struggle as the central task", promptly shifting the work focus of the party and the state to economic construction. Since then, China's reform and opening up has been advancing at great speed.

China's reforms began with economic reform and first achieved breakthroughs in rural areas. Some farmers in places such as Anhui and Sichuan spontaneously took action to have farm output quotas fixed by household, to delegate production responsibility to households, and devolved production responsibility to groups. Deng Xiaoping gave timely support and guidance to the momentum of reform emerging in the countryside, noting that "after the relaxation of rural policies, some places where it was appropriate to engage in fixing farm output quotas by household did so, with very good results and rapid transformation"[44].

In September 1980, the CPC Central Committee issued the document *Several Issues Pertaining to Further Strengthening and Improving the Agricultural Production Responsibility System* which, while stressing the need to further improve the collective economy, pointed out that implementing the fixing of farm output quotas by households under the leadership of production teams was dependent on the socialist economy and would not deviate from the socialist track, and that there was therefore no danger of restoring a capitalist path. On New Year's Day 1982, the Central Government's Document No. 1 approved the *Minutes of the National Conference on Rural Work*, which clearly pointed out that the various responsibility systems then in force, including the small section of contracted work at fixed rates of pay, professional contracting for joint production for pay, pay according to productivity levels, fixing farm output quotas by household and by groups, and delegating production responsibility to households and groups, all constituted systems of responsibility for production in a socialist collective economy. With the support and impetus of the central government, the percentage of production teams that fixed farm output quotas by households and delegated production responsibility to households quickly rose from 50% in 1980 to 86.7% in June 1982.

In parallel with the reforms in the countryside, reform of the urban economy also began on a pilot basis, mainly through the gradual expansion of enterprise autonomy, the decentralisation of enterprise management, the separation of government and enterprises, and the implementation of comprehensive reform of the urban economy, achieving remarkable results. Reforms of the employment system, the distribution system and the financial system were also gradually carried out.

As reform progressed, major breakthroughs began to be made in opening up to the outside world. In this regard, the establishment of Special Economic Zones (SEZs) constituted an innovative practice in opening up to the outside world. In May 1980, the CPC Central Committee and the State Council decided to set up SEZs in Shenzhen, Zhuhai, Shantou and Xiamen. Former frontier towns and a deserted fishing village were quickly transformed into a frontier region for the introduction of foreign investment and advanced technology, developing into fledgling modern cities in a matter of years.

In October 1984, the 3rd Plenary Session of the 12th CPC Central

Committee deliberated and adopted the *Decision on Economic Reform*[45], proposing that China's socialist economy would be a planned commodity economy based on public ownership, thereby breaking through the traditional notion of pitting a planned economy against a commodity economy. This constituted a new development in Marxist political economics and provided new theoretical guidance for comprehensive economic reform.

In March 1985, the CPC Central Committee made a decision on reform of science and technology-related systems, and in May a decision on reform of the education system. In November 1986, the CPC Central Committee and the State Council decided to implement the *State High-Tech Development Plan* (that is, the *863 Program*), which further promoted the development of science and technology in China.

The deepening of reforms stimulated new steps in the process of opening up to the outside world. In May 1984, the CPC Central Committee and the State Council decided to open up 14 coastal port cities, including Dalian, Tianjin, Qingdao, Shanghai, Ningbo and Guangzhou. From 1985 onwards, economic open zones were opened in the Yangtze River Delta, the Pearl River Delta, southeast Fujian and the Bohai Sea Rim, and Hainan was approved as a province and an SEZ. The process of opening up to the outside world continued to expand and the rapid development of the coastal zone in turn gave a strong impetus to the reform and opening up, and economic construction of the whole of China.

Reform and opening up are the most distinctive features of the new period in China's development. Reform and opening up began at the 3rd Plenary Session of the 11th CPC Central Committee, was comprehensively implemented after the 12th CPC National Congress, and continued to deepen after the Thirteenth National Congress. It is because of reform and opening up that the national landscape underwent a historic and profound change, with remarkable achievements in all areas of the economy, politics, ideology, culture, national defence and foreign affairs. The achievements in economic construction were particularly remarkable, with GDP, gross industrial and agricultural output, state revenue and the average income of urban and rural residents reaching roughly double in 1986 what they were in 1978. The tremendous achievements of reform and opening up, and the profound changes that took place made the majority of party members, cadres and the masses gradually realise that the line and policy of reform and opening up set by the Party Central Committee was correct and that the series of strategic plans for reform and opening up were correct, increasing their approval of the party and its approach to governance, and strengthening their determination and confidence to follow the party on the road of socialism with Chinese characteristics.

The great practice of reform and opening up eloquently proved that reform and opening up constituted an important asset enabling the party and the people to make great strides in catching up with the times and was the only way to uphold and develop socialism with Chinese characteristics, a key manoeuvre to determine the fate of contemporary China and to achieve the great rejuvenation of the Chinese nation.

Reform and opening up did not go smoothly and after the 3rd Plenary Session of the 11th CPC Central Committee was constantly subject to interference from both the "left" and the right. In particular, as the process of reform and opening up was comprehensively implemented and continued to deepen, the problems brought about by reform and opening up multiplied, and debate on the nature of the reform and opening up process became more and more intense. In the early 1980s, the most salient challenges posed by reform and opening up to the party's governance were as follows.

First, serious criminal activities such as smuggling and trafficking, corruption and bribery, speculative fraud, and theft of state and collective property increased significantly, and were still quite rampant in a few areas and among a few people. These serious criminal activities corrupted and are still corrupting the ranks of cadres, damaging the muscle of the party, the government, the army and the credibility of the country, poisoning people's minds, polluting the social climate, undermining economic construction, hindering the correct implementation of the policies of opening up to the outside world and revitalising the economy internally, affecting social stability and doing great harm to the future of China's socialist cause.

Second, some problems arose in the development of the SEZs, which led to censuring and criticism of the SEZs and had a serious impact on the ideology of the majority of party members and cadres. Many people were bewildered by the new problems and matters that emerged in the course of reform and opening up, even raising the question of whether it was right for China to follow socialism or capitalism. International public opinion and the masses of cadres in China still had some doubts about whether reform and opening up would be continued and were worried that there would be problems with its direction in the future.

Third, corrupt ideas of the bourgeoisie and other exploitative classes were seeping in, and bourgeois liberalisation as a kind of *zeitgeist* gradually gave rise to a wave of political activities whose fundamental aim was to overthrow the leadership of the CPC and to deny the socialist system. This reflects the fact that in the primary stage of socialism, the ideology of bourgeois liberalisation will persist for a long time, and the process of eliminating interference and influence from the ideology of bourgeois liberalisation will persist throughout the primary stage of socialism.

In response to the above problems, the CPC implemented a series of targeted measures, carrying out a series of activities. Firstly, the party determined to combat serious economic crime. At the end of 1981, a letter of petition entitled *Smuggling Activities Rampant in Some Areas of Guangdong*, issued by the Central Commission for Discipline Inspection, drew the attention of the commission's leading comrades. In January 1982, the CPC Central Committee issued an *Urgent Notification* and decided to launch a nationwide struggle against serious criminal activities in the economic sector. In April 1982, the CPC Central Committee and the State Council issued the *Decision on Combating Serious Criminal Activities in the Economic Sector*, and a nationwide struggle to combat criminal activities in the economic sector was launched across the board. By 1986, after more than four years of tireless efforts, a major victory had been achieved in the fight against serious economic crime. The struggle against serious economic crimes constituted an important aspect of the Central Committee's series of major decisions to "grasp reform and opening up with one hand and punish corruption with the other" and was instrumental in implementing the policy of reform and opening up, safeguarding the zeal of cadres and the masses for reform, and strengthening the cadres' and masses' concept of the legal system and their ability to resist the corrosive capacity of corrupt ideology. Deng Xiaoping commented that, "While working to combat economic crimes, opening up to the outside world and revitalising the domestic economy can be correctly oriented"[46].

Second, expansive opening up continued. From 22 January to 17 February 1984, Deng Xiaoping visited the Shenzhen, Zhuhai and Xiamen SEZs, as well as Guangzhou and Shanghai, at a time when there were difficulties in advancing SEZ construction. In Zhuhai, he wrote a dedicatory inscription stating that "Zhuhai SEZ is good" and later wrote an inscription for Shenzhen stating that, "The development and experience of Shenzhen proves that our policy of establishing SEZs is correct." After returning to Beijing, Deng Xiaoping talked with several senior ranking comrades in the Central Government and said that, "In our construction of SEZs and implementing a policy of opening up, there is a guiding principle which must be clear, namely, not to restrain but to release. The SEZs are windows, being windows for technology, windows for management methods, windows for knowledge, and windows for foreign policy"[47]. Deng Xiaoping's southern tour and his affirmation of the SEZs ushered in new opportunities for opening up to the outside world, and a multi-level, focused, fully integrated and interconnected pattern of opening up to the outside world gradually took shape, made up of SEZs, coastal open cities, coastal open economic zones and inland areas of the country.

Third, a struggle against bourgeois liberalisation was conducted. In October 1983, at the 2nd Plenary Session of the 12th CPC Central Committee, Deng Xiaoping clearly stated in response to the problem of bourgeois liberalisation that on the ideological front the party must not become embroiled in spiritual pollution. The essence of spiritual pollution is the spreading of all kinds of corrupt and decadent ideas of the bourgeoisie and other exploiting classes, and the spreading of a distrust of socialism, the communist cause and the CPC leadership. Spiritual pollution is so harmful that it has the capacity to harm China and mislead the people. He pointed out that modern Western bourgeois culture must be analysed, discerned and criticised in terms of its ideological content and methods of expression using Marxism, and should not be ignorantly esteemed amidst a flood of fascination. Deng Xiaoping demanded that party committees at all levels effectively strengthen their leadership on the ideological front. In accordance with the spirit of this plenary session, a struggle against spiritual pollution, that is, against bourgeois liberalisation, was launched throughout China in the ideological and cultural field.

Fourth, the construction of socialist spiritual civilisation was strengthened. In September 1986, in order to strengthen the construction of spiritual civilisation, the 6th Plenary Session of the 12th CPC Central Committee adopted the *Resolution of the CPC Central Committee on the Guiding Principles for the Construction of Socialist Spiritual Civilisation* (hereinafter referred to as the *Resolution*). From the height of the overall scheme of socialist modernisation, the *Resolution* elaborated on the strategic position and fundamental tasks of the construction of socialist spiritual civilisation, emphasising the need to cultivate socialist citizens with ideals and morals who are educated and disciplined, unite all the peoples of China with the common ideal of building socialism with Chinese characteristics, and improve the ideological, moral, and scientific and cultural quality of the entire Chinese nation. The *Resolution* pointed out that socialist spiritual civilisation guided by Marxism is an important feature of socialist society, providing spiritual impetus and intellectual support for the development of material civilisation and an ideological guarantee for the correct direction of its development, and that improving construction in this area constitutes a major issue pertaining to the success or failure of socialism. Comprehensive reform and opening up to the outside world led to the advancing of new and higher demands for the construction of spiritual civilisation and constituted a historically significant test of whether spiritual civilisation would be able to adapt to such demands, strongly resist the corrupt ideas of capitalism and feudalism, and prevent various dangers of disorientation. The *Resolution* emphasised that bourgeois liberalisation, namely, the rejection of the socialist system and the advocacy of the capitalist system, is fundamentally contrary to the interests of the people and historical trends, and is resolutely opposed by the general public[48]. Deng Xiaoping also made it clear that to engage in liberalisation would be to lead China onto the path of capitalism. A combination of not resisting this *zeitgeist*, plus the great disorder that would inevitably infiltrate China as a result of opening up, would amount to an attack on the socialist Four Modernisations that could not be ignored. This is why he also said that, "opposing liberalisation is not only an issue now, but it will remain one for 10 to 20 years". In March 1987, Deng Xiaoping added that it would not only remain an issue for 10 to 20 years but also for "a further 50 years". The *Resolution* adopted at the 6th Plenary Session of the 12th CPC Central Committee was the party's first programmatic document on the construction of spiritual civilisation, providing the general guidelines for the healthy development of spiritual civilisation in China. The above initiatives both uphold the socialist direction of reform and opening up, and also play a role in safeguarding reform and opening up.

After taking power, Marxist parties must focus on economic construction, uphold reform and opening up, and constantly improve the living standards of the people through the liberation and development of productivity. This is dictated by the governance aims of Marxist parties and is also a realistic requirement for consolidating the parties' governance position. The overall purpose of reform and opening up is to consolidate the socialist system and the leadership of the party, and develop productivity under the party's leadership and the socialist system. The "Four Upholds" and reform and opening up are interdependent.

In the course of reform, opening up and modernisation, it is only by profoundly understanding the historical necessity of reform and opening up, consciously grasping the regularity of reform and opening up, and firmly shouldering the great responsibility of deepening reform and opening up that it is possible to remain sober-minded, eliminate all kinds of interference, and unswervingly implement reform and opening up to its completion.

(IX) A NEW UNDERSTANDING OF THE OVERSEAS GOVERNANCE SITUATION: PEACE AND DEVELOPMENT CONSTITUTE THE TWO MAJOR ISSUES IN THE CONTEMPORARY WORLD

Correctly assessing the international situation, grasping the lifeline of the times, and making full use of the state of global development is not only the basis for formulating foreign policy but also an important factor in formulating domestic policy. Since the 3rd Plenary Session of the 11th CPC Central Committee, the party has concentrated its efforts on reform, opening up and socialist modernisation based on a new understanding of the state of governance overseas. In the new period of reform and opening up, the party's judgment of the international situation and its understanding of the issue of war and peace have changed. The original view that war is inevitable and imminent has changed, and the belief has come that it is possible to strive for a longer-term peace and that it is possible that no large-scale world war will break out for a long time. This constitutes a major shift in the party's perspective. Of this Deng Xiaoping said, "It was based on such a judgment that we formulated the policy of a single-minded approach to construction in 1978"[49].

After the 3rd Plenary Session of the 11th CPC Central Committee, the party led the nation to set the two-stage goal of reaching the level of moderate prosperity by the end of the 20th century, and then attaining the level of moderately developed countries within the first 30 to 50 years of the following century. To this end, the Party Central Committee stressed that, "the achievement of the goals of these two stages is dependent on two conditions, one being a peaceful international environment, and the other a stable and united domestic political climate that will enable us to implement socialist construction in an orderly manner with effective leadership"[50]. In order to single-mindedly implement socialist modernisation in the new era of reform and opening up, a peaceful international environment was an absolute necessity. As Deng Xiaoping emphasised, "we are faced with the task of developing and escaping from backwardness. For this we hope there will be a peaceful international environment. We hope there will be peace for at least 50 to 70 years".

For quite a long time after the founding of new China, against the backdrop of the Cold War, the judgement of Chinese leaders of the international environment and the characteristics of the development of the times was not free from the dominance of Lenin's idea of "war and revolution". They believed that the danger of war was always present due to the existence of the root causes of the imperialist wars, even at one time believing that the danger of a major war was imminent and preparing for imminent civil war and major and nuclear war.

The PLA was also on the brink of war for many years, making it difficult to modernise the army and national defence in a planned manner in accordance with peacetime requirements. In this connection Deng Xiaoping once said, "Our view in the past was always that war is inevitable and imminent. I myself propagated this view for many years." He believed that this judgment had resulted in much time being wasted.

In the 1980s, US-Soviet rivalry was at a stalemate, impacting the entire world, and the atmosphere of global tension was generally easing. After the 3rd Plenary Session of the 11th CPC Central Committee, China's leaders began to change their views on the issue of war. While still insisting that "world war is inevitable", they no longer considered it to be "imminent" and thought it possible to try to delay the outbreak of war. In January 1980, Deng Xiaoping said at a meeting of central cadres, "The 1980s are very important years, both internationally and domestically. It is difficult to predict what problems will occur internationally, but it can be said that they will be very turbulent and crisis-ridden years. Of course, we are confident that if the anti-hegemonic struggle is carried out effectively then it will be possible to delay the outbreak of war and secure peace for a little longer"[51]. In March 1981, when he was briefed by his army comrades, he also stated, "I don't think a major war will be fought for several years to come. Neither hegemony of the US or the Soviet Union would dare to start a war in the first place. We should not fret and create artificial tension." In November 1982, when meeting with visitors from Japan, he stressed that, "the danger of war is always there but it does not look like there will be a war in the near future"[52].

In the mid-1980s, the CPC Central Committee further observed the international situation, reconceptualised and made a new judgment on the prospects for war and peace. Building on the belief of the previous period that war could be delayed, they proposed that a world war could actually be avoided if work were done well. In November 1984, when meeting with foreign visitors, Deng Xiaoping said, "The only two countries in the world today that have the power to fight a major war are the US and the Soviet Union, both of which have the ability to destroy each other and the world. As a result, they do not dare to go to war easily." When Deng Xiaoping met with Austrian President Kirchschläger in September 1985, he also stated that, "although there is still a danger of war, it can be avoided if we get it right. If war is not fought in this century, there will be more hope for peace in the next century. We are switching from pessimism to optimism on the issue of war. But, of course, there is no room for complacency; peace must be striven for to be won"[53]. This fundamentally changed the party's perception that a world war was inevitable and imminent, and also changed its perception of war and peace.

In June 1985, Deng Xiaoping formally proposed at an enlarged meeting of the CMC that it was possible there would not be a large-scale world war for a relatively long period of time, that there was hope for maintaining world peace and declared that the party had changed its original view that the danger of war was imminent. Based on this judgment, the CMC decided to shift the guiding ideology of military construction from the past pro-war state based on "fighting an early, large-scale and nuclear war" to a track of peacetime construction and took decisive measures, putting forward a plan to reduce military posts by 1 million.

It was at this time that the Party Central Committee, based on its judgment that war could be delayed and on its new understanding of the issue of war and peace, advanced the concept that "peace and development are the two major themes in the contemporary world".

In May 1984, Deng Xiaoping was the first to make it clear that there were many problems in the world at that time, with two of them being the most salient. One was the issue of peace and the second was the North-South issue[54]. In October 1984, he further clarified this matter, stating that, "two major international issues are very salient; one is the issue of peace, and the other is the North-South issue. There are many other problems but none of them have such global and strategic significance like these two issues, impacting the overall international situation"[55]. In March 1985, he also clearly stated that, "The truly great problems in the world now, the strategic problems with a global dimension, are the issue of peace and the economic issue, or rather the issue of development. The issue of peace is an East-West issue, and the issue of development is a North-South issue. In a nutshell, the problems revolve around the four words North, South, East and West"[56].

In June 1985, at an enlarged meeting of the CMC, Deng Xiaoping spelt out more clearly the two major strategic shifts in China's foreign policy. The first shift, he said, was the party's understanding of the issue of war and peace. He said that in the preceding few years the party had carefully observed the situation and concluded that the danger of world war still existed but that the growth of the world's forces for peace exceeded the growth of those for war; it was possible, he said, that there would not be a large-scale war for a relatively long time and that there was hope for the possibility of maintaining world peace. The second shift was in China's foreign policy. In the past, in response to the threat of Soviet hegemony, the party had had a so-called "one-line" strategy but now it had changed this strategy, which constituted a major shift. In April 1986, the State Council's *Report on the Seventh Five-Year Plan*, approved at the Fourth Session of the Sixth NPC, comprehensively expounded the main thrust and basic principles of China's independent and peaceful foreign policy from 10 aspects, summarising the adjustments of China's foreign policy since reform and opening up, and drawing conclusions. With this the adjustment of China's foreign policy was basically complete.

On the basis of the above understanding, the 14th Party Congress convened in October 1992 established that, "peace and development are the two major themes of the contemporary world" based on the 12 propositions of the theory of building socialism with Chinese characteristics and stressed that, "peace and development are the two major themes of the contemporary world, and we must uphold an independent and peaceful foreign policy and strive for a favourable international environment for the modernisation of China." The party's judgment that "peace and development are the two major themes of the contemporary world" has been of great significance to China's internal affairs, national defence and foreign affairs.

In terms of the economy, the party made the major decision to shift the work focus of the party and the state to economic construction and has always insisted on putting economic construction at the centre of all work, making full use of the favourable international environment, learning from advanced science, technology and management experience from around the world, and speeding up the pace of socialist modernisation. In terms of national defence, in line with the comprehensive implementation of reform and opening up, and based on the development of, and changes in, the international situation, the Party Central Committee made a series of judgments that conformed with reality. A strategic change in the guiding ideology of defence construction was achieved, which was conducive to the concentration of the party's efforts for reform and opening up, and socialist modernisation. In terms of foreign affairs, scientifically grasping the changeable nature of the international situation, reformulating a correct, strategic approach to foreign affairs, policies and strategies, and pioneering new conditions in foreign affairs, won a favourable international environment for the long-term governance of the party.

A correct judgment and accurate grasp of the international situation has a direct impact on both domestic and foreign affairs. The CPC has closely followed the changes in the international situation, kept firm hold of the salient theme of peace and development, formulated a correct, strategic approach to foreign affairs, opened the door to friendship and cooperation between China and the rest of the world, learnt from advanced science, technology and management experience from around the world, and accelerated the pace of socialist modernisation. This has won a favourable international environment for the long-term governance of the party and created new conditions for governance in an open environment.

(X) THE THEORY OF THE PRIMARY STAGE OF SOCIALISM AND THE BASIC LINE: LAYING THE THEORETICAL FOUNDATIONS FOR A NEW PATH OF GOVERNANCE

From October to November 1987, the party's 13th National Congress, on the basis of taking stock of the historical experience since the founding of new China and the practice of reform and opening up during the 3rd Plenary Session of the 11th CPC Central Committee, elaborated the theory of the primary stage of socialism in a more systematic manner, and clearly outlined and comprehensively expounded the party's basic line during the primary stage of socialism. This laid the theoretical foundation for the further development of China's socialist modernisation, and reform and opening up, as well as the theoretical cornerstone for the new path of governance after the 3rd Plenary Session of the 11th CPC Central Committee.

Whether or not China's basic national conditions are correctly understood and whether or not the party's basic line is correct has a bearing on the success or failure of reform and opening up, and socialist construction. Before the 3rd Plenary Session of the 11th CPC Central Committee, one of the fundamental reasons for the mistakes made by the party in uniting and leading the whole party and the whole nation in implementing socialist construction lay in the fact that some of the tasks and policies proposed went beyond the primary stage of socialism.

In June 1981, the *Resolution on Several Historical Issues of the Party Since the Founding of the PRC*, adopted at the 6th Plenary Session of the 11th CPC Central Committee, put forward for the first time, on the basis of the lessons learned from China's socialist construction, the view that "China's socialist system is still in its primary stage"[57]. In September 1982, the report of the 12th CPC National Congress further stated that "China's socialist society is still in the primary stage of its development" and pointed out that the fundamental characteristic of this stage was that "material civilisation is still underdeveloped"[58].

As comprehensive reforms were implemented, the Resolution of the CPC Central Committee on the *Guiding Principles for the Construction of Socialist Spiritual Civilisation*, adopted at the 6th Plenary Session of the 12th

CPC Central Committee in September 1986, laid the foundation for the systematic formation of the theory of the primary stage of socialism by taking the concept of the primary stage of socialism as its rationale and discussing issues such as the strategic status and fundamental tasks of the construction of spiritual civilisation.

In February 1987, when talking with several senior comrades from the Central Committee about the preparations for the 13th National Congress, Deng Xiaoping proposed that "the report of the 13th National Congress should set out theoretically what socialism is and make clear whether or not our reforms constitute socialism. It should affirm the necessity of the Four Upholds, of opposing bourgeois liberalisation, and of reform and opening up, and make it more clear from a theoretical point of view"[59]. Deng Xiaoping's speech clarified the theme and central task of the 13th National Congress and indicated the appropriate orientation for its convening.

From 25 October to 1 November 1987, the 13th National Congress was held. The most prominent contribution of this congress was the introduction of the theory of the primary stage of socialism and its basic line, which constituted the result and summary of the party's renewed understanding of socialism and China's national conditions based on the practice of socialist construction in China after the 3rd Plenary Session of the 11th CPC Central Committee.

The Congress took the primary stage of socialism as the basis for its thesis and clearly pointed out that a correct understanding of the historical stage in which Chinese society stood at that time was the primary issue in building socialism with Chinese characteristics and the basic foundation for formulating and implementing correct lines and policies. China, stated the congress, is indeed in the primary stage of socialism.

This assertion implied two things. First, Chinese society is already a socialist society, and it was vital to uphold and not depart from socialism; second, Chinese socialist society is still in its primary stage, and it is crucial to start from this reality but not seek to go beyond it. Under the specific historical conditions of modern China, not recognising that the Chinese people can embark on the road to socialism without going through the stage of full capitalist development constitutes a mechanistic theory on the issue of revolutionary development and a major source of right-leaning errors of understanding. But to think that the primary stage of socialism can be traversed without a huge development of productivity is also an empty fantasy on the issue of revolutionary development, and a major source of "leftist" errors of understanding. The primary stage of socialism that China is in is not a general reference to the initial stage that any country will go through to enter socialism but refers specifically to the particular stage that China must go through to build socialism within the context of backward productivity and an underdeveloped commodity economy. From the basic completion of the socialist transformation of private ownership of the means of production in the 1950s to the basic achievement of socialist modernisation, China would be in the primary stage of socialism for at least a hundred years[60].

The 13th CPC National Congress made a profound analysis of Chinese society at that time, pointing out that, on the one hand, the socialist economy based on public ownership of the means of production, the socialist political system of the people's democratic dictatorship and the guiding position of Marxism in the field of ideology had been established, and with that the system of exploitation and the exploiting classes themselves had been eliminated, the country's economic strength had grown tremendously and there had been considerable development in education, science and culture. On the other hand, the congress pointed out, the population was large, the economic base was underdeveloped, and the per capita GDP was still lagging behind the rest of the world. The backwardness of productivity meant that, in terms of socio-economic relations, the degree of socialisation of production necessary for the development of socialist public ownership was still very low, the commodity economy and the domestic market were still very underdeveloped, and the socialist economy was still immature and imperfect. In terms of the superstructure, the set of economic and cultural conditions necessary for the construction of a high degree of socialist democracy was far from being met.

On the basis of a profound analysis of China's national conditions, the 13th National Congress systematically articulated the party's basic line in the primary stage of socialism which is ， namely ， to lead and unite the people of all of China's ethnic groups, to focus on economic construction, to uphold the Four Cardinal Principles, to uphold reform and opening up, to be self-reliant, to be entrepreneurial and to strive to build China into a rich, strong, democratic and civilised socialist modern country. This basic line is referred to as "one central task and two basic points", meaning a focus on economic construction and upholding both the Four Cardinal Principles and reform and opening up.

Based on the theory of the primary stage of socialism, the 13th National Congress further defined the basic guidelines for future economic construction, reform of the economy and the political system, and party building, and planned the basic blueprint for China's socialist construction, and reform and opening up. The basic line of "one central task and two basic points" proposed by the 13th National Congress constitutes a continuation, enrichment and development of the line since the 3rd Plenary Session of the 11th CPC Central Committee, was in line with China's national conditions and was absolutely correct. The most basic implications of the road to socialism with Chinese characteristics were thereby established. Practice has proven that the implementation of this basic line constitutes the fundamental guarantee of victory in all socialist endeavours; departing from it would lead to all kinds of mistakes being made.

The correct line comes from a proper assessment of China's national conditions. On the basis of previous explorations, the 13th National Congress summed up the fresh experience of reform and opening up, and systematically expounded the theory of the primary stage of socialism, resulting in a big step forward in the understanding of the primary stage of socialism.

Proposing the theory of the primary stage of socialism not only provided both within and outside the party a clearer understanding of the long-term, complex and arduous nature of China's socialist construction but also provided a powerful ideological weapon for preventing and redressing "leftist" and rightist interference, enhancing the consciousness of all party members in implementing the party's basic line in the primary stage of socialism, and constant advancement of the great cause of China's modernisation, and reform and opening up. It also constituted another major contribution of the Chinese communists to the theory of scientific socialism. The theory of the primary stage of socialism and the party's basic line distinctly reflected China's basic national conditions and the historical stage China was in, outlined the party's basic political assertions and basic tasks, and constituted the general basis for all the policies and guidelines formulated by the party. Recognising China's basic national conditions and the historical stage it was in, and moving forward in line with the established lines and policies, were the fundamental reasons why the party was able to unite and lead the people of China to achieve a series of historic achievements since the outset of reform and opening up. After the political turmoil of 1989, Deng Xiaoping had stressed more than once that, "the line, guidelines and policies since the 3rd Plenary Session of the 11th CPC Central Committee must continue to be implemented, and even the wording must not be changed. The political report of the 13th National Congress was adopted by the party congress, and not one iota of it can be altered"[61]. This fully demonstrates the importance of the theory of the primary stage of socialism and the party's basic line, as well as the party's determination and confidence in upholding the theory of the primary stage of socialism and the party's basic line.

(XI) AN IN-DEPTH CONSIDERATION OF CHINA'S DOMESTIC POLITICAL TURMOIL AND THE LOSS OF COMMUNIST PARTIES' GOVERNANCE POSITION IN THE SOVIET UNION AND EASTERN EUROPE

In the late 1980s and early 1990s, against the backdrop of the Western countries' intensified peaceful evolutionary strategy against socialist countries, there was serious political turmoil in China, followed by a wave of anti-China efforts ignited by some Western countries, led by the US, to exert political pressure and impose economic "sanctions" on China. The practice of socialism in Eastern European countries also encountered major setbacks, resulting in dramatic changes there and the collapse of the Soviet Union occurring in quick succession; socialist governments which countless communists had worked for at the cost of their blood and lives went completely to waste. The emergence of these storms and setbacks caused great shock in China and overseas, and in order to safeguard and consolidate its position of governance the CPC seriously reflected on these matters and sought to identify the crux of the problem to avoid committing the same disastrous mistakes.

On 9 June 1989, when receiving senior military cadres from the martial law forces in Beijing, Deng Xiaoping reflected deeply on the political turmoil occurring within China and pointed out, "the turmoil was bound to come sooner or later. This is determined by the international climate and China's own microclimate. It was bound to come and is not subject to the will of the people. The outbreak of this incident is well worth pondering over and prompts us to consider the past and the future very soberly." He raised two major questions that required serious consideration. The first question was whether the line, guidelines and policies formulated by the 3rd Plenary Session of the 11th CPC Central Committee, including the "three steps" of China's development strategy, were correct. Was the correctness of the line, guidelines and policies formulated by the party in doubt in the wake of that political storm? Was the party's goal a "leftist" goal? Should the party continue to maintain the same goal as the objective of its future struggles? The second question was whether the "one central task and two basic points" outlined by the 13th National Congress was correct. Or were the two basic points, namely the Four Upholds and reform and opening up, wrong? In response to these two questions, Deng Xiaoping categorically stated that the line, guidelines and policies formulated by the 3rd Plenary Session of the 11th CPC Central Committee, including the "three-step" development strategy, were not wrong, that it would not be right to say that the party's strategic objectives were wrong just because of this incident, and that the "one central task and two basic points" outlined by the 13th National Congress were not wrong. The Four Upholds are not wrong in themselves, [he said], but if a mistake had been made it was that the Four Upholds had not been adhered to consistently enough. There was also nothing wrong with the basic point of reform and opening up either. If anything was inadequate, [he said], it was the extent of reform and opening up. With regard to China's subsequent development, Deng Xiaoping firmly pointed out that the basic lines, guidelines and policies the party had originally formulated should continue to be implemented with unwavering determination. As for the problems and shortcomings of reform and opening up, he made a dialectical analysis, emphasising that, "the achievements of 10 years of reform and opening up should be fully assessed", "but today, looking back, there are obvious shortcomings; we have not grasped our tasks equally firmly with both hands; the hand firmly gripping and the one not so are not mutually suited or compatible". He also sternly pointed out that, "the biggest mistake of the past decade has been education, and here I am mainly talking about ideological and political education, not simply for schools and young students, but education for the people in general. There has been very little education about hard work and entrepreneurship, about the type of country China is and the type of country it will become; this is a great failing on our part". Therefore, he said, "we should unswervingly implement the line and set of guidelines and policies formulated since the 3rd Plenary Session of the 11th CPC Central Committee and carefully take stock of our experience. We should continue to uphold what is right, correct what has gone wrong and strengthen what is inadequate. In short, we must take stock of the present and envision the future"[62]. This major speech of Deng Xiaoping preliminarily summarised the lessons learnt from the party's leadership of reform and opening up after the 3rd Plenary Session of the 11th CPC Central Committee and pointed out the right direction for further upholding and developing socialism with Chinese characteristics.

After the political turmoil of 1989, Western countries, led by the US, imposed 'sanctions' on China. In the face of all kinds of Western pressure, the CPC's position was firm, and on 16 June 1989, Deng Xiaoping pointed out in a conversation with Jiang Zemin and others that, "the whole imperialist Western world is seeking to make all socialist countries abandon the socialist path and eventually be integrated under the rule of international monopoly capitalism and into the orbit of capitalism. Now we have to resist this countercurrent, and the banner of our values must be clear". "Now that international public opinion is pressurising us but we are unruffled and are not enticed by them"[63]. On July 2, when meeting with Brent Scowcroft, special envoy of the US president, Deng Xiaoping further pointed out that China would never allow anyone to interfere in its internal affairs and would never concede, regardless of the consequences. China's internal affairs were to be managed by China and whatever disaster were to come, China would be able to bear it and would never concede. On 4 September, Deng Xiaoping pointed out in a conversation with senior comrades from the Central Committee that, "China must have a collective leadership publicly recognised as proponents of reform and opening up", that "reform and opening up must never be abandoned", and "we must engage sincerely in reform and opening up; it cannot be done behind closed doors". He also said, "First of all, China itself must not mess around but sincerely and genuinely carry on with reform and opening up. Without reform and opening up there is no hope". "We must uphold our image of independence, refusing to believe in fallacies and fearing no one", and "China must definitely follow to the end the socialist path it has chosen. No one will be able to crush us. As long as China does not collapse, one fifth of the world's population will be upholding social-ism. We have full confidence in the prospects of socialism." Deng Xiaoping also pointed out, "With regard to the international situation, to sum up, there are three crucial phrases: first, observe calmly; second, hold your ground; third, handle situations calmly. We must not rush and then nobody will be able to rush us. We must be calm, calm and calm again, fully devote ourselves to our work and do one thing well - take care of our own affairs"[64].

During the time of the dramatic changes in Eastern Europe and the collapse of the Soviet Union, the CPC focused on solving domestic issues while also keeping a close eye on the changes in the international situation. Faced with the extremely complex international situation, Deng Xiaoping repeatedly emphasised the need to maintain stability and uphold reform and opening up, and proposed a series of guiding principles. These were "observe calmly, hold your ground, handle situations calmly, conceal your strengths and bide your time, know your weaknesses and keep them concealed, never claim leadership, and be adept". Deng Xiaoping said, "Now that the old pattern of things is changing and the new pattern has not yet been formed, our foreign policy is still twofold: the first is to oppose hegemonism and power politics, and maintain world peace; the second is to establish a new international political order and a new economic order. In concrete terms, we still have to persist in dealing with all countries, and no matter how the Soviet Union changes, we have to unhurriedly develop relations, including political relations, with them on the basis of the five principles of peaceful coexistence without engaging in ideological arguments. When talking with senior comrades from the Central Committee in December 1990, Deng Xiaoping, in response to the claim that some countries in the Third World wanted China to take a leading role after the dramatic changes in the Soviet Union, clearly stated, "We must not take a leading role; refusing this role is one of our fundamental national policies. We cannot afford to take a leading role; our strength is not sufficient for this. There is absolutely no benefit in our taking a leading role, and many of our initiatives will be lost. China will always be on the side of the Third World; China will never claim hegemony and China will never take a leading role"[65].

In accordance with the guidelines proposed by Deng Xiaoping, the Party Central Committee made a basic judgement on the international situation and concluded that the world at that time was in a period of great historical change. The polarisation of the Cold War had come to an end and the world was moving towards multipolarity as forces regrouped. Although the international situation at that time was turbulent and full of contradictions, he said that peace and development were still the two major themes of the world. In accordance with this judgment, the Central Government made it clear that it would continue to implement its basic foreign policy since reform and opening up, persist in opposing hegemonism and power politics, and develop friendly relations with all countries in the world on the basis of the five principles of peaceful coexistence. In accordance with the strategic and tactical guidelines put forward by Deng Xiaoping, the Party Central Committee remained unperturbed, resisted pressure and maintained its determination, successfully broke free from Western "sanctions", appropriately responded to the dramatic changes in the Soviet Union, upheld and safeguarded the overall context of reform and opening up, and defended the great cause of socialism with Chinese characteristics.

Faced with a complex situation after experiencing domestic political turmoil and the international situation after the dramatic changes in Eastern Europe and the collapse of the Soviet Union, and at a major historical juncture when China was facing the question of its future direction, the CPC, standing in a strategic position to consider the development challenges of the era and full of confidence in reform and opening up, and socialism with Chinese characteristics, profoundly considered and elaborated on a series of major theoretical and practical issues concerning the future prospects of the party and the country. In this the CPC unswervingly adhered to the party's basic line and unswervingly upheld and developed socialism with Chinese characteristics, further promoted reform and opening up, vigorously strengthened the construction of the party itself, and opened up a new dimension of understanding the communist party's governance law, which was all of great significance in ensuring the prosperity and long-term stability of the causes of the party and the state.

(XII) DENG XIAOPING'S SOUTHERN TOUR SPEECHES: PROFOUND ANSWERS TO A SERIES OF MAJOR QUESTIONS ON CPC GOVERNANCE

From 18 January to 21 February 1992, Deng Xiaoping visited Wuchang, Shenzhen, Zhuhai and Shanghai, delivering some important speeches. Deng Xiaoping's southern tour speeches incisively analysed the international and domestic situation, scientifically summarised the basic practice and experience of the party since the 3rd Plenary Session of the 11th CPC Central Committee, clearly answered many major cognitive issues that had long troubled and shackled people's thinking and gave clear answers to a series of major questions about CPC governance. From 9 to 10 March that year, the Politburo held a plenary session to discuss Deng Xiaoping's southern tour speeches, which were considered to be of major and far-reaching significance not only for current reform and construction, and for the opening of the 14th CPC National Congress but also for the whole cause of socialist modernisation and construction.

In the spring and summer of 1989, political turmoil occurred in China and the party and government relied on the people and defended socialist state power, safeguarded the fundamental interests of the people and ensured that reform and opening up, and modernisation would continue to advance. In December 1991, the Soviet Union, the world's first socialist state, collapsed in an instant without war or invasion by foreign aggressors. The disintegration of the Soviet Union, coupled with the dramatic changes in Eastern European countries from 1989 on, led to many socialist countries changing their ideological affiliation and the international communist movement fell to a low ebb. This major change and restructuring of the world posed a major challenge to the governance of the CPC and had a huge impact on China.

On the one hand, the world became multi-polar and Western countries intensified their struggle for, and penetration of, former socialist countries while some developing countries seized the opportunity of the accelerated process of economic globalisation and exhibited strong development momentum. At the same time, despite thwarting Western "sanctions", China still faced serious challenges.

On the other hand, this complex situation caused confusion in the minds of a considerable number of cadres and the masses. Some people lacked confidence in the future of socialism, some wavered from the party's basic line, and some raised the question of whether it was right for China to follow socialism or capitalism, and were worried that the market economy, the creation of SEZs and the development of the non-public ownership economy would lead to capitalism. These doubts and worries boiled down to the question of whether the party's basic line of "one central task and two basic points" should still be upheld and whether it was right to persist with the reform and opening up of China.

Faced with such a complex international and domestic situation, at a critical moment and important juncture in China's reform and opening up, 88-year-old Deng Xiaoping embarked on a tour of southern China to deliver targeted speeches on a series of major theoretical and cognitive issues in China's reform and development. These included many major issues pertaining to the CPC's governance.

First, he emphasised, the line, guidelines and policies of reform and opening up should be upheld without wavering. In response to people's worries and doubts concerning China's reform and opening up, Deng Xiaoping pointed out in no uncertain terms that, "The key to upholding the line, guidelines and policies since the 3rd Plenary Session of the 11th CPC Central Committee is to uphold 'one central task and two basic points.' If we do not uphold socialism, and reform and opening up, and develop the economy and improve people's livelihoods, then we are at death's door. We must submit to the basic line for a century and not be shaken. Only if we uphold this line will the people believe and support us. Whoever wants to change the line, guidelines and policies since the Third Plenary Session, the people will not agree, and that person will be defeated." Deng Xiaoping used the results of reform and opening up to prove the correctness of the party's basic line and the necessity of upholding it. He said, "Without the fruits of reform and opening up, we would not have been able to break through the barriers created by 'June Fourth'[66]. How is it that our country has been able to be so stable since 'June Fourth'? It is because we have carried out reform and opening up, promoting economic development and improving people's lives. Therefore, military and state power, must all uphold this path, this system, and these policies." Deng Xiaoping said, "The fact that our country has developed so rapidly in these short 10 years, to the delight of the people and gaining the attention of the world, is proof enough of the correctness of the line, the guidelines and the policies since the Third Plenary Session. No one could change these even if they wanted to. No matter how people may debate and argue, this will never change - the need to uphold this line, and these guidelines and policies." Deng Xiaoping emphasised, in relation to the practice of rural reform, that "the basic policy of urban and rural reform must remain stable for a long time", and "don't do anything which would make people feel the policy has changed. It is with this one unchanging line that China has great hope."

Second, he clearly answered many of the major theoretical questions that had long troubled and shackled people's thinking on the question of the nature of socialism and the appropriate method for its construction. In response to the question of whether it was right for China to follow socialism or capitalism in reform and opening up, Deng Xiaoping hit the nail on the head by saying that, "if reform and opening up does not move forwards and does not dare to break through, then, in the final analysis, we are afraid that we will take the capitalist road. The reason why some hesitate to advance reform and opening up, and dare not enter uncharted waters is because they fear it would mean introducing too many elements of capitalism and, therefore, following the capitalist path. The crucial point is the question of whether it was right for China to follow socialism or capitalism. The criterion for judgment should be mainly whether it is conducive to the development of the productivity of a socialist society, whether it is conducive to the enhancement of the comprehensive national power of a socialist country, and whether it is conducive to the improvement of people's living standards." Regarding the relationship between planning and the market, and the nature of socialism, he pointed out, "Whether there is more planning or more market is not the essential difference between socialism and capitalism. A planned economy does not equate to socialism because capitalist economies are also planned. Likewise, a market economy does not equate with capitalism because socialist economies also have markets. Both planning and the market are economic tools. The essence of socialism is to liberate and develop productivity, eradicate exploitation, eliminate polarisation and ultimately achieve common prosperity."

Third, he proposed seizing the opportunity to develop the economy, stressing that only development is the unchanging principle to be upheld. Deng Xiaoping said, "Nowadays, some neighbouring countries and regions are developing faster than us economically. If we do not develop or develop too slowly, then once people make comparisons there will be a problem. Therefore, if development is possible, we must not hinder it; regions in China which are already ready for this must do it as quickly as possible. As long as there is commitment to efficiency, quality and an export-oriented economy, there is nothing to worry about. Low speed is tantamount to stagnation or even backwardness. We have to seize the opportunity, and now is indeed a good opportunity." He advocated that China's economic development should strive to move to a higher level every few years, saying that, "It seems that we should always seize the opportunity to accelerate our development for a few years at a certain stage and thereafter continue to move forward after problems have been identified and promptly dealt with." He said this not to encourage an unrealistically high speed of development but to emphasise that, "it is better to be solid and pragmatic, to be efficient and to develop in a steady and coordinated manner." But, at the same time, he pointed out that, "for a large developing country like ours, the economy has to develop faster and it cannot always be entirely calm and steady. We have to pay attention to ensuring a stable economy and coordinated development but stability and coordination are also relative, not absolute; only development is the unchanging principle to be upheld." His perspective was that, "from our own experience over these few years, it is possible to move up a level in terms of economic development every few years." "From international experience, some countries have had periods of rapid development or a number of phases of rapid development, in the course of their development. This was the case in Japan, South Korea and some countries and regions in Southeast Asia. Now that we have suitable domestic conditions and a favourable international environment, coupled with the advantage of the socialist system of being able to concentrate our efforts on carrying out large-scale projects, it is necessary and achievable to implement several stages of faster and more effective development in the long process of modernisation in the future. All we need for this is to have this lofty ambition!" At the same time, Deng Xiaoping stressed that for faster economic development it was necessary to rely on science and technology and education. He said, "Science and technology are the primary productive force", "science must be promoted and only in science is there hope", and "in the field of high technology, China must also take its place in the world".

Fourth, he proposed that it was necessary to grasp our tasks equally firmly with both hands. Deng Xiaoping emphasised that at the same time as taking firm hold of reform and opening up, it is also necessary to grasp the struggle against all kinds of criminal activities and build socialist spiritual civilisation. He pointed out, "in order to combat all kinds of criminal activities and eradicate all kinds of abhorrent phenomena, we must not have a loose grip", and "since opening up, some corrupt forces have also come in, and abhorrent phenomena have emerged in some parts of China, such as drug abuse, prostitution and economic crimes. Attention must be paid to getting a firm grip on these, and resolutely cracking down on and combating them, and they must not be allowed to develop." He also said that, "Corruption must be opposed throughout the whole process of reform and opening up, and for cadres and CPC members, honest politics should be strongly embraced as a major concern. It is still necessary to rely on the legal system and it must be made more reliable. In short, as long as our productivity develops, we maintain a certain pace of economic growth and uphold this approach of grasping tasks equally firmly with both hands, then it will be possible to implement the construction of socialist spiritual civilisation." Deng Xiaoping emphasised that throughout the process of reform and opening up, care must always be taken to uphold the Four Cardinal Principles. He cautioned that, "The consequences of widespread bourgeois liberalisation are extremely serious. It took more than 10 years to build the SEZs into what they are now but they can collapse overnight. They can collapse easily but are difficult to build. If we don't pay attention when the first signs of trouble appear, something will go wrong." He said, "It is a fundamental point of Marxism to rely on the dictatorship of the proletariat to defend the socialist system." "Using the power of the people's democratic dictatorship to consolidate the people's power is a righteous act and there is nothing wrong about it. We have only been engaged in socialism for a few decades and are still in the primary stage. It will take a long period of history to consolidate and develop the socialist system; it will take several generations or a dozen generations, even dozens of generations of our people struggling persistently, and we must not lower our guard."

Fifth, he said that a correct political line depends on a correct organisational line to ensure that China's affairs can be conducted effectively, that socialism and reform and opening up can be upheld, that the economy can develop faster and that the party can govern the country for a long time; as he said, in some way the people are the key. Deng Xiaoping stressed the need to educate China's army, its dictatorial institutions, CPC members, and the people and youths well. He pointed out that, "if China has problems, then the source still lies within the communist party. We have to approach this problem with soberness, pay attention to training people, and select people with both integrity and talent into work teams according to the criteria of 'revolutionisation, rejuvenation, intellectualisation and specialisation". When we talk about submitting to the party's basic line for a century and having longlasting stability, it all comes down to this one line. This is what is really at stake." "That is, we should elect people who are recognised by the people as upholding reform and opening up, and who have a track record of political achievements, and boldly put them into the new leadership structure, so that the people will sense our sincerity in carrying out reform and opening up. The people want to see how we actually practise things. As soon as the people see that socialism is better and that reform and opening up are better, our cause will last forever!" Deng Xiaoping also stressed the need to make more progress in finding young people to join work teams. He said, "Now we must also continue to select people, younger comrades, and help nurture them." "We have to select people and, after we have selected them, then help to nurture them, so that more young people can be raised up. Once they have grown up, we will be relieved."

Sixth, he said that socialism is bound to replace capitalism after a long process of development; this is an irreversible general trend in the historical development of society but the road to get there is tortuous. In response to some people's lack of confidence in the future prospects of socialism, Deng Xiaoping firmly believed that, "the number of people in the world agreeing with Marxism will increase because Marxism is scientific." He said, "How many dynastic restorations have occurred in the centuries since capitalism replaced feudalism? So, in a certain sense, some kind of temporary restoration is also a regular phenomenon that is difficult to avoid completely. In some countries there are serious complications and socialism seems to be weakened but as the people undergo hardship and learn from it they will push socialism to develop in a healthier direction. Therefore, do not be alarmed and do not think that Marxism has disappeared, is useless and has failed. That will never happen!"

In his southern tour speeches, Deng Xiaoping also made some other important points. For example, he said, "Revolution is the liberation of the productive forces, and reform is also the liberation of productive forces." "In the past, it was incomplete to speak only of developing the productive forces under socialist conditions and not of also liberating them through reform. Both the liberation of productive forces and the development of productive forces should be articulated in their entirety." An example of another point he made is when he said, "Reform and opening up should be more daring and dare to try new things, and not be timid and restrained. If you get it right, you must try boldly and venture boldly." "Without a little bit of spirit to break through, without a little bit of spirit to 'take risks', without a breath of energy and strength, it will not be possible to follow a good path, to follow a new path, and it will not be possible to pursue new things." And another point he made was that "the right can ruin socialism, and the 'left' also has the capacity to ruin socialism. China should be wary of the right but mainly focus on guarding against the 'left'"[67].

Deng Xiaoping's southern tour speeches constituted a political mandate and briefing given by Deng Xiaoping to the third generation of the party's central leadership, as well as to the entire party and the people of China at a major historical juncture. They also incisively analysed the international and domestic situation at the time, scientifically summarised the party's governance practice and basic experience since the 3rd Plenary Session of the 11th CPC Central Committee, and provided a profound theoretical answer to many major cognitive issues that had long troubled and shackled people's thinking. They demonstrated not only Deng Xiaoping's high sense of historical responsibility for the party's cause but also the CPC's firm belief in following the path of socialism with Chinese characteristics, and constituted a glorious landmark chapter in the history of socialist thought. These speeches of Deng Xiaoping broke the spell that had long held people in shackles, greatly enlightened and liberated people's minds, and advanced China's reform and opening up into a new historical phase.

(XIII) DENG XIAOPING THEORY: A PROFOUND REVELATION OF THE COMMUNIST PARTY'S GOVERNANCE LAW

After the 3rd Plenary Session of the 11th CPC Central Committee, the second generation of the party's central leadership, with Comrade Deng Xiaoping at its core, gradually created and formed Deng Xiaoping Theory under historical conditions characterised by prevailing peace and development. This was achieved in the course of China's reform and opening up, and socialist modernisation on the basis of summing up the historical experience of China's socialist victories and setbacks, and drawing on the historical experience of the rise and fall and success and failure of socialism in other countries. Deng Xiaoping Theory, which focuses on the basic question of the nature of socialism and the appropriate way to construct it, provided the first relatively systematic answer to a series of basic questions on how to build, consolidate and develop socialism in an economically and culturally backward country like China, and inherited and developed Marxism with new ideas and perspectives.

The 15th CPC National Congress was held in Beijing from 12 to 18 September 1997. The greatest contribution of this congress was the establishment of Deng Xiaoping Theory as the guiding ideology of the whole party. The Constitution of the 15th CPC National Congress clearly stipulated that the CPC takes Marxism-Leninism-Mao Zedong Thought and Deng Xiaoping Theory as its guide to action. Deng Xiaoping Theory is the product of integrating the basic principles of Marxism-Leninism with contemporary Chinese practice and the characteristics of the period. It constitutes the inheritance and development of Mao Zedong Thought under new historical conditions, a new stage in the development of Marxism in China, the manifestation of Marxism in contemporary China, and the crystallisation of the collective wisdom of the CPC, guiding the cause of China's socialist modernisation constantly forward[68]. This is the unshakeable conclusion that the CPC has drawn from history and reality.

The 15th CPC National Congress formally established Deng Xiaoping Theory as the party's guide, which constituted a historic decision made by the CPC, after nearly 20 years of successful practice in reform and opening up, and socialist modernisation, on the basis of the 3rd Plenary Session of the 11th CPC Central Committee and the 12th and 13th National Congresses and, in particular, the 14th CPC National Congress.

At the 3rd Plenary Session of the 11th CPC Central Committee, the party made the major decision to implement reform and opening up, starting the historic transformation from "taking class struggle as the central task" to focusing on economic construction, from rigidity and semi-rigidity to comprehensive reform, from a closed or semi-closed state to opening up to the outside world, and commencing a new period of reform and opening up, and socialist modernisation. Through the 3rd Plenary Session of the 11th CPC Central Committee a series of important ideologies and views began to be put forward, including the theories of the party's ideological line, of the party's work priorities, of the fundamental tasks and main contradictions of socialism, of the socialist democratic legal system, and of socialist reform and opening up. Thereby the framework of Deng Xiaoping Theory began to take shape.

At the 12th CPC National Congress, Deng Xiaoping proposed in his opening speech that "integrating the universal truths of Marxism with China's concrete reality, following our own path and building socialism with Chinese characteristics, constitutes the basic conclusion we have drawn from our long historical experience". The 12th National Congress compared the great historical turnaround marked by the 3rd Plenary Session of the 11th CPC Central Committee with the great historical trans-formation marked by the Zunyi Conference and proposed that "under new historical conditions and in the process of great new practices, we should accumulate new experiences, create new theories and advance Marxism-Leninism and Mao Zedong Thought". The theme of this new theory was "building socialism with Chinese characteristics"; in other words, Deng Xiaoping Theory shaped this theme.

At the 13th National Congress, the CPC stated that "there have been two historic leaps" in the integration of Marxism with practice in China. "The second leap occurred after the 3rd Plenary Session of the 11th CPC

Central Committee, when the Chinese communists, on the basis of summing up both positive and negative experiences over the preceding 30 years since the founding of the PRC, and on the basis of studying international experience and the state of the world, began to find a path for building socialism with Chinese characteristics and brought about a new stage of socialist construction". It was stressed that Deng Xiaoping "made a significant contribution" to the formation and development of the line since the 3rd Plenary Session of the 11th CPC Central Committee, and that the series of scientific theoretical perspectives developed by the CPC in philosophy, political economics and scientific socialism preliminarily answered the basic questions of the stages, tasks, dynamics, conditions, composition and international environment of China's socialist construction, "configuring the outline of the theory of building socialism with Chinese characteristics"[69].

At the 14th CPC National Congress, the CPC explicitly pointed out that the "second generation of central leadership with Comrade Deng Xiaoping at its core" formed at the 3rd Plenary Session of the 11th CPC Central Committee had begun "another great revolution" and that Deng Xiaoping, as the chief architect of China's socialist reform and opening up, and modernisation, had "demonstrated great political courage to pioneer a new path for socialist construction and great theoretical courage to open up new horizons for Marxism, making a major historic contribution to the establishment of the theory of building socialism with Chinese characteristics"[70].

The 14th CPC National Congress established the partywide guiding position of "Comrade Deng Xiaoping's theory of building socialism with Chinese characteristics" and gave a systematic, accurate and complete overview of nine aspects of Deng Xiaoping's theory of building socialism with Chinese characteristics.

With regard to the development path of socialism, it was emphasised that China should pursue its own path, not take books as dogma and not copy foreign models but, using Marxism as a guide, take practice as the sole criterion for testing truth, emancipate the mind, seek truth from facts, respect the initiative of the masses and build socialism with Chinese characteristics.

With regard to the stage of development of socialism, the scientific assertion was made that China was still in the primary stage of socialism, stressing that this constituted a long historical stage of at least one hundred years, and that all guidelines and policies must be formulated on the basis of this basic national condition, and must not be detached from reality and seek to leapfrog this stage.

With regard to the issue of the fundamental task of socialism, it was pointed out that the essence of socialism was to liberate and develop productive forces, eradicate exploitation, eliminate polarisation and ultimately achieve common prosperity. It was stressed that the main contradiction in China's society in that era was between the growing material and cultural needs of the people and backward social production, and that the development of the productive forces must be given primary importance, with economic construction at the centre of all efforts, to promote overall social progress. It was also said that, in the final analysis, the merits and demerits of all aspects of work should be judged by whether they are conducive to the development of the productive forces of socialist society, the enhancement of the comprehensive national strength of a socialist country, and the improvement of the people's living standards. Science and technology are the primary productive force, and economic construction must depend on scientific and technological progress and the improvement of the quality of labourers.

With regard to the dynamics of socialist development, it was stressed that reform also constitutes a revolution and the liberation of the productive forces, and is the only path to modernisation in China, and that rigidity and stagnation provide no way forward. The objective of economic system reform was to establish and refine the socialist market economy on the basis of upholding the system of public ownership and distribution according to work as the main feature, supplemented by other economic components and distribution methods. The objective of political system reform was to develop socialist democratic politics, with the refinement of the system of people's congresses and the system of multi-party cooperation and political consultation under the leadership of the CPC as the main elements. In line with the reform and development of the economy and politics, the aim was to build socialist spiritual civilisation with "ideals, morality, culture and discipline".

With regard to the external conditions for socialist construction, it was pointed out that peace and development were the two major themes of the contemporary world and that it was necessary to persist with an independent and peaceful foreign policy, and to strive for a favourable international environment beneficial for China's modernisation. It was stressed that opening up to the outside world was essential for reform and construction, and that all the advanced civilisational achievements attained by all countries in the world, including capitalist developed countries, should be absorbed and utilised for the development of socialism, and that closure would only lead to backwardness.

With regard to the issue of the political guarantee for socialist construction, emphasis was placed on upholding the socialist path, the people's democratic dictatorship, the leadership of the CPC and Marxism-Leninism and Mao Zedong Thought. These Four Cardinal Principles are essential to the establishing of the nation and constitute a guarantee for the healthy development of reform and opening up, and modernisation while also having been further enriched in the process of reform and opening up, and modernisation.

With regard to the strategic steps of socialist construction, it was proposed that the basic achievement of modernisation should be carried out in three steps. In the long process of modernisation, it was vital to seize the opportunity to strive for a number of stages of faster and more effective development, and move up a step in the process every few years. Socialism does not mean poverty but simultaneous affluence is also impossible. However, it is necessary to permit and encourage some people in some regions to become affluent first, so as to propel more and more regions and people to gradually reach common prosperity.

With regard to the leadership and supporters of socialism, it was stressed that the CPC, as the vanguard of the working class, is the leading core of the socialist cause and that the party must adapt to the needs of reform and opening up, and modernisation, constantly refine and strengthen its leadership in all aspects of work, and improve and strengthen its own construction. The work style of the ruling party and the relationship between the party and the people is a matter of life and death for the party. It was vital to rely on the masses of workers, farmers and intelligentsia, on the unity of the people of all ethnic groups, and on the broadest united front of all socialist workers, patriots who support socialism and patriots who support the reunification of the motherland. The PLA, led by the party, is the defender of the socialist motherland and a major force in building socialism.

With regard to the reunification of the motherland, the creative concept of "one country two systems" was put forward. Under the premise of one China, the main part of the country adheres to the socialist system, while Hong Kong, Macau and Taiwan will maintain their original capitalist systems for a long time, so as to promote the completion of the great undertaking of the peaceful reunification of the motherland in accordance with this principle.

The points above demonstrate that Deng Xiaoping Theory had become systematised and reached maturity.

In February 1997, Deng Xiaoping passed away. In his eulogy at the memorial service of Deng Xiaoping, Jiang Zemin stressed that the most valuable legacy Comrade Deng Xiaoping left to China was the theory of building socialism with Chinese characteristics that he founded and the party's basic line regarding the primary stage of socialism that was formulated under the guidance of this theory[71]. In September of the same year, the 15th CPC National Congress made the decision to raise aloft the great banner of Deng Xiaoping Theory. This Congress officially used the concept of "Deng Xiaoping Theory" and wrote it into the party constitution as the party's guiding ideology.

History and practice have amply proven that Deng Xiaoping Theory, which integrates Marxism with contemporary Chinese practice and the characteristics of the times, is the correct theory to guide the Chinese people to triumphantly achieve socialist modernisation in the course of reform and opening up. The reason why Deng Xiaoping Theory is scientific and correct lies in its revealing of, and response to, the communist party's governance law.

Deng Xiaoping Theory upholds emancipation of the mind and seeking truth from facts, and embraces the legacy of the previous generations while also breaking through old-fashioned ways on the basis of new practice, opening up a new realm of Marxism. Seeking truth from facts is the essence of Marxism-Leninism, of Mao Zedong Thought and of Deng Xiaoping Theory. In 1978, Deng Xiaoping's speech *Emancipating the Mind, Seeking Truth from Facts, Uniting as One and Looking to the Future* was a manifesto for breaking free from the shackles of the "Two Whatevers" after the end of the Cultural Revolution at a critical historical juncture when China was determining the appropriate direction to take, and opened up a new path and a new era, and created a new theory for building socialism with Chinese characteristics. Deng Xiaoping's southern tour speeches in 1992 constituted another manifesto for emancipating the mind and seeking truth from facts, at a critical historical juncture during the severe test of political turmoil both within China and internationally, which adhered to the theory and line of the party since the 3rd Plenary Session of the 11th CPC Central Committee, profoundly answering many cognitive issues that had long fettered people's thinking, and advancing reform and opening up, and modernisation to a new stage. In the new situation as China approached the new century, facing many difficult issues that the nation had never encountered before, Deng Xiaoping Theory demanded strengthened and enhanced firmness and awareness of emancipating the mind and seeking truth from facts, based on the fundamental criteria of the "Three Beneficials", namely whether something is beneficial for developing the productivity of a socialist society, whether it is beneficial for strengthening a socialist country's comprehensive national power, and whether it is beneficial for raising the people's living standards, and continuously broke new ground in developing China's new context.

Deng Xiaoping Theory upholds the basic achievements of the theory and practice of scientific socialism, grasps the fundamental question of the nature of socialism, profoundly reveals the essence of socialism, and raises the understanding of socialism to a new scientific level. The various twists and turns and mistakes experienced by Chinese socialism before reform and opening up, and some of the confusion encountered in its progress since reform and opening up, all ultimately originate in a failure to fully understand this issue. The historical transformation from bringing order out of chaos to comprehensive reform, from "taking class struggle as the central task" to a focus on economic construction, from a closed or semi-closed state to reform and opening up, and from a planned economy to a socialist market economy, is the process of gradually clarifying this fundamental issue.

Deng Xiaoping Theory upholds observing the world with the broad vision of Marxism, making correct analyses and new scientific judgments on the characteristics of the present era and the overall international situation, on the successes and failures of other socialist countries, on the successes and failures of developing countries in their pursuit of development, and on the dynamics and contradictions in the development of developed countries. The world is changing drastically and rapidly, and in particular rapid scientific and technological progress has profoundly changed and continues to change contemporary economic and social life and the world itself, with the result that no Marxist in any country can afford not to take it seriously. It was in the light of this very situation that Deng Xiaoping Theory defined the CPC's party line and international strategy, requiring the party to understand, inherit and develop Marxism with a new perspective, stressing that only this constitutes true Marxism and that being hidebound by convention can only lead to backwardness or even failure.

Deng Xiaoping Theory formed a new scientific system for the construction of the theory of socialism with Chinese characteristics. This theory links together the fields of philosophy, political economics and scientific socialism, covers the economy, politics, science and technology, education, culture, ethnicity, the military, foreign affairs, the united front and party building, and constitutes a relatively complete scientific system. It provided preliminary answers for the first time in a relatively systematic manner to a series of fundamental questions about the path of development of Chinese socialism, the stages of development, the fundamental tasks, the driving force of development, external conditions, political guarantees, strategic steps, party leadership and strength, and the reunification of the motherland.

Great practice gives birth to great theory, and great theory promotes great practice. In a context where peace and development have become the central theme of the times, in the practice of China's reform and opening up, and modernisation, and based on the historical experience of China's socialist victories and setbacks, and on the historical experience of the rise and fall, and success and failure of other socialist countries, Deng Xiaoping Theory firmly grasped the fundamental question of the nature of socialism and the appropriate way to construct it. It deepened with a new vision the understanding of the communist party's governance law, the laws of socialist construction and of human social development, and created a new situational context for party governance, providing scientific guidance for promoting socialist modernisation and ensuring the long-term stability of the party and the country.

2

EXPANDING A NEW PATH OF GOVERNANCE IN DEVELOPING THE SOCIALIST MARKET ECONOMY

After the 4th Plenary Session of the 13th CPC Central Committee, the third generation of the party's central leadership, with Comrade Jiang Zemin at its core, withstood heavy pressure and overcame various challenges at a critical historical juncture when the situation at home and abroad was changing rapidly. They also firmly upheld socialism with Chinese characteristics, established the reform objectives and basic framework of the socialist market economy, formulated the party's basic principle of the primary stage of socialism, put forward the basic strategy of the rule of law, promoted the new great project of party construction, formed the major ideology of the "Three Represents", and successfully propelled the great cause of socialism with Chinese characteristics into the 21st century. In continuing the process of reform and opening up, the Party Central Committee, with an eye on the practice of socialist modernisation and the fundamental requirements of human social development, explored the communist party's governance law by applying the positions, viewpoints and methods of Marxism, opening up new horizons of Marxism and expanding new paths of governance in the development of a socialist market economy.

(I) FIRMLY DEFENDING AND DEVELOPING SOCIALISM WITH CHINESE CHARACTERISTICS IN THE FACE OF SEVERE TESTS

At the end of the 1980s, the global situation was complex and changeable. The political turmoil in the Soviet Union and the socialist countries of Eastern Europe was intensifying, Western political leaders threatened that capitalism would "win without a fight" against socialism, the *zeitgeist* of bourgeois liberalisation was growing and spreading in China, and the contradictions and problems accumulated in the course of reform and opening up came to the fore. The spring and summer of 1989 saw political turmoil in Beijing and some other cities in China. From the second half of 1989 until 1991, there were dramatic changes in Eastern Europe and subsequently the Soviet Union collapsed. This inflicted a strong political shock on China. Socialist China came to a crucial point in its history, and the CPC and the people faced a severe test. In the face of the complex and changeable situation in China and abroad, the Party Central Committee, with Comrade Jiang Zemin at its core, relied closely on the whole party and the people of China, held high the great banner of building the theory of socialism with Chinese characteristics, took a firm and clear-cut stand, assessed the situation and made appropriate plans, powerfully answered the question of whether it was possible to uphold socialism and how to do so, steered the cause of socialism with Chinese characteristics on the right course, and laid the political groundwork for expanding the new path of governance.

Shortly after the domestic political turmoil had occurred, and before the tensions and uneasiness in the country had subsided, the 4th Plenary Session of the 13th CPC Central Committee was held from 23 to 24 June 1989. The plenary session analysed the nature and causes of the political turmoil in China, made a preliminary summary of the lessons learnt, clarified the party's guidelines and tasks for that period and the subsequent period, and made adjustments to the membership of the party's central organs. Jiang Zemin was also elected General Secretary of the Central Committee. He pointed out in his speech that, "This time, the party's central leadership organs have made some personnel changes but the line and basic policies since the 3rd Plenary Session of the 11th CPC Central Committee remain unchanged and must continue to be implemented. On this most fundamental issue, I would like to say two things very clearly: one is to be steadfast and unwavering; the other is to implement them fully and consistently"[1]. These two phrases express the determination to unswervingly promote reform and opening up, and socialist modernisation, and at the same time to capture the key essence of the matter, which was of great significance in helping the masses of party members, cadres and the people to comprehensively understand and consciously implement the party's line, guidelines and policy since the 3rd Plenary Session of the 11th CPC Central Committee, and in ensuring the healthy development of China's reform and opening up, and modernisation along the path of socialism with Chinese characteristics.

Faced with the pressure of 'sanctions' imposed by Western countries, Jiang Zemin declared clearly at a conference to celebrate the 40th anniversary of the founding of the PRC on 29 September 1989, "Our socialist cause has been consolidated and developed in the process of breaking the isolation, blockade and provocations of hostile foreign forces against China. The Chinese people have never and will never capitulate to any foreign pressure and will never give up their socialist path and national independence in exchange for handouts from others". "We must be more determined to integrate the universal truths of Marxism with China's concrete reality, follow our own path and build socialism with Chinese characteristics"[2]. It is very unwise and fundamentally impossible to attempt to ostracise or isolate China. No economic sanctions can in any way shake our determination to revitalise China and adhere to the path of socialism, nor can they in any way shake our firm principle of living in friendship with all peoples of the world.

In December 1990, in order to further sum up the lessons learned from China's socialist construction, the *Proposal of the CPC Central Committee on the Formulation of the Ten-Year Plan for National Economic and Social Development and the Eighth Five-Year Plan* deliberated on and adopted at the 7th Plenary Session of the 13th CPC Central Committee, gave a scientific overview of the basic theory and practice of building socialism with Chinese characteristics since the founding of new China, especially since the 3rd Plenary Session of the 11th CPC Central Committee, and concisely summarised them in 12 basic principles. Those principles are as follows:

- Upholding the people's democratic dictatorship led by the working class and based on the alliance of workers and peasants, constantly refining the system of people's congresses, the system of multiparty cooperation and political consultation under the leadership of the CPC, constantly consolidating and developing a broad patriotic united front, and striving to strengthen socialist democracy and the socialist legal system.

- Upholding the development of social productivity as the fundamental task of socialism, concentrating on modernisation, and constantly raising the material and cultural living standards of the people.

- Through reform, constantly improving the socialist economic, political, and other management systems to fully mobilise the initiative, enthusiasm and creativity of central and local government, enterprises and the working people.

- Adopting various methods, including developing foreign economic and trade relations, and utilising foreign investment and introducing advanced technology, and continuing to open up to the outside world by organising SEZs and economic open zones, and implementing the necessary special policies and flexible measures.

- Persisting with an ownership structure in which multiple economic components coexist and socialist public ownership constitutes the main feature, fully optimising the role of the individual economy, the private sector and other economic components as a useful complement to the public-sector economy, and strengthening correct management and leadership of these areas.

- Actively developing a socialist planned commodity economy, integrating the planned economy with market regulation, and striving to promote the sustained, stable and coordinated development of the national economy.

- Implementing a distribution system in which distribution according to work is the main feature and which is supplemented by other forms of distribution, allowing and supporting some people and regions to become prosperous first through honest labour and legitimate operations, then encouraging those who have become prosperous first to help those who have not done so yet, in order to facilitate the gradual achievement of common prosperity for the entire population and all regions of China.

- Upholding Marxism-Leninism-Mao Zedong Thought as the guide, inheriting and carrying forward China's outstanding cultural heritage, drawing on and absorbing all the outstanding cultural achievements of the humanity, to continuously improve the ideological, moral, scientific and cultural quality of China as a whole, and build a socialist spiritual civilisation;

- Establishing and developing socialist ethnic relations of equality and mutual assistance, unity and cooperation, and common prosperity, upholding and refining the system of ethnic regional autonomy, opposing ethnic discrimination, oppression and division.

- Promoting the gradual achievement of the great cause of the unification of China in accordance with the concept and practice of "one country, two systems".

- Upholding an independent and peaceful foreign policy, developing friendly relations with all countries on the basis of the five principles of peaceful coexistence, opposing hegemonism and power politics, and supporting the just struggles of oppressed nations and peoples, safeguarding world peace and promoting human progress.

- Upholding the leadership of the CPC, constantly improving the system of party leadership, and leadership style and methods, and strengthening the party's political, ideological, theoretical and organisational construction so that the party will always be the strong leading core of the socialist cause.

These 12 principles cover all aspects of politics, economics, ideology, culture, ethnicity, international relations and party construction, and indicated the direction and path for building socialism with Chinese characteristics, as well as articulating a series of guidelines and policies for building socialism with Chinese characteristics, fully reflecting the party's basic line of "one central task and two basic points". They also demonstrate that the CPC achieved a new leap forward in its understanding of the intrinsic laws of socialist construction and achieved new results in its exploration of the road to socialist construction in China.

On 1 July 1991, at a conference to celebrate the 70th anniversary of the founding of the CPC, Jiang Zemin summarised the main experiences of China's revolution, construction and reform by reviewing the process of the CPC's struggles. He pointed out that, "the 70 years of the CPC are 70 years of the party's increasing development and strengthening, 70 years of the party leading the Chinese people to pioneer a new chapter in their history, and 70 years of the great victory of Marxism in China". Overall, in those 70 years, the party had led the people of all of China's ethnic groups to do three major things for the social progress of China. The first was to complete the task of the anti-imperialist and anti-feudal new democratic revolution, which brought an end to the history of China's semi-colonial and semi-feudal society. The second was to eliminate the system of exploitation and the exploiting classes, and to establish a socialist system. The third was to pioneer a path for building socialism with Chinese characteristics and gradually achieving socialist modernisation, which is still a work in progress. These three things have completely transformed China. He summed up the rich experience accumulated by the party over the preceding 70 years in a nutshell which was, namely, to integrate the basic principles of Marxism with the concrete reality of the Chinese revolution and construction, and for China to choose its own path. He also stressed that, "the solemn mission of today's Chinese communists is to uphold the party's basic line, unite and lead the people of all China's ethnicities along the road of building socialism with Chinese characteristics, to rely on themselves and, through hard work and entrepreneurship, to build China into a prosperous, strong, democratic and civilised modern socialist country"[3].

In October 1992, the 14th CPC National Congress amended the *Constitution of the CPC* in light of the major changes in the domestic and international situation, and the tasks of the party and, for the first time, the party's basic line regarding the primary stage of socialism was formally enshrined in the party constitution on the basis of the clarification that China was in the primary stage of socialism. At the same time upholding the party's basic line was added to the party constitution as a basic requirement for party building and leadership, stressing that, "The party as a whole must unify its ideology and actions with the theory of building socialism with Chinese characteristics and the party's basic line, and uphold them in the long term without wavering. It is necessary to unite reform and opening up with the Four Cardinal Principles, to fully implement the party's basic line and to oppose all misguided tendencies of 'left' and right, being vigilant about the right but mainly guarding against the 'left' "[4]. This was of great significance to the CPC in unifying the ideology and actions of the entire party, adhering unwaveringly to the party's basic line, and seizing greater victory in the cause of socialism with Chinese characteristics.

In the face of the downturn of the world socialist movement after the collapse of the Soviet Union and the dramatic changes in Eastern Europe, the Party Central Committee, with Comrade Jiang Zemin at its core, persisted in maintaining the direction of socialism, steadfastly adhered to the party's basic line and continued to walk along the path of socialism with Chinese characteristics. In an interview with the *Washington Times* in October 1991, Jiang Zemin pointed out that, "Chinese socialism is neither the Soviet model nor the Eastern European model but it is socialism with uniquely Chinese characteristics. The decision to follow this path is a historic choice made by the Chinese people after more than 100 years of struggle and fumbling around"[5]. In November 1993, during a meeting with Fidel Castro, First Secretary of the Central Committee of the Communist Party of Cuba and President of the Cuban Council of State, Jiang Zemin stressed, "After the collapse of the Soviet Union and the dramatic changes in Eastern Europe, some people in the West put about the idea that Marxism-Leninism had become obsolete and that socialism would disappear from the face of the earth. But we believe that the future of socialism is still bright". "We should integrate the basic principles of Marxism with the concrete reality of our own countries and concentrate on conducting our countries' affairs, especially economic construction, so that the living standards of the people can continue to rise and the superiority of socialism can be fully reflected. Only in this way will we be able to consolidate and develop socialism and stand in an unshakeable position"[6]. These views powerfully countered the *zeitgeist* that sought to sway the future prospects of Chinese socialism, set the record straight, dispelled doubts and confusion, and played an important role in unifying the ideology and willpower of the whole party and all the people of China to explore a path for successful socialist reform.

In the face of a very complicated situation at home and abroad, and the severe test of serious twists and turns in world socialism, the CPC firmly adhered to the line adopted since the 3rd Plenary Session of the 11th CPC Central Committee, emancipated the mind, sought truth from facts, advanced with the times, pioneered and innovated, and succeeded in overcoming unprecedented, enormous challenges. The party stabilised the general situation of reform and development, and defended and developed socialism with Chinese characteristics, opening up a new horizon in the development of Marxist theory and advancing the cause of socialism with Chinese characteristics into a new historical phase.

(II) SOLVING DILEMMAS IN CPC GOVERNANCE: INTEGRATING SOCIALISM WITH A MARKET ECONOMY

The question of whether a market economy could be developed in the context of socialism was once a major theoretical and practical issue that socialist countries had difficulty in breaking through. Many people within China and overseas asserted that it was impossible to integrate socialism with a market economy, and that either the socialist system would stifle market dynamics, or the market economy would evolve a socialist system. Some even talked nonsense saying that socialism with Chinese characteristics that has engaged in a market economy is in essence capitalism with Chinese characteristics. Indeed, Chinese communists were faced with the great test of how to integrate the advantages of the basic socialist system with those of a market economy and find a concrete way to establish a socialist market economy.

The decision regarding the kind of target model to set for the reform of China's economy was a major issue with a bearing on the overall situation of reform and opening up, and modernisation. Traditional views held that a market economy is something unique to capitalism and that a planned economy is the basic feature of a socialist economy. Since the 3rd Plenary Session of the 11th CPC Central Committee, as reform progressed, the party gradually shook off this notion and formed a new understanding, which played an important role in promoting reform and development.

The 12th CPC National Congress proposed that a planned economy should be the core feature with market regulation as a supplement. The 3rd Plenary Session of the 12th CPC Central Committee pointed out that a commodity economy was an insurmountable stage of socioeconomic development and that China's socialist economy was a planned commodity economy based on public ownership. The 13th CPC National Congress proposed that the system of a socialist planned commodity economy should be one in which planning and the market were intrinsically integrated. After the 4th Plenary Session of the 13th Central Committee, it was proposed that an economic system and operational mechanism combining a planned economy and market regulation should be established to adapt to the development of a planned commodity economy. However, in the process of exploring the question of the target model for China's economic reform, the party was subjected to interference from various quarters. In the face of all the difficulties and challenges, the Party Central Committee, calm and composed, rose to the challenge, persisted with reform and development, overcame numerous obstacles and opened up a new path for the socialist market economy.

After the political turmoil of 1989, there were still major disagreements within the party and in domestic theoretical circles as to whether or not China should persist with market-oriented economic reform. The market economy and market-oriented reforms were once the subject of criticism by certain theorists. The Party Central Committee considered that major issues such as the direction of reform should be studied, making arrangements to listen extensively to the views of all parties. In July 1990, the Politburo Standing Committee several times invited comrades in charge of economic work to study economic issues and, between October and December 1991, Central Government leaders invited some economists and diplomats to discuss theoretical issues relating to the construction of socialism with Chinese characteristics, holding 11 symposia in succession. In their speeches at the symposia, comrades at the conference all emphasised market-oriented reform. Jiang Zemin stressed at the symposia that planning and the market were the core issues in determining how to build socialism with Chinese characteristics and sought to find an integrated approach to planning and the market.

At that time, the debate on the relationship between socialism and the market economy was not limited to the CPC and China's domestic theoretical circles. In September 1991, former British Prime Minister Margaret Thatcher, who was visiting China, argued that socialism and the market economy were not compatible, that it was impossible to have a market economy under socialism, and that a capitalist system and privatisation would be necessary in order to have a market economy[7]. Margaret Thatcher was known for pushing privatisation during her administration and her views can be said to represent mainstream Western thinking. Jiang Zemin disagreed with Margaret Thatcher's views and had discussions with her.

In early 1992, Deng Xiaoping gave his southern tour speeches, in which he expressed his views on the correct understanding of the mutual relationship between planning and the market. He pointed out that a planned economy does not equate to socialism, since capitalism also has economic planning, and that a market economy does not equate to capitalism, since socialism also has markets. Both planning and the market are economic instruments. The essential difference between socialism and capitalism is not whether there is more planning or a more open market. This assertion fundamentally removed the shackles of the idea that a planned economy and a market economy are domains of the basic system of society and provided a fundamental principle for the party to finally solve the problem regarding what should be the target model of China's economic reform.

In March 1992, Jiang Zemin presided over a meeting of the CPC Central Committee Politburo and fully affirmed the important guiding significance of Deng Xiaoping's southern tour speeches, stressing that both planning and the market are economic instruments, and that good use should be made of these instruments to accelerate the development of a socialist commodity economy. We should boldly absorb and draw on all the achievements of civilisation created by human society and the advanced business and management methods of modern countries, including developed Western countries. On 1 April, Jiang Zemin phoned Chen Jinhua, then director of the State Commission for Restructuring the Economy and asked him to organise research into the relationship between planning and the market. Jiang Zemin said, "Now the reform and opening up is at a very important juncture, and everyone is waiting and a little anxious to see what should be done next. So, let the State Commission for Restructuring the Economy research this thoroughly and make recommendations to the central government"[8]. On 15 April, Chen Jinhua invited the regional directors of the commission in five provinces, namely Guangdong, Jiangsu, Shandong, Liaoning and Sichuan, to Beijing for special discussions on the next steps of reform, with the main topic being the relationship between planning and the market. There the participants from the five provinces clearly proposed the "establishment and development of a socialist market economy". After the meeting, Chen Jinhua wrote a report and handed it directly to Jiang Zemin and Li Peng. On 30 April, the Politburo Standing Committee convened a meeting and proposed that the 14th CPC National

Congress should take a step forward in establishing the relationship between planning and the market, this being a major issue related to the overall situation of reform and opening up, and modernisation. On 28 May, the Politburo Standing Committee formally decided to make a new statement on the relationship between planning and the market at the 14th CPC National Congress.

On 9 June 1992, Jiang Zemin gave a speech entitled: *Deeply understanding and fully implementing the spirit of Comrade Deng Xiaoping's important speech and accelerating and enhancing economic construction and reform and opening up* at an advanced course for provincial and ministerial-level cadres held at the CPC Central Committee's Party School. The speech reviewed the process of the party's understanding of the issue of planning and the market, and their mutual relationship since the 3rd Plenary Session of the 11th CPC Central Committee. Regarding views put forward in the discussion on establishing a new economic system, such as "establishing a socialist commodity economy that integrates planning and the market", "establishing a socialist planned market economy" and "establishing a socialist market economy", Jiang Zemin said, "In my personal opinion, I am inclined to use the term 'socialist market economy'"[9]. In his speech, he elaborated on the characteristics of the new socialist economic system in terms of ownership structure, distribution system and economic operation mechanism, outlining the basic characteristics of the socialist market economy. This important theoretical breakthrough was widely endorsed and supported by the older generation of revolutionaries. On 12 June, Deng Xiaoping told Jiang Zemin, who was visiting him, that he was in favour of using the term "socialist market economy". The CPC Central Committee then consulted 30 provinces, autonomous regions and municipalities, as well as the Central Government and various departments of the State Council, who all unanimously agreed on the term "socialist market economy". This marked the unification of the party's thinking on the establishment of a socialist market economy.

In October 1992, Jiang Zemin stated in his report to the 14th CPC National Congress that, "the development of practice and the deepening of understanding require us to make it clear that the goal of China's economic reform is to establish a socialist market economy to facilitate the further liberation and development of productivity"[10]. This was the party's official goal in proposing the reform of China's economy. The report of the 14th CPC National Congress further elaborated on the basic requirements for the establishment of a socialist market economy, stating: "The socialist market economy we want to establish will enable the market to play a fundamental role in the allocation of resources under the macrocontrol of the socialist state, so that economic activities follow the requirements of the law of value and adapt to changes in supply and demand. It will allocate resources to the more efficient sectors through the function of price leverage and competition mechanisms, and give enterprises pressure and incentives to fight for their survival, strengthen themselves and utilise the strengths of having a market which is more responsive to various economic signals to promote timely coordination of production and demand. At the same time, we must recognise that the market has its own weaknesses and negative aspects, and we must strengthen and improve the state's macroeconomic control. We must vigorously develop a unified national market, further expand the role of the market and, in accordance with the requirements of objective laws, apply good economic policies, economic regulations, planning, steering and the necessary administrative management to guide the healthy development of the market"[11]. The report of the 14th CPC National Congress focused on the wisdom of the whole party, and comprehensively and scientifically expounded the positive role of the socialist market economy, indicating that the establishment of a socialist market economy demonstrated the consensus and will of the whole party.

In March 1993, the First Session of the Eighth NPC accepted the CPC Central Committee's proposal and agreed to write the "socialist market economy system" into Article 7 of the amendment to the *Constitution* of the PRC, thereby establishing the socialist market economy in the form of a fundamental law in China.

In November 1993, in accordance with the significant decision of the 14th CPC National Congress, the 3rd Plenary Session of the 14th CPC Central Committee discussed the issue of establishing a socialist market economy, and deliberated and adopted the *Decision of the CPC Central Committee on Several Issues Concerning the Establishment of a Socialist Market Economy* (hereinafter referred to as the *Decision*). The *Decision* concretised the objectives and basic principles of economic reform put forward by the 14th CPC National Congress and constructed the basic framework of the socialist market economy.

The *Decision* states that it is necessary to:

- Adhere to the policy of having public ownership as the main mechanism, with the joint development of multiple economic components, further transform the operational mechanisms of SOEs, and establish a modern enterprise system adapted to the requirements of the market economy, having clear property rights, powers and responsibilities, marked by the separation of government and enterprises, and scientific management.

- Establish a unified and open market system across China, achieve close integration between urban and rural markets, and interconnect domestic and international markets to promote the optimal distribution of resources.

- Transform the government's role in managing the economy, establish a sound system of macroeconomic control based on indirect means, and ensure the healthy operation of the national economy.

- Establish an income distribution system that gives priority to efficiency and fairness, with the distribution of labour as the main feature, and encourage some people in some regions to become prosperous first and follow the path of common prosperity.

- Establish a multilevel social security system, and provide urban and rural residents with social security that is appropriate to China's national conditions, so as to promote economic development and social stability.

These aspects constitute an interlinked and mutually constraining organic whole and the basic framework of the socialist market economy, demonstrating the solidification of the aim of establishing a socialist market economy.

The establishment of a socialist market economy constituted an unprecedented and pioneering undertaking, since there was no precedent in the world for a market economy under socialist conditions. Former US Secretary of State Henry Kissinger said that if China were to succeed, then it would present a philosophical proposition to both capitalism and socialism. The Chinese communists conducted lengthy explorations to establish an economic system suited to China's reality. The 14th CPC National Congress set the reform goal of establishing a socialist market economy, organically combining the socialist market economy with the basic socialist system. This was to be done by integrating the strengths of the basic socialist system with the strengths of the market economy, making full use of the advantages of the market, such as being more responsive to various economic signals, giving full play to the basic role of the market in the distribution of resources, while also overcoming the weaknesses and negative aspects of the market economy, such as blindness and spontaneity, through macrocontrol, so that the superiority of the socialist system can be more optimally utilised. The facts have proven the superiority of the socialist market economy, and the establishment of a socialist market economy in China constitutes a historic contribution made by the CPC to the development of Marxism, an important pillar of socialism with Chinese characteristics, and the result of the party's deepening understanding of the laws of socialist construction.

(III) CORRECTLY HANDLING CERTAIN MAJOR RELATIONSHIPS IN SOCIALIST MODERNISATION

Deng Xiaoping's 1992 southern tour speeches and the 14th CPC National Congress marked a new stage of accelerated development of China's reform and opening up, and socialist modernisation. In the practice of leading reform and opening up, and socialist modernisation, the CPC has encountered many contradictions and difficulties in the process of establishing a socialist market economy, and some new situations and problems have emerged. In order to adapt to the new situation and solve the new problems, the CPC proposed 12 major relationships in socialist modernisation that should be handled adeptly and correctly, and these are also some of the major issues that need to be clearly resolved by communist party governance under a socialist market economy.

After the 14th CPC National Congress, the party further emancipated the mind and led the people of all ethnicities in China to continue to stride forward along the road of socialism with Chinese characteristics, making great achievements in all fields. The national economy developed rapidly, comprehensive national power increased significantly, the socialist market economy was gradually established, various social undertakings achieved remarkable development and the living standard of the people improved significantly. In the course of accelerating reform and development, some new contradictions and problems gradually came to light, such as friction and clashes between China's old and new systems in the process of institutional transformation, lagging reform of China's SOEs, and difficulties in production and operation in the process of reform and opening up, weakness of the agricultural base, inflation and state financial difficulties, poor efficiency and serious waste caused by a large-scale economy, rapid population growth and employment pressures, widening of the regional development gap, as well as the growth of certain instances of corruption in the economy and social life. These contradictions and problems, having a bearing on China's overall situation, affected and restricted the entire process of socialist modernisation.

In the face of such a situation and task, the CPC integrated Deng Xiaoping's ideology on how to correctly handle a series of major relationships in China's reform and development with China's concrete realities, and considered in depth a number of major relationships in socialist modernisation.

On 28 September 1995, Jiang Zemin delivered a speech at the 5th Plenary Session of the 14th CPC Central Committee, focusing on 12 major and comprehensive relationships that must be dealt with in the construction of socialist modernisation. He pointed out that the correct handling of these major relationships should be guided by a general approach, which was to take Deng Xiaoping's theory of building socialism with Chinese characteristics and the party's basic line as guidance, and clarified the principles which should be upheld in view of the new contradictions and problems with comprehensive ramifications encountered in modernisation and construction under the conditions of a socialist market economy. The aim, he said, was to diligently grasp objective laws, unify the party's understanding, unite the people of all China's ethnicities, mobilise all positive elements and accelerate socialist modernisation, all on the basis of taking stock of historical experience.

With regard to the correct handling of the relationship between reform, development and stability, Jiang Zemin pointed out that reform, development and stability are inseparably interlinked. A holistic view of the whole situation must be taken, and plans carefully made, comprehensively grasping the intrinsic relationship between reform, development and stability, to achieve mutual coordination and reinforcement. He said we must integrate a sense of urgency to speed up reform and development with a spirit of scientific pragmatism, fully consider the favourable conditions and potential difficulties in all aspects of the economy and society, so as to promote reform and development in the midst of political and social stability, and achieve long-term political and social stability in the midst of reform and development.

With regard to the correct handling of the relationship between speed and efficiency, Jiang Zemin said that China's modernisation must follow the principle of unity between speed and efficiency, and correctly handle the relationship between the two. China is a developing country and the key to achieving modernisation and narrowing the gap with developed countries is to develop a national economy that has both higher speed and better efficiency.

With regard to the correct handling of the relationship between economic construction and population, resources and the environment, Jiang Zemin believed that in the process of modernisation, it is necessary to make the achievement of sustainable development a major strategy. Population control, conservation of resources and protection of the environment must be given an important place, so that population growth will be compatible with the development of social productivity, and economic construction will be coordinated with resources and the environment to achieve a virtuous cycle.

With regard to the correct handling of the relationship between the primary, secondary and tertiary industries, Jiang Zemin pointed out that with the development of the economy, the industrial structure must inevitably be constantly optimised and upgraded, gradually forming a reasonable structure of the primary, secondary and tertiary industries that is in line with the level of social productivity. The main problems at the time, he said, were that the agricultural base was weak, the quality of industry was not high, the development of the tertiary sector was lagging behind, and the relationship between the primary, secondary and tertiary sectors was not yet coordinated. In the future, he said, we must vigorously strengthen the primary sector, adjust and improve the secondary sector, and actively develop the tertiary sector.

With regard to the correct way to handle the relationship between the eastern, and central and western regions of China, Jiang Zemin said, "The issue of the widening gap in the economic development of the eastern, and central and western regions must be taken seriously and handled correctly. Addressing the regional development gap and persisting with coordinated regional economic development is a strategic task for future reform and development".

With regard to correctly handling the relationship between market mechanisms and macrocontrol, Jiang Zemin proposed that, "fully utilising the role of market mechanisms and strengthening macrocontrol are both basic requirements for the establishment of a socialist market economy; they are both indispensable and must not be separated or, worse still, set in opposition to each other.

With regard to the correct handling of the relationship between the public sector of the economy and other economic components, Jiang Zemin stressed that, "having the public sector as the economic mainstay and the joint development of various economic components is a policy that we must uphold in the long term. It is determined by China's socialist system and the level of development of productivity at the present stage. Upholding the status of public ownership as the mainstay is a fundamental principle of socialism and the basic hallmark of China's socialist market economy. This principle must be upheld throughout the process of reform and opening up, and modernisation. While actively promoting the development of the state-owned economy and the collective economy, we will allow and encourage the development of the non-public economy, such as individual, private and foreign investment, and properly guide, strengthen supervision and regulate these in accordance with the law, so that they can become a necessary complement to the socialist economy".

With regard to the correct handling of the relationship between the state, enterprises and individuals in income distribution, Jiang Zemin pointed out that, "in income distribution, it is necessary to uphold the principle of distribution according to work as the mainstay and the co-existence of various modes of distribution, reflecting the priority of efficiency and taking into account fairness, and integrating the interests of the state, enterprises and individuals".

With regard to the correct handling of the relationship between broadly opening up to the outside world and persisting with self-reliance, Jiang Zemin said, "Broadly opening up to the outside world on the basis of self-reliance is a principle we must uphold in the long term. As a large socialist country like ours engages in modernisation, we must successfully handle the relationship between broadly opening up to the outside world and upholding self-reliance, establishing our standpoint on a foundation of relying on our own strength. Independence does not mean closing our country to international engagement, and self-reliance does not mean blind xenophobia. Independence and self-reliance by no means equate to engaging in construction after closing up the country and closing the door to the outside but, rather, to raising up opening up to the outside world to a new and higher level.

With regard to the correct handling of the relationship between the central government and local levels, Jiang Zemin believed that, "fully utilising both central and local initiatives is an important principle in China's political and economic life, directly related to national and ethnic unity, and the coordinated development of the national economy. Neither local nor sectoral interests that undermine overall national interests of the country should be allowed to exist. The general principle should be that there should be unity reflecting the overall interests but also flexibility taking into account local interests under the guidance of the principle of unity, and there should be centralisation to maintain the state's macroregulatory powers but also to give the necessary power to the localities under the guidance of centralisation".

With regard to the correct handling of the relationship between the construction of national defence and economic construction, Jiang Zemin emphasised that, "the modernisation of national defence is an important part of China's socialist modernisation and strengthening the construction of national defence constitutes a basic guarantee for national security and economic development. The construction of national defence and military construction must be based on economic construction and be subordinate to the general situation surrounding national economic construction. The state must support and strengthen the construction of national defence as needed and as possible.

With regard to the correct handling of the relationship between the construction of material and spiritual civilisation, Jiang Zemin pointed out that, "the construction of material and spiritual civilisation should be made a goal of unified struggle, and it is necessary to unswervingly uphold the approach of grasping both and grasping both firmly. Under no circumstances should we sacrifice spiritual civilisation in exchange for temporary economic development"[12].

Jiang Zemin's discourse on the 12 major relationships constitutes a profound summary of China's successful experience in reform and opening up, and socialist modernisation, and a concrete expression of the laws of socialist construction with Chinese characteristics. These treatises display the following main features throughout.

First, they are global in nature. Socialist modernisation is a huge systemic project with a multitude of tasks and complex contradictions. The 12 major relationships take a holistic approach to modernisation, comprehensively revealing the contradictions and problems encountered in economic and social development, and covering all aspects of socioeconomic and political life.

Second, they are strategic. The 12 major relationships and the basic principles and methods for correctly handling these relationships are fundamental and comprehensive issues that have a bearing on the success or failure of socialist modernisation, and also constitute scientific decisions and important guarantees for achieving the strategic objectives of the "three-step development strategy".

Third, they are full of dialectics, in that the 12 major relationships and the aspects within each relationship are prominent, while avoiding one-sidedness and are full of materialistic dialectic ideology.

Jiang Zemin once said that of the 12 relationships he had spoken about in relation to China's construction, there are, in brief, three. He said that, "The first is that we must properly handle the relationship between reform, development and stability, the second is that we must properly handle the relationship between the socialist market economy and macro-control, and the third is that we must coordinate the speed and efficiency of our construction"[13].

The core of the 12 major relationships discussed by Jiang Zemin is to uphold one basic policy and achieve two kinds of transformation. In other words, upholding the basic policy of 'one central task and two basic points' and accomplish the transformation of the economic system from the traditional planned economy to a socialist market economy and the transformation of the mode of economic growth from an extensive to an intensive one. Among these 12 major relationships, the most important and fundamental one is the correct handling of the relationship between reform, development and stability. This is the overarching and fundamental relationship and constitutes a fundamental issue of programmatic importance in China's socialist modernisation.

As early as March 1994, when addressing the Shanghai delegation at the Second Session of the Eighth NPC, Jiang Zemin proposed the importance of grasping the relationship between reform, development and stability. He pointed out that, "In order to accomplish the bigger picture of the work of the party and the state, the key is to correctly handle the relationship between reform, development and stability. While striving to deepen reform, expand openness and promote development, we must also pay attention to maintaining a stable social and political environment, strive to promote reform and development in the midst of stability, and ensure long-term social stability by way of reform and development. Reform, development and stability are like three closely related strategic pieces on the chessboard of China's modernisation. If each piece is played well and promotes the others, the overall situation will be vibrant but if one piece is not played well, the other two pieces will fall into difficulty and there will be setbacks across the board. Therefore, grasping the relationship between reform, development and stability is an important leadership skill in the context of modernisation"[14].

The correct handling of the relationship between reform, development and stability has a bearing on the success or failure of reform and opening up. Reform, development and stability are the three important pivots of China's socialist modernisation. Reform is a powerful driving force for economic and social development, development is the key to solving all economic and social problems, and stability is a prerequisite for reform and development. As long as the relationship between these three is handled properly, it is possible to control the overall situation and ensure smooth economic and social development. But if they are not handled properly, there will be suffering and a price will be paid for this.

Reform, development and stability are inextricably and intrinsically linked. Development is the hard truth. The key to solving all China's problems is relying on domestic development. Development is indispensable for strengthening comprehensive national power and improving people's livelihoods, for consolidating and improving the socialist system and maintaining stability, for resisting the pressure of hegemonism and power politics, and safeguarding national sovereignty and independence, and for fundamentally breaking away from economic backwardness and becoming a member of the global community of modernised countries. Reform is the driving force to further liberate and develop productivity. Reform means the self-improvement and development of the socialist system. Its decisive role is not only to solve some major problems in current economic and social development and to promote the liberation and development of social productivity but also to lay a solid foundation for the sustainable development of China's economy and the long-term stability of the country. Stability is the prerequisite, and a stable political and social environment is necessary for development and reform. During the period of economic restructuring, people's ideology and mindset must be transformed, the interests of various parties will change significantly, and various conflicts may become prominent. Therefore, maintaining stability is of great practical significance. Without a stable political and social environment, there is no way to accomplish anything, and it will be difficult to implement any beneficial plans or programmes.

In his report to the 15th CPC National Congress in 1997 and his speech at the conference commemorating the 20th anniversary of the 3rd Plenary Session of the 11th CPC Central Committee in 1998, Jiang Zemin reiterated the importance of correctly handling the relationship between reform, development and stability, stressing that it was necessary to harmonise the strength of reform, the speed of development and the extent of society's tolerance thereof, to promote reform and development in the context of social and political stability, and achieve social and political stability in the context of reform and development.

In October 2000, at the 5th Plenary Session of the 15th CPC Central Committee, Jiang Zemin, with an eye on avenues for new practice, further stressed that, "the relationship between reform, development and stability must be correctly handled so that the advancement of reform is both proactive and prudent". He also said that, "Everyone should firmly implement the Central Government's line, guidelines and policies, strive to coordinate their own work with these in practical terms and accomplish their work creatively, think about the concerns of, and urgently address the difficulties of, the masses and make plans to meet their demands, resolutely solve various urgent problems related to the overall situation of reform, development and stability affecting the production and life of the masses, in order to improve the practical activities of our work style to win the trust of the people"[15]. In November of the same year, Jiang Zemin also stated at the Central Economic Work Conference, "Constantly improving people's livelihood is the ultimate manifestation of our party's objective to serve the people wholeheartedly and what is required by the 'Three Represents'. It is also the key link in handling the relationship between reform, development and stability. As the living standards of the people continue to improve, the promotion of reform will receive more widespread support, and the foundations of our party's governance will be further consolidated"[16]. This statement advanced the assertion that improving people's livelihood constitutes the key link in the correct handling of the relationship between reform, development and stability. Practice has proven that only by firmly grasping this key link is it possible to harmonise the strength of reform, the speed of development and the degree of stability, integrate the fundamental and long-term interests of the people with local and immediate interests, and grasp the intrinsic relationship between reform, development and stability from a holistic perspective.

The party went on to make many important decisions and implemented a series of strategic plans based on the 12 major relationships on which Jiang Zemin elaborated that must be dealt with in socialist modernisation. For example, in handling the relationship between eastern China and the central and western regions of China, Jiang Zemin formally put forward the strategic idea of the Great Western Development Strategy in his speech at the party leaders' meeting at the Second Session of the Ninth NPC and the Second Session of the Ninth National Committee of the CPPCC in March 1999. In September of the same year, the 4h Plenary Session of the 15th CPC Central Committee explicitly proposed that the state should implement the Great Western Development Strategy, emphasising the need to support the accelerated development of the central and western regions and minority areas by prioritising measures such as the construction of infrastructure and increasing financial transfers. In dealing with the relationship between expanding and opening up to the outside world and adhering to the principle of self-reliance, the CPC established accession to the WTO as a major step in China's comprehensive opening up to the outside world. After hard talks and challenging negotiations, the Fourth WTO Ministerial Conference unanimously adopted the *Decision on China's Accession to the WTO* in November 2001, whereby China formally became a WTO member, and China's opening up to the outside world entered a new phase.

In response to a series of major problems faced in socialist modernisation, the party proposed to correctly handle the 12 major relationships pertaining to socialist modernisation on the basis of new practical experience and drawing on the lessons of history. This constituted an overview and summary of the experience of China's socialist modernisation since the outset of reform and opening up, an enrichment and deepening of socialism with Chinese characteristics in the context of new practice and development, and a correct reflection of the vivid practice and objective laws of socialist modernisation, and it brought about a further refinement of the understanding of the laws of socialist construction.

(IV) DEVELOPING THE BASIC LINE OF THE PRIMARY STAGE OF SOCIALISM IN THE FIELDS OF ECONOMICS, POLITICS AND CULTURE

In September 1997, the 15th CPC National Congress summed up the party's guidelines, policies and practical experience since the 3rd Plenary Session of the 11th CPC Central Committee on the basis of a profound understanding of the basic national conditions in the primary stage of socialism in accordance with Deng Xiaoping Theory and the party's basic line, proposed the party's basic programme at the primary stage of socialism, and clarified the basic features and requirements of building socialism with Chinese characteristics in terms of economics, politics and culture. This constituted a further deepening of the party's understanding of socialism with Chinese characteristics and a strategic arrangement and plan of action for successfully propelling socialism with Chinese characteristics into the 21st century.

After the 3rd Plenary Session of the 11th CPC Central Committee, in the process of leading reform and opening up, and socialist modernisation and of forming and implementing the party's basic line in the primary stage of socialism, the second generation of the party's central leadership with Comrade Deng Xiaoping at its core made many incisive and profound treatises on building an economy, politics and culture in line with socialism with Chinese characteristics. As early as September 1979, in a speech at the conference to celebrate the 30th anniversary of the founding of the PRC which was then endorsed at the 4th Plenary Session of the 11th CPC Central Committee, Ye Jianying advanced the goal and task of fully achieving socialist modernisation. Deng Xiaoping went on to reiterate this in his subsequent speech, stating that "Our country has entered a new period of socialist modernisation. We must reform and refine the socialist economic and political systems, develop a high degree of socialist democracy and a complete socialist legal system, while substantially increasing social productivity. We must raise the scientific and literacy level of the whole nation, develop a refined and colourful cultural life and build a high degree of socialist spiritual civilisation, while also building a high degree of material civilisation"[17]. Later, Deng Xiaoping repeatedly stressed that there were many tasks to be completed in order to build socialism with Chinese characteristics, and that it was necessary to persist with the comprehensive development and progress of socialist society premised on a focus on economic construction; it was not acceptable to focus on one and neglect the other. In accordance with the actual state of Chinese society at that time, he proposed the strategic policy of "doing two jobs at once and attaching equal importance to each", requiring that in the process of reform and opening up, and modernisation, the party should be devoted to reform and opening up at as well as to fighting crime, to economic construction at the same time as to the democratic rule of law, and to material civilisation at the same time as to spiritual civilisation. He stressed the need to uphold the approach of doing two jobs at once and attaching equal importance to each.

In October 1987, the party's 13th National Congress systematically expounded the theory of the primary stage of socialism for the first time and clearly outlined the party's basic line in the primary stage of socialism, namely, "one central task and two basic points". As an important part of the party's basic line, "building China into a rich, strong, democratic and civilised socialist modern state" clearly defined the goal of the party's struggle. This 'trinity' of objectives comprising wealth and strength, democracy, and civilisation, embodied the economic, political and cultural requirements for building socialism with Chinese characteristics. All the efforts made by the party to unite and lead the people of China are aimed at achieving this hard-fought goal.

After the 4th Plenary Session of the 13th CPC Central Committee, by consistently adhering to the party's basic line, the party further elaborated on the concept of building an economy, politics and culture in line with socialism with Chinese characteristics. On 1 July 1991, in his speech at a conference to celebrate the 70th anniversary of the founding of the CPC, Jiang Zemin advanced the concept that building socialism with Chinese characteristics includes the 'trinity' of a socialist economy, politics and culture with Chinese characteristics, based on the lessons learned from China's reform and opening up, and modernisation as well as the rise and fall of some other socialist countries. He pointed out that the economy, politics and culture in line with socialism with Chinese characteristics constitute an organic, unified and inseparable whole, and that the construction of the economy, politics and culture in line with socialism with Chinese characteristics must adhere to the general policy of reform and opening up, premised on adhering to the Four Cardinal Principles. This constituted a further exploration of the path of socialism with Chinese characteristics by the party and laid the foundation for deepening the party's understanding of socialism with Chinese characteristics.

In September 1997, on the historic occasion of propelling the cause of socialism with Chinese characteristics fully into the 21st century in his report to the 15th CPC National Congress, Jiang Zemin comprehensively expounded the basic objectives and interrelationships of the economy, politics and culture in the context of building socialism with Chinese characteristics, put forward the party's basic programme for the primary stage of socialism, and enriched and developed the party's basic line.

Jiang Zemin proposed that the whole party should unswervingly adhere to the party's basic line in the primary stage of socialism and unite the Four Cardinal Principles with the two basic points of reform and opening up, all of which have a focus on economic construction, on the foundation of the great practice of building socialism with Chinese characteristics. This constitutes the CPC's most valuable experience in the past 20 years and the most reliable guarantee for the successful advancement of our cause. It is vital to be wary of the right but mainly to prevent errors of the "left", to maintain sober thinking, to overcome all kinds of interference, and to adhere to Deng Xiaoping Theory and the basic line without wavering. With regard to the goal of building a rich, strong, democratic and civilised socialist modern state, it is necessary to further clarify what constitutes a socialist economy, politics and culture in line with Chinese characteristics at the primary stage of socialism, and how to build said economy, politics and culture, in accordance with this theory and basic line.

Jiang Zemin pointed out that building a socialist economy with Chinese characteristics means to develop a market economy under socialist conditions and to continuously liberate and develop productivity. This requires upholding and refining a basic economic system mainly characterised by socialist public ownership and where a multiownership economy develops together, upholding and refining the socialist market economy so that the market plays a fundamental role in the allocation of resources under the macroeconomic control of the state, upholding and refining multiple modes of distribution mainly characterised by distribution according to work and allowing some people in certain regions to become affluent first, providing impetus for, and helping others to, become affluent next, and gradually moving towards common prosperity, and upholding and refining the opening up of the country to the outside world, actively participating in international economic cooperation and competition. This would all ensure the sustained rapid and healthy development of China's economy, and ensure that China's people together share the fruit of economic prosperity.

Jiang Zemin stressed that building a political system in line with socialism with Chinese characteristics means to develop socialist democratic politics in accordance with the rule of law under the leadership of the CPC and on the basis that the people are the masters of their own country. This requires upholding and refining the people's democratic dictatorship led by the working class and based on the alliance of workers and peasants, upholding and refining the system of people's congresses, and the system of multiparty cooperation and political consultation led by the CPC, and the system of regional ethnic autonomy, and developing democracy, improving the legal system and building a socialist state under the rule of law. Achieving social stability necessitates an honest and efficient government, unity and harmony among all of China's ethnic groups, and a lively political situation.

Jiang Zemin also pointed out that building a culture in line with socialism with Chinese characteristics means to be guided by Marxism, to cultivate citizens with ideals and morality who are cultured and disciplined, and to develop a national, scientific and popular socialist culture oriented toward modernisation, globalism and the future. This requires persistence in arming the party with Deng Xiaoping Theory and educating the people, striving to raise the ideological and moral quality of the whole nation and the level of education, science and culture, upholding an orientation of serving the people and socialism, and the policy of letting a hundred flowers bloom and a hundred schools of thought contend with an emphasis on construction and prospering learning, art and literature. Building socialist spiritual civilisation that is based on Chinese reality necessitates inheriting the best traditions of Chinese history and culture, and drawing on the beneficial achievements of foreign cultures.

Jiang Zemin further stressed that the basic objectives and policies of building an economy, politics and culture in line with socialism with Chinese characteristics are organic, unified and inseparable, and constitute the party's basic programme in the primary stage of socialism. This programme constitutes a major feature of Deng Xiaoping Theory, implementation of the party's basic line in economic, political and cultural terms, and a summary of the party's most significant experiences in the course of the preceding years.

The basic programme of the party in the primary stage of socialism, as put forward at the 15th CPC National Congress, constitutes the basic objectives and basic policies for the primary stage of socialism, and its theoretical cornerstone is the theory of the primary stage of socialism. On the basis of the 13th and 14th CPC National Congresses, the 15th CPC National Congress elaborated on the basic characteristics of the primary stage of socialism. It pointed out that the primary stage of socialism is the historical phase marked by the gradual emergence from underdevelopment and the basic achievement of socialist modernisation, and by the gradual transformation from an agricultural country with a large proportion of the population engaged in agriculture and relying mainly on manual labour to an industrialised country where the majority of the population are not engaged in agriculture and which incorporates modern agriculture and modern services industries. It also stated that this primary stage of socialism is marked by a gradual transition from a predominantly natural or semi-natural economy to a more market-oriented economy, from a population where a large proportion are illiterate or semi-illiterate and a state marked by backwardness in science, education and culture, to having more developed science, technology, education and culture. It further stated that this historical phase is marked by a gradual transition from a state where a large proportion of the people are poor and have a relatively low standard of living to a state where the people as a whole are relatively affluent, and is one where the significant disparity in regional economic and cultural development is gradually reduced by way of continuous development. It is, it was further stated, the phase in history when, through reform and exploration, a more mature and dynamic socialist market economy, a socialist democratic political system and other systems are established and refined, a phase when the general public firmly establish the common ideal of building socialism with Chinese characteristics, strive unremittingly with determination and a proactive stance, struggle arduously, build up the country through thrift and hard work, and make great efforts to build spiritual civilisation while also building material civilisation, and a phase when the gap with the advanced countries of the world is gradually narrowed and the great rejuvenation of the Chinese nation is achieved on the basis of socialism.

This historical process will take at least a hundred years. The consolidation and development of the socialist system itself will take much longer, requiring generations, a dozen generations, or even dozens of generations of persistence in relentless struggle. In order to uphold the party's basic programme at the primary stage of socialism, it is necessary always to be established in China's national conditions in the primary stage of socialism, concretely analyse the state and characteristics of China's economy, politics, culture and other aspects, persist with the approach which holds that all policies must start from and conform to China's realities in the primary stage of socialism, and not depart from reality and seek to skip ahead by adopting some "leftist" methodologies.

The party's basic programme for the primary stage of socialism is based on the goal of the struggle to "build China into a rich, strong, democratic and civilised socialist modern state", and spells out what is meant by establishing an economy, politics and culture in line with socialism with Chinese characteristics in the primary stage of socialism, and also how to build said economy, politics and culture. It points out the basic objectives and policies in the three major areas of the economy, politics and culture.

With regard to the party's basic line, the party's basic programme constitutes a relatively concrete arrangement of ideas, and with regard to the party's specific objectives and specific policies in each specific area of work a relatively high-level arrangement of ideas. The combination of the party's basic line and the party's basic programme has enabled the party to form a system of basic objectives and basic policies that serve the goal of struggle, making the direction and ideology of socialism with Chinese characteristics clearer, and the path and methods more concrete. In order to uphold the party's basic programme in the primary stage of socialism, it is necessary to adhere unswervingly to the party's basic line in the primary stage of socialism and unite the Four Cardinal Principles, and reform and opening up focused on economic construction with the whole process of building socialism with Chinese characteristics.

The party's basic programme for the primary stage of socialism clearly answered the question surrounding the nature of socialism in its primary stage and how to build it in this stage, enriching and developing socialism with Chinese characteristics. The chief issue surrounding socialism with Chinese characteristics itself pertains to "the nature of socialism and the appropriate way to construct it". After the 3rd Plenary Session of the 11th CPC Central Committee, the historical process of reform and opening up implemented by the party was also a process of continuous exploration and in-depth consideration of socialism with Chinese characteristics in practice. On the basis of the party's past practical experience and understanding, the 15th CPC National Congress put forward the party's basic programme for the primary stage of socialism, answering, at the level of basic objectives and policies, the question surrounding the nature of socialism in its primary stage and how to build it in this stage. The party's basic programme for the primary stage of socialism constitutes the basic blueprint for building socialism with Chinese characteristics, clearly setting out for the CPC various tasks, the goals for which to struggle, and guiding principles. Adhering to the party's basic programme during the primary stage of socialism plays an important role in gaining a deeper understanding of socialism with Chinese characteristics, upholding the party's basic line without wavering, clarifying the party's goals and tasks at the primary stage of socialism, unifying the ideology of the entire party, and uniting and leading the whole nation in the struggle to build China into a modern socialist country.

The programme of a political party stipulates the current and future goals for which that party will struggle and constitutes the fundamental symbol of the party's values, the path it will take and the policy and strategy to which it will adhere. The formulation of a correct programme is of vital importance to a working-class party and the cause it leads. The introduction of the party's basic programme for the primary stage of socialism made the party's basic objectives and policies for the primary stage of socialism more authoritative and raised a distinctive banner for mobilising and organising the whole party and the whole of China to comprehensively promote socialism with Chinese characteristics in the new century.

(V) ADVANCING THE GREAT NEW PROJECT OF PARTY BUILDING WITH A FOCUS ON TWO HISTORICAL ISSUES

After the 14th CPC National Congress, the Party Central Committee with Comrade Jiang Zemin at its core actively explored and achieved important results pertaining to strengthening the objectives, tasks and means of the party's construction under the conditions of a socialist market economy, not only raising the party's construction to the lofty status of a "great new project" but also focusing on two historical issues facing the ruling party, endeavouring to construct the party's working pattern to ensure that the party always plays a leading role in the great cause of building socialism with Chinese characteristics.

The 1990s saw the collapse of the US-Soviet bipolar international system, the initial formation of a multipolar pattern, continuously intensifying economic competition and the accentuation of national security issues. The development of socialism was hit hard by the dramatic changes in Eastern Europe and the collapse of the Soviet Union, and the competition between socialism and capitalism became increasingly challenging. Meanwhile in China, reform and opening up, and socialist modernisation continued to move forward, and in 1992, the 14th CPC National Congress decided to establish a socialist market economy, whereupon the traditional planned economic system began to be transformed into a socialist market economy, leading to great changes in China's economic life and social relations. Internally within the party a series of new changes occurred in the party's own situation, and the construction of the party's ideology, politics, organisation and work style was faced with many new situations and problems. In such a complex and profoundly changing environment within China and overseas, and within the party itself, determining the best approach to consolidating the party's governance position and strengthening the party's leadership presented a major issue for the CPC.

In order to improve party building, the Party Central Committee had to have a clear and comprehensive understanding of the situation faced by the construction task and also of the state of the party. As early as 1 July

1991, Jiang Zemin pointed out in his speech at a conference to celebrate the 70th anniversary of the founding of the CPC that, "under new historical conditions, our party must not only continue to stand the test of governance but also faces the test of reform and opening up, and developing a commodity economy, and the test of opposing peaceful evolution"[18]. In September 1994, the *Decision of the CPC Central Committee on Several Major Issues Concerning Strengthening Party Building* adopted at the 4th Plenary Session of the 14th CPC Central Committee specifically analysed new problems encountered in party building, stating that, "reform and opening up have injected new vitality into party building while, at the same time, party building has also encountered many complex situations", and "our work has not yet adapted to the new situation. In some places and within some units, the party does not manage itself, party governance is not strict, discipline is lax and organisation is disorganised while there are also various problems in ideology, organisation and work style that cannot be ignored. In particular, certain negative factors and corruption are growing and spreading within the party, seriously harming party members and the ranks of cadres"[19].

On 1 July 2001, in his speech at a conference celebrating the 80th anniversary of the founding of the CPC, Jiang Zemin analysed the changes that had taken place in the party, stating, "In the course of 80 years of development, our party's membership, the party's status and environment, and the tasks it has been charged with, have all undergone significant changes. Our party has changed from one which led the people in their struggle to seize national power into one which leads the people to take control of national power and exercise long-term governance, and from one which led national construction under a state of external blockade into one which leads national construction under the conditions of comprehensive reform and opening up"[20]. In November 2002, Jiang Zemin further advanced the concept of the historical orientation of the party in his report to the 16th CPC National Congress, stating, "Through revolution, construction and reform, our party has changed from being a party which led the people in their struggle to seize national power to being one which leads the people to take control of national power and exercise long-term governance, and from being one which led national construction under external blockade and implemented a planned economy to being one which leads national construction in the context of opening up to the outside world and developing a socialist market economy"[21].

These two major changes constitute a scientific judgement of the CPC's historical orientation. The change in the party's historical orientation not only exposes it to the tests of long-term governance and of reform and opening up but also to the test of developing a socialist market economy. These tests have brought with them many deep-rooted theoretical and practical problems. These include problems such as, for example, how to guide the masses of party members, cadres and the people to understand correctly the objective laws of social development and to strengthen their determination and confidence in following the path of building socialism with Chinese characteristics, how to keep the nature and aims of the party unchanged as before, and how to foster even closer ties between the party and the people. Only by making scientific analyses of these major theoretical and practical problems, and by proposing feasible solutions is it possible to drive forwards party building more effectively.

In September 1994, the 4th Plenary Session of the 14th CPC Central Committee was convened, which adopted the *Decision of the CPC Central Committee on Several Major Issues Concerning Strengthening Party Building*. The *Decision* elevated party building to the level of a "great new project" and clearly set out the general objective of party construction in the new period. This objective was, "Under the changing conditions of the contemporary world and in the midst of the great changes resulting from reform and opening up, and modernisation in contemporary China, to build the party into a Marxist party armed with the theory of building socialism with Chinese characteristics, and which wholeheartedly serves the people, is fully consolidated ideologically, politically and organisationally, is able to withstand a wide range of risks, and is always at the forefront of the times"[22]. This general objective, proposed on the basis of summing up domestic and international historical experience, including the lessons learned from the dramatic changes in the Soviet Union and Eastern Europe, and the fresh experience of enhancing party building since the reform and opening up, incorporated the party's guiding ideology, nature and purpose, as well as the general requirements of party building, and reflected the CPC's new understanding of the laws of its own construction in a focused manner. Focusing on this general objective, the *Decision* proposed that while continuing to fully implement the Party Central Committee's arrangements regarding ideological and work style construction, it would also particularly address the issue of upholding and improving democratic centralism, with particular emphasis on institutional construction. It focused on three aspects of organisational construction, namely, consolidating and strengthening the party's grassroots organisations, enabling them to become the bastions of combat capable of uniting and leading the masses in implementing reform and opening up, and modernisation, nurturing and tempering the party's senior and mid-level leading cadres, and forming competent and dynamic leadership which walks along the path of socialism with Chinese characteristics, and is adept at studying new situations and solving new problems. At the plenary session, Jiang Zemin emphasised that, "if these three aspects of work are done well, the party's organisation will be stronger and more consolidated, and it will be able to ensure organisationally that the second strategic goal is achieved, so that China will be able to step into the 21st century more smoothly"[23].

In September 1997, the 15th CPC National Congress made further arrangements for party construction on the basis of the 4th Plenary Session of the 14th CPC Central Committee. In his report to the 15th CPC National Congress, Jiang Zemin pointed out that the key for comprehensively propelling the party's cause into the 21st century lay in upholding, strengthening and improving the leadership of the party, and further building the party. Focusing intently on the fundamental question of the nature of the party which should be built and how to build it, he elevated party building to the level of a "great new project", stating that, "In the new century, the Party Central Committee is leading the party as a whole to continue to promote this great new project, which is to build the party into a Marxist party, armed with Deng Xiaoping Theory, which wholeheartedly serves the people, is fully consolidated ideologically, politically and organisationally, is able to withstand a wide range of risks, is always at the forefront of the times, and leads the whole nation in building socialism with Chinese characteristics. The whole party should follow the general objective of the great new project, comprehensively strengthen party building ideologically, organisationally and in terms of work style, continuously raise the level of its leadership and governance, constantly enhance its ability to fight corruption and forestall moral degeneration, and lead the people to accomplish new historical tasks with a new look and stronger fighting power"[24]. Jiang Zemin emphasised that ideological construction constitutes the primary task of party building, that Marxism-Leninism and Mao Zedong Thought, and Deng Xiaoping Theory constitute the fundamental guiding ideology in the founding of the CPC and the PRC, and that it was necessary for the party to uphold the ideological line of emancipating the mind and seeking truth from facts, and to be brave and adept at theoretical innovation according to the requirements of practice. He emphasised that it was necessary to consolidate the party organisationally to provide a strong guarantee for the accomplishment of the party's political line, to strengthen and improve the construction of the party's work style and to maintain vibrant connections with the people and also that, in order to govern the country, it was first necessary to govern the party and that party governance must be strict. He also emphasised that it was necessary to uphold the principle of treating both the symptoms and the root causes of problems and uphold comprehensive treatment, and to strive to prevent and solve the problem of corruption at source. In the face of the new situation in the new century, in order to ensure that the ship of socialist modernisation with Chinese characteristics would always follow the correct course, the construction of the CPC must be further advanced. The report of the 15th CPC National Congress comprehensively elaborated on the general objectives and overall arrangements for the great new project of party building, was in line with the development trends of the times and the requirements of China's social progress, and reflected the urgent need for party building in practice under the new historical conditions.

In accordance with the practical requirements of party building, Jiang Zemin raised the two major historical issues facing governance in his speech at the conference celebrating the 80th anniversary of the founding of the CPC on 1 July 2001. He pointed out that it was always necessary for the party to consciously strengthen and improve its construction, constantly enhance its creativity, cohesion and fighting power, and perpetuate its vitality and vigour. The CPC is the key to the effective conducting of China's affairs. We must, he said, continue to focus on the basic questions of the kind of party which should be built under new historical conditions and how to build it, further address the two historic issues of improving the party's governability, and leading and improving its ability to fight corruption, forestall moral degeneration and withstand risk, enriching the basic essence of the great new project of party building and raising the CPC's understanding of the laws of party building to a new level.

These two major historical issues raised by the party captured the key issues of the great new project of party building and ascertained the focal point for promoting the great new project of party building. The first issue pertains to solving the problem whereby the needs of the new situation and new tasks are not met, in order to maintain and develop the party's progressiveness. The second pertains to solving the problem whereby the requirements of advancing the cause of socialism with Chinese characteristics and building a moderately prosperous society are not met, in order to constantly safeguard the purity of the party, so that the CPC would always possess the power of truth and constantly enhance its integrity. Solving these two historic issues is a long-term and arduous task, which is of great significance to the CPC in advancing the great new project of party building, continuously improving the party's leadership and level of governance, and enhancing the party's cohesiveness and fighting power.

The ability to continuously improve the level of the party's governability and leadership under the conditions of reform and opening up, and the development of a socialist market economy, and to consolidate the party's governance position and foundation, is a historical issue that must be resolved in order to advance the great new project of party building. From the 1990s onwards, a number of major political parties around the world with experience of long-term governance lost their positions of power, leading many to ponder this situation deeply. Although the reasons for the loss of power of these ruling parties are very complex and the circumstances vary, common factors included neglecting the construction of party governability, failing to respond correctly to changes in the international and domestic situation, failing to effectively solve the problems of domestic economic and social development, and the constant growth and spread of corruption which led to serious disengagement from the masses and resulted in fundamental changes in the hearts and minds of the people. In this context Jiang Zemin pointed out, "Our party is the ruling party, and the leadership of the party must be reflected in its governance. We must strengthen our awareness of governance and improve our governance capabilities"[25]. He also said, "Whether our work can be done well, whether we can always take the initiative amid fierce international competition, and whether our cause will ultimately succeed, depends to a large extent on our party's level of leadership and governability"[26]. The construction of governability is a fundamental area of party building since it came to power. Improving the party's governability and level of governance is a necessary requirement for accelerating and advancing China's socialist modernisation, and establishing and refining the socialist market economy.

The ability to constantly enhance the party's capacity to fight corruption and forestall moral degeneration under the conditions of reform and opening up, and the development of a socialist market economy, and to safeguard the nature and purpose of the party, constitutes another historical issue that must be addressed in order to advance the great new project of party building. In this regard, Jiang Zemin pointed out that, "The phenomenon of corruption is a virus that invades the healthy muscles of the party and state organs. If we take it lightly and allow it to flourish, we will bury our party, our people's power and our great cause of socialist modernisation"[27]. The Party Central Committee objectively analyses the state of the anti-corruption struggle, continuously increases the intensity of the fight against corruption, organically combines the fight against corruption with reform, development and stability, and relies on its own strength and the support of the people in an effort to reduce passive corruption to a minimum. The CPC always grasps the initiative in the fight against corruption, grasps the overall situation of the fight against corruption, enhances the relevance and efficacy of the fight against corruption, and greatly enhances the ability to fight corruption and forestall moral degeneration.

To improve the party's governability and leadership under the conditions of reform and opening up, and the development of a socialist market economy, it is necessary to adhere always to the ideological line of emancipating the mind and seeking truth from facts, promote the spirit of advancing with the times, and maintain the party's progressiveness and creativity. To this end a correct political line and strategic and phased development goals in the economic, political, social and cultural fields must be formulated under the guidance of a correct ideological line and, in accordance with the realities and development trends of society, and national and party conditions, corresponding and flexible policies and strategies must be adopted to mobilise the people's enthusiasm, initiative and creativity to participate in the great cause led by the party. At the same time, efforts must also be made to foster highly educated and ambitious ranks of cadres, so that they will possess the theories, policies, knowledge and work standards to meet the requirements of developing times and situations, and the ability to manage the market economy, the ability to act according to scientific laws, and the mastery of scientific leadership styles and methods.

The key to improving the party's ability to fight corruption and forestall moral degeneration, and to be resilient to risks is to maintain vibrant connections between the party and the people. Historical experience has repeatedly proven that the greatest danger to the ruling party is being detached from the people. Since the start of the period of reform and opening up, ideas such as loving ease, hating work and coveting pleasure have multiplied among some party members and cadres, and formalism and a bureaucratic work style have become serious problems while the phenomenon of using power for personal gain and taking bribes to bend the law have continued despite repeated prohibition. If these phenomena are not effectively curbed, there is a danger that the party and the country will be ruined. Efforts must be made to carry forward the party's fine work style of linking theory with practice, close contact with the masses and conducting criticism and self-criticism in the light of new realities while, at the same time, summing up new practical experience and striving to cultivate a new style of work. In order to treat the fight against corruption as a systematic project and uphold an approach of treating both the symptoms and the root causes, education must be the foundation, the legal system the guarantee and supervision the key. It is necessary to constantly eradicate the soil in which corruption breeds and spreads through deepening reforms.

Party building is a major asset of the CPC in leading the revolution, construction and reform to continuous victory. If the party is to stay at the forefront of the times, always implement strong leadership in carrying out socialist modernisation, always uphold the vanguard nature of the working class and the aim to serve the people wholeheartedly during broad and profound historical changes, and always grasp the initiative in fierce international struggles, then it is vital to consistently strengthen party building and regard promotion of the great new project as the party's sacred responsibility. The Party Central Committee, with Comrade Jiang Zemin at its core, summed up its experience, followed the past and heralded the future and, based on a clear understanding of the characteristics of the times and the historical orientation of the party and the governance mission it shouldered, creatively promoted the great new project of party building, which is an objective requirement for the CPC to carry out social revolution, an inevitable requirement for it to guard against hazards and challenges, and a fundamental requirement for it to achieve long-term governance.

(VI) A NEW UNDERSTANDING OF GOVERNANCE METHODS AND STRATEGIES

After the 14th CPC National Congress, the party inherited and developed Deng Xiaoping's ideology regarding democracy and the rule of law, elevated the rule of law to the level of governance strategy, and constantly improved governance methods with regard to the strategy of the rule of law, such that the party's governance theory became increasingly mature, its governing strategy more refined and its level of governance constantly improved.

A modern national system of governance is built on the basis of the rule of law, which constitutes an important support for the governance of a ruling party and the prosperity of a nation, and a fundamental guarantee for long-term national stability. In the history of new China, the nation has suffered serious setbacks such as the Great Leap Forward and the People's Commune Movement, and, in particular, made the mistake of the Cultural Revolution, which had long-term and far-reaching implications, all because it did not correctly handle the relationship between law and policy.

After the 3rd Plenary Session of the 11th CPC Central Committee, Deng Xiaoping summed up the lessons learned from both positive and negative experiences at home and abroad, and stressed in his speech entitled *Emancipating the Mind, Seeking Truth from Facts, Uniting as One and Looking to the Future* that the legal system must be strengthened in order to safeguard people's democracy. He said that there must be a legal foundation, compliance with the law, strict law enforcement and investigations of violations. The relationships between the rule of law and the rule of man, and between the party and the government should be resolved through reform of the political system, so as to ensure the long-term stability of the country and prevent the recurrence of the longlasting and comprehensive mistake of the Cultural Revolution.

The Party Central Committee, with Comrade Jiang Zemin at its core, also responded to historical developments and the will of the people, elevating the construction of the legal system to a more prominent position in the work of the whole party and nation. In October 1992, Jiang Zemin pointed out in his report to the 14th CPC National Congress that, "without democracy and the rule of law there can be no socialism and no socialist modernisation. We should make marked progress in developing socialist democracy and improving the socialist legal system in order to consolidate and develop a stable social and political environment, and ensure the smooth implementation of economic construction, and reform and opening up." He also emphasised that, "great importance is attached to the construction of the legal system. Strengthening legislative work, especially urgently formulating and improving laws and regulations that safeguard reform and opening up, strengthen macroeconomic management and regulate microeconomic activity, is an urgent requirement for establishing a socialist market economy"[28].

In December 1994, the CPC Central Committee conducted a lecture on legal knowledge, and there Jiang Zemin pointed out in his speech that the purpose of constructing a socialist legal system and implementing the rule of law was to build China into a prosperous, strong, democratic and civilised modern socialist state. The management of all affairs in accordance with the law is enshrined in the general outline of the CPC constitution and the national constitution. Leading cadres learning the law will not only help popularise legal knowledge, and educate and motivate the whole party to learn and abide by the law and act in accordance with the law, but also help promote the establishment of a socialist market economy and the construction of a national legal system to ensure the smooth implementation of reform and opening up, and modernisation.

In February 1996, Jiang Zemin delivered a speech at a lecture on the legal system organised by the CPC Central Committee, to present strengthening construction of the socialist legal system and the rule of law as important guidelines for the CPC and the state in managing social affairs. He pointed out that, "strengthening construction of the socialist legal system and the rule of law is an important aspect of Deng Xiaoping's theory of building socialism with Chinese characteristics and an important policy of our party and government in managing state and social affairs"[29]. Implementing and upholding the rule of law means to gradually put each aspect of the state's work on a trajectory to legalisation and to bring about the legalisation and standardisation of China's political, economic and social life. It means that the masses of the people manage the affairs of the state, economic and cultural undertakings and social affairs through various approaches and forms in accordance with the provisions of the constitution and laws under the leadership of the party, and also means to gradually achieve the institutionalisation and legalisation of socialist democracy. Just over a month later, the Fourth Session of the Eighth NPC incorporated "the rule of law and the construction of a socialist state under the rule of law" as a basic policy in the *Ninth Five-Year Plan for National Economic and Social Development and the Long-range Objectives to 2010.*

In September 1997, the 15th CPC National Congress defined the rule of law as the party's basic strategy in leading the people to govern the country and made the rule of law and the construction of a socialist state under the rule of law an important part of the political system reform. The report of the 15th CPC National Congress refers to the "further expansion of socialist democracy, improving the socialist legal system, the rule of law, and the construction of a socialist state under the rule of law", and further states that, "the rule of law constitutes the CPC's basic strategy in leading the people to govern the country, an objective need for the development of a socialist market economy, an important symbol of social civilisation and progress, and an important safeguard for China's long-term stability"[30]. The adoption of the rule of law as a basic strategy constituted a major decision made, and a new goal set, by the party on national governance, and demonstrated that the construction of a socialist democratic political system in China had reached a new level.

After the basic strategy of the rule of law was proposed, the party further enriched and developed the basic strategy of the rule of law, according to the requirements of strengthening socialist ideology and moral development, in the context of the practice of leading the people to govern the country by the rule of law.

In March 1996, when attending the Second Plenary Session of the PLA Delegation at the Fourth Session of the Eighth NPC, Jiang Zemin pointed out in his speech that socialist spiritual civilisation constitutes an important part and essential feature of building socialism with Chinese characteristics. When the construction of spiritual civilisation is complete, it can provide strong spiritual impetus and intellectual support for economic construction. Under the historical conditions of the constant deepening of China's reform and opening up, and modernisation, it is of great significance to place the building of socialist spiritual civilisation and a democratic legal system in a more prominent position. He said that throughout the process of socialist modernisation, it is necessary for all to unswervingly implement Deng Xiaoping's strategic idea of "doing two jobs at once and attaching equal importance to each" and attach great importance to the building of spiritual civilisation, while vigorously promoting the building of material civilisation.

In February 2000, Jiang Zemin emphasised in a speech during an inspection tour in Guangdong that building socialism with Chinese characteristics includes the development of both material and spiritual civilisation, and that coordinated economic and social development, and overall progress must be achieved. In order to implement the construction of party culture style and clean politics, education and management, and rule by virtue and the rule of law, a two-pronged approach must be adopted. When education is good, moral governance is strengthened, and the ideological and political quality of cadres and their level of spirituality is improved, then it is possible to firmly prevent and reduce the incidence of misconduct. When management is good and the rule of law is strengthened, then it is possible to plug the loopholes that lead to crime and punish those guilty of misconduct in accordance with the rules, which can also serve as a warning and function as an educational instrument for the masses of cadres and the general public.

In January 2001, Jiang Zemin pointed out in his speech at the National Propaganda Ministry Conference that, "In the process of building socialism with Chinese characteristics and developing a socialist market economy, we must persistently strengthen construction of the socialist legal system and rule the country according to law while, at the same time, persistently strengthening the construction of socialist morality and rule the country by virtue. For the governance of a country, the rule of law and rule by virtue have always been complementary and mutually reinforcing. Both are indispensable and neither can be neglected. The rule of law pertains to political construction and political civilisation while rule by virtue pertains to ideological construction and spiritual civilisation. The two are different in scope but their status and functions are both very important. We should closely integrate construction of the legal system with construction of morality and the rule of law with rule by virtue"[31]. In this way the rule of law and rule by virtue were organically integrated.

As components of the political superstructure, both law and morality are important means of maintaining social order and regulating people's thoughts and behaviour, and they are interrelated, complementary and mutually reinforcing. The rule by law constitutes an important guarantee for rule by virtue, and rule by virtue is an important foundation for the rule by law. Closely integrating the construction of both the rule of law and of morality is conducive to improving the legal awareness and moral quality of citizens, and results in the internalising of their moral sentiments into behavioural standards. The rule of law regulates the behaviour of members of society with the authority and compulsion of the law while rule by virtue raises the ideological understanding and moral consciousness of members of society with the persuasiveness and charisma of morality, and the two complement each other to form China's basic governance strategy.

While adhering to the basic strategy of the rule of law, the party established the organic unification of upholding the leadership of the party, the sovereignty of the people and the rule of law as important elements in the development of socialist democratic politics and the construction of socialist political civilisation. In this regard Jiang Zemin pointed out that, "The most fundamental thing in developing socialist democratic politics is to organically unify adherence to the leadership of the party, the sovereignty of the people and the rule of law"[32]. The law constitutes the common expression of the position of the party and the will of the people, and the institutionalisation and legalisation of people rights. Party leadership is the fundamental safeguard of the sovereignty of the people and the rule of law. Without party leadership, China would only be a scattered mess and its ethnic groups would lack cohesion. Our party's leadership of the country is in accordance with the law, ensuring that China will operate and develop on a trajectory of democracy and the rule of law. The sovereignty of the people is the essential requirement of socialist democratic politics. Socialist laws must be formulated through the processes of the people's democracy and implemented through the supervision of the people's democracy; democracy and the rule of law have always been inseparable. The organic unity between party leadership, the sovereignty of the people and the rule of law ensures the long-term stability and practical implementation of the party's basic line and basic programme in accordance with the legal system, and ensures that the party always plays the core leading role in the overall situation and the coordination of all parties.

On this foundation, and in light of the continuous development of the socialist market economy, the party has explored and reflected on how to refine the approach to party leadership and method of governance in accordance with the principle of considering the overall picture and coordinating all parties in order to further strengthen and refine the system of party leadership.

In May 2001, during an inspection tour to Anhui Province, Jiang Zemin pointed out that adopting the correct leadership style and leadership methods is a capability that must be possessed by the CPC, as a Marxist party and as a ruling party that leads the people to keep up with the times and constantly forge ahead. In the face of the new situation and new tasks, how to further improve leadership style and methods to achieve innovation in these constitutes a major issue currently faced in party building and political system reform [33].

In November 2002, Jiang Zemin in his report to the 16th CPC National Congress further emphasised the need for reform and improvement of the party leadership and governing methods. This has an overall effect on promoting the construction of socialist democratic politics. The party's leadership is mainly political, ideological and organisational leadership, and it implements the party's leadership of the state and society by formulating general policies, proposing legislation, recommending important cadres, implementing ideological propaganda, utilising the function of party organisations and party members, and upholding governance according to the law. And this indeed indicated the right direction for the CPC to further improve party leadership and governing methods.

The question of how to govern the country and how to better safeguard and bring to fruition the fundamental interests of the greatest number of people constitutes a major theoretical and practical issue that the party is constantly exploring. On the basis of profound summaries of experiences of national governance in all places and throughout history, the party put forward the basic strategy of integrating the rule of law and rule by virtue, and explored ways to improve the party's leadership and governing methods, achieving heartening results. This constitutes the application and development of the party's strategic thinking of "doing two jobs at once and attaching equal importance to each", the refinement of regular understanding of building socialism with Chinese characteristics, and the enrichment and development of the Marxist doctrine of the state, and has played an important role in helping the party to create a new situation of reform and opening up, and modernisation in the new century, and to achieve the long-term stability and development of the Chinese nation.

(VII) THE MAJOR IDEOLOGY OF THE 'THREE REPRESENTS': A FURTHER DEEPENING OF THE UNDERSTANDING OF THE COMMUNIST PARTY'S GOVERNANCE LAW

The way in which the party can always maintain its nature as the vanguard of the working class and better represent the interests of the greatest number of people under the conditions of opening up to the outside world and developing a socialist market economy, and the way to always ensure that all party comrades act in accordance with the goals of the party's struggle and in the highest interests of the country and the people, and maintain and strengthen the party's strong solidarity and high degree of unity under the further development of the trend of diversification of social and economic composition, forms of organisation, modes of employment, stakeholder relations and distribution, are major theoretical and practical issues pertaining to the strengthening of party building under new historical conditions. It was in the process of correctly answering these questions that the party formed the major ideology of the "Three Represents", thereby achieving the progressive advance of the guiding ideology of Marxism with the times and further deepening its understanding of the communist party's governace law.

On 20 February 2000, Jiang Zemin attended the mobilisation meeting of the "Three Emphases" education for leading cadres in Gaozhou City, Guangdong Province and delivered a speech in which he put forward the requirement of the "Five Always" for party building, stating that, "We must make the party always maintain the vanguard nature of the working class, always represent the interests of the greatest number of people, always be the representative of society's advanced productive forces, always lead the people of all of China's ethnic groups to promote the development of society's productive forces, and always play the role of a strong leading core, and we must also further build the party ideologically, organisationally and in terms of work style, in the light of new historical conditions"[34]. On 25 February, he first put forward the scientific assertion of the "Three Represents" when he chaired a symposium on party building in Guangzhou, stating that, "Our party has won people's support because it has always represented the development requirements of China's advanced productive forces, the direction of China's advanced culture and the fundamental interests of the greatest number of Chinese people during the various historical periods of revolution, construction and reform, and has struggled tirelessly to bring about the fundamental interests of the country and the people through the formulation of correct lines, guidelines and policies"[35].

In May 2000, Jiang Zemin stressed the significance of the Three Represents when he chaired a seminar on party building in Shanghai, saying that always implementing the Three Represents constitutes "the foundation of our party, the basis of our governance, and the source of our strength". In October of the same year, at the 5th Plenary Session of the 15th CPC Central Committee, Jiang Zemin further clarified that, "the requirements of these Three Represents are based on the nature and purpose of our party and its historical experience and practical needs", and "are the basic guidelines for our party to strengthen party building in the new era"[36].

On 1 July 2001, in his speech at the conference celebrating the 80th anniversary of the founding of the CPC, Jiang Zemin reviewed and summarised the glorious history and basic experience of the party over the preceding 80 years, systematically expounded the scientific meaning of the major ideology of the Three Represents, and profoundly answered the major issues that need to be resolved in order to strengthen and improve party building under the new historical conditions. With the major ideology of the Three Represents at its core, the speech connected the communist party's ruling law, the laws of socialist construction and the laws of human social development, and expounded a series of rich and profound perceptions regarding socialism with Chinese characteristics.

On 31 May 2002, Jiang Zemin delivered a speech at the graduation ceremony of the provincial and ministerial-level cadres' training course at the Central Party School, in which he elaborated on the fundamental requirements for implementing the major ideology of the Three Represents. He pointed out that the key to implementing the major ideology of the Three Represents was to keep up with the times, the core aim was to maintain the party's progressiveness, and the essence was to uphold the concept of governing for the people.

In November 2002, the 16th CPC National Congress, on the basis of summing up the basic experience since the 4th Plenary Session of the 13th Central Committee, comprehensively and systematically revealed the background, practical basis, historical status, spiritual essence, guiding significance and fundamental requirements of the important thought of the Three Represents, and wrote the important thought of the Three Represents, together with Marxism-Leninism, Mao Zedong Thought and Deng

Xiaoping Theory, into the party constitution as a guiding thought of the party.

The major ideology of the Three Represents is a scientific theory formed by the Chinese communists, mainly represented by Comrade Jiang Zemin, in the practice of building socialism with Chinese characteristics, which deepens the understanding of the nature of socialism and the appropriate way to construct it, and how to build the party, and accumulates new and valuable experience in governing the party and the country. It constitutes the inheritance and development of Marxism-Leninism, Mao Zedong Thought and Deng Xiaoping Theory, reflecting the new requirements for the work of the party and the state arising from the developments and changes in the contemporary world and in China, and it constitutes a powerful theoretical weapon for strengthening and improving party building and promoting the self-improvement and development of Chinese socialism, the crystallisation of the collective wisdom of the CPC, and the guiding ideology that the party must adhere to in the long-term.

The major ideology of the Three Represents is a unified whole, interlinked and mutually reinforcing. Only the development of advanced productivity can create the necessary material conditions for the development of advanced culture and satisfying the fundamental interests of the greatest number of people. Only the development of advanced culture can provide spiritual impetus and intellectual support for the development of advanced productivity and provide the best spiritual food for the people. Satisfying the fundamental interests of the greatest number of people is the fundamental purpose of developing advanced productivity and advanced culture, and provides inexhaustible impetus for the further development of advanced productivity and advanced culture. The major ideology of the Three Represents embodied the unity of productivity and socioeconomic relations, of the economic base and the superstructure, the unity of the construction of material, political and spiritual civilisation, the unity of the economy, politics and culture, and the unity of respecting the objective laws of social development and fully utilising the subjective initiative of the makers of history.

As an important part of the theoretical system of socialism with Chinese characteristics, the major ideology of the Three Represents constitutes a theoretical summary of the practical experience of China's socialist modernisation and deepened the party's understanding of the communist party's governance law, the laws of socialist construction and the laws of human social development. The major ideology of the Three Represents reflects the basic propositions of Marxist dialectical materialism and historical materialism in a comprehensive and complete manner. Among these propositions, advanced productivity being the fundamental driving force of human social development, advanced culture the fundamental guarantee of comprehensive social progress, and serving the fundamental interests of the greatest number of people, together constitute the fundamental purpose of social development and progress. The combination of the three organically unites the ultimate determining role of the productive forces, the countervailing force of the superstructure on the economic base and the historical subjectivity of the people, and constitutes a concentrated exposition of the Marxist worldview, methodology and values, as well as of the nature and purpose of the communist party. This elaboration clearly underscores the requirement for the communist party to be progressive, advancing from the pursuit of a certain ideal social form in the future to the pursuit of the dynamics of social advancement and mechanisms for its formation, thereby creatively building a bridge between the future and reality. It closely integrates the long-term goals of the party's struggle with its current tasks, and the pursuit of ideals by advanced elements with the immediate interests of the general people, reflecting the unity of the party's supreme and minimum agendas, and the unity of the party as the vanguard of the Chinese working class with the vanguard of the Chinese people and the Chinese nation. It is under the guidance of this major ideology that the party integrated the exploration of the laws of socialist construction and the communist party's governance law into one substance, attaining the level of new understanding of the laws of human social development and on the basis of new practice and opening up a wide space for the advancement of Marxist theory apace with the times.

Theoretical maturity is an important foundation and sign of political maturity. Lenin once said that without theory, the party would lose its right to exist and would inevitably be doomed to political bankruptcy sooner or later. The kind of governance theory the party puts forward and the kind of governing philosophy it follows relates not only to party building but also to China's future prospects. The major ideology of the Three Represents summarised the party's historical experience and reflected its understanding of the communist party's governanc law, enabling the party to develop a new path of governance in the development of a socialist market economy. The major ideology of the Three Represents also made a significant contribution to Marxist theory on the construction of a ruling party and provided theoretical guidance for advancing the great new project of party building and advancing the development of socialism with Chinese characteristics.

3

ADHERING TO AND DEVELOPING A NEW PATH OF GOVERNANCE IN THE PROCESS OF BUILDING A MODERATELY PROSPEROUS SOCIETY IN ALL RESPECTS

After the 16th CPC National Congress, the Party Central Committee, with Comrade Hu Jintao as its General Secretary, adhered to the guidance of Deng Xiaoping Theory and the major ideology of the Three Represents, seizing and making good use of an important period for strategic opportunities. The committee actively promoted practical, theoretical and institutional innovation, upheld people-oriented, comprehensive and coordinated sustainable development, built a socialist harmonious society, accelerated the construction of ecological civilisation, formed the general composition of the cause of socialism with Chinese characteristics, focused on safeguarding and improving people's livelihoods, promoted social justice, promoted the building of a harmonious world, advanced the construction of the party's governability and progressiveness, formed a scientific concept of development, successfully upheld and developed socialism with Chinese characteristics from a new historical starting point, and pioneered and developed a new path of governance in the great practice of building a moderately prosperous society in all respects.

(I) A MODERATELY PROSPEROUS SOCIETY: THE INITIAL ACHIEVEMENT OF THE CPC'S PHASED GOVERNANCE OBJECTIVES

Achieving moderate prosperity is the goal of China's economic construction work in the 20th century, and a phased objective of the party's governance. At the end of the 20th century, the CPC achieved the second step of its "three-step" modernisation strategy in the process of deepening reform, expanding openness and tackling various risks and challenges, and people's livelihoods generally reached the level of moderate prosperity. This constituted a great achievement made by China's reform and opening up, laying a solid foundation for the Party Central Committee, with Comrade Hu Jintao as General Secretary, to lead the whole party and nation to build a moderately prosperous society and accelerate socialist modernisation.

In the 1980s, the second generation of the party's central leadership, with Comrade Deng Xiaoping at its core, established an ambitious blueprint for the "three steps" of China's economic development in the context of history and the overall situation, and established achieving a moderately prosperous standard of living for the people as the second step of modernisation. In the 1990s, the third generation of the party's central leadership, with Comrade Jiang Zemin at its core, put forward a "new three-step" development strategy at a major historical juncture, making further plans to achieve the third step of modernisation in the first 50 years of the 21st century.

In 1995, China's GDP reached more than Rmb576 billion, and the original target of quadrupling the 1980 level by 2000 was achieved five years ahead of schedule. In 1997, the target of quadrupling per capita GDP was also achieved three years ahead of schedule. In 2000, the second-step goal of people's livelihoods reaching a moderately prosperous level in all respects was achieved on schedule. China's GDP exceeded US$1 trillion for the first time, reaching Rmb10.02 trillion, foreign exchange reserves reached US$165.6 billion, ranking second in the world, per capita disposable income of urban residents rose to Rmb6,256 and per capita consumption expenditure rose to Rmb5,027, per capita disposable income of rural residents rose to Rmb2,282 and per capita consumption expenditure rose to Rmb1,714, and the total number of people in China still in poverty in terms of food and clothing was reduced to 28.2 million nationwide.

In November 2002, the 16th CPC National Congress declared, "Through the joint efforts of the whole party and people of all ethnic groups in China, we have triumphantly achieved the goals of the first and second steps of the "three-step" modernisation strategy, with the people's livelihoods having reached a moderately prosperous level in all respects. This is a great victory for the socialist system and a new milestone in the history of the development of the Chinese nation"[1].

Proposing a new phased objective after achieving the phased objectives of governance constitutes a highly effective methodology of the party in uniting and leading the people towards continuous victory. The 16th CPC National Congress, based on a scientific judgement of the historical mission shouldered by the party and its governance position, drew up an ambitious blueprint for building a moderately prosperous society in all respects, including economically, politically and culturally, in accordance with the requirements of comprehensively pioneering a new context for socialist modernisation.

The 16th CPC National Congress, starting from the basic national conditions of the primary stage of socialism, had a sober understanding of the level of moderate prosperity that people's lives had reached in all respects. The congress pointed out that the level of moderate prosperity that China had then attained was still at a low level, was not comprehensive and very unevenly developed. This was seen in the following ways. China's productivity, science and technology, and education were still lagging behind, and there was still a long way to go to achieve industrialisation and modernisation. The urban-rural economic dualism had not yet changed, the trend of widening regional disparities had not yet been reversed, and a large number of people were still poor. The total population was continuing to increase while the proportion of the elderly population was also rising, and the pressure on employment and social security was increasing. The conflicts between ecosystems, natural resources and socioeconomic development were becoming increasingly prominent. China was still under pressure from the dominance of developed countries economically and in terms of science and technology. The economic system and management systems in other sectors still lacked refinement. There were also still some problems that could not be ignored in the construction of democracy and the legal system, as well as in the construction of ideology and morality. It would take, stated the congress, a long period of hard struggle to consolidate and improve on the level of moderate prosperity achieved by that time.

Based on this understanding, the 16th CPC National Congress made the major judgement that the first two decades of the 21st century would constitute an important period of strategic opportunity that China must grasp tightly, and that great progress could be made if this were done. The congress emphasised that, in accordance with the development goals set out at the 15th CPC National Congress for the periods up to 2010, up to 100 years after the founding of the CPC in 1921 and up to 100 years after the founding of new China in 1949, China should concentrate its efforts in the first 20 years of this century on the comprehensive construction of a higher level of moderately prosperous society benefiting more than one billion people, so that the economy would become more developed, democracy more robust, science and education more progressive, culture more prosperous, society more harmonious and people's lives more prosperous. This is the stage of development crucial to achieving the third-step strategic objective of modernisation and is also the key stage for refining the socialist market economy and opening up more to the outside world. After this stage of construction, it will be necessary to continue to struggle for a few more decades to build China into a prosperous, strong, democratic and civilised socialist country by the middle of this century.

Based on the above overall strategic plan, the 16th CPC National Congress put forward specific plans for building a moderately prosperous society in all respects. First, on the basis of optimising the structure and improving efficiency, the government would strive to quadruple the level of GDP from the year 2000 by 2020, and significantly enhance China's comprehensive national power and international competitiveness. Industrialisation would be basically achieved, and a sound socialist market economy and a more dynamic and open economic system would be established. The proportion of the urban population would increase substantially, and the trend of widening disparity between industrial and agricultural workers, urban and rural areas and geographical regions would be gradually reversed. The social security system would be more robust, social employment would be more adequate, there would be an increase in household assets, and people would lead more affluent lives.

Second, socialist democracy would be more refined, the socialist legal system would be further enhanced, the basic strategy of the rule of law would be fully implemented, and the political, economic and cultural rights and interests of the people would be tangibly respected and safeguarded. Grassroots democracy would be more robust, social order better, and people would live in peace and work happily.

Third, the ideological and moral, scientific and cultural, and health quality of all ethnic groups would be significantly improved, and a relatively robust modern national education system, system of science and technology, and cultural innovation, and system of national fitness and healthcare would be formed. The people would enjoy access to good education, upper secondary education would be basically universalised, and illiteracy would be eliminated. A learning society would be formed in which all people learn and lifelong learning is encouraged, promoting people's all-round development.

Fourth, the capacity for sustainable development would be enhanced, ecosystems would be improved, the efficiency of resource usage would be significantly increased, harmony between humans and nature would be promoted, propelling society as a whole onto a civilised development path for the development of production, affluence and eco-friendliness[2].

The goal of building a moderately prosperous society in all respects established by the 16th CPC National Congress is the goal of the comprehensive economic, political and cultural development of socialism with Chinese characteristics and a goal that is unified with accelerated modernisation. The goal of building a moderately prosperous society in all respects is in line with the theme of pioneering and developing socialism with Chinese characteristics since the 3rd Plenary Session of the 11th CPC Central Committee, with the national conditions of China at the primary stage of socialism and the reality of socialist modernisation, and with the expectations of hundreds of millions of people, and is conducive to presenting a good international image of China, and to mobilising and uniting the masses of Chinese people in their unremitting struggle to build China into a prosperous, strong, democratic and civilised modern socialist country.

On the basis of the goal of building a moderately prosperous society in all respects established at the 16th CPC National Congress, the 17th CPC National Congress adapted to the firm steps already taken towards the goal of building a moderately prosperous society in all respects, responded to the new expectations of the people of all China's ethnic groups to lead a better life, grasped the trends and laws of socioeconomic development, upheld the basic programme formed by the basic objectives and policies for the economic, political, cultural and social construction of socialism with Chinese characteristics, and set out new and higher demands for China's development. These were, namely, enhancing the coordination of development and striving to achieve excellent and rapid economic development, expanding socialist democracy and better safeguarding people's rights and interests and social justice, strengthening cultural construction and significantly improving the quality of civilisation of all China's ethnic groups, accelerating the development of social affairs and comprehensively improving people's living standards, building an ecological civilisation, and basically forming an industrial structure, growth pattern and pattern of consumption that conserves energy and resources, and protects ecosystems[3].

The 17th CPC National Congress pointed out that by 2020, when the goal of building a moderately prosperous society in all respects would have been achieved, China, a large developing socialist country with an ancient civilisation and a long history, would be a country where industrialisation will have been basically achieved, where comprehensive national power will have been significantly enhanced, and where the overall size of the domestic market is among the highest in the world, a country where the level of people's prosperity has generally increased, where the quality of life has been significantly improved and which has good ecosystems, a country where people enjoy fuller democratic rights, and have higher quality civilisation and spiritual goals, a country with more refined systems in all aspects, and a more vibrant but stable and united society, and a country that is more open to the outside world and more affable and which makes greater contributions to human civilisation.

After achieving a moderately prosperous standard of living in all respects at the end of the 20th century, the CPC again put forward the new governance objective of building a moderately prosperous society in all respects at the 16th and 17th CPC National Congresses in accordance with the development of the cause of socialism with Chinese characteristics and the wishes of the general public. The fact that the party has repeatedly proposed and achieved its phased objectives fully reflects the party's governance ability and level of governance, being able to control the overall situation, elevate standards and determine the direction to pursue, and reflects the party's original intention and mission to serve the people wholeheartedly. The goals of achieving a moderately prosperous standard of living overall for the Chinese people and building a moderately prosperous society in all respects are key aspects of China's "three-step" strategy for economic development and are of great significance to the party in uniting and leading the entire party and nation to achieve the great rejuvenation of the Chinese nation.

(II) SOLVING PROMINENT GOVERNANCE PROBLEMS AND CONTRADICTIONS THROUGH SCIENTIFIC DEVELOPMENT

After the 16th CPC National Congress, based on China's basic national conditions at the primary stage of socialism and the characteristics of the new stage of China's development, the Party Central Committee, with Comrade Hu Jintao as General Secretary, scientifically analysed the new changes in the international and domestic situation, profoundly grasped the new issues and contradictions facing China's development in the process of building a moderately prosperous society in all respects, and solved the prominent problems and contradictions arising in the course of governance through scientific development. In particular, through the struggle against SARS (severe acute respiratory syndrome), the committee accelerated the historical process of actively exploring new thinking on development and firmly propelled socioeconomic development onto the path of scientific development.

In early 2003, the rapid spread of the SARS epidemic overwhelmingly exposed the weaknesses and prominent problems in China's socioeconomic development. In mid-to-late February that year, the SARS epidemic became endemic in local areas of Guangdong Province, and later proliferated and spread in northern China in early March. By mid-to-late April, the outbreak had spread to 26 provinces, autonomous regions and municipalities across the country. Apart from mainland China, outbreaks also occurred in more than 30 countries and regions around the world. The SARS epidemic posed a serious threat to people's health and safety, and had a severe impact on socioeconomic development.

In accordance with the situation at the time but also with a long-term perspective, the Party Central Committee, on the basis of a comprehensive analysis of the situation, required all regions and departments to hold an overall and strategic viewpoint, correctly grasped and handled the relationship between combating SARS and promoting economic development, upheld an approach of putting the top priority on people's health and safety, made the significant decision not to relax their grasp on the battle against SARS with one hand and not to waver in their focus on economic construction with the other,

and used development to solve the prominent contradictions and problems arising in economic life.

Under the strong leadership of the Party Central Committee, all regions, departments, units and sectors of society were united, worked together and overcame difficulties. In the fight against SARS, the masses of cadres and workers on all fronts held fast to their posts and worked hard to maintain the positive momentum of accelerated economic growth. Through relentless efforts, the SARS outbreak was effectively contained, and in June 2003, the WHO announced that the travel advisory against Beijing had been lifted. China achieved a major milestone victory in the fight against SARS.

In July 2003, Hu Jintao pointed out in his speech at the National Conference on the Prevention and Control of SARS that mankind always advances and overcomes one ordeal after another. A wise nation, he said, will learn much more from disasters and mistakes than from normal times[4]. The occurrence and spread of SARS was a sudden disaster but this prompted the party and the government to consider the prominent contradictions and problems affecting socioeconomic development. As a result, through the struggle against SARS, the party came to realise more profoundly than in the past that China's socioeconomic development, and urban and rural development were not yet sufficiently coordinated, that the development of public health was lagging behind and the public health system contained deficiencies, that emergency response mechanisms were not robust and that China's capacity to handle and manage crises was not strong, that some places and departments lacked the preparation and ability to deal with emergencies, and the work style of a very small number of party members and cadres was not practical and they did not work effectively or take appropriate initiative in emergency situations. The party and the government thereby came to a deep understanding that in order to build a moderately prosperous society in all respects and to develop a new context in pioneering socialism with Chinese characteristics, they had to scientifically grasp the characteristics of China's stage of development, profoundly consider and resolve the question of the kind of development China should achieve and the means of development, and pay more attention to the comprehensive, coordinated and sustainable development of the economy and society.

In October 2003, the *Decision of the CPC Central Committee on Several Issues Concerning Improvement of the Socialist Market Economy* adopted at the 3rd Plenary Session of the 16th CPC Central Committee, put forward for the first time in its entirety the concept of "upholding a people-oriented approach and establishing a comprehensive, coordinated and sustainable concept of development". It also proposed for the first time the "Five Coordinations", namely, 'the coordination of urban and rural development, of regional development, of socioeconomic development, of the harmonious development of human beings and nature, and of domestic development and opening up to the outside world"[5] as a requirement for China's socioeconomic development and as a concrete way to implement the scientific concept of development.

In March 2004, Hu Jintao delivered a speech at the Central Government Symposium on Population, Resources and Environment, clearly explaining and scientifically defining for the first time the essence and basic requirements of the scientific concept of development, taking the Five Coordinations as the basic content and fundamental requirements of the "coordinated development" scientific concept of development.

In October 2006, the *Decision of the CPC Central Committee on Several Major Issues in Building a Socialist Harmonious Society* adopted by the 6th Plenary Session of the 16th CPC Central Committee set out the objectives and main tasks of building a socialist harmonious society and made the Five Coordinations the basic principle and requirement for building a socialist harmonious society.

In October 2007, in his report to the 17th CPC National Congress, Hu

Jintao further reiterated and elaborated on the basic substance, spiritual essence, theoretical system and basic requirements of the scientific concept of development. On the basis of the Five Coordinations, he also proposed to coordinate the relationships between central and local government, individual and collective interests, local and national interests, and current and long-term interests, to fully mobilise the initiative of all parties. At the same time, these coordinations were elevated to the level of methodology, and became an important guideline for China's socioeconomic development as the concrete essence of the fundamental "overall coordination and balance" method of implementing the scientific concept of development.

The Five Coordinations profoundly embodied the inherent requirements of comprehensive, coordinated and sustainable socioeconomic development, and is the entry point for, and means of, implementing the scientific concept of development. The Five Coordinations fundamentally encompassed the five main contradictions in the process of building a moderately prosperous society in all respects, adhering to the key points while balancing all aspects to the greatest possible extent, focusing on strengthening the weaknesses in socioeconomic development, and achieving a positive interaction between different aspects, which is all of great significance in solving the prominent problems and contradictions in governance through scientific development and advancing China's socioeconomic development.

In leading the process of building a moderately prosperous society in all respects, an important aspect of the CPC's efforts to promote scientific development is coordinating urban and rural development. Coordinating urban and rural development means accelerating urban development while paying more attention to rural development, solving the "Three Rural Issues", resolutely implementing the policy of industry repaying agriculture and cities supporting rural areas, gradually changing the economic structure of urban-rural economic dualism, gradually narrowing the gap between urban and rural development, implementing comprehensive socioeconomic development in rural areas, implementing a strategy of urban areas leading rural ones, industry promoting agriculture, urban-rural interaction and coordinated development, and achieving the sustainable development of agriculture and the rural economy. To this end, the party advanced the concept of the "Two Tendencies", namely, that "Looking at the developmental history of some industrialised countries, at the initial stage of industrialisation, it is a universal tendency for agriculture to support industry and provide accumulation for industry but after industrialisation has reached a certain level it is also a universal tendency for industry to repay agriculture and for cities to support rural areas, so as to achieve the coordinated development of industry and agriculture and of urban and rural areas". And, in accordance with the requirement of coordinating urban and rural development, it also means to persist with making solving issues pertaining to agricultural, rural areas, and farmers the top priority of the work of the whole party and, while tapping deeply into the developmental potential of agriculture and rural areas, to constantly increase support for agricultural development, utilise the role of cities in propelling and driving rural areas and the role of industry in supporting and repaying agriculture, pursuing an approach of coordinated development with urban-rural interaction and the mutual promotion of industry and agriculture.

The 16th CPC National Congress established the goal of building a moderately prosperous society in all respects but the unbalanced economic development of China's urban and rural areas, and urban-rural economic dualism, was still prominent. This was a major issue on which China's socioeconomic development had to focus. Hu Jintao proposed persisting with the coordination of urban and rural socioeconomic development, paying more attention to rural areas, caring for farmers, and supporting agriculture, and placed solving the problems of agriculture, rural areas and farmers in a more prominent position, consciously focusing on building a moderately prosperous society in all respects in rural areas[6].

In December 2003, the CPC Central Committee and the State Council issued the *Opinions on Several Policies for Promoting Increased Incomes for Farmers*, emphasising, in accordance with the requirements of coordinating urban and rural socioeconomic development, adherence to the policy of giving more, taking less and loosening control, adjusting the structure of agriculture, expanding employment for farmers, accelerating scientific and technological progress, deepening rural reform, increasing agricultural investment, and strengthening support and protection for agriculture, and striving to achieve relatively rapid growth in farmers' incomes and reverse the widening income gap between urban and rural residents as soon as possible.

In September 2004, Hu Jintao pointed out in his speech at the 4th Plenary Session of the 16th CPC Central Committee that, after decades of development, China had generally reached a stage of development where industry was promoting agriculture and urban areas were leading rural ones[7].

In October 2005, the 5th Plenary Session of the 16th CPC Central Committee clearly put forward the major strategic task of building a new socialist countryside, specifying the development of production, affluence, social etiquette and civility in rural areas, clean and tidy villages and democratic management as the goals of, and requirements for, building the new socialist countryside. In December of the same year, the CPC Central Committee and the State Council issued the document *Several Opinions on Promoting the Construction of a New Socialist Countryside,* which made arrangements for the construction of the new socialist countryside.

In order to promote agricultural development and build the new socialist countryside, since 2004, the Central Government has issued the *Document No. 1* on the "Three Rural Issues" every year, with topics such as promoting the increase of farmers' incomes, improving comprehensive agricultural production capacity, promoting the construction of a new socialist countryside, developing modern agriculture, strengthening the construction of rural infrastructure, promoting stable agricultural development and sustainable income for farmers, increasing efforts to coordinate urban and rural development, accelerating water conservation reform and development, and promoting scientific and technological innovation in agriculture. The distinctive features of these *Document No. 1s* have been accelerating the construction of the new socialist countryside, promoting the integration of urban and rural economic development, and promoting the growth of sustainable income for farmers.

With the development of the rural economy, the party and the government also implemented a series of significant measures to effectively reduce the burden on farmers. On 29 December 2005, the 19th meeting of the Standing Committee of the 10th NPC decided to repeal the *Regulations of the PRC on Agricultural Tax.* With this, Chinese farmers bade farewell to the "imperial grain tax" which had been in place for more than 2,600 years. According to statistics, after the full abolition of agricultural taxes in 2006, the national rural tax reform reduced the burden of farmers by Rmb125 billion per year, with a per capita reduction of more than Rmb140 and an average reduction rate of 80%, compared with comparable statistics in 1999 before the tax exemption, thereby fundamentally reversing the heavy burden on farmers.

As the party leads the process of building a moderately prosperous society in all respects, coordinating regional development is also an important aspect of promoting scientific development. Coordinating regional development means actively implementing the country's overall strategy for regional development, encouraging the eastern regions of China to take the lead in development and promoting the rapid rise of the central region while more actively promoting the Great Western Development Strategy and revitalising old industrial bases such as the northeastern region of China, so as to achieve the comprehensive and coordinated development of all regions. Coordinated regional development is not only a major economic issue but also a major political one, and is not only related to the overall situation of modernisation but also to social stability and China's long-term stability. The Party Central Committee clearly defined the strategic composition of promoting coordinated regional development in accordance with the actual situation of regional development and the requirements of comprehensively promoting modernisation, namely "upholding the promotion of the Great Western Development Strategy, revitalising old industrial bases such as the northeastern region of China, promoting the rapid rise of the central region, encouraging the eastern region to accelerate its development, and forming a new pattern of interaction between eastern, central and western China, characterised by complementing each other's strengths, mutual reinforcement and mutual development".

In January 2000, the CPC upheld its commitment to coordinated regional development and began to implement the Great Western Development Strategy. Through unremitting efforts, important progress was made in the development of infrastructure in western China. Among them, the focused launch of landmark projects such as the Qinghai-Tibet Railway, the West-to-East Electricity Transmission Project and the West-East Gas Transmission Project gave strong impetus to the economic development and social progress of western China. The 16th CPC National Congress made arrangements to support China's old industrial bases, such as the northeastern region, to accelerate their restructuring and transformation. Then in October 2003, the 3rd Plenary Session of the 16th CPC Central Committee proposed the revitalisation of China's old industrial bases such as the northeast. In the same month, the CPC Central Committee and the State Council issued *Several Opinions on Implementing the Strategy for Revitalising the Northeast Region and Other Old Industrial Bases*. Then in September 2009, the State Council issued *Several Opinions on Further Implementing the Strategy for Revitalising the Northeast Region and Other Old Industrial Bases*. Under the combined effect of a series of policy measures, the economic development of China's three northeastern provinces, namely Liaoning, Jilin and Heilongjiang, was significantly accelerated, and the construction of a number of major infrastructure projects related to the long-term development of the region was steadily promoted, facilitating the revitalisation and development of old industrial bases such as the northeastern region.

In September 2004, in order to solve the problems limiting the development of central China, the 4th Plenary Session of the 16th CPC Central Committee clearly proposed promoting the rapid rise of the central region. In April 2006, the CPC Central Committee and the State Council issued

Several Opinions on Promoting the Rapid Rise of Central China. In August 2012, the State Council issued *Several Opinions on Vigorously Implementing the Strategy of Promoting the Rapid Rise of Central China*. With this the reform and development of central China took new steps, with the regional strengths coming from the interconnection and interaction of eastern and western China further highlighted and the capacity for sustainable development significantly improved.

The state continued to support the pioneering development of eastern China and, on the basis of continuing to utilise SEZs and the model of the reform and opening up of the Shanghai Pudong New Area, the State Council approved the Tianjin Binhai New Area as a national comprehensive reform pilot zone in 2006. The state also actively promoted the development and opening up of key regions such as the Yangtze River Delta and the west coast of the Taiwan Strait, and advanced guidelines on further promoting the reform and opening up, and socioeconomic development of the Yangtze River Delta region. The restructuring of the economic structure of eastern China was accelerated, and the pace of change in the mode of development and industrial upgrading was significantly accelerated.

With the implementation of the above-mentioned development strategy, coordinated regional development achieved noticeable results. The central and western regions and the northeastern region demonstrated accelerated development. In 2011, the central and western regions' share of the country's GDP was 22.1% and 21.2% respectively, 3.2 and 3.8 percentage points higher than in 2002. The development and opening up of advanced regions was further promoted and new regional growth poles continued to emerge. The SEZs, Shanghai Pudong New Area and Tianjin Binhai New Area took new steps in their development and opening up, and the three major metropolitan areas of the Yangtze River Delta, the Pearl River Delta and Beijing-Tianjin-Hebei continued to be the "three engines" of China's economic development. Chengdu, Chongqing, Wuhan and the Changsha-Zhuzhou-Xiangtan City cluster played the required role of central cities as nationally approved comprehensive reform pilot zones. The three large economic zones of the Beibu Gulf in Guangxi, Guanzhong-Tianshui and Chengdu-Chongqing developed with powerful momentum and have become a new dynamic force in China's regional development.

In leading the process of building a moderately prosperous society in all respects, another important aspect of the CPC's promotion of scientific development is the coordination of socioeconomic development. Integrating socioeconomic development means that while vigorously promoting economic development, it is necessary to pay more attention to social development, accelerate the development of science and technology, education, culture, health, sports and other social undertakings, constantly meet people's needs in terms of spiritual culture, health and safety and other aspects, and integrate accelerated economic development with the promotion of social progress. As people's material living standard continues to rise, so does their demand for spiritual culture, and health and safety, which increases the demand for joint socioeconomic development.

Since the outset of reform and opening up, the CPC has always upheld a focus on economic construction and has made great achievements in economic development, resulting in a substantial increase in comprehensive national power and people's living standards. However, on the whole, there has existed a problem of "one leg being long and the other short" in economic development and the development of social undertakings. The development of the institutions of public education, public health, scientific and technical innovation, and culture, as well as those of social assistance, social security, social crisis management and other social institutions are lagging behind, and the ambitious cause of building a moderately prosperous society in all respects rightly includes the development and progress of these aspects.

After the SARS epidemic in 2003, China undertook the largest public health system construction since 1949, and basically built a relatively well-functioning disease prevention and control system, and an emergency medical care system covering both urban and rural areas. In May 2003, an executive meeting of the State Council adopted the *Regulations on Emergency Response to Public Health Emergencies*. In September of the same year, the National Development and Reform Commission and the Ministry of Health issued the *Plans for the Construction of Medical Care Systems for Public Health Emergencies* to establish an early warning and emergency response mechanism for public health emergencies. The construction of public health facilities was vigorously strengthened, with emphasis on the construction of disease prevention and control networks at the provincial, municipal (local) and county levels.

After the 16th CPC National Congress, and in accordance with the request of the congress to "closely formulate a general plan for cultural system reform", the reform of cultural construction and cultural system were set as major agenda items as an important part of overall reform. In early 2003, the Central Propaganda Department, together with the Ministry of Culture, the State Administration of Radio, Film and Television, the State General Administration of Press and Publications and other relevant departments, drew up the *Pilot Programme for Cultural System*

Reform. In December 2005, on the basis of summing up the experience of the pilot cultural system reform, the CPC Central Committee and the State Council issued the *Opinions on Deepening Cultural System Reform*, which comprehensively elaborated on the significance, guiding ideology, principle requirements, and objectives and tasks of further promoting cultural system reform. In March 2006, a national conference on cultural system reform was held in Beijing which newly identified 89 regions and 170 units nationwide to carry out pilot cultural system reform. The changes in institutional mechanisms stimulated the intrinsic vitality of cultural units in various regions and the market competitiveness of cultural industries was greatly enhanced.

Science and technology play an important supporting role in socioeconomic development and in October 2007 the strategies of reinvigorating China through science and education, strengthening the nation through human resource development and sustainable development, were incorporated into the report of the 17th CPC National Congress as the three basic strategies for developing socialism with Chinese characteristics. In February 2006, June 2010 and July 2010 respectively, the State Council issued the *National Medium to Long-term Scientific and Technological Development Plan (2006-2020)*, the *National Medium to Long-term Human Resource Development Plan (2010-2020)* and the *National Medium to Long-term Educational Reform and Development Plan (2010-2020)*. China has vigorously strengthened its independent innovation capacity in accordance with the arrangements of the Party Central Committee and the State Council, and investment in scientific and technological R&D has continued to increase, thereby further improving the system of technological innovation, which is enterprise-oriented, market-guided and marked by the integration of industry, academia, and research. Under the impetus of this innovation strategy, a number of major achievements have been made in independent innovation at the forefront of major disciplines and in highly competitive strategic areas, and major breakthroughs have been achieved in manned space engineering, lunar exploration projects and supercomputers.

In October 2005, the 5th Plenary Session of the 16th CPC Central Committee considered and adopted the *Proposal on the Formulation of the 11th Five-Year Guidlines for National Economic and Social Development*. Based on this proposal, the *State Council formulated the (Draft) Outline of the 11th Five-Year Guidelines for the National Economic and Social Development of the PRC*. In March 2006, the 4th Session of the 10th NPC considered and adopted the *Outline of the Guidelines*. From that time onwards, the "plans" for national economic and social development, which had been pursued for more than 50 years, were replaced by "guidelines" for the first time.

This difference in terminology marked the beginning of a major shift from government-led to market-led macroeconomic operations in China, with the government shifting its focus from making directive plans to providing strategic and forward-looking guidelines, and from direct participation in economic development to providing public goods and regulating the macroeconomy.

In the process of leading the construction of a moderately prosperous society in all respects, coordinating the harmonious development of man and nature is also an important aspect of promoting scientific development. Coordinating the harmonious development of humans and nature means attaching great importance to issues concerning resources and ecosystems, correctly handling the relationship between economic construction, population growth and resource utilisation, and the protection of ecosystems, enhancing the capacity for sustainable development and stimulating the whole of society to embark on a path of civilised development characterised by productive development, affluence and eco-friendliness. The harmonious development of humans and nature constitutes one of the major objectives of building a moderately prosperous society in all respects and a fundamental plan related to the survival and long-term development of the Chinese nation. The Party Central Committee adheres to the basic national policies of family planning, environmental protection and resource conservation, the unification of socioeconomic development with environmental protection and ecological construction, the simultaneous development and conservation of resources, coordinated planning and systematic environmental governance and construction, reliance on scientific and technological progress to promote environmental protection and governance, and protection of the environment and ecology in accordance with the law, and deepening reforms and innovating mechanisms to promote sustainable development institutionally and in terms of mechanisms.

In the 21st century, along with the rapid development of the economy, ecological damage and environmental pollution have become increasingly severe, and the construction of ecological civilisation has been more greatly prioritised by the party and the state, gradually becoming one of their major strategies. In June 2003, the Party Central Committee established a forestry development strategy based on ecological construction, clearly proposing "to establish a national system of ecological security mainly characterised by forest vegetation and a combination of trees and grass, and to build an eco-civilised society with beautiful mountains and rivers"[8]. In October 2005, the 5th Plenary Session of the 16th CPC Central Committee proposed to accelerate the construction of a resource-saving and environmentally-friendly society and to promote the coordination of economic development with population, resources and the environment. In October 2006, the 6th Plenary Session of the 16th CPC Central Committee set "a significant improvement in the efficiency of resource usage and a marked improvement in ecosystems" as one of the goals and main tasks of building a socialist harmonious society. In October 2007, for the first time, the 17th CPC National Congress made "the construction of an ecological civilisation" a strategic task and a new requirement for building a moderately prosperous society in all respects. This actually clarified the relationship between the construction of ecological civilisation and economic, political, cultural and social construction, and laid the foundation for the formation of the "Five-Sphere" integrated plan of socialism with Chinese characteristics.

Another major aspect of the party's efforts to promote scientific development in the process of leading the construction of a moderately prosperous society in all respects is to coordinate domestic development with opening up to the outside world. Coordinating domestic development and opening up to the outside world means effectively dealing with the relationship between domestic development and the international environment, by both making good use of favourable external conditions and utilising China's own strengths, using both international and domestic markets and resources to integrate the expansion of domestic demand with the expansion of external demand, and the use of domestic capital with the use of foreign capital, and striving to achieve coordination between domestic reform and development, and opening up to the outside world.

The 16th CPC National Congress proposed the requirement to "improve the socialist market economy". In October 2003, the 3rd Plenary Session of the 16th CPC National Congress deliberated and adopted the Decision of the CPC Central Committee on *Several Issues Concerning the Improvement of the Socialist Market Economy*. The Decision made a series of new breakthroughs in the theory of economic reform, such as proposing for the first time to adapt to the trend of the continuous development of economic marketisation and further enhance the vitality of the public ownership economy, by vigorously developing a mixed ownership economy with the participation of state capital, collective capital and non-public capital, and achieving investment diversification, so that the shareholding system becomes the main means of achieving public ownership, proposing for the first time to "establish a modern system of property rights with clear attribution, clearly defined rights and responsibilities, strict protection and unhindered circulation", which is an important basis for building a modern enterprise system, and proposing for the first time to "establish a system conducive to gradually changing the structure of urban-rural economic dualism", which demonstrates bright prospects for the final resolution of urban-rural dualism through urbanisation and the corresponding reform of the household registration system.

After the 16th CPC National Congress, the party continued to deepen economic reform while actively promoting opening up to the outside world and continuously pioneering a new context for opening up to the outside world. In October 2005, the 5th Plenary Session of the 16th CPC Central Committee proposed to "implement a mutually beneficial and win-win opening-up strategy", continuously enhancing the level of opening up to the outside world and strengthening the party's capacity to promote development in the context of expanded opening up. In accordance with the decision and arrangements made by the Party Central Committee, China conscientiously fulfilled its commitment to join the WTO and actively carried out various areas of work during the transition period. At the same time, the foreign-related economy was further deepened, and the facilitation of trade and investment was promoted, foreign trade operation rights were liberalised, tariffs were significantly reduced, non-tariff measures such as import quotas and licenses were abolished, and the opening up of financial, commercial and telecommunications services was continuously expanded. The structure of import and export commodities was gradually optimised, and the quality of foreign investment utilised was further improved. The implementation of the "going out" strategy also took solid steps, and mutually beneficial cooperation in the foreign economy achieved significant results.

After the 16th CPC National Congress, in the context of deepening reform and expanding opening up, the party took timely measures to address new situations and problems arising in the development of the national economy and vigorously strengthened macro-control. By promoting reforms in key areas and key links and strengthening macro-control, the Party Central Committee prevented major economic volatility and maintained steady and rapid economic development. Through the joint efforts of all parties, macro-control achieved noticeable results, some prominent contradictions in economic operations were alleviated, and the national economy maintained a positive trend of accelerated growth, optimised structure and improved efficiency. From 2003 to 2007 China's GDP growth rate reached or exceeded 10% for five consecutive years and the stability of its economic development increased significantly. China's economic output rose from sixth to fourth place in the world in terms of the World Bank's ranking of major exchange rate factors, making this one of the fastest periods of growth since the outset of reform and opening up.

After the 17th CPC National Congress, the Party Central Committee paid close attention to the unfolding of the international financial crisis, carefully analysed the risks and impacts of the financial crisis on China's economic development, united and led the whole party and the whole of China to be firm and confident, cope calmly, rise to the challenge, overcome the difficulties together and turn challenges into opportunities. It also adopted a series of policies and measures to promote stable and rapid economic development and achieved remarkable results, successfully withstanding the major test of the impact of the international financial crisis. In 2011, China's share of the global economy increased to around 10%, and its average annual contribution to global economic growth exceeded 20%. The process of the party's response to the international financial crisis was also a process of deepening reform and expanding opening up. The Party Central Committee emphasised the importance of always integrating the promotion of development and the deepening of reform, and through continuous promotion of reform, not only better utilised the fundamental role of the market in the allocation of resources institutionally but also formed a system of macro-control conducive to scientific development, so as to provide a strong impetus and institutional guarantee for socioeconomic development.

How to deal with the relationship between "good" and "rapid" economic development has always been a major theoretical and practical issue in China's socialist construction. After the 16th CPC National Congress, with the rapid expansion of China's whole economy, the rapid development of industrialisation, urbanisation, marketisation and internationalisation, and the rapid increase in domestic residents' income and the continuous rapid upgrading of consumption patterns, the one-sided emphasis on the economic growth rate was no longer appropriate. Particularly conspicuous is the fact that the "extensive" pattern of economic growth, which for many years was dominated by "speed" and was propped up by high consumption of energy and resources, resulted in serious environmental pollution and ecological damage, severely limiting the sustainable development of China's economy and society. In October 2006, Hu Jintao in his speech at the 6th Plenary Session of the 16th CPC Central Committee elaborated in depth on "firmly promoting sound and rapid economic development". The Central Economic Work Conference held in December of the same year further proposed that, "good and rapid development is an essential requirement for the full implementation of the scientific concept of development", and that "efforts should be made to coordinate speed, quality and efficiency, to coordinate consumption, investment and exports, and to coordinate population, resources and environment, so as to truly achieve good and rapid development". Since then, the concept of "good and rapid" has been used as a major guideline for economic development by the party and the state, gradually replacing the idea of "rapid and good" which had been upheld for many years. The change from "rapid and good" to "good and rapid", although only amounting to a change in the order of the words "good" and "rapid", nevertheless reflects a significant adjustment in thinking regarding China's economic development and a deeper understanding of the nature of socialist development with Chinese characteristics.

Based on China's national conditions, the party scientifically judged the reality of China's development, firmly grasped the prominent problems facing China's development, proposed the scientific concept of development as its guiding ideology, and promoted the sound and rapid development of China's economy and society and the scientific development of the economy and society in accordance with the requirements of the "Five Coordinations". The party's ability to lead the entire party and the people of China in implementing reform and opening up has continued to grow, demonstrating that the party's governance ability has gradually increased, and that its philosophy of governance has continued to develop in the course of its practice of leadership in building a moderately prosperous society in all respects.

(III) STRENGTHENING THE CONSTRUCTION OF GOVERNANCE ABILITY

The construction of governance ability has been a fundamental aspect of party building since it came to power. In the face of profound changes in global, national and party conditions, the Party Central Committee, with Comrade Hu Jintao as its General Secretary, closely integrated the management of state affairs, adhered to the main party line of constructing governance ability and advanced construction, comprehensively promoted the great new project of party building, further strengthened the party's core leadership role and effectively promoted the development of the party and the national cause.

At the turn of the century the world entered a new phase, the international situation underwent profound changes, the trends of global multipolarisation and economic globalisation continued to develop in a complicated manner, scientific and technological progress was rapid, competition for comprehensive national power was becoming increasingly fierce, various ideologies and cultures were clashing with each other, various contradictions were convoluted and tangled, the strategic plots of hostile forces to Westernise and divide China remained unchanged, and China was still under pressure from the dominance of developed countries in economics, technology and other aspects. China's reform and development were also at a critical stage, domestic reform, development and stability were difficult and onerous tasks, the interrelations of social interests were more complex, new situations and problems were emerging, and a period of opportunity for development and of prominent contradictions existed at the same time. In addition, the party's governance environment and conditions, governance objectives and tasks, governing methods and approaches, as well as the situation of party members and the ranks of cadres also underwent profound changes, and, in the face of the new situation and new tasks, there still remained many imperfections in the party's leadership style, governing methods, leadership system and work mechanisms, and these problems all impacted the effectiveness of the party's governance. Under this kind of domestic and international situation, if the CPC were to unite and lead the people of China to achieve the ambitious goal of building a moderately prosperous society in all respects and to continuously pioneer a new context for the cause of socialism with Chinese characteristics, then it would be vital to comprehensively promote the great new project of party building, attach great importance to and urgently promote the building of the party's governance ability and raise it to a new level in every way.

In November 2002, the 16th CPC National Congress proposed "strengthening the construction of the party's governance ability and improving the party's leadership and governance" as a major strategic task, requiring party committees and leading cadres at all levels in the face of profound changes to continuously improve their ability to judge situations scientifically, to manage the market economy,

to deal with complex situations, to govern according to the law, and to be in full control of the overall situation.

In September 2004, in accordance with the requirements of the 16th CPC National Congress, the 4th Plenary Session of the 16th CPC Central Committee deliberated and adopted the *Decision of the CPC Central Committee on Strengthening Construction of the Party's Governance Ability.* The *Decision* summarised and elaborated on the main experiences of the party's governance, stating that it is necessary for the party to persist with progressive advance in its guiding ideology, using the development of Marxism to guide new practice, with promoting the self-improvement of socialism, enhancing its vitality and vigour, with grasping development as the party's first priority in governing and rejuvenating China, making development the key to solving all China's problems, with establishing the party for the sake of the public and governing for the sake of the people, always maintaining vibrant connections between the party and the people, with governance which is scientific, democratic and in accordance with the law, constantly refining the party's leadership and governance methods, and with strengthening the construction of the party in the spirit of reform, constantly enhancing the party's creativity, cohesion and fighting strength.

It was emphasised that these experiences constitute important guiding principles for strengthening the construction of the party's governance ability and must be adhered to in practice in the medium to long term, and continue to be enriched and refined. The *Decision* further clarified the guiding ideology, overall objectives and main tasks for strengthening the construction of the party's governance ability under new circumstances. It was pointed out that in order to strengthen construction of the party's governance ability, the process must be guided by Marxism-Leninism and Mao Zedong Thought, Deng Xiaoping Theory and the major ideology of the Three Represents, with the core approach being the maintenance of the vibrant connections between the party and the people, the key being the construction of ranks of high-quality cadres, the focus being on reforming and refining the system of party leadership and work mechanisms, on the foundation of strengthening the party's grassroots organisations and the ranks of party members.

This guiding ideology constitutes a theoretical overview of the party's practice of strengthening the construction of its governance ability and reflects the requirements of succession and timeliness. It was proposed that, through the efforts of the whole party, it should become a ruling party that is always established for the sake of the public and governs for the sake of the people, a ruling party that governs scientifically, democratically and according to the law, a ruling party that is realistic and pragmatic, pioneering and innovative, diligent and efficient, clean and honest and ultimately a Marxist ruling party that always achieves the Three Represents, that forever maintains progressiveness, and that withstands all kinds of storms and tests, in order to lead the people of all China's ethnic groups to achieve national prosperity, the revitalisation of China's ethnic groups, social harmony and the happiness of the people. This overall objective clarified the major issues of for whom the party governs, how it governs and on what basis it should govern, and points out the fundamental direction for strengthening the construction of the party's governance ability.

It was emphasised that the main task of strengthening construction of the party's governance ability going forwards was to "continuously improve its capacity to manage the socialist market economy, develop socialist democracy and politics, build an advanced socialist culture and a harmonious socialist society, cope with the international situation and handle international affairs" in accordance with the requirement of promoting the coordinated development of socialist material, political and spiritual civilisation. Construction of capacity in these five areas covering economic, political, cultural, social and diplomatic affairs as well as national sovereignty, security and territorial integrity, constitute arrangements for strengthening the party's overall governance ability. The *Decision* also emphasised that the party's ruling position is not innate, nor is it guaranteed permanence. It is not easy for a proletarian party to seize power and it is even more difficult to hold power firmly, especially for a long time. Therefore, the CPC must be vigilant in peacetime, enhance its consciousness of hardship, draw deeply from the lessons of the successes and failures of some of the world's ruling parties, and more consciously strengthen construction of its governance ability, in order always to govern and hold power firmly for the sake of the people[9].

In order to strengthen construction of the party's governance ability, it is most crucial to uphold governance which is scientific, democratic and in accordance with the law. This is the inevitable conclusion of the party's successful experience of governance and is a major issue that the party must closely grasp and seriously address in order to govern and hold power firmly for the sake of the people, as well as being a fundamental requirement for strengthening construction of the party's governance ability under new circumstances.

In order to uphold scientific governance, the CPC must continue to strengthen its exploration and understanding of the communist party's governance law, the laws of socialist construction and the laws of human social development, and its exploration and understanding of the laws of the party's construction itself, so as to constantly improve its ability to lead the cause of socialism with Chinese characteristics with scientific thinking, systems and methods.

In order to uphold democratic governance, the CPC must further implement the aim to serve the people wholeheartedly, uphold governance for the people and by the people, develop democracy within the party, develop socialist democratic politics, fully mobilise the enthusiasm, initiative and creativity of the people, and constantly transform the wisdom and strength of the people into a powerful force for the advancement of its cause.

In order to uphold governance in accordance with law, the CPC must always adhere to the basic strategy of governance according to the law, uphold the basic approach of governance according to the law, refine the socialist legal system, build a socialist state under the rule of law, enhance the concept of the legal system, act strictly in accordance with the law, and continuously promote the institutionalisation and legalisation of the management of all state affairs.

Upholding governance which is scientific, democratic, and in accordance with the law constitutes an organic and unified whole, the core of which is to govern well for the people and to hold power firmly. Only by upholding governance which is scientific, democratic and in accordance with the law can the party more effectively address the new situations and problems encountered in the course of governance, more effectively respond to the new challenges and tests facing the operation of governance, more effectively solve the major problems and complex contradictions facing reform and opening up, and modernisation, and more effectively fulfil the solemn mission entrusted to it by the people and the epoch.

In order to strengthen construction of the party's governance ability, it is necessary to focus on the party's progressiveness and build the party well. Progressiveness constitutes the fundamental characteristic of Marxist parties and also their very life and strength. Implementing advanced party building means to promote the party's ideological, organisational, work style and institutional construction, so that the party's theories, line, guidelines and policies will be in line with the development trends of the times and the requirements of China's social development and progress, and reflect the interests and aspirations of the people of all of China's ethnic groups so that party organisations at all levels will continuously improve their creativity, cohesion and fighting strength, always play the role of a leading core and the bastions of combat, so that the masses of party members will continuously improve their own qualities and always serve as pioneers so that the party will maintain its quality of progressive advance, always walk at the forefront of the times, continuously improving its governance ability, consolidating its ruling position and completing its governance mission.

The 16th CPC National Congress made the decision to carry out educational activities for the maintenance of the progressiveness of communist party members. After the 16th CPC National Congress, the Party Central Committee selected 19 units to carry out pilot projects, thereby accumulating experience. The 4th Plenary Session of the 16th CPC Central Committee further advanced requirements for the development of educational activities on progressiveness. In November 2004, the CPC Central Committee issued the *Opinions on the Partywide Implementation of Educational Activities for Maintaining the Progressiveness of Communist Party Members Mainly Focused on the Practice of the Major Ideology of Three Repre-*

sents and made arrangements for educational activities on progressiveness.

In January 2005, Hu Jintao delivered a public lecture on the topic of maintaining the progressiveness of communist party members in the new era, requiring all party members to actively participate in educational activities on progressiveness, in particular requiring leading cadres to play an exemplary role, and for the first time proposed the major proposition of "the construction of the party's progressiveness". Hu Jintao reviewed the longstanding theory and practice of the party's construction of progressiveness and emphasised that strengthening the construction of the party's progressiveness has always been a fundamental aspect of construction for the survival, development and growth of the party. This construction, he said, must be closely linked with accomplishing the party's historical tasks and is even more arduous in the context of governance, especially long-term governance, and constitutes a long-term task and perennial issue for strengthening and improving party building.

From January 2005, the party conducted an 18-month educational campaign on maintaining the progressiveness of communist party members, focused on the practice of the major ideology of the Three Represents. The Party Central Committee emphasised that the educational campaign on progressiveness should fully implement a Scientific Outlook on Development with a focus on the practice of the major ideology of the Three Represents and, focusing on the study and implementation of the party constitution and concentrating on achieving results and public satisfaction, work hard to improve the quality of party members, strengthen grassroots organisations, serve the people and promote all areas of work. This progressiveness educational campaign was a major initiative by the party to arm the whole party with the development of Marxism under the conditions of reform and opening up, and the development of the socialist market economy, and constituted an important instance of the practice of strengthening the construction of the party's governance ability and progressiveness in a key period of building a moderately prosperous society in all respects and the acceleration of socialist modernisation. Through the progressiveness educational campaign, the masses of party members received a profound experience of Marxist education and their role as pioneers and exemplars was further utilised.

The construction of governance ability is the connecting point between the great cause of socialism with Chinese characteristics and the great new project of party building. Strengthening the party's governance ability is related to the success or failure of the cause of socialism with Chinese characteristics, the future prospects of the Chinese nation, the survival or demise of the party, and the long-term stability of China, reflecting the party's assessment of circumstances, sense of vigilance in peacetime and responsibility to govern for the people and benefit the people in times of crisis. In order to strengthen construction of the party's governance and to fulfil the historical task of governing and rejuvenating China, the party needs to integrate new realities, constantly explore and improve institutional mechanisms, approaches and means conducive to governance which is scientific, democratic and in accordance with the law, and constantly understand and grasp the laws of governance, so as to not only propel the cause of the party and the people forward but also to continuously lead the party's governance practice to move from the realm of necessity to the realm of freedom.

(IV) PROPOSALS FOR BUILDING A HARMONIOUS SOCIALIST SOCIETY

After the 16th CPC National Congress, the Party Central Committee, with Comrade Hu Jintao as its General Secretary, proposed the major strategic goal of building a harmonious socialist society from the overall layout of the cause of socialism with Chinese characteristics and the construction of a moderately prosperous society in all respects, so that the overall layout of the cause of socialism with Chinese characteristics would develop from the "trinity" of economic, political and cultural construction to the "four-sphere plan" of economic, political, cultural and social construction.

Achieving social harmony has always been a social ideal for which mankind has striven and is a long-term and never-ending goal. Chinese civilisation has always focused on social harmony, emphasising solidarity and mutual assistance. The Chinese have long advanced the idea that "harmony is precious", pursuing harmony between heaven and humans, interpersonal harmony, harmony between mind and body, and aspiring to an ideal society where "all are mutually attached, all are equal and the world is fair". The party made the building of a harmonious socialist society a major strategic objective by making a scientific judgment of the situation facing China's development, effectively addressing the major challenges at home and abroad, and analysing the historical mission that the party itself has taken on. From a domestic perspective, it determined that building a socialist harmonious society is an inevitable requirement for seizing and making good use of the important period of strategic opportunity and achieving the ambitious goal of building a moderately prosperous society in all respects. From an international perspective, it determined that building a harmonious socialist society is an inevitable requirement for grasping the complex and changing international situation and responding vigorously to the various challenges and risks emerging from the international environment. From the perspective of the mission that the party has undertaken, it determined that building a harmonious socialist society is an inevitable requirement for consolidating the social basis of party governance and accomplishing the historical task of party governance.

In November 2002, the report of the 16th CPC National Congress, when elaborating on the goal of building a moderately prosperous society in all respects, put forward the requirement of achieving a more harmonious society, emphasising that building a society with a higher degree of moderate prosperity requires more economic development, more robust democracy, more progress in science education, more cultural prosperity, more social harmony and a more prosperous life for the people. It also stressed that efforts should be made to form a political climate in which all people do their best, each is provided for, and all live in harmony. This is the first time in history that "a more harmonious society" was explicitly mentioned as a major objective for the party to strive for in a report from a party congress.

After the 16th CPC National Congress, the Party Central Committee, in light of the new changes in the international and domestic situations, comprehensively analysed the opportunities and challenges facing China's development and deepened its understanding of the important position and role of social harmony in the cause of socialism with Chinese characteristics. In September 2004, the 4th Plenary Session of the 16th CPC Central Committee clearly advanced the major strategic task of building a harmonious socialist society, identifying improving the party's ability to build a harmonious socialist society as an important element in strengthening the construction of the party's governance ability and proposing the basic requirements for building a harmonious socialist society. The plenary session stressed that the formation of a society in which all people do their best, each is provided for and all live in harmony, is an inevitable requirement for consolidating the social basis of the party's governance and achieving the historical task of the party's governance, and that it is necessary to adapt to the profound changes in Chinese society and give priority to the building of a harmonious society.

In February 2005, Hu Jintao pointed out in his speech at a seminar for leading cadres at the provincial and ministerial levels on the improvement of their ability to build a harmonious socialist society that, in accordance with the basic principles of Marxism and the practical experience of China's socialist construction, and with the new requirements of China's socioeconomic development in the new stage of the new, and the new trends and characteristics emerging in Chinese society, the harmonious socialist society the party must build should be a society characterised by democracy and the rule of law, fairness and justice, honesty and fraternity, full vitality, stability and order, and harmony between humans and nature. Democracy and the rule of law means socialist democracy being fully developed, the basic strategy of the rule of law being effectively implemented, and the positive elements of all parties being widely mobilised. Fairness and justice means the interests of all parties in society being properly coordinated, internal conflicts among the people and other social conflicts being correctly handled, and social equity and justice being effectively safeguarded and achieved. Honesty and fraternity means that everyone in society helps each other, all are honest and trustworthy, and all the people live in equality and fraternity, and interact harmoniously. Full vitality means that all creative aspirations conducive to social progress are respected, creative energies are supported, creative talents are utilised and creative achievements are affirmed. Stability and order means that the social organisation mechanisms are robust, social management and social order are good, the people live and work in peace and happiness, and social stability and unity are maintained. Harmony between humans and nature means that production is developed, people's lives are affluent, and the ecology is in good condition. These basic features of a harmonious socialist society are interrelated and interact with each other, and need to be comprehensively grasped and manifested in the process of building a moderately prosperous society in all respects[10].

In October 2005, the 5th Plenary Session of the 16th CPC Central Committee identified the building of a harmonious socialist society as a major task that must be firmly grasped to implement the Scientific Outlook on Development and put forward work requirements and policy measures to this end. The *Proposal of the CPC Central Committee on the Formulation of the 11th Five-Year Guidelines for National Economic and Social Development* adopted by the plenary session states that the promotion of social harmony is an important goal and requirement for the development of China. The *Proposal* stated that it was necessary to act in accordance with the requirement of being people-oriented by solving practical problems of immediate interest to the people, paying more attention to coordinated socioeconomic development, accelerating the development of social undertakings and promoting comprehensive human development, that it was necessary to pay more attention to social equity so that all the people of China could enjoy the fruit of reform and development, and that it was necessary to pay more attention to construction of democracy and the legal system, correctly handle the relationship between reform, development and stability, and maintain social stability and unity[11].

In October 2006, in order to further promote the building of a harmonious socialist society, the 6th Plenary Session of the 16th CPC Central Committee adopted the *Decision of the CPC Central Committee on Several Major Issues Concerning the Building of a Harmonious Socialist Society*. The *Decision* pointed out that social harmony constitutes an essential attribute of socialism with Chinese characteristics and an important safeguard of national prosperity, of the revitalisation of China's ethnic groups and the happiness of the people. Building a harmonious socialist society is a major strategic task in terms of the overall composition of the cause of socialism with Chinese characteristics and the overall situation of building a moderately prosperous society in all respects.

The *Decision* set out the goals and main tasks for building a harmonious socialist society by 2020, namely:

- further refining the socialist democratic legal system, fully implementing the basic strategy of the rule of law and ensuring respect for, and protection of, people's rights and interests;

- gradually reversing the widening development gap between urban and rural areas, and between regions, basically forming a reasonable and orderly pattern of income distribution, generally increasing household assets, and increasing the level of people's affluence;

- maintaining an adequate system of social employment and basically establishing a social security system covering both urban and rural residents;

- establishing a more complete system of basic public services and a greater improvement in the level of government management and services

- significantly improving the ideological, moral, scientific, cultural and health quality of all China's ethnic groups, and further developing good ethical practices and harmonious interpersonal relations;

- significantly enhancing the creative vitality of the whole society and basically building an innovative country;

- further perfecting social management systems and achieving good social order;

- significantly increasing the efficiency of resource usage and notably improving the condition of ecosystems;

- achieving the goal of building a society with a higher degree of moderate prosperity in all respects which benefits more than one billion people and striving to create a context in which all the people do their best, each is provided for and all live in harmony[12].

For the party to build a harmonious socialist society, it must correctly understand and deal with the major relationships in China's economic, political, cultural and social fields that involve the overall work of the party and the state and, most fundamentally, correctly handle the interests of all parties. In the process of building socialism with Chinese characteristics, the fundamental interests of the people of all China's ethnic groups are the same, and the party represents the fundamental interests of the Chinese general public. At the same time, it is also vital to see that, on the basis of the unanimity of the fundamental interests of all the people of China, different parties, classes and groups also have various kinds of specific interests. The party must correctly handle various relationships on the basis of socioeconomic development, maintain overall balance with a comprehensive plan, and actively guide and form synergies to unite and bring the whole of Chinese society closer together to struggle jointly to promote social harmony and achieve the development goals of the party and the state.

In July 2006, Hu Jintao delivered a speech at the National Conference on United Front Work in which he presented his views on the correct understanding and handling of major relationships in five areas involving the overall situation of the work of the party and the state. He said, "Today, I would like to focus on relationships between the political party, ethnic relations, religious relations, class relations, and relations between compatriots at home and abroad. These are some of the major relationships in the political and social spheres that involve the overall situation of the work of the party and the state", and "to correctly understand and handle these five major relationships, and to maintain and promote harmony in these five major relations relates to the overall situation of the cause of socialism with Chinese characteristics, the process of building a harmonious socialist society, and the prosperity and long-term stability of the party and the country"[13].

Hu Jintao pointed out that the relationship between the CPC and democratic parties should be correctly understood and handled, and the political landscape characterised by multi-party cooperation under the leadership of the CPC should be consolidated and developed. The political landscape of multi-party cooperation, led by the CPC and featuring multi-party participation, governance by the CPC, and multi-party participation in politics, embodies the essential requirements of China's socialist democratic politics and constitutes a political strength of China's socialist system. The fundamental approach to consolidating and developing China's socialist party relations and to achieving long-term harmony in China's inter-party relations, is upholding pursuit of the path of socialist political development with Chinese characteristics, and the key lies in upholding and refining the system of multi-party cooperation and political consultation under the leadership of the CPC. Not only must leadership of the CPC be upheld but the unity and cooperation of multiple parties must also be promoted. Not only must the party's governance ability be improved but the role of democratic parties in political participation and discussion must also be utilised. Not only must importance be attached to the ideological guidance of democratic parties but their democratic supervision must also be sincerely accepted. Not only must the great new project of party building be comprehensively promoted but democratic parties must also be actively supported in strengthening their own construction. This is all so that construction of the ruling party and that of the participating parties can be mutually reinforcing, in order that they may all be better unified in the historical process of multi-party cooperation and together initiate great undertakings.

In his speech Hu Jintao also stressed the need to correctly understand and handle the relationship between China's various ethnic groups, especially the Han and ethnic minorities, in order to promote the common unity and struggle of all ethnic groups, and their common prosperity and development. The socialist ethnic relations characterised by equality, unity, mutual assistance and harmony embody the basic pattern of the unity in diversity of the Chinese nation and the fundamental interests of the big family of the Chinese nation. Equality is the cornerstone of socialist ethnic relations while unity is its main thread, mutual assistance is its safeguard and harmony is its essence. In order to correctly understand and handle ethnic relations in China, the most fundamental aspect is to constantly uphold ethnic equality, strengthen ethnic unity, promote mutual assistance between ethnic groups and foster ethnic harmony. To this end it is necessary to firmly grasp the theme of the common unity and struggle of all China's ethnic groups and their common prosperity and development, fully bring out the strengths of the system of ethnic regional autonomy, fully implement laws on ethnic regional autonomy, accelerate the socioeconomic development of ethnic minorities and ethnic areas, strengthen and maintain ethnic unity, and resolutely prevent and combat all kinds of divisive and destructive activities carried out by hostile forces within China and abroad which exploit ethnic issues.

Hu Jintao pointed out that it is necessary to correctly understand and handle the relationship between the religious and non-religious masses, and between those who believe in different religions, and actively guide religions to adapt to socialist society. The key to conducting religious work competently under the new situation is to comprehensively understand and conscientiously implement the party's basic policy on religious work.

To this end it is necessary to implement the party's policy of the freedom of religious belief in a comprehensive and correct manner, uphold political unity and cooperation, and respect for the beliefs of others, and strive to achieve consensus among the masses of religious believers on such important issues as supporting the leadership of the CPC and the socialist system, ardently loving the motherland and safeguarding its unity, and promoting social harmony. It is also necessary to uphold the management of religious affairs in accordance with the law, protect lawful activities and put a stop to unlawful ones, and combat crime, in order to ensure that religious activities are conducted in a standardised and orderly manner. It is further necessary to uphold the principle of independence and self-management, and to help and support the various religious groups in strengthening their own construction. Religions should be actively guided to adapt to socialist society so that the masses of believers can be united to the greatest extent possible under the ambitious goal of building a moderately prosperous society in all respects.

In his speech Hu Jintao also emphasised the need to correctly understand and handle the relationship between various social strata, and to promote and achieve the harmonious coexistence and common development of the whole of society. To this end, he said, it is necessary to scientifically analyse and accurately grasp the profound changes that have occurred in the structure of China's social strata, comprehensively take into account and achieve the interests of people from all social strata, and fully utilise the role of all social strata in promoting socioeconomic development. It is also necessary to uphold the policy of full respect, extensive contact, unity strengthening, enthusiastic help and active guidance, earnestly and competently implement work with people of the new social strata, respecting the fruit of their labour and their entrepreneurial spirit, pooling their intelligence and wisdom, and guiding them to be qualified builders of the cause of socialism with Chinese characteristics.

Hu Jintao pointed out that the relationship between compatriots in mainland China, Hong Kong and Macau, and Taiwan and overseas Chinese should be correctly understood and handled, and the great unity of China's sons and daughters at home and abroad should be strengthened under the banner of patriotism. Adherence to the policies of "one country, two systems", "Hong Kong people ruling Hong Kong", "Macanese people ruling Macao" and a high degree of autonomy is the fundamental guarantee for the promotion of long-term prosperity and stability of Hong Kong and Macau, as well as for the promotion of harmonious coexistence and common development between the mainland and Hong Kong and Macau. Therefore, it is necessary to conduct affairs in strict accordance with the constitution and the basic law of the SARs, support the chief executives and the governments of the SARs to govern in accordance with the law, pay attention to and support Hong Kong and Macau in developing their economies and improving people's livelihoods, and strengthen exchanges and cooperation between the mainland and Hong Kong and Macau. It is also necessary to strengthen work with the people of Taiwan, enhance solidarity with compatriots in Taiwan, and expand and deepen cross-strait personnel exchanges, and economic and cultural exchanges, and cooperation. It is further necessary to aim to bring together the hearts, wisdom and strength of the Chinese diaspora, and persist in safeguarding the fundamental interests of overseas Chinese and returned diaspora as the starting point and end point of overseas Chinese work, so that overseas Chinese will have a growing sense of identity and pride in the motherland, and the fine tradition of ardently loving the motherland and rejuvenating China will be passed on from generation to generation.

The party's proposal to build a harmonious socialist society requires the whole party to more consciously strengthen the building of a harmonious socialist society in the great practice of building socialism with Chinese characteristics so that the construction of socialist material, political and spiritual civilisation, and the building of a harmonious society will develop comprehensively. The building of a harmonious socialist society is organically unified with the building of a socialist material, political and spiritual civilisation. They are inseparably and closely related and also have their own special domains and laws. Building a socialist material, political and spiritual civilisation can provide a solid foundation for building a socialist harmonious society and, in turn, building a socialist harmonious society can provide important conditions for the construction of a socialist material, political and spiritual civilisation.

The party's proposal to build a socialist harmonious society constitutes not only a scientific summary of China's experience in reform and opening up, and socialist modernisation but also a strategic initiative to improve the party's governance ability, implement the Scientific Outlook on Development and better promote China's socioeconomic development in the context of the new domestic and international situation. The proposal to build a socialist harmonious society reflected the party's new understanding of the laws of the development of the socialist cause with Chinese characteristics, and the party's new understanding of the laws of governance, governance ability, governance strategy and governance methods, and provides important ideological guidance for the party to firmly seize and make good use of the period of important strategic opportunity and achieve the ambitious goal of building a moderately prosperous society in all respects.

(V) STRIVING FOR AN EXTERNAL GOVERNANCE ENVIRONMENT CONDUCIVE TO PEACEFUL DEVELOPMENT: PROMOTING THE CONSTRUCTION OF A HARMONIOUS WORLD

Identifying the kind of world China should promote the construction of is a major issue related to China's achievement of peaceful development, as well as a major issue for the global configuration and international order. As it entered the new century, the party made a scientific judgment on the characteristics of an era of great development, change and adjustment taking place in the world at that time, accurately grasped the trend of development of China's increasingly close ties with the world, responded to the global *zeitgeist* of seeking peace, planning development and promoting cooperation, consistently followed the path of peaceful development, actively promoted the building of a harmonious world and strove for the peaceful development of the external governance environment.

Since the founding of new China, and especially since the start of reform and opening up, the CPC has responded to the *zeitgeist*, seized historical opportunities, upheld the close integration of domestic and international work, and promoted the remarkable achievements of China's diplomacy. The party and the government have:

- Responded calmly to a series of international emergencies related to China's sovereignty and security, overcome various risks and challenges from the international arena, resolutely safeguarding national interests and national dignity, and persisting with the correct direction of reform and opening up, and modernisation;

- Improved and developed relations with the major international powers, pioneering a new situation of mutual trust, friendship and cooperation with China's neighbours, consolidating solidarity and cooperation with the majority of developing countries, and actively participating in multilateral diplomacy and summit diplomacy, thereby securing a favourable international and regional political environment for China's modernisation;

- Continuously expanded China's opening up to the outside world, actively participating in international economic and technological cooperation and competition, making full use of "two markets and two resources", and promoting the continuous improvement of China's comprehensive national power and international competitiveness;

- Resumed the exercise of sovereignty over Hong Kong and Macau, and maintained their prosperity and stability, making a historic breakthrough in the process of completing the reunification of the motherland;

- Held high the banner of peace and development, actively participating in international affairs, promoting the cause of human progress, and playing an active role in maintaining world peace and regional stability, and promoting common development, playing the positive role they should play.

Since the late 1980s and early 1990s, the world has entered a period of great change and transformation. The former world order has disintegrated, and a new world order has yet to be formed. The composition of international forces and interests has undergone new changes and many new features have emerged in international politics, economics, culture, science and technology, and military and other fields. The main international developmental trends are as follows.

First, peace and development are still the main issues of the age but neither of them has been resolved. On the one hand, the world's desire for peace, the people's desire for cooperation, countries' desire for development and societies' desire for progress constitute an unstoppable historical trend. The forces safeguarding peace in the world are developing and the factors constraining war are also growing. On the other hand, factors leading to traditional and non-traditional security threats are intertwined, ethnic and religious conflicts, and local conflicts arising from border and territorial disputes break out sporadically, the danger of terrorism is on the rise, uncertainties affecting world peace and development are on the rise, and the former unjust and unreasonable international political and economic order has not fundamentally changed.

Second, the global configuration is developing towards multipolarity but the contradictions and struggles between unipolarity and multipolarity are becoming increasingly intense. Since the end of the Cold War, the world's major powers have all been growing and declining, and they are both mutually dependent and mutually constraining, thereby promoting the development of multipolarity and helping to check hegemonism and power politics. However, hegemonism and power politics have new expressions and have developed in new ways, with some countries pursuing a policy of strength and unilateralism by virtue of their strong economic, technological and military power. They advance "pre-emptive" military strategies, are intensifying their strategies for achieving global hegemony and are in the midst of a new round of strategic expansion. As a consequence, the multipolarisation of the world will be a tortuous and complex process.

Third, the trend of economic globalisation is developing further but the economic risks and challenges faced by developing countries are also increasing. The trend of economic globalisation and the development of science and technology have facilitated the accelerated flow and distribution of commodities, technology, information and especially capital on a global scale, promoted economic and technological exchanges and cooperation between countries, and brought new opportunities and favourable conditions for the development of all countries. However, the trend of economic globalisation has also brought severe tests to some countries, especially developing countries, and the gap between the Global North and the Global South has further widened, making the task of economic development and safeguarding economic security more arduous for developing countries.

In the face of a diverse and complex world, and the unprecedented and historic changes taking place in the world, China proposes that greater attention must be paid to harmony, emphasises and promotes harmony, and advocates the building of a harmonious world characterised by lasting peace and common prosperity, which is the common aspiration of all peoples in the world and an inevitable requirement for the development of human society.

In April 2005, Hu Jintao clearly stated at the Asian-African Summit in Jakarta that, "we Asian and African countries should become partners who learn from each other and complement each other's strengths and weaknesses. We should carry forward the fine tradition of the 1955 Asian-African Bandung Conference of seeking common ground while putting differences aside, advocate the spirit of openness and tolerance, respect the diversity of civilisations, religions and values, respect the freedom of each country to choose its social system and development model, promote the friendly coexistence, dialogue on an equal footing, development and prosperity of different civilisations, and together build a harmonious world"[14].

In July 2005, the Russian and Chinese heads of state incorporated the expression "harmonious world" in the *Joint Statement of the Russian Federation and the PRC on the International Order in the 21st Century*, stating that the two countries were determined to work tirelessly together with other interested countries to build a world of development and harmony, and to become an important and constructive force in a secure world system.

In September 2005, Hu Jintao delivered a speech entitled *Working for a Harmonious World Characterised by Lasting Peace and Common Prosperity* at the UN 60th anniversary summit, in which he comprehensively and systematically expounded the major ideology of building a harmonious world. Hu Jintao pointed out that the diversity of civilisations constitutes a fundamental feature of human society and an important driving force for the progress of human civilisation. He said that throughout human history, various civilisations have made positive contributions to the progress of human civilisation in their own ways. It is only through the existence of differences that all civilisations can learn from each other and improve together - seeking uniformity would only lead to the loss of momentum and the rigidity and decline of human civilisation. The only difference between civilisations is the length of their history and none is superior or inferior to another. Differences in history, culture, social systems and development models should not be an obstacle to exchanges between countries, let alone a reason for mutual confrontation. Hu Jintao proposed that we should respect the right of each country to choose its own social systems and development path, learn from each other instead of deliberately rejecting each other, complement each other's strengths instead of relying on a single authority, and promote the revitalisation and development of each country in accordance with its national conditions. He also proposed that we should strengthen dialogue and exchange between civilisations, learn from each other's strengths and complement each other's weaknesses in the context of competitive comparison, develop together in seeking common ground while preserving differences, and strive to eliminate mutual doubts and misunderstandings, so as to make humanity more harmonious and enrich the world. He further proposed that we should uphold the diversity of civilisations in a spirit of equality and openness, promote the democratisation of international relations, and work together to build a harmonious world in which all civilisations are compatible and inclusive[15].

In October 2007, the 17th CPC National Congress proposed that "people of all countries should work together to promote the construction of a harmonious world of lasting peace and common prosperity". The congress report pointed out that to promote the building of such a world, it is necessary for countries to:

- respect each other politically, engage in dialogue on an equal footing and jointly promote the democratisation of international relations;

- cooperate with each other economically, complement each other's strengths and jointly promote economic globalisation in the direction of balanced, inclusive and win-win development;

- learn from each other culturally, seek common ground while preserving differences, respect the diversity of other countries and jointly promote the prosperity and progress of human civilisation;

- develop mutual trust in terms of security and strengthen cooperation, uphold peaceful means rather than war to resolve international disputes, and jointly safeguard world peace and stability;

- and help each other with regard to environmental protection, working together to promote it, and together take good care of our home planet on which humanity depends for survival[16].

After the 17th CPC National Congress, promoting the building of a harmonious world became an important standpoint of the party and the state. The Chinese government actively advocated in various diplomatic settings for the construction of a harmonious world, articulating key concepts and initiatives for building a harmonious world of lasting peace and common prosperity. These are as follows:

Promoting the construction of a harmonious world requires a commitment to the harmonious coexistence of all nations. All countries should abide by the universally recognised international law and basic norms of international relations, respecting each other's sovereignty and territorial integrity, pursuing non-aggression and non-interference in each other's internal affairs, and respecting and safeguarding the right of each country to choose its own social system and development path. They should also uphold multilateralism, promote the democratisation of international relations, and guarantee the equal rights of all countries to participate in international affairs. They should encourage and support the peaceful resolution of disputes and conflicts through dialogue, consultation and negotiation, opposing the arbitrary use of force or the threat of force, as well as strengthen cooperation on the basis of equality to jointly address global challenges.

Promoting the construction of a harmonious world requires a commitment to the harmonious development of a global economy. All countries should prioritise and take effective measures to promote economic globalisation in the direction of balanced, inclusive and win-win development, strive to alleviate development imbalances and eliminate poverty. All countries should also actively promote regional and global economic cooperation, work together to solve problems arising from global economic development and maintain economic security, as well as replace mutual unreceptiveness with mutual openness and strive to establish an open, fair and regulated multilateral trading system to achieve complementarity of advantages and mutual benefit, for the benefit of all countries.

Promoting the construction of a harmonious world requires a commitment to the harmonious progress of different civilisations. All countries should safeguard global diversity and the diversity of development models, persist with dialogue and exchanges on an equal footing, and advocate an open and inclusive view of civilisation, so that different civilisations can complement each other's strengths in competition and develop together by seeking common ground while preserving differences. The differences in cultural traditions, social systems, values and development paths of various countries should be acknowledged and should not be used as an excuse to speak ill of the internal affairs of other countries, let alone attribute some of the problems and contradictions that exist in the world to any one civilisation, nationality or religion. All countries should also strive to lead all civilisations and all peoples in the world to work together to advance the noble cause of human peace and development.

Promoting the construction of a harmonious world is both an inevitable requirement for China to adhere to the path of peaceful development and an important condition for achieving peaceful development. Promoting the construction of a harmonious world is in line with the fundamental interests of the Chinese people and reflects the common aspirations of all peoples. China needs harmonious external relations and a stable external environment if it is to follow the path of peaceful development and maintain stable economic and social development. Promoting the construction of a harmonious world has demonstrated the party's high level of effectiveness in responding to domestic and international developments and scientific judgement of the challenges and opportunities facing China's development, creating a favourable external environment for China's development and securing a peaceful governance environment for the party.

(VI) UNDERSTANDING AND SUMMING UP THE EXPERIENCE OF 30 YEARS OF GOVERNANCE IN REFORM AND OPENING UP

In 2008, China's reform and opening up reached its 30th anniversary. In the preceding 30 years, under the leadership of the party, the whole party and all the people of China were united in their struggle to make great strides in catching up with the trends of the times, steadily embarking on a broad road towards prosperity and well-being. Socialism with Chinese characteristics was full of vigour and vitality, and the Chinese nation stood tall in the East with unprecedented majesty. At that special point in time when reform and opening up was entering its 30th year, reviewing and summarising the historical experience of governance in reform and opening up was of great significance with regard to the firm adherence to the path of socialism with Chinese characteristics pioneered since the 3rd Plenary Session of the 11th CPC Central Committee and continuing to promote reform and opening up, and the cause of socialist modernisation from a new historical starting point.

In October 2007, the 17th CPC National Congress summarised the valuable experience of the party in the historical process of reform and opening up, in the form of the "Ten Integrations", as follows. The party has integrated adherence to the basic principles of Marxism with the promotion of the Sinicization of Marxism, has integrated adherence to the Four Cardinal Principles with adherence to reform and opening up, has integrated respect for the people's innovative spirit with strengthening and refining the leadership of the party, has integrated adherence to the basic system of socialism with the development of a market economy, has integrated promoting changes in the economic base with the promotion of reforms in the superstructure, has integrated developing the productive forces with the improvement of the ethnic qualities of the whole nation, has integrated the improvement of efficiency with the promotion of social equity, has integrated adherence to independent action with participation in economic globalisation, has integrated the promotion of reform and development with the maintenance of social stability, and has integrated the promotion of the great cause of socialism with Chinese characteristics with the promotion of the great new project of party building. Through this the party has attained valuable experience of freeing a large developing country with a population of more than one billion people from poverty, of accelerating the accomplishment of modernisation and of consolidating and developing socialism[17].

In December 2008, Hu Jintao, in his speech at the conference commemorating the 30th anniversary of the 3rd Plenary Session of the 11th CPC Central Committee, systematically summarised the valuable experience accumulated in the great creative practice of reform and opening up over the preceding 30 years, and further elaborated on the Ten Integrations outlined by the 17th CPC National Congress.

He said, "it is necessary to integrate adherence to the basic principles of Marxism with the promotion of the Sinicisation of Marxism, to emancipate the mind, seek truth from facts, pursue progressive advance, and to provide theoretical guidance for reform and opening up with theoretical innovation based on practice. The key to the great success of China's reform and opening up in the past 30 years is that the party has not only adhered to the basic principles of Marxism but also continuously promoted the Sinicisation of Marxism in accordance with contemporary Chinese practice and the development of the times, forming and developing the theoretical system of socialism with Chinese characteristics, including Deng Xiaoping Theory, the major ideology of the Three Represents and the scientific outlook on development, which gave great vitality to contemporary Chinese Marxism.

"We must integrate adherence to the Four Cardinal Principles with adherence to reform and opening up, to firmly grasping a focus on economic construction, and to always maintaining the correct direction of reform and opening up. Over the past 30 years, we have unswervingly adhered to the party's basic line, not only ensuring the correct direction of reform and opening up with the Four Cardinal Principles but also giving the Four Cardinal Principles a new contemporary essence through reform and opening up, persisting with unifying the Four Cardinal Principles, and reform and opening up marked by a focus on economic construction with the great practice of developing socialism with Chinese characteristics. As a result, socialism with Chinese characteristics has firmly taken hold and stood firm amidst the profound changes in the world today and in contemporary China, making socialism with Chinese characteristics a manifestation of socialism full of vitality and vigour.

"We must integrate respect for the people's spirit of initiative with strengthening and improving the leadership of the party, uphold governance for the people, rely closely on the people and effectively benefit them, and embody the party's core leadership role in the process of fully bringing out the people's role in the creation of history. Over the past 30 years, we have adhered to the Marxist scientific principle that states that the people create history, sincerely represented the fundamental interests of China's general public, relied closely on the people, and mobilised their initiative, proactiveness and creativity to the greatest extent possible. We have drawn wisdom from the people, strengthened and improved the leadership of the party, enabling the party to be fully trusted and supported by the people, and always play a leading role, gathering great strength and providing a fundamental political guarantee for reform and opening up, and socialist modernisation.

"We must integrate adherence to the basic socialist system with the development of a market economy, bring into play the superiority of the socialist system and the effectiveness of the market in distributing resources, so that the whole of society is filled with the creative energy of reform and development. Over the past 30 years, we have both upheld the basic socialist system in the midst of profound and extensive changes, and creatively developed a market economy under socialist conditions, so that economic activities comply with the requirements of the law of value. We have constantly liberated and developed social productivity, strengthened comprehensive national power, raised people's living standards and more effectively accomplished the central task of economic construction. The establishment and improvement of the socialist market economy is the party's historic contribution to Marxism and socialism.

"We must integrate the promotion of changes in the economic base with the promotion of reforms in the superstructure to continuously promote political system reform, and to provide institutional guarantees and legal safeguards for reform and opening up, and socialist modernisation. Over the past 30 years, we have actively promoted both economic and political system reform, developed socialist democracy, built a socialist state under the rule of law, ensured the sovereignty of the people, continuously promoted the adaptation of China's socialist superstructure to the economic base, as a result of which socialist democracy has shown more vigorous vitality.

"We must integrate the development of social productivity with the improvement of the quality of civilisation of the entire nation, promote the coordinated development of material and spiritual civilisation, and more consciously and proactively promote the great development and great prosperity of culture. Over the past 30 years, we have prioritised both material development, namely, the development of social productivity, and human development, namely, the improvement of the quality of civilisation of the entire nation, upheld a firm grasp of both material and spiritual civilisation, integrated the rule of law with rule by virtue, armed people with scientific theories, guided them with correct opinions, shaped them with noble sentiments and inspired them with excellent works, and focused on cultivating citizens with ideals and morals who are educated and disciplined. We have continuously improved the ideological, moral, scientific and cultural quality of the whole nation, provided strong spiritual impetus and intellectual support for reform and opening up, and socialist modernisation, and created an environment of favourable public opinion.

"We must integrate increasing efficiency with the promotion of social equity, achieve the sharing of the fruits of reform and development by the general public on the basis of economic development, and promote the building of a harmonious socialist society. Over the past 30 years, we have not only prioritised enhancing social vitality and promoting economic development through improving efficiency but also prioritised promoting social harmony through achieving social equity on the basis of economic development, upholding a people-oriented approach. We have focused on solving the most direct and practical interests of most concern to the people, focusing on developing social causes, improving the income distribution system, safeguarding and improving people's livelihoods, and taking the road to common prosperity. We have striven to create a context in which all the people do their utmost, each is provided for, and all live together in harmony, so as to create a favourable social environment for reform and opening up, and socialist modernisation.

"We must integrate independence with participation in economic globalisation, coordinate China's two overall situations, namely, the domestic and international contexts, and contribute to the noble cause of promoting human peace and development. Over the past 30 years, we have not only greatly cherished and unswervingly safeguarded the right of the Chinese people to independence and autonomy, which they have earned through long struggle, but also upheld the basic national policy of opening up to the outside world. We have always closely examined the development of China and the world from the perspective of the interconnectedness of the international and domestic situations, considered and formulated China's developmental strategy, persisted with an independent and peaceful foreign policy, the road of peaceful development, and a mutually beneficial win-win strategy of openness, promoted the building of a lasting peace, common prosperity and a harmonious world, striven for a favourable international environment for China's development, and made an important contribution to world peace and development.

"We must integrate the promotion of reform and development with the maintenance of social stability, persist with the unity of reform efforts, speed of development and social affordability, and ensure social orderliness and unity, harmony and stability. Over the past 30 years, we have not only vigorously promoted reform and development but also correctly handled the relationship between reform, development and stability, and insisted that reform be the driving force, development be the goal and stability be the premise. We have made continuous improvements in people's livelihoods a key link in handling the relationship between reform, development and stability, promoted reform and development in the context of social stability, and promoted social stability through reform and development, and in the current broader context of widespread and profound changes in the world and in contemporary China, we have always maintained the broad stability of society.

"We must integrate the promotion of the great cause of socialism with Chinese characteristics with the promotion of the great new project of building the party, strengthen the party's governability and construction of progressiveness, and improve the level of the party's leadership and governance, its ability to fight corruption and forestall moral degeneration, and its resilience to risks. Over the past 30 years, we have not only promoted the party building by closely focusing on advancing the cause of socialism with Chinese characteristics but also advanced the cause of socialism with

Chinese characteristics by strengthening and improving party building. We have responded to new changes in global, national and party conditions, clarified the party's historical orientation, upheld the standpoint that the party should be managed by the party and governed strictly, insisted on strengthening the party's self-construction through the spirit of reform and innovation, continuously improved the party's governability, maintained and developed the party's progressiveness, continuously enhanced the party's class base and expanded its mass base, continuously improved its ability to fight corruption and forestall moral degeneration and resilience to risks, always maintaining vibrant connections between the party and the people, so that the party will always be the strong leading core of the cause of socialism with Chinese characteristics."

The report of the 17th CPC National Congress and Hu Jintao's speech at the conference commemorating the 30th anniversary of the 3rd Plenary Session of the 11th CPC Central Committee summed up the valuable experience of the "Ten Integrations", thereby constituting both a profound summary of historical experience and a concentrated embodiment of theoretical innovation. These Ten Integrations vividly illustrated the valuable experience of how, in the practice of reform and opening up, the CPC has upheld and developed Marxism and socialism, comprehensively promoted the cause of socialism with Chinese characteristics, coordinated China's two overall situations, namely the domestic and international contexts, and strengthened and improved the leadership of the party. They also profoundly revealed the key aspects of, and fundamental factors in, the success of China's reform and opening up in terms of the unity of history and logic, theory and practice.

The success of China's reform and opening up is ultimately due to the integration of the basic principles of Marxism with China's concrete realities and the pioneering, upholding and development of socialism with Chinese characteristics.

In October 2007, the report of the 17th CPC National Congress, on the basis of summarising the valuable experience of the Ten Integrations, further emphasised that the fundamental reason for all the achievements and progress the party has made since the start of reform and opening up all comes down to the fact that the CPC carved out the path of socialism with Chinese characteristics and formed its theoretical system.

In July 2011, Hu Jintao pointed out in his speech at the conference celebrating the 90th anniversary of the founding of the CPC that, after 90 years of struggle, creation and accumulation, the achievements that the party and the people must greatly cherish, uphold in the long term, and continuously develop, are having carved out the path of socialism with Chinese characteristics, formed the theoretical system of socialism with Chinese characteristics, and established a socialist system with Chinese characteristics.

In November 2012, the 18th CPC National Congress further expanded the historical experience of reform and opening up, attributing the fundamental reason for all the achievements and progress made since the start of reform and opening up to "carving out the path of socialism with Chinese characteristics, the formation of the theoretical system of socialism with Chinese characteristics, and the establishment of a socialist system with Chinese characteristics". It also emphasised that this constitutes "a fundamental achievement of the party and the people after 90 years of struggle, creation and accumulation, which must be greatly cherished, always adhered to and continuously developed".

The path of socialism with Chinese characteristics consists of building a socialist market economy, socialist democratic politics, advanced socialist culture, socialist harmonious society and socialist eco-civilisation under the leadership of the CPC, based on China's basic national conditions and with a focus on economic construction, upholding the Four Cardinal Principles and reform and opening up, liberating and developing social productivity, building a socialist market economy, socialist democratic politics, advanced socialist culture, socialist harmonious society and socialist ecological civilisation. It consists of promoting comprehensive human development, gradually achieving the common prosperity of the people as a whole and building a prosperous, strong, democratic, civilised and harmonious modern socialist state.

The theoretical system of socialism with Chinese characteristics is a scientific theoretical system comprised of Deng Xiaoping Theory, the major ideology of the Three Represents and a Scientific Outlook on Development, and constitutes adherence to, and development of, Marxism-Leninism and Mao Zedong Thought.

The socialist system with Chinese characteristics is comprised of the fundamental political system of people's congresses, the basic political system of multi-party cooperation and political consultation under the leadership of the CPC, the systems of ethnic regional autonomy and grass-roots mass autonomy, the socialist legal system with Chinese characteristics, the basic economic system mainly characterised by public ownership whereby a variety of ownership systems develop together, and the specific economic, political, cultural, social and other institutions based on these systems.

The path of socialism with Chinese characteristics constitutes the route to realisation, the theoretical system of socialism with Chinese characteristics the guidelines for action, and the socialist system with Chinese characteristics the fundamental guarantee. These three are unified in the great practice of socialism with Chinese characteristics, and this is the most distinctive feature of the party's leadership of the people in the long-term practice of the construction of socialism.

On the occasion of 30 years since the start of reform and opening up, the party profoundly summed up its historical experience of the governance of reform and opening up, the main purpose of which is to call on the whole party, the whole army, and all the people of China to hold high the great banner of socialism with Chinese characteristics, uphold reform and opening up, continue to emancipate the mind and continuously advance the cause of socialism with Chinese characteristics to achieve the great rejuvenation of the Chinese nation. The historical experience of 30 years of reform and opening up has shown that reform and opening up is the key choice to determine the fate of contemporary China and is the only way to develop socialism with Chinese characteristics and achieve the great rejuvenation of the Chinese nation, that only socialism can save China and only reform and opening up can develop China, socialism and Marxism, and that reform and opening up is in line with the heart of the party and the people and the *zeitgeist*, the direction and path of reform and opening up are completely correct, the results and achievements are undeniable, and stagnation or retrogression would be a blind alley.

(VII) THE SCIENTIFIC OUTLOOK ON DEVELOPMENT: FURTHER DEVELOPMENT OF THE UNDERSTANDING OF THE COMMUNIST PARTY'S GOVERNANCE LAW

The party's adeptness at promoting theoretical innovation in the light of the fresh experience of practice, and persistence in utilising the results of theoretical innovation to guide new practice, constitutes a fundamental guarantee for the development of the cause of socialism with Chinese characteristics. In accordance with new development requirements, the party Central Committee with Comrade Hu Jintao as its General Secretary, persisting in taking Deng Xiaoping Theory and the major ideology of the Three Represents as its guide, profoundly understood and answered the major questions regarding the kind of development which would be most suited to China's national conditions and the appropriate methods of development under the new situation, forming a Scientific Outlook on Development which is people-oriented, comprehensive, coordinated and sustainable, developed the CPC's philosophy of governance and deepened the party's understanding of the communist party's governance law, the laws of socialist construction and of human social development.

After the 16th CPC National Congress, the Party Central Committee, with Comrade Hu Jintao as its General Secretary, accurately grasped the general trend of world development and China's basic national conditions in the primary stage of socialism, thoroughly studied the phased characteristics of China's development, and gradually formed its Scientific Outlook on Development in the process of studying new situations and solving new problems. This outlook was proposed, on the basis of a systematic summary of China's successful experience of reform and opening up, and socialist modernisation, and drawing lessons learned from the development process of other countries, incorporating an overview of the key lessons learned from the victory over the SARS epidemic, all against the backdrop of the new century, when China entered a new stage of building a moderately prosperous society in all respects, and when global, national and party conditions were undergoing profound changes. This outlook profoundly revealed the objective laws of economic and social development and intensively reflected the party's new understanding of development.

In April 2003 during an inspection tour to Guangdong, Hu Jintao proposed adherence to a comprehensive outlook on development. He pointed out that in the new stage of the new century, the eastern part of China, including Guangdong, was at a new starting point of development, facing new opportunities, challenges and tasks, and that it was necessary to clearly understand the situation at the time and further enhance the party's sense of historical responsibility and mission to accelerate, take the lead in, and coordinate development. Hu Jintao proposed that it was necessary to adhere to a comprehensive outlook on development and continuously increase China's strengths in innovation by promoting the coordinated development of the three civilisations.

In July 2003 at the National Work Conference on the Prevention and Control of SARS, Hu Jintao proposed that it was necessary to more robustly adhere to a development outlook focused on comprehensive, coordinated and sustainable development. He pointed out that promoting coordinated socioeconomic development is an inevitable requirement for building socialism with Chinese characteristics and for building a moderately prosperous society in all respects. With regard to development being the party's first priority in governing and rejuvenating China, the development referred to here by no means refers only to economic growth. Rather it is necessary to achieve comprehensive social development on the basis of economic development, with a focus on economic construction. It is necessary for the party to more robustly adhere to an outlook on development focused on comprehensive, coordinated and sustainable development, more consciously uphold the promotion of the coordinated development of the socialist, political and spiritual civilisations, promote comprehensive human development on the basis of socioeconomic development, and uphold the promotion of harmony between mankind and nature. In the process of promoting development, the party should not only focus on economic indicators but also on human, resource and environmental indicators, not only increase investment to promote economic growth but also increase investment to promote social development and protect resources and the environment. All regions of China and all departments should further prioritise the promotion of coordinated socioeconomic development, further reflect this prioritisation in development guidelines and further implement it in work arrangements, constantly improving self-awareness and proactiveness of cadres at all levels in the promotion of coordinated socioeconomic development. Research on some major issues related to coordinated socioeconomic development should be strengthened, scientific solutions should be formulated and then they should be gradually and increasingly implemented.

In August and September 2003, Hu Jintao explicitly used the concept of a "Scientific Outlook on Development" during an inspection tour to Jiangxi, proposing that a Scientific Outlook on Development which is coordinated, comprehensive and characterised by sustainable development should be firmly established.

In October 2003, the 3rd Plenary Session of the 16th CPC Central Committee adopted the *Decision of the CPC Central Committee on Several Issues Concerning Refining the Socialist Market Economy*, which put forward the Scientific Outlook on Development in its entirety for the first time. The *Decision* called for "adherence to a people-oriented approach and establishing a comprehensive, coordinated and sustainable outlook on development", emphasising the promotion of reform and opening up, and modernisation "in accordance with the requirements of coordinated urban-rural development, coordinated regional development, coordinated socioeconomic development, the coordinated harmonious development of human beings and nature, and the coordination of domestic development and opening up to the outside world".

In February 2004, the CPC Central Committee held a special study session for leading cadres at the provincial and ministerial levels on the establishment and implementation of the Scientific Outlook on Development. This constituted an important initiative taken by the Party Central Committee to promote the establishment and implementation of the Scientific Outlook on Development by the entire party. In March, Hu Jintao pointed out in his speech at the Central Government Symposium on Population, Resources and Environment that adhering to a development outlook which is people-oriented, comprehensive, coordinated and sustainable is a major strategic concept that is guided by Deng Xiaoping Theory and the major ideology of the Three Represents, and is based on the overall development of the party and the state in a new stage and a new century. Hu Jintao also comprehensively elaborated on the scientific essence, basic requirements and guiding significance of the Scientific Outlook on Development.

In October 2007, the 17th CPC National Congress gave a comprehensive and systematic exposition of the Scientific Outlook on Development in terms of its historical context, scientific and spiritual essence, and fundamental requirements. The report of the 17th CPC National Congress pointed out that the Scientific Outlook on Development is based on China's basic national conditions in the primary stage of socialism, and summarises China's practice of development, draws on foreign development experience, and adapts to new development requirements. The Scientific Outlook on Development constitutes a continuation and development of the major ideology on development by the three generations of the party's central leadership group, a concentrated embodiment of the Marxist worldview and methodology on development, a scientific theory that is in line with Marxism-Leninism and Mao Zedong Thought, Deng Xiaoping Theory and the major ideology of the Three Represents but is also characterised by progressive advance, an important set of guidelines for China's economic and social development, and a major strategic concept that must be adhered to and implemented in the development of socialism with Chinese characteristics. The report stressed that, in order to continue to build a moderately prosperous society in all respects and develop socialism with Chinese characteristics in the new stage of development, it was necessary to uphold Deng Xiaoping Theory and the major ideology of the Three Represents as a guide, and thoroughly implement the Scientific Outlook on Development. The report puts forward clear requirements for the in-depth implementation of the Scientific Outlook on Development from four aspects, which were always adhering to the party's basic line, actively building a harmonious socialist society, continuing to deepen reform and opening up, and effectively strengthening and improving party building[18]. On the basis of the 17th CPC National Congress the 18th CPC National Congress held in November 2012 elevated the Scientific Outlook on Development to the level of guiding ideology of the CPC and incorporated it into the party constitution. The establishment of the historical status of the Scientific Outlook on Development and the determination of the Scientific Outlook on Development as the party's guiding ideology constitutes an important decision and historic contribution made by the 18th CPC National Congress.

As a major theoretical achievement of the party, the Scientific Outlook on Development, as the party's guiding ideology, is rich in content and its essence is profound. The first key point of the Scientific Outlook on Development is development. Development is of decisive significance in building a moderately prosperous society in all respects and accelerating socialist modernisation. It is vital to firmly grasp economic construction as the focus, persist in concentrating the party's attention on construction, single-mindedly pursue development, and continuously liberate and develop social productivity. The strategies of invigorating China through science and education, human resource development and sustainable development must be implemented better, by focusing on grasping the laws of development, the concept of innovative development, methods of transformative development, and solving development problems, improving the quality and efficiency of development, achieving robust and rapid development, and laying a solid foundation for the development of socialism with Chinese characteristics. It is also necessary to strive to achieve scientific development that is people-oriented, comprehensive, coordinated and sustainable, achieve harmonious development characterised by the organic unification of all undertakings and the unity and harmony of members of society, and achieve peaceful development that not only develops itself through safeguarding world peace but also safeguards world peace through its own development.

The core of the Scientific Outlook on Development is the concept of being people-oriented. Upholding a people-oriented approach means aiming to achieve comprehensive human development, seeking and promoting development starting from the fundamental interests of the people, continuously meeting the growing material and cultural needs of the people, effectively protecting the economic, political and cultural rights, and interests of the people, and ensuring that the fruits of development benefit all the people. Serving the people wholeheartedly is the fundamental aim of the party, and all its struggles and work are for the benefit of the people. It is necessary to always take achieving, safeguarding and developing the fundamental interests of the general public as the starting and end points of all the work of the party and the state, to respect the central position of the people, fully bring out the people's innovative spirit, protect the rights and interests of the people, walk along the path of common prosperity and promote all-round human development so that development is for the people and depends on the people, and that the fruits of development are enjoyed by the people.

The basic requirement of the Scientific Outlook on Development is comprehensive, coordinated and sustainable development. Comprehensive development means promoting economic, political and cultural construction in a comprehensive manner, and achieving economic development and overall social progress, all with a focus on economic construction. Coordinated development means coordinating urban and rural development, regional development, socioeconomic development, the harmonious development of humans and nature, and domestic development, opening up to the outside world and promoting the coordination of productivity and socioeconomic relations, the economic base and the superstructure, and promoting the coordination of all aspects of economic, political and cultural construction. Sustainable development means promoting harmony between humans and nature, achieving coordination between economic development and population, resources and the environment, and upholding the path of civilised development in which production develops, livelihoods are affluent and the ecology is in a good condition, so as to ensure the sustainable development of each successive generation. In accordance with the overall composition of the cause of socialism with Chinese characteristics, it is necessary to comprehensively promote economic, political, cultural and social construction, and to promote the coordination of all aspects of modernisation, as well as the coordination of socioeconomic relations with productivity and the superstructure with the economic base. Adherence to a civilised development path characterised by the development of production, affluence and a good ecology, building a resource-saving and environmentally-friendly society, and achieving the unity of rapid development, and structural quality and efficiency, as well as the coordination of economic development with population, resources and the environment, enabling the people to produce and live within a good ecological environment, and achieve sustainable socioeconomic development.

The fundamental method of the Scientific Outlook on Development is overall coordination and balance. This means correctly understanding and properly handling the major relationships in the cause of socialism with Chinese characteristics, coordinating urban and rural development, regional development, socioeconomic development, the harmonious development of humans and nature, and domestic development and opening up to the outside world, coordinating the relationship between the central and local governments, and coordinating individual and collective interests, local and national interests, and current and long-term interests, in order to fully mobilise the initiative of all parties. It also means taking into account China's two overall situations, namely the domestic and international contexts, establishing a global perspective, strengthening strategic thinking, and being adept at grasping development opportunities and addressing risks and challenges within the changing international situation, so as to create a favourable international environment. Therefore, it is necessary to take an overall view of the situation and make comprehensive guidelines but also to take firm hold of the main work impacting the overall context and the prominent issues that concern the interests of the public and make efforts to advance and achieve breakthroughs.

The most distinctive spiritual aspect of the Scientific Outlook on Development is the emancipation of the mind, seeking truth from facts, progressive advance and being pragmatic. The entire process of the Scientific Outlook on Development, namely the emancipation of the mind, seeking truth from facts, progressive advance, and being pragmatic, and each of its components and major viewpoints all connect together and embody the spiritual qualities of the emancipation of the mind, seeking truth from facts, progressive advance and being pragmatic, and they all uphold the basic principles of Marxism. It also brings new ideas and reflects the unity of perseverance and development, and of continuity and innovation, making people feel deeply the powerful vitality of Marxism, which is evolving with the times, practice and scientific development.

The Party Central Committee, with Comrade Hu Jintao as its General Secretary, developed the Scientific Outlook on Development in the process of promoting reform and opening up, and modernisation. In terms of its theoretical origin, the Scientific Outlook on Development is derived from the perspectives of Marxism-Leninism and Mao Zedong Thought, Deng Xiaoping Theory and the major ideology of the Three Represents on development. In terms of its practical basis, it constitutes a scientific summary of the historical experience of China's socialist construction, in particular the fresh experience since the 16th CPC National Congress. In terms of its historical context, it was formed by profoundly grasping the international situation and global development trends, drawing on the lessons learned from the development of other countries and the beneficial achievements of foreign theories of development. In terms of its practical basis, it was proposed on the basis of a profound analysis and grasp of the characteristics and requirements of the current stage of China's development. The Scientific Outlook on Development involves all aspects of productivity and socioeconomic relations, the economic base and the superstructure, and cuts across all aspects of the great cause of socialism with Chinese characteristics and the great new project of party construction. It constitutes a concentrated embodiment of the Marxist worldview and methodology on development, a major achievement of the Sinicisation of Marxism and a guiding ideology that must be upheld in the long term in the development of socialism with Chinese characteristics, providing scientific theoretical guidance for building a moderately prosperous society in all respects and accelerating the promotion of socialist modernisation.

4

THE SECOND MIRACLE CREATED BY CPC GOVERNANCE

THE GREAT LEAP OF THE CHINESE NATION FROM STANDING UP TO BECOMING AFFLUENT

After the 3rd Plenary Session of the 11th CPC Central Committee, the party correctly understood and determined the new governance environment, formulated and established scientific governance objectives, shifted the work focus of the party and the state to economic construction, united and led all the people of China to implement the great new revolution of reform and opening up, and pioneered and expanded a new path for governing and rejuvenating China. The Chinese nation has made a great leap from standing up to becoming affluent. Between 1978 and 2012, China's socioeconomic development underwent sweeping changes, with productivity rising dramatically, people's living standards improving significantly, comprehensive national power growing continuously, the national spirit being completely renewed, and the Chinese nation achieving a great leap from standing up to becoming rich. This is the second miracle created by the party's governance, and it is also a miracle in the history of global development.

The key to achieving the great leap of the Chinese nation from standing up to becoming rich is reflected in the word 'affluence', reflecting the fact that productivity was greatly developed and the living standards of the people were greatly improved, with the result that the livelihoods of Chinese people achieved a historic leap from inadequate subsistence to sufficiency to moderate prosperity. Before the 3rd Plenary Session of the 11th CPC Central Committee, the Chinese people had not yet completely solved the problem of inadequate subsistence. In March 1979, at the party's theoretical work retreat, Deng Xiaoping elaborated on two major characteristics of China at that time, stating that, "One was that the economic base was underdeveloped. The long period of destruction brought about by imperialism, feudalism and bureaucratic capitalism had made China a poor and backward country. ...... China is still now one of the poorer countries in the world. ...... The second one is that there is a large population and little arable land. The country now has a population of over 900 million, of which 80% are farmers. ...... food, education and employment have all become serious problems"[1]. In 1976, rural commune members nationwide received a share of only Rmb63.3 from the collective income, 140 million people nationwide had an average food ration of less than 150kg in 1977, and 250 million people were living in rural poverty. Deng Xiaoping also said, "After decades of revolution and more than 30 years of socialism, as of 1978 the average monthly wage for workers was only Rmb40 or Rmb50 and most rural areas were still in poverty"[2]. It was precisely because of the backwardness of the productive forces and the poverty of the people that the 3rd Plenary Session of the 11th CPC Central Committee made the historic decision to shift the work focus of the party and the state to economic construction and to implementing reform and opening up. By formulating and implementing such major development strategies as the "three steps" and the "new three steps", and by focusing on economic construction and single-mindedly pursuing development, the party has enabled China to make rapid progress in a period of more than 30 years, completely throwing off the label of "the sick man of Asia", and casting poverty and backwardness into the depths of the Pacific Ocean, and to make the experience of inadequate subsistence nothing more than a historical memory.

The historic leap achieved in the lives of the Chinese people from inadequate subsistence to overall moderate prosperity was achieved one step at a time, steadily and surely, and in the course of hard struggle. In just nine years, from 1978 to 1987, the 13th CPC National Congress solemnly declared that after the 3rd Plenary Session of the 11th CPC Central Committee, "the GDP, state revenue and the average income of urban and rural residents have all roughly doubled in nine years", and that, "the vast majority of the one billion people reached above the level of subsistence". Another 14 years later, in March 2001, the of the *Government Work Report*, deliberated and adopted at the Fourth Session of the Ninth NPC, solemnly declared that "the people's livelihoods have continued to improve and generally reached the level of moderate prosperity". In other words, the livelihoods of the Chinese people finally made the leap from subsistence to general prosperity. In 2000, China's per capita GDP and GNP both exceeded US$800. The market was rich in commodities, the consumption level of the population was rising, and the consumption patterns and living conditions of the people had improved considerably. The shortage of commodities that had long plagued the Chinese people was basically ended, and there were significant changes in the relationship between market supply and demand. The "Eight Seven" poverty alleviation targets were basically achieved, and the proportion of the rural population in poverty was significantly reduced. Urban employment channels were broadened, and various forms of employment developed rapidly. A social security system was preliminarily established, and the system of endowment insurance, unemployment insurance and minimum living security for urban residents was gradually extended.

After the 16th CPC National Congress in 2002, the party made new achievements in uniting and leading the people of China in their common struggle to achieve the goal of quadrupling the GDP of the year 2000 by 2020, and to comprehensively build a society with a higher level of moderate prosperity benefiting more than one billion people. According to the *Statistical Monitoring Report on the Process of Building an Affluent Society in all Respects in China (2011)*, which was formulated and issued by the relevant national departments, by 2010, progress in building a moderately prosperous society in all respects was smooth, with the degree of achievement increasing from 59.6% in 2000 to 80.1% in 2010. The degree of achievement in all six major areas of building a moderately prosperous society in all respects had increased significantly. Significant achievements had been made in economic development, with the degree of achievement increasing from 50.3% in 2000 to 76.1% in 2010. The degree of social harmony had gradually improved, from 57.5% in 2000 to 82.5% in 2010. The people's quality of life had also improved significantly, with the degree of achievement increasing from 58.3% in 2000 to 86.4% in 2010. The democratic legal system had also been gradually improved, with the degree of achievement increasing from 84.8% in 2000 to 93.6% in 2010. Cultural and educational undertakings had also developed steadily, with the degree of achievement increasing from 58.3% in 2000 to 68.0% in 2010. The situation of resources and environmental protection was in good shape too, with the degree of achievement increasing from 65.4% in 2000 to 78.2% in 2010[3].

From 1978 to 2012, every policy the party proposed, every strategy it implemented and every reform it introduced was always focused on the liberation and development of productivity, on socioeconomic development and on the improvement of people's living standards. The history of those more than 30 years was fundamentally about changing the old face of China's poverty and backwardness and achieving the real prosperity of the Chinese people. In 2012, China's per capita GDP reached Rmb38,354, and the Engel coefficient for urban residents was 37.1%, close to the level of middle-income countries. The per capita living space in urban and rural areas was 32.9 sqm and 37.1 sqm respectively. Urban residents owned 21.5 domestic cars per 100 households. The educational level of the nation also increased significantly, with the average number of years of education for people aged 15 or above reaching more than nine. The basic endowment insurance for urban and rural residents achieved full coverage, with 790 million people covered by various endowment insurance schemes. The level of national health also further improved, with average life expectancy reaching 75 years.

The great leap from standing up to becoming affluent was also reflected in the country's strength, as China's comprehensive national power also grew significantly, its sway in the world's political and economic affairs becoming stronger, and its voice in international affairs greater. First, China's economic output continued to rise to new heights, its comprehensive national power and international competitiveness transformed from weak to strong, and it successfully achieved the historic leap from a low-income economy to a middle-income economy. China's GDP jumped from Rmb364.5 billion in 1978 to nearly Rmb52 trillion in 2012; 1978 saw China rank 10th in the world in terms of economic output, in 2008 it surpassed Germany to rank third in the world, and in 2010 it surpassed Japan to rank second in the world, becoming the world's second largest economy after the US. China has steadily solved the problem of feeding more than 1.4 billion people by relying on its own strength. China's output of major agricultural and industrial products ranked first in the world, major scientific and technological innovations of advanced levels in the world were constantly emerging, high-tech industries were flourishing, breakthroughs had been made in the construction of infrastructure such as water conservancy, energy, transport and communications, the construction of eco-civilisation was constantly being promoted, and urban and rural areas had begun to take on a new look. Extensive and in-depth international cooperation had accelerated China's economic development and made significant contributions to the development of the global economy, making it one of the most important forces driving the development of the global economy.

Next, China has continuously expanded its opening up to the outside world and successfully achieved a great historical turnaround from a closed or semi-closed state to all-round opening up. This has led to China's increasing dependence on the world, and China has become increasingly inseparable from the world and vice versa. China adheres to the basic national policy of opening up to the outside world, opens its doors for construction, continuously expands the breadth and depth of its opening up to the outside world, and accelerates the development of an open economy. From the establishment of SEZs to the opening up of coastal, riverine, border and inland areas to accession to the WTO, from large-scale "bringing in" to "going global" in big strides, the extent of utilisation of the international and domestic "two markets and two resources" has been significantly improved, and international competitiveness has been continuously enhanced. In 2012, the value of China's total imports and exports reached US$386.71 billion, 186 times higher than the 1978 level and ranking first in the world in terms of total goods exports. Also, in 2012, the actual use of overseas foreign direct investment amounted to US$111.7 billion, ranking first amongst developing countries for many years, while net FDI (foreign direct investment) amounted to US$87.8 billion, and the reserves of outward direct investment reached US$531.9 billion at the end of the year.

Again, China is playing an increasingly important role in international organisations such as the UN, the World Bank and the WTO, in international counter-terrorism, in tackling global warming, in maintaining peace and stability in relevant regions, and in addressing issues related to global hotspots, delivering an increasingly resounding Chinese voice on the international stage and contributing more and more Chinese wisdom and strength on global issues.

In November 2012, the report of the 18th CPC National Congress highly appraised China's economic and social development achievements since the 16th CPC National Congress, emphasising, "Over the past decade, we have made a series of new historic achievements, laying a solid foundation for building a moderately prosperous society in all respects. China's economic output has jumped from sixth to second place in the world, social productivity, economic, scientific and technological strength have risen to a high level, people's living standards, income levels and levels of social security have risen to a high level, China's comprehensive national power, international competitiveness and international influence have risen to a high level, and the national landscape has undergone new and historic changes"[4]. It can be said that this is also a lofty summary of China's international status, image and influence over the preceding 30 years of reform and opening up.

The most fundamental aspect in the achievement of the historic leap of the Chinese nation from standing up to becoming affluent is the pioneering of, adherence to and development of socialism with Chinese characteristics and finding the path of socialism with Chinese characteristics, which is the sure way to achieve the great rejuvenation of the Chinese nation. This also constitutes the greatest achievement of the Chinese nation in the process from standing up to becoming affluent. Socialism with Chinese characteristics has been the theme of all the party's theory and practice since reform and opening up, and socialism with Chinese characteristics is the fundamental reason for all its achievements and progress. Since the start of reform and opening up, the CPC has deepened its understanding of socialism with Chinese characteristics in the course of reform and opening up, and the practice of socialist modernisation, raising the great banner of socialism with Chinese characteristics ever higher, establishing Deng Xiaoping Theory, forming the major ideology of the Three Represents and the Scientific Outlook on Development.

For the first time, Deng Xiaoping Theory systematically and preliminarily answered a series of basic questions on how to build, consolidate and develop socialism in a relatively economically and culturally backward country like China, raising the understanding of socialism to a new scientific level and playing a seminal role in the conception and formation of socialism with Chinese characteristics. The major ideology of the Three Represents is the party's foundation, the basis of its governance and the source of its strength, and it reflects the new requirements for the work of the party and the state arising from the development and changes in the contemporary world and China. It constitutes a powerful theoretical weapon for strengthening and improving the party building and promoting the self-improvement and development of Chinese socialism, which has pointed the way for the party to achieve long-term governance in the context of a socialist market economy and to unite more than one billion Chinese people around the party to struggle for the cause of socialism with Chinese characteristics. The Scientific Outlook on Development is the concentrated manifestation of the Marxist worldview on, and methodology for, development, provides a new scientific answer to the major questions surrounding the type of development the party should pursue and how to achieve development under the new situation, and opens up a new horizon for the development of contemporary Chinese Marxism. The second generation of the party's central leadership with Comrade Deng Xiaoping as its core successfully pioneered socialism with Chinese characteristics, the third generation of the party's central leadership with Comrade Jiang Zemin as its core successfully propelled socialism with Chinese characteristics into the 21st century, and the Party Central Committee with Comrade Hu Jintao as its general secretary successfully upheld and developed socialism with Chinese characteristics from a new historical starting point. It is under the scientific guidance of Deng Xiaoping Theory, the Three Represents and the Scientific Outlook on

Development that socialism with Chinese characteristics has continued to make glorious achievements and has shown unprecedented vigour and vitality.

In November 2012, the 18th CPC National Congress profoundly summarised the 90-year history of the party, in particular the great practice of socialism with Chinese characteristics, further systematically answered the question of what the essence of socialism with Chinese characteristics is and how to build it, and enriched and deepened the party's understanding of the laws of socialism with Chinese characteristics. It developed the basic essence of socialism with Chinese characteristics from the concept of "two-in-one" to the concept of a "trinity", meaning from the path and theoretical system of socialism with Chinese characteristics to the path, theoretical system and systems of socialism with Chinese characteristics, which are all unified in the great practice of socialism with Chinese characteristics. It also developed the overall composition of socialism with Chinese characteristics from a "trinity" and a "four-sphere" plan to a "five-sphere" plan, meaning from the "trinity" of the material, political and spiritual civilisation proposed at the 15th CPC National Congress, to the "four-sphere" plan of economic, political, cultural and social construction proposed at the 17th CPC National Congress, and then further to the "five-sphere" plan of economic, political, cultural, social and eco-civilisation construction proposed at the 18th CPC National Congress. On the basis of the party's basic theory, line, programme and experience advanced following the 3rd Plenary Session of the 11th CPC Central Committee, the congress also put forward eight basic requirements that must be firmly grasped in order to build socialism with Chinese characteristics which, together with the party's basic theory, line, programme and experience, formed the "Five Basics" pattern of the party's strategy for guiding socialism with Chinese characteristics.

These major theoretical innovations and regular understanding constitute not only an important embodiment and an important part of the Chinese nation's achievement of the great leap from standing up to becoming affluent but they also provided solid theoretical support and a powerful ideological weapon for achieving this leap.

History and reality have fully proven that socialism with Chinese characteristics constitutes the dialectical unity of the theoretical logic of scientific socialism and the historical logic of China's social development, scientific socialism rooted in Chinese soil, reflecting the will of the Chinese people and adapted to the requirements of China and the development progress of the times, that it constitutes the only way to build a moderately prosperous society in all respects, to build China into a rich, strong, democratic, civilised, harmonious and beautiful modern socialist power, and to achieve the great rejuvenation of the Chinese nation, and that it constitutes the most essential, fundamental and important achievement in achieving the great leap of the Chinese nation from standing up to becoming affluent.

The great leap of the Chinese nation from standing up to becoming affluent has led to an unprecedented rise in the self-confidence, pride and cohesion of the entire Chinese nation, and a fundamental change in the spirit of the Chinese people as a whole, from which an open and confident China full of vitality and hope has come to stand tall in the East. From the perspective of the entire journey of the great rejuvenation of the Chinese nation, getting affluent is the pivotal link between standing up and getting strong. After standing up, if China fails to open up new paths of governance in a timely manner to liberate and develop productivity, then it will eventually be unable to stand firmly or continue to stand. Likewise, if China does not become affluent and if there is no great development of productivity and no significant increase in comprehensive national power, then it will not have the socioeconomic foundation or the capital and stamina to become strong. No matter from which perspective it is viewed, the second miracle created by the governance of the CPC, namely the great leap made by the Chinese nation from standing up to becoming affluent, is worthy of writing about in great volumes.

PART IV
A NEW REALM OF UNDERSTANDING OF THE LAWS OF COMMUNIST PARTY GOVERNANCE

Since the 18th CPC National Congress, the Party Central Committee, with Comrade Xi Jinping at its core, has united and led the Chinese people to focus closely on achieving the struggle goal of the "Two Centenaries" and the Chinese dream of the great rejuvenation of the Chinese nation, raising the flag, planning the layout, overcoming difficulties and strengthening the foundation, opening up new frontiers in the management of state affairs and pioneering a new context for the development of party and state affairs. In the new great practice of managing state affairs, Xi Jinping, with the great political wisdom, theoretical courage and responsibility of a statesman and strategist, delivered a series of important speeches on reform, development and stability, internal and foreign affairs, and national defence, and on party, state and military governance. He put forward a series of new concepts, ideas and strategies, forming Xi Jinping Thought on Socialism with Chinese Characteristics for a New Era, which has come to constitute a new exploration, deepening and development of the CPC on the communist party's governance law.

The Party Central Committee with Comrade Xi Jinping at its core has deepened and developed the communist party's governance law, which distinctly reflects the coherent integration of the historical, theoretical and practical logic of the CPC's leadership of China's revolution, construction and reform, and opened up a new frontier in the Sinicisation of Marxism, a new frontier in socialism with Chinese characteristics, and a new frontier in the construction of the communist party. This deepening and development is of both great practical and far-reaching historical significance, having significance both for China and for the world.

1

ADVANCING NEW ISSUES OF PARTY GOVERNANCE IN THE NEW ERA

The 18th CPC National Congress was a crucial congress held at a decisive point in China's progress towards the completion of a moderately prosperous society in all respects and also formed a bridge serving as the historical transition from the past into the future. The 18th CPC National Congress and the subsequent election of a new central leadership group with Comrade Xi Jinping as General Secretary at the 1st Plenary Session of the 18th CPC Central Committee marked a new historical stage in the CPC's exploration and development of the communist party's governance law.

(I) THE NEW HISTORICAL ORIENTATION OF PARTY GOVERNANCE: SOCIALISM WITH CHINESE CHARACTERISTICS ENTERS A NEW ERA

Historical orientation is the position of objective matters in the development of history. The party's historical orientation is the position of the party in the development of the times and history. Recognising the party's historical orientation is the basic premise for the party to formulate correct theories, lines, guidelines and policies, and likewise for the party to explore, deepen and develop the communist party's ruling law.

After the dawn of the 21st century, there were significant changes both within China and overseas, which brought new opportunities for the CPC to deepen and develop the communist party's governance law while at the same time posing new challenges. Based on this situation, the 16th CPC

National Congress stated, "Through revolution, construction and reform, our party has changed from a party that led the people in their struggle to seize national power to a party that is leading the people to firmly hold national power and exercise long-term governance, and from a party that led national construction in the context of an external blockade and implementing a planned economy, to a party that has led national construction in the context of opening up to the outside world and developing a socialist market economy"[1]. It was in this historical context that the party, looking at the history, current situation and future of China and the world, accurately grasped the characteristics of the times and the tasks of the party, scientifically formulated and correctly implemented the party's lines, guidelines and policies, diligently studied and resolved the issues of promoting China's social progress and strengthening party buiding, and led the cause of party governance to gain a series of major victories in the first decade of the 21st century.

After this the wheels of history kept rolling forward and the second decade of the 21st century was fast approaching. The CPC celebrated the 90th anniversary of its founding, and the historical orientation of the party's governance saw new changes and took on many new characteristics. Xi Jinping later noted, "We must prepare for a great struggle with many new historical characteristics" and "the concept of 'new historical characteristics' has a profound meaning and constitutes an important judgment derived from a comprehensive examination and judgment of the major trends in the development of China's two overall situations, namely the domestic and international contexts"[2]. This constitutes a sober understanding of the new historical orientation of the CPC.

In the second decade of the 21st century, the multipolarisation of the world and economic globalisation are still the main features of global affairs. On the one hand, the dominant themes of this age of peace and development have not changed, with world multipolarisation, economic globalisation, cultural diversification and social informatisation undergoing profound development, and new and more development opportunities are before us. On the other hand, the deep-rooted impact of the international financial crisis will remain for a considerable period of time and complicated changes in geopolitical relations, increasingly fierce economic competition, and never-ending plots to westernise and divide China are also before us. Just as Xi Jinping pointed out, "many international storms are not unrelated to the 'colour revolutions' instigated by some Western countries"[3], and the external environment has become more unstable and uncertain.

From a national perspective, the transition from the first to the second decade of the 21st century was also a time of "great divergence" between Chinese and foreign economic development. While the growth of the world's major economies slowed down significantly or even faced recession, China's economy maintained a fairly high growth rate and was the first to rally, becoming an important engine of recovery for the global economy. China's economic output made a historic leap forward. In 2010, before the start of the second decade of the 21st century, China's GDP surpassed that of Japan to become the second highest in the world. Socioeconomic development was positive but it was also necessary to face various problems head-on. On the one hand, China had a strong material base, abundant human resources, vast market space and huge development potential, and the long-term positive fundamentals of the economy had not changed, and as Xi Jinping said, "we are closer to achieving the goal of the great rejuvenation of the Chinese nation than at any other time in history, and more confident and capable of achieving this goal than at any other time in history"[4]. On the other hand, China's basic national condition of still being in the primary stage of socialism remained unchanged, the problem of unbalanced and unsustainable development was still prominent, the civilisational quality of the people and their level of social civilisation needed to be improved, the construction of the rule of law needed to be strengthened and the online environment of public opinion needed further attention. While socialism with Chinese characteristics had made significant achievements, it also faced new situations and new tasks such as economic transformation and upgrading, social transformation and development, and reform to tackle thorny problems.

The second decade of the 21st century saw the 90th anniversary of the founding of the CPC. On the one hand, through 90 years of tempering by fire and hammer, the party has become stronger and more popular among the masses, further proving that it is a party that has always upheld the nature, ideals, purpose and struggle goals of a Marxist party, a party that has united and led the people in their unremitting struggle, making great achievements in revolution, construction and reform, that has constantly promoted theoretical innovation and armed itself with theory, and that has attached great importance to its own construction, withstood various tests, and matured and strengthened itself. Indeed, the party has always been the core force leading the socialist cause. On the other hand, as of 2011 the party had been established for 90 years and had been in power for more than 60 years so the issue of how to maintain youthful vitality and how to maintain the purity of progressiveness was a very practical one. At the 90th anniversary of its founding the party had more than 80 million members and more than 4 million grassroots party organisations so the issue of how to ensure the unity and consistency of the party was also very important. "The long march is always ongoing", and the fact that the party faces many dangers and many tests shows that "the results achieved in the construction of party style and clean government are only preliminary and phased"[5]; it is impossible to finish the job in one go. There is still a long way to go to strengthen the party's self-construction.

These matters all point to one thing, namely, that socialism with Chinese characteristics has entered a new era. This constitutes both a new historical orientation for China's development and a new historical orientation in the CPC's exploration of the communist party's governance law. In this new era, China has entered a new stage of development, with new changes in its development environment and conditions, and new changes in its goals and tasks. China has moved from a period of "underdevelopment" to a one of "post-development". In the new era, the main contradiction in Chinese society has been transformed into the contradiction between the people's constantly growing need for a better standard of living, and unbalanced and insufficient development. Economic construction remains the central work of the party and the state but more attention should be paid to improving the quality of development and to grasping comprehensive development. In the new era, the CPC and the Chinese people are moving towards new struggle goals, the Chinese nation is taking a great leap from standing up to becoming affluent to becoming strong, and is about to build a moderately prosperous society in all respects and embark on a new journey to build a modern socialist country in all respects.

The new goals of the new era predestined the CPC's exploration and deepening of the communist party's governance law after the 18th CPC National Congress and in the second decade of the 21st century. They were implemented in the process of solving the new problems of the new era and achieving more optimal development, and in the historical process of continuing to promote reform and opening up, and transforming the mode of economic development. This is the basic historical background of the CPC's deepening and development of the communist party's governance law since the 18th CPC National Congress.

(II) ESTABLISHING A NEW THEME OF UPHOLDING AND DEVELOPING SOCIALISM WITH CHINESE CHARACTERISTICS

The 18th CPC National Congress was held triumphantly from 8 to 14 November 2012 at a critical period when the transformation of China's mode of economic development and measures to bring about the elimination of the negative impact of the international financial crisis were underway. At the congress, Hu Jintao delivered a report entitled *Firmly March on the Path of Socialism with Chinese Characteristics and Strive to Complete the Building of a Moderately Prosperous Society in All Respects*. The theme of the 18th CPC National Congress was: holding high the great banner of socialism with Chinese characteristics, taking Deng Xiaoping Theory, the major ideology of the Three Represents and the Scientific Outlook on Development as guidance, emancipating the mind, reforming and opening up, gathering strength, overcoming difficulties, firmly marching on the path of socialism with Chinese characteristics, and striving to complete the building of a moderately prosperous society in all respects.

The 18th CPC National Congress reviewed and summarised the work of the preceding five years, the struggle and historic achievements since the 16th CPC National Congress, established the historical status of the Scientific Outlook on Development, and achieved the progressive advance of the party's guiding governance ideology. On the basis of a clear guiding ideology, the 18th CPC National Congress elaborated and expanded on the rules of governance of the communist party on many levels, the core of which was the establishment of the new theme of upholding and developing socialism with Chinese characteristics.

The 18th CPC National Congress emphasised that the road to socialism with Chinese characteristics, the theoretical system of socialism with Chinese characteristics and the socialist system with Chinese characteristics constitute the fundamental achievements of the party and the people over 90 years of struggle, creation and accumulation, and must be more greatly cherished, consistently upheld and constantly developed. Upholding and developing socialism with Chinese characteristics became the main line throughout the 18th CPC National Congress and therefore one of the main lines for the party to deepen and develop the communist party's governance law with a new historical orientation.

Focusing on the main line of socialism with Chinese characteristics, the 18th CPC National Congress clarified the scientific essence of the road to socialism with Chinese characteristics, the theoretical system of socialism with Chinese characteristics and the socialist system with Chinese characteristics, as well as the interlinking nature of these, emphasising that the road to socialism with Chinese characteristics is the pathway to realisation, the theoretical system of socialism with Chinese characteristics is the guide to action, the socialist system with Chinese characteristics is the fundamental guarantee, and that the three are unified in the great practice of socialism with Chinese characteristics, which is the most distinctive feature of the party's leadership of the people in their long-term practice of building socialism[6]. The report of the 18th CPC National Congress points out that the general basis for building socialism with Chinese characteristics is the primary stage of socialism, the general composition is the "five-sphere" socialist economic, political, cultural, social and eco-civilisation construction, and the general task is to achieve socialist modernisation and the great rejuvenation of the Chinese nation. Socialism with Chinese characteristics not only adheres to the basic principles of scientific socialism but also furnishes distinctive Chinese characteristics in accordance with the conditions of the times, deepens the understanding of the communist party's governance law, the laws of socialist construction and of human social development with a new vision. It systematically answers the fundamental question surrounding the kind of socialism which should be built and how to build socialism in a large East Asian country like China with a large population and an underdeveloped economic base, based on the integration of theory and practice which enabled China to develop rapidly and its people's living standards to rise swiftly. The 18th CPC National Congress further advanced the basic requirements that must be firmly grasped in order to win a new victory in socialism with Chinese characteristics, among which the primacy of the people, the liberation and development of social productivity, the promotion of reform and opening up, the safeguarding of social justice, and the road to common prosperity must all be upheld, all of which are closely related to economic reform and development.

The 18th CPC National Congress, "gave prominence to the construction of eco-civilisation, integrating it into all aspects and processes of economic, political, cultural and social construction, striving to build a beautiful China and achieve the sustainable development of the Chinese nation". It thereby clarified the "five-sphere" integrated plan of the cause of socialism with Chinese characteristics, marking a new stage in China's socialist modernisation and reflecting a new dimension in the CPC's management of state affairs, fully demonstrating that the party is constantly summing up its experience in socialist construction, deepening its understanding of the laws of socialist construction, enriching its practice in the management of state affairs, and constantly improving its governance ability.

Focusing on the new theme of upholding and developing socialism with Chinese characteristics, the 18th CPC National Congress clearly defined the CPC's subsequent goals for governing and rejuvenating China, namely, building a moderately prosperous society in all respects and comprehensively deepening reform and opening up. In order to ensure that the ambitious goal of building a moderately prosperous society in all respects would be achieved by 2020, and in accordance with the actual nature of China's socioeconomic development and on the basis of the goals of building a moderately prosperous society in all aspects established by the 16th and 17th CPC National Congresses, the 18th CPC National Congress put forward new requirements to be diligently achieved. These new requirements were, namely, sustained and healthy economic development, continuous expansion of people's democracy, significant enhancement of cultural soft power, overall improvement in people's living standards, and significant progress in building a resource-saving and environmentally-friendly society. Among these, the concrete targets for sustainable and healthy economic development were to make significant progress in transforming China's mode of economic development, by achieving double the 2010 GDP level and per capita income of urban and rural residents on the basis of a marked strengthening of the balance, coordination and sustainability of development. The contribution of scientific and technological progress to economic growth has risen sharply and China has joined the ranks of innovative countries. Industrialisation has been basically achieved, the level of informatisation has been significantly raised, the quality of urbanisation has been significantly improved, the modernisation of agriculture and the construction of a new socialist countryside have been effective, and a mechanism for coordinated regional development has been basically formed. China's level of opening up to the outside world has been further improved and the country's international competitiveness has been significantly enhanced.

The 18th CPC National Congress also stressed that to build a moderately prosperous society in all respects, it was necessary to use greater political courage and wisdom, lose no time in deepening reforms in major areas, resolutely eliminate all ideologies, mindsets and shortcomings in institutional mechanisms that hinder scientific development, build a system that is systematic and complete, scientific and standardised, and operates effectively, and make various systems more mature and better established. At the same time, the report of the 18th CPC National Congress specifically pointed out that, "the evolving situation, the pioneering of the cause and the expectations of the people all require us to comprehensively promote the great new project of party building in the spirit of reform and innovation, and comprehensively improve the scientific level of party building"[7]. The 18th CPC National Congress laid out the requirement that, "The entire party must remember that only by being rooted among the people and benefiting them will the party always be invincible; only by being vigilant in peacetime and daring to forge ahead will the party always be at the forefront of the times".

The overall composition of socialism with Chinese characteristics and the new struggle goals show that the CPC has become more mature in its philosophy on the development of the cause of socialism with Chinese characteristics in the new historical period. The concept of being people-oriented and serving the people shines through the spirit of the 18th CPC National Congress, in that the approach of "doing more to improve the lives and address the concerns of the people" reflects everywhere the party's aim of serving the people wholeheartedly, and that when the people express their views, the ruling party answers. These are the new themes for upholding and developing socialism with Chinese characteristics in the new era, fully reflecting the belief in and ideals of the Marxist theory of historical materialism and the consistent belief in the CPC, and also heralding the new concept of governance of the new central leadership group after the 18th CPC National Congress, and constituting a continuation, lesson and innovation in the process of moving forward. After the 18th CPC National Congress, the Party Central Committee with Comrade Xi Jinping at its core, united and led the entire party and the people of all China's ethnic groups to hold high the great banner of socialism with Chinese characteristics, opening up a great struggle with many new historical characteristics and a brand-new journey to explore, deepen and develop the communist party's governance law. This latter-day subject of communist party governance in human history reveals a broader and deeper vision of time and space.

(III) FURTHER CLARIFICATION OF THE GOVERNANCE MISSION: ACHIEVING THE CHINESE DREAM OF THE GREAT REJUVENATION OF THE CHINESE NATION

After the 18th CPC National Congress, Xi Jinping and the party's new central leadership group were innovative and enterprising, determined and proactive, and soon opened up a new context in all aspects of the management of state affairs, demonstrating a new style of governance. Shortly after the closing of the 18th CPC National Congress, on 29 November 2012, Xi Jinping, Li Keqiang, Zhang Dejiang, Yu Zhengsheng, Liu Yunshan, Wang Qishan, Zhang Gaoli and other leading comrades of the central government visited the exhibition *The Road to Rejuvenation* at the National Museum of China. In a major speech delivered during the visit, Xi Jinping clearly put forward and elaborated on the struggle goal of the Chinese dream, stressing that achieving the great rejuvenation of the Chinese nation has been the greatest dream of the Chinese nation since the mid-19th century, and that he firmly believed that the goal of building a moderately prosperous society in all respects by the 100th anniversary of the founding of the CPC, the goal of building a rich, strong, democratic, civilised and harmonious socialist modern state by the 100th anniversary of the founding of new China, and the dream of the great rejuvenation of the Chinese nation would definitely be achieved.

After that, Xi Jinping made a number of important statements on the Chinese dream, systematically putting forward a series of new ideas, perspectives and assertions on the Chinese dream for the great rejuvenation of the Chinese nation. On 17 March 2013, in his speech after being elected national president for the first time, Xi Jinping pointed out that it was vital to deeply understand that achieving the Chinese dream means to achieve national prosperity, the revitalisation of China's ethnic groups and the happiness of the people, and that the Chinese dream is ultimately the people's dream and must be achieved by relying closely on the people, and must be continuously implemented for the people's benefit, and to unswervingly follow the Chinese path, carry forward the Chinese spirit, gather China's strength and continue to work for the people's welfare, forming a bridge between the past and the future, and continuing to courageously advance toward achieving the Chinese dream of the great rejuvenation of the Chinese nation. These important ideas and assertions had a powerful impact at home and abroad, fully reflecting the new central leadership group's firm confidence in socialism with Chinese characteristics and their responsibility toward the country, China's ethnic groups and the people, and became a major political declaration for the CPC to lead the Chinese nation toward prosperity and great rejuvenation. Making the accomplishment of the Chinese dream of the great rejuvenation of the Chinese nation the struggle goal of the CPC further clarified the essence and extent of the CPC's governance mission.

In terms of essence, the introduction and systematic elaboration of the Chinese dream of achieving the great rejuvenation of the Chinese nation made the goals and tasks to be accomplished by the CPC clearer and more specific, thereby reinforcing and highlighting the unique attributes and exclusivity of the CPC's governance mission itself, namely, in the new era, to achieve the Chinese dream of the great rejuvenation of the Chinese nation. And the Chinese dream of realising the great rejuvenation of the Chinese nation, as Xi Jinping pointed out, "is to achieve national prosperity and strength, the revitalisation of China's ethnic groups and the happiness of the people"[8]. These are the goals and tasks to be accomplished by CPC governance, and they alone constitute the concentrated visionary threshold for exploring the communist party's governance law in the new era for which there is no alternative.

It is important to note in particular that the happiness of the people occupies an important place in the Chinese dream. This is determined by the nature and aims of the communist party, and is fundamental to its governance as distinct from that of parties of the exploiting classes. Xi Jinping pointed out that, "The Chinese dream is the dream of the nation and the dream of every Chinese person"[9]. The people are the main focus of the Chinese dream. Socialism allows everyone to enjoy the opportunity to excel in life, to make their dreams come true, and to grow and progress with the motherland and with the times. By bringing together the aspirations of all the people of China for a happy life, the Chinese dream prompts the people to advance bravely. On the other hand, the Chinese dream also depends on the labour and creativity of the people as a whole in order to achieve it. Xi Jinping emphasised that, "The Chinese dream is ultimately the people's dream, which must be realised by relying closely on the people and must constantly be for their benefit"[10]. As Deng Xiaoping once said, "Empty talk misleads the country but practical work rejuvenates the nation". If more than 1.4 billion people work together to build the Chinese dream, the power to realise the dream will be immensely strong and the Chinese nation, which has undergone hardships but goes on growing forever, will be able to cross the proverbial river and accomplish the dream. Consequently, it is possible for the dreams of every Chinese person to come true in the historical logic of the words of Xi Jinping that "only when the country and China's ethnic groups are well will everyone be well".

In terms of extent, the introduction and systematic elaboration of the Chinese dream of achieving the great rejuvenation of the Chinese nation made the path for the CPC to accomplish its governance mission clearer and more concrete, thereby enriching and expanding the method and substance of the CPC's governance. In other words, it relates to how, in the new era, the CPC is to achieve the Chinese dream, how it is to govern well, and how it invigorates the country and enriches the people. In this regard, Xi Jinping stressed that to achieve the Chinese dream, it is necessary to adhere to the Chinese way, enhance the Chinese spirit and gather Chinese strength. This important assertion reveals the pathway to achieving the CPC's governance, its spiritual pillar and the strength on which it is to rely.

The major strategic ideology of achieving the Chinese dream of the great rejuvenation of the Chinese nation more closely links the struggle and exploration of the Chinese people since the mid-19th century, the struggle goal of the Two Centenaries, and upholding and developing socialism with Chinese characteristics, with the accomplishment of the great rejuvenation of the Chinese nation and the CPC's governance mission. This is a new exploration and an important innovation by the Chinese communists of the communist party's governance law. It not only makes it clear to the Chinese people that achieving the great rejuvenation of the Chinese nation is a higher goal than achieving modernisation, reflecting the high confidence of the CPC in China's future development, but also more closely links the CPC's governance mission, objectives and performance to the future prospects of China's ethnic groups, reflecting the fact that the future development of the party, the country, China's ethnic groups and the people are closely bound together in unity and destiny. It also reflects the CPC's high sense of responsibility and solemn mission toward the country, China's ethnic groups and the people.

(IV) THE PEOPLE'S ASPIRATION FOR A BETTER LIFE IS THE GOAL OF THE PARTY'S STRUGGLE

On 15 November 2012, just after the conclusion of the 1st Plenary Session of the 18th CPC Central Committee, in his first speech to Chinese and foreign journalists after becoming general secretary, Xi Jinping pointed out sincerely that, "our people love life and look forward to better education, more stable jobs, more satisfying income, more reliable social security, a higher level of medical and health services, more comfortable living conditions and a better environment. They expect their children to grow up, work, and live better than they themselves have". He solemnly proclaimed to the people of China and other countries, "The people's aspiration for a better life is the goal of our struggles"[11]. This presented a new governance issue for the CPC. The communist party comes from the people and is rooted in the people, and its insistence on establishing the party for the public and governing for the people constitutes the fundamental difference between the communist party and all political parties of the exploiting classes. In the words of Wen Jiabao, "Only when you put the people at the heart will the people let you take the stage". Although these words seem straightforward, they indicate the essence of the communist party's governance law. On 8 September 1944, Mao Zedong delivered his famous speech *Serve the People* at Zhang Side's memorial service, saying, "Our communist party, and the Eighth Route Army and the New Fourth Army led by the communist party, are the combat ranks of the revolution. These combat ranks of ours are entirely for the liberation of the people and work thoroughly for the interests of the people"[12]. He also said, "All of us working cadres, regardless of our position, are the servants of the people, and everything we do is in the service of the people"[13].

Although the reasoning is clear, in some countries in the world and at some times, the ruling communist party has not really implemented the governance concept of establishing the party for the public and governing for the people, thereby losing its governance position. It is in this sense that Xi Jinping admonished the party, saying "At all times and under all circumstances, the position of sharing the same destiny with the people must not change, the aim of serving the people wholeheartedly must not be forgotten, and the historical materialist view that the masses are the real heroes must not be lost". This means that serving the people wholeheartedly constitutes the "entire mission" and *raison d'être* of the CPC, and that firmly establishing and consciously practising the party's tenets is a political character that all communist party members must possess.

The times are developing and changing, and so are the interests of the people and the demands on the ruling party to safeguard the people's interests. As we enter a new era, the people have a clearer and more practical need to lead a better life, based on solving the problem of subsistence and escaping from the deprivation of material and cultural life. This has presented new requirements for the communist party's governance, namely, "to always put the people in the highest place in our hearts, always serve them wholeheartedly, and always work hard for their interests and happiness"[14].

After the 18th CPC National Congress, Xi Jinping and the new central leadership group fully practised the governance orientation of making people's aspiration for a better life the goal of their struggle, and strived to achieve, safeguard and develop the fundamental interests of the general public. In the period following the 18th CPC National Congress, in response to the security issues arising from development, Xi Jinping particularly emphasised that development should respect the safety of people's lives, and focus on safeguarding and improving people's livelihoods. In June 2013 he provided the direction that, "Human lives are at stake and development must not come at the expense of human lives. This must be treated as a red line that must not be crossed"[15]. Improving people's livelihoods is the purpose of development and the demand for this is constantly increasing. Xi Jinping attached great importance to this and proposed to work successfully with regard to people's livelihoods according to the thinking of "holding the bottom line, highlighting priorities, refining systems and guiding public opinion". "Holding the bottom line" means to focus on protecting the basic livelihoods of low-income people and to successfully provide subsidies for college students living in hardship. "Highlighting priorities" means to pay attention to stabilising and expanding employment, especially to encourage entrepreneurship and employment, and to create jobs through multiple channels. "Refining systems" means to uphold a policy of full coverage, basic protection, and being multi-layered and sustainable, to strengthen the construction of urban and rural livelihood protection systems, continue to improve the methods of transfer and succession of endowment insurance, and raise the level of coordination. It also means to continue to strengthen the construction and management of affordable housing and accelerate the transformation of shantytowns. "Guiding public opinion" means promoting the formation of a good climate of public opinion and life expectancy, and guiding the general public to establish for themselves the concept of improving their lives through becoming affluent by their own efforts, so that improving people's livelihoods is both the direction of of party and government work and the goal of the people's own struggle.

(V) PREPARING FOR AND IMPLEMENTING A GREAT STRUGGLE WITH MANY NEW HISTORICAL CHARACTERISTICS

The 18th CPC National Congress clearly proposed that, "the development of socialism with Chinese characteristics is a long and arduous historical task, and great struggles with many new historical characteristics must be prepared for and implemented"[16]. This was the position advocated by Xi Jinping when he chaired the drafting of the report for the 18th CPC National Congress[17]. After that, Xi Jinping repeatedly pointed out that, "we are engaged in a great struggle with many new historical characteristics"[18] and "we must prepare to carry out a great struggle with many new historical characteristics". This assertion with "profound connotations" speaks to the new situation and new tasks facing the CPC in the new era of governance and is an important reflection of the communist party's governance law in the new historical period.

The communist party is a Marxist party that dares to engage in struggle. The CPC, in particular, has made it its great trait to dare to struggle. In the history of the development of human civilisation, there has never been a shortage of political groups, model figures and vivid examples who have dared to struggle, both in ancient and modern times, in China and overseas, and regardless of nationality. But never has there been a political party or group like the CPC that has faced such daunting challenges and risks in the context of struggle, paid so much in blood and in the self-sacrificing of lives in such a moving way, where the characters and model that emerged were so many, which has lasted so long, and whose results and achievements have been so remarkable. On the great journey to achieve national independence and people's liberation, the Chinese communists dared to struggle and win, completing the New Democratic Revolution and establishing the PRC. On the great journey to carry out socialist revolution and construction, they dared to fight and struggle, and made great achievements in socialist revolution and construction. On the great journey of reform and opening up, and the pioneering and development of socialism with Chinese characteristics, they dared to break through and to experiment with new approaches, and created a miracle in the history of human social development. It can be said that the history of the CPC's development over the past century and its 70-year history of national governance is the history of the struggles of the Chinese communists. Generations of Chinese communists have passed on the burning torch of their work to the next generation, advanced in wave upon wave, and struggled while soaked in their own blood, uniting and leading the Chinese people to compose the magnificent poem of the great rejuvenation of the Chinese nation.

After the 18th CPC National Congress, Xi Jinping and the new central leadership group made daring to struggle a distinctive feature of their governance, and carried forward and promoted this great characteristic. In the period following the 18th CPC National Congress, the Party Central Committee and Xi Jinping not only prepared for, but actually engaged in, many "great struggles". For instance, in the fight against corruption, the CPC implemented a large-scale campaign unprecedented since the founding of new China to "fight tigers"(corrupt senior officials), "swat flies" (corrupt low-ranking bureaucrats) and "hunt foxes" (fugitives abroad suspected of major economic crimes). Faced by a number of countries stirring up trouble in the South China Sea, the Party Central Committee and Xi Jinping also clearly demonstrated China's practical action to firmly defend China's national sovereignty. In addition, in the face of a highly leveraged and risky economic situation, the Party Central Committee and Xi Jinping steadfastly carried out supply-side structural reforms and implemented a struggle to deleverage and prevent risks. These behavioural measures and powerful actions with a realistic orientation fully reflect the major ambitious strategy of the Party Central Committee, with Comrade Xi Jinping at the core, to govern and rejuvenate China, and its responsibility to manage state affairs.

With the further enrichment and development of its governance practice, the Party Central Committee became more mature in its achievement of, and philosophy on, implementing great struggles. At the Politburo's Democratic Life Meeting at the end of 2016, Xi Jinping further pointed out that "in the face of the new situation and new challenges, it is necessary to carry forward the spirit of struggle, both daring to struggle and also struggling successfully"[19]. In October 2017, the 19th CPC National Congress systematically elaborated on the great struggle from a theoretical perspective, juxtaposing the implementation of the great struggle with the accomplishment of great dreams, the construction of great projects and the promotion of great undertakings, configuring the main elements of the historical mission of the CPC in the new era and forming a complete theoretical system. The implementation of the great struggle and the governance mission of the CPC have since been organically unified in theory and practice.

The governance cause of the communist party is an unprecedented and ground-breaking one, and there is no precedent for success to be followed in the governance cause of the CPC. The mission of the CPC to achieve the great rejuvenation of the Chinese nation will encounter many new problems at all stages of its development, and it must always promote the resolution of various conflicts and problems in a spirit of struggle characterised by forging ahead and enterprise. Of course, the word "struggle" in the spirit of struggle advocated by the communist party does not mean, in the vulgar philosophical sense, fighting or contention between different people, groups or organisations for the sake of different interests, and it is absolutely not another instance of "taking class struggle as the central task". Rather it means that in the new journey of focusing on economic construction, the party must not lose the mindset of daring to face up to contradictions and the truth, and must dare to make all-out efforts, do good work, and overcome practical difficulties. Without this, the communist party's great governance work will suffer setbacks.

2

THE 'FOUR COMPREHENSIVES'

A NEW STRATEGIC DESIGN FOR THE PARTY'S MANAGEMENT OF STATE AFFAIRS

In the period following the 18th CPC National Congress, the Party Central Committee, with Comrade Xi Jinping at its core, took up the baton of history, built on the successive struggles of the party and the people since the founding of new China, and continued to plan the great task of governing and rejuvenating China on the path of socialism with Chinese characteristics, successfully "cracking" the new issue of the communist party's governance law in the new era. On this basis, the answers to the new issues of communist party governance in the new era have been implemented in an orderly manner in the governing practice of the Party Central Committee with Comrade Xi Jinping as the core. The "Four Comprehensives", the new strategic layout of the CPC's management of state affairs, configured the main elements of the answers to the new issues of governance.

From the proposition of the 18th CPC National Congress to "build a moderately prosperous society in all respects", to the arrangements of the 3rd Plenary Session of the 18th CPC Central Committee to "comprehensively deepen reform", to the call of the 4th Plenary Session of the 18th CPC Central Committee for "the comprehensive rule of law" to the concluding conference of the campaign for mass line education and practice declaring there would be a "comprehensive promotion of strict party governance", and then to Xi Jinping's first reference to the "strict party governance" during his survey in Jiangsu in December 2014 along with the proposition of the comprehensive building of a moderately prosperous society in all respects, the comprehensive deepening of reform, and the comprehensive development of the party, the strategic composition of the "Four Comprehensives" was clearly revealed. In February 2015, in his speech at a special seminar for major leading cadres at the provincial and ministerial levels to study and implement the spirit of the 4th Plenary Session of the 18th CPC Central Committee and comprehensively promote the rule of law, Xi Jinping clearly put forward for the first time the strategic composition of the Four Comprehensives. The Four Comprehensives strategy was derived from the practical needs of China's development and from the ardent expectations of the people and was proposed to promote the resolution of the prominent contradictions and problems facing China. They are based on the overall situation of the management of state affairs, grasp the key to reform, development and stability, and lead the master-plan of China's development, establishing the strategic direction, key areas and main objectives of the CPC's governance and rejuvenation of China under the new situation.

(I) BUILDING A MODERATELY PROSPEROUS SOCIETY IN ALL RESPECTS AND ACHIEVING SOCIALIST MODERNISATION: A NEW PLAN FOR GOVERNANCE OBJECTIVES

The CPC is a party that attaches great importance to the selection and setting of strategic objectives. During various historical periods when it led and promoted revolution, construction and reform, it has put forward inspirational goals in accordance with the wishes of the people and the development needs of its cause, and united and led the broad masses of people to strive for these. After a long-term and unremitting struggle, China has entered a new stage of development in which it has built a moderately prosperous society in all respects and accelerated its socialist modernisation. The report of the 18th CPC National Congress clearly advanced the new requirements for achieving the struggle goal of building a moderately prosperous society in all respects, planning an ambitious development blueprint for China by 2020, and clearly declaring that the construction of a moderately prosperous society in all respects will be accomplished by the time of the centenary of the CPC's founding, and that a rich, strong, democratic, civilised and harmonious modern socialist state will have been built by the time of the centenary of the founding of new China. The planning of this goal brought the party's governance more closely in line with the future prospects of the nation and clearly indicated the governance mission and role of the CPC in the new era.

Achieving the goal of building a moderately prosperous society in all respects is a key step towards achieving the Chinese dream of the great rejuvenation of the Chinese nation and is the primary goal of the CPC in the new era of governing and rejuvenating China. The core of building a moderately prosperous society in all respects lies in its comprehensiveness. This comprehensiveness is reflected in the fact that the population coverage is comprehensive. It is a comprehensive moderate prosperity with no distinction between regions and that leaves no one behind, so this comprehensiveness is reflected in the fact that the geographical coverage is comprehensive.

This comprehensive moderate prosperity is one which ensures "the cadres are clean, the government is clean, and the politics is sober" and "finds the greatest possible agreement on the wishes and demands of society as a whole", where "urban-rural dualism is broken down and a better home for farmers to live happily is built", where "China's material and spiritual strength are enhanced and the material and spiritual lives of the people of all China's ethnic groups are improved", which "enables the people to sense fairness and justice in every judicial case" which, as Xi Jinping said, "enables people to enjoy the natural landscape, retain their love of nature, and maintain a sense of nostalgia" and which "opens up new horizons in national defence and military construction in the spirit of reform and innovation" and "provides strong support for the realisation of the Chinese dream". The 18th CPC National Congress made it clear that the objectives of building a moderately prosperous society in all respects include sustained and healthy economic development, continuous expansion of people's democracy, significant enhancement of cultural soft power, overall improvement in people's living standards, and significant progress in building a resource-saving and environmentally-friendly society.

From 2016, China entered the implementation period of the 13th Five-Year Guidelines for National Economic and Social Development and the decisive stage of the first of the Two Centenaries struggle goals of building a moderately prosperous society in all respects and achieving the CPC's struggle goal of governing and rejuvenating China.

After 30 more years of struggle to build a moderately prosperous society in all respects, the party will basically have achieved modernisation and have built China into a modern socialist power by the 100th anniversary of the founding of new China. This was the basic content of party literature on the second of the Two Centenaries struggle goals before the 19th CPC National Congress. The 19th CPC National Congress made a comprehensive analysis of the international and domestic situation and the conditions of China's development, and made a two-stage strategic arrangement for the period from 2020 to the middle of this century, the time when the second of the Two Centenaries goals is to be achieved, putting forward new specific goals.

The first stage, from 2020 to 2035, on the basis of building a moderately prosperous society in all respects, will be the basic achievement of socialist modernisation after a further 15 years of struggle. By then, the following will have happened. China's economic, scientific and technological strength will have risen significantly and be at the forefront of all innovative countries, and the people's right to equal participation and development will be fully guaranteed. The system characterised by the state, government and society being governed by the rule of law will basically have been built, various institutions will have been further refined, and the modernisation of the national governance system and governance ability will have been basically achieved. China's level of social civilisation will have reached new heights, its cultural soft power will have been significantly enhanced, and the influence of Chinese culture will be more extensive and in-depth. The people's livelihoods will be more affluent, the proportion of middle-income groups will have increased significantly, the gap between urban and rural regional development, and residents' living standards will have narrowed significantly, the equalisation of basic public services will have been basically achieved, and the common prosperity of the people as a whole will have taken a solid step forward. The modern social governance pattern will have been basically formed, society will be vibrant, harmonious and orderly, China's ecosystems will have fundamentally improved and the goal of building a beautiful China will have been basically achieved[1].

In the second stage, from 2035 to the middle of this century, on the basis of the basic achievement of modernisation, the party will struggle for a further 15 years to build China into a rich, strong, democratic, civilised, harmonious and beautiful modern socialist power. By that time, China's material, political, spiritual, social and eco-civilisations will have been comprehensively upgraded, and its national system of governance and governance ability will have been modernised. China will be a leading country in terms of comprehensive national power and international influence, the common prosperity of the people as a whole will have been basically achieved, the people of China will enjoy a happier and more prosperous life, and the Chinese nation will stand taller among the nations of the world[2].

Building a moderately prosperous society in all respects and achieving socialist modernisation, as the goal for the CPC's governance, is the starting and end point for comprehensively deepening reform, ruling the country in accordance with the rule of law and strict party governance, and occupies the leadership position in the strategic layout of the Four Comprehensives. The strategic layout of the CPC's governance in the new era is being gently implemented in the planning for the goals of building a moderately prosperous society in all respects and achieving socialist modernisation.

(II) COMPREHENSIVELY DEEPENING REFORM: PROMOTING MODERNISATION OF THE NATIONAL SYSTEM OF GOVERNANCE AND GOVERNANCE ABILITY

In order to demonstrate his determination to continue to promote reform and open up, Xi Jinping visited Shenzhen, Zhuhai, Foshan and Guangzhou, the frontiers of China's reform and opening up, on his first inspection trip outside Beijing from 7 to 11 December 2012, and conducted in-depth investigations and research in rural areas, enterprises, communities, army units and research institutes. He emphasised that, "reform and opening up is the source of vitality for the development and progress of contemporary China, an important and highly effective methodology for our party and people to make great strides to catch up with the times, and the only way to uphold and develop socialism with Chinese characteristics". This demonstrated to other countries and to the people of China the strong determination and firm will of the party's new central leadership group to "unceasingly implement reform and opening up". At the end of December, shortly after returning to Beijing from Guangdong, Xi Jinping presided over the second collective study of the Politburo of the 18th CPC Central Committee, the theme of which was to review and study the history of China's reform and opening up, and to unswervingly continue to promote it. In April 2013, during informal discussions with Chinese and foreign entrepreneurs attending the 2013 annual meeting of the Bo'ao Forum for Asia, Xi Jinping once again declared unequivocally that, "China's open door will not be closed", "China will raise the level of openness of its economy on a broader scale, broader areas and at a deeper level", and that China "resolutely opposes any form of protectionism"[3].

In the period after that, the party's new central leadership group took the reform of the administrative approval system and the transformation of government functions as an area of breakthrough to be seized and launched a series of successive and major reform measures in the fields of taxation, finance, prices, investment financing, livelihood protection, social management, eco-civilisation construction, agriculture and rural areas. As a result, some prominent contradictions and problems that had long restricted socioeconomic development began to be solved.

Based on ideological preparation and practical exploration, the *Decision of the CPC Central Committee on Several Major Issues Regarding Comprehensively Deepening Reform*, deliberated and adopted at the 3rd Plenary Session of the 18th CPC Central Committee in November 2013 put forward a systematic plan and specific requirements for comprehensively deepening reform. Thereby the CPC further clarified its strategic intent of using reform and opening up as the "key move" to govern and rejuvenate China, and elevated reform and opening up to the level of "comprehensive deepening" in the new era, achieving a series of major breakthroughs in reform theory and policies, and forming a strategic format for the comprehensive deepening of reform.

The content and practice of the comprehensive deepening of reform is implemented closely based on general objectives. Xi Jinping pointed out that, "the general objective of comprehensively deepening reform must be understood and grasped in its entirety; it is a whole composed of two parts". "The former part sets out the fundamental orientation, and our orientation is the path of socialism with Chinese characteristics and no other", and "the latter part sets out the distinctive orientation of refining and developing the socialist system with Chinese characteristics under the guidance of the fundamental orientation. It is only when both parts are presented together that they constitute a complete whole. To state only the second part and not the first is incomplete and incomprehensive"[4]. The reasoning and method of reform is to uphold "thinking which is strategic, dialectical, characterised by the rule of law, systematic, representative of the baseline and innovative", to deal with "the relationships between emancipating the mind and seeking truth from facts, between overall promotion and key breakthroughs, between top-level design and improvising by trial and error, between boldness and steady steps, and between reform, development and stability", to "promote reform correctly, accurately, and in an orderly and coordinated manner", and to make precise efforts and move at a steady pace[5].

The direction of socialism with Chinese characteristics is the fundamental basis, root and soul of the comprehensive deepening of reform, and is also the fundamental conclusion drawn by the CPC from the historical experience of both positive and negative aspects of the governance of communist parties in various countries. In the process of governing China and comprehensively deepening reform, the CPC must not make subversive mistakes on fundamental issues and must maintain its strategic determination and the correct course of reform. On this basis, the CPC clearly set the modernisation of the national system of governance and governance ability as another strategic goal of modernisation, following on from the Four Modernisations. This is both an objective requirement for the reform process itself to expand forward, reflecting the deepening and systematisation of the CPC's knowledge of reform, and also a new requirement for CPC governance in the new era, reflecting the CPC's new understanding of the communist party's governance law.

On 30 December 2013, the Central Leading Group for Comprehensively Deepening Reform, headed by Xi Jinping, was established to be responsible for the overall design, coordination, promotion and supervision of the implementation of reform. In order to grasp reform in various fields, the Central Leading Group for Comprehensively Deepening Reforms set up several special groups for the reform of the economy and eco-civilisation, the democratic legal system, the cultural system, the social system, the system of party building and the system of discipline inspection, in order to "coordinate and deal with major reform issues of an overall, long-term, interregional and intersectoral nature". Since then, the comprehensive deepening of reform has deepened and advanced step by step.

(III) COMPREHENSIVELY RULING CHINA IN ACCORDANCE WITH THE LAW: FURTHER MANIFESTING THE BASIC STRATEGY OF THE PARTY LEADING THE PEOPLE TO GOVERN THE COUNTRY

The 18th CPC National Congress put forward the goal for the governance and rejuvenation of China to build a moderately prosperous society in all respects, and the 3rd Plenary Session of the 18th CPC Central Committee made a top-level design for the governance "key move" of comprehensively deepening reform. To achieve this goal of governing and rejuvenating China and to implement this top-level design, it was necessary to provide reliable protection on the basis of the rule of law. In October 2014, one year after launching the comprehensive deepening of reform, the 4th Plenary Session of the 18th CPC Central Committee deliberated and adopted the *Decision of the CPC Central Committee on Several Major Issues Concerning Comprehensive Promotion of the Rule of Law*. Thereby, the comprehensive rule of law was incorporated into the strategic design of the CPC's governance in the new era.

The 4th Plenary Session of the 18th CPC Central Committee and the *Decision* designed a general blueprint, roadmap and construction plan for comprehensively promoting the rule of law and building a socialist state under the rule of law. The *Decision* answered the question of the unity of the rule of law from the angle of top-level design from the perspectives of the party leadership, the sovereignty of the people, the organic unity of the rule of law, and the integration of the rule of law and rule by virtue. It also answered the question of the coordination of the rule of law with regard to the "five major systems of the rule of law", the "three joint promotions" and the "three integrated constructions", from the perspective of national governance. It also answered the question of the systemic nature of the rule of law with regard to "scientific legislation, strict law enforcement, impartial justice and universal compliance with the law" from the perspective of the participating subjects. In particular, on the fundamental issue of the relationship between the party leadership and the rule of law, the *Decision* clarified the fact that that the CPC is the leading core of the cause of socialism with Chinese characteristics and is in a position to oversee the overall situation and coordinate all parties, and also emphasised that the socialist rule of law must uphold the party leadership and that the party leadership must rely on the socialist rule of law[6]. Deepening understanding of the rule of law constitutes precisely the self-transcendence and self-improvement of the ruling party in the process of governance.

With the deployment and arrangements of the 4th Plenary Session of the 18th CPC Central Committee, the governance concept of comprehensively promoting the rule of law and accelerating the building of a socialist state under the rule of law was concentratedly manifested in the CPC's governance practice. After the 4th Plenary Session of the 18th CPC Central Committee, the CPC upheld the leadership of the party as the fundamental guarantee, accelerated improvement of the leadership system of the comprehensive rule of law, and starting from China's realities fully utilised its political advantages, complied with the laws of the rule of law, progressively advanced its concepts and innovative institutional mechanisms, and comprehensively deepened its practice of implementing the rule of law. The party upheld the full implementation of the constitution as the primary task, and effectively strengthened implementation and supervision of the constitution. It also strictly implemented the provisions of the constitution, improved the mechanism for reviewing constitutionality with Chinese characteristics, and ensured that unconstitutional acts are redressed and pursued in a timely manner.

On 1 November 2014, the 11th meeting of the 12th NPC Standing Committee voted to adopt the *Decision on the Establishment of National Constitution Day*, establishing 4 December as National Constitution Day through legislation and providing for the implementation of constitutional propaganda and education activities through various means. In February 2015, at a special seminar organised by the CPC Central Committee for leading cadres at the provincial and ministerial levels to study and implement the spirit of the 4th Plenary Session of the 18th CPC Central

Committee to comprehensively promote the rule of law, Xi Jinping delivered a major speech emphasising that the belief, determination and actions of leading cadres at all levels are of great importance in comprehensively promoting the rule of law, and in order to comprehensively promote the rule of law it was necessary to win over the "key minority" of leading cadres. Leading cadres should be models of respect for the law, taking the lead in respecting the rule of law and the laws of China, be models of learning the law, taking the lead in understanding China's laws and mastering them, be models of abiding by the law, taking the lead in complying with the law and defending the rule of law, and be models of using the law, taking the lead in enforcing the rule of law and acting in accordance with the law[7]. On 1 July of the same year, the 15th meeting of the 12th NPC Standing Committee voted to adopt the *Decision on the Implementation of the Constitutional Oath System*, which provides for the public taking of the constitutional oath when state employees assume office.

In the five years between the 18th and 19th CPC National Congresses, the state enacted or amended 48 laws, including the *National Security Law*, the *Administrative Procedure Law*, 42 administrative regulations, 2,926 local regulations and 3,162 other regulations, making the socialist legal system with Chinese characteristics more complete. In December 2014, the seventh meeting of the Central Leading Group for Comprehensively Deepening Reform deliberated and adopted the *Pilot Programme for the Establishment of Circuit Courts of the Supreme People's Court* and the *Pilot Programme for the Establishment of People's Courts and People's Procuratorates Across Administrative Regions*, further advancing a new round of judicial system reform. In March and December 2015, the CPC Central Committee and the State Council successively issued the *Guiding Opinions on Implementing the Power List System of Local Government Departments at All Levels* and the *Outline for the Implementation of the Construction of a Government Which Upholds the Rule of Law (2015-2020)*, whereby the construction of a government which upholds the rule of law entered a new stage. In November 2015, the 18th meeting of the Central Leading Group for Comprehensively Deepening Reform deliberated and adopted the *Guiding Opinions on Furthering Reform of the Urban Law Enforcement System and Improving Urban Management*, whereby reform of the administrative law enforcement system was further advanced. In March 2016, the CPC Central Committee and the State Council transmitted the *Seventh Five-Year Guidelines of the Central Propaganda Department and the Ministry of Justice on Publicity and Education on the Rule of Law Among Citizens (2016-2020)*, whereby the building of a society governed by the rule of law took new steps.

The comprehensive rule of law is a systematic project ,and a new and profound revolution in the field of the communist party governance. It will have a significant and direct impact on adherence to and development of the path of the socialist rule of law with Chinese characteristics, building a socialist legal system with Chinese characteristics, and promoting modernisation of the national system of governance and governance ability, as well as providing a strong guarantee for the success of communist party governance. It will also have a significant and far-reaching impact on the exploration of new strategies and thinking for the communist party's leadership of the people in governing China under modern conditions.

(IV) COMPREHENSIVE STRICT GOVERNANCE OF THE PARTY: STRENGTHENING THE FOUNDATIONS FOR THE LONG-TERM STABILITY OF THE PARTY AND THE STATE

In December 2014 during his research trip to Jiangsu, Xi Jinping emphasised that it was necessary to "coordinate the building of a moderately prosperous society in all respects, comprehensively deepen reform, promote the rule of law, govern the party strictly, and propel reform and opening up and socialist modernisation to a new level"[8]. This is the first time that the CPC advanced a precise explanation of the Four Comprehensives in its entirety in the context of the overall strategic management of China.

In the face of difficult and complex situations and tasks, after the 18th CPC National Congress the Party Central Committee with Comrade Xi Jinping at its core always upheld the principle that the party should be responsible for managing itself, steadfastly promoted the comprehensive strict governance of the party, and always put the great self-revolution of the party in a prominent position. With a clear mindset that, in the words of Xi Jinping, "iron must harden itself", the party promoted a brand-new party and political culture and, with the strong will to tackle disease with powerful medicine and a firm hand, and strike with power and great courage, the spirt of the party and the people was greatly lifted.

As early as November 2012, at a meeting with Chinese and foreign journalists at the beginning of his tenure after the 18th CPC National Congress, Xi Jinping described his responsibility to the nation, the people and the party as being ruling the party strictly and making the party a strong leadership core at all times. He said, "Our responsibility, together with that of all our party comrades, is to insist that the party should manage itself and govern it strictly, and to effectively solve the prominent problems that exist in the party"[9]. In December 2012, the Politburo of the CPC Central Committee deliberated and adopted eight provisions on improving work style and keeping in close contact with the masses. The eight provisions, which are just over 600 words long, set out rules for strengthening work style construction without being overcautious and using unimaginative or empty slogans, and faced up to practical issues, putting forward specific requirements. This is the first starting point for the Party Central Committee, with Comrade Xi Jinping at its core, to gain deep insight into the problems within the party and grasp the overall strict governance of the party. Xi Jinping took the lead in making a commitment and issuing a call to action, stating that, "To build a clean party style, we must start with the leading cadres, and from among the leading cadres we must first start with the party's central leadership. As the saying goes, if you are not correct yourself, how can you correct others?" He also said, "The rules act as a constraint, so must be strict", and "If we are a little uncomfortable and uneasy, the people will be a little more comfortable, a little more satisfied and feel better about us. This is also a new form and a new climate"[10]. The majority of party members and cadres were ideologically and politically aligned with the Party Central Committee with Comrade Xi Jinping at its core and took the implementation of the eight provisions of the Central Committee as a major political task to be grasped. As the saying goes, "Small moves drive great change", and so the eight provisions of the Central Committee have become the brilliant signature feature of the CPC's grasp of the overall strict governance of the party, and signature words to change the CPC's party style and China's social climate.

After this, from June 2013 to October 2014, the Party Central Committee organised the party's mass line education and practical activities focused on being pragmatic, practical and uncorrupted for the people, adhering to the general requirements of metaphorically "looking in the mirror, grooming their apparel, bathing and curing maladies", focusing on formalism, bureaucratism, hedonism and extravagance that have emerged during the party's long period of governance. In the spirit of rectification, they conducted a major investigation, overhaul and clean-up of neglected internal party ideology, the ills of work style and disgraceful conduct, and explored a set of effective practices to solve the problems of the governing party's work style by relying on the party's own strength and the active participation of the people. In April 2015, the Party Central Committee launched the "Three Stricts and Three Steadies" special education, seizing on the "key minority" of leading cadres above the county level to seriously rectify unstrict and unsteady tendencies using the Three Stricts and Three Steadies, and promote the progressiveness and purity of the whole party in the context of governance. From February 2016 onwards, the Party

Central Committee organised the "Two Studies, One Action" study and education among all party members, and in February 2017 made major arrangements to promote the normalisation and institutionalisation of the Two Studies, One Action study and education, promoting the expansion of intra-party education starting from the "key minority" to the majority of party members, and from centralised education to regular education.

After the 18th CPC National Congress, with the introduction of the eight provisions of the Central Committee as the starting point, the construction of work style as the point of breakthrough, the strict discipline of the party and the maintenance of party unity as the driving force, and the "fighting tigers", "swatting flies" and "hunting foxes" as the handle of which to grasp hold, the strategic thinking of the CPC on the overall strict governance of the party has continued to mature in practice. The core issue in the overall strict governance of the party is to always maintain vibrant connections between the ruling communist party and the people, and the party's progressiveness and purity, and the focus is on strictly governing officials, correcting the culture and fighting corruption, and strictly disciplining the party, while the goal is to enhance the party's ability to purify, refine, renew and improve itself, so as to ensure that the party is always a strong leadership core for the cause of socialism with Chinese characteristics. Within the concept of the comprehensive strict governance of the party, "comprehensiveness" constitutes the foundation, the close integration of ideological party building and institutional party governance, the organic unity of constructing rules and regulations, and implementing them, and a two-way interaction which is both top-down and bottom-up. "Strictness" is the main line, so education, standards, discipline, punishment and the system must all be strict, hence the word "strict" runs through the whole process and every aspect of managing and governing the party. "Management" and "governance" are the key, and "management" and "governance" pertain to political, ideological, organisational, work style, discipline, and institutional construction, as well as fighting corruption and advocating probity. They also pertain to the integration of the ideological construction of the party and its institutional governance, strict intraparty political life, strict management of cadres, continuous and in-depth improvement of work style, serving to supervise the people, and grasping the specific tasks relating to the rules of party governance.

In the strategic design of the CPC's governance, the most fundamental thing in coordinating promotion of the Four Comprehensives is to uphold the leadership of the party without wavering. The leadership of the party is the soul of the Four Comprehensives and the commander of the army in terms of strategy. If the party is ruled strictly across the board and a strong leadership core is forged, it will provide direction for coordinated promotion of the Four Comprehensives and prevent subversive mistakes on major issues. It will also be possible to continuously strengthen and improve the party leadership, provide political assurance for coordinated promotion of the Four Comprehensives, and build consensus and strength for the party's governance mission in the new era.

3

THE NEW CONCEPT OF DEVELOPMENT

A NEW UNDERSTANDING OF THE LAWS OF DEVELOPMENT IN CHINA

Development is the first priority of the party in governing and rejuvenating China. The loss of power by communist parties in some countries in the late 1980s and early 1990s was ultimately due to a failure to address the issue of development. For China, which is still in the primary stage of socialism and is the largest developing country in the world, development is the key to solving all of the nation's problems and to the CPC's governance of China. In the face of the new circumstances and problems encountered in China's development, such as the country's economy entering the reality of a new normal, the Party Central Committee with Comrade Xi Jinping at its core put forward a new concept of development, which elevated the party's understanding of the laws of China's development to a new level and provided theoretical guidance and a guide to action for opening up a new horizon for China's development, propelling it to a higher level.

(I) A MAJOR JUDGMENT THAT ECONOMIC DEVELOPMENT HAS ENTERED A NEW NORMAL

From the launch of reform and opening up to 2010, China's economy maintained a sustained rapid rate of growth for 32 years, creating a miracle in the history of global economic growth. However, China's economic growth slowed significantly after 2010, with GDP growth falling from 10.4% in 2010 to 9.3% in 2011, 7.7% in 2012, 7.7% in 2013, 7.4% in 2014, 6.9% in 2015, 6.7% in 2016 and 6.9% in the first half of 2017. At the same

503

time, China's development was notably unbalanced, uncoordinated and unsustainable, environmental resources and population constraints were strengthened, traditional comparative advantages weakened and, in the context of a continued downturn in international markets and slowing domestic demand growth, the contradiction of oversupply in some industries become increasingly pronounced and there was a general overcapacity in traditional manufacturing industries. Since then, China's economy has demonstrated new trends and how these new trends are perceived will determine the economic development strategy to be adopted and impact whether healthy economic development can be sustained.

It was under the guidance of this historical context and the goal of building a moderately prosperous society in all respects established by the 18th CPC National Congress that the Party Central Committee launched a new exploration and in-depth consideration of the major issues of China's economic development. In December 2012, shortly after the 18th CPC National Congress, Xi Jinping pointed out during an inspection tour to Guangdong that, "accelerating the promotion of the strategic restructuring of the economy is utterly essential and demands immediate action. International competition has always been a competition in terms of time and speed. Whoever moves fast can seize the first opportunity and control the high ground and initiative while whoever moves slowly will lose the opportunity and be left behind by others"[1]. Also in December 2012, the Central Economic Work Conference analysed the specific changes in the essence and conditions of China's period of strategic opportunity in terms of the international environment, stating that "the opportunities we face are no longer the traditional ones of simply integrating into the global division of labour system, expanding exports and accelerating investment but new ones that force us to expand domestic demand, improve our capacity for innovation and promote a change in the mode of economic development"[2].

Based on a scientific analysis of the new features of China's new stage of economic development, a new summary and judgment of China's economic development by the Party Central Committee and Xi Jinping gradually took shape. In October 2013, while attending the APEC Business Leaders Summit, Xi Jinping outlined the main features of China's economic development at that time, emphasising that "China's economy has already entered a new stage of development and is undergoing profound modal changes and structural adjustments"[3]. In December 2013, the Central Economic Work Conference made the important judgment that China's economy was in a specific situation referred to as the "three overlapping periods: the period of changing gears in economic growth, the painful period of structural adjustment, and the digestion period of previous stimulus policies"[4]. In May 2014, Xi Jinping first used the concept of the "new normal" during his inspection tour in Henan Province. He stated that, "We should enhance our confidence, start from characteristics of the current phase of China's economic development, adapt to the new normal, and maintain a stable mindset in terms of strategy"[5]. On July 29 of the same year, at a forum for non-party figures held by the central government, Xi Jinping, when asked about the economic situation at that time, again referred to the new normal, stressing that it was necessary "to correctly understand the characteristics of the current phase of China's economic development, further enhance confidence, adapt to the new normal and jointly promote sustainable and healthy economic development"[6].

From the strategic judgment on the important strategic opportunity period for China's development, to the accurate grasp of the new characteristics and changes in the stage of development, to the introduction of the new normal of economic development, it is clear to see that the strategic judgment made by the central government that economic development had entered a new normal is in line with the international economic situation and China's domestic economic realities. It is not a simple interpretation of the decline in the growth rate of China's economic development but a new historical positioning of the stage of China's economic development. In this regard, Xi Jinping emphasised that, "We propose to accurately grasp and actively adapt to the new normal of economic development which is a judgment made by adapting to changes in the international and domestic environment, and dialectically analysing the characteristics of the current phase of China's economic development. To accurately grasp the new changes and characteristics of the different stages of China's development, to make the subjective world better conform to the objective reality, and to decide on the working approach in accordance with the reality, is a working method that we must keep in mind"[7].

As soon as the new normal of economic development was proposed, it attracted widespread domestic and international attention. But how to understand the new normal was a matter of opinion. In November 2014, at the opening ceremony of the APEC Business Leaders Summit, Xi Jinping analysed three aspects of the new normal of China's economic development, saying "First, there has been a shift from a high rate of growth to a medium-to-high rate of growth. Second, the economic structure is constantly being optimised and upgraded, with the tertiary sector and consumer demand gradually becoming the main aspect; the gap between urban and rural areas is gradually narrowing, the proportion of residents' income is rising, and the fruits of development are benefiting the wider public. Third, there is a shift from being factor-driven and investment-driven to being innovation-driven"[8]. On this basis, in December 2014, the Central Economic Work Conference made a comprehensive and systematic elaboration of the new normal of economic development. The conference analysed the trending changes in nine aspects of China's economy, including consumer demand, investment demand, exports and balance of payments, production capacity and industrial organisation, the relative advantages of production factors, the characteristics of market competition, resource and environmental constraints, the accumulation and resolution of economic risks, resource allocation patterns and macrocontrol methods. From this the conference made the important judgment that China's economy is evolving towards a more advanced form, a more complex division of labour and a more rational structure. From this it drew the major conclusions of the "Four Shifts" that China's economic development under the new normal was undergoing, namely that, "the growth rate is shifting from a high growth rate of about 10% to a medium-to-high growth rate of about 7%, the mode of economic development is shifting from extensive growth based on scale and speed to intensive growth based on quality and efficiency, the structure of the economy is shifting from a predominantly incremental expansion to an adjustment of stocks, and the momentum of economic development is shifting from traditional growth points to new growth points"[9].

The "Nine Trending Changes", "One Stage of Evolution" and "Four Shifts" accurately define the new long-term, prevalent and regular characteristics of China's economic development, and also profoundly reveal the historic changes in the shape, structure and dynamics of China's economy and point to the future direction of China's economic development. At this meeting of the Central Economic Work Conference, Xi Jinping concluded that, "China's economic development has entered a new normal, which is an inevitable reflection of the characteristics of the current phase of China's economic development and is not subject to human will. Recognising the new normal, adapting to it and leading it is the great logic of China's economic development in the current and future period"[10]. The new normal has consequently become the logical base of China's economic development strategy for the current and future periods, and a major achievement of the CPC's understanding in exploring the laws of governance.

(II) UPHOLDING A PEOPLE-CENTRED DEVELOPMENT IDEOLOGY

In the process of the communist party leading the development of China and its society, the question of "for whom" the party governs and "on whom" development depends is a question of fundamental importance, determining the direction of development and the direction of the communist party's governance. Making the people the decisive force in the advancement of the communist party necessarily requires that the development led by the party should be for the people and depend on the people. Marx and Engels clearly pointed out in the *Communist Manifesto* that, 'All previous historical movements were movements of minorities or in the interest of minorities. The proletarian movement is the self-conscious, independent movement of the immense majority, in the interest of the immense majority"[11]. The 19th CPC National Congress emphasised that, "The founding aspiration and mission of the Chinese communists is to work for the happiness of the Chinese people and the rejuvenation of the Chinese nation"[12]. Xi Jinping also further stated that, "Always being with the people and struggling for their interests constitutes the fundamental difference between Marxist parties and other political parties"[13]. Xi Jinping also repeatedly stressed that to uphold and develop socialism with Chinese characteristics it is necessary to uphold the primacy of the people and an approach which puts the people first, which does all for the sake of the people and in all ways depends on the people, and which places the interests of the people above all else. All these important treatises clearly express the fact that upholding the position of the people, an approach which puts the people first, and the interests of the people above all, and upholding the approach of people-centred development constitutes the fundamental position of the CPC in governing and rejuvenating China and leading development.

On the basis of its stance to uphold the position of the people, the CPC has continued to develop and mature its people-centred ideology of development. As early as November 2012, at the 1st Plenary Session of the 18th CPC Central Committee, Xi Jinping pointed out that, "to test the effectiveness of all our work, we must ultimately see whether the people have really been benefited and whether their lives have really been improved, which is the essential requirement for upholding the establishment of the party for the sake of the public and governance for the sake of the people, and is an important guarantee for the continuous development of the cause of the party and the people". Over the past few years, he has repeatedly stressed this principle, requiring all party comrades to always put the people in the highest place in their hearts, to make upholding the position of the people their fundamental political stance, to give top priority to the interests of the people, and to constantly propel forward the cause of working for the benefit of the people. In October 2015, the 5th Plenary Session of the 18th CPC Central Committee first proposed "upholding a people-centred ideology of development". At this session Xi Jinping stressed that, "we must never forget to uphold a people-centred approach and make enhancing the well-being of the people, promoting comprehensive human development, and making steady progress toward common prosperity the starting and end point of economic development. We must firmly adhere to this fundamental position when we arrange economic work, formulate economic policies and promote economic development".

Under the guidance of this series of major ideologies, the party has embodied a people-centred ideology of development in all aspects of leading socioeconomic development. The Party Central Committee and Xi Jinping have further advanced four requirements for implementing the people-centred ideology of development, as follows. First, it is necessary to uphold the primacy of the people, respond to the people's aspiration for a better life, and continuously achieve, safeguard and develop the fundamental interests of the general public, so that development will be for the sake of the people and will depend on the people, and the fruits of development will be shared by the people. Second, it is necessary to improve the quality and efficiency of economic development, produce more material and spiritual products of higher quality, and continuously meet the growing material and cultural needs of the people, all through deepening the drive for reform and innovation. Third, it is necessary to comprehensively mobilise human initiative, proactiveness and creativity to create a stage and environment for workers, entrepreneurs, innovative talent and cadres at all levels from all sectors and disciplines to facilitate the playing of their roles. Finally, it is necessary to uphold the basic socialist economic system and the system of distribution, adjust the pattern of income distribution, refine the redistribution adjustment mechanism mainly characterised by taxation, social security and transfer payments, safeguard social equity and justice, and address income disparity, so that the fruits of development will benefit all the people of China in a greater and fairer way.

In the concrete practice of governance, the party and the state have adhered to a people-centred ideology of development, focusing on safeguarding and improving people's livelihoods, promoting the continuous improvement of people's material and cultural living standards and sustained new progress in education, labour, medical care, elderly care and housing. Since the 18th CPC National Congress, the proportion of state financial expenditure spent on education has always remained above 4% of GDP and the number of new jobs in urban areas has averaged over 13 million annually, reaching 65.24 million in five years, and the registered unemployment rate in urban areas has remained at the low level of 4.1% or less. In addition, people's living standards have continued to improve rapidly, with a national per capita disposable income of 23,821 yuan in 2016, which was up 44.3% from 2012, with an average annual real growth rate of 7.4%. Furthermore, by 2017, when the 19th CPC National Congress was held, the number of people covered by basic medical insurance had exceeded 1.3 billion, universal medical insurance had basically been achieved, and the level of social security had steadily improved[14]. With the implementation of the people-centred ideology of development, the general public's recognition of, support for, and participation in party governance has continuously increased, and the party's governance base has been consolidated and developed.

(III) INTRODUCING A NEW CONCEPT OF DEVELOPMENT

The concept of development is a summary and distillation of the objective laws of economic and social development and a reflection of the ruling party's philosophy of governance on the issue of development. After the 18th CPC National Congress, the Party Central Committee and Xi Jinping responded to the new requirements of the times and practical develop-ment, made the major judgment that economic development had entered a new normal, upheld the people-centred ideology of development and clearly put forward a new concept of development marked by innovation, coordination, eco-friendliness, opening up and mutual benefit at the 5th Plenary Session of the 18th CPC Central Committee, leading a historic change in the overall situation of China's development and adding another major connotation to the CPC's laws of governance.

In October 2015, Xi Jinping proposed and comprehensively elaborated the five major development concepts of innovation, coordination, eco-friendliness, opening up and shared development at the 5th Plenary Session of the 18th CPC Central Committee. When he presided over the drafting of the *Proposal of the CPC Central Committee on Formulation of the 13th Five-Year Plan for National Economic and Social Development* (hereinafter referred to as the *Proposal*), he emphasised that, "First of all, it is necessary to clarify the kind of development concept which should be established. This is because the development concept is of a strategic, programmatic and guiding nature, and is the concentrated embodiment of our thinking on development, and the direction and focus of development. If the development concept is right, the goals and tasks will be more straightforward to set, and it will also then be more straightforward to establish appropriate policy initiatives"[15]. Xi gave a comprehensive elaboration of the five major concepts of development at the 2nd General Congress of the 5th Plenary Session of the 18th CPC Central Committee. The *Proposal* adopted at the 5th Plenary Session of the 18th CPC Central Committee further developed the elaboration of the five major concepts of development.

Upholding innovative development means that innovation must be placed at the heart of overall national development, and innovation in all aspects, including theoretical, institutional, scientific and technological, and cultural innovation, must be continuously promoted, so that innovation can permeate all the work of the party and the state and becomes common practice across the whole society. It also means that it is necessary to establish the foundation of development on innovation, form an institutional structure that promotes innovation, and mould a guiding development that is more innovation-driven and gives greater play to first-mover advantages. The *Proposal* puts forward seven focus points for innovative development, namely cultivating new development momentum, expanding a new space for development, further implementing innovation-driven development strategy, vigorously promoting agricultural modernisation, building a new industrial system, building new institutions for development, and innovating and improving macrocontrol methods. Innovative development focuses on solving the problem of development momentum.

Upholding coordinated development requires firmly grasping the overall design of the cause of socialism with Chinese characteristics, correctly handling the major relationships in development, focusing on promoting the coordinated development of urban and rural areas, promoting coordinated socioeconomic development and the simultaneous development of a new type of industrialisation, informatisation, urbanisation and agricultural modernisation, focusing on enhancing China's soft power while strengthening its hard power, and continuously strengthening the overall nature of development. To enhance the coordination of development, it is necessary to broaden the space for development within the context of coordinated development and strengthen the momentum of development in areas of weakness. The *Proposal* points out the need to implement coordinated development in four areas, presented as the "Four Promotions", namely the promotion of coordinated regional development, coordinated urban-rural development, the coordinated development of material and spiritual civilisation, and the integrated development of economic construction and national defence construction.

510

Coordinated development focuses on solving the problem of unbalanced development.

Upholding eco-friendly development requires adherence to the basic state policy of conserving resources and protecting the environment, upholding sustainable development, resolutely following the path of the civilised development of productive development, affluence and a good ecology, accelerating the construction of a resource-saving and environmentally-friendly society, forming a new pattern of development and modernisation characterised by the harmonious development of humans and nature, promoting the construction of a beautiful China and making new contributions to global ecological security. The *Proposal* points out the need to implement eco-friendly development in six areas, namely, promoting the harmonious coexistence of humans and nature, accelerating the construction of the main functional zones, promoting low-carbon and circular development, comprehensive conservation and efficient use of resources, environmental governance and building a solid ecological security barrier. Eco-friendly development focuses on solving the problem of the harmonious coexistence of humans and nature.

Upholding development characterised by opening up requires following the trend of China's deep economic integration into the global economy, pursuing a strategy of opening up which is mutually beneficial and of a win-win nature, developing an economy with a greater degree of openness, actively participating in global economic governance and the supply of public goods, increasing China's institutional clout in global economic governance, and building a broad community of interests. In order to create a new context of opening up to the outside world, it is necessary to enrich the connotation and raise the level of opening up to the outside world, and to collaboratively promote strategic mutual trust, economic and trade cooperation, and people-to-people exchanges in a concerted effort to form a deeply integrated pattern of mutually beneficial cooperation. The *Proposal* makes arrangements in five areas for development marked by opening up, namely, refining the strategic composition of opening up to the outside world, forming a new system for opening up to the outside world, promoting the construction of the "Belt and Road" Initiative, deepening cooperation and development between the mainland, and Hong Kong and Macau, and the mainland and Taiwan, and actively participating in global economic governance. The focus of development marked by opening up is to solve the problem of domestic and international linkages in development.

Upholding shared development requires upholding the concept that development is for the people and depends on the people and that the fruits of development are for the mutual benefit of the people, in order to make more effective institutional arrangements to give the people as a whole a greater sense of access to shared development, strengthen the momentum of development, enhance the unity of the people and make steady progress toward common prosperity. In accordance with the requirements of participation by all, endeavour by all and enjoyment by all, it is necessary to adhere to the bottom line, highlight priorities, refine systems, and guide expectations, focus on fair opportunities, safeguard the basic livelihood of the people, and achieve the common progress of all people towards a moderately prosperous society in all respects. The *Proposal* aims to implement shared development in seven areas, namely, increasing the provision of public services, implementing poverty eradication projects, improving the quality of education, promoting employment and entrepreneurship, narrowing the income gap, and establishing a fairer and more sustainable social security system and promoting the construction of a healthy China. Shared development focuses on solving the problem of social equity and justice.

Among these five development concepts, innovation and development are at the forefront and leading position of the new concept of development. As Xi Jinping pointed out, "we must make innovation the first driving force leading development", "place innovation at the heart of China's overall development, continuously promote innovation in all aspects, including theoretical, institutional, scientific and technological, and cultural innovation, so that innovation can permeate all the work of the party and the state and become a common practice across the whole of society"[16]. In the *Proposal* adopted by the 5th Plenary Session of the 18th CPC Central Committee, the word "innovation" appears 71 times. Therefore, to grasp innovation is to grasp development, to seek innovation is to seek the future, and to have innovation is to have hope. Xi Jinping also pointed out that, "Upholding development marked by innovation, coordination, eco-friendliness, opening up and which is of a shared nature, constitutes a profound change that concerns the overall situation of China's development. These five development concepts are interlinked and mutually reinforcing and are an intrinsically linked collective that must be implemented in a unified manner. None may be neglected and none of them are interchangeable. If any one of the development concepts is not implemented properly, the whole development process will be affected"[17].

In March 2016, the 4th Session of the 12th NPC reviewed and approved the *Outline of the 13th Five-Year Guidelines for Economic and Social Development of the PRC (draft)* proposed by the State Council in accordance with the *Proposal of the CPC Central Committee on the Formulation of the 13th Five-Year Guidelines for National Economic and Social Development*. The new development concept was accordingly elevated to the level of national development concept.

The new concept of development is a comprehensive, fundamental, directional and long-term guiding concept that has a significant and direct guiding role in solving development problems, enhancing development momentum and building up development advantages. Therefore, the introduction of the new development concept constitutes a new understanding of development by the CPC and a new leap, as well as a deepening and refinement of the communist party's governance law. It is not only a scientific guide to lead profound changes in the overall development of China but also an important model for better development worldwide, especially for developing countries to achieve successful development.

(IV) INTEGRATED PROMOTION OF THE 'FIVE-SPHERE' INTEGRATED PLAN

The 18th CPC National Congress clearly advanced the understanding that to build socialism with Chinese characteristics the general foundational concept is that China is in the primary stage of socialism, the general integrated plan is Five-Sphere in nature, and the general task is to achieve socialist modernisation and the great rejuvenation of the Chinese nation. These so-called "Three General" summaries succinctly outline the logical framework of the CPC's governance in the new era. After the 18th CPC National Congress, Xi Jinping repeatedly stressed the need to uphold and develop socialism with Chinese characteristics and to promote the Five-Sphere Integrated Plan in the integrated promotion of economics, politics, culture, society and eco-civilisation, so as to lay a solid material foundation for the great rejuvenation of the Chinese nation. The integrated promotion of the Five-Sphere Integrated Plan has become the basic composition of the CPC's governance and rejuvenation of China and an important element in the management of state affairs.

In fact, the CPC has a long history of thinking about the "general composition", and in 1982 the 12th CPC National Congress put forward the idea of building a socialist material and spiritual civilisation, which in effect put forward the idea of a 'Two-in-One' general composition. In CPC literature, the first time the concept of a general composition was explicitly put forward was in the *Resolution on the Guidelines for the Construction of Socialist Spiritual Civilisation*, adopted at the 6th Plenary Session of the 12th

CPC Central Committee in 1986. In 1997, the report of the 15th CPC National Congress pointed out that socialism with Chinese characteristics constitutes the organic unity of the socialist market economy, socialist democratic politics and advanced socialist culture, in effect establishing the general composition of a "Trinity". In 2007, the 17th CPC National Congress established the general composition of the Four-Sphere plan for economic, political, cultural and social construction. In 2012, the 18th CPC National Congress raised the construction of eco-civilisation to the level of the general composition of the cause of socialism with Chinese characteristics, thereby expanding the general composition of the cause of socialism with Chinese characteristics to being Five-Sphere in nature. The addition of the construction of eco-civilisation to the general composition is of great practical and far-reaching historical significance in accelerating the transformation of the mode of economic development, walking along the path of the civilised development of productive development, affluence and good ecology, forming a spatial pattern, industrial structure, mode of production and way of life that conserves resources and protects the environment, building a resource-saving and environmentally-friendly society, striving to build a beautiful China and achieving the sustainable development of the Chinese nation. The development of the CPC's thinking on the general composition fully illustrates that the party's arrangements for the cause of socialism with Chinese characteristics correspond to the party's goals and are closely related to the party's philosophy and practice of governance.

After the 18th CPC National Congress, the Party Central Committee with Comrade Xi Jinping at its core, attached great importance to the coordinated promotion of the Five-Sphere integrated plan, and made it mutually reinforcing and integrated with the coordinated promotion of the strategic composition of the Four Comprehensives, to with the coordination and promotion of the "Four Comprehensive" strategic layout. They emphasised that the five major development concepts should be used to lead the five major constructions and to continuously pioneer a new context for the construction of a socialist economy, politics, culture, society and eco-civilisation with Chinese characteristics.

In terms of economic construction, China's economic restructuring began to bear fruit, gradually shifting from a large-scale growth mode to an intensive one and from low-to-medium-quality growth to high-quality growth, with the level of economic growth gradually stabilising, the income level of the working masses constantly rising, and economic strength and comprehensive national power being greatly enhanced.

In terms of political construction, China made significant strides in building democracy and the rule of law, the system of the organic unity of the leadership of the party, the sovereignty of the people and the rule of law was comprehensively strengthened, the institutional mechanism of the system of party leadership was improved, socialist democracy continued to develop, and intraparty democracy became more widespread. The socialist system of the rule of law with Chinese characteristics was increasingly refined, and the concept of the rule of law was significantly strengthened throughout society. The reform of the national supervisory system was fully implemented, and the reform of the administrative system, the judicial system, and the construction of a system of checks and supervision of the exercise of power were effectively implemented.

In terms of cultural construction, taking core socialist values as the guide, China persisted with prioritising societal benefits and strove to achieve the unity of societal benefits and economic efficiency. The construction of ideology, morality and social integrity were strengthened, cultural products and services were significantly enriched, and the role of culture in leading current trends, the education of the people, serving society and the promotion of development was fully utilised. The core values of socialism and the excellent Chinese traditional culture were continuously passed on and promoted, and the construction of a strong socialist cultural state was solidly advanced. Core socialist values and the strengths of Chinese traditional culture were continuously handed down and promoted, and the construction of a state with a strong socialist culture was solidly promoted.

In terms of social construction, people's lives continued to improve, a large number of initiatives to benefit the people were put into practice and decisive progress was made in the battle against poverty. Education was comprehensively developed, and education in the central and western regions of China and rural areas was significantly strengthened. People's employment status continued to improve, a social security system covering urban and rural populations was basically established, and the construction of subsidised housing was steadily promoted. The system of social governance was further refined, the general social situation remained stable and national security was comprehensively strengthened.

In terms of the construction of eco-civilisation, the self-awareness and proactiveness of the whole party and nation in implementing eco-friendly development were significantly enhanced, the formation of a system of eco-civilisation was accelerated, the intensity of energy and resource consumption was substantially reduced, major ecological protection and restoration projects progressed smoothly, ecosystem governance was significantly strengthened, and the environmental situation in China was improved. Significant progress was made in the construction of an eco-civilisation, from ideological transformation to theoretical innovation, from overall design to system construction, and from institutional reform to the promotion of work.

(V) INTRODUCTION AND IMPLEMENTATION OF 'TARGETED POVERTY ALLEVIATION'

After the 18th CPC National Congress, the CPC, with a high sense of historical responsibility and a solemn governance mission, placed the development of poverty alleviation in a prominent position in its management of state affairs and took it as the biggest civil wealth project. The party increased investment in poverty alleviation, innovated ways to alleviate poverty, implemented targeted poverty alleviation and the eradication of poverty, and waged a battle against poverty, achieving important results.

At the end of December 2012, shortly after the end of the 18th CPC National Congress, Xi Jinping pointed out during his study tour of poverty alleviation work in Fuping County in Hebei Province that, "without moderate prosperity in rural areas, and in particular without moderate prosperity in deprived areas, it cannot be said that a moderately prosperous society in all respects has been built,"[18] and that, "in order to help our fellow countrymen to escape poverty and become affluent there must be clear targets and we must grasp the situation at the level of individual households ...... to make sure we have a good idea what is actually happening"[19]. On 3 November 2013, while on a research trip to examine poverty alleviation work in Xiangxi, Hunan Province, Xi Jinping made it clear that poverty alleviation work, "should be planned scientifically, adapted to local conditions, and seize key points, and be increasingly precise, effective and sustainable"[20], "should be practical realistic and tailored to local conditions"[21] and "should have clear targets in poverty alleviation and avoid chanting profound slogans setting overly ambitious goals"[22]. In mid-September and early October 2013, when Li Keqiang chaired two executive meetings of the state council to study poverty alleviation work, he put forward specific requirements for targeted poverty alleviation and the work of the national poverty database. In April 2013, Wang Yang conducted a research and inspection tour of poverty alleviation work in Gansu Province, proposing that in order to promote poverty alleviation and development work in the new era, it was necessary to establish a working mechanism for targeted poverty alleviation. In December 2013, the General Office of the CPC Central Committee and the General Office of the State Council issued the *Opinions on Innovative Mechanisms for Solidly Promoting Poverty Alleviation and Development in Rural Areas*, which clearly put forward requirements for the work of establishing a targeted poverty alleviation mechanism and improving the mechanism whereby cadres are stationed in villages in order to help them. Consequently, "targeted poverty alleviation" was established as a regular task and an important institutional arrangement in the context of the party's governance.

After that, Xi Jinping gave further systematic guidance and elaboration on the implementation of targeted poverty alleviation and eradication, taking into account new issues and situations in poverty alleviation work in various regions and departments. On 19 January of that year, Xi Jinping emphasised during his inspection tour in Yunnan that, "Poverty alleviation and development is the key work of our first centennial goal, and it is also the most arduous task. Now that we are only five or six years away from achieving a moderately prosperous society in all respects, time is running out; we must increase our sense of urgency with regard to poverty alleviation and development, truly work hard and not just chant profound slogans, and we must not let the deprived areas and those suffering from deprivation fall behind. With clearer goals, more powerful initiatives and more effective action, we must implement targeted poverty alleviation and eradication, and improve the precision of project arrangements and the use of funds to hit the core issues head on so that the poor can really benefit"[23]. On 13 February, Xi Jinping hosted a forum in Yan'an, Shaanxi Province on poverty alleviation in the old revolutionary areas of Shaanxi, Gansu and Ningxia, and particular commented that, "Implementing the requirements of targeted poverty alleviation, achieving clear goals, tasks, responsibilities and initiatives, and putting money to the exact needed use will play a real role in uprooting poverty"[24]. In June, at a seminar for comrades in charge of some provincial, regional and municipal party committees in Guizhou, Xi Jinping pointed out that poverty alleviation and development in China had "entered a period when great effort is required to break down very difficult strongholds", and that, "the most important determining factor in the success of poverty alleviation and development is its being targeted in nature". All locales should be targeted in their provision of support, project arrangements, use of funds, measures for households, assigning specific people (the first secretary) to specific villages, and in terms of precise effectiveness of poverty alleviation have strategic thinking, make practical moves and see real results. It is necessary to uphold the application of policies suited to specific groups of people and specific places, targeting the causes of poverty suited to the specific types of poverty, and differentiating between different situations, so as to administer the right solution and precise measures with targeted treatment, and not seek to simply apply random measures indiscriminately, make quick judgments based on inadequate information or be careless. It is necessary to implement the action plan of the "Four Somes" according to local conditions through support for production and employment development for some, migrant relocation and resettlement for some, underwriting the policy of subsistence allowance for some and medical assistance to support some, to achieve targeted poverty alleviation"[25]. In November, at the Central Work Conference on Poverty Alleviation and Development, Xi Jinping again emphasised that, "Targeted poverty alleviation is for the purpose of targeted poverty eradication. A timetable should be set to achieve an orderly exit [from poverty], preventing both the ills of procrastination and impetuousness. A buffer period should be set to implement the policy of removing counties from the poverty list and ensuring they do not return to it. We must implement rigorous assessment, and verify and accept their removal in accordance with the relevant criteria for this. We must work for this from one house to the next, ensure the people all experience poverty alleviation, and ensure that all together escape poverty and all likewise acknowledge it"[26].

Under the scientific decision-making and arrangements of the Party Central Committee and Xi Jinping, poverty alleviation and development work after the 18th CPC National Congress took on a new dimension, and decisive progress was made in the battle for targeted poverty alleviation and eradication. A total of more than 60 million people in poverty across China were steadily lifted out of poverty, and the rate of poverty incidence dropped from 10.2% to less than 4%, which constitutes the greatest achievement in the history of poverty alleviation in China. China became the country with the largest number of people to have escaped poverty, and the first country in the world to accomplish the UN's Millennium Development Goals. This achievement is worthy of being noted in the annals of human social development and proves to the world that the CPC has mastered governance ability and possesses superior governance abilities.

4

RESOLUTE IN THE FACE OF CHANGES UNPRECEDENTED IN A CENTURY, SAFEGUARDING NATIONAL INTERESTS AND NATIONAL SECURITY

Safeguarding national interests and national security is an important element of the communist party's governance. In the face of changes unprecedented in the preceding century, the Party Central Committee, with Comrade Xi Jinping at its core, put forward and upheld an overarching concept of national security, upheld the supremacy of national interests, keeping as its objective the security of the people and political security as its fundamental basis. It integrated external and domestic security, homeland and national security, traditional and non-traditional security, and individual and common security, improved the system of national security, strengthened the construction of national security capacity, resolutely safeguarded national sovereignty, security and development interests, promoted the construction of the Belt and Road, and promoted the building of a community with a shared future for mankind. This series of major ideas and initiatives accurately grasped the new features and trends of China's changing internal and external environment, especially the external security environment, facing the governance of the CPC in the new era, and enriched and expanded the essence of the communist party's governance law.

(I) UPHOLDING THE STRATEGIC JUDGMENT THAT 'PEACE
AND DEVELOPMENT REMAIN THE KEY THEME OF THE
TIMES'

Correctly understanding and grasping the key theme of the times is a very important issue, a basic foundation for the ruling communist party in formulating various domestic and foreign policies, and it pertains to the overall strategy of socialist countries and their people's livelihoods. Similarly, responding to the *zeitgeist* and recognising the key theme of the times is a basic starting point for the ruling CPC in formulating China's domestic development strategy as well its strategic approach to foreign affairs and foreign policy, and is one of the important lessons of contemporary China's development.

Since the outset of reform and opening up, the CPC has made the strategic judgement that, in the words of Xi Jinping, "peace and development are the key themes of the times", which has provided the theoretical basis for the party to formulate correct strategic methodologies, reversing the inherent notion that war is inevitable and imminent, and enabling the party to focus its efforts on economic construction and achieving a shift in the focus of the party's work. It was also with a clear grasp of the changing theme of the times that China entered a new period of comprehensive great development after the 1990s. More importantly, under this theme of the times, the CPC gradually formed and developed socialism with Chinese characteristics, achieving unprecedented success in the field of communist party governance.

After the 18th CPC National Congress, in the face of "changes unprecedented in a century" now seen in the contemporary world, Xi Jinping pointed out at the Central Conference on Work Relating to Foreign Affairs in November 2014 that understanding the general situation of the world "requires a global vision and a grasp of the pulse of the age, and it requires seeing the changeable situation in the world today accurately, clearly and thoroughly; we must discover the essential substance of the great abundance of phenomena and, in particular, recognise long-term trends"[1].On the basis of a profound analysis of the general trends of global development and the evolution of the international landscape, the Party Central Committee amply surmised the complexity of the development and evolution of the international landscape and moreover observed that the forward momentum of the trend of multipolarisation in the world would not change. They also amply surmised the complicated nature of global economic adjustments and moreover observed that the course of economic globalisation would not change, amply surmised the acuteness of international contradictions and struggles, and moreover observed that peace and development would continue to be the key theme of the times, amply surmised the long-term nature of the struggle for international order, and moreover observed that the direction of change of the international system would not change, and amply surmised the uncertainties in China's regional political environment, and moreover observed that the overall prosperity and stability of the Asia-Pacific region would not change. These scientific assertions by the Party Central Committee and Xi Jinping provided China with somewhat of a telescopic sight and basis for understanding realities in the midst of international chaos and for grasping the appropriate direction in which to proceed in the midst of global changes.

In January 2013, Xi Jinping, presiding over the third collective study session of the Politburo of the 18th CPC Central Committee, which focused on unswervingly pursuing the path of peaceful development, pointed out that throughout world history, foreign aggression and expansion by force has ultimately led to failure. Global prosperity and stability constitute an opportunity for China, and China's development also constitutes an opportunity for the world. China upholds pursuit of the path of peaceful development but must not give up its legitimate rights and interests or sacrifice its core national interests. As China takes the path of peaceful development, so must all other countries, and only when all countries take this path can they develop together and can nations live in peace with each other. This understanding clearly indicated the development path that China should choose under the strategic premise that peace and development remain the key theme of the times[2].

On the basis of a systematic summary of the evolution of the external environment and China's development practices, the 19th CPC National Congress in October 2017 made the judgment that the world is in a period of great development, change and adjustment, and that peace and development remain the key themes of the times. The CPC made such a strategic judgment on the basis that global multipolarisation, economic globalisation, social informatisation and cultural diversification of the world are developing in depth, the changes in the global system of governance and international order are accelerating, the interconnection and interdependence of countries is deepening, power is becoming increasingly balanced internationally, and the general trend of peaceful development is irreversible. At the same time, the world is facing noticeable instability and uncertainty, global economic growth is not adequate, the gap between the rich and the poor is becoming increasingly serious, regional flashpoints are emerging, terrorism, cyber security, major infectious diseases, climate change and other non-traditional security threats continue to spread, and humanity faces many common challenges[3].

This means that, fundamentally speaking, the fact that the key theme of the times is peace and development has not changed but its essence and the way it is achieved has nevertheless changed. In this regard, the CPC's understanding and grasp of the situation is sharp and discerning, and also constantly being enriched and improved. Peace no longer only refers to the absence of a worldwide war but also includes non-traditional aspects of security such as international terrorism, national separatist forces and cyber security. Regional conflicts and wars have also become some of the most important factors affecting world peace. The essence of the notion of development has also become richer, pointing more to the comprehensive and balanced development of all sectors and elements, including economic development, and the joint development and prosperity of all countries in the course of development. In line with these changes, since the 18th CPC National Congress, China has held high the banner of peace, development, cooperation and mutual benefit, firmly committed to maintaining world peace and promoting common development, adding the aspects of "cooperation" and "mutual benefit" to the key theme of the times of peace and development, and grasping the key theme of the times more accurately. This has provided fundamental guidance for the CPC in safeguarding national security and national interests in the context of a very turbulent era, a fast-changing world, and a complex governance environment.

(II) RESOLUTELY SAFEGUARDING CHINA'S NATIONAL SOVEREIGNTY, SECURITY AND DEVELOPMENT INTERESTS

The 18th CPC National Congress in 2012 clearly stated that, "we are determined to safeguard China's national sovereignty, security and development interests, and will never yield to any external pressure", clearly highlighting the CPC's will and determination to firmly safeguard China's national interests. The 19th CPC National Congress in 2017, while comprehensively and systematically summarising the glorious achievements made by the CPC in the governance of China since the 18th CPC National Congress, frankly and objectively put forward the challenges and risks facing the CPC in the new era. In the opening part of the report of the 19th CPC National Congress, it is clearly stated that, "At present, the situation at home and abroad is undergoing profound and complex changes, and China's development is still in an important period of strategic opportunity, with both a very bright future and very serious challenges. All comrades across the party must look far ahead, be vigilant in peacetime, be brave in change and innovation, and never become rigid or stagnate"[4]. In the report, the concept of Comprehensive National Security is once again emphasised, where it is stated that, "Integrating development and security, enhancing awareness of worries and being vigilant in peacetime is one of the party's major principles in its management of state affairs"[5]. Resolutely safeguarding China's national sovereignty, security and development interests is incorporated into the CPC's governance vision as an important aspect of the CPC's governance.

National sovereignty, security and development interests are the most important cornerstones of national development and the most fundamental guarantee of the wellbeing of the people. The term "national security" first appeared in the report of the CPC National Congress in 1992 and since then the number of references to "security" in national party congress reports has gradually increased.

The word "security" was mentioned six times in the 15th CPC National Congress report, 14 times in the 16th CPC National Congress report, 23 times in the 17th CPC National Congress report and 36 times in the 18th CPC National Congress report. The report of the 19th CPC National Congress also mentioned "security" 55 times, including 18 references to "national security". In addition, the report of the 19th CPC National Congress contains nine references to "risks", seven to "challenges", 15 to "contradictions", 17 to "stability" and 44 to "governance". These figures show that the Party Central Committee, with Comrade Xi Jinping at its core, has come to pay more attention than ever to security issues. Xi Jinping emphasised that, "It is necessary to uphold national interests above all else, have the security of the people as our aim, political security as the foundation, integrate external and domestic security, homeland and national security, traditional and non-traditional security, and individual and common security, refine the system of national security, strengthen the construction of national security capacity, and resolutely safeguard China's national sovereignty, security and development interests"[6].

After the 18th CPC National Congress, the CPC comprehensively strengthened its governance capabilities, especially its ability to manage risks, and improved risk prevention and control mechanisms in various areas, becoming adept at handling various complex contradictions and overcoming various difficulties and obstacles along the way, firmly grasped the initiative in its work and resolutely safeguarded China's national sovereignty, security and development interests with a firm determination to govern.

In safeguarding China's national sovereignty, the CPC has taken a firm stand and adopted active and effective means to resolutely defend the dignity of China's sovereignty and territorial integrity. China has become increasingly stronger in its will to defend its sovereignty and is demonstrating its determination and will to defend its sovereignty through appropriate and timely displays of military power and will never compromise on the important tools for concessions on the issue of sovereignty. China has actively responded to Japan's provocations by gradually normalising its patrols in the waters of the Diaoyu Islands since 2013, and by implementing development and construction on islands and reefs in the South China Sea since 2014, actively declaring its sovereignty to the rest of the world and strengthening effective control. China has also sent a message to others that it will defend its territorial sovereignty through, amongst others, strong statements, displays of sophisticated weapons and conducting military drills. In July 2016, Xi Jinping emphasised in an important speech at the conference celebrating the 95th anniversary of the founding of the CPC that, "the Chinese people neither believe in evil nor are afraid of evil, neither provoke trouble nor are afraid of trouble, and no foreign country should expect us to trade our core interests or to swallow the bitter fruit of harming China's sovereignty, security and development interests"[7]. Following the standoff between China and India in Donglang which started on 18 June 2017, the Chinese government took a firm stance and forced India to withdraw all personnel and equipment back across to the Indian side of the border on 28 August.

In safeguarding China's national security, the CPC has focused on priorities, grasped the overall picture and provided leadership, upheld preparation for worst-case scenarios, strengthened risk awareness, and upheld the leadership of the party in all work. It has also upheld the socialist system to ensure the security of the party's governance. It has firmly established the "Four Consciousnesses" and the "Four Matters of Confidence", kept a clear mind, resolutely prevented and resisted "colour revolutions", and resolutely curbed the infiltration and subversive activities of hostile Western forces. It has also strengthened its ideological work and firmly grasped its leadership role and voice in the field of ideology.

The CPC has resolutely opposed all activities that seek to split up China, intensively combated the "three forces" of religious extremism, ethnic separatism and terrorism, and effectively curbed all kinds of plots and actions which infringe on China's homeland security. It has upheld the basic economic system of socialism with Chinese characteristics without wavering, continuously refined the socialist market economy, fought the battle to prevent and resolve financial risks, resolutely guarded the baseline of ensuring no systemic financial risks exist, and maintained and safeguarded economic security. The CPC has also vigorously promoted the construction of a peaceful China, improved the three-dimensional system of public security and protection, raised the overall level of social governance and safeguarded public security. As well as upholding an approach marked by self-reliance and independent innovation, accelerating breakthroughs in core technologies in the information field, strengthening cyber security and protection for critical information infrastructure, enhancing early warning and monitoring of cyber security, and safeguarding cyber security.

In safeguarding national development interests, the CPC has persisted with coordinating development interests and security, ensuring that security is provided for wherever national interests are concerned, effectively safeguarding the security of China's overseas interests, protecting the safety and legitimate rights and interests of Chinese citizens, organisations and institutions overseas, and protecting China's overseas financial, oil, mineral, maritime and other commercial interests. In particular, the evacuation operation in Yemen in March 2015 was the first time that the Chinese government had ever used a warship to berth directly at a foreign port to carry out an evacuation mission, and the first time that a special operation was undertaken to evacuate foreign nationals in a dangerous location. As Saudi Arabia and other countries launched air strikes against Houthi targets in Sana'a and other places in Yemen, in order to protect the lives and property of Chinese citizens, the Chinese navy's 19th Escort Task Group rushed to Yemen on 26 March 2015 to carry out its mission to evacuate Chinese citizens, as ordered by President Xi Jinping and the CMC. By 7 April, China had evacuated a total of 613 Chinese citizens from Yemen and assisted in the safe evacuation of a total of 279 foreign citizens from 15 countries[8].

(III) PROMOTING THE BUILDING OF A COMMUNITY WITH A SHARED FUTURE FOR MANKIND TO TRANSFORM THE SYSTEM OF GLOBAL GOVERNANCE

Promoting the building of a community of human destiny constitutes the core and quintessence of Xi Jinping's ideology on foreign affairs in the context of socialism with Chinese characteristics for a new era, and also the deepening and expansion by the Party Central Committee with Comrade Xi Jinping at its core of the related content of the communist party's governance law on foreign affairs. It also constitutes the most recent fruit of the exploration of the laws of human social development by contemporary Chinese communists.

After the 18th CPC National Congress, China entered a critical stage in achieving the great rejuvenation of the Chinese nation. It is particularly important for the CPC and the Chinese people to understand the major trends of world development and keep up with the *zeitgeist*. How to position China in relation to the world and keep up with the times is a question that the ruling CPC must ponder over and answer in depth. The introduction of Xi Jinping's concept of building a community with a shared future for mankind has greatly deepened the party's understanding of this issue. Following the 18th CPC National Congress in 2012, when it was first proposed to "advocate for the awareness of a community with a shared future for mankind", Xi Jinping delivered a speech at the Moscow State Institute of International Relations in March 2013, in which he for the first time elaborated in-depth on the concept of a community with a shared future for mankind on the international stage. He pointed out that, "in this world, countries are becoming more interconnected and interdependent than ever before; all people live in the same global village and in the same space and time where history and reality intersect, and they increasingly constitute a community with a shared future where all people are mutually interdependent"[9]. In September 2015, when participating in the general debate of the 70th session of the UN General Assembly, Xi Jinping systematically elaborated on how to build a community with a shared future for mankind from five aspects, namely, "building a partnership marked by equality, mutual consultation and understanding", "creating a security context marked by justice, co-building and mutual benefit", "seeking prospects for open, innovative, inclusive and mutually beneficial development", "promoting exchanges of civilisations that are harmonious but different and also inclusive", and "constructing an ecosystem that respects nature and eco-friendly development"[10]. In January 2017, Xi Jinping delivered a keynote speech entitled *Co-building a Community with a Shared Future for Mankind* at the European headquarters of the UN in Geneva, once again comprehensively and systematically elaborating on the concept of a community with a shared future for mankind. The concept of building a community with a shared future for mankind, on which he has repeatedly elaborated, reverberated strongly and drawn positive responses from the international community[11]. In February and March 2017, *Building a Community with a Shared Future for Mankind* was included for the first time in a UN resolution and a UN Security Council resolution respectively.

Xi Jinping's key remarks on building a community with a shared future for mankind and the reaction of the international community show that promoting the building of a community with a shared future for mankind is not diplomatic rhetoric but a way to link China's development with that of the rest of the world, to integrate the interests of the Chinese people with the common interests of all peoples, to jointly address global challenges and to strive to contribute to global development. Obviously, promoting the building of a community with a shared future for mankind is a product of the CPC's enlargement of its own governance vision, which distinctly reflects the global vision of the contemporary Chinese communists and China's global outlook that unites its own development with that of the world.

In order to promote the building of a community with a shared future for mankind, it is necessary to uphold the concept of global governance based on mutual consultation, co-building and mutual benefit, and to actively participate in the reform and construction of the system of global governance. After the 18th CPC National Congress, the Politburo successively conducted two collective study sessions on global governance, on 12 October 2015 and 27 September 2016 respectively. Xi Jinping also delivered a major speech, pointing out that promoting changes in the system of global governance is a matter for the attention of all in the international community, and that it is necessary to adhere to the principles of mutual consultation, co-building and mutual benefit, so that ideas on changes in the system of global governance can be translated into consensus among all parties and lead to the formation of concerted action. Based on this foundation, Xi Jinping stressed at the 19th CPC National Congress in October 2017 that, "we must advocate for the democratisation of international relations, insist on the equality of all countries regardless of their size, strength and level of wealth, support the UN in playing an active role, and support the enlargement of the representation and voice of developing countries in international affairs[12]. Under the strong leadership of the Party Central Committee with Comrade Xi Jinping at its core, China has upheld the balancing of rights and duties in the light of its own national conditions and has not only actively participated in global governance and taken the initiative to assume international responsibilities but also tried its utmost and acted within its strengths. In line with its active participation in the reform and construction of the system of global governance, the CPC has paid special attention to enhancing China's capacity to participate in global governance in the course of its administration, strengthening the construction of a pool of human resources for global governance, striving to enhance the capacities of the state and human resource pool for formulating regulations, setting agendas, guiding public opinion through propaganda, and integration and coordination, striving to contribute Chinese wisdom and strength to the reform and construction of the system of global governance.

(IV) PROMOTING 'BELT AND ROAD' CONSTRUCTION

An important platform and path to promote the building of a community with a shared future for mankind is to promote construction of the "Belt and Road" and to promote international cooperation for the Belt and Road. The major initiative of building the Silk Road Economic Belt and the 21st Century Maritime Silk Road constitutes a major strategic decision made by Xi Jinping to promote common global prosperity and build a community with a shared future for mankind by profoundly considering the future prospects of mankind and the development trends of China and the world. It has opened up a new horizon for China to participate in and lead global opening up and cooperation, and constitutes a major milestone in the history of global development, as well as a landmark in expanding the vision of communist party governance and deepening the communist party's governance law.

In September 2013, Xi Jinping proposed in his speech at Nazarbayev University in Kazakhstan that, "In order to make the economic ties of we Eurasian countries closer, mutual cooperation even deeper and the space for development even wider, we can use innovative cooperation models to jointly build the Silk Road Economic Belt"[13]. This was the first time that the concept of the "Silk Road Economic Belt" appeared in the minds of the people. Less than a month later, in a speech to the Indonesian parliament, Xi Jinping proposed for the first time the joint construction of a 21st century Maritime Silk Road, and at the same time proposed the establishment of the Asian Infrastructure Investment Bank, sending a further clear signal to the world that China was indeed promoting a new strategy for opening up. In November of the same year, "promoting construction of the Silk Road Economic Belt and the Maritime Silk Road, and forming a new model of all-round opening up" was written into the *Decision of the CPC Central Committee on Several Major Issues Relating to Comprehensively Deepening Reform*, which was deliberated on and adopted at the 3rd Plenary Session of the 18th CPC Central Committee, constituting a major decision and arrangement of the Party Central Committee with Comrade Xi Jinping at its core to comprehensively deepen reform. In June 2014, at the Sixth Ministerial Meeting of the China-Arab States Cooperation Forum in Beijing, Xi Jinping formally used the term Belt and Road for the first time, and also for the first time systematically elaborated on the spirit of the Silk Road and the principles that should be adhered to in building the Belt and Road[14]. With this, construction of the Belt and Road began to attract global attention as a new initiative, a new model of cooperation and a programme for common prosperity and development.

In order to build consensus and promote construction of the Belt and Road, Xi Jinping and other leading comrades of the central government have, on various occasions such as the G20 State Leaders' Summit, Informal Meetings of APEC Leaders, the Heads of State Council (HSC) of the Shanghai Cooperation Organisation, the BRICS Summit, as well as the World Economic Forum, the Bo'ao Forum for Asia, the Forum on China-Africa Cooperation and the China-Arab States Cooperation Forum, engaged in frank and in-depth dialogue and communication with all parties concerned to enhance strategic mutual trust, reduce mutual suspicion and build broad consensus to promote construction of the Belt and Road. In November 2014, the CPC Central Committee and the State Council issued the *Strategic Plan for Construction of the Silk Road Economic Belt and the 21st Century Maritime Silk Road*, making comprehensive arrangements to promote construction of the Belt and Road. In May 2017, the Belt and Road Forum for International Cooperation was held, where guests from various sectors from more than 100 countries gathered in China to discuss cooperation in building the grand scheme of the Belt and Road. This constituted both a review of the achievements of the Belt and Road construction and a re-launch to build consensus further.

In October 2017, the 19th CPC National Congress incorporated construction of the Belt and Road in its report. Xi emphasised the need to focus on construction of the Belt and Road to form a model of opening up with domestic and international linkages between land and sea, and mutual assistance between east and west, and the need to actively promote international Belt and Road cooperation to create a new platform for international cooperation and provide further momentum to joint development. After the 19th CPC National Congress, and with a view to putting into practice the concept of a community with a shared future for mankind, Xi Jinping profoundly elaborated on the idea and policy proposition of making the Belt and Road into a supremely broad platform for international cooperation in line with the trend of economic globalisation at the CPC in Dialogue with World Political Parties Summit and the first meeting of the Central Foreign Affairs Commission.

Under the leadership of the Party Central Committee with Comrade Xi Jinping at its core, Belt and Road construction has progressed rapidly and achieved fruitful results. Since the introduction of the Belt and Road Initiative, more than 80 countries and international organisations have signed cooperation agreements with China, creating a new context for international cooperation. From 2013 to 2017, China's total trade in goods with countries and regions along the Belt and Road exceeded US$5 trillion, FDI exceeded US$70 billion, Chinese enterprises promoted the construction of 75 economic and trade cooperation zones in countries and regions along the Belt and Road, paying US$2.2 billion in host country taxes and fees, creating 210,000 jobs, and Chinese FDI gradually became an important engine driving the growth of global FDI[15]. The first China International Import Expo, held in Shanghai in November 2018, provided new opportunities for countries around the world to increase exports, built a new platform for sharing the dividends of China's development and injected new momentum into global economic growth.

By promoting Belt and Road construction, China has won high praise from the international community. With the energetic implementation of Belt and Road construction, the CPC has expanded its governance vision, enriched the content of its governance, and achieved new results in exploring the communist party's governance law while also providing important lessons for countries, peoples and political parties across the world which wish to accelerate development whilst also maintaining their independence.

(V) UPHOLDING THE CONCEPT OF COMPREHENSIVE NATIONAL SECURITY

With the interplay of two historic processes, namely China's rapid development and profound changes occurring in the world, China's national security is in a period of comprehensive expansion and profound change, with the essence and extension of national security richer, its spatial and temporal scale wider, internal and external factors more complex, and the effects of the interlinkage of various threats and challenges more prominent, than ever before. As the great cause of socialism with Chinese characteristics continues to advance and the great struggle with many new historical characteristics continues to unfold, there will be a marked increase in the occurrence of both various foreseeable and unpredictable risk factors. The closer the critical historical moment of achieving the great rejuvenation of the Chinese nation comes, the more important it is to make enhancing our awareness of unexpected developments, being vigilant in peacetime and safeguarding national security a major principle and important task that the communist party always adheres to in its governance and on which it keeps a firm grip. This is an important safeguard for consolidating the ruling position of the communist party, improving its governance performance and achieving its governance mission.

Since the 18th CPC National Congress, the Party Central Committee, with Comrade Xi Jinping at its core, has stood at a new starting point for governing and rejuvenating China, accurately grasped the new features, objectives and tasks of the development of China's national security context, grasped the basic laws of national security, and creatively proposed and continuously enriched the development of the concept of comprehensive national security. On 15 April 2014, Xi Jinping put forward the concept of comprehensive national security when presiding over the First Plenary Session of the Central National Security Commission. On 25 April of the same year, Xi Jinping emphasised the implementation of the concept of comprehensive national security when presiding over the 14th Politburo Collective Study Session and made arrangements for implementation. On 1 July 2015, the 15th meeting of the Standing Committee of the 12th NPC adopted the *National Security Law of the PRC*, establishing 15 April every year as National Security Education Day for all of China. In January 2016, in a speech at a seminar for major leading cadres at provincial and ministerial levels to study how to implement the spirit of the 5th Plenary Session of the 18th CPC Central Committee, Xi Jinping further made implementation of the concept of comprehensive national security a prerequisite for implementing the new outlook on development, stating that "without security and stability, development is out of the question"[16].

After that, the discourse on, and arrangements relating to, the concept of comprehensive national security by the Party Central Committee and Xi Jinping became richer and more comprehensive. On the occasion of the first National Security Education Day for all of China on 15 April 2016, Xi Jinping spoke about advocacy and education pertaining to national security, stating, "We must uphold the approach that national security is all for the people and all depends on them, mobilise the whole party and all of society to work together, gather great strength to safeguard national security, strengthen the social foundation of national security, and prevent and resolve various types of security risks, continuously improving the people's sense of security and happiness"[17]. In February 2017, at a symposium on national security, Xi Jinping put forward clear requirements for specific work to implement the concept of comprehensive national security, stating "We should focus on political, economic, homeland, public, and cyber security and other aspects of security. We should improve the system of three-dimensional public security control, raise the overall level of social governance, and pay attention to investigating and resolving contradictions and disputes at the source. We must strengthen the governance of production safety in key sectors such as transportation, firefighting and hazardous chemicals, and curb the occurrence of serious accidents. We must build a firm line of defence for cyber security, improve the level of cyber security, strengthen the protection of critical information infrastructure, increase the strength of R&D of core technologies and guidance of marketisation, strengthen early warning and monitoring of cyber security, ensure the security of big data, and achieve all-weather and holistic awareness and effective protection. We must actively shape the external security environment, strengthen cooperation in the area of security, and guide the international community to jointly safeguard international security. We must increase our capacity for the construction of the material, technological equipment, human resources, legal and institutional safeguards needed to maintain national security, and better adapt to the needs of national security work"[18].

On this basis, the 19th CPC National Congress incorporated "upholding the concept of comprehensive national" into Xi Jinping Thought on socialism with Chinese characteristics for a new era, making it one of the 14 basic strategies for adhering to and developing socialism with Chinese characteristics in the new era, and proposing that "national security is a major cornerstone in the peace and stability of China, and safeguarding national security is the fundamental interest of all the people of China"[19]. The congress also incorporated "upholding the concept of comprehensive national security and resolutely safeguarding national sovereignty, security and development interests"[20] into the Party Constitution revised and adopted by the 19th CPC National Congress. As a result, the concept of comprehensive national security became a programmatic ideology for pursuing the path of national security with Chinese characteristics and pioneering a new frontier in national security work, as well as a new and important element of the communist party's governance.

5

COMPREHENSIVELY STRENGTHENING PARTY LEADERSHIP

The party is the leader of all things in the party, government, military, people, and education for the whole of China. The CPC is the strong leading core of the cause of socialism with Chinese characteristics and the highest force of political leadership. Only by always upholding the leadership of the party in all its work is it possible for the party and society as a whole to achieve ideological unity, political solidarity and unanimity of action at a higher level, and further enhance the party's creativity, cohesiveness and fighting strength, and provide fundamental political assurance for the success of building a moderately prosperous society in all respects and winning the great victory of socialism with Chinese characteristics in the new era. As Xi Jinping has said, "The most essential feature of socialism with Chinese characteristics is the leadership of the CPC, which is also the greatest strength of this system"[1]. This important assertion by General Secretary Xi Jinping has enriched and developed the Marxist doctrine of party building, profoundly reflecting a new level of understanding of the fundamental relationship between party leadership and socialism with Chinese characteristics, and profoundly reflecting a new dimension in the CPC's exploration of the communist party's governance law.

(I) STRENGTHENING THE AUTHORITY AND CENTRALISED LEADERSHIP OF THE PARTY CENTRAL COMMITTEE

The CPC is a whole organised according to its own programme and constitution and in accordance with the system of democratic centralism. Therefore, the party as a whole must safeguard the Central Committee, which is elected by the party's national congress, and uphold the centralised and unified leadership of the party. After the 18th CPC National Congress, in accordance with the provisions of the party's constitution and in response to the problems within the party, the Central Committee required the entire party, especially leading cadres at all levels, to firmly establish political consciousness, consciousness of the whole situation, consciousness of the core and also of the line, and to consciously maintain a high degree of consistency with the Party Central Committee in thought, politics and action. This constituted a major decision to safeguard the authority of the Party Central Committee and the party's centralised and unified leadership over the whole situation, starting from the overall situation of the party's leadership.

In January 2014, at the 3rd Plenary Session of the 18th Central Commission for Discipline Inspection, Xi Jinping pointed out that, "The party is the leading core of all our undertakings ...... the Central Committee, the Politburo, and the Standing Committee of the Politburo are the leading decision-making core of the party. The decisions and arrangements made by the Party Central Committee must be implemented by the party organisation, propaganda, united front, and political and legal departments, by the party organisations of the NPC, government, CPPCC, courts and procuratorates, and by the party organisations of business units and peoples' groups, amongst others"[2]. Under the guidance of Xi Jinping's series of major ideological discourses, the authority of the Party Central Committee has been effectively safeguarded and strengthened, and the centralised and unified leadership of the party has been strengthened and implemented on a wider scale and at a higher level, becoming a major innovation in the governance practice of the CPC.

Since the 18th CPC National Congress, the Central Government has set up a series of leading groups, including the Central Leading Group for Comprehensively Deepening Reform, the Central Leading Group for Cyber Security and Informatisation, and the CMC Leading Group for Enhancing Defence and Military Reform, with Xi Jinping personally serving as the head of many of these groups to comprehensively strengthen the leadership of economic, political, cultural, social, eco-civilisation, and military and defence construction. Major work and decisions in the overall development of the party and the country is coordinated at the central level, and the role of the core of the party leadership has been fully utilised. The establishment of these leading groups constitutes a restructuring of the power structure of the Standing Committee of the Central Politburo, which not only strongly promotes democracy in decision-making but also effectively guarantees the efficiency of decision-making, and plays an important role in safeguarding the authority of the Party Central Committee and promoting comprehensive and profound reform. For four consecutive years, the Standing Committee of the Central Politburo and the Central Politburo itself listened to reports on the work of the NPC Standing Committee, the State Council, the CPPCC, the Supreme People's Court and the party group of the Supreme People's Procuratorate and reports on the work of the Central Secretariat. This constitutes another important institutional arrangement to safeguard the centralised and unified leadership of the party since the 18th CPC National Congress, and is of great significance, playing a very important role as a model for the whole party.

In June 2015, the CPC Central Committee issued the *Regulations on the Work of the Party Groups of the CPC (Pilot)*, which further provided clear regulations on the establishment, duties, organisational principles, and deliberations and decisions of party groups, and became the general guidelines for the establishment and operation of party groups. In December 2015, the CPC Central Committee issued and implemented the newly revised *Regulations on the Work of Local CPC Committees*, proposing that the party committees (party groups) of all regions and departments enhance their level of reporting to the Party Central Committee and that this become the standard. In September 2015, in response to the weakening, dilution, deflation and marginalisation of the party's leadership in SOEs to varying degrees, the General Office of the CPC Central Committee issued the *Opinions on Upholding the Leadership of the Party and Strengthening the Party Building in the Midst of Deepening SOE Reform*. In October 2016, at the National Conference on SOE Party Building, Xi Jinping stressed that upholding the leadership of the party and strengthening party building constitutes the "root" and "soul" of SOEs. In October 2017, after the 19th CPC National Congress, the CPC Central Committee issued *Several Provisions of the CPC Central Committee Politburo on Strengthening and Safeguarding the Party's Centralised and Unified Leadership*, and in November 2017 the CMC issued the *Opinions on the Comprehensive and In-depth Implementing the Responsibility System of the Military Commission Chairman*, taking the strengthening of the authority and centralised and unified leadership of the Party Central Committee to a new level. The Party Central

Committee successively convened the National Conference on Propaganda and Thought Work, the Symposium on Literary and Art Work, the Symposium on Public Opinion Work, the Symposium on Cyber Security and Informatisation Work, the Central Conference on Urban Work, the Central Conference on United Front Work, the Central Conference on the Work of Party Groups and Organisations, the National Conference on SOE Party Building Work, the National Conference on the Ideological and Political Work of Universities, the All-Army Political Work Conference, and the National Conference on the Work of Party Schools. Xi Jinping personally attended the meetings and delivered important speeches, putting forward requirements for all aspects of work and further strengthening the centralised and unified leadership of the party over all aspects of work.

During this period, the Party Central Committee strictly enforced political discipline and resolutely eliminated ambitious and conspiratorial individuals such as Zhou Yongkang, Bo Xilai, Sun Zhengcai, Guo Boxiong, Xu Caihou and Ling Jihuan, eliminating major political hazards and safeguarding the centralised party unity. The Party Central Committee made efforts to strengthen the internal supervision of the party and achieve full coverage through inspection and field-posting of relevant politicians, pushing party organisations at all levels to align themselves with the Party Central Committee. The discipline inspection and supervision organs at all levels implemented the Party Central Committee's request to put strict political discipline and rules at the forefront, enhanced accountability mechanisms, highlighted political responsibility, and pointed out superficial obeisance and other issues, ensuring that the entire party would act in accordance with orders and in unison, resolutely upholding the authority of the Party Central Committee, and powerfully safeguarding its centralised and unified leadership.

In October 2016, the 6th Plenary Session of the 18th CPC Central Committee deliberated and adopted *Some Guidelines on Political Life Within the Party Under the New Situation* and the *Regulations on Supervision Within the CPC*, formally introducing the concept of "the Party Central Committee with Comrade Xi Jinping at its core" and establishing Comrade Xi Jinping as the core of the Party Central Committee and the core of the entire party. The enormity of the CPC's governance task, the glory of its mission and the great responsibility it bears are unparalleled by any other political party in the world, including any communist parties that have ever been in governance. Without the core of the Party Central Committee and the core of the entire party, there would be no authority or centralised leadership of the Party Central Committee, and it would not be possible to achieve its governance mission. Resolutely safeguarding Comrade Xi Jinping's position as the core of the Party Central Committee and the core of the entire party is a matter impacting the future prospects of the party and China itself, and is in the fundamental interests of the entire nation. With the establishment of Comrade Xi Jinping's core position as the hallmark of the party, profound results have been achieved in strengthening the authority, and centralised and unified leadership of the Party Central Committee.

(II) COMPREHENSIVELY PROMOTING PARTY BUILDING WITH ITS POLITICAL CONSTRUCTION AS THE OVERARCHING PRIORITY

For a period of time, some places and departments were lax and over-lenient in terms of party management, resulting in a serious weakening of party leadership, lack of party building and a lack of rigour in party governance, with lax political and organisational discipline becoming a major concern for the party and the policies of the central government becoming difficult to implement in some places. Under such circumstances, the presence of the political construction of the party as the overarching priority necessary to promote party building became an urgent requirement in order to promote comprehensive party building, put forward party building, and led the whole party in implementing an effective and innovative exploration. On 16 November 2012, at the first meeting of the Politburo of the 18th CPC Central Committee, Xi Jinping emphasised that, "The Politburo should take the lead in abiding by the party's organisational principles and the guidelines for political life within the party, understand the rules and observe discipline". On 22 January 2013, at the 2nd Plenary Session of the 18th CPC Central Committee Central Commission for Discipline Inspection, Xi Jinping focused on elaborating on the issue of the strict political discipline of the party, emphasising that, "For strict party discipline, the first priority is to implement strict political discipline"[3]. On 23 October 2014, at the 2nd General Congress of the 4th Plenary Session of 18th CPC Central Committee, Xi Jinping further stated, "Is the communist party still called the communist party if it is not political? …… Problems with the politics of cadres are no less harmful to the party than problems with corruption, and in some cases even more serious than corruption"[4]. He also summarised the phenomenon of some party members and cadres, especially leading cadres, disregarding the party's political discipline and political rules as "Seven Fundamental Areas of Concern", calling on the party as a whole to always be vigilant and constantly cross-check them. On 13 January 2015, at the 5th Plenary Session of the 18th CPC Central Committee Central Commission for Discipline Iinspection, Xi Jinping put forward the "Five Musts" for observing political discipline and rules. At the 6th Plenary Session of the 18th CPC Central Committee Central Commission for Discipline Inspection in January 2016, Xi Jinping also proposed "always being clear on politics"[5]. At the same time as this, on 29 January 2016, the Politburo clearly proposed the "Four Consciousnesses" for the first time.

Under the leadership of strict political discipline and strict political life within the party, significant progress has been constantly made in the party's political construction, and a systematic ideological and theoretical system has been gradually formed. Party organisations at all levels have comprehensively implemented the party's basic line, upheld the systems of Three Conferences and One Lesson, democratic appraisal of party members and regular analysis of party spirit, and made efforts to solve the problems of the failure to implement party activities in accordance with regulations and low-quality, superficial and ineffective party life. Party members and leading cadres have strictly implemented the system of double organisational life meetings, attending both the organisational life meetings of the party branches and groups in their units and the democratic life meetings held separately by party leaders and cadres. The quality of democratic life meetings and organisational life meetings has been effectively improved. In the practical activities of the party's mass line education, the Politburo Standing Committees each chose a county as a contact point and participated in special democratic life meetings in person, fully exercising its role as a model and propelling education and practice to greater depth. The Party Central Committee specifically sent supervisory groups to tour all areas and departments to provide strict supervision and guidance.

On this basis, and based on the need to deepen the comprehensive strict governance of the party and solve prominent problems within the party, the Central Politburo made a decision in February 2016 that the 6th Plenary Session of the 18th CPC Central Committee would conduct a special study on comprehensive strict party governance. In October 2016, the 6th Plenary Session of the 18th CPC Central Committee deliberated and adopted *Several Guidelines on Political Life Within the Party under the New Situation*, which is connected with and has a common origin with *Some Guidelines on Internal Party Political Life* adopted in 1980 but has also evolved with the times and developed in an innovative way. These guidelines systematically summarised the new initiatives, experiences and achievements of the party in recent years, especially since the 18th CPC National Congress, in terms of comprehensive strict governance, and formed a new institutional arrangement that clarified the direction, objectives, principles, tasks and initiatives for strengthening and regulating the political life of the party under the new situation. In January 2017, the CPC Central Committee issued *Several Provisions on the Democratic Life Meetings of Leading Party Members and Leading Cadres of Party Organs Above the County Level*, providing institutional safeguards for further adherence to, and improvement of, democratic life meetings. As a result, democracy within the party was further expanded. Respecting the subjective status of party members, safeguarding their democratic rights, and implementing their right to information, participation, election and supervision, guaranteeing that all party members equally enjoy the rights and fulfil the obligations of party members as stipulated in the party constitution, led to the upholding of democratic and equal comradeship within the party. The approach of encouraging party members to participate in and discuss party affairs, and broadening the channels for them to express their views created within the party a political atmosphere marked by democratic discussion.

While prioritising the political party building, ideological, organisational, work style and disciplinary party building was also vigorously strengthened. The Party Central Committee, with Comrade Xi Jinping at its core, placed ideological construction in a prominent position, promoting the firm establishment of the Four Consciousnesses among party members and cadres, and consolidating the ideological foundation for the party to continue to move forward without forgeting its original aspirations. The seriousness of the party's internal political life and the purification of the party's political ecology were elevated to the level of being an issue pertaining to the party's survival, and all parties generally reflected the fact that the party's positive spirit increased significantly, and its culture improved significantly. This also led to an upturn in social morale, accumulating strong positivity in support of the cause of the development of the party and the state. The party adhered to the principle of party management of cadres, strengthened its role in the leadership and checking of party organisations, implemented standards specifying what is expected of good cadres in the new era, and established a correct orientation regarding employment. At the same time, it thoroughly implemented a strategy of giving priority to the development of human resources, deepened reform of the institutional mechanism for the development of human resources, and tightened the cohesion of various human resources around the party. It upheld placing the demand for strict standards on cadres, managing them with strict measures and constraining them with strict discipline, creating a set of "combination punches" to govern officials strictly, and making significant strides in the strict governance of officials.

In deepening the advancement of the fight against corruption, in the five years between the 18th and 19th CPC National Congresses, more than 280 cadres at the central management level, 8,600 cadres at the bureau level and 660,000 cadres at the county level were investigated, and overwhelming momentum in the fight against corruption was formed and consolidated at this time[6]. The party has focused on forming close vibrant ties between the party and the people, taking the formulation and implementation of the Eight-point Regulation of the Centre as the entry point, and focused on solving prominent problems strongly reacted to by the people, so as to promote fundamental change in the party's culture and style of government. The party also effectively strengthened the construction of grassroots party organisations and party members, firmly and effectively developed party members and strictly managed education, coordinated the promotion of the construction of grassroots party organisations, made up for the shortcomings of grassroots party construction work, guided party organisations and members in the work of serving the central government and the people, and further established the clear orientation of placing major emphasis on the grassroots. The party also raised the building of the party's system of internal regulations to an unprecedented level, formulating and revising 88 central party regulations, which accounts for about 47% of the 188 central party regulations currently in force[7].

On the basis of the fruitful results achieved in party building, the 19th CPC National Congress proposed that, "great struggles, great projects, great undertakings and great dreams are closely linked, interconnected and interact with each other; among these the decisive role is played by the great new project of partybuilding", and "the party's political construction must be prioritised overall with the party's constitution as the fundamental guideline"[8]. This fully reflected Xi Jinping's profound understanding of the importance of political party building and his profound grasp of the laws of party governance, and constitutes the latest theoretical innovation integrating the Marxist doctrine of party building with the great practice of party building in the new era of socialism with Chinese characteristics, as well as a new summary and overview of the historical experience of the CPC in its own construction and a new result of the exploration of the communist party's governance law.

(III) FURTHER REFINEMENT OF THE INSTITUTIONAL MECHANISMS FOR UPHOLDING THE PARTY'S LEADERSHIP

The overall leadership of the party is not abstract but rather concrete. Since the 18th CPC National Congress, the Party Central Committee with Comrade Xi Jinping at its core has, in its exploration of the laws of governance, not only achieved the important result of strengthening the overall leadership of the party but has also implemented the overall leadership of the party into every aspect of the management of state affairs and reflected it in the design, arrangement and operation of the organs, institutions and systems of state power, ensuring the full coverage of the party's leadership.

The key to upholding the overall leadership of the party is to uphold the party's core position in overseeing the overall situation and coordinating all parties. This is a prominent feature of the superiority of China's socialist political system. In February 2015, at a seminar for major leading cadres at the provincial and ministerial levels to study and implement the spirit of the 4th Plenary Session of the 18th CPC Central Committee to comprehensively promote the rule of law, Xi Jinping further emphasised that, "One of the prominent features of the superiority of China's socialist political system is the core leadership role of the party in overseeing the overall situation and coordinating all parties, figuratively speaking, [as Confucius said] 'the stars cup themselves around the moon', and this 'moon' [being revered by all] is the CPC. In the big [grand strategy of the] [Chinese] chess game of the national system of governance, the Party Central Committee is the 'general' [king piece] who sits in the middle of the board, with the chariots, horses and cannons each displaying their strengths, thereby clearly portraying the big picture of a chess game. If China emerges as a fragmented and scattered force on the board, not only can the goals we have set not be achieved but there will also certainly be disastrous consequences"[9].

On the basis of the party's clear position as the core leadership for China's overall context and coordination of all parties, the party has endeavoured to establish a sound institutional mechanism for its leadership of major work. Under the leadership of the Politburo and its Standing Committee, the party's central decision-making deliberative and coordinating body has been optimised to be responsible for the top-level design, general composition, coordination and overall promotion of major work. At the same time, the party has ensured that the deliberative and coordinating bodies of other parties dovetail with the establishment and adjustment of the Party Central Committee's deliberative and coordinating bodies, so as to ensure that orders are followed and work is carried out efficiently. It has strengthened the leading position of the party's organisations at the same level as each other, ensured that party committees (party groups) set up in state organs, business units, mass organisations, social organisations, enterprises and other organisations are subject to the unified leadership of the party committee and reported regularly on their work, so as to ensure that the party's guidelines, policies and confirmed arrangements are implemented in organisations at the same level as each other, and accelerated the establishment of sound organisational structures for the party in new socioeconomic organisations, so that wherever the party's work progresses, party organisations are also covered.

In order to systematically ensure the authority and centralised leadership of the Party Central Committee, the committee has reaffirmed and improved the system of requesting reports. In accordance with the party constitution and *Several Guidelines on Political Life Within the Party Under the New Situation, Regulations on Supervision Within the CPC, Regulations on the Work of CPC Local Committees, Regulations on the Work of CPC Party Groups (Pilot), Regulations on CPC Work Organs (Pilot), Several Provisions of the Politburo of the CPC Central Committee on Strengthening and Maintaining the Centralised and Unified Leadership of the Party* and other institutional provisions, all comrades in the Politburo of the Central Committee report annually in writing to the Party Central Committee and the General Secretary. Also, the Central Secretariat and the Central Commission for Discipline Inspection, the Party Group of the NPC Standing Committee, the Party Group of the State Council, the Party Group of the National Committee of the CPPCC, the Party Group of the Supreme People's Court and the Party Group of the Supreme People's Procuratorate report annually to the Standing Committee of the Central Committee Politburo and the Politburo itself. In this way the party committees (party groups) of all regions and departments have strengthened their approach in reporting to the Party Central Committee. The Party Central Committee has to be consulted and reported to in a timely manner when studying major matters or making major decisions that affect the overall situation, and special reports have to be made on the implementation of important decisions of the Party Central Committee. In the event of sudden and major problems and issues in the course of work, the Party Central Committee has to be consulted and reported to in a timely manner. If the situation is urgent and must be dealt with on the spot, then the work must be done to the highest standard and then swiftly reported.

In order to strengthen the centralised and unified leadership of the Party Central Committee, Xi Jinping personally headed several leading groups after the 18th CPC National Congress, including the Central

Leading Group for Comprehensively Deepening Reform, the Central Leading Group for Cyber Security and Informatisation, the CMC Leading Group for Deepening National Defence and Military Reform, the Central Leading Group on Financial and Economic Affairs, and the Central Leading Group for Foreign Affairs, so that he could oversee the overall management of China's affairs and comprehensively strengthen the leadership of economic, political, cultural, social, eco-civilisation, and military and defence construction, and foreign affairs.

In March 2018, the central government initiated the deepening of reform of party and state organs, bringing to a climax initiatives to improve the institutional mechanisms for the overall leadership of the party. As an important manifestation of upholding and strengthening the overall leadership of the party on a practical level, deepening reform of the party and state organs was dedicated to building party and state institutional roles which are systematic and complete, scientific and standardised, and efficient, forming a system of party leadership that oversees China's overall context and coordinates all parties, a system of government governance with clear responsibilities and administration in accordance with the law, a world-class system of armed forces with Chinese characteristics, a system of mass organisation that reaches out to a wide range of people and serves the masses, and a system of work which promotes coordinated action and synergy among the NPC, the government, the CPPCC, supervisory organs, the judiciary, the procuratorial organs, people's organisations, enterprises and institutions, and social organisations under the unified leadership of the party. Judging from the effectiveness of the reform, the institutional mechanism for the party's leadership of all work has basically been achieved in terms of institutional functions, and the relationship between the institutional functions of the party, the government and the military under the conditions of the party's long-term governance has been resolved. As a result the party's leadership has been implemented in all aspects and sectors in exercising the duties of the party and state organs, which has better adapted to the requirements of the development of socialism with Chinese characteristics in the new era, and also better met the needs of the CPC in power.

(IV) IMPROVING THE PARTY AND STATE SUPERVISORY SYSTEM

The greatest challenge facing the long-term rule and overall leadership of the communist party is the supervision of power. In order to achieve a breakthrough with regard to this difficult issue and break out of the historical cycle, it is necessary to explore an effective path to achieve self-purification. Since the 18th CPC National Congress, the Party Central Committee with Comrade Xi Jinping at its core, has made significant decisions and arrangements to deepen reform of the national supervisory system, focusing on refining and strengthening the party and state supervisory system, and walked along a new path to solve the so-called "Goldbach's Conjecture" of national governance, namely self-monitoring under the long-term governance of the communist party.

After the 18th CPC National Congress, the Party Central Committee achieved a breakthrough regarding the difficult issue of accountability in theory and practice. The Central Committee clarified the "Two Responsibilities" for the construction of party culture and clean government, namely, that the party committee is responsible for the main body and the Central Commission for Discipline Inspection is responsible for supervision. In January 2014, at the 3rd Plenary Session of the 18th Central Commission for Discipline Iinspection, Xi Jinping classified the main responsibilities for the construction of party culture and clean government into five areas, basically listing the main responsibilities, requiring party committees at all levels to take the initiative to take responsibility for selection and employment, correcting culture and discipline, education and supervision, case investigation and handling, and leading from above, so that the implementation of key responsibilities would drive the implementation of overall responsibilities. The central government requires discipline inspection and supervisory organs to focus on the construction of party culture and clean government and the anti-corruption struggle, focus closely on accountability for supervision and discipline, and deepen the "Three Turns", returning the work which they should not be in charge to the main department responsible for it, so as not to overstep, not to miss something, and not to make an erroneous judgment.

The Central Committee has advanced progressively to promote reform of the dual leadership system of the party's discipline inspection work, proposing the "Two Mains", namely, the investigation and handling of corruption cases in the main by the leadership of the senior discipline inspection committee, with the handling of clues, and case investigation and handling, being required to be reported to the senior discipline inspection committee while also reporting to the party committee of the same level, and also the nomination and inspection of secretaries and deputy secretaries of the discipline inspection committee at all levels to be in the main conducted by the senior discipline inspection committee in conjunction with the organisational department. The development and implementation of methods for the nomination and inspection of heads and deputy heads of discipline inspection teams assigned by the Central Commission for Discipline Inspection, the secretaries and deputy secretaries of discipline inspection committees of provinces, autonomous regions and municipalities, and enterprises under Chinese control has reinforced the predominance of system leadership in terms of the two major powers of personnel and case handling. The significant increase in the number of letters of complaint and denunciation of malefactors, cases filed and concluded, and the number of people disciplined by the party and the government showed that there was less interference and disquiet in investigating and handling corruption cases, and the supervisory authority and initiative of the discipline inspection committees at all levels was significantly increased.

During this period, the Party Central Committee vigorously promoted the deepening of the reform of the national supervisory system and its pilot work, which became an important element in improving the party and state supervisory system. In January 2016, Xi Jinping delivered an important speech at the 6th Plenary Session of the 18th Central Commission for Discipline Iinspection, pointing out that the proportion of party members in China's civil service ranks exceeded 80%, and the proportion of party members among leading cadres at or above the county level exceeded 95%, and that party supervision and state supervision have a high degree of internal consistency and complementarity. Discipline and inspection are the sharpest tools for governing the party in a comprehensive and strict manner, and state supervision is the most direct and effective method of supervising public power. Co-location of offices can strengthen the effectiveness of the supervision and governance of the party and the state, so that party governance according to rules and regulations and governing the country according to the rule of law can mutually promote and complement each other. Xi emphasised the need to uphold the party's unified leadership of the construction of party culture, and clean government and anti-corruption work, to expand the scope of supervision, integrate supervisory forces, improve the organisational structure of state supervision, and form a system of state supervision with comprehensive coverage of state organs and their civil servants[10]. From June to October 2016, Xi Jinping chaired six meetings of the Central Leading Group for Comprehensively Deepening Reform, meetings of the Politburo Standing Committee and meetings of the Politburo to make arrangements and give instructions for promoting reform of the national supervisory system, stating the direction for deepening reform of the system. In October 2016, the 6th Plenary Session of the 18th CPC Central Committee juxtaposed the supervisory organs with the NPC and the government for the first time, stressing that, "party committees at all levels should provide support and ensure that the NPC, government, supervisory organs and judicial organs at the same level supervise state organs and public officials in accordance with the law"[11].

In accordance with the timetable and roadmap set by the Party Central Committee,

the General Office of the CPC Central Committee issued the *Pilot Programme on Reform of the National Supervisory System in Beijing, and Shanxi and Zhejiang Provinces* in November 2016, establishing supervisory committees at all levels in the three provinces and municipalities to implement pilot reforms of the national supervisory system, focusing on trialling and exploration of practice in terms of institutional mechanisms and institutional construction, in order to accumulate experience for nationwide implementation. Through bold exploration and proactive innovation, the three pilot provinces and municipalities developed much rich experience that can be replicated and expanded. When Xi Jinping visited Shanxi in June 2017, he noted, "You have put a lot of effort into the pilot reforms of the national supervisory system, and the strengths of the system are being converted into governance effectiveness, in order that the fruits of these reforms will be effectively exploited"[12]. On the basis of the work carried out for the pilot reforms, in October 2017, the General Office of the CPC Central Committee issued the *Pilot Programme for the Nationwide Implementation of Reform of the National Supervisory System*. Subsequently, the 30th meeting of the Standing Committee of the 12th NPC adopted the decision to implement the pilot work of reforming the national supervisory system nationwide. The Central Commission for Discipline Inspection and all regions resolutely implemented the requirements of the party Central Committee and advanced the formation of supervisory committees at all levels in a swift, steady, firm and orderly manner. On 24 November 2017, the Qingshan District Supervisory Committee in Baotou City, Inner Mongolia Autonomous Region was established and began operations, becoming the first banner (county or district) level supervisory committee to be established and begin operations after the comprehensive implementation of the work of the pilot reforms of the national supervisory system. Since then, the pace of the formation of supervisory committees across China has been continuing to accelerate. On 25 February 2018, with the official establishment of the Supervisory Committee in Daxin County, Chongzuo City, Guangxi Zhuang Autonomous Region, the formation of all provincial, municipal and county-level supervisory committees across China was completed within a three-month period, laying a solid foundation for the formation of the National Supervisory Commission (NSC).

In October 2017, Xi Jinping stated in his report to the 19th CPC National Congress the need to "deepen reform of the national supervisory system, implement the pilot work nationwide, form national, provincial, municipal and county-level supervision committees, and co-locate them with the party's disciplinary and inspection organs, to achieve full coverage of the supervision of all public officials exercising public power"[13]. Xi Jinping subsequently also delivered a series of major speeches at the 1st, 2nd and 3rd Plenary Sessions of the 19th CPC Central Committee and the 2nd Plenary Session of the 19th Central Commission for Discipline Iinspection, giving important instructions on deepening reform of the national supervisory system and providing fundamental guidelines for the formation of national, provincial, municipal and county-level supervisory committees.

In March 2018, the 1st session of the 13th NPC adopted constitutional amendments and the Supervision Law of the PRC, thereby giving birth to the National Supervisory Commission and its leadership, achieving the major creation of state institutions and the party and state supervisory system, and forming a national supervisory system with Chinese characteristics. Accordingly, the National State Supervision Commission of the Central Commission for Discipline Inspection unified the establishment of a fixed agency known as the CCDI-NSC (Central Commission for Discipline Inspection-National Supervisory Commission). If a new department is established or renamed, the name of the agency is changed accordingly. The soundness of the party and state supervisory system has adapted to the evolving situation, enabling the party's internal supervision to be effectively strengthened, covering all party organisations and members, and truly locking power into an institutional cage. This constitutes a new contribution made by the CPC to explore and deepen the communist party's governance law.

(V) ENHANCING THE PARTY'S LEADERSHIP AND INFLUENCE IN THE FIELD OF IDEOLOGY

After the 18th CPC National Congress, in the face of the increasingly complex situation in the field of ideology, the CPC vigorously strengthened its leadership of ideological work, promoted key themes and spread positivity, consolidating the ideological unity of the whole party and society.

In August 2013, the National Conference on Propaganda and Thought Work was convened, where Xi Jinping delivered an important speech, profoundly expounding a series of major theoretical and practical issues related to the long-term development of propaganda and ideological work, and clearly defining the directional objectives, key tasks and basic guidelines for propaganda and ideological work under the new situation. Xi Jinping emphasised that economic construction is the central work of the party and ideological work is an extremely important work of the party[14]. He said that only if economic construction continues to achieve success and the people continue to benefit will ideological work have a solid material basis, and only by effectively grasping ideological work will central works have an ideological guarantee, and will a strong spiritual impetus to lead society, unite people and promote development be formed. In order to implement the main responsibility of ideological work, he said, it is necessary to hold high the great banner of socialism with Chinese characteristics, firmly establish confidence in the path, theory, system and culture of socialism with Chinese characteristics, and ensure that the party and the state always advance triumphantly in the right direction. This meeting made arrangements and deployments for the whole party to effectively fulfil its main responsibility for ideological work.

In order to enhance the party's leadership and influence in the field of ideology and strengthen its guidance and leadership of the work of literature and art, Xi Jinping attended the Symposium on Literary and Art Work on 15 October 2014 and delivered an important speech. He pointed out that for literature and art to reflect the voice of the people well, it must uphold the fundamental direction of serving the people and serving socialism. This is a basic requirement put forward by the party for the literary and artistic front and is also the key to determining the future prospects of China's literary and artistic endeavours. Only by firmly establishing a Marxist view of literature and art, and truly putting the people at the centre, can literature and art exert the greatest positive energy. To be people-centred means to take meeting the spiritual and cultural needs of the people as the start and end point of literature and art, and work related to them, to take the people as the subjects of literary and artistic expression, to take the people as the connoisseurs and judges of the aesthetics of literature and art, and to take serving the people as the duty of literary and artistic workers. General Secretary Xi Jinping required that party committees at all levels should prioritise the work of literature and art on their agenda, implement the party's guidelines and policies on literature and art, and grasp the correct direction for the development of literature and art, as well as select and strengthen the leadership of literary and artistic units and create a good environment conducive to literary and artistic creation[15]. This historic meeting and Xi Jinping's important speech creatively answered a series of major questions of fundamental and directional importance for the prosperity and development of literature and art, and made comprehensive arrangements for effective work in literature and art under new historical conditions.

After that the party steadily implemented major initiatives to strengthen its leadership of ideological work. In January 2015, the National Propaganda Ministry Conference stressed that propaganda work should grasp the correct orientation, uphold leading by values, tell a good Chinese story, strengthen legal management, strive for innovation and progress, strengthen the system of responsibility for ideological work led by the party committee, firmly grasp leadership and influence in the field of ideology, improve the capacity and level of leading public opinion, and enhance China's cultural soft power. In April of the same year, the Central Propaganda Department and three other departments jointly issued the *Opinions on Strengthening Grassroots Propaganda, and Ideological and Cultural Work*, effectively strengthening grassroots propaganda, and ideological and cultural work and promoting the implementation of various tasks to strengthen the party's leadership over ideological work. In September, the CPC Central Committee Politburo deliberated and adopted the *Opinions on Prospering and Developing Socialist Literature and Art*, which further elaborated on and made arrangements for important issues such as upholding a people-centred creative orientation, and strengthening and improving the party's leadership of literature and art work. In October, the General Office of the CPC Central Committee and the General Office of the State Council issued the *Opinions on Reforming the National System of Awards for Literature and Art*, which regulated accreditation to support excellence and guide innovation. In January 2016, the Central Propaganda Department and five other departments jointly issued the *2016-2017 National Guidelines for the Training Work Plan for Core and Management Literary and Artistic Cadres*, training 130,000 literary and art workers in two years. In 2015 alone, nearly 70,000 literary and art workers and volunteers participated in more than 2,000 thematic practical activities, directly serving more than 3 million people at the grassroots level[16].

News and public opinion work constitute another important element of the party's ideological work. In February 2016, Xi Jinping, in a major speech at the party's Symposium on Press and Public Opinion Work, profoundly expounded the significance, duty and mission, basic guidelines and practical path for successfully carrying out press and public opinion work. Xi Jinping pointed out that the party's press and public opinion work is an important aspect of the party's work and is a major matter in the management of state affairs and in establishing the nation and bringing peace and stability. He proposed that the duties and mission of the party's press and public opinion work are to hold high the banner and lead the way, focus on central issues and serve the greater good, unite the people and inspire them, lead social trends, transform the people and gather strength, clarify falsehoods and distinguish right from wrong, and connect China with foreign countries and communicate with the world. In order to assume this responsibility and mission, [he said] it is necessary to prioritise political orientation, firmly adhere to party principles, to the Marxist concept of journalism, to the correct orientation of public opinion, and to an emphasis on positive publicity[17]. Xi Jinping's major speech brought the work of news and public opinion into the party's vision of governance, specifying the direction and path for improving the competence of news and public opinion work from the position of the management of state affairs. In April of the same year, at the National Symposium on Cyber Security and Informatisation Work, Xi Jinping also focused on building a good internet ecology, utilising the role of the internet in guiding and reflecting public opinion, and made comprehensive plans for firmly grasping the dominant power of internet communication and successfully implementing ideological work.

In order to study and promote the innovative development of China's philosophical and social science work, Xi Jinping gave a major speech at the symposium on philosophical and social science work in May 2016. There he pointed out that it was necessary to follow the idea of being based in China and drawing on foreign countries, drawing on history and grasping the realities of the contemporary era, caring for humanity and facing the future, and also to focus on building philosophical and social sciences with Chinese characteristics, fully reflecting Chinese characteristics, style and dignity in the guiding ideology, and systems of discipline, academia and discourse[18]. In May 2017, in accordance with the spirit of this symposium, the CPC Central Committee issued the *Opinions on Accelerating the Construction of Philosophical and Social Sciences with Chinese Characteristics*, making comprehensive deployments and arrangements for the innovative development of major areas such as accelerating the construction of philosophical and social sciences with Chinese characteristics.

During this period, the central government also made arrangements to strengthen the ideological work of higher education institutions and party schools, issuing the *Opinions on Further Strengthening and Improving the Propaganda and Ideological Work of Higher Education Institutions under the New Situation* and the *Opinions of the CPC Central Committee on Strengthening and Improving the Work of Party Schools under the New Situation* in January and December 2015 respectively, clearly setting out the task of consolidating the role of party schools and higher education institutions at all levels as important positions for the party's ideological work.

This series of important ideas and major initiatives by the Party Central Committee enabled the party to firmly grasp the leadership, management and influence of ideological work in terms of ideological understanding, methods and means, and institutional mechanisms, greatly reversing the negative and passive situation which had existed in the field of ideology for some time, and greatly enhancing the level of the party's leadership and governance ability in the field of ideology.

(VI) THE REVOLUTIONARY RESHAPING OF THE PLA: UPHOLDING AND PERFECTING THE ABSOLUTE LEADERSHIP OF THE PARTY OVER THE MILITARY

National defence and military construction constitute important components of the general composition of the cause of socialism with Chinese characteristics, an important element of the CPC's management of state affairs, and an important element of the communist party's governance law. After the 18th CPC National Congress, in accordance with the changing situation, the Party Central Committee with Comrade Xi Jinping at its core led the PLA to achieve a revolutionary and holistic reshaping and to create a new situation for strengthening and rejuvenating the army.

On 15 November 2012, the day after the closing of the 18th CPC National Congress, Xi Jinping presided over the first executive meeting of the new CMC and clearly declared, "We must always think of the party and the people, China's national sovereignty, security and territorial integrity, and national defence and military construction, always be at our work, do our duty conscientiously, work hard and effectively, never betray the trust of the party and the people, and never fall short of the expectations of all officers and soldiers"[19]. In December 2012, Xi Jinping gave an important speech during a work tour in the Guangzhou Military Region, [stating that], "Achieving the great rejuvenation of the Chinese nation is the greatest dream of the Chinese nation in modern times. It can be said that this dream is the dream of a strong nation, and for the army, it is also the dream of a strong army"[20]. In March 2013, at a plenary session of the PLA delegation at the 1st session of the 12th NPC, Xi Jinping further stated, "Building a people's army that listens to the party's commands, is capable of winning battles and has an excellent work style constitutes the party's goal of strengthening the army under the new situation"[21]. Xi Jinping's series of important discourses on the dream of a strong army captured the prominent contradictions facing the construction of the people's army and became the party's general strategy and requirements for strengthening and governing the army under the new situation.

In order to further promote the implementation of the fundamental principle of the absolute leadership of the party over the army and to ensure that the fundamental aim of the PLA would remain unshaken, the first All-Army Political Work Conference since the turn of the century, commonly known as the "New Gutian Meeting", was held in Gutian, Fujian Province, in October 2014 in accordance with the personal decision of Xi Jinping. Xi Jinping attended the meeting and delivered a major speech and profoundly analysed 10 prominent problems in ideology, politics, and work style among the troops, especially among leading cadres. He emphasised that in the face of profound changes in the situation within China and overseas, and the test of deepening national defence and military reform, political work in China's military should only be strengthened and must not be weakened, should only advance and must not be stagnant, should only be active and must not respond passively, and also emphasised that the most urgent matter at the time was to firmly and comprehensively establish the four fundamental areas of ideals and beliefs, party spirit and principles, the standard of fighting strength, and the prestige of political work, focusing on five key areas of work[22]. This conference and Xi Jinping's important speech further clarified the guiding principles, key tasks and practical requirements for the political work of the PLA under the new situation and became an important pivotal moment for the party in upholding and refining the absolute leadership of the party over the army and reshaping the PLA in the new era. At the end of 2014, the Party Central Committee transmitted to the whole party and army the *Decision on Several Issues Concerning the Political Work of the Army under the New Situation*, which profoundly explained the extreme importance, necessity and urgency of strengthening and improving the political work of the army and focused on demonstrating the important results of the New Gutian Meeting.

At the same time, the historic task of deepening the reform of national defence and the military was also being carried out in earnest. The 3rd Plenary Session of the 18th CPC Central Committee incorporated national defence and military reform into the general composition of the comprehensive deepening of reform in China, specifically pointing out the three major directions for the reform of national defence and military reform, namely, deepening the adjustment and reform of the military establishment, promoting the adjustment and reform of the military policy system, and promoting the in-depth development of military-civilian integration. In March 2014, Xi Jinping proposed at the first meeting of the CMC's

Leading Group on Deepening Defence and Military Reform upholding the study of reform with the goal of strengthening the military, leading reform with the goal of strengthening the military and promoting reform in connection with the goal of strengthening the military. In July 2015, Xi Jinping presided over the executive meeting of the CMC and the meeting of the Politburo Standing Committee of respectively to deliberate and screen the *General Programme for Deepening National Defence and Military Reform*. On 3 September, at a conference marking the 70th anniversary of the victory of the Chinese people's War of Resistance Against Japanese Aggression and the World Anti-Fascist War, Xi Jinping announced that China would reduce the number of its military personnel by 300,000. In October, Xi Jinping again chaired an executive meeting of the CMC, which deliberated and adopted the Implementation Plan for Reform of the Leadership and Command System. In November, the reform work conference of the CMC was held, where Xi Jinping issued a mobilisation order to win the battle to deepen the reform of national defence and the military, to comprehensively implement the strategy of reforming and strengthening the army, and to unswervingly follow the path of strengthening the army with Chinese characteristics. The CMC subsequently issued the *Opinions on Deepening the Reform of National Defence and the Military*.

In 2016, holistic and revolutionary reforms of national defence and the military were launched on all fronts, focusing on the implementation of revolutionary changes in the command structure. The Central Committee took the restructuring and reform of the CMC as the highest priority, transforming the four headquarters into 15 functional departments, thoroughly dismantling the system of large military regions and continental armies, establishing five major theatre commands, forming a new leadership structure for the army, and setting up a rocket force and strategic support forces. They established a new leadership management system characterised by "the CMC being in charge of the headquarters, the theatre commands being in charge of warfare, and the military services being in charge of construction", forcefully grinding down many stubborn issues and solving many prominent problems that had existed for a long time but that it had not been possible to solve all along, and accomplishing many great undertakings which the Central Committee had wanted to accomplish for many years but had not been able to. At the same time, breakthroughs were made in the adjustment and reform of the military policy system, and substantial steps were taken in the development of military-civilian integration. The comprehensive implementation of the strategy of reforming and strengthening the army achieved landmark results and won key victories.

Along with the deepening of national defence and military reforms, the Party Central Committee and Xi Jinping upheld the approach of ruling the army strictly and in accordance with the law, severely punishing corruption in the army, continuously increasing efforts to correct culture and discipline, and recreating a good image of the PLA. From the 18th to the 19th CPC National Congresses, more than 4,000 cases were opened and reviewed across the whole military, with disciplinary action taken against more than 13,000 people[23], and major cases such as Guo Boxiong, Xu Caihou and Gu Junshan were seriously investigated and dealt with, effectively curbing the momentum of corruption from spreading. In October 2013, the CMC established an inspection system and carried out inspection work throughout the army, and, by the end of 2015, completed full inspection coverage of all major army units. The overwhelming momentum of the construction of clean politics in the military and party culture and the anti-corruption struggle was established and gradually consolidated.

The completion of the revolutionary reshaping of the PLA safeguarded and implemented the CMC Chairman responsibility system, purified the political ecology of the PLA ideologically, politically and organisationally, achieved a new system, structure, pattern and appearance for the PLA, firmly upheld and refined a series of fundamental principles and systems related to the absolute leadership of the party over the military, and laid the foundation for comprehensively promoting the modernisation of national defence and the military from a new historical starting point. This constitutes another major contribution made by the CPC to the expansion and deepening of the communist party's governance law.

6

THE HISTORICAL MISSION OF THE CPC IN GOVERNING CHINA IN THE NEW ERA

The 19th CPC National Congress was held triumphantly from 18 to 24 October 2017, building on the tremendous achievements made by the party since its 18th CPC National Congress. This was a very important congress of the CPC held at the decisive stage of building a moderately prosperous society in all respects and at a critical period when socialism with Chinese characteristics entered a new era. The congress clearly proposed that the historical mission of the CPC in the new era is to achieve the great dream of the great rejuvenation of the Chinese nation, and issued a political manifesto to the whole party and whole nation to unite and lead the people of all China's ethnic groups to unswervingly follow the path of socialism with Chinese characteristics, to be victorious in building a moderately prosperous society in all respects and to win the great victory of socialism with Chinese characteristics in the new era. Anchored to the 19th CPC National Congress, the CPC embarked on a new journey to govern China in the new era of socialism with Chinese characteristics and to explore the communist party's governance law.

(I) CHANGES IN THE MAIN CONTRADICTIONS IN CHINESE SOCIETY PLACE NEW DEMANDS ON PARTY GOVERNANCE

The 19th CPC National Congress, on the basis of an in-depth study and extensively listening to the views of all concerned, made new progressive statements on the current main contradictions in Chinese society, emphasising that, "socialism with Chinese characteristics has entered a new era, and the main contradictions in Chinese society have transformed into the contradiction between the people's constantly growing need for a better life, and unbalanced and inadequate development"[1]. The 19th CPC National Congress clearly indicated the transformation of the main contradictions in Chinese society, signalling the opening of a new chapter in the history of the CPC's governance. After the development of 40 years of reform and opening up, China's level of social productivity had generally improved significantly, and its social productivity had become world-class in many respects. China's GDP had ranked a steady second in the world since 2010. Agricultural and industrial productivity had increased significantly, and the productivity of more than 220 major industrial and agricultural products ranked a steady first in the world, with some products even experiencing a large surplus[2]. This shows that China's longstanding economy characterised by shortages and inadequate supply was fundamentally transformed, and it was no longer in line with reality to speak of "backward social production".

At the same time, people's living standards had risen significantly and their aspirations for a better life had become stronger. Not only have they come to have higher demands for material and cultural life but they also have growing demands for democracy, rule of law, equity, justice, security and the environment. Since the outset of reform and opening up, China has steadily solved the problem of providing adequate subsistence for more than one billion people, has generally achieved moderate prosperity, and will soon complete the building of a moderately prosperous society in all aspects. The standard of living of the Chinese people has continued to rise to new levels, with per capita GDP growing from around US$156 in 1978 to over US$8,000 in 2016, reaching the level of upper middle-income countries[3].

At the same time, the level of social security in China has improved greatly, and a social security system covering both urban and rural areas has been basically established while many other aspects of livelihood protection have also improved significantly. As people's living standards continue to rise, their needs diversify, becoming multi-level and multi-faceted, and they expect better education, more stable jobs, more satisfactory incomes, more reliable social security, higher levels of medical and health services, more comfortable living conditions, a more beautiful environment, and a richer spiritual and cultural life. The people's consciousness of democracy, equity, rule of law, participation, supervision and the protection of their rights constantly increases. This shows that the needs of the people have gone beyond the realm and level of material culture in terms of scope and focus, and that mere talk about "material cultural needs" no longer truly and comprehensively reflects the aspirations and demands of the people. There are many factors affecting the satisfaction of people's needs for a better life but the main problem from which all other problems are ultimately generated or derived is unbalanced and insufficient development. Uneven development mainly refers to the lack of balance in the development of various sectors and aspects in various regions, which restricts the improvement of the national development level. Insufficient development mainly refers to the fact that some regions, sectors and aspects are still underdeveloped, and the task of development yet to be achieved is very significant. The problems of unbalanced and inadequate development constrain each other, bring about many social contradictions and problems, and are the main source of various social contradictions which are intertwined at the present stage. Development is a dynamic process, and the problem of imbalance and insufficiency will always exist, but when unbalanced and insufficient development becomes the key aspect of the main social contradictions after a certain stage, efforts must be made to understand and solve them.

Seizing the key points to drive the overall work is a basic requirement of materialistic dialectics, and is also a methodology advocated and adhered to by communists, and constitutes an important lesson drawn by the CPC during its history of revolution and governance. The nearly century-long history of the CPC is a practical process of constantly recognising and resolving social contradictions under different historical orientations, thereby driving history forward. After the completion of the socialist transformation, the main social contradiction in China has always been the contradiction between the growing material and cultural needs of the people and backward social production. The Eighth CPC National Congress and the 6th Plenary Session of the 11th CPC Central Committee successively confirmed this. The new judgments and statements of the 19th CPC National Congress both changed significantly from the past and yet also maintained continuity with the past, from "material and cultural needs" to the "need for a better life", and from solving the problem of "backward social production" to "unbalanced and inadequate development", reflecting the unique features of this stage of China's development, as well as the direction and path of the development of the cause of the party and the state. This constituted a historic change in the overall situation. Seeking to resolve how to focus on solving the problem of unbalanced and inadequate development, to vigorously improve the quality and efficiency of development, better meet the growing needs of the people in the economic, political, cultural, social and ecological fields, and better promote the all-round development of people and social progress, all on the basis of the continued promotion of development, has not only advanced new requirements for the CPC's governance but also added new connotations to the communist party's governance law.

(II) THE 'FOUR GREATS' AND A NEW HISTORICAL MISSION

The 19th CPC National Congress profoundly elaborated the historical mission of the CPC in the new era, pointing out that achieving the great rejuvenation of the Chinese nation is the greatest dream of the Chinese nation in modern times. Today, we are closer to, more confident in, and more capable of, achieving the goal of the great rejuvenation of the Chinese nation than at any other time in history. As the old saying goes, the closer one is to completing a task, the tougher it gets. Likewise, the great rejuvenation of the Chinese nation can by no means be achieved lightly or with the mere beating of a gong. The entire party must be prepared to make even more arduous and difficult efforts[4]. On this basis, the report of the 19th CPC National Congress distinctly proposes the fact that in order to achieve great dream in the new era, it is necessary to engage in a great struggle, build a great project and advance a great cause. This is a clear answer to the question surrounding the kind of main line on which CPC governance will centre in order to move forward and develop in the new era of socialism with Chinese characteristics.

In order to achieve this great dream, it is necessary to engage in a great struggle with many new historical characteristics. The 18th CPC National Congress in 2012 clearly proposed that, "the development of socialism with Chinese characteristics is a long-term and arduous historical task, and it is necessary to prepare to engage in a great struggle with many new historical characteristics"[5]. Subsequently, the "great struggle with many new historical characteristics" was incorporated into the CPC's governance philosophy. The 19th CPC National Congress in 2017 required all party comrades to more consciously uphold the leadership of the party and China's socialist system, and resolutely oppose all words and deeds that weaken, distort or deny the leadership of the party and China's socialist system, to safeguard the interests of the people more consciously, and resolutely oppose all acts that harm the interests of the people and are detached from the masses, to engage more consciously in the *zeitgeist* of reform and innovation, and resolutely achieve breakthroughs in all persistent and chronic problems, to more consciously safeguard national sovereignty, security and development interests, and resolutely oppose all acts that split the motherland, and undermine national unity and social harmony and stability, and to more consciously guard against all kinds of risks, and resolutely overcome all difficulties and challenges that arise in the political, economic, cultural and social fields, and in the natural world. [The congress highlighted that] communists should be fully aware of the long-term nature, complexity and enormity of this great struggle, carry forward the spirit of struggle, improve their capacity for handling this struggle and continuously seize new victories in this great struggle.

In order to achieve this great dream, it is necessary to promote the great new project of party building. In October 1939, Mao Zedong called party building a "great project" in his *Message to the Communist Party*, and in September 1994, the 4th Plenary Session of the 14th CPC Central Committee proposed the "great new project" of party building. Subsequently, the 15th CPC National Congress in September 1997 clearly put forward the general objective of comprehensively promoting the great new project of building the CPC for the new century. The 19th CPC National Congress in 2017 stated that history has proven, and will continue to prove, that without the leadership of the CPC, Chinese national rejuvenation can be nothing but an empty dream. If the CPC is to remain always the vanguard of the times and the backbone of the Chinese nation, and if it is to always remain the ruling Marxist party, it must always be up to the mark and comprehensively promote the great new project of building the party.

In order to achieve the great dream, it is necessary to advance the great cause of socialism with Chinese characteristics. Socialism with Chinese characteristics has been the theme of all the party's theory and practice in the new era since the 12th CPC National Congress in 1982, when it put forward the major proposition of "building socialism with Chinese characteristics". Then, the 18th CPC National Congress in 2012 refined and summed up the path, theoretical system and [overall] system of socialism with Chinese characteristics. The 19th CPC National Congress in 2017 further pointed out that the path of socialism with Chinese characteristics is the only way to achieve socialist modernisation and create a better life for the people, that the theoretical system of socialism with Chinese characteristics is the correct theory to guide the party and the people to achieve the great rejuvenation of the Chinese nation, that the socialist system with Chinese characteristics is the fundamental institutional guarantee for the development and progress of contemporary China, and that socialist culture with Chinese characteristics is a powerful spiritual force to inspire the whole party and the people of all China's ethnic groups to advance courageously.

The Great Struggle, the Great Project, the Great Cause and the Great Dream are closely linked, interlinked and interacting, and are harmonised and unified in the great practice of the CPC's governance of China in the new era. Among these four, the decisive role is played by the great new project of building the party. In order to accomplish the new task of governance and achieve the historical mission of the new era, it is necessary for all party comrades to more consciously uphold the Four Greats and continuously promote them.

(III) PROMOTING A GREAT SOCIAL REVOLUTION THROUGH THE GREAT SELF-REVOLUTION OF THE PARTY

On 25 October 2017 when meeting with Chinese and foreign journalists after the 1st Plenary Session of the 19th CPC Central Committee, Xi Jinping said, "Practice has fully proven that the CPC is capable of leading the people in carrying out a great social revolution and also in carrying out a great self-revolution"[6]. This was the first time that the CPC explicitly formulated the "Theory of the Two Revolutions". At a seminar on 5 January 2018 for new Central Committee members, alternate members and leading cadres at the provincial and ministerial levels to study and implement Xi Jinping Thought on Socialism with Chinese Characteristics for a New Era and the spirit of the 19th CPC National Congress, Xi Jinping further pointed out that, "socialism with Chinese characteristics in the new era is the fruit of the great social revolution carried out by the people under the leadership of the party, and it is also the continuation of the great social revolution carried out by people under the leadership of the party, which must be consistently implemented" and "in order to carry out the great social revolution of upholding and developing socialism with Chinese characteristics in the new era, our party must be brave enough to carry out self-revolution and build the party even stronger"[7]. Xi Jinping's series of important statements systematically expounded the essence and intrinsic relationship of the Theory of the Two Revolutions, which has become an important achievement of the CPC's theoretical innovation, and is certain to leave a strong and indelible mark in the history of the exploration of the communist party's governance law.

Carrying out social revolution and self-revolution is a concentrated expression of the original aspirations and historical mission of the CPC, and of its political and social functions as a political party. Being "revolutionaries" constitutes the most distinctive aspect of the identity of communists and is their never-changing political role. In times of war, when the communists led the people to seize power, it was a revolution. In times of peace, when the communists led the people to carry out socialist transformation and construction, it was also a revolution. At a turning point in history, when the party led the people to launch the spectacular reform and opening up, it was a revolution. Under the new historical conditions of socialism with Chinese characteristics entering a new era, the party led the people to carry out great struggles, implement great projects, advance great causes and achieve great dreams. This was also a revolution, and a broader and more profound great revolution.

After the 18th CPC National Congress in 2012, the Party Central Committee with Comrade Xi Jinping at its core promoted historic changes and made all-round achievements in party and state undertakings. These changes and achievements were based on the major topical issue of the time regarding the kind of socialism with Chinese characteristics which was to be upheld and developed, and also how to uphold and develop socialism with Chinese characteristics in the new era, in order to promote and develop socialism with Chinese characteristics from a new historical starting point. Therefore, socialism with Chinese characteristics in the new era constitutes a new outcome of the great social revolution implemented by the people under the leadership of the CPC, a continuation of the great social revolution implemented by the people under the leadership of the party, and a continuation with an even more important new quality and new meaning.

The 19th CPC National Congress in 2017 explicitly adopted the strategic composition of the Five-Sphere Integrated Plan and the Four Comprehensives as the guiding principle and made comprehensive strategic arrangements for China's socioeconomic development as well as the strict party governance. Socialism with Chinese characteristics constitutes a cause led by the party and is also the cause of hundreds of millions of Chinese people themselves. It is necessary to uphold the principle that development is for the people, and depends on them, and that the fruits of development are to be shared by the people and focus on promoting the well-being of the people. This is the fundamental start and end point of the great social revolution of the new era. In order to lead the great social revolution in the new era, the CPC faces "Four Tests" and "Four Risks", which raises the issue that in order to lead the great social revolution in the new era well, the party must also lead its great self-revolution well. This requires the party to continue to uphold the policy that the party should manage the party and govern it in a comprehensive and strict manner, to build the party up and to complete the party's task of self-revolution, in order to make the party the strong leading core of the cause of socialism with Chinese characteristics.

If the CPC is to continue to carry out the great social revolution and thereby achieve its historical mission and task of governance in the future, it must always maintain the political nature and determination of revolutionaries, always maintain its revolutionary spirit and will, and strive to "carry out well the great social revolution of upholding and developing socialism with Chinese characteristics in the new era". And only by promoting a great social revolution with a great self-revolution, making the party always remain the vanguard of the times and the backbone of the nation, and always maintain the unchanging nature of a Marxist ruling party, ensuring that the party unites and leads the people to effectively face major challenges, resist major risks, overcome major resistance and resolve major contradictions, will the great social revolution led by the party continue to triumph.

7

XI JINPING THOUGHT ON SOCIALISM WITH CHINESE CHARACTERISTICS FOR A NEW ERA

THE SCIENTIFIC GUIDANCE OF THE CPC'S GOVERNANCE OF CHINA

The 19th CPC National Congress formally established Xi Jinping Thought on Socialism with Chinese Characteristics for a New Era as the guiding ideology that the CPC must uphold in the long term, achieving another progressive advance in the party's guiding ideology. This constituted a strategic decision of great significance made by the party under new historical conditions, a historic development of Marxism by contemporary Chinese communists, and a historic contribution to the enrichment and deepening of the communist party's governance law.

(I) THE PRACTICAL AND THEORETICAL FOUNDATION GENERATED BY XI JINPING THOUGHT ON SOCIALISM WITH CHINESE CHARACTERISTICS FOR A NEW ERA

The CPC has always attached great importance to the construction of ideology and theory. The progressive advance in the party's ideology is an important theoretical characteristic of Marxism, and whether the guiding ideology of a political party can advance progressively is a matter of the success or failure of that party's cause. As an advanced political party, the party must, on the one hand, consciously adapt its ideology and theory to correctly reflect the changing objective reality. On the other hand, it must also constantly, dynamically and consciously guide new practice with this scientific theory that keeps abreast of the times. This means that in order for the cause of the party and the country to avoid stagnation, there must first be no stagnation in theory or ideology. One of the fundamental reasons why the CPC has continued to make glorious achievements in its long history of leading the people to carry out revolution and governance is that it has paid special attention to integrating the basic principles of Marxism with China's concrete reality and the characteristics of the times, always upholding the continuous development of Marxism in practice and developing Marxism to guide practice, thereby propelling the cause of the party ever forwards.

After a long period of hard work, socialism with Chinese characteristics entered a new era after the 18th CPC National Congress, constituting a new historical orientation of China's development. The new era has put forward new requirements for all aspects of CPC governance which are manifested in new goals, mechanisms and measures for the work of the party and the state in various sectors, posing a group of questions that constitute the "Main Questions of the Age". These focus on the major questions of the times surrounding the kind of socialism with Chinese characteristics to be upheld and developed, and how to uphold and develop socialism with Chinese characteristics in the new era. In the process of systematically answering these major questions of the times and many practical questions, Xi Jinping Thought on Socialism with Chinese Characteristics for a New Era was born and developed.

At the same time, the world is in a period of great development, change and adjustment, and is undergoing major changes unprecedented in a century. In this historical context, the Party Central Committee with Comrade Xi Jinping at its core has led China closer to the centre of the world stage than ever before. The influence of China's development philosophy and path has increased significantly, China's voice in the international arena has grown significantly, Chinese culture is increasingly showing its unique value, and China is playing an important role as a builder of international peace, a contributor to global development and a defender of the international order. It is in this international environment that Xi Jinping Thought on Socialism with Chinese Characteristics for a New Era has been nurtured, enriched and developed.

Since the 18th CPC National Congress, the party has faced a new situation and new tasks in its construction. The Party Central Committee with Comrade Xi Jinping at its core has led the whole party with the courage for self-revolution to correct party culture, discipline and to fight corruption, with the result that management of the party since the 18th CPC National Congress has achieved a profound transformation from "relaxed and soft" to "strict and resolute". The party's political ecology has significantly improved, its unity and solidarity have been more consolidated, the relationship between the party and the people has improved significantly, and the party as a whole has taken on a new and powerful vitality. Xi Jinping Thought on Socialism with Chinese Characteristics for a New Era, again formed and developed under the historical conditions of the profound revolutionary forging the party has undergone since the 18th CPC National Congress, constitutes an important achievement of the party's self-purification, self-refinement, self-innovation and self-improvement.

Xi Jinping Thought on Socialism with Chinese Characteristics for a New Era constitutes the inheritance and development of Marxism-Leninism and Mao Zedong Thought, Deng Xiaoping Theory, the major ideology of the Three Represents, and the Scientific Outlook on Development. It also constitutes the latest achievement of Marxism in China, the crystallisation of the practical experience and collective wisdom of the party and the people, and an important part of the theoretical system of socialism with Chinese characteristics[1]. Marxism-Leninism and Mao Zedong Thought are the important foundations of Xi Jinping Thought on Socialism with Chinese Characteristics for a New Era, while Deng Xiaoping Theory, the Three Represents and the Scientific Outlook on Development are the important sources of Xi Jinping Thought on Socialism with Chinese Characteristics for a New Era.

The theoretical innovations made by the Chinese communists, mainly represented by Comrade Xi Jinping, have always been innovations led by upholding Marxism. Although Xi Jinping Thought on Socialism with Chinese Characteristics for a New Era was formed in a different historical period and faced with different historical tasks from Marxism-Leninism and Mao Zedong Thought, Deng Xiaoping Theory, the major ideology of the Three Represents and the Scientific Outlook on Development, these all fully adhere to the basic principles of Marxism and the positions, views and methods that permeate them, and they all unswervingly adhere to the lofty ideals of communism, the standpoint of the people, and the world-view and methodology of dialectical and historical materialism, constituting a system of scientific thought with a common origin.

At the same time, Xi Jinping Thought on Socialism with Chinese Characteristics for a New Era is also very much abreast of the times. It pays special attention to using Marxism to observe, interpret and lead the times, profoundly understanding and accurately grasping the changes in Chinese society and the historical mission of the CPC in the new era, scientifically formulating strategic arrangements for the development of socialism with Chinese characteristics in the new era, advancing the modernisation of Marxism, and opening up new realms of Marxism, of socialism with Chinese characteristics, of national governance and party governance and management. It has greatly enriched and developed Marxism-Leninism and Mao Zedong Thought, and likewise the theoretical system of socialism with Chinese characteristics.

(II) THE PARTY'S SYSTEMATIC OVERVIEW OF A NEW SCIENTIFIC THEORY

There was a process by which the scientific theory of Xi Jinping Thought on Socialism with Chinese Characteristics for a New Era was formed and recapped. For a period of time after the 18th CPC National Congress, a series of major speeches, discourses and ideological and theoretical views put forward by Xi Jinping were referred to in the press and media as "the spirit of Xi Jinping's major speeches", "the spirit of a series of major speeches by General Secretary Xi Jinping", "the spirit of Comrade Xi Jinping's major speeches", "the spirit of Comrade Xi Jinping's series of major speeches", or "Comrade Xi Jinping's major discourses" or "Xi Jinping Thought on Governance", among others[2]. From the second half of 2013, the official name for this was gradually standardised in the *People's Daily* and other newspapers as "the spirit of the series of major speeches by General Secretary Xi Jinping"[3]. In October 2014, the concept of the spirit of the series of major speeches by General Secretary Xi Jinping was written into the *Decision of the CPC Central Committee on Several Major Issues Regarding Comprehensively Promoting the Rule of Law* adopted at the 4th Plenary Session of the 18th CPC Central Committee. This was the first time that this concept appeared in the party's central documents. After the 5th Plenary Session of the 18th CPC Central Committee in October 2015, concepts such as "Xi Jinping's New Ideas and Strategies for the Governance of China" or "General Secretary Xi Jinping's New Ideas and Strategies for the Governance of China" began to appear in the press. In October 2016, the Communiqué of the 6th Plenary Session of the 18th CPC Central Committee used the concept of the spirit of the series of major speeches by General Secretary Xi Jinping, and new ideas and strategies for the governance of China for the first time. A year later, at the 19th CPC National Congress, Xi Jinping Thought on Socialism with Chinese Characteristics for a New Era was officially proposed as the name of this scientific theory.

Xi Jinping Thought on Socialism with Chinese Characteristics for a New Era is very rich in content, covering various fields and aspects such as reform, development and stability, domestic and foreign affairs, and national defence, and governance of the party, the state and the military. The report of the 19th CPC National Congress systematically summarises the main contents of this major strategic thought in the "Eight Clarifications" and "Fourteen Upholds" outlined below.

The Eight Clarifications, namely, clarify that:

- the overall task of upholding and developing socialism with Chinese characteristics is to achieve socialist modernisation and the great rejuvenation of the Chinese nation, and to build a rich, strong, democratic, civilised, harmonious and beautiful modern socialist power in two steps by the middle of the century on the basis of building a moderately prosperous society in all respects;
- the main contradiction in Chinese society in the new era is the contradiction between the people's growing need for a better life, and unbalanced and inadequate development, and that consequently it is necessary to uphold a people-centred ideology of development and continuously promote the all-round development of the people and the common prosperity of all people;
- the general composition of the cause of socialism with Chinese characteristics is Five-Sphere and its strategic composition is the Four Comprehensives, and emphasising firm confidence in the path, theory, institutions and culture thereof;
- the overall goal of comprehensively deepening reform is to refine and develop the socialist system with Chinese characteristics and to promote modernisation of the national system of governance and governance ability;
- the overall goal of comprehensively promoting the rule of law is to build a socialist rule of law system with Chinese characteristics and a state built on the socialist rule of law;
- the party's goal of having a strong military in the new era means building a people's army that follows the party's orders, is capable of winning battles and has a work culture, and building the people's army into a world-class army;
- great-power diplomacy with Chinese characteristics should promote the building of a new type of international relations and the building of a community with a shared future for mankind;
- the most essential characteristic and the greatest strength of the socialist system with Chinese characteristics is the leadership of the CPC, and that the party is the supreme force of political leadership, putting forward the general requirements for party building in the new era, and underscoring the important position of political construction in party building.

The Fourteen Upholds, namely, uphold leadership of the party in all work, a people-centred approach, the comprehensive deepening of reform, the new concept of development, the sovereignty of the people, the comprehensive rule of law, the system of core socialist values, the protection and improvement of people's livelihoods in the midst of development, the harmonious coexistence of humans and nature, the concept of comprehensive national security, the absolute leadership of the party over the PLA, "one country, two systems" and promoting reunification of the motherland, promoting the building of a community with a shared future for mankind, and strict party governance.

From the Eight Clarifications and Fourteen Upholds, it can be seen that Xi Jinping Thought on Socialism with Chinese Characteristics for a New Era has made significant theoretical breakthroughs, innovations and developments, and constitutes a complete, logical and mutually interlinked scientific ideological and theoretical system with a series of major ideological standpoints which are original and strategic. The main founder of this ideology is Xi Jinping. Xi Jinping has been the main leader of the development of the party and the state since the 18nth CPC National Congress, the main proposer of a series of ground-breaking new concepts, ideas and strategies, and has played a decisive role and made a decisive contribution to the creation of Xi Jinping Thought on Socialism with Chinese Characteristics for a New Era. This is the conclusion reached by history and by practice.

(III) ESTABLISHING THE GUIDING POSITION OF XI JINPING THOUGHT ON SOCIALISM WITH CHINESE CHARACTERISTICS FOR A NEW ERA

The 19th CPC National Congress clearly outlined and put forward Xi Jinping Thought on Socialism with Chinese Characteristics for a New Era, highly appraised its historical status and guiding significance, established it as the guiding ideology that the CPC must adhere to in the long term and wrote it into the party constitution, achieving the progressive advance of the party's guiding ideology. This constitutes the most significant theoretical innovation, the most important political achievement and the most far-reaching historical contribution of the 19th CPC National Congress. In March 2018, on behalf of the common will of the entire party and the people of all China's ethnic groups, the 1st Session of the 13th NPC separately enshrined Xi Jinping Thought on Socialism with Chinese Characteristics for a New Era in the constitution, achieving the transformation of this ideology from the party's guiding ideology to the national guiding ideology and achieving progressive advance in the national guiding ideology. In this way, the CPC and the Chinese people clearly established Xi Jinping Thought on Socialism with Chinese Characteristics for a New Era as the guiding ideology and raised it high as a banner.

The establishment of Xi Jinping Thought on Socialism with Chinese Characteristics for a New Era as the guiding ideology of the party is an inevitable choice of history, of the party and the people, and of socialism with Chinese characteristics as it enters a new era. The report of the 19th CPC National Congress states that, "Since the 18th CPC National Congress, changes in the situation at home and abroad and the development of various undertakings in China have presented us with a major issue of the times, which is that, from the integration of theory and practice, we must systematically answer the basic questions surrounding the kind of socialism with Chinese characteristics to uphold and develop in the new era and how to uphold and develop it. This includes the basic questions surrounding the overall goals, tasks, general composition, strategic composition, direction and mode of development, the impetus for development, strategic steps, external conditions and political guarantees for upholding and developing socialism with Chinese characteristics in the new era, as well as conducting theoretical analysis of, and giving policy guidance on, various aspects including the economy, politics, rule of law, science and technology, culture, education, people's livelihoods, ethnicity, religion, society, eco-civilisation, national security, national defence and military, 'one country, two systems' and the unification of the motherland, united front, foreign affairs and party building in the light of the new practice, which is conducive to better adherence to, and development of, socialism with Chinese characteristics"[4].

It is around this major issue of the times that the CPC has upheld Marxism-Leninism and Mao Zedong Thought, Deng Xiaoping Theory, the major ideology of the Three Represents and the Scientific Outlook on Development as its guidance, upheld the emancipation of the mind, seeking truth from facts, progressive advance, being pragmatic and realistic, dialectical materialism and historical materialism, and closely integrated the new conditions of the times and practical requirements. With a brand new vision and deepened understanding of the communist party's governance law, the laws of socialist construction and the laws of human social development, the CPC has conducted painstaking theoretical explorations and made significant theoretical innovations, forming Xi Jinping Thought on Socialism with Chinese Characteristics for a New Era, and establishing its guiding position throughout the party and across the whole of China.

Therefore, establishing Xi Jinping Thought on Socialism with Chinese

Characteristics for a New Era as the guiding ideology that the party and state must uphold in the long term is a historical choice made by the entire party and the people of all Chinese ethnic groups based on a profound understanding of the scientific truth and macro-strategy of this ideology, and is of great and far-reaching significance for unifying ideological understanding, uniting force for progress and clarifying the way forward in order to better conduct great struggles, build great projects, advance great causes and achieve great dreams. In particular, it is of special significance for the development of the CPC's management of state affairs to establish the guiding position of Xi Jinping Thought on Socialism with Chinese Characteristics for a New Era. The CPC is at a critical point in the history of its governance, in that it is about to achieve its first centenary struggle goal and move towards its second centenary struggle goal and is closer than at any other time in history to achieving the goal of the great rejuvenation of the Chinese nation. However, success in governance is not self-appointed or simply something to wait for, and the road ahead is not smooth, requiring constant preparation to deal with major challenges, protect against major risks, overcome major resistance and resolve major contradictions. Scientific theory is a powerful ideological weapon for adhering to the right direction and overcoming difficulties and hardships. Only by establishing the guiding position of Xi Jinping Thought on Socialism with Chinese Characteristics for a New Era can the CPC be more confident about achieving its ambitious blueprint and constantly strengthening its courage to overcome difficulties, only then can it continuously implement scientific decisions and effective measures to promote socioeconomic development, and only then can it avoid forgetting its original aspirations and continue to move forward, and make new governance achievements worthy of the times, of the people of China, and of history.

At the same time, the success of the party's governance also depends on the success of the party's management and governance of itself. Since the 18th CPC National Congress, the Party Central Committee with Comrade Xi Jinping at its core, has comprehensively strengthened the leadership of the party and promoted the comprehensive strict governance of the party, resulting in historic achievements in party building and winning the hearts and minds of the party and the people. However, it should also be soberly seen that solving the various problems within the party is certainly not something which can be achieved overnight, and the Four Tests and Four Risks which the party faces are long-term, complex and severe, and comprehensive strict party governance will always be an ongoing task. Xi Jinping Thought on Socialism with Chinese Characteristics for a New Era has enriched and developed the Marxist doctrine of party building, providing scientific guidance for achieving the correct management, strong governance and effective building of the party. Only by establishing the guiding position of Xi Jinping Thought on Socialism with Chinese Characteristics for a New Era can the party continuously enhance its firmness and awareness in self-management and comprehensive strict self-governance, and ensure its thinking and measures for managing and governing the party are more scientific, stricter and more effective to ensure that the party always remains the strong leading core of the cause of socialism with Chinese characteristics.

(IV) INTEGRATING XI JINPING THOUGHT ON SOCIALISM WITH CHINESE CHARACTERISTICS FOR A NEW ERA INTO ALL ASPECTS OF PARTY GOVERNANCE

Xi Jinping Thought on Socialism with Chinese Characteristics for a New Era constitutes a guide for action for the whole party and the whole of China to strive to achieve the great rejuvenation of the Chinese nation and is the fundamental guarantee for the CPC to achieve its governance mission and complete its governing tasks. It must be upheld and continuously developed in the long term.

The value of theories lies in its guiding for practice. The practical value of Xi Jinping Thought on Socialism with Chinese Characteristics for a New Era is that it is realistic and has a long-term impact and will be more fully manifested with the development of practice. In the five years from the 18th to the 19th CPC National Congress, with great political courage and taking strong responsibility, the CPC put forward a series of new ideas, concepts and strategies, introduced a series of major guidelines and policies, and launched a series of major initiatives and pushed forward a series of major tasks, solving many longstanding problems that had not been solved and accomplishing many unprecedented major achievemments, promoting the cause of the party and the state have to undergo historic changes, and making historic achievements in reform and opening up, and socialist modernisation. The most important and crucial factor in these historic achievements lies in the strong leadership of the Party Central Committee with Comrade Xi Jinping at its core, and in the scientific guidance of Xi Jinping Thought on Socialism with Chinese Characteristics for a New Era. Looking to the future, if the CPC is to lead the people to win victory in comprehensively building a moderately prosperous society, start a new journey of building a modern socialist country, and win the great victory of socialism with Chinese characteristics in the new era, it must incorporate Xi Jinping Thought on Socialism with Chinese Characteristics for a New Era in all aspects of the whole governance process, and must unswervingly arm itself, guide its practice and promote its work all with this major ideology.

In order to incorporate Xi Jinping Thought on Socialism with Chinese Characteristics for a New Era into all aspects of the whole governance process, it is necessary to implement the Eight Clarifications and Fourteen Upholds of Xi Jinping Thought on Socialism with Chinese Characteristics for a New Era. This is the party's basic path and strategy for implementing adherence to and development of socialism with Chinese characteristics in the new era. In the practice of governance, the whole party should take the initiative to adapt to the changes in the main contradictions in Chinese society, deeply understand and grasp laws, formulate scientifically correct lines, guidelines and policies for use in guiding and promoting various tasks, and pioneer, innovate, struggle and work hard in accordance with the excellent blueprint already drawn up and the ambitious goals already set. It is necessary to implement Xi Jinping Thought on Socialism with Chinese Characteristics for a New Era in the vivid practice of winning the victory of comprehensive prosperity and seizing the great victory of socialism with Chinese characteristics in the new era. It is necessary to focus closely on the coordinated promotion of the Five-Sphere integrated plan and the strategic composition of the Four Comprehensives, uphold a people-centred ideology of development, take the new development concept as the leader and, taking the new concept of development as the guide, promote sustained healthy socioeconomic development, and let the people have a greater sense of access and wellbeing. It is necessary to put the basic strategy of Xi Jinping Thought on Socialism with Chinese Characteristics for a New Era into practice in the work of comprehensively deepening reform and striving to overcome difficulties. It is necessary to establish a problem-based orientation, have firm confidence in victory, dare to take on arduous challenges and pass through treacherous waters, in order to resolutely break through the fetters of ideology and the mindset that do not meet the requirements of timely progress, resolutely break down the strongholds of solidified interests, resolutely remove the obstacles of institutional mechanisms in all sectors, and strive to continue to make new breakthroughs in solving the major problems of reform, development and stability, and the prominent problems strongly reported by the people. It is necessary to implement Xi Jinping Thought on Socialism with Chinese Characteristics for a New Era and the basic strategy in the comprehensive strict governance of the party and in the promotion of the party's self-revolution. With the political construction of the party as the leader, it is necessary to comprehensively strengthen the political, ideological and organisational construction of the party as well as the construction of the party's work style and discipline, implement institutional construction in the midst of all this, carry out a profound anti-corruption struggle, continuously improving the quality of party building, and build the party into a more vigorous and stronger entity, so that the party's governance ability and level of leadership will continuously improve.

The new era gives birth to new ideas, and new ideas lead the new era and guide new practices. This is the internal logic and development process of the interaction between Xi Jinping Thought on Socialism with Chinese Characteristics for a New Era and the new era of socialism with Chinese characteristics; these are mutually supportive and work together. The learning and implementation of these will "transform scientific ideology and theory into a powerful material force for understanding the world and transforming it, in order to better uphold and develop socialism with Chinese characteristics"[5]. This is the conclusion drawn from history and practice. Under the guidance of Xi Jinping Thought on Socialism with Chinese Characteristics for a New Era, socialism with Chinese characteristics will certainly demonstrate a stronger and more convincing power of truth, the CPC will certainly achieve new success in governance with a more energetic pace, and the communist party's governance law will reach a new realm.

(V) A SCIENTIFIC SUMMARY OF THE PARTY'S GOVERNANCE EXPERIENCE DURING 40 YEARS OF REFORM AND OPENING UP

On 18 December 2018, the party and state held a general conference to celebrate the 40th anniversary of reform and opening up, at which Xi Jinping delivered a major speech, summarising and refining the historical essence and main experiences of the party in governing and rejuvenating China over the previous 40 years of reform and opening up. This was in the form of the "Ten Perpetual Adherences" and "Nine Valuable Lessons", and he used highly evocative language to issue a great call to the entire party and all the people of China to comprehensively deepen reform and opening up, and make unremitting efforts to realise the great dream.

Over the preceding 40 years of reform and opening up, under the leadership of the party, hundreds of millions of Chinese people created the astounding Chinese miracle, and the CPC made remarkable achievements in governance. In those 40 years, China's gross domestic product grew from Rmb367.9 billion to Rmb82.7 trillion in 2017, with an average annual growth rate of 9.5% in real terms, much higher than the world economy's average annual growth rate of around 2.9%. China's share of global GDP rose from 1.8% at the beginning of reform and opening up to 15.2%, contributing more than 30% to global economic growth over those many years. The total import and export of goods grew from US$20.6 billion to over US$4 trillion, and total overseas FDI exceeded US$2 trillion, with total outward investment reaching US$1.9 trillion[6]. National per capita disposable income increased from Rmb171 to Rmb260,000, and the middle-income group experienced sustained expansion. The number of people in poverty was reduced by a cumulative total of 740 million people, and the incidence of poverty fell by 94.4 percentage points[7]. The problems of hunger, lack of food and clothing, and hardship that had plagued the Chinese people for thousands of years were now, on the whole, permanently gone. Why has China's development been so successful? Why has the CPC's governance been this successful? The focus of the entire international community is on these questions.

The CPC gave a systematic summary and answer to these questions on the occasion of the 40th anniversary of reform and opening up. In his speech at the conference celebrating the 40th anniversary of reform and opening up, Xi Jinping profoundly expounded the historical essence of the 40 years of reform and opening up and the basic laws of onward development, namely, the "Ten Perpetual Adherences", and profoundly summarised the historical experience of the glorious achievements made in the preceding 40 years, namely, the "Nine Valuable Lessons".

The great achievements of reform and opening up have attracted worldwide attention. What factors have driven these achievements, and what are the qualitative factors behind them? Xi Jinping pointed out clearly in this regard that there are laws governing the development of history but people are not completely passive in this process. As long as the general trend of historical development is grasped, the opportunity for historical change is seized, and hard work is conducted to forge ahead, human society can move forward in a more optimal manner. Since the outset of reform and opening up, how has the CPC advanced in its cause of governing and rejuvenating China? It is through the Ten Perpetual Adherences.

Over the preceding 40 years, the CPC always adhered to the emancipation of the mind, to seeking truth from facts, to progressive advance, and to being pragmatic and realistic, as well as adhering to the guiding position of Marxism without wavering, and to the basic principles of scientific socialism without wavering. It always adhered to an approach of focusing on economic construction, and constantly liberating and developing social productivity, to the path of socialist political development with Chinese

574

characteristics, constantly deepening political system reform and developing socialist democratic politics, and to developing an advanced socialist culture. It always adhered to an approach of safeguarding and improving people's livelihoods in the course of development, to environmental protection, conservation of resources, and promoting eco-civilisation construction, and to the absolute leadership of the party over the military. It always adhered to promoting peaceful reunification of the motherland, to an independent and peaceful foreign policy, and to strengthening and improving party leadership.

The practice of the preceding 40 years fully proved that the path, theory, system and culture of socialism with Chinese characteristics pioneered by the CPC since the 3rd Plenary Session of the 11th CPC Central Committee, united and led by the people of all China's ethnic groups, are completely correct, and that the basic theory, line and strategy of the CPC are too. The practice of the preceding 40 years fully proved that China's development has provided successful experiences and bright prospects for a vast number of developing countries in their modernisation and constitutes a powerful force for world peace and development, and a major contribution of the Chinese nation to the progress of human civilisation. The practice of the preceding 40 years fully proved that reform and opening up is an important and highly effective methodology for the party and the people to make great strides in catching up with the times, a necessary path for upholding and developing socialism with Chinese characteristics, and a key move in determining the fate of contemporary China, as well as a key move in achieving the struggle goal of the Two Centenaries and the great rejuvenation of the Chinese nation. Only by responding to historical trends, actively adapting and seeking change can China keep pace with the times. Although different historical periods have different stages and tasks, the governance position and mission of the CPC is ongoing, as is the historical process of reform and opening up. As Xi Jinping pointed out, "The valuable experience accumulated in the 40 years of reform and opening up is a precious spiritual asset for the party and the people, and has extremely important guiding significance for upholding and developing socialism with Chinese characteristics in the new era, which must be cherished, adhered to in the long term, and constantly enriched and developed in practice"[8].

In order to gain a deeper understanding of the historical necessity of reform, to grasp more consciously the laws of the governance and rejuvenation of China by the communist party, and to shoulder more firmly the great responsibility of achieving the historical mission of the communists, the party has systematically summarised and scientifically refined the

Nine Valuable Lessons from 40 years of reform and opening up. These are as follows: it is necessary to uphold the party's leadership of all work and constantly strengthen and improve it; to uphold a people-centred approach and continuously achieve the people's aspirations for a better life; to uphold the guiding position of Marxism and constantly promote theoretical innovation based on practice, uphold the path of socialism with Chinese characteristics and constantly adhere to and develop socialism with Chinese characteristics; to uphold the refinement and development of the system of socialism with Chinese characteristics and constantly bring out and strengthen the advantages of China's system; to uphold development as the first priority and continuously strengthen China's comprehensive national power; to uphold the broadening of openness and continuously promote the building of a community with a shared future for mankind; to uphold strict party governance and continuously improve the party's creativity, cohesion and fighting power; and to uphold dialectical materialism and a historical materialistic worldview and methodology, and correctly handle the relationship between reform, development and stability.

History has always given people the strength to draw wisdom and continue to move forward in the course of exceptional years. Summing up and refining the party's experience in governance over the preceding 40 years of reform and opening up at the pivotal moment of the 40th anniversary of reform and opening up, the Party Central Committee and Xi Jinping gave an emphatic call to, "Fully implement reform and opening up, continuously achieve the people's aspiration for a better life, and create a new and greater miracle for the Chinese nation in the new era, as well as create a new and greater miracle that will impress the world"[9]. And the fundamental task of the contemporary Chinese communists is to, under the strong leadership of the Party Central Committee with Comrade Xi Jinping at its core, take Xi Jinping Thought on Socialism with Chinese Characteristics for a New Era as its guide, comprehensively deepen reform and opening up, strive to seize the great victory of socialism with Chinese characteristics in the new era, create new achievements in party governance, and create new glory for the great rejuvenation of the Chinese nation.

8

THE THIRD MIRACLE CREATED BY CPC GOVERNANCE

USHERING IN A GREAT LEAP OF THE CHINESE NATION FROM BECOMING AFFLUENT TO BECOMING STRONG

In the new era, the Chinese communists have integrated the basic principles of Marxism with the specific reality of China in the new era, united and led the people to carry out great struggles, build great projects, promote great undertakings and achieve great dreams, stimulated the party and the state to make all-round and ground-breaking historical achievements, undergo profound rearrangements and fundamental historical changes, and ushered in the great leap of the Chinese nation from getting rich to becoming strong. This constitutes the third miracle created by the CPC in its governance after it led the Chinese people and the Chinese nation to make the great leap from being the "sick man of East Asia" to standing up, and from standing up to becoming affluent.

"Becoming strong" is the practical struggle goal of socialist modernisation, the basic pursuit for the great rejuvenation of the Chinese nation, and the most ardent expectation of the people of all China's ethnic groups for the future and destiny of their socialist country, and therefore the most important goal of the CPC in governing and rejuvenating China. In this regard, Xi Jinping pointed out that, "Achieving the great rejuvenation of the Chinese nation is the greatest dream of the Chinese people in modern times. We call this the Chinese dream, and it has the basic connotation of achieving national prosperity, the revitalisation of China's ethnic groups, and the happiness of the people"[1]. After the 18th CPC National Congress, the Party Central Committee with Comrade Xi Jinping at its core, raised a banner and planned strategies, and in its ground-breaking practice of governance under new historical conditions, formed Xi Jinping Thought on Socialism with Chinese Characteristics for a New Era, which has promoted historic changes in the cause of the party and the state. The great magnitude, scope, effectiveness and far-reaching impact of the governance achievements embodied in these changes are of great significance in the history of the CPC, the development of the PRC, the development of the Chinese nation, and the history of the communist party governance, for opening up new horizons.

After the 18th CPC National Congress, socialism with Chinese characteristics entered a new era. The CPC has driven and led the people of China in a great social revolution by way of a great self-revolution, and the party and the state have broken new ground across the board. The Party Central Committee with Comrade Xi Jinping at its core, has steadfastly strengthened the party's leadership across the board, greatly enhancing the party's cohesion, fighting strength, leadership and appeal. It has steadfastly implemented the new concept of development and built a modern economy, making significant achievements in economic construction and continuously improving the quality and efficiency of development. It has also steadfastly deepened reform across the board, making comprehensive efforts in reform and multi-point breakthroughs, and advancing in depth, significantly improving the national system of governance and the modernisation of the governance ability of the party. It has unswervingly and comprehensively promoted the rule of law, and the party's ability to use the law to lead and govern China has been significantly enhanced. It has firmly strengthened the party's leadership of ideological work, comprehensively promoted the party's theoretical innovation, made significant progress in ideological and cultural construction, and consolidated the ideological unity of the party and society as a whole. It has also firmly promoted social construction, raised the level of protection and improvement of people's livelihoods, continuously improved people's lives, and further consolidated the social governance system. Furthermore, it has also unswervingly promoted the construction of eco-civilisation and made significant strides in building a beautiful China. It has unswervingly promoted the modernisation of the national defence and military forces, and achieved a revolutionary reshaping of the people's army, unswervingly promoted great diplomacy with Chinese characteristics, forming an all-round, multi-level and three-dimensional diplomatic layout, and creating favourable external conditions for China's development. It has also unswervingly promoted the comprehensive strict governance of the party, investing in solving prominent problems that are most strongly reflected by the people and most threatening to the party's governance base, as well as significantly enhancing the party's capacity for self-purification, self-refinement, self-innovation and self-improvement, further consolidating the party's governance and mass foundations.

After the 18th CPC National Congress, China's economy shifted from high-speed growth to high-quality development and, through building a modern economy and a strong country in terms of science and technology, space flight, the internet, transportation, digital technology and an intellectual society, the vision is gradually becoming a reality. China is firmly established as the world's second-largest economy, the world's top manufacturing and goods trading country, and the top foreign exchange reserve holder, and is the largest contributor to global economic growth. The CPC is striving to resolve the contradictions between the people's growing need for a better life and the reality of unbalanced and inadequate development, continuously promoting the all-round development of people and the common prosperity of all people, and as a result the people's sense of attainment and happiness is constantly increasing. China has become increasingly powerful in science and technology. High-performance computers, manned spaceflight, lunar exploration projects, quantum communications, the Beidou satnav system, crewed deep-submergence and other cutting-edge technological achievements have been successively launched, while China's high-speed railways have also been built overseas, and China's self-developed large-scale aircraft has successfully made its maiden flight. China's circle of friends in the international community is growing larger, and its international influence, appeal and impact on shaping developments have increased significantly. The number of approved member countries of the Asian Infrastructure Investment Bank (AIIB) has reached 87, while the number of countries, regions and international organisations participating in the Belt and Road has steadily increased, the number of cooperation agreements signed and implemented has also increased, and the concept of building a community with a shared future for mankind has gained global recognition[2]. Under the strong leadership of the Party Central Committee with Comrade Xi Jinping at its core and the guidance of Xi Jinping Thought on Socialism with Chinese Characteristics for a New Era, the governance and rejuvenation of China by the CPC is entering a new historical stage, the great motherland is marching from strength to strength and the Chinese nation is fast approaching rejuvenation. Not only are we closer to the goal of the great rejuvenation of the Chinese nation than at any other time in history, and more confident and capable of achieving this goal than at any other time in history, but we are also more capable and have more potential than any other working-class party that has ever ruled and any other communist party that is now in power to deepen and expand the communist party's governance law to a new level of effectiveness and a new realm.

The achievement of this miracle of governance is the result of the strong leadership of the Party Central Committee, the result of the unity and struggle of the entire party and the people of all China's ethnic groups, and the result of the dedication and commitment of party organisations at all levels, and the masses of party members and cadres to their duties. The most important thing is that the CPC has the strong leadership of the Party Central Committee with Comrade Xi Jinping at its core and a leader as eloquent as General Secretary Xi Jinping as the core of the Party Central Committee and the core of the entire party. It is precisely because the Party Central Committee with Comrade Xi Jinping at its core has been brave enough to face up to the historic issues raised by the development of the times and practice, and with extraordinary vigour and a tenacious spirit of struggle, and has led the party and the people of China to carry out a great struggle with many new historical characteristics, that this series of profound changes and consequently the prosperous development of the CPC's governance has occurred.

In this great leap forward, the CPC has led the people in a few brief and extremely unusual years, to closely integrate the new conditions of the times and practical requirements, deepened its understanding of the communist party's governance law, the laws of socialist construction and human social development with a brand-new vision, and from the integration of theory and practice systematically answered the major question surrounding the kind of socialism with Chinese characteristics which should be upheld and developed in the new era, and how to uphold and develop socialism with Chinese characteristics. This gave birth to Xi Jinping Thought on Socialism with Chinese Characteristics for a New Era, which provides unlimited possibilities, opens up a wide space and establishes a fundamental guarantee for the CPC to achieve more and greater governance achievements in the future.

Communist party governance is an incomparably great and arduous undertaking in human society. On the road ahead, communists will encounter new situations and problems, and will have to deal with various predictable and unpredictable risks and challenges. And yet history does not end there. In the late 1980s, the Japanese American scholar Francis Fukuyama put forward the so-called theory of the "end of history", regarding the end of the Cold War as this end of history. However, China's rapid development has proved that the theory of the end of history, which originated from Western centrism, was a serious misjudgment. China has declared the bankruptcy of the end of history and of the unilinear view of history, in which all countries ultimately end up with the Western institutional model. As long as communists in all countries raise high the correct banner and take the right path, uphold a scientific approach to Marxism, understand more fully the practical and open nature of Marxism, and neither dogmatise Marxism nor detach from, deviate from or deny it, then communists will certainly achieve new successes in their governance cause, and more and more people in the world will believe in Marxism and trust in communist party governance.

Similarly, as long as we Chinese communists are rooted in the social soil of the Chinese land and, based on China's own social practice, closely integrate the basic principles of Marxism with Chinese reality and the characteristics of the times, uphold the reliance on using Marxist positions, views and methods to study and solve various major theoretical and practical problems, constantly instil into Marxism a new contemporary connotation and vitality, and constantly promote the Sinicisation and periodisation of Marxism, then we will certainly be able to constantly overcome difficulties and achieve new governance results and make a new "great leap" under the guidance of contemporary Chinese Marxism and 21st century Marxism, namely Xi Jinping Thought on Socialism with Chinese Characteristics for a New Era, and make a new and greater contribution to deepening and exploring the communist party's governance law.

CONCLUSION

THE NEW CONCEPT OF DEVELOPMENT: A NEW UNDERSTANDING OF THE LAWS OF DEVELOPMENT IN CHINA

1

LEADERSHIP IN GOVERNANCE

UPHOLDING AND STRENGTHENING THE OVERALL LEADERSHIP OF THE PARTY

The question of leadership has always been an important issue in the Marxist concept of political parties. The proletarian party is a party with a mission to achieve the full liberation and comprehensive development of mankind as its struggle goal. Its strong consciousness of being a historical subject, its responsibility to put the world first and its value of doing everything for the people have determined that a proletarian party naturally possesses the value and appeal of comprehensive leadership in the historical process of transforming the old world and building a new one. One of the most fundamental and valuable experiences accumulated by the CPC in the periods of revolution, construction and reform through which it has passed is to always uphold and strengthen the overall leadership of the party. The 19th CPC National Congress pointed out that the most essential feature and greatest strength of socialism with Chinese characteristics is the leadership of the CPC. General Secretary Xi Jinping emphasised that the party is the leader of everything pertaining to China's government, military and people throughout the entire country. The CPC is the strong leading core of the cause of socialism with Chinese characteristics and the supreme force for political leadership in China, and the leadership of the party must be firmly and consciously upheld in all fields and sectors. Only by consistently upholding the overall leadership of the party is it possible to achieve ideological and political unity, as well as unity of action, at a higher level throughout the entire party and society, further enhance the party's creativity, cohesion and fighting strength, and provide fundamental political guarantees for the successful construction of a moderately prosperous society in all respects and winning the great victory of socialism with Chinese characteristics in the new era. Upholding and strengthening the overall leadership of the party in the new era constitutes a profound summary of the logic of historical development, a highly condensed version of the logic of socialism with Chinese characteristics in practice, and a diligent exploration of the communist party's governance law and the laws of socialist construction.

(I) UPHOLDING AND STRENGTHENING THE OVERALL LEADERSHIP OF THE PARTY IS AN INEVITABLE REQUIREMENT OF INTEGRATING THE BASIC PRINCIPLES OF SCIENTIFIC SOCIALISM WITH CHINA'S REALITY

Upholding and strengthening the overall leadership of the party constitutes the dialectical unity of a theoretical, historical and practical logic of a proletarian party. In the *Communist Manifesto* and other works, Marx and Engels expounded the idea of the dictatorship of the proletariat, that is, the party representing the interests of the proletariat, namely, the communist party, should hold state power, and made it the basic principle of scientific socialism. Marxism tells us that the leadership of a proletarian party is necessary for the working class to fulfil its historical mission and tasks, to achieve human freedom and emancipation, and to make communism a reality. It is a basic principle of the Marxist concept of political parties that a proletarian party must uphold the supreme leadership of the party over state power. Looking at the history of the development of the proletariat, generally speaking, the power of the proletariat has been weak at the beginning of revolutionary movements, which meant that the proletariat could only form alliances with other classes. With the development of the revolution and the establishment of proletarian parties, the progressiveness of the proletariat becomes increasingly evident. The proletariat consequently had to maintain its independence in alliances and fight for leadership, both as a tactical necessity and in order to strengthen its revolutionary forces. In addition to leadership in the revolutionary alliance, the proletariat must also assume leadership within its own class and in mass movements. For this reason, Marx and Engels proposed that the party was "the centre and core of the workers' union" and Lenin emphasised that the party was "the highest form of class union of the proletariat". In terms of revolutionary practice by the proletarian class, the Russian October Revolution of 1917 established the world's first socialist state. When a proletarian party first comes to power in a large country, the first question it faces pertains to the kind of party system it should adopt. The Marxist answer to this question is that whatever party system is adopted in a socialist country, the leadership of the communist party must be upheld, and there can be no rotation of two or more parties in power as in capitalist countries. In countries with a multi-party system, the relationship between the communist party and the other parties is not one of confrontation or reciprocity but one of leadership and acceptance of leadership. Looking at the history of the world socialist movement and the practice of the CPC in leading China's revolution, and construction and reform over the past hundred years, it can be seen that the important reason for the collapse of the Soviet Union was its departure from the basic principles of scientific socialism and its abandonment of the leadership of the CPSU, while China's success lies in its adherence to the direction of scientific socialist development in relying on the leadership of the CPC as a winning and highly effective methodology.

Upholding and strengthening the overall leadership of the party is the inevitable result of China's socio-historical development in modern times and constitutes a correct summary of experience and an important political principle that has been proven in practice to ensure the continuous success of China's revolution, construction and reform. In this regard Deng Xiaoping once pointed out, "In a large country like China, it is impossible to envisage the unification of the ideology, strength and forces of hundreds of millions of people to build socialism without a party comprising members with a high degree of consciousness, discipline and self-sacrifice that can truly represent and unite the people, and without such a party having unified leadership; without these elements the country would be divided and achieve nothing"[1]. In 1921, the CPC was born out of the violent movements of Chinese society in the modern era, the fierce struggle of the Chinese people against feudal rule and foreign aggression, and the integration of Marxism-Leninism with the Chinese workers' movement. As soon as it was founded, the CPC took on with no second thoughts the historic responsibility of leading the people of China to seek national independence and liberation, and to achieve national prosperity and the people's happiness. In the historical process of revolution, construction and reform, it was the people who chose the CPC, and China completely brought to an end the history of semi-colonial and semi-feudal society, completed the most extensive and profound social transformation ever undertaken by the Chinese nation, started the great new revolution of reform and opening up, pioneered the path of socialism with Chinese characteristics and achieved great achievements in socialist modernisation. The profound trajectory of history clearly shows that without the communist party, there would be no new China and without the communist party, there would be no great leap of the Chinese nation from standing up to becoming affluent and then to becoming strong. This is the most fundamental conclusion that the Chinese people have drawn from their long struggle.

(II) RESOLUTELY SAFEGUARDING THE AUTHORITY AND CENTRALISED LEADERSHIP OF THE PARTY CENTRAL COMMITTEE

In order to uphold and strengthen the party's overall leadership, the first and foremost matter is to resolutely safeguard the authority and centralised leadership of the Party Central Committee. Establishing and safeguarding the leading core of the proletarian party has always been a fundamental standpoint of the Marxist doctrine of party building. Marx and Engels, as the founders of the proletarian party, repeatedly stressed the importance of upholding the centralised and unified leadership and authority of the Party Central Committee. For example, the *Communist Manifesto* which they drafted for the world's first proletarian party, clearly requires that members accepted into the league "must swear unconditional obedience to the resolutions of the [Communist] League"[2], in effect emphasising the centralised leadership and authority of the Communist League as a central committee. Engels wrote a special essay, *On Authority*, in which he profoundly expounded the importance of upholding the centralised leadership and authority of the party. He said, "On the one hand, there is a certain authority, however it is formed, and on the other, a certain obedience, both of which we are obliged to accept, regardless of the material conditions under which social organisation and the circulation of production and products take place. It is absurd... to speak of the principle of authority as something absolutely bad and of the principle of autonomy as something absolutely good"[3].

It is not difficult to see that, in their practice of leading the proletarian revolution, Marx and Engels placed special emphasis on the centralisation and authority of the proletarian party and stressed that the centralised unity and central authority of the party were the fundamental guarantee for the victory of the proletarian revolution. In his practice of leading the CPR in revolutionary struggle and construction, Lenin also placed great emphasis on upholding the centralised and unified leadership of the party and upholding the authority of the Party Central Committee. Around 1900, in response to the claims of some radical intellectuals in the country that they did not want any authority, Lenin stressed that the Party Central Committee must have authority and that party members must submit to the authority of the Party Central Committee, and that "to refuse to submit to the leadership of the central authorities is to refuse to remain in the party and to destroy it"[4].

Upholding the authority and centralised leadership of the Party Central Committee is a unique and powerful political strength that the CPC has developed during the historical process of revolution, construction and reform. Looking at the history of the CPC, it can be seen that the formation of a strong central leadership group in practice and the safeguarding of the authority of this collective has been an important and highly effective methodology for the victory of the revolution and the achievements of construction. Before the Zunyi Conference, the failure to form a mature central leadership within the party resulted in serious setbacks to the party's cause as a result of repeated poor decision-making. It was after the Zunyi Conference that the party began to form an authoritative and correct leadership with Comrade Mao Zedong at its core, and the party's revolutionary cause averted danger. In response to Zhang Guotao's serious mistake of disobeying the unified leadership of the Central Committee and attempting to set up another Central Committee, Comrade Mao Zedong reiterated the "Four Obediences", demanding that party members and party organisations at all levels must obey the centralised and unified leadership of the Party Central Committee, stressing that, "all party comrades must be united around the Central Committee, and any act that undermines unity is evil"[5]. It can be said that it was with the Seventh CPC National Congress that the leadership authority of the Party Central Committee with Comrade Mao Zedong at its core was established throughout the whole party and the whole army, and that only then was the victory of China's revolution ushered in. After the founding of new China, it was also only under the centralised, unified and authoritative leadership of the Party Central Committee with Comrade Mao Zedong at its core, that the party was able to lead the people of China to complete the socialist transformation, establish the socialist system and begin exploring the path of socialist construction. After the 3rd Plenary Session of the 11th CPC Central Committee, Comrade Deng Xiaoping pointed out that, "the Central Committee must have authority",[6] and that only under the centralised, unified and authoritative leadership of the Party Central Committee could the cause of reform and opening up be carried out in a guided and orderly manner. Without this it would have been difficult to coordinate the conflicting interests of various regions and departments, to unify the will of the whole party and to ensure the implementation of central policies. Looking back on the great achievements made since the 18th CPC National Congress, the party has been able to lead the people of all China's ethnic groups to carry out many pioneering tasks, especially solving many difficult problems that had long needed solving but had not been, and to accomplish many great things that had long needed to be accomplished but had not been. The reason for this ultimately lies in the fundamental establishment of the authority of the centralised and unified leadership of the party with Comrade Xi Jinping at its core, the fundamental reversal of the weakening of the party's leadership, the lack of party building and the ineffectiveness of strict governance of the party, and the individualism, decentralism, sectarianism and selfish departmentalism that had existed in the party for some time being reversed for all to see, creating a political climate where orders are enforced and prohibitions are observed. Practice has fully proven that the authority, and centralised and unified leadership of the Party Central Committee, constituting a great political strength, has powerfully ensured the scientific formulation of major decisions and arrangements, the efficient implementation of various guidelines and policies, and the rational response to major challenges, promoting the new development of socialism with Chinese characteristics and opening up a new era of socialism with Chinese characteristics.

In contemporary China, in order to resolutely safeguard the authority and centralised leadership of the Party Central Committee, the most important aspect is to resolutely safeguard the core position of Xi Jinping in the Party Central Committee and the party as a whole. To this end it is necessary to earnestly enhance political awareness, awareness of the overall situation, of the core, and of alignment, and consciously maintain a high degree of consistency with the Party Central Committee with Comrade Xi Jinping at its core, achieving a high degree of ideological agreement, resolutely safeguarding the core politically, consciously obeying the core in terms of organisation, and following the core closely in action. To maintain a high degree of ideological consistency with the Party Central Committee means to deeply understand and accurately grasp Xi Jinping Thought on Socialism with Chinese Characteristics for a New Era, employing this to observe matters, judge the situation, analyse and solve problems, and use it to arm the mind, guide practice and promote work. To maintain a high degree of political consistency with the Party Central Committee means to always maintain a high degree of political alertness and acumen, have a firm political stance, uphold the correct political direction, always be of one mind with the Party Central Committee, be absolutely loyal to the Party Central Committee, and truly be politically credible, hard-working and reliable. To maintain a high degree of organisational consistency with the Party Central Committee means that under all circumstances, it is necessary to consciously stay within the party organisation, always remember the duties and responsibilities of party members, and fully believe in the organisation and trust the Party Central Committee. To maintain a high degree of consistency in action with the Party Central Committee means to consciously emulate the Party Central Committee and General Secretary Xi Jinping, to align with the party's basic theories, line and strategies, and implement the Four Consciousnesses in every word and action, and embody them in all duties.

(III) REFINING THE INSTITUTIONAL MECHANISMS FOR UPHOLDING THE PARTY'S OVERALL LEADERSHIP

Upholding and strengthening the party's overall leadership is a concrete requirement, not empty or abstract. It requires the provision of a set of institutional arrangements, and a sound and powerful institutional guarantee, a solid organisational basis and an effective working system to effectively bring into play the greatest strength of the system of socialism with Chinese characteristics, the leadership of the CPC, so as to ensure that the party's system for exercising leadership over the state and society is strengthened and refined, and that it better assumes the party's historical mission and major responsibilities. To this end the following are required.

Refining the institutional mechanisms for the overall leadership of the Party Central Committee.

In order to uphold the overall leadership of the party and safeguard the core party's core leadership position, it is first necessary to uphold the centralised and unified leadership of the Party Central Committee. The all-round leadership of the Party Central Committee over the work of the party and the state covers all aspects and fields of reform, development and stability, internal and foreign affairs, national defence, and governance of the party, state and the military, and is reflected in the overall design of the Five-Sphere integrated plan and the coordinated promotion of the strategic composition of the Four Comprehensives. In order to establish a sound institutional mechanism for the party's leadership of major work, under the leadership of the Politburo and its Standing Committee, it is necessary to optimise the party's central decision-making deliberative and coordinating body to be responsible for the top-level design, general composition, integrated coordination and overall promotion of major work. The deliberative and coordinating bodies in other areas are aligned with the establishment and adjustment of the Party Central Committee's deliberative and coordinating bodies to ensure that orders are followed and work is carried out efficiently. In order to strengthen the leading position of party organisations at the same level, party committees (party groups) established in state organs, units, mass organisations, social organisations, enterprises and other organisations are under the unified leadership of the party committee that approves their establishment, and report regularly on their work to ensure that the party's policies and decision-making are implemented in organisations at the same level. To this end it is necessary to accelerate the establishment of sound party organisational structures in new socioeconomic organisations, so that wherever the work of the party progresses, it is covered by the party's organisation.

Continuously deepening the reform of party and state institutions

Deepening reform of party and state institutions is an inevitable requirement for improving the party's governance ability and leadership, and constitutes a profound change to promote modernisation of the national system of governance and governance ability. By deepening reform of party and state institutions, efforts are made to solve problems pertaining to institutional mechanisms for the party's leadership of all work in terms of institutional functions, and to solve the problem of the relationship between the institutional functions of the party, government and military within the context of the party's long-term governance, so as to implement leadership of the party in all aspects and parts of the performance of duties by party and state organs. To this end it is necessary to build a system of party and state institutions and functions that is systematic, scientific, standardised and efficient, form a scientific system of party leadership, a system of government management of state affairs with clear responsibilities and administration in accordance with the law, a system of armed forces with Chinese characteristics and which is world class, and a system of group work that reaches out to a wide range of people and serves the masses. It is also necessary to promote coordinated action and enhanced synergy among the NPC, the government, the CPPCC, supervisory organs, judicial organs, procuratorial organs, people's organisations, enterprises and institutions, and social organisations under the unified leadership of the party, so as to better meet the requirements of socialist development with Chinese characteristics in the new era.

• • •

Strict implementation of democratic centralism.

The system of democratic centralism is the fundamental organisational and leadership system of the party and state. It regulates the relationship between the CPC and organs of state power, administrative organs, supervisory organs, judicial organs and people's organisations, and between party members, between party members and organisations, lower and higher-level organisations, and the whole party and the Central Committee. The sound and careful implementation of the specific systems of democratic centralism institutionalises, standardises and scientificises the relations between these parties. Always upholding the "Four Obediences", namely, the obedience of individual party members to the party organisation, the obedience of the minority to the majority, the obedience of lower-level organisations to higher-level organisations, and the obedience of all party organisations and members to the party's national congress and Central Committee. These Four Obediences embody both democracy and centralisation, and constitute a general summary of the order of political life within the party. The leading organs of the party are always elected. Party committees at all levels are elected by the party's congresses at the same level, are accountable to and report on their work to the congresses, and are subject to the supervision of the congresses. Collective leadership is always upheld. The party constitution stipulates that the party committees at all levels shall adopt a system combining collective leadership and individual division of labour. All major issues should be discussed collectively by the party committee and decisions made in accordance with the principles of collective leadership, democratic centralism, individual consideration and plenary decisions. Committee members should perform their duties effectively in accordance with collective decisions and division of labour. Collective leadership constitutes the concrete embodiment of democratic centralism in the system of party leadership and is a key link in the implementation of democratic centralism. It is important to give full play to the initiative of the lower-level party organisations and to establish a system whereby the higher-level organisations seek the views of the lower-level organisations before making important decisions relating to them, so as to link and unify the leadership of, and support for, the lower-level organisations. It is important to take care to respect minority views. Party members may express their views freely and equally within the party and should be tolerant of different opinions. As long as the minority submits to the verdict of the majority, the minority should be allowed to maintain their own opinions and should never be discriminated against because they are a minority or because they have different opinions. It should be ensured that the activities of party leaders are supervised by the party and the people, while maintaining the trust of all leaders who represent the interests of the party and the people.

(IV) IMPROVING THE PARTY'S ABILITY AND DETERMINATION TO SET THE DIRECTION, PLAN THE OVERALL SITUATION, DETERMINE POLICIES AND PROMOTE REFORMS

In order to uphold and strengthen the party's overall leadership, it is necessary to both have mastery of politics and be highly competent. It is necessary to focus on improving the party's ability and determination to orientate itself, plan the overall situation, set policies and promote reform, and be adept at handling various complex contradictions and overcoming various untold dangers and difficulties, so as to firmly grasp the work initiative.

Orientation has a bearing on the fundamental overall situation and determines long-term prospects. The party leadership's first and foremost role is to raise the flag. For the party to provide orientation means to hold high the great banner of socialism with Chinese characteristics, adhere to Xi Jinping Thought on Socialism with Chinese Characteristics for a New Era as guidance, promote social revolution and self-revolution with a high degree of consciousness, consistently uphold and develop socialism with Chinese characteristics, consistently promote the great new project of party building, consistently enhance the awareness of unexpected developments and guard against risks and challenges. It is necessary to further enhance confidence in the path, theory, system and culture of socialism with Chinese characteristics, raise political awareness, maintain strategic determination, have a clear-cut stand in the face of major rights and wrongs, be clear-headed in the face of major storms and turmoil, and always stand firm in the right direction of socialism with Chinese characteristics. It is necessary to uphold the authority and centralised leadership of the Party Central Committee, firmly implement the party's political line, strictly abide by political discipline and rules, and maintain a high degree of consistency with the Party Central Committee with Comrade Xi Jinping at its core in terms of political stance, direction, principles and path. It is also necessary to enhance sensitivity, improve synergy, effectively find and handle problems just taking root or already prevalent in reform and development, so as to anticipate and forestall problems.

Planning for the bigger picture reflects both the ideological and working methods of dialectical materialism and historical materialism, as well as ways of thinking prevalent in China's excellent traditional culture. General Secretary Xi Jinping has repeatedly emphasised that those who do not plan for the overall situation should not plan for just an individual area. Those who are good at seeing the big picture, make large-scale plans, consciously thinking and doing work in the context of the general situation. This means firmly establishing a sense of the big picture and consciously putting work into the context of the big picture to think, position, and arrange matters, in order to achieve a correct understanding of the big picture, and consciously comply with, and resolutely maintain, the big picture. It means to be good at grasping the crux of the matter, capturing the main contradictions and the main aspects of the contradictions, succeeding with a single move and not being careless. It means being good at grasping local interests in the context of overall interests, and not just seeing the trees without seeing the woods. It means unifying immediate needs with long-term plans, not seeking quick success and seizing every opportunity. It also means together solving specific problems and deep-seated problems, rather than just being sporadically reactive as each individual problem crops up. To this end it is necessary to always have the big picture in mind, grasp the full context, and focus on major matters, having a temperament marked by gaining a clear view from a lofty position, and also having the broadmindedness that success does not have to belong only to oneself. It means planning for different scenarios, moving in response to situations which transpire, following trends, and constantly enhancing the scientific, systematic and foreseeable nature of the work.

Setting policy constitutes the litmus test reflecting the nature and purpose of the ruling party, and is an indicator of the level of governance. In promoting socioeconomic and development, it is always necessary to uphold a people-centred outlook, focus on solving the contradiction between the people's constantly growing need for a better life, and unbalanced and inadequate development, grasp the most direct and practical interests of the masses, and formulate practical and effective policy measures. Persisting in seeking truth from facts means starting from reality, coming to the masses from a position of understanding the masses, carrying out extensive research and study, and analysing specific problems, to make policy decisions and program initiatives conform to practical realities, reflecting objective laws and solving practical problems. The most important thing is to have a firm grasp of decision-making, strengthen the analysis of, and conclusions regarding, the state of the world, China, the party and the people, refine the decision-making process, enhance awareness of the rule of law, avoiding reliance on subjective decision-making but also not falling short of minimal standards, and strive to achieve scientific, democratic and lawful decision-making.

Promoting reform to enhance development momentum.

Reform and opening up is a key move in determining the fate of contemporary China and in achieving the struggle goal of the Two Centenaries and the great rejuvenation of the Chinese nation. Now the comprehensive deepening of reform has entered a new stage so it is necessary to make every effort and maintain determination, dare to take on tough challenges and pass through dangerous waters, further emancipate the mind, liberate and develop social productivity, and liberate and enhance social vitality. It is also necessary to vigorously carry forward the spirit of reform and innovation, and self-revolution, promote the re-liberation of ideas and the restart of reform, and achieve new breakthroughs from a new starting point of comprehensively deepening reform. It is further necessary to focus on promoting the modernisation of the national system of governance and governance ability, adapting to the basic characteristic of China's economy which has shifted from the stage of high-speed growth to the stage of high-quality development, scientifically determine ideas on reform and development, formulate measures for reform and development, dare to take charge, be competent and capable, and to open up a new chapter and pioneer a new path in practice. It is vital to encourage innovation at the grassroots level, advocate pioneering new works before others do, strengthen the thorough research, scientific summary, promotion, and publicising of successful experiences of reform, promote the formation of a stronger and more energetic atmosphere of innovation and creativity, and gather strength to unswervingly promote reform and opening up.

2

THE GUIDING IDEOLOGY OF GOVERNANCE

THE BANNER PROVIDES THE DIRECTION AND THE EMBODIMENT

Establishing the correct guiding ideology for governance is a common problem faced by any ruling party since the emergence of political parties in modern times. The guiding ideology of a ruling party is the central expression of the kind of "ism" it believes in and the kind of party philosophy it upholds. This is true of both bourgeois and proletarian parties. Since the birth of Marxism in 1848, all proletarian parties have taken Marxism as their theoretical basis and guide to action.

On the importance of establishing Marxism as the guiding ideology of the ruling proletarian party, Engels pointed out long ago that, "Our party has the great merit of having a new scientific point of view as the basis of its theory..."[1]. The CPC is a proletarian party founded under the guidance of Marxism-Leninism. When Mao Zedong spoke of holding high the banner of Marxism, he pointed out that, "Doctrine is like a banner; only when the banner is up will everyone have something to count on and know where to go."[2] In this regard Jiang Zemin pointed out that, "The issue of the banner is of vital importance. The banner provides direction and is the embodiment."[3] And in his speech at the Conference to Celebrate the 95th Anniversary of the Founding of the CPC, General Secretary Xi Jinping discussed in depth the vital importance of adhering to the guiding position of Marxism, stressing that, "the guiding ideology is the spiritual banner of a political party. In these 95 years, the reason why the CPC has been able to accomplish the arduous task that has been impossible for all political forces in recent times lies in always taking the scientific theory of Marxism as its guide to action, and in its persistence in constantly

597

enriching and developing Marxism in practice."[4] The practice of the international communist movement has proven time and again that the ruling communist party must uphold Marxism as the theoretical basis and guide for action in governing and rejuvenating a country.

(I) UPHOLDING THE GUIDING POSITION OF MARXISM

Unshakeable adherence to the guiding position of Marxism is determined by the intrinsic characteristics of Marxism and the nature of the proletarian party. First, Marxism is a great tool for the proletariat and its political parties to understand the world. It reveals the laws of nature, human society and the development of thought, points out the law of historical development whereby capitalism is bound to perish and socialism is bound to triumph, indicates the direction of human society, and provides proletarian parties with ideological leadership and a scientific world view and methodology. Second, Marxism is a correct summary of the practical activities of proletarian parties. It is a fundamental rule of Marxist development to pay close attention to the development of social practice and to the new topics and challenges of social reality. As the science guiding the communist movement, once it is grasped by the proletarian parties, it makes regular predictions about the revolutionary movement, increases the consciousness of action, and becomes a great material force for advancing the revolutionary movement. Lenin once pointed out that the inexorable appeal of this theory to socialists all over the world lies in the fact that it integrates rigorous and high-level scientificity and revolutionary essence, and it does not do so accidentally but rather integrates these inherently and inseparably within the theory itself. The reason why the communists did not yield in the face of ferocious enemies and did not waver in the face of heavy difficulties was that they had revolutionary theory as their strong spiritual pillar and guide. Scientific theory gave them confidence and strength, the conviction that what they were fighting for was a just cause and the belief that communism would prevail.

Once again, the proletarian party was established in accordance with Marxist theory, and its theoretical basis and ultimate goal are all Marxist. Therefore, upholding the guiding position of Marxism is the only way for the proletarian party to develop and grow, and the communist party can only maintain its progressiveness and ensure the socialist direction of the country if it clearly upholds Marxism as its guide in the process of governance. And to shake and abolish the guiding position of Marxism would shake the legitimacy of the party and its ruling base. This is the most painful lesson in the history of the world socialist movement and was the

598

fundamental cause of the dramatic changes in the Soviet Union and Eastern Europe. The dissolution of the CPSU and the disintegration of the Soviet Union were the result of the CPSU's gradual abandonment of the guiding position of Marxism, especially after Mikhail Gorbachev came to power and put forward his "new thinking" on reform, introducing a set of so-called humane democratic socialist reform programmes, the core of which was the abandonment of the guiding position of Marxism and the implementation of pluralism in guiding ideology. Therefore, the CPC has repeatedly stressed that, "old ancestors must not be lost", namely, that Marxism must never be abandoned.

(II) UPHOLDING THE LOCALISATION OF MARXISM

In the preface to the 1872 German edition of the *Communist Manifesto*, Marx and Engels state that, "the general principles laid down in the manifesto are, on the whole, as correct today as ever… The practical application of the principles will depend, as the manifesto itself states, everywhere and at all times, on the prevailing historical conditions."[5] This insightful statement has profoundly clarified the scientific principle that adherence to, and application of, Marxism must be based on objective reality. In other words, it means integrating the basic principles of Marxism with the realities of the country in question and the characteristics of the times to create a socialist theory with national characteristics that follows the basic principles of Marxism and is in line with the specific realities of the country.

Upholding the integration of theory and practice and starting everything from the practical aspects is the fundamental way for the ruling party to achieve the localisation of Marxism. In this regard, Marx pointed out that, "the extent to which a theory is implemented in a country always depends on the extent to which it meets the needs of that country."[6] The extent to which a theory meets the needs of a country depends not on the theory itself but on an objective grasp of the practical needs of that country. The history of the international communist movement shows that the first socialist state established by Lenin under the Bolshevik Party was the result of integrating the universal principles of Marxism with the realities of Russia from the starting point of the country's actual situation. After the deterioration of its relations with the Soviet Union and under the severe situation of political isolation and economic blockade by the Soviet Union, Yugoslavia, taking into account the actual situation in the country, explored a path of socialist development centred on self-government for itself and was the first to break away from the Soviet model, based on the Marxist idea that the emancipation of the working class should be fought for by itself, the idea of establishing a free association of producers and the idea that self-government is a necessary step in the transition to an advanced form of socialist ownership of the means of production. After Mao Zedong proposed the proposition of the sinicisation of Marxism in 1938, the CPC, after a long period of continuous exploration, achieved two historic leaps in integrating Marxism-Leninism with the concrete reality of Chinese revolution, construction and reform, and found the correct road to national liberation, socialist construction and socialism with Chinese characteristics, creating Mao Zedong Thought, Deng Xiaoping Theory, the major ideology of the Three Represents, the Scientific Outlook on Development and Xi Jinping Thought on Socialism with Chinese Characteristics for a New Era, thereby achieving the sinicisation of Marxism.

Marxism is a doctrine of continuous development. As the development of practice never ends, the understanding of truth and theoretical innovation also never ceases to advance. Engels said long ago that, "Marx's whole world view is not a doctrine but a method. It offers not ready-made dogma but a point of departure for further research and a methodology for such research"[7]. In the process of founding Marxism, Marx and Engels constantly developed their ideas. After the publication of the *Communist Manifesto*, Marx and Engels continued to revise and refine their theories, continuously systematising and scientificising Marxism. After the death of Marx and Engels, Lenin carried their banner high and formed Leninism, achieving the transformation of Marxism from theory to practice. Today, the breadth and depth of the changes of the times and the development of socialism are far greater than the classic Marxist writers could have imagined at the time. As Deng Xiaoping said, "Marx must not be asked to provide ready-made answers to the problems that have arisen more than a hundred, or hundreds of, years after his death. ...... True Marxist-Leninists must recognise, inherit and develop Marxism-Leninism in the light of the present situation"[8]. Therefore, development constitutes a vivid embodiment of the essential attributes and scientific nature of Marxism, as well as the way it exists. The guiding governance ideology of the communist party must uphold theoretical innovation based on practice and constantly develop Marxism.

In order to promote the theoretical innovation of the guiding governance ideology of the communist party it is necessary to accurately grasp the characteristics of the times. Time is the mother of ideology, and practice is the source of theory. The progress of the times and the development of society put theory in constant danger of becoming detached from reality. In the first half of the 20th century, the themes of the times were war and revolution, while in the second half, the themes of the times were peace and development. The 21st century has seen the emergence of new features such as political multipolarity, economic globalisation, cultural pluralism and social informatisation. In the face of the new international environment, it is undoubtedly the right choice to actively adjust internal and external policies in order to gain the initiative in international competition. In order to consolidate its ruling position and win the trust of the people, the ruling communist party must accurately judge the historical orientation of the party and the socialist cause, accurately judge the main social contradictions, adapt to the changes in the international situation, seize opportunities and accelerate development. The key to China's remarkable achievements over the past 40 years of reform and opening up lies in the fact that in the 1980s Deng Xiaoping grasped the global trend that the power of peace was growing and the danger of war still existed, established a guiding ideology centred on economic construction, and started the journey of reform and opening up, and socialist modernisation. From an international perspective, if the ruling party of a country fails to progressively advance in its guiding governance ideology, does not have a global vision and moves against the tide of global trends, it is bound to fall into passivity and close itself off to the world.

In order to uphold theoretical innovation based on practice, it is necessary to constantly emancipate the minds. Taking practice as the basis and the problems themselves as the guide and responding to the call of the times is the key to achieving progressive advance in guiding. Every time the guiding governance ideology advances progressively, it is as a result of the urgent needs of the times and of the actual situation. When the theme of the times and the historical conditions in which some of the principles in Marxist theory are reflected change, then it is necessary to start from new objective reality, answer new questions, make new conclusions, and then develop Marxism. When the contradictory relationship between theory and practice, upholding and development emerges, how to innovate and develop theories based on the changing development of practice, and on the basis of adherence to the basic positions, views and methods of Marxism, becomes the key to resolving this contradictory relationship. In solving the contradictions, it is necessary to emancipate the mind from the shackles of anachronistic concepts, practices and institutions, and to prevent rigidity of thought. Only then can problems encountered on the way be solved with developing theory and can new horizons of Marxist development be continuously opened up.

(III) PREVENTING BOTH DOGMATIC AND EMPIRICAL TENDENCIES

Both dogmatism and empiricism misinterpret and distort Marxism from its essence. Marx and Engels not only founded Marxism, the scientific theory of proletarian revolution, and the proletarian parties, the Communist League and the International Workingmen's Association, but also pioneered the history of the struggle against the opportunism of the "left" and the right in the building of proletarian parties and revolutionary struggle. Engels summed up the opportunism of the "left" and the right, which essentially misinterpreted Marxism, as Marxism in words and anti-Marxism in deeds. Engels pointed out that opportunism is a bourgeois and petty-bourgeois ideology in disguise performed within the party, and that opportunists distort, falsify and blunt Marxism under the banner of Marxism in an attempt to make Marxism fit the demands of the bourgeoisie. Consequently, opportunism is Marxist in word and anti-Marxist in deed, nominally representing the interests of the working class but in fact representing the interests of the bourgeoisie. "Left"-leaning opportunism has dogmatised Marxism and rendered it lifeless, while right-leaning opportunism has obliterated and weakened the revolutionary nature of Marxism, "advocating a socialism that overrides the class interests of the workers and class struggle, and attempts to reconcile the interests of the two struggling classes in a higher humanity", turning Marxism into a theory acceptable to both the proletariat and the bourgeoisie[9].

Therefore, when a communist party is in power and adheres to Marxism as its guide, it must resolutely oppose and prevent two misguided tendencies in its approach to Marxism, neither dogmatising Marxism nor creating another set of rules apart from Marxism. In response to the errors of the "left" and right in the Russian Social Democratic Party and the international communist movement, Lenin first put forward the scientific proposition of the "fight on two fronts" against the "left" and the right. He explained in depth that the common feature of the errors of the "left" and right was that they were detached from Marxism in theory and from practical struggle in action. The difference is that right-leaning opportunists deny the guiding role of the universal principles of Marxism in the revolutionary struggle of the proletariat, while "left"-leaning opportunists absolutise and dogmatise Marxism and deny the different features of the practical struggle. In the history of the international communist movement, both of these misguided tendencies have brought losses to the socialist revolution and construction. The most painful lesson is that after the CPSU came to power, especially during the reign of Stalin, excessive emphasis was placed on certain aspects of Marxism-Leninism to the neglect of others, leading to subjective, one-sided and absolutist errors. Theoretical flaws inevitably lead to errors in practice, and one of the reasons why Stalin made such mistakes as the widening of the purges of counter-revolutionary elements in the later period of his life was his one-sided understanding and subjective interpretation of Leninism, and his one-sided emphasis on anti-rightism at the expense of anti-"leftism", which led to the mistake of extreme leftism.

It was in summing up the "leftist" mistakes in the history of the CPC, which had once dogmatised the Soviet experience and the instructions of the Comintern, and the departure from Marxism and the loss of revolutionary principles in the later period of the great revolution, committing the right-leaning error of compromising with the KMT, which caused great losses to the Chinese Revolution, that the Chinese communists, represented mainly by Comrade Mao Zedong, creatively applied the basic principles of Marxism-Leninism and integrated them with the concrete practice of the Chinese revolution to form Mao Zedong Thought, finding the correct path to achieve victory in the Chinese revolution.

In the period after the 3rd Plenary Session of the 11th CPC Central Committee, in response to the fact that some comrades in the party showed a certain degree of incomprehension and even resistance to the party's line, guidelines and policy, on the other hand, a very small number of people, under the banner of reform and opening up, distorted the ideological essence of the emancipation of the mind and arbitrarily expanded the mistakes of the party and Mao Zedong in an attempt to deny the leadership of the party and the socialist system. In this regard, Deng Xiaoping clearly pointed out that, "we must criticise the wrong ideas of the 'left' as well as those of the right", and "if [errors of the] 'left' appear, we should oppose the 'left', and if [errors of the] right appear, we should oppose the right". In early 1992 during his southern tour speeches, Deng Xiaoping further pointed out that, "the right can ruin socialism, and the 'left' also has the capacity to ruin socialism. China should be wary of the right but mainly focus on guarding against the 'left'."[10] Since the 18th CPC National Congress, the Party Central Committee, with Comrade Xi Jinping at its core, has repeatedly stressed that, 'Marxism-Leninism and Mao Zedong Thought must not be lost; if we lose them, we lose our fundamental [essence]."[11] This refers to upholding the basic principles of Marxism without wavering and opposing the misguided tendency to treat Marxism dogmatically or to deviate from its direction.

Historical experience has taught us that the most important thing in preventing these two misguided tendencies in the guiding governance ideology of the communist party is to establish a mechanism for preventing and correcting errors. In terms of the system of party leadership and organisational structure, the party's core leadership position should be further consolidated and the relationship between the party and the government, and governance mechanisms should be improved. In terms of the leadership system, the basic systems such as democratic centralism should be improved and implemented, so that the operational mechanism and operating procedures of democratic centralism can be scientificised, institutionalised and standardised.

3

THE PATH OF GOVERNANCE

UPHOLDING AND DEVELOPING A SOCIALIST SYSTEM IN LINE WITH NATIONAL CONDITIONS AND SOCIALISM THAT MEETS CONTEMPORARY NEEDS

Every ruling party is faced with choices pertaining to the path of governance. This is true of a bourgeois party in power, and it is also true of a proletarian party in power. After the birth of the world's first socialist country, the Soviet Union chose a different path of development from that of other European countries. After the second world war, the Communist Party of Yugoslavia led its people to the path of autonomous socialism while in the mid-1950s, the Polish United Workers' Party also put forward the idea of "a socialist path suited to the specific conditions of Poland". In December 1978, the 3rd Plenary Session of the 11th CPC Central Committee marked the beginning of China's reform and opening up, as China embarked on the path of socialism with Chinese characteristics. The scientific conclusion reached by these ruling communist parties after repeated explorations was to "to follow the country's own path to socialism".

(I) ADHERENCE TO THE DIRECTION OF SCIENTIFIC SOCIALISM - THE FUNDAMENTAL DIRECTION OF THE RULING COMMUNIST PARTY

Direction is fundamental, has a bearing on the overall situation and deter- mines long-term [outcomes], while direction determines the path and the path determines destiny; the question of direction is the most fundamental issue. Historical experience tells us that the fundamental direction of a communist party's governance is scientific socialism. Scientific socialism is a critique and transcendence of capitalism. Human society is a process of the negation and movement from a lower to a higher stage. This has been true of the primitive, slave-owning, feudal, capitalist and socialist societies experienced so far. Capitalist society has evolved from feudal society and has created great social wealth, advanced social civilisation and historic social change unparalleled in previous human societies. As Marx and Engels said, "The bourgeoisie has played a very revolutionary role in history" and "the bourgeoisie has created more and greater productive forces in its less than a hundred years of class rule than all the productive forces created in all past generations".[1]

Just as capitalism inevitably replaced feudalism, so socialism inevitably replaced capitalism, because capitalism has inherent contradictions and shortcomings that are difficult to resolve on its own. The cyclical nature of its economic crises has caused enormous destruction and waste of social productivity, brought massive unemployment, falling wages and other types of disastrous suffering to the working people, and intensified the contradictions between the proletariat and the bourgeoisie. On the basis of the fierce struggle between the proletariat and the bourgeoisie, Marx and Engels drew the basic conclusion that the demise of the bourgeoisie and the victory of the proletariat are equally inevitable, and thereby founded scientific socialism.

Genuine proletarian parties are established in accordance with Marxist theory. Applying the principles of scientific socialism to carry out socialist revolution and socialist construction, and ultimately achieve communism is the historical mission of proletarian parties after they come to power, and it is also the fundamentally correct direction for the governance of communist parties. The historical experience of the international communist movement shows that in order for a communist party to uphold scientific socialism after it comes to power, it must always uphold the leadership of the party in all its work. In the political life of a socialist country, only by adhering to the leadership of the party can the proletariat form a powerful force, put forward correct goals, programmes, tasks and policies, rid itself of the influence of various errors brought by *zeitgeist* and reactionary forces, maintain the ideological and theoretical purity of the party, and ensure the correct direction of the proletarian revolutionary movement. Here the public ownership of the means of production must be practised. In a socialist society, public ownership of the means of production is the mainstay, and this is also the most essential feature of socialism. The main means of production are together owned by the working people, and the purpose of production is to meet the material and cultural needs of the people as a whole. This is so that the people's initiative for production can be fully mobilised and the rapid development of productivity can be promoted, and at the same time the state can use unified planning to coordinate the relations between the various sectors of production, organise and guide the planned and proportional development of the entire national economy, eliminate production anarchy and avoid the cyclical economic crises of capitalist society. A system of distribution according to work where each does their utmost must also be implemented. This system constitutes a product of socialist public ownership, a fundamental negation of the system of exploitation, and a great advance in history. According to this principle, labour becomes the means by which the working class creates a better life for itself and they no longer work for capitalists, thereby inspiring the people to produce and to build socialism. The dictatorship of the proletariat must also be implemented so that the working people become the masters of the state and society. In a socialist state, democracy is practised for the masses of working people and dictatorship is practised for enemies. The people enjoy a wide range of democratic rights in the political life of the state, and the working people become the masters of the state and have the right to participate in the management of all economic and cultural affairs of the state, while the state also provides legal guarantees for the exercise of democratic rights by the people. This cannot be achieved in any country where a bourgeois party is in power.

(II) BASED ON NATIONAL CONDITIONS - A PRACTICAL REQUIREMENT FOR COMMUNIST PARTY GOVERNANCE

Being grounded in national conditions and starting everything from the actual reality is the core essence of adhering to and developing Marxism. As Marx said once when he was young, "Correct theory must be articulated and developed in context and in accordance with existing conditions"[2]. Lenin, who led the Bolshevik Party to integrate the universal principles of Marxism with the concrete practice of the Russian Revolution, to achieve the victory of the October Revolution and establish the world's first socialist state, summed up the experience of the October Revolution saying, "It is inevitable that all peoples will gravitate toward socialism but all peoples will not go there in exactly the same way; in this or that form of democracy, in this or that form of the dictatorship of the proletariat, and in terms of the speed of the socialist transformation of all aspects of social life, each nation will have its own characteristics."[3] This tells us that after a proletarian party comes to power, it must determine which socialist path that state will take in accordance with the characteristics of the times, national conditions and the needs of the people.

Why must the choice of socialist path start from the reality of the country? Because any theory is a product of specific historical conditions, and to copy theoretical principles out of the context of that particular era and national conditions is bound to be a historical mistake. Marxist doctrine is not a dogma or a set formula but rather a guide for action. Marxism arose in Western Europe in the 1840s, and Marx and Engels in their time could only have made a principled vision of socialist society, only theoretically exploring the starting point and general direction of the further development of future society. The specific laws governing the development of socialist societies in different countries were yet to be explored by future generations through practice. Scientific socialism is bound to evolve with the times, with practice and with science. So, at the 10th CPR Congress after the victory of the October Revolution, Lenin first addressed the question of the necessity of a special path of transition to socialism in Russia, where small producers were in the majority, stating that, "In our country, the first characteristic ...... is that the proletariat in our country is not only a minority but a tiny minority; the peasantry constitutes the majority", and "there is no doubt that the introduction of a socialist revolution in a country where small peasant producers form the majority of the population must be carried out through a series of special methods of transition which would be totally unnecessary in a developed capitalist country where employed workers in industry and agriculture form the majority".[4] Based on a profound analysis of Russia's national conditions, Lenin led the Soviet government to implement a wartime communist system which achieved good results in restoring and developing the country's economy.

It was China that was most successful in choosing the correct path to socialism based on its own national conditions. In this connection, Mao Zedong emphasised that, "clearly identifying China's national conditions is the basic foundation for identifying all revolutionary problems."[5] As soon as it was founded, the CPC made socialism its goal and dream. After the founding of new China and after the CPC became the ruling party, with regard to the question of which path to take in socialist revolution and socialist construction, and drawing on lessons from history surrounding following the path of others, Mao proposed learning from the Soviet Union, created new theories, wrote new works, and carried out the "second integration" of the basic principles of Marxism-Leninism and China's actual situation, and conducted arduous exploration. The most prominent and greatest contribution of Mao Zedong's life is that he led the CPC and the Chinese people to find the correct path for the New Democratic Revolution, completed the task of anti-imperialism and anti-feudalism, established new China and the basic socialist system, and accumulated experience and provided the conditions for exploring the path of socialism with Chinese characteristics. In the new era of reform and opening up, Deng Xiaoping clearly put forward the proposition of China "taking its own path and building socialism with Chinese characteristics", and found the correct path for socialist revolution and construction in China, establishing the road of socialism with Chinese characteristics. Since the 18th CPC National Congress, General Secretary Xi Jinping has repeatedly stressed that "only the person who wears a shoe knows whether it fits or not." By this he meant that it was necessary to base everything on China's national conditions, repeatedly experiment, and continue to explore a path of socialist development in line with China's national conditions. He also pointed out that the CPC's insistence on independently choosing its own path did not start only with reform and opening up, but from the founding of the party and the country. This is precisely what the party did after the founding of new China, otherwise it would not have fallen out with its "big brother", the Soviet Union. It is only because the CPC did not walk with any crutches that it was able to stride forward and stand firmly on its own feet, and the dramatic changes in Eastern Europe and the collapse of the Soviet Union had no major impact on China. China is on its own path, with an incomparably broad stage, an incomparably rich historical heritage and an incomparably strong determination to move forward.

In order to choose the path of socialism based on a country's own national conditions, it is necessary to integrate the basic principles of Marxism with the country's specific reality. This means liberating and developing social productivity, focusing on the practical problems of socialist modernisation, on what is being done, on the application of Marxism, on theoretical thinking about practical problems, and on new practices and new developments, building a socialist market economy, socialist democratic politics, advanced socialist culture, a socialist harmonious society and socialist eco-civilisation, promoting the all-round development of people, gradually achieving common prosperity for the people as a whole, and building a rich, strong, democratic, civilised, harmonious and beautiful socialist modern state, all on the basis of adherence to the basic principles of Marxism under the leadership of the CPC and based on China's national conditions with economic construction at the centre.

There is no way to talk about Marxism in isolation from a country's reality and the development of the times.

In order to walk along the path of socialism with national characteristics, China's experience shows that it is neither right to take the old path of closure and rigidity nor the evil path of changing flags and banners but rather it is necessary to uphold Marxism as the guide and independently choose the path of socialist development with national conditions and needs as the starting point. It is necessary to focus on economic construction, uphold reform and opening up, continuously raise the material and cultural living standards of the people, and build a strong modern socialist power. It is also necessary to establish and refine a socialist theoretical system, a socialist system and a socialist culture with national characteristics. The socialist theoretical system is the guide to action on the path of socialism, the socialist system is the fundamental guarantee of the country's development and progress, and the socialist culture is the powerful spiritual force that inspires the party and the people to move forward courageously. By upholding confidence in the path, theory, system and culture, it is possible to propel forward the cause of socialism with national characteristics.

(III) RESPONDING TO THE *ZEITGEIST* - THE REQUIREMENT OF THE TIMES FOR COMMUNIST PARTY GOVERNANCE

"The global current is broad and powerful; if you go with it, you will prosper but if you go against it, you will perish." Engels long ago pointed out that, "we can only know [reality] under the conditions of our time, and we can only know it in accordance with the extent of the scope of these conditions."[6] This tells us that in order to uphold and develop socialism in line with a country's national conditions, it is necessary to establish a scientific world view, follow the mainstream, trends and direction of development of the times, follow the objective laws of how things develop, establish a global vision, and walk along an autonomous path in the context of the general background and pattern of the *zeitgeist*. Looking at the history of the world, the development of political parties, the rise of great powers and the 500-year history of socialism in the world, we can see that all countries that have generally developed rapidly and had an important influence in the world were countries that led the *zeitgeist*, stood at the head of the tide of the times and seized historical opportunities. The Industrial Revolution, launched in Britain in the 1860s, ushered in an era of replacing manual labour with machines, and Britain, which was the first to complete this industrial revolution, soon became the world's dominant power. The reason why the Soviet Union rose rapidly after establishing itself as a socialist state and developed into a global superpower was also due to the skill of the ruling CPSU in seizing the historical opportunities offered by the global situation; 1929-1933 saw a serious economic crisis in the capitalist world. In order to escape from the economic crisis and solve their own immediate problems, capitalist countries had to temporarily relax their economic and political siege of the Soviet Union and were willing to provide technical assistance to the Soviet Union in order to obtain capital and employment opportunities. The CPSU led the party and people to seize the opportunity for development given by the global capitalist economic crisis and vigorously imported advanced technology and human resources from the West, effectively contributing to the rapid development of Soviet society while in turn launching an attack on the capitalist system. As two sharply opposed social systems, a strong institutional crisis arose within the capitalist countries, and many people began to doubt the liberal economic system of capitalism. At a time when the *laissez-faire* capitalist economy was in the midst of the worst disaster in its history, the socialist planned economy practised by the CPSU stood alone in the midst of the global economic depression, and Soviet-style social welfare became a powerful attraction for the lower and middle classes in capitalist countries, with capitalism being challenged as never before. Faced with the challenge of the Soviet socialist system and the rising labour movement at home, capitalist countries had to implement new policy adjustments. Among the policy adjustments made by capitalist countries, the influence of the great attraction of the state-owned economy led by the CPSU led to increased government intervention in the economy, certain concessions to the working masses and corresponding policies to improve labour relations and social welfare, resulting in Roosevelt's "New Deal" in the US. Zbigniew Brzezinski later said that at that time socialism under the leadership of the CPSU had had a powerful impact on capitalist countries and the world as a whole, and that communism was no longer a "ghost" but was seen as an "auspicious historical omen"[7].

The *zeitgeist* has different connotations in different historical periods. In the 18th century it represented the industrial revolution, in the 20th century it represented the broad spread of Marxism around the world and the establishment of socialist systems, and in the 21st century it represents peace, development, cooperation and mutual benefit. If the communist party is to shoulder the historical mission given to it by the times, it must scientifically understand the characteristics of the times and thereby grasp the features and laws of the times. Time, as a historical process, is not fixed but an extremely complex process of constant development and change. In the process of historical development, there may be several different stages of development. At each stage the basic contradictions that determine the nature and basic characteristics of the era still exist but the manner of expression of these contradictions, the interrelationship between them and the main contradictions that play a dominant role, change and, consequently, the essence of the era develops, and the theme of the era changes. Following the 1960s and 1970s, the global situation underwent new changes, with the launch of a new scientific and technological revolution which drove tremendous productivity development. The structure of the capitalist economy also underwent great changes, and its self-regulating capacity was enhanced. Economic strength and comprehensive national power became the most important condition for the major powers to win in global competition, and the arms race and the threat of war became the greatest constraint to world development, especially economic development. As a result, the fight for, and maintenance of, world peace became the common demand of a wider range of countries and social strata, and considerations of war and revolution gradually weakened, and peace and development gradually rose to become the theme of the times. Under such circumstances, any ruling party must do its utmost to adapt to and meet the various opportunities and demands brought about by this great change, otherwise it will fail to keep pace with the times and lag behind the tide of historical development. Looking at the countries where communist parties were in power during this period, an important reason for the dramatic changes in the Soviet Union and Eastern Europe, where the ruling communist parties lost power and the countries were no longer "red", was that the ruling parties in these countries did not adapt to the changes of the times and follow a socialist path that was in line with their own national conditions, but were frozen in the rigid Soviet model. In stark contrast to the situation in these countries, the CPC, after the 3rd Plenary Session of the 11th Central Committee, reconceptualised the international environment and the international situation, changed its previous view that war was inevitable, and realised that the theme of the times was gradually changing from the past one of revolution and war to peace and development. In this connection, Deng Xiaoping clearly pointed out on 4 March 1985 that, "peace and development are the two major issues of the contemporary world" and that "one of the really big issues in the world now, among the strategic issues with a global dimension, is the issue of peace, and another is the economic or development issue."[8] The change in the theme of the times has had a tremendous impact on the direction and content of China's socialist modernisation, and the CPC has sensitively responded to the requirements of the change in the theme of the times by proposing theories, lines, guidelines and policies for building socialism with Chinese characteristics, and scientifically formulating strategies and tactics for achieving socialist modernisation, guiding all the people of China to focus mainly on how to develop the economy, improve comprehensive national power and raise the living standards of the people, achieving brilliant results which have attracted global attention. This is the result of both a profound understanding of the essence of socialism and a correct understanding of the changing theme of the times.

In order to conform to the trend of the times, it is necessary to be at the forefront of the times and move in step with the development of the times. In order to be at the forefront of the times, it is fundamental to have a profound understanding of the times, which requires emancipation of the mind and the establishment of new ideas that are in harmony with the spirit of the times. In this connection, Xi Jinping pointed out, "Throughout the world, change is the trend, the direction of travel of peoples' hearts, and constitutes a vast and turbulent historical trend which, if followed leads to prosperity and if resisted leads to demise. In leading a great undertaking like ours, which is unprecedented and rare in the world, the most intolerable thing is to be rigid in thinking and stuck in our ways. The development of practice never ends and emancipation of the mind never ends; reform and opening up is always a work in progress and until it is finished, there can be no stopping or going back." From the historical experience of the international communist movement, the core of responding to the *zeitgeist* is to employ the spirit of innovation and constantly solve the new problems of the times. In the past, the socialist construction of various socialist countries has generally developed along the following path. Politically, class struggle was taken as the central task, and in terms of ownership, the approach of "large and communal" was pursued. In terms of distribution, egalitarianism was practised in the name of distribution according to work, and in terms of economics, a planned economy which was in essence a natural economy and a product economy, were pursued. By engaging in self-imposed closures and confrontation between the two systems in external relations, the objective pursued was not actually the development of productivity but the so-called advancement of socioeconomic relations and the purity of society. The path of socialism with Chinese characteristics which the CPC led the people to establish has freed socialist development from the constraints of a certain model and the mechanical adaptation of previous theories, and has created a form of realisation that better reflects the essence of socialism and gives better play to its potential in accordance with the specific conditions of the country and the development requirements of the times, making it creative and diverse, and more capable of development and of adapting to changes in the environment.

The opening up of a new path in China began in the 1970s, when the Chinese communists, mainly represented by Comrade Deng Xiaoping, summed up the positive and negative experiences since the founding of new China, emancipated the mind, sought truth from facts, achieved the shift of the centre of the CPC's work to economic construction, implemented reform and opening up, opened up a new period in the development of the socialist cause, clarified the basic issues of building, consolidating and developing socialism in China, gradually formed the line, guidelines and policy for building socialism with Chinese characteristics, and successfully pioneered socialism with Chinese characteristics. Through unremitting efforts, the Chinese communists, represented mainly by Comrade Jiang Zemin, defended socialism with Chinese characteristics in the face of a very complicated domestic and international situation and the severe test of serious complications in world socialism, deepened their understanding of the nature of socialism and the appropriate way to build it, as well as the appropriate kind of party to build and how to build it, established the reform objectives and basic framework of the socialist market economy, established the basic economic and distribution systems in the primary stage of socialism, pioneered a new context for comprehensive reform and opening up, promoted the great new project of party building, and successfully propelled socialism with Chinese characteristics into the 21st century. The Chinese communists, mainly represented by Comrade Hu Jintao, continued to work hard and, in accordance with the new requirements of development, profoundly understood and answered the major questions surrounding the kind of development which should be achieved and how to achieve it under the new situation, successfully upholding and developing socialism with Chinese characteristics from a new historical starting point. Since the 18th CPC National Congress the CPC, mainly represented by Comrade Xi Jinping, has responded to the development of the times and systematically answered the major contemporary issues regarding the kind of socialism with Chinese characteristics to uphold and develop, and how to uphold and develop it in the new era, from a combination of theory and practice, successfully writing a new chapter of socialism with Chinese characteristics. The path of socialism with Chinese characteristics not only answers new questions of the times but also establishes a model for the continuous refinement and development of socialism according to changing conditions. It is the spiritual banner of the Chinese communists, making an original Chinese contribution to the development of Marxism, providing the spiritual force for the great rejuvenation of the Chinese nation, and contributing Chinese wisdom and solutions to the cause of socialism and to the building of a better world. It expands the pathways of developing countries to modernisation and offers a brand-new choice to those countries and nations in the world that wish to accelerate their development while maintaining their independence.

4

THE FUNDAMENTAL TASK OF GOVERNANCE

DEVELOPMENT IS THE BASIS AND KEY TO SOLVING ALL PROBLEMS

The history of human society is the history of the continuous development of productivity. "The means of labour are not only a measure of the development of human labour but also an indicator of the social relations by which labour is carried out"[1]. Rubbing wood to make fire illuminated the journey from ape to man, the iron plough opened the way to agrarian civilisation, the steam engine sounded the trumpet of the industrial age, and the computer keyboard pounded out the powerful sounds of the information age. The development of productivity ultimately determines the changes in the face of society, the renewal of social structures and the progress of social civilisation. Marxism holds that the fundamental aim of a proletarian party in leading the people to seize power and establish a socialist system is to liberate and develop productivity and ultimately achieve communism. Therefore, after coming to power, a genuine Marxist party must unswervingly make development the first priority in governing and rejuvenating a country, and persist with the liberation and development of social productivity. Deng Xiaoping once profoundly pointed out that, "There are many tasks of socialism but the fundamental one is to develop productivity, to manifest its superiority over capitalism on the basis of developing productivity, and to create the material basis for achieving communism"[2]. Summing up the experience of the CPC in more than 70 years of governance, especially the successful experience since the outset of reform and opening up, one inevitable conclusion which can be drawn is that, in order to always uphold the progressiveness of the party

616

and consolidate the party's ruling position, it is necessary to firmly grasp the theme of development, unite and lead the people to struggle hard and forge ahead for economic development and social progress, sincerely safeguard and achieve the fundamental interests of the general public, and constantly meet the growing needs of the people for a better life. Only then will the people truly support the party and will the party's ruling base be more consolidated. This is related to the fundamental question of for whom the communist party governs, how it governs and whether it can govern in the long term, and is an important law of communist party governance. As the 19th CPC National Congress pointed out, "development is the basis and key to solving all China's problems."

(I) UPHOLDING THE FOCUS ON ECONOMIC CONSTRUCTION

Economic construction is a fundamental measure of the state to maintain and improve the people's livelihoods, ensure the development and progress of the state and the nation, and maintain social stability. Marxism holds that in the process of movement of the basic contradictions in society, productivity is the starting point of the whole process, that is, the development of productivity determines the change in socioeconomic relations, and the development of productivity to a certain extent inevitably causes change in these relations. It also holds that changes in socioeconomic relations as the basis of the economy in turn inevitably drive changes in the superstructure, thereby causing the change of social relations and social form. Therefore, after the armed seizure of power by the proletarian party, the focus of the party's work had to be shifted to economic construction. This is the inevitable result of the contradictory movements of productivity and socioeconomic relations, the economic base and the superstructure, and constitutes a historical law of the development and victory of the proletariat's struggle for liberation. In this regard, Marx pointed out long ago that achieving communism required, "tremendous growth and high development of productivity", and that without this, "there would only be poverty and the universalisation of extreme poverty and, in the case of extreme poverty, the struggle for necessities would have to be resumed, and all that is banal and filthy would return and take over once more"[3]. After the victory of the October Revolution in Russia, Lenin stated in his Address to the Third All-Russian Congress of Trade Unions in April 1920 that, "The whole attention of the CPSU administration is now concentrated on the question of building a peaceful economy"[4]. At the end of 1920, at the Eighth All-Russian

Congress of Soviets, Lenin again elaborated on the question of the transformation of the main tasks of the party and state. He said, "The economic tasks and economic front are now again brought before us as the main and fundamental task and battlefront"[5]. The practice of socialism has repeatedly proven the truth and foresight of Marxist theory.

As a Marxist party, the CPC attaches great importance to the liberation and development of productivity and has made "focusing on economic construction" an important element of the party's basic line in the primary stage of socialism. China began to build socialism on the basis of the legacy of a semi-colonial and semi-feudal society, with a relatively backward economy and culture. On the eve of the founding of new China, Mao Zedong made a profound statement at the Second Plenary Session of the Seventh CPC National Congress on the gradual shift of the focus of work to economic construction after the party's national victory, stating that, "From the first day we take over the city, our eyes must be directed toward the restoration and development of the city's undertakings in production. It is important to avoid blindly clawing for things and forgetting the central task"[6]. After the founding of new China, the Eighth CPC National Congress decided to shift the focus of the party's work to economic construction, that the fundamental task of the party and the state was to develop productivity, and that the main contradiction in the primary stage of socialism was between the growing material and cultural needs of the people and backward social production. Unfortunately, after the Eighth CPC National Congress, this correct understanding was not upheld, thereby leading to the gradual establishment of class struggle as the basic line for the entire phase of socialist history. After the 3rd Plenary Session of the 11th CPC Central Committee, Deng Xiaoping repeatedly required the whole party to firmly grasp economic construction as the focus, stating, "The tasks of modernisation are multifaceted, and all aspects need to be integrated and balanced without a focus on any one aspect. But ultimately, economic construction must still be the focus. If we move away from a focus on economic construction, there is a danger of losing the physical base. All other tasks must be subordinated to this focus and revolve around it, never interfering with or attacking it"[7]. After the 14th CPC National Congress, Jiang Zemin repeatedly stressed that, "The key to upholding the party's basic line without wavering is to uphold a focus on economic construction without wavering"[8]. And then in his report to the 17th CPC National Congress, Hu Jintao pointed out that focusing on economic construction "is a fundamental requirement for our party and China to prosper and develop, and enjoy long-term peace and stability"[9].

Since the 18th CPC National Congress, Xi Jinping has pointed out that, "focusing on economic construction is the key to China's prosperity, and development is the party's first priority in governing and rejuvenating China, and the basis and key to solving all China's problems"[10]. Since the founding of new China, especially since the outset of reform and opening up, China has undergone radical changes, its economy and society have developed rapidly, its comprehensive strength has increased significantly, and the Chinese people have embarked on a broad path to prosperity and well-being. The fundamental reason for this lies in upholding the strategic mindset that development is the top priority and the first priority of economic construction.

Proactively adapting to, grasping and leading the new normal of economic development and achieving the high-quality development of China's economy are fundamental requirements for upholding a focus on economic construction in the new era. The entry of China's economy into a new normal constitutes a major strategic judgment made by the Party Central Committee since the 18th CPC National Congress through a comprehensive analysis of the cycles of global economic growth and the phased characteristics of China's development as well as the interaction between these aspects. An accurate grasp of the general logic of China's economic development is the starting point for effective economic work in the present era. The basic feature of China's economic development in the new era is the shift from the stage of high-speed growth to that of high-quality development, which is an inevitable requirement in order to adapt to the changes in the main contradictions in Chinese society. In order to promote the high-quality development of China's economy, it is necessary to take the promotion of supply-side structural reform as the main theme of economic work, build a modern economy, enabling the market to play a decisive role in resource allocation, accelerating the formation of an indicator system, a policy system, a standard system, a statistical system, and a performance evaluation and political performance assessment system, which all promote high-quality development, thereby establishing and refining the institutional environment.

(II) UPHOLDING COMPREHENSIVE SOCIAL DEVELOPMENT

A socialist society is one which develops and progresses comprehensively. It is the great mission of us communists to promote the comprehensive development of people and society, and this is also the purpose and final destination of socialist and communist development. The Marxist concept of social development reveals that the progress of human society is an objective process of moving from a lower to a higher civilisation, and from a society of one-sided development to a society of comprehensive development. Marx astutely pointed out that, "all peoples, whatever their historical circumstances, are destined to follow this path - so that in the end they all reach an economic form which guarantees the very high development of the productivity of social labour and, at the same time, the most comprehensive development of each individual producer"[11]. The society with the economic form to which Marx was referring is socialist society. In his study of the historical development of human society, Engels once famously put forward the "central axis principle". He pointed out that, "the further the field we study is from the economy, the closer it is to purely abstract ideology, the more we find it manifesting itself as a contingent phenomenon in its own development, and the more curved its curve becomes. If you draw the central axis of the curve, you will find that the longer the period examined, the wider the scope examined, the closer this axis is to parallel with the axis of economic development"[12]. "Parallel" here can be understood as comprehensive or coordinated development. In the view of the founder of Marxism, the comprehensive development of a socialist society is in accordance with the general law of human social development, whereas the highly unbalanced or deformed development of a capitalist society violates this law and therefore this society is eventually replaced by a socialist one. After the victory of the October Revolution, Lenin put forward the major ideology of the comprehensive construction of socialism on the basis of the practical experience of socialism in Russia, which had lasted only a few years. Lenin famously said that, "Marxists - were the first socialists to raise the question of the necessity of analysing not only the economic aspects of social life but all aspects of social life"[13].

The Chinese communists inherited and developed the theories of the classic Marxist writers on social development and in different historical periods have put forward a concept of development marked by the characteristics of different eras. During the War of Resistance Against Japanese Aggression, when national conflicts were the main social contradiction of the time, Mao Zedong pointed out that, "we communists, for many years, have been struggling not only for China's political and economic revolution but also for China's cultural revolution", comprehensively putting forward and discussing the idea that the economy, politics and culture must develop in a coordinated manner and promote each other. In some sense, this gave direction to the development of the Chinese revolution at a high level, which can be said to be the comprehensive view of development of that era[14]. During the period of socialist construction, he also put forward the idea of comprehensive, balanced and coordinated development in his speech *On the Ten Major Relationships*. After the 3rd Plenary Session of the 11th CPC Central Committee, Deng Xiaoping once purposefully pointed out that, "while building a high degree of material civilisation, we should raise the scientific and cultural level of the whole nation, develop an exquisite and richly colourful cultural life, and build a high level of socialist spiritual civilisation"[15]. He also put forward the idea of "comprehensive reform", stating that "reform is comprehensive reform, including reform of the economic system and the political system, and corresponding reform in various other areas"[16]. After the 14th CPC National Congress, Jiang Zemin also pointed out that, "a socialist society is a society marked by all-round development and progress"[17]. After the 16th CPC National Congress, Hu Jintao made a further profound announcement of the meaning of comprehensive development, stating "The overall layout of the cause of socialism with Chinese characteristics has been clearly developed from the three prongs of socialist economic, political and cultural construction to the four-sphere plan of socialist economic, political, cultural and social construction"[18], and elaborated on the concept of comprehensive and coordinated development in major strategic ideology such as the Scientific Outlook on Development. Since the 18th CPC National Congress, Xi Jinping has responded to the new requirements of the times and practical development by proposing the strategy composition of the Four Comprehensives and the new development concept of "innovation, coordination, eco-friendliness, opening up and mutual benefit", which has led to historic changes in China's overall development. The 19th CPC National Congress clearly drove forward the cause of socialism with Chinese characteristics in the context of the Five-Sphere integrated plan in terms of economics, politics, culture, society and eco-civilisation, which is a mission statement for further promoting all-round human development and social progress. The rich development of the CPC's theory on comprehensive social development reflects the theoretical innovation of integrating Marxist theory on comprehensive development with the actual socioeconomic development of contemporary China, as well as the consistency and commonality of the CPC's thinking on social development.

In order to uphold social development in the new era, it is necessary to persist with the strategic composition of the integrated promotion of the Five-Sphere integrated plan and coordinated promotion of the Four Comprehensives in order to implement the new development concept. With socialism with Chinese characteristics entering a new era, China's development has been characterised by phases, and the main social contradictions have undergone historic changes that pertain to the overall situation. In order to meet the growing needs of the people for a better life, it is necessary to focus on solving the problem of unbalanced and insufficient development on this basis of continuously promoting development.

In accordance with the arrangements of the 19th CPC National Congress, only by implementing the new development concept and building a modern economy can higher-quality, more efficient, more equitable and more sustainable development be achieved. Only by improving the sovereignty of the people and developing socialist democratic politics can the will of the people be manifested, their rights and interests safeguarded, and their creativity stimulated. Only by firmly asserting cultural confidence and promoting the prosperity of socialist culture is it possible to stimulate the vitality of cultural innovation and creativity of all the people of China. Only by raising the level of protection and improvement of people's livelihood and strengthening and innovating social governance is it possible to make people's sense of access, well-being and security more substantial, secure and sustainable. Only by accelerating reform of the system of eco-civilisation and building a beautiful China is it possible to form a new pattern of modernisation and construction for the harmonious development of humans and nature.

(III) UPHOLDING PROMOTION OF PEOPLE'S WELL-BEING AS THE FUNDAMENTAL PURPOSE OF DEVELOPMENT

Promoting the people's welfare is an essential requirement of the CPC which was founded for the public and governs for the sake of the people. Leading the people to create a better life is the party's unswerving struggle goal. The fundamental aim of the party in uniting and leading the people of all China's ethnic groups to implement a great social revolution is to enable the people to live a good life. As early as 1934, Mao Zedong said, "All the problems of the practical life of the masses are issues to which we should pay attention. If we pay attention to these problems, solve them and meet the needs of the masses, we will really become the organisers of their lives and the masses will really rally around us and enthusiastically endorse us"[19]. All the work of the party must always give the highest priority to the interests of the people, must take the fundamental interests of the broadest number of people as the highest standard, doing more to improve the lives and address the concerns of the people, and persist in taking the smaller concerns of the people as our own great concerns, all from a starting point of the people's concerns and with the aim of bringing them satisfaction.

Protecting and improving people's livelihoods is the fundamental purpose of promoting development. "There are constants in the governance of a country but the benefit of the people is the main focus". Development implemented by the CPC is people-centred, and the people are the agents of development and its biggest beneficiaries. If development fails to meet people's expectations and to provide the masses with tangible benefits, such development becomes meaningless and cannot be sustained. In this regard, Xi Jinping pointed out, "the people-centred development ideology is not an abstract and esoteric concept, and it should not remain only in words and stop at ideological linkages, but rather be reflected in all aspects of socioeconomic development"[20]. It is necessary always to uphold the principle that development is for the people and depends on the people, and that its fruit is to be shared by the people. It is also necessary to ensure that all people have a greater sense of access to shared development on the basis of promoting sustained and healthy economic development, so that the superiority of the socialist system can be fully manifested and the all-round development of the people and their common prosperity as a whole can be continuously promoted.

Grasping the people's livelihood is also a part of grasping development. The CPC has always made an organic link between promoting economic development and improving people's livelihoods. Economic development is the material basis for improving people's livelihoods, and without it there is no sustainable foundation for improving the people's livelihoods. At the same time, it is also necessary to see that people's livelihoods are the "compass" for good socioeconomic development work, and that the continuous improvement of people's livelihoods can not only effectively solve the worries of the masses and mobilise people's initiative to develop production but also enhance expectations regarding social consumption, expand domestic demand, generate new economic growth points, and provide strong endogenous power for economic development, transformation and upgrading. The government should also promote social consumption expectations, expand domestic demand, generate new economic growth points and provide strong internal power for economic development, transformation and upgrading. Therefore, it is necessary both to lay a solid material foundation for the continuous improvement of people's livelihoods through economic development, and also to create more effective demand for economic development through the continuous improvement of people's livelihoods, so as to achieve a virtuous cycle between the two. The transformation of the main contradiction in Chinese society into the contradiction between the people's growing need for a better life, and unbalanced and inadequate development has created new requirements for continuing to safeguard and improve people's livelihoods in the course of development. Efforts should be made to address the problem of unbalanced and inadequate development, improve the quality and efficiency of development, and better meet the growing needs of the people in terms of the economy, politics, culture, society and eco-civilisation.

5

THE DRIVING FORCE OF GOVERNANCE

REFORM AND OPENING UP CONSTITUTES A GREAT REVOLUTION

It is a basic law of human social development that socioeconomic relations must adapt to productivity and the economic base must adapt to the superstructure. When socioeconomic relations do not adapt to productivity and the superstructure does not adapt to the economic base, matters must be resolved through political revolution or reform or improvement. In the situation where a working-class party has gained power and a socialist system has been established, there are no fundamental contradictions or conflicts between productivity and socioeconomic relations, or between the economic base and the superstructure, and the resolution of any contradictions is not carried out through political revolution but through reform. Opening up is also reform. Reform and opening up is a requirement for the movement of the basic contradictions of socialist society and the fundamental driving force for the self-refinement and development of the socialist system. In order to gain a deeper understanding and grasp of the communist party's governance law, it is necessary to study the major issues of reform and opening up.

(I) REFORM AND OPENING UP IS THE FUNDAMENTAL DRIVING FORCE BEHIND THE DEVELOPMENT OF SOCIALIST SOCIETY

Throughout the history of the international communist movement, the understanding of the basic contradictions of socialist society and dynamics of its reform has undergone a long and complicated process. Due to historical limitations, Marx and Engels focused their research on the question of the dynamics of the development of socialist society regarding how to promote the emergence of socialist society, rather than how to develop socialist society. They generally believed that once socialism was achieved, the fundamental contradictions inherent in capitalism could be resolved. They also anticipated that the development of socialist society, as one of the forms of human society, would likewise follow the laws of movement of the basic contradictions of society. Engels pointed out that, "so-called 'socialist society' is not something that remains static but should be seen, like any other social system, as a society that is constantly changing and reforming"[1]. But this genius prophetic assertion has yet to be further confirmed and tested in the concrete practice of socialism.

After the October Revolution in Russia, Lenin, faced with the new situation that had arisen, creatively put forward his unique insight into the dynamics of socialist social development. He believed that under socialist conditions, "confrontation will disappear, contradictions will remain"[2] and that "every step forward and every step forward and upwards in the development of productivity and culture must in future be accompanied by an improvement and transformation of our Soviet system"[3]. Due to Lenin's early death, it was not possible for this sparkling idea to unfold into a systematic scientific theory.

In 1936, when the socialist transformation of the Soviet Union was largely completed and all classes and strata of Soviet society worked in unity to accomplish the great achievements of socialist industrialisation under the leadership of the CPSU, society as a whole took on a completely new look from the past. Putin once commented on this, saying "The planned economy had the definite advantage of being able to concentrate the country's resources on the most important tasks. For example, the solution to the problem of health security for the people of the USSR was unquestionably the work of the communist party." The notion that the Soviet model was a rigid, stagnant and bad system from its inception is not historically accurate. In the face of the great achievements and the new situation of CPSU governance, Stalin believed that in Soviet socialist society socioeconomic relations and productivity, and the superstructure and the economic base were perfectly suited to each other, and that the "moral and political unity" of Soviet society was the driving force of the development of Soviet socialist society. Although this reveals the fundamental difference between socialist society and capitalist society in terms of the dynamics of development, and is not without its rational elements, the denial of the existence of the basic contradictions of human society in socialist society, and consequently of the contradictions between classes and strata, led people to feel, consciously or subconsciously, that socialist society is only harmonious and free of contradictions, that it is a perfect society and that there is no need for any reform or improvement. In retrospect, Soviet society, which had just become socialist, was very far from a mature and established socialism, and it was only through socialism's own "constant changes and reforms" that it could gradually approach its ambitious goal. Of course, the exploration of the communist party's governance law is a never-ending historical process, and Stalin's views represent merely one stage of awareness in the historical process of communist party governance, constituting a reference for future generations to continue their search. Therefore, it is not right to be too critical of those who have gone before.

After Stalin's death, the CPSU, especially during Brezhnev's 18 years in power, became increasingly conservative and rigid, and stopped reforming, effectively abolishing reform. Instead, the term "perfection" was used. This largely delayed the development of reforms and ultimately led to stagnation and the accumulation of social problems in the Soviet Union. After the 24th CPSU National Congress in 1971, even the word "reform" was no longer allowed to be used but rather "refine". This delayed the development of reform to a large extent and eventually led the Soviet Union to stagnation and caused social problems to become ingrained.

With regard to the tragedy that followed in the Soviet Union, some people with a Western view of history have argued that the socialist system created by Lenin and Stalin was wrong from the start and led the world astray. This is utterly absurd. The superiority of any system or institution is determined by certain conditions in time and space, and when those conditions change, the reform of institutional mechanisms must follow, otherwise that system will be eliminated by history. Just as the downfall of the late Qing dynasty cannot be attributed to Huang Taiji, who laid the foundation for the greatness of the Qing court, Shunzhi, who created a prosperous era for the Qing dynasty, or Kangxi, who created a new era of prosperity for the Qing dynasty, neither can some of the subversive mistakes of the late Soviet Union be attributed simply to Lenin and Stalin, the pioneers of the Soviet socialist system. The fundamental question here is whether the successors to the CPSU had the courage and ability to carry out reforms after the serious shortcomings of the Soviet socialist system had been exposed, and to this history has answered in the negative. Current Russian president, Vladimir Putin, who is a witness to history, has pointed out starkly that, "the collapse of the Soviet Union did not have to happen and that reform measures could have been implemented at that time", arguing that the main reason for the collapse of the Soviet Union was the responsibility of the CPSU leaders at that time. This points out the crux of the tragedy of the CPSU and the Soviet Union.

The CPC is a good reference in terms of its approach to the major issue of socialist reform. After the CPC ascended to power, its approach to building socialism began with learning from the Soviet Union. China's socialist transformation had its own unique approach but in its model of socialist goals, it copied the Soviet Union's highly centralised planned economy and extremely pure system of public ownership. This played a positive role in the early stages of China's industrialisation in concentrating its efforts on the effective implementation of 156 heavy industrial projects and laying the foundations of industrialisation. However, as China's economy grew in size and economic relations became more complex, the drawbacks of this system, which was rigid and uninspiring due to its excessive centralisation, began to be exposed, hindering the further development of productivity. With the revelation of the problems of socialist construction in the Soviet Union at the 20th CPSU National Congress in February 1956, the CPC became keenly aware that the method of construction of socialism in China could not be completely copied from the Soviet Union but must follow its own path. Mao Zedong pointed out through in-depth consideration that the basic contradictions of socialist society were still the contradictions between productivity and socioeconomic relations, and between the economic base and the superstructure, and that these contradictions could be constantly resolved through the self-adjustment and refinement of the socialist system itself. For the first time in the history of the world socialist movement, this laid the solid theoretical foundation for China's socialist reforms and for China to find its own path of construction. The Chinese communists, mainly represented by Comrade Mao Zedong, made painstaking explorations to this end, and even made serious mistakes and errors, but on the whole the Chinese economy was not able to break out of the framework of the Soviet model at that time. In a speech before the 3rd Plenary Session of the 11th CPC Central Committee, Deng Xiaoping pointed out that, "In terms of the general situation, our national system, including institutions and systems and so on, basically comes from the Soviet Union ...... There are so many institutional issues that need to be reconsidered"[4]. In that context the party made the decision to implement reform and opening up at the same time as it shifted the focus of work of the party and the state. In this regard,

628

Deng Xiaoping warned, "If reforms are not implemented now, our modernisation and socialist cause will be buried"[5]. He called for, "a fundamental change in the economic system that fetters the development of productivity, the establishment of a vibrant and dynamic socialist economy, and promotion of the development of productivity; this is reform'[6].

The greatest reward of China's reform and opening up is the creation, upholding, and development of socialism with Chinese characteristics. Reform and opening up is the only way to develop socialism with Chinese characteristics. On the basis of the same institutional "template" as the Soviet Union, socialism with Chinese characteristics has gradually taken on distinctive and clear features through constant "change", and Chinese society has accordingly unleashed enormous energy and new vitality. In the historical process of promoting reform and opening up, the Chinese communists, mainly represented by Comrade Deng Xiaoping, pioneered socialism with Chinese characteristics and founded Deng Xiaoping Theory. The Chinese communists, mainly represented by Comrade Jiang Zemin and Comrade Hu Jintao, upheld and developed socialism with Chinese characteristics, and formed the major ideology of the Three Represents and the Scientific Outlook on Development. The Chinese communists, mainly represented by Comrade Xi Jinping, have systematically answered the major issue of the times regarding the kind of socialism with Chinese characteristics to uphold and develop, and how to uphold and develop it in the new era, and founded Xi Jinping Thought on Socialism with Chinese Characteristics for a New Era. Guided by the banner of socialism with Chinese characteristics, the CPC has united and led the people in their unremitting struggle, propelling China to the forefront of the world in terms of economic, scientific, technological and national defence strength and comprehensive national power, bringing unprecedented changes to the appearance of the party, the country, the people, the army and the Chinese nation. Consequently, the Chinese nation has made a great leap from standing up and becoming affluent to becoming strong. The creation, upholding and development of socialism with Chinese characteristics marked the emergence of a new path of socialist construction in the world, following on from Soviet socialism. This has enabled scientific socialism to emerge with great vitality in 21st-century China and has raised high the great banner of socialism with Chinese characteristics around the world. The continuous development of the path, theory, system and culture of socialism with Chinese characteristics has expanded the potential pathways of developing countries toward modernisation, providing a brand-new choice for those countries and peoples in the world that wish to accelerate development while maintaining their independence, and contributing Chinese wisdom and Chinese approaches to solving mankind's problems. As we can see from the journeys of Chinese and Soviet socialism, which set out on the same path but encountered different outcomes, timely socialist reform and opening up determines the future prospects of the ruling communist party in socialist countries. As Xi Jinping said, "Reform and opening up is the key move that has determined the fate of contemporary China"[7] and "reform and opening up is a powerful driving force for the development of China, socialism and Marxism"[8]. This important statement is of general significance to a ruling communist party.

(II) ADHERING TO THE CORRECT DIRECTION OF REFORM AND OPENING UP FROM START TO FINISH

The fundamental requirement for adhering to the correct direction of reform and opening up is to integrate adherence to socialism with adherence to reform and opening up, and to neither take the old path of closure and rigidity nor the evil path of turning away from socialism. The question of direction is crucial. The kind of reform direction to adhere to determines the nature and ultimate success or failure of reform and has a great impact on the ruling communist party.

Upholding the direction of socialism is the rightful meaning of reform and opening up as the self-refinement and development of socialism. The core aspect here is upholding and improving the leadership of the party and upholding and refining the socialist system. Without the leadership and rule of the communist party, there would be no socialism, and without socialism, there could be no talk of socialist reform and opening up. There must be political principles and bottom lines pertaining to what and how to change in the process of reform, and the leadership of the party must be upheld to ensure that the socialist system does not degenerate or become deformed. The Soviet Union had not initiated reform in the true sense for a long time, and it had accumulated a large number of contradictions and problems, so that by the mid-1980s, the Soviet economy and politics were in a pre-crisis predicament. In this case, the CPSU could have stayed the course with the path of socialist reform under the leadership of the party, as China did at the end of the Cultural Revolution in China, but some people with ulterior motives took the opportunity to direct the goal of reform towards the destruction of the Soviet socialist system, turning "reform" into "redirection". Mikhail Gorbachev later claimed that he had long since lost faith in the vitality of scientific socialism and wanted to transform the CPSU with "Western European-style social democratic ideas". In 1985, shortly after taking over as General Secretary of the CPSU, Gorbachev proposed "humane and democratic socialism", shifting the goal of reform to the Nordic countries. Under his guidance Marxism was removed as the guiding force, as was the legal position of the CPSU as the ruling party and effective control of the public sector economy was also removed, causing serious disruption in the ideological, political and social life of the Soviet party and state, leading the country's economy to continue to deteriorate and collapse. Six short years later, the CPSU lost power, the country fell apart and the gains of socialist construction that the CPSU had painstakingly accumulated over 70 years were completely lost. Some commentators have analysed the reasons for Gorbachev's change of direction, and he later made some apparently remorseful reflections after that, but one thing is certain, and that is that although he had been strongly nurtured and reappointed by the CPSU, he was not a true Marxist and a reliable successor to socialism. This is evident from his heartfelt confessions about the fall of the CPSU and the collapse of the Soviet Union, saying, "When I left the Kremlin, hundreds of journalists thought I would cry. I did not cry because the main purpose of my life had been achieved, and for a true statesman the aim is not to defend his power and position but to advance the country's progress and democracy". This shows how important it is for the supreme power of the ruling party in a socialist country to be in the hands of genuine Marxists; once the sceptre of reform falls into the hands of "two-faced people" who are superficially glamorous but inwardly disloyal to the party and who use the banner of "reform" to sell their own agenda and stir up public sentiment with false statements, then the future of socialism and the ruling position of the communist party will be untenable.

From the very beginning of China's reform and opening up, the CPC has clearly established the basic principles of adhering to the path of socialism, the dictatorship of the proletariat (the people's democratic dictatorship), the leadership of the communist party and Marxism-Leninism and Mao Zedong Thought, which have been written into the party's basic line, enshrined in the party constitution and enshrined in the national constitution. This all clearly indicates that the Four Cardinal Principles are the foundation of the country and that reform and opening up is the road to strengthening China which must always be adhered to unwaveringly and consistently. In the process of reform and opening up, the party has promptly countered bourgeois liberalisation tendencies that deny socialism and the leadership of the party, taken decisive action to quell domestic political turmoil that "subverts the country and the party", remained highly vigilant and taken resolute precautionary measures against Western countries' "peaceful evolution" strategy of Westernisation and division of China, and their attempts to instigate "colour revolutions", resolutely corrected and stopped the misguided tendency of weakening party leadership that has emerged in China within the party, pursued political responsibility for those leading cadres who are not resolute and effective in upholding the Four Cardinal Principles and opposing bourgeois liberalisation, and taken resolute measures to deal with those "two-faced" people who are found to be disloyal to the party, who only pay lip service to the cause and are duplicitous, and who are conspiratorial in their political ambitions. Since the 18th CPC National Congress, in response to a situation where the leadership of the party had been neglected, diluted or weakened for "a period of time", the Party Central Committee with Comrade Xi Jinping at its core has been comprehensively ruling the party in a strict manner, reforming and refining the institutional mechanism for upholding the leadership of the party, upholding democratic centralism, strictly enforcing the party's political discipline and rules, resolutely fighting against all kinds of misguided tendencies that are morally at odds with the party, and comprehensively strengthening the leadership of the party. The CPC has led reform and opening up, managed the market economy in the midst of its development, and resolved dangers and trials, thereby not only providing a strong guarantee for the healthy development of reform and opening up, and socialist modernisation but also consolidating its ruling position.

Preventing "backtracking" and going backwards in the process of reform and opening up is another major issue that must be dealt with in order to uphold the correct direction of reform and opening up. In the course of China's reform and opening up, some people are stuck in their past dogmatic understanding of certain principles and books of Marxism, or in their past unscientific or even completely distorted understanding of socialism, or in incorrect ideas and policies from before reform and opening up, or even in opposition to reform and opening up, doubting and denying reform and opening up, believing that reform and opening up will lead to the path of capitalism and considering comrades who advocate reform and opening up as "capitalists". This kind of ideology, which on the surface appeared to safeguard socialism, could in reality only lead to the death of socialism. The CPC is always on high alert against such tendencies. In 1992, Deng Xiaoping gave his Southern Tour speeches in which he severely criticised the tendency and viewpoint of following the old ways of the past, stating clearly that there was a danger of the right burying socialism but also of the "left" doing likewise. China, he said, should be vigilant against the right but mainly be careful to guard against the "left". The CPC has repeatedly demanded that it must adapt to the development of practice, test everything by practice and consciously liberate its ideological understanding from the shackles of anachronistic concepts, practices and institutions, from the false and dogmatic understanding of Marxism, and from the shackles of subjectivism and metaphysics. Since the 18th CPC National Congress, Xi Jinping has repeatedly made serious criticisms of conservative and rigid ideas, pointing out that, "China is a large country and we must not make subversive mistakes on fundamental issues that are irreversible and irreparable once they occur. At the same time, nothing should as a result be left untouched or unchanged, for that would be rigid, closed and conservative"[9]. He required maintaining the spirit of courageous change and innovation, never becoming stagnant or rigid, breaking through the barriers of ideology and mindset, and through the fences of solidified interests, and continuously making new breakthroughs in comprehensively deepening reform. Under the correct leadership of the CPC, China's reform and opening up has continued to eliminate all kinds of interference and has always followed the right course in braving rough seas.

(III) CORRECTLY HANDLING THE RELATIONSHIP BETWEEN REFORM, DEVELOPMENT AND STABILITY

The above all pertains to the question of how to take reform forward, and if the approach is not right, even the best reforms cannot be implemented and may even topple a government. In a general sense, reform has always been an extremely difficult and perilous task. Throughout the history of China and the world, there have been many successful revolutions while successful reforms have been rare, and those that have failed in reforms have been numerous. There have been many failed reforms, such as the changes in law by Shang Yang (4th century BC) and Wang Anshi (11th century AD) in the distant past, and the Hundred Days Reform as recently as 1898. The famous American political scientist Samuel P. Huntington once compared reform and revolution, stating that the path of reformers is a difficult one, and that the problems they face are more difficult than those of revolutionaries. The reformer, he said, must fight on both sides, facing opposition from both conservative and revolutionary sides. To win, he does have to fight a war with multiple fronts, a war with a myriad of participants, where the enemy on one front may be an ally on another. Huntington also argued that not only must reformers be better at manipulating social forces than revolutionaries but they must also be more sophisticated in their control of social change. The question of how to prioritise the various forms of reform is much more acute for reformers than for revolutionaries. Consequently, he said, reformers must be more politically skilled than revolutionaries, and a successful revolutionary need not be a political mastermind but a successful reformer must be a first-class politician[10]. Huntington's argument is not accurate but he does give a relatively objective assessment of the risks of reform and the difficult situation of reformers. Only when reformers are adept at navigating complex contradictions and dealing correctly with difficult issues can they lead reforms to success.

History has shown that under communist rule, without competence to manage reforms, without choosing the right approach to reform, if the wrong path to reform is chosen, and if there is impatience and impetuousness, something can go wrong. In 1990, Gorbachev and others set up a Soviet Union-wide 500-day plan for the transition to a market economy in an attempt to completely transform the planned economy into a market economy in a relatively short period of time, which directly caused a decline in productivity, a shortage of supply and the devaluation of the rouble to the brink of collapse. The 500-day plan formed an important economic backdrop to the fall of the CPSU and the collapse of the Soviet Union. The Russian Federation, which inherited the Soviet legacy, introduced even more radical reforms from Western economic advisers, known as "shock therapy", which also proved to be unsuccessful and plunged the Russian economy into an unprecedented crisis, leading directly to the dissolution of the government of Yegor Gaidar in December 1992.

It is not our intention to dismiss radical approaches to reform, including "shock therapy", out of hand. Such reforms have worked wonders in some smaller countries, as in the case of Bolivia's anti-crisis measures in the mid-1980s with strong US support, and such successes cannot be ruled out in the future. However, for socialist countries under the rule of a communist party, especially large socialist countries like the Soviet Union and China, it is necessary to determine a sound and effective reform strategy and methods in the light of the country's own realities.

From the practice of China's reform and opening up over the past 40 years, it can be seen that the correct handling of the relationship between reform, development and stability and the adoption of gradual reform have been important lessons gained from the success of China's reform. As early as at the outset of reform and opening up, Deng Xiaoping repeatedly pointed out that it is necessary to be bold in carrying out reforms and taking steady steps. If mistakes are made, changes must be made quickly but the key is to be good at summing up experience. It is necessary to "feel one's way across the river by touching the stones". The Party Central Committee clearly required that, "the steps of reform should be positive and steady, resolutely changing those which come into view, changing things one by one, piloting approaches not yet experienced, and not attempting to finish the job in one go"[11]. Although China has also made mistakes in "achieving breakthroughs" in price reform, in general, China's reform has basically followed the policy of first introducing the easy and then the difficult, and gradually advancing from easy to difficult.

In terms of the objectives of reform, market factors were first introduced at the beginning of the reform, with the planned economy as the mainstay and market regulation as a supplementary approach. When conditions were ripe, the reform objective was to establish a socialist market economy. After entering the new era, the overall goal of deepening reform has been to refine and develop the system of socialism with Chinese characteristics and to promote the modernisation of the national system of governance and governance ability. In terms of the order of reform, rural reform was carried out first, followed by urban reform, and reform of the economy was carried out first, followed by reform of the political system. Also, the opening up of coastal areas was implemented first, followed by opening up in inland areas. Further, reform of various forms of economy, namely "system outsiders", were carried out first, followed by the reform of SOEs, 'system insiders', and so on. At a certain stage of reform, a holistic approach to reform was adopted which brought key breakthroughs. In terms of the implementation of specific reform measures, these were first piloted and then gradually rolled out, such as the reform of shareholding, which began in 1984 and was only gradually rolled out after the 15th CPC National Congress in 1997.

In adjusting the interests of all parties to reforms, efficiency and fairness were given equal importance, and the interests of all parties were comprehensively coordinated and balanced. Whether or not people's livelihoods were improved was taken as the criterion for measuring the rights and wrongs of the reform, and whether or not the reforms were acceptable to the masses was taken as the main indicator for promoting the reform. Thereby, the party strove to adapt the reforms to be acceptable to the masses, meeting the expectations of the masses for reform as far as possible, taking into account the immediate and local interests of the masses. In this way quality of life was constantly improved. With regard to damage brought to the people's immediate interests caused by the reforms, the party and the government also made it possible to compensate people to a certain extent within the scope of the policies. The implementation of these measures effectively mitigated against the social shocks that might have been caused by reform and opening up, and continued to deepen reform and opening up.

This approach to reform was summed up by party leaders in the mid-1990s as "gradual" reform, saying, "Our direction of reform and opening up is correct, our conviction is firm, our steps are steady, our approach is gradual, and our achievements are enormous"[12]. According to the Party Central Committee, "This gradual reform avoided social unrest caused by unclear circumstances and inappropriate initiatives, and provided a guarantee for steady progress and the smooth achievement of goals"[13]. Gradual reform became the best choice for the reform of the Chinese economy and also the consensus of theoretical and academic circles as well as Chinese society as a whole. After the 18th CPC National Congress, in the face of a complex situation whereby China's reform entered a period of particularly hard work and more dangerous waters, as well as the daunting task of comprehensively deepening reform, while emphasising the need to "dare to take on hard challenges, wade through water containing dangerous hidden reefs, and attack persistent and chronic problems that have existed for years"[14], Xi Jinping also highlighted the importance of a steady pace, stating, "reform is a step-by-step process. We must be bold enough to make a breakthrough but we must also take one step at a time steadily but surely"[15]. He also said, "Opening up should also be carried out gradually, tackling easy issues first and then difficult ones, using the successful experience of one unit or place to drive the work of many, thereby growing to have great impact"[16]. Xi Jinping thereby proposed a series of important requirements and made strategic plans for comprehensively deepening reform, leading the way in the steady and comprehensive deepening of reform in the new era.

In conclusion, reform and opening up is an inevitable requirement and choice for communist party governance. The CPC has accumulated a wealth of experience in reform and opening up, and has deepened its understanding of the communist party's governance law, with reform and opening up becoming the hallmark of China's path and Chinese experience. There is no precedent in the history of mankind in a large socialist country with a population of over a billion people for reform and opening up that has lasted for 40 years and is yet still set to continue. Only an advanced and strong Marxist ruling party like the CPC can lead its people to achieve such miraculous feats. China's path and experience belong to China and also to the world. Since China embarked on the new path of reform and opening up, and achieved success, a number of other socialist countries have also drawn on China's experience and successively implemented reform and opening up, resulting in vibrant socioeconomic development. Looking to the future, we are confident that the world socialist movement will continue to develop in synergy with reform and opening up, that the socialist system will be "reformed" to become more mature and established, and that the ruling communist party will be inspired by reform and opening up to become more powerful and vital.

6

GOVERNANCE ORGANISATION AND LEADERSHIP SYSTEMS

UPHOLDING DEMOCRATIC CENTRALISM

All political parties are faced with the question of what kind of organisational principles and organisational and leadership systems to build to govern themselves. All ruling parties also face the question of the kind of organisational principles, and organisational and leadership systems to use to govern their country. So, since the communist party is a Marxist party and a proletarian party, what kind of organisational principles, and organisational and leadership systems does it adopt to build and govern itself, and what kind of organisational principles, and organisational and leadership systems does it adopt to govern the country after it comes to power? Looking at the history of the international communist movement, after Lenin established the Russian Social Democratic Labour Party (RSDLP) and led the founding of the Third International, the vast majority of communist parties in the world (both those in power and those not in power) established democratic centralism as the fundamental organising principle and the fundamental organisational and leadership system of communist parties. Moreover, this principle and system also became the most important political and organisational discipline of the communist party. Thereafter, whether or not the party is built and governed in accordance with democratic centralism became an important marker differentiating Marxist parties from other parties.

(1) DEMOCRATIC CENTRALISM IS THE BIGGEST SUPERIORITY OF THE COMMUNIST PARTY GOVERNANCE SYSTEM

Democratic centralism is the fundamental organising principle of Marxist parties. The Communist League was the first Marxist political party ever established. When Marx and Engels guided the establishment of the Communist League, they emphasised the integration of democracy and centralism as the basic principle of the League's activities. From the actual situation in those years when Marx and Engels guided the Communist League and the First and Second Internationals, it can be seen that while they stressed the issue of expanding and promoting democracy within the party, they also stressed the issue of strengthening centralisation and unity. The emphasis varied at different times. Lenin inherited and developed Marx's ideas on party building, and when he led the RSDLP and founded the Third International, he clearly put forward the scientific concept of democratic centralism and established it as the organisational principle and system of the communist party, implementing this principle in the practice of party building and management, governing the country and leading coordination of the activities and relations of the national parties of the Comintern. All the communist parties of the Comintern were established in accordance with the organisational principle of democratic centralist organisation. The CPC is a party with Marxism-Leninism as its guiding ideology, and it was guided and assisted in its creation by the Comintern, which passed a resolution at its Second Congress to join the Comintern and become a branch of the Third International[1]. Therefore, although the concept and expression of democratic centralism did not appear in the party programme or the party constitution from the First to the Fourth CPC National Congresses, it can be said that the CPC took democratic centralism as its organisational principle and discipline in building and managing the party as soon as it was founded, and it has always implemented the spirit and ideology of democratic centralism in the work of the party. In the history of the CPC, democratic centralism was formally enshrined in the party's constitution from the Fifth CPC National Congress onwards. In June 1927, the Politburo of the CPC Central Committee held a meeting and made the *Decision on the Third Amendment to the Constitution of the CPC* in accordance with the mandate of the Fifth CPC National Congress, clearly stating that, "the guiding principle of the party committee is democratic centralism"[2]. Since then, the party constitution adopted at each of the CPC's National Congresses has included democratic centralism in the party constitution, always making specific provisions and clear requirements for upholding democratic centralism. The CPC has enriched and developed democratic centralism.

After establishing democratic centralism as the party's organising principle, during the various periods of revolution, construction and reform the party continuously deepened its understanding of the scientific essence and status of democratic centralism in accordance with its own practice and achieved fruitful theoretical results. In 1938, in his report to the party's expanded Sixth Plenary Session of the Sixth CPC Central Committee, Mao Zedong reiterated the four basic party disciplines, namely, individual obedience to the organisation, majority rule, subordination to superiors, and partywide obedience to the Central Committee. After the Seventh CPC National Congress, the CPC wrote these Four Obediences into the party constitution as the basic principle of democratic centralism and the most important political discipline. The Party Constitution of the Seventh CPC National Congress summarised democratic centralism as "centralisation on the basis of democracy and democracy under the leadership of centralisation". In July 1957, Mao Zedong proposed the creation of "a political climate in which there is both centralisation and democracy, discipline and freedom, unity of will and a carefree, vibrant and dynamic mood"[3]. The Party Constitution of the Eighth CPC National Congress followed the definition of democratic centralism in that of the Seventh CPC National Congress, replacing "democracy under the leadership of centralisation" with "democracy under centralised guidance". Although there is only a minor difference, namely, between "leadership" and "guidance", the connotation has changed significantly. After the 3rd Plenary Session of the 11th CPC Central Committee, the CPC creatively applied the principle of democratic centralism to formulate basic guidelines and specific systems for regulating the political life of the party and for handling intra-party relations, establishing a distinctive feature of the party's organisational construction. Summing up the lessons of history, the Party Constitution of the 12th CPC National Congress clearly states that "the party is a unified whole organised according to its own programme and constitution, and in accordance with democratic centralism". This assertion has been reiterated in subsequent revisions of the party constitution by successive party congresses[4]. The Party Constitution of the 14th CPC National Congress made upholding democratic centralism one of the several basic requirements of party building, stating that:

"democratic centralism constitutes the integration of democracy under centralisation and centralised guidance on the basis of democracy. It is both the fundamental organising principle of the party and the application of the mass line in the life of the party. Democracy within the party must be fully employed, and the initiative and creativity of party organisations at all levels, and of the masses of party members must be brought into play. Correct centralisation must be practised to ensure that the whole party acts in unison and that the party's decisions are carried out promptly and effectively"[5].

Subsequent CPC National Congresses up to the Party Constitution adopted at the 19th CPC National Congress all advanced these requirements. The democratic centralism established by the CPC is the fundamental organisational principle of the party, and its main content is reflected in the following aspects:

- the leading organs of the party are democratically elected;
    - formulation of the party's lines, guidelines and policies, as well as the party's rules and regulations, must carry out the "mass line of doing everything for the masses, relying on the masses, coming from the masses and going to the masses";
    - individual obedience to the organisation, majority rule, subordination to superiors, and partywide obedience to the Central Committee;
    - strengthening organisational discipline and implementing the equality of all in the face of party discipline;
    - the party must carry out criticism and self-criticism correctly in its political life, engage in ideological struggle over issues of principle, uphold the truth and correct mistakes;
    - the party's leading organs at all levels must implement the principle of integrating collective leadership and the division of labour, and prohibit any form of personality cult;
    - leading organs at all levels must always maintain close contact with the masses, listen to the views of subordinate organisations and the masses, and accept supervision by party members and the masses.

Democratic centralism is a unique political, organisational, institutional and working advantage of communist parties. After Lenin established democratic centralism as the organising principle of communist parties, this principle came to play an important role in the construction of communist parties around the world. The reason why the RSDLP was able to lead the Russian people to victory in the October Socialist Revolution and successfully defend itself against foreign imperialist armed intervention with only a few hundred thousand members, and why the All-Union Communist Party (AUCP) was able to lead the Soviet people to victory in the second world war and the war against fascism, and successfully defend socialism with only a few million members, was all inseparably related to the democratic centralism practised by the Soviet party. Democratic centralism gave the communist party its great strength. When a communist party is strong and unified, and becomes the leading core of the united struggle of the people in a country, its power is all-surpassing and invincible. One of the major reasons why the CPC has been able to grow continuously from small to large and from weak to strong, and to go from victory to victory, is also very much related to its adherence to, and implementation of, democratic centralism. The history of the CPC shows that democratic centralism is the party's greatest institutional advantage. In the history of the CPC there have been two great historical turning points, one being the Zunyi Conference and the other the 3rd Plenary Session of the 11th CPC Central Committee. One turn took place during the new democratic revolution and the other during the socialist revolution and construction. Both great turning points constituted life-or-death moments in the history of the CPC. Looking back and taking stock of these two important meetings in the history of the CPC to identify the reason why they were held successfully, we can see that they would not have worked without the organising principle of democratic centralism. From the contents and agenda of the Zunyi Conference and the central work conference which prepared for the 3rd Plenary Session of the 11th CPC Central Committee, it can be seen that the two different ideologies and propositions at the conference were so hotly contested that the party would have split without democratic centralism as an institutional, and political and organisational guarantee. History shows that democratic centralism is a highly effective methodology and valuable political asset of the communist party. As Xi Jinping pointed out, "This system organically integrates the full development of democracy within the party and the correct implementation of centralisation, which not only maximises the creative energy of the party as a whole but also unifies the party's ideology and actions; it effectively prevents and overcomes the decentralism of deliberation without decision and decision without action, and is a scientific, reasonable and efficient system"[6]. "Democratic centralism is our party's fundamental organisational and leadership system. It correctly regulates the internal life of the party and the basic guidelines for handling intra-party relations. It is also a scientific, rational and efficient system that reflects and embodies the interests and aspirations of all party comrades and the whole nation, and ensures the correct formulation and implementation of the party's line, guidelines and policies. Therefore, it is our party's greatest institutional advantage"[7]. If the communist party is to build and manage the party well, and if it is to hold power and govern well for the people, it must consistently uphold this fundamental organisational principle, and maintain and bring into play this greatest institutional advantage of the communist party.

(II) THE KEY TO IMPLEMENTING DEMOCRATIC CENTRALISM IS TO HANDLE WELL THE RELATIONSHIP BETWEEN DEMOCRACY AND CENTRALISATION

Managing the relationship between democracy and centralisation is crucial. History has proven that democratic centralism is good. However, the most crucial thing in implementing democratic centralism is to handle the relationship between democracy and centralism well. If this relationship is handled well, the cause of the party and the state will flourish, but if not, then the cause of the party and the state will suffer and be destroyed. This has also been proven by numerous historical facts. In the early years of Soviet history, Lenin upheld well the principle of democratic centralism and set a shining example for the CPC in the implementation of this organisational system. On the eve of the October Revolution, when the conditions were ripe for the proletariat to seize power, would an armed uprising be launched? Should the new Soviet government fight for a respite and sign the Treaty of Brest-Litovsk with Germany when it was threatened by internal and external enemies? At that time, there were many dissenting voices within the party and even opposition. Lenin's proposal for an armed uprising was twice rejected by the Party Central Committee and his proposal to sign the Treaty of Brest-Litovsk was attacked by some as constituting a "forfeiting of sovereignty and national humiliation"[8]. However, Lenin took great pains to persuade others repeatedly and eventually gained the support of the majority of the people. By the Soviet period, starting with Stalin, this principle and system was gradually undermined within the Soviet party. All CPSU leaders after Stalin engaged in personal dictatorship until Gorbachev even abandoned and abolished this principle and system. For a long time, some leaders of the communist parties in Eastern Europe also practised "patriarchy" and personal dictatorship, which seriously affected the normal political life of their party and correct decision-making on some major issues, resulting in the serious consequences of being out of touch with reality, detached from the masses and making wrong decisions. The lessons are profound! The CPC has had successful experiences in dealing with the relationship between democracy and centralisation but it has also learned from its mistakes. Before the Zunyi Conference, the main leaders of the CPC, Chen Duxiu and Wang Ming, engaged in "patriarchy" and personal dictatorship, and pursued right-leaning opportunism and "left-leaning" dogmatism, as a result of which the unity of the party was seriously undermined, and the revolutionary cause suffered great losses. After the Zunyi Conference, the party established Mao Zedong as the leader of the party and the Red Army, and the party adhered to and implemented democratic centralism, thereby averting danger for the party and the Red Army and leading the Chinese people to continuously break new ground. The period from the Seventh to the Eighth CPC National Congresses was one of the periods when the CPC managed the relationship between democracy and centralisation relatively well. The CPC adhered to the principles and systems of democratic centralism, formulated correct lines, guidelines and policies, unified the party as never before, mobilised the initiative of all parties, and successively achieved great victories in the new democratic revolution, the socialist revolution and construction. However, after the criticism against advances in 1958 and the "anti-rightist movement" in 1959, the democratic life of the party and the state gradually became abnormal, and paternalistic phenomena such as autocratic rule, one person making decisions on major issues, personality cult, and the supremacy of the individual over the organisation continued to grow[9]. Democratic centralism was destroyed, especially during the Cultural Revolution, which went to extremes and caused great disasters to the party, the state and the people. After the 3rd Plenary Session of the 11th CPC Central Committee, the party broke through the shackles of the Two Whatevers, emancipated the mind and sought truth from facts, restored and re-established the correct ideological, political and organisational lines of the party, restored normal political life within the party, and continuously developed and refined democratic centralism. This provided an important political and institutional guarantee for the consolidation of the party's unity and the formulation of the party's correct lines, guidelines and policies, and their implementation in practice. History demonstrates what Deng Xiaoping once profoundly pointed out, when he said that "When democratic centralism is poorly implemented, the party can degenerate, and so can the state and socialism themselves"[10].

Democracy and centralisation are dialectically unified. In the principles and systems of democratic centralism, there are two important concepts and key words. One is democracy and the other is centralisation. Democracy emphasises the development of democracy and the centralisation of collective wisdom and the wisdom of the whole party. Centralisation emphasises correct centralisation, bringing together the will of the whole party and forming a collective force. Democracy is the premise and foundation of correct centralisation, and centralisation is the inevitable requirement and destination of democracy. The two are complementary, intrinsically unified and inseparable. Democratic centralism is the organic integration of democracy and centralisation and "it is democratic and centralised, that is to say, centralised on the basis of democracy and democratic under the guidance of centralisation"[11]. Centralisation is based on democracy, and the results of democracy are reflected through centralisation. Democracy and centralisation are mutually dependent and inseparable, an organic unity where the two complement and bring out the best in each other. Historical experience has shown that in implementing the principles and systems of democratic centralism, one has to take the middle point between the two ends of the spectrum, and any ideology or practice that favours one side is incorrect and wrong, and will lead to mistakes and negative consequences. A bias toward democracy will lead to "great democracy", anarchy and weakness, whereas a bias toward centralisation will lead to personal arbitrariness, "patriarchy" and even autocracy. From a static perspective, democratic centralism consists of two opposing aspects, democracy and centralisation; without democracy, there is no centralisation, and without centralisation, there is also no democracy. Deng Xiaoping once discussed this issue in this way, "The organising principle of our party is a combination of a high degree of democracy and a high degree of centralisation, bringing into play the spirit of the principle of democratic centralism proposed by Lenin. A party cannot do without centralisation; without centralised leadership from the central committee and party committees at all levels, the party will have no fighting strength. If this kind of centralisation is not based on a high degree of democracy, then it is also a sham. By promoting democracy, and criticism and self-criticism throughout the party, the will of the entire party can truly be centralised and the unity of all can truly be achieved"[12]. From a dynamic point of view, the two aspects of democratic centralism, democracy and centralisation, are in contradictory movement and are unified in movement. In terms of the process of implementing democratic centralism for decision-making, any decision begins with a high degree of democracy under correct guidance and ends with a high degree of centralisation on the basis of full democracy. This process is fully consistent with the Marxist epistemology of practice, knowledge, and then practice and knowledge again, and with the implementation of the party's mass line of "everything for the masses, relying on the masses, coming from the masses and going to the masses". Democratic centralism is the embodiment of Marxist epistemology in the party system and the application of the party's mass line in the internal life of the party. In the long run, this process is cyclical and recurring, inexhaustible and unending. Therefore, on the one hand, it is important to maintain and develop internal party democracy. *The Constitution of the CPC* clearly stipulates that, "Democracy within the party must be fully developed, the dominant status of party members respected, the democratic rights of party members safeguarded, and the initiative and creativity of party organisations at all levels and of party members at large unleashed"[13]. In addition, from the lessons of history and reality it can be seen that in the CPC's implementation of democratic centralism there "has not only been the problem of the key leader being dictatorial due to the insufficient promotion of democracy but also the problem of the leadership team being weak due to an insufficient level of correct centralisation, with the former being relatively more prominent"[14]. This is also broadly true in terms of the implementation of democratic centralism in the communist parties of other countries. On the other hand, it is necessary to be adept at implementing correct centralisation, pay attention to the development of scientific decision-making procedures, strictly enforce the party's political discipline and rules, and maintain the unity and centralised leadership of the party. It "prevents deliberation without decision and decision without action"[15]. It prevents weakness and disorganisation and an inability to cooperate. Consequently, it is necessary to resolutely abandon liberalism, decentralism, and individualism, never allow a schism of policies from above and countermeasures from below, never permit orders not to be implemented, never permit that which is prohibited, and never permit devaluation, personal choice, and flexibility in the process of implementing the Party Central Committee's decisions and arrangements.

(III) ESTABLISHING AND REFINING AN INSTITUTIONAL SYSTEM WITH DEMOCRATIC CENTRALISM AT ITS CORE

The implementation and enforcement of democratic centralism must be guaranteed by an internal system of party regulations and systems. Democratic centralism is a good principle and system of the communist party but it is only a grand principle and system. In order to ensure it does not become deformed in the course of its implementation and enforcement, and to give full play to its role, it is necessary to establish a whole system of institutions and implement this good principle and system in detail. In summing up some of the blunders that occurred in the CPC during the

Chinese socialist revolution and construction, Deng Xiaoping clearly emphasised that, "the problems in the systems of leadership and organisation are fundamental, comprehensive, long-term, and pertain to stability". He also said, "A good system in these areas can prevent malefactors from running amok at will, whereas a bad system can prevent good people from doing good things in a satisfactory way and can even go the other way."[16] The CPC has profoundly summarised the lessons learned from both positive and negative experiences of socialist countries around the world, and profoundly summarised its own historical experience and fresh experience, proposing to continuously improve the level of scientificisation and standardisation of the construction of democratic centralism, and establish and refine the institutional system with democratic centralism at its core. Xi Jinping stressed that democratic centralism is the party's fundamental organisational principle and leadership system, and all the CPC's principles, systems and regulations constitute the concretisation and expansion of democratic centralism." In order to uphold and implement democratic centralism, it is necessary to "improve and conscientiously implement the various specific systems of democratic centralism" and to "urgently establish and improve the specific systems of democratic centralism, make efforts to build a system of democratic systems within the party, effectively promote the concretisation and proceduralisation of democratic centralism, and truly put the major principles of democratic centralism into practice."[17] What are the features of the institutional system established and refined by the CPC with democratic centralism at its core? To summarise, it is a series of intra-party regulations formed with the party constitution as the root, democratic centralism as the core, and with guidelines, regulations and rules in support. The party's system of regulations has seven levels, in terms of substance, procedure, supervision, safeguards, senior and subordinate relationships, and interrelationships. The first is the party constitution, which is the fundamental law of the party and the basis for all party regulations. The second is the guidelines while the third is the regulations, the fourth is the rules, the fifth is the provisions, the sixth is the methods, and the seventh is the by-laws. Since the 18th CPC National Congress, the CPC Central Committee has carried out a comprehensive tidying-up of all party regulations and has formulated two consecutive five-year guidelines for the formulation of central party regulations, specifying the requirements for their creation, amendment, abolition and interpretation. Now several clusters of systems have been formed in the CPC's system of internal regulations and rules, with guidelines and regulations at the head, supplemented by supporting rules, provisions, measures and by-laws as refinements. As of the end of August 2018, there were approximately 4,200 party regulations in force. Of these, more than 4,100 are rules, provisions, measures and by-laws[18]. They play an important role in the implementation of the basic main regulations and enhance the relevance and operability of the main regulations. With democratic centralism at the core, the establishment and refinement of the party's system of regulations means that the principles and spirit of democratic centralism must be implemented and reflected in the formulation of all the party's regulations, with democratic centralism as the political basis for the formulation of party regulations. It means giving full play to the leading and central role of the party in the governance of the country, in maintaining an overview and coordinating all parties. It also means correctly handling the relationship between the party committee and the NPC, the government, the CPPCC, the judiciary and people's organisations, and ensuring the systems of the party's leadership of state power and state affairs, upholding and refining the system of multiparty cooperation and political consultation under the leadership of the CPC, and giving full play to the strengths of the political party system with Chinese characteristics, as well as strengthening and improving the work of the party's social groups and give full play to the role of trade unions, the Communist Youth League, women's federations and other people's groups in reaching out to and serving the masses.

The implementation of democratic centralism must improve scientific and democratic decision-making mechanisms. It is necessary to uphold the integration of collective leadership and the division of responsibility and make decisions in accordance with the principles of collective leadership, democratic centralism, individual consultation and making decisions through meetings. Major matters should be studied collectively. Major matters pertaining to overall economic and social development must be discussed collectively by the team of leaders on the basis of in-depth investigation and research, and extensive listening to opinions of others, and decided in accordance with the principle of majority rule. Decisions on important issues are subject to a vote. The differing opinions of the minority shall be carefully considered. If arguments arise on an important issue and the two sides are close in number, the decision should be suspended, except in urgent cases when the majority view must be implemented first. Public opinion should be fully and accurately reflected. Leading cadres at all levels should often go to the grassroots and the masses to understand the situation on the ground. This will help to broaden the channels for the people to participate in decision-making, implement the people's right to be informed and to make suggestions in decision-making, and consciously accept the people's supervision. Experts should be consulted on major matters. For those major matters that are highly professional and technical, the role of experts, scholars, and advisory and research institutions should be given full play. Major matters closely related to the interests of the public should be publicised and their opinions should be heard. Except for matters involving core state secrets, the decision-making process and implementation should be made public and communicated to the public through the media in a timely manner.

The implementation of democratic centralism must guarantee the democratic rights of party members. Party members are the cells of the party's body and the main body through which the party acts. In order to uphold democratic centralism and improve the party's democratic system, it is necessary to safeguard the central position of party members and improve the system for safeguarding their democratic rights. In order to form a complete set of standardised, effective and useful systems for safeguarding the democratic rights of party members, to create democratic and equal comradeship within the party, a political atmosphere conducive to democratic discussion, and an institutional environment for democratic supervision, it is necessary to put into practice the right to information, the right to participate, the right to vote, and the right to supervision of party members. The open system of party affairs should be improved to guarantee party members' right to information. The ways for party members to participate in party affairs should be opened up to safeguard their right to participate. The party's internal electoral system should be refined to safeguard the right of party members to vote. The supervision mechanism within the party should be strengthened to safeguard the right of party members to supervision.

The implementation of democratic centralism must strengthen supervision and intensify party discipline. As Mao Zedong pointed out, "As a member of the party, iron discipline must be enforced." He also said, "The Party is a union of the best elements of the people, and everyone is consciously willing to be disciplined, that is, to acknowledge the party programme and constitution, to obey the party resolutions and to be willing to sacrifice themselves"[19]. It is necessary to improve the system of supervision within the party, as well as strengthen the supervision of party organisations at higher levels over those at lower levels, as well as party members and leading cadres. Intra-party supervision should be integrated with state supervision and mass supervision, and coordinated with legal, democratic, financial audit, judicial, and public opinion supervision to form a coordinated supervision force. It is necessary to strengthen inspection supervision and effectively implement the strict rule of the party, as well as improve the ability to implement inspections in accordance with regulations and discipline, and promote the institutionalisation and standardisation of inspection work. It is necessary to innovate institutional mechanisms and establish sound mechanisms for organisational leadership, coordination, reporting and feedback, rectification and implementation, team building and other work. It is necessary to seize the "key minority", crack difficult issues of supervision, and to improve rules of procedure and decision-making procedures to prevent procedures from becoming empty and simply a matter of going through the motions. Party discipline, especially political discipline, should be strictly enforced. Party members should maintain a high degree of consistency with the Party Central Committee in terms of political stance, direction, principles and path. A system of seeking guidance and reports should be established, and major issues and important matters should be provided with guidance and reports in a timely manner. It is necessary to hold good Democratic Life Meetings, which are an important vehicle of democratic centralism. By holding good Democratic Life Meetings and carrying out frequent criticism and self-criticism, it will be possible to promptly overcome incorrect and erroneous ideas and consciousness within the party and promptly correct tendencies and behaviour that deviate from the principles and system of democratic centralism.

7

GOVERNANCE METHODS

SCIENTIFIC GOVERNANCE, DEMOCRATIC GOVERNANCE AND LEGAL GOVERNANCE

The question of what kind of governance and how to govern is an important issue that Marxist parties have been exploring since their emergence, especially after they gain state power. In its practice of governing since the founding of new China, especially since the outset of China's reform and opening up, the CPC has explored and developed a method of governance that is in line with China's national conditions, namely, to govern scientifically and democratically, and in accordance with the law. This method of governance reflects the deepening of the CPC's understanding of the communist party's governance law and a scientific summary of the CPC's experience in both the positive and negative aspects of long-term governance, the CPC's sober understanding of its own historical position and the historical mission it has undertaken, as well as the party's high degree of consciousness of closely integrating the promotion of the great new project of party building with the promotion of the great cause of socialism with Chinese characteristics. Scientific and democratic governance and governance by law are interlinked and dialectically unified. Scientific governance is the basic premise, democratic governance is the basic content, and governance by law is the basic way.

(I) SCIENTIFIC GOVERNANCE IS A PREREQUISITE FOR THE SUCCESS OF MARXIST PARTIES IN GOVERNMENT

Governing scientifically means upholding the scientific theories of Marxism as guidance, continuously exploring and following the communist party's governance law, and the laws of socialist construction and human social development, and organising and leading the people to build socialism together with scientific ideas, systems and methods.

Numerous historical facts prove that a political party, especially a Marxist ruling party, cannot depart from scientific ideological and theoretical guidance for a moment if it wants to stay ahead of the times and continuously improve its governance ability. The CPC has been in power for a long time and has continued to break new ground, which has been fundamentally through the scientific guidance of Marxism-Leninism and the theoretical innovations of Chinese Marxism, comprised of Mao Zedong Thought, Deng Xiaoping Theory, the major ideology of the Three Represents, the Scientific Outlook on Development and Xi Jinping Thought on Socialism with Chinese Characteristics for a New Era. The guiding ideology of the CPC not only upholds the position, viewpoint and methods of Marxism, the basic principles of Marxism and the basic principles of scientific socialism but, at the same time, does not start from books, concepts and abstract principles but, rather, is based on practice, starts from China's actual situation, emancipates the mind, seeks truth from facts, advances with the times and is pragmatic. It has also provided the fundamental guidelines for the scientific formulation and implementation of the party's theories and policies, as well as the scientific design, organisation and implementation of all governance activities. In accordance with the needs of the times and practice, a series of new ideas, perspectives and assertions have been innovatively and continuously put forward, giving scientific ideological leadership to the governance of China and providing fundamental guidelines for the scientific formulation and implementation of the party's theories, line, guidelines and policies, as well as the scientific design, organisation and implementation of the operation of governance. Marxism-Leninism and the theoretical innovations from the sinicisation of Marxism are the banner of the CPC and the Chinese people. With this banner, the CPC and the Chinese people have gained a distinctive ideological and spiritual hallmark characterising this era, the unity of the party has had an ideological foundation and a "common language", the people of China have been led forward in the correct direction. The CPC's scientific governance has been guided by scientific theories in the past and is bound to continue to break new ground in the future under the guidance of 21st-century Marxism and contemporary Chinese Marxism, namely, Xi Jinping Thought on Socialism with Chinese Characteristics for a New Era.

Institutional issues are fundamental, holistic, stable and long-term in nature. A scientific system of governance can effectively prevent arbitrariness and blindness in the operation of governance, reduce the cost of governance and improve its efficiency. After a long struggle, the CPC led the Chinese people to establish a national and political system suitable for China's national conditions, which laid a solid foundation and created the fundamental prerequisites for the establishment and development of a scientific system of governance. In the practice of reform and opening up, the CPC has led the people to continuously promote the self-improvement and development of the socialist system, forming a set of interconnected and interlinked systems in various fields, including the economic, political, cultural and social spheres, to ensure the continuous development of the cause of socialism with Chinese characteristics. Institution building never happens overnight. Today, a major historical task before the CPC and the Chinese people is to promote a more mature and established socialist system with Chinese characteristics, so as to provide a more complete, stable and effective system for the development of the cause of the party and the state, for the happiness and well-being of the people, for social harmony and stability, and for China's long-term stability. One aspect of this is the modernisation of the national system of governance and governance ability. National governance ability is the ability to use the national system to manage all aspects of social affairs, including reform, development and stability, internal affairs, foreign affairs and national defence, as well as the ability to govern the party, the state and the military. The national system of governance and governance ability are an organic whole and complement each other, and with a scientific national system of governance, a high level of governance ability can be nurtured, and the effectiveness of the national system of governance can be given full play only when the national governance ability is continuously improved. The key to solving the various problems of contemporary China and achieving the various goals set, depends on the modernisation of the national system of governance and governance ability. Promoting the modernisation of the national system of governance and governance ability requires timely updating of the concept of governance, in-depth reform of the system of governance, enrichment and improvement of the system of governance, and efforts to improve governance ability, so that the national system of governance will be institutionalised, scientificised, standardised and proceduralised, and those who govern the country will be adept at using rule-of-law thinking and the legal system to govern the country, thereby transforming the institutional strengths of various aspects of socialism into effectiveness in governing the country.

The scientific method of governing is the concrete embodiment of the ruling ideology and system of governance of the Marxist ruling party in the practice of governance, and it is also an effective way to improve the party's level of governance ability. The CPC's governance method is closely related to the party's leadership method. The party's leadership method includes the party's governance method and determines the party's method of governance - the party's method of governance is the central core of the party's leadership method and is the most important manifestation of the leadership method. In the practice of governance, the CPC is faced with an unprecedented breadth and depth of development and an unprecedented complexity of various interests, which requires the party to grasp the direction of development, formulate development strategies, coordinate the work of various parties, coordinate various interests, rationalise major relationships and promote socioeconomic development from a holistic perspective. In the face of new situations and problems, upholding a scientific approach to governance requires giving full play to the party's central leading role of taking the overall picture and coordinating all parties. The party's role of taking the overall picture and coordinating all parties is not only an important principle of the CPC's leadership but also an important principle of the CPC's adherence to democratic centralism, and a scientific conclusion drawn from a summary of the CPC's historical experience. The so-called overall picture means that party committees at all levels should focus their main efforts on grasping the direction, discussing major issues and managing the overall situation, concentrating on major issues of an overall, strategic, fundamental and forward-looking nature, grasping the political direction, deciding on major matters, arranging important personnel appointments and dismissals, firmly grasping ideological and political work, safeguarding social and political stability, and effectively implementing the party's political, ideological and organisational leadership in all fields. The so-called coordination of all parties means that the party committee should start from the requirement of promoting holistic overall work, coordinate the relationship between the party committee, the NPC, the government and the CPPCC, and arrange the work of the discipline inspection, organisation, publicity, united front, political and legal affairs, armed forces and people's groups, so that all parties can perform their respective duties and responsibilities, and cooperate with each other, thereby forming a synergy. Practice has proven that by adhering to the party's scientific method of governance by taking the overall picture into account and coordinating all parties, the initiative and proactiveness of all parties can be mobilised and the wisdom and strength of all parties can be brought together.

(II) DEMOCRATIC GOVERNANCE IS AN ESSENTIAL REQUIREMENT FOR THE GOVERNANCE OF MARXIST PARTIES

The core issue of democratic governance is the correct understanding and handling of the relationship between the ruling party and the people, which means upholding the principle of governance for and by the people, supporting and ensuring the sovereignty of the people, upholding and refining the people's democratic dictatorship, upholding and refining democratic centralism, promoting people's democracy through the development of intraparty democracy, uniting all forces that can be united, mobilising all positive elements, and strengthening the broadest patriotic united front. The basic essence of democratic governance is not only a scientific answer to the democratic nature of party governance but also a profound revelation of the way in which the communist party achieves governance, and it embodies both the fundamental purpose, and the source, of motivation for communist party governance.

Democratic governance is determined by the nature of the Marxist ruling party. The fundamental question that any ruling party must first address pertains to who the intended beneficiary of governance is and on whom it relies, and this is also the fundamental basis for judging the nature of the ruling party. The CPC is the vanguard of the Chinese working class, the Chinese people and the Chinese nation, and the leading core of the cause of socialism with Chinese characteristics. The party has no special interests of its own except the interests of the people. In this regard Comrade Xi Jinping profoundly pointed out that, "The highest interest and core value of our communist party members is to serve the people wholeheartedly and sincerely for the benefit of the people. Party members and cadres should always think about and act on why they joined the party, what they do as cadres, and their legacy; they should never seek their personal interests or those of a minority but always hold fast to the spiritual home of communists who wholeheartedly serve the people"… 'we must put the interests of the people first at all times"… and "We should always put the people in the highest position in our hearts, remember that responsibility is an extremely serious matter, and always prioritise the people's safety and well-being." The nature of the communist party determines that only whe it relies closely on the people, always upholds the fundamental Marxist viewpoint of doing everything for the masses, trusting the masses and relying on the masses, and insists on taking the achievement, safeguarding and development of the fundamental interests of the general public as the fundamental start and end points of all governance operations, can it continue to gain the support and endorsement of the people and lay a solid mass foundation for democratic governance.

Democratic governance is determined by the historical position of the people. Marxism holds that the people are the driving force behind the advance of history and social development, and the creators of all material and spiritual assets. The historical status of the people determines that democratic governance requires the ideological establishment of the people's dominant status. The history of the CPC shows that the party has its roots, its bloodline and its strength in the people. In planning development, the people are the most knowledgeable about the actual situation, and in promoting reform, the biggest force to rely on is also the people. In the management of state affairs, only by consulting the people in the field and asking them for advice is it possible to grasp what the people think and expect, draw together the people's hearts and minds, and create a new context for reform and development. The grassroots constitute the biggest classroom, and the masses are the best teachers. Their life is the most profound and they are the wisest people. The historical status of the people determines that democratic governance requires respect for the people's innovative spirit in its actions. In summing up the experience of CPC governance, a very important point is that it has always taken the masses as the source of wisdom and strength, and always deeply rooted the growth of its political wisdom and the enhancement of its governance expertise in the creative practice of the people.

Democratic governance is not only regulated and guaranteed by a series of legal institutions but also embodied and implemented by a series of methods and measures. This requires the ruling party to constantly adapt to the new changes in the party's historical orientation and mission, its governing environment and governance ranks, to uphold progressive advance, to constantly reform and refine the party's leadership style and governance method, leadership system and working mechanisms, and to provide institutional safeguards for democratic governance. In practice, it is necessary to further improve the democratic system, constantly enhance the capacity to develop socialist democratic politics, and vigorously promote the institutionalisation, standardisation and proceduralisation of socialist democratic politics. It is also necessary to vigorously develop intraparty democracy, establish and improve the various systems of intraparty democracy, guarantee the democratic rights of party members, and use intraparty democracy to provide the impetus for the people's democracy. It is also necessary to uphold the organic unity of party leadership, the sovereignty of the people and the rule of law, as well as to uphold and refine the system of people's congresses and gradually establish a sound system for ensuring the sovereignty of the people. It is necessary to vigorously promote the widespread, multi-layered and institutionalised development of consultative democracy, further expand grassroots democracy, expand the orderly political participation of citizens, enrich the forms of achieving democracy, and guarantee the people's right to exercise democratic elections, decision-making, management and supervision through various channels in accordance with the law.

(III) GOVERNANCE IN ACCORDANCE WITH THE LAW IS THE BASIC GOVERNANCE METHOD FOR MARXIST PARTIES

Governance in accordance with the law is the CPC's basic strategy in upholding the rule of law. The CPC has always emphasised that the party leads the people in formulating and implementing the constitution and laws, and that the party itself must operate within the scope thereof, truly ensuring that the party leads in legislation, ensuring law enforcement, supporting justice and taking the lead in abiding by the law. The level of the rule of law in the institutionalisation, standardisation and procedural operation of state and social life is an important indicator of the modernisation of the national system of governance and its governance ability. The governance of the CPC in accordance with the law has concentratedly reflected the CPC's progressive advance and institutional innovation in the way it governs the country under new historical conditions, and has highlighted the proactiveness, creativity and criticality of the ruling party in leading the construction of the rule of law in China.

Governance in accordance with the law requires firmly establishing and promoting the socialist concept and spirit of the rule of law. The concept and spirit of the rule of law are the soul of the rule of law, relate to the fundamental nature of the rule of law, and to the basic questions surrounding which path to take, which principles to grasp, and the right direction in which to advance. In order to firmly establish and promote the socialist concept and the spirit of the rule of law, it is necessary to enhance the consciousness and firmness in taking the path of the rule of law that suits the country's reality. The kind of rule of law path a country takes and the kind of rule of law system it builds depends on the country's fundamental nature, basic national conditions and cultural traditions. The CPC emphasises that to uphold the path of socialist rule of law with Chinese characteristics, it is necessary to set up its rule of law platform clearly, raise the banner of the rule of law higher, and release correct and clear signals to the whole society. In order to firmly establish and promote the socialist concept and spirit of the rule of law, it is necessary to enhance the consciousness and firmness in comprehensively promoting the rule of law under the leadership of the communist party. The leadership of the CPC is the most essential feature of socialism with Chinese characteristics and the most fundamental guarantee of the socialist rule of law. The relationship between the party's leadership and the rule of law is the core issue in the construction of the rule of law, and the question of whether or not to uphold the party's leadership is the dividing line that distinguishes China's rule of law path from the Western rule of law model. So it is necessary to enhance the consciousness and firmness in constructing the rule of law for the people, relying on the people, benefiting the people and protecting the people. The people are the main body and source of strength of the rule of law, and in order to comprehensively promote the rule of law, it is necessary to uphold the primacy of the people and truly achieve the construction of the rule of law for the people, rely on the people, benefit the people and protect the people. It is also necessary to enhance the consciousness and firmness in upholding the supremacy of the constitution and the law, and the equality of all people before the law. Advocating and enforcing the rule of law will truly make laws and regulations the norm of social life and the standard for the conduct of the people. So it is necessary to enhance consciousness and firmness in upholding the integration of the rule of law and rule by virtue. The rule of law and rule by virtue are like "two axles of a car" and the "two wings of a bird", in that they go hand in hand and are both vital. It is necessary to have a deep understanding of the dialectical relationship between the rule of law and rule by virtue, strengthen awareness of the rule of law on one hand and rule by virtue on the other, vigorously promote core socialist values and traditional virtues, better nourish the spirit of the rule of law with morality, and create a good human environment for the rule of law.

Governance in accordance with the law requires constantly improving the ability to think and act in accordance with the law. The vitality and authority of the law lie in its implementation. The important issue around governance in accordance with the law is putting it into practice, ensuring unity of knowledge and action, to effectively reflect the concept and spirit of the rule of law in the practice of work, and to constantly improve the ability to use rule-of-law thinking and methods to solve problems.

With regard to upholding the use of rule-of-law thinking and methods to consider issues and make decisions, the law is the basic guarantee for effective and correct decision-making. The CPC emphasises improvement of decision-making mechanisms in accordance with the law, establishes public participation, the testimony of experts, risk assessment, reviews of legality and collective discussion and decision as the legal procedure for major administrative decisions, and establishes a permanent system of accountability for major decisions and a mechanism for reversal of liability, which will have a positive impact on forming the habit of making decisions and acting in accordance with the law. Upholding the use of rule-of-law thinking and methods deepens reform and promotes development. This is done by promoting reform on the track of the rule of law, paying more attention to optimising the leading and normative role of the rule of law, consciously condensing reform consensus on the basis of the rule of law, and being adept at using the rule of law to resolve reform risks, so that reform initiatives are based on law. Reform achievements that have proven to be effective in practice should be crystallised in law in a timely manner while reform initiatives that are not yet ripe for practice, and require early and pilot implementation, should be authorised in accordance with statutory procedures. Laws and regulations that do not meet the requirements of reform should be amended and repealed in a timely manner to ensure that reform operates within the framework of the rule of law. The CPC also emphasises upholding the use of the rule of law thinking and methods to resolve contradictions and maintain stability, actively adapting to the requirements of modernising governability, further strengthening the authoritative position of the rule of law in safeguarding the rights and interests of the masses and reconciling interests, strengthening the protective role of the rule of law in resolving social contradictions and maintaining harmony and stability, actively promoting multilevel and multidisciplinary governance in accordance with the law, and continuously improving the level of the rule of law in social governance. [The CPC further emphasises] upholding the use of rule-of-law thinking and methods to strictly manage and rule the party, further strengthen the awareness of managing and ruling the party in accordance with rules and discipline, upholding the party charter as the basis, focus on the interface with national laws, refine the system of intraparty regulations and improve the implementation thereof, ensuring that party rules and discipline are stricter than national laws, and the requirements for party members and cadres are stricter than those for ordinary citizens, and truly put into practice the requirements of managing the party in accordance with rules and discipline, and strictly managing and ruling the party.

Governance in accordance with the law requires upholding the use of power in accordance with the law and consciously accepting supervision. The relationship between power and law should be handled well, so that power can be used in accordance with the law, impartially and with integrity. The premise for using power in accordance with the law is to grasp the boundaries of power. Power is bestowed by the party and the people, and is not unlimited but subject to party discipline and national law. In upholding the use of power in accordance with the law, it is important to grasp the basic requirement that "legal authority must be exercised but not without authority"[1], with power consciously used within the constraints of the law and within the context of the institutional cage. The principle of using power in accordance with the law means upholding fairness and impartiality, which are the lifeline of the rule of law and the basis of governance and the use of power. The key to upholding the use of power in accordance with the law is to establish a correct concept of power, correctly handle the relationship between situation and law, profit and law, and power and law, effectively and fairly use power and handle matters, and resolutely oppose the use of power for personal gain and attaining private ends by abusing public position. The key to using power in accordance with the law is to consciously accept supervision. Those having power must be responsible, the use of power must be subject to supervision, and violations of the law must be prosecuted. In order to uphold the use of power in accordance with the law, measures should be adopted to promote open government, and in order to uphold the principle of openness being the norm and a lack of openness being the exception, openness surrounding decision-making, implementation, management, services and results should be promoted. Efforts should be made to raise awareness and change the concept of power, such that it becomes normal to exercise power in the "spotlight" and work under a "magnifying glass"; those in power must consciously accept the supervision of all areas of society, resolutely overcome obstacles aimed at avoiding supervision, resolutely prevent the phenomenon of artificial manipulation, and ensure that power is exercised in broad daylight.

8

THE BASIS OF GOVERNANCE

THE PEOPLE ARE THE COMMUNIST PARTY'S FOUNDATION, BLOODLINE AND SOURCE OF STRENGTH

Human history shows that the basis of social development is in the economy, the manifestation of economic issues is in politics, and political gains and losses are found in the hearts of people. [As Mencius said,] "He who wins the hearts of the people wins the world, and he who loses the hearts of the people loses the world." This is an unchanging law of the historical development of human society, and there is no exception to this rule in any time or place. The greatest politics of a ruling party takes place in the hearts and minds of the people. Any political party represents the interests of a certain class, stratum and group, and has its own class base and mass base for ruling. The communist party is a party of the working class, and it represents the interests of the working class and the broad masses of the people. Therefore, its class base is the working class and its mass base is the broad mass of the people.

(I) THE MASSES OF THE PEOPLE ARE THE DRIVING FORCE BEHIND THE ADVANCEMENT OF SOCIAL HISTORY

History is made by the people, and this is a fundamental principle of Marxism. Is there a law for the development of human society? Before the birth of Marxism, all politicians, thinkers, historians, and others said that there was no law. They believed that people are conscious and that consciousness is erratic. Different people, different groups and different classes produce different consciousnesses, form a different type of will and demonstrate different effects. As a result, social history is chaotic and disorderly. The establishment of Marx's historical materialism revealed for the first time the objective laws of human social development. According to Marx, productivity determines socioeconomic relations and the economic base determines the superstructure. The socioeconomic relations have a certain opposing effect on productivity and the superstructure on the economic base. The contradiction between them is the basic contradiction of human society, and the contradictory movement between them determines the direction of development of human society and its condition. The emergence of the capitalist mode of production has made the history of human society truly "world history". So what is the role of the people in the historical development of human society? Do heroic figures make history? Or do the people make history? Marx believed that the masses constitute the main body of historical activity, the creators of the material and spiritual wealth of society, and the ultimate decisive force in driving the advance of history and social change. He pointed out that, "the activities and ideas of history are the ideas and activities of the 'masses'" and that "historical activity is the activity of the masses, and as historical activity deepens, the ranks of the masses will inevitably expand"[1]. Engels also pointed out that the real driving force behind the development of history is, "the motivation which leads the masses, an entire nation of people, and whole classes of people in that nation, to act", and that they are "not short bursts and fleeting flames but lasting actions which cause major historical changes"[2]. Marx also said that, "No revolution can be accomplished by a political party; only the people can accomplish it"[3]. He also stressed that, "it is not the national system that creates the people but the people that create the national system"[4]. In leading the Russian people in the process of implementing socialist revolution and construction, Lenin also emphasised that, "vibrant and creative socialism is created by the people themselves"[5]. "The strength of a nation lies in the consciousness of the masses. A nation has strength only when the masses know everything, are able to judge everything, and are consciously engaged in everything"[6]. "We are, after all, a drop in the ocean among the people, and we can only manage if we express the ideas of the people correctly. Otherwise, the communist party will not be able to lead the proletariat, and the proletariat will not be able to lead the masses, and the whole apparatus will fall apart"[7]. In the historical process of revolution, construction and reform, the CPC has, in the light of China's actual situation, continuously promoted the sinicisation of Marxism, and, in the practice of building and managing the party and governing China, has persisted with the approach of integrating the basic principles of Marxism with China's reality and the characteristics of the times, constantly enriched and developed Marxist-

Leninist ideology on the historical status and role of the people, determined the correct programmes of action and development strategies, and mobilised the initiative, proactiveness and creativity of hundreds of millions of people to build socialism.

The source of the communist party's strength is the people. The communist party is made up of the advanced elements of the proletariat, it comes from the people, grows out of the people and is part of the people. Its historical mission is to work for the welfare and happiness of the people, for the liberation and rejuvenation of the nation, and for global peace and development. Its basic task is to organise, mobilise and educate the masses so that the people will come to identify their own interests, unite in the struggle to achieve their interests and to build a better society. As Deng Xiaoping pointed out, "The political parties of the working class do not regard the people as their own tool but consciously identify themselves as a kind of tool of the people in a particular historical period for the accomplishment of a particular historical task"[8]. The completion of historical missions and tasks culminates in the eradication of classes, the disappearance of political parties and the demise of the state. So what have the communist parties around the world done since the emergence of Marxist parties, that is, communist parties? The greatest thing they have done, in a nutshell, is to usher in a new era of socialist revolution and construction. 1871 saw the first attempt by the proletariat to seize power with the revolution of the Paris Commune in France. The triumph of the October Socialist Revolution in Russia in 1917 ushered in a new era in human history. The emergence of a large number of socialist countries in Eastern Europe after the second world war, and especially the founding of the PRC in 1949, strengthened the world's peaceful democratic and socialist camp, broke through the eastern front of imperialism, changed the ratio of forces in the international Cold War, and had a wide and far-reaching impact on the world. After the October Revolution, the CPR [later renamed the AUCP and then CPSU], united and led its people to overcome unimaginable difficulties, and worked hard to achieve great socioeconomic construction, in a very short period of time its economic output becoming the first in Europe and second in the world. The Chinese people, under the leadership of the CPC, overthrew the "three mountains" of imperialism, feudalism and bureaucratic capitalism that had been opressing the people through 28 years of bloody struggle, and achieved the great victory of the new democratic revolution. After the founding of new China, the CPC also led the Chinese people in implementing socialist revolution and construction, establishing a relatively complete industrial system and national economy, and solving the problem of feeding hundreds of millions of people. In particular, the 3rd Plenary Session of the 11th CPC Central Committee in 1978 made the historic decision to focus on economic construction and implement reform and opening up, and pioneered, upheld and developed socialism with Chinese characteristics. Over the past few decades, China's economy and society have developed rapidly, its economic, scientific and technological strength and comprehensive national power have increased significantly, its global influence, appeal and capacity to shape [global affairs] have increased significantly, and the living standards of its people have improved significantly. China's economic output has steadily ranked second in the world since 2010, and it has now become the world's largest manufacturer, the largest trader of goods, and the largest foreign exchange reserve holder. At a time when the world economy is experiencing a depression and the outlook is bleak, China's economy is "the light at the end of the tunnel" and "in a league of its own". At a time when the international communist movement has suffered setbacks and is at a low ebb, the banner of scientific socialism is flying high in China, which has become the mainstay of socialism in the world. Under the leadership of the communist party, through revolutionary construction and through the period of reform and opening up, these countries have created and are creating miracles in the world and great human exploits. Where, then, does its strength come from? Historical facts show that the majestic power to change the world comes from the people. All this proves the correctness of historical materialism and the incontrovertible truth of Marxism that "the masses are the real heroes".

(II) THE PEOPLE'S STANDPOINT IS THE FUNDAMENTAL COMMUNIST PARTY MEMBERS' STANDPOINT

Serving the people wholeheartedly is the fundamental aim of the communist party. Without the people, the communist party will achieve nothing. The communist party cannot be separated from the people and must depend on them, and this is determined by the nature and purpose of the communist party. Marx and Engels clearly pointed out in the Communist Manifesto that, "All movements in the past involved a minority of people or were for the benefit of a minority. The movement of the proletariat is an independent movement of the vast majority, for the benefit of the vast majority"[9]. "At all stages of development through which the struggle between the proletariat and the bourgeoisie has passed, the communists have always represented the interests of the movement as a whole" and "the communists are not a unique party in opposition to the other workers' parties. They do not have any interests different from those of the proletariat as a whole"[10]. Why does the communist party have such a nature? It is determined by the historical position and historical mission of the working class, the class base of the communist party. Since the 1840s, with the emergence of big industry, the class situation in society has changed profoundly. Of all the classes opposed to the bourgeoisie, only the proletariat has truly become a revolutionary class because it is a product of big industry itself; the other classes are increasingly declining and dying out with the development of big industry. Therefore, the interests of the communist party are the interests of the working class, the interests of the broad mass of the people. Mao Zedong pointed out that, "the communist party is a party that works for the good of the nation and the people; it has absolutely no selfish interests of its own"[11]. At the Seventh CPC National Congress in 1945, the principle of "serving the people" was written into the party's constitution, clearly stating that "Chinese communists must have the spirit of serving the Chinese people wholeheartedly". In his political report to the congress, Mao Zedong also strongly emphasised, "serve the people wholeheartedly, and do not be detached from the masses for a single moment, do everything in the interests of the people, not in the interests of individuals or small groups, and be accountable to the people and to the leading organs of the party; these are our point of departure"[12].

Since then, the CPC has clearly defined "serving the people" as the purpose of the party in its own constitution and has consistently embodied it in all its work. In 2017, the Constitution of the CPC, adopted at the 19th CPC National Congress, made it clear that, "the party has no special interests of its own except the interests of the working class and the broad masses of the people"[13]. Everything for the people and everything by depending on the people has become the start and end point of all the work of the communist party, and its sacred duty and obligation, and serving the people wholeheartedly has become the fundamental purpose of the communist party. The communist party emphasises the purpose of serving the people wholeheartedly and this cannot be discounted at all and does not contain the least impurity. After the founding of new China, when confronted with the phenomenon of party members and cadres taking credit for themselves, being complacent and seeking enjoyment, Mao Zedong stressed that, "the communist party is about struggle, about serving the people wholeheartedly and not half-heartedly or with anything less than the whole heart and mind"[14]. Marx is the great ancestor of the communist party. Marxism is vast and profound but it boils down to one phrase, namely, seeking liberation for the people. Therefore, it is a natural, unchanging and fixed reality that the communist party should be founded for the public and govern for the sake of the people. This purpose of the communist party is an important mark that distinguishes it from any other political party of the exploiting classes. Serving the people is a value of the communist party, affinity with the people is the most distinctive character of Marxism, the people's sentiment is the sentiment of the communists, and their position is the fundamental position of the communists. In this regard it is important to emphasise that the communist party's party spirit and affinity the people are highly unified, completely consistent and inseparable. To uphold the people's standpoint is also to uphold the party spirit.

Communists must always keep the people's well-being at heart. To uphold the people's standpoint and serve them, the communist party must work tirelessly for the good aspirations of the people. To uphold the people's standpoint and serve them is not something that can be achieved overnight or once and for all. In this regard, the communist party and socialist countries have experience as well as lessons for others. The CPSU's long-term neglect of the improvement of people's lives had serious consequences later on. If, back then, under special circumstances, everything was for the revolution and everything was for the war, the Soviet masses would still have been able to persevere and endure the difficulties in their lives. However, when such circumstances changed, their attitudes and choices changed accordingly. After the end of the second world war, with the threat of foreign enemies largely removed, it became difficult for the masses to accept the continued demand for long-term sacrifices from the people in order to compete with the US for hegemony. Relevant information shows that, on the one hand, the Soviet Union's consumer goods for the masses were of poor quality and in short supply. The time people spent each year queuing for food and daily necessities such as toothpaste and toilet paper was equivalent to the annual working hours of 15 million labourers. The people's feelings and trust in the CPSU were lost and exhausted in this unbearably long wait. On the other hand, many leaders and cadres could easily obtain delicious food and imported goods from special shops without having to queue up and lacked a personal sense of the plight of the masses and the urgency to improve people's lives. Some of them even criticised the "bourgeois ideology" of the people's desire for a rich material and cultural life while they were still full of wine and food[15].

Similar problems were found in the decision-making of the communist parties in Eastern Europe, as was the case with the Polish and Hungarian Crises of 1956. From 1957 in China the party began to make "leftist" mistakes in its decision-making. The Great Leap Forward caused damage to the cause of the party and the country, and the Cultural Revolution was even more leftist and brought about internal disorder. As the economy did not develop rapidly and the people's livelihoods did not improve for a long time, the people became discontented with the party and the government. Deng Xiaoping later pointed out sharply in this regard that, "Socialism has to eradicate poverty. Poverty is not socialism, still less is it communism." …. "If we do not implement reforms now, our modernisation and socialist cause will be buried"[16]. It was against this historical background that China's reform and opening up was initiated. Reform and opening up has enabled China to truly develop and become vibrant. Over the past 40 years of reform and opening up, absolute poverty in rural China has been reduced from 770 million people to 5.51 million at the end of 2019, and from 97.5% of the total rural population to 0.6%. With a total of 70% of the global poverty reduction, China has made a huge contribution to the cause of human poverty reduction. From 1978 to 2017, the per capita disposable income of Chinese residents increased 22.8 times in real terms on an inflation-adjusted basis. History tells us that an absence of concern for the people and the neglect of the interests of the masses were important reasons why the CPSU and the communist parties of Eastern European countries were abandoned by their people. In contrast, focusing on economic construction at the centre, liberating and developing social productivity, developing the economy and constantly improving people's livelihoods are the fundamental reasons why the CPC has gained great prestige among the people and received their heartfelt support and strong backing.

With regard to upholding a people-centred ideology of development, in the practice of reform and opening up, especially since the 18th CPC National Congress, the CPC has continuously deepened its understanding of the status and role of the people in social and historical development, enriched and developed Marxist ideology and theory on the people, put forward the people-centred ideology of development, and used it to guide the practice of reform and development, achieving tremendous theoretical, practical and institutional results. In this regard, Xi Jinping pointed out, "There are constants in ruling a country but benefiting the people is the main focus." The people-centred development ideology is not an abstract and esoteric concept and should not remain only in words and stop at ideological links but be reflected in all aspects of socioeconomic development"[17]. He has also repeatedly emphasised that to uphold and develop socialism with Chinese characteristics, it is necessary to uphold the supremacy and primacy of the people, do all for the sake of the people with everything depending on the people, exalting the interests of the people above all. It is also necessary to make the promotion of the people's well-being, of all-round human development and steady progress toward common prosperity the start and end point of our work. The core point of these important statements is to uphold the standpoint and supremacy of the people. The people-centred ideology of development put forward by the CPC upholds the basic principles of Marxism, sums up the lessons learned from both positive and negative experiences of socialist countries and the fresh experience of China in the practice of reform and opening up, reflects the essential characteristics of socialism with Chinese characteristics and embodies the values and principles of scientific socialism. It solves the problem of who to trust, who to depend on and who to serve, in terms of epistemology, methodology, historical outlook and values. To put this idea into practice, it is necessary to uphold the principle that power is used for the people, love is given for the people and benefit is sought for the people, that development is for the people and depends on them, and that the fruits of development are shared by the people. This is a major political issue that upholds the fundamental stance of the communist party. Therefore, in contemporary China, in order to achieve the struggle goals of Two Centenaries, to build a moderately prosperous society in all respects and to achieve the Chinese dream of the great rejuvenation of the Chinese nation, whether it be innovation-driven, energising reform initiatives or the integration of urban-rural construction, or regional, economic and social, material and spiritual civilisation construction, or whether it be tackling environmental pollution, meeting people's expectations for a good ecology, or coordinating the relationship between efficiency and equity, making a "bigger cake" and sharing it more fairly, it is necessary to uphold the people-centred ideology of development, the value and concept of the supremacy of the people, and the distinctive orientation of solving livelihood-related issues.

(III) ALWAYS MAINTAIN THE FLESH-AND-BLOOD TIES BETWEEN THE COMMUNIST PARTY AND THE PEOPLE

Privilege and passive corruption are corrosive agents in the relationship between the party and the people. The history of socialism in the world has shown that the communist party gained power and the position of governance by the support of the people, and the communist parties in the Soviet Union, Eastern Europe and other socialist countries lost their ruling position or even died out because they lost the support of the people. Both positive and negative historical experiences fully illustrate that the support or otherwise of the people and the backwardness of the human heart are decisive factors in the rise or fall of communist parties. The period from

1921 to 1926 was the best period of party and political life in the Soviet Union, and the period when the Soviet Union was better prepared for its rapid rise to power. After Lenin's death, the phenomenon of Soviet party cadres becoming disconnected from the masses gradually developed, and became more and more serious, to the extent that a privileged class was gradually formed and consolidated in the life of the party and the state. The results of research show that "the powerful class at the union and local levels during the Soviet period numbered about 750,000 people, and if their relatives were added, there were about 3 million people, or 1.5% of the total population"[18]. The system of privilege caused a huge rift in the relationship between the party and the cadres in the late Soviet Union, and the interests of the people were increasingly unprotected. The privileges were extended even further by the dictatorship of individuals and the destruction of the socialist legal system, and the leading cadres were eventually transformed from "servants of the people" to "masters of the people". As a result, its decline was inevitable. Before the collapse of the Soviet Union, the then Academy of Social Sciences of the USSR conducted a survey showing that the vast majority of Soviet people did not believe that the CPSU represented their interests. Rather, they believed that the CPSU represented the interests of the party cadres and the bureaucratic class[19]. The CPSU lost its ruling position after 74 years in power when it had nearly 20 million members. 'To date, one finds no record in either central or local historical archives of resistance from all levels of the party when hostile forces outlawed the communist party, no record of CPSU members assembling in an organised manner to stage any large-scale protests in defence of their district, city or oblast committees, nor any record of the masses of the people taking action to support or show solidarity for the CPSU, or of any organised action by the people in support of them"[20]. When the Soviet Union collapsed, the people had long since abandoned the CPSU in their own minds, and with it, the CPSU lost its foundation for survival. In some Eastern European countries, communist parties lost their position of governance, and one of the main reasons for this was also the serious disengagement of the party from the masses and the passive corruption that occurred. Kadar, the leader of the Hungarian Socialist Workers' Party, once said that there were two major tests for communists. The first was the difficult test when communists faced the enemy alone, which was very hard because they had to risk their lives. Many have heroically withstood this test. The other was the test of assuming power. Certain people failed in the second test because they began to think that they were omnipotent and so began to disengage from the masses for whom they had fought for so long. There were more and more petty despots around the country and in all areas of life, and dictating orders became the dominant method of maintaining their ruling position[21]. There is some truth in his view. The CPC attaches great importance to the relationship between the party and the people, comparing the relationship between the party and the people to the relationship between fish and water, flesh and blood, public and servant, and so on. The reason why the CPC led the revolution, the Agrarian Revolutionary War, the War of Resistance Against Japanese Aggression and the War of Liberation, and was able to pioneer a new context in the revolution, explore a revolutionary path with Chinese characteristics and achieve victory in China's new democratic revolution was the result of the vigorous persistence of the people. In the War of Liberation, the Huaihai Campaign was a major battle fought by the armies led by the KMT and CPC parties. At that time, the PLA had only 600,000 men, while the KMT army had nearly 800,000 men, representing a huge contrast in power. However, on the other hand, the PLA was backed by 5.43 million people who supported the front. Wherever the battle was fought, the food trolleys of the people were wheeled out in support. Chen Yi once fondly said that the Huaihai Campaign was advanced by the people with trolleys. During the period of national economic restructuring after the Great Leap Forward, the people responded to the call of the CPC Central Committee to streamline the workforce and completed the daunting task of reducing the urban population by 26 million in just two years. State council Premier Zhou Enlai, who organised and led the work, said at the time that this was, "equal to a medium-sized country moving house, which is unprecedented and can be called a miracle"[22]. In order to accelerate the socialist revolution and construction in China, the masses shed blood and sweat during those fiery times and wrote a magnificent epic of self-reliance and hard struggle. In the course of reform and opening up, the Chinese people have boldly explored and practised, moreover, they have pushed through thorns and briers, pioneered and innovated, and walked along a new path of socialism with Chinese characteristics. In the face of the global and difficult issue of corruption, the CPC has been brave enough to revolutionise itself and resolutely oppose corruption and privileges. Since the 18th CPC National Congress, the party has raised its flag and drawn its sword, done all it can to treat ills, removed cancerous growths and eliminated corruption, making achievements that have caught the world's attention and won the world's praise and the heartfelt support and affection of the general public. The historical facts, both positive and negative, show that in order for the communist party to maintain the purity of its progressiveness and not degenerate, it must have a clear-cut stand, and firmly oppose privilege and corruption.

With regard to consistently implementing the party's mass line, the mass line is the lifeline and fundamental working line of the communist party. Communist parties all over the world, including the CPSU, the communist parties of Eastern European countries (workers' parties) and the CPC, are all products of the confrontation between labour and capital at a certain stage of socioeconomic development since the 1840s. They were not created within a representative system and their existence has no so-called "legitimacy". Therefore, during the revolutionary period before it takes power, a communist party cannot be separated from the support of the working class and the masses of the people for a single moment and could not survive without it. Lenin attached particular importance to the links between the party and the masses during the period when the party was founded and made many statements about strengthening relations between the party and the masses. Stalin also attached great importance to this problem in his early days, once using the relationship between the ancient Greek mythological hero Antaeus and Mother Earth as a metaphor for the inseparable relationship between the communist party and the people, stressing that the communist party would not survive without the people just as the hero Antaeus would not survive without Mother Earth. As communist parties (workers' parties) in the Soviet Union and Eastern Europe took power one after another, the phenomenon of detachment from the masses began to occur, and later developed to an increasingly serious extent. The CPC attaches great importance to close links with the masses and regards it as one of the distinguishing marks that differentiates it from any other political party[23]. The concept of the mass line was introduced by the CPC leadership in 1928, and Mao Zedong gave a complete and systematic exposition of the mass line in 1943. Since then, upholding and implementing the mass line has become a fine work style and tradition of Chinese communists. The basic essence of the CPC mass line is in five phrases given in the *Constitution of the CPC*, namely, "All for the masses, all depending on the masses, coming from the masses, going to the masses, and turning the correct ideas of the party into the conscious actions of the masses"[24]. These five phrases respectively elaborate on the dialectical unity of their interdependence and mutually reinforcing nature in terms of their standpoints, methods and goals, and they have become the basic guidelines for the fundamental working line of the Chinese communists. History has repeatedly proven that when the party's mass line is well implemented, the relationship between the party and the people will be close and the party's cause will be victorious and develop, but when the party's mass line is poorly implemented, the relationship between the party and the people will be damaged and the party's cause will suffer setbacks. Under the new historical conditions, if the communist party is to govern for a long time and to hold power and rule well for the people, it must maintain the vibrant connections between the party and the people, and to maintain such ties it must implement the party's mass line in the practice of governance. Whether or not the party can always maintain and develop the vibrant connections between the party and the people, and whether or not it can always uphold and implement the party's mass line, depends on the support or opposition of the people and is related to the survival of the party and the country.

9

A COMMON IDEOLOGICAL BASIS FOR GOVERNANCE

BUILDING A SOCIALIST IDEOLOGY WITH STRONG COHESION AND THE POWER TO LEAD

In *The German Ideology*, Marx and Engels insist that, "the ideology of the ruling class is in every age the dominant ideology"[1]. This is a profound revelation of the law of state governance in human society. For the communist party to govern, following this law means that the doctrine espoused and the values advocated by the communist party should be incorporated into all areas of ideology. This is so that it will have strong cohesion and the power to lead society as a whole, and become the ideological basis for the unity of society as a whole and for forging ahead.

(I) CONSOLIDATING THE COMMON IDEOLOGICAL BASIS OF THE WHOLE SOCIETY IS AN IMPORTANT CONDITION FOR PARTY GOVERNANCE

Under the conditions of communist party governance, the common ideological basis of the whole society can only be Marxism and its localised scientific theories. The extent to which the ideological theories of the communist party are accepted by society is an important indicator of the consolidation of the communist party's governance position. The seizure and consolidation of power by the CPSU constituted a great victory under the guidance of Marxism and Soviet (Russian) Marxism-Leninism. Marxism-Leninism became not only a conscious practice of the Soviet people but also a strong belief shared by the whole society. Without the support of such a strong faith and belief, it would have been impossible to break through a strong and strict imperialist system, and build socialism in a country and consolidate it in the long-term. Russian scholars have commented on the Soviet Union under Stalin that, "In terms of ideology and theory, in the sphere of social consciousness one can describe it in one word - ironclad. People believed in social justice, in their own future and in the future of their country. It seemed that it would never have been possible to destroy such a society, let alone even shake it up"[2]. This "ironclad" situation changed radically in later years. In the mid-1980s, Gorbachev, from a social-democratic standpoint, judged the CPSU's leadership of social thought as simply a "spiritual monopoly" and "ideological authoritarianism", and advocated ideological pluralism and liberalisation. This led to the spread and proliferation of ideas other than Marxism-Leninism, especially Western bourgeois ideology, and the loss of faith within and outside the party, which ultimately led to the defeat of the CPSU and the disintegration of the USSR. It has been proven that the disintegration of a regime often begins in the realm of ideology, and that while political upheaval and regime change may happen overnight, the evolution of ideology is a long-term process. When ideological defences are breached, it is difficult to guard other defences. When the party and the country are in disarray, they both die, and the ideology is the first to be disrupted and the soul the first to die.

One important reason why the CPC has achieved its governance position and remained in power for so long in an ancient country with a civilisation stretching back more than 5,000 years and a great Eastern power is that history and the people have chosen the CPC to lead and govern, and have also chosen the ideological theory of the CPC as the ideological basis of society as a whole and the pillar of the national spirit. This can be seen more clearly in the history of Chinese thought, especially in the evolution of modern Chinese thought. One of the major reasons for the continuity of the Chinese nation as a unified state for most of the time since the Qin and Han dynasties was that Chinese culture, with Confucianism as its main spiritual pillar, was used by the feudal rulers of all dynasties as the theoretical basis for maintaining their rule. In China from the 1840s, however, with the introduction of Western bourgeois doctrines, the status of Confucianism was fundamentally shaken. The ideological chaos, disagreements and lack of conformity in society as a whole were a major cause of the warlordism and frequent warfare of the modern era. For the Chinese nation to be reunited and revitalised, a new leadership force had to emerge, as well as a new theory that transcended traditional Chinese thought and Western bourgeois thought. For any political group to stand at the centre of the Chinese political scene and achieve power, it must also first reunite the Chinese nation ideologically. The CPC, founded after the

October Revolution in Russia, integrated Marxism with Chinese reality, including the culture of the Chinese nation, to form Mao Zedong Thought. This scientific theory not only became the guiding ideology of the CPC but was also gradually accepted by the Chinese people as the Chinese revolution developed, and as the Chinese nation gathered under the banner of Mao Zedong, the party moved from partial to national governance and China once again became a highly centralised and unified state. The theoretical creation of the CPC constituted one of the greatest ideological changes and spiritual awakening of the Chinese nation after the decline of Confucianism, and the Chinese people were transformed from being spiritually passive to spiritually active. On the foundation of Mao Zedong Thought, the CPC has continued to promote the process of sinicisation of Marxism. This includes Deng Xiaoping Theory, the major ideology of the Three Represents, the Scientific Outlook on Development and Xi Jinping Thought on Socialism with Chinese Characteristics for a New Era, all of which constitute manifestations of Chinese Marxism at different times and the inheritance and development of Mao Zedong Thought. Marxism-Leninism and Mao Zedong Thought, Deng Xiaoping Theory, the major ideology of the Three Represents, the Scientific Outlook on Development and Xi Jinping Thought on Socialism with Chinese Characteristics for a New Era are not only written into the party constitution but also into the national constitution, establishing their supreme status as the guiding ideology in the political life of the party and the state.

The CPC has always been highly conscious of the importance of maintaining its own scientific theories. Mao Zedong pointed out clearly at the very beginning of the CPC's governance that, "The core force leading our cause is the CPC. The theoretical basis guiding our thinking is Marxism-Leninism". Deng Xiaoping regarded the Four Cardinal Principles, including adherence to Mao Zedong Thought, as fundamental to the founding of the country, and Jiang Zemin and Hu Jintao both discussed them in depth. Jiang Zemin pointed out that, "If a party, a country and a nation, especially a large party such as ours and a country as large as this with such a large population, were not to have correct theory as their guide and not to have a strong spiritual pillar based on correct theory, then our party, country and nation would be inconceivable; they would become entirely incohesive, with no possibility for cohesion, fighting strength and creativity, and would not have a bright future"[3].

On the basis of these remarks, Xi Jinping further made it a fundamental task of ideological work to "consolidate the guiding position of Marxism in the field of ideology and the common ideological basis for the unity and struggle of the whole party and whole nation". These Two Consolidations further point out the fundamental requirements for consolidating the ideological foundation under the conditions of communist party governance, namely that Marxism, the ideological theory of the communist party, must be taken as the guiding ideology of social ideology and the common ideological foundation of society as a whole, and that social ideology and culture may be pluralistic, but the guiding ideology of the state and the common ideological foundation of society must not be. The introduction of the Two Consolidations signifies that the CPC has reached a new level of understanding of the laws of ideological work and the laws of governance.

As China enters a new era, consolidating the position of Marxism in the political life of the party and the country means using the latest achievement of the sinicisation of Marxism, contemporary Chinese Marxism and 21stcentury Marxism - Xi Jinping Thought on Socialism with Chinese Characteristics for a New Era - as the guiding ideology and common ideological basis for the whole of Chinese society. This is an inevitable requirement for the CPC to govern China in the new era and for the Chinese nation to usher in the great leap from standing up and getting rich to getting strong and achieving the Chinese dream of the great rejuvenation of the Chinese nation.

(II) PRESERVING ITS OWN HISTORY IS AN IMPORTANT QUALIFICATION FOR THE PARTY TO SETTLE DOWN AND PROCEED WITH ITS CAUSE

Reality is a continuation of history and history is the basis for reality. The place of any country, party or regime in reality is based on its role in history. All countries and governments focus on preserving their historical roots. To deny the history of a state, party and government also inevitably means to shake or even destroy the basis and inevitability of their real existence. For a political party, especially a Marxist party, the preservation of its own history is a major issue that concerns the consolidation of the foundations of the party's governance.

Our ancestors recognised early on the significant role of history in consolidating power. Mencius said, "Confucius made the Spring and Autumn Annals, and the rebellious ministers and traitors were afraid". Gong Zizhen, a thinker of the late Qing Dynasty, profoundly pointed out that, "to destroy a nation, one must first remove its history; to destroy a senator's square and corrupt a man's discipline, one must first remove his history; to destroy a man's talent and annihilate his teaching, one must first remove his history; to exterminate a man's ancestors, one must first remove his history." The seriousness of the destruction of the state, the destruction of power, the defeat of discipline, the destruction of talent, the annihilation of teaching and the extermination of ancestors profoundly reveals the great significance of preserving history for rulers and demonstrates the profound wisdom of the Chinese nation in governance.

Many countries and political groups around the world today, despite the plurality of their guiding ideologies and the irreconcilability of their political battles, share common claims and demands regarding the understanding of history. The US, for example, which has been a nation for just over 200 years, has set a uniform national standard for the national education of its own history, emphatically stating that without history a society has no common memory of its historical beginnings, its core values, and the impact of past decisions on the present, without history no reasonable examination of political, social or moral issues in society can be made, and without historical knowledge and enquiry based thereon, people cannot become well-informed and discerning citizens. And in South Korea, for example, in addition to making its own history a compulsory subject at all levels of schooling from primary school onwards, it has also set up a national examination to assess Korean historical competence, so that only those who pass this "national examination" on history at the appropriate level can take the corresponding national examinations for civil servants, teachers and lawyers, and can enter the country's ruling elite. The aim of this is also to create a unified historical understanding of the country. All of this reflects, in one way or another, the commonality of governance in human societies.

It is difficult for a country and society with a divided understanding of its own history to maintain its unity in the long term; it is difficult for a government and political party with a negative attitude toward its own history to claim a bright future. The CPSU and the Soviet Union are examples of this. The reasons for the collapse of the CPSU and the disintegration of the Soviet Union were, of course, multifaceted but the negation of its own history and the abandonment of Stalin's "sword" and then Lenin's "sword" were important aspects. In this regard, Xi Jinping pointed out profoundly, "Why did the Soviet Union disintegrate? Why did the CPSU collapse? An important reason was the fierce struggle in the ideological sphere, the total denial of the history of the Soviet Union and that of the CPSU, the denial of Lenin and Stalin, and historical nihilism"[4]. This lesson deserves great attention.

The CPC has become more mature in dealing with its own historical issues. After entering the new period of reform and opening up, with the complete repudiation of the Cultural Revolution and the full-scale implementation of bringing order out of chaos, the erroneous *zeitgeist* of the comprehensive denial of the history of the party, especially the history of new China, the so-called "de-Maoisation" of the party's history in the denial of the historical status of Mao Zedong and the scientific value of Mao Zedong Thought began to spread. Deng Xiaoping, keenly aware of the seriousness of this problem, clearly pointed out that, "Comrade Mao Zedong's merits come first and his mistakes come second". He said dropping the banner of Mao Zedong Thought "effectively negates the glorious history of our party"[5], and emphasised that, "if we really engage in 'non-Maoisation', we will be making a historical mistake"[6]. Regarding the view that the party's leadership and ruling position should be denied on the grounds that the party had made mistakes in history, the *Resolution on Several Historical Issues of the Party Since the Founding of the PRC*, adopted at the 6th Plenary Session of the 11th CPC Central Committee in 1981, profoundly pointed out that, "The party leadership is not without mistakes but the close unity of the party and the people will certainly be able to redress such mistakes. No one can use the fact that the party has made mistakes as a reason to weaken, get rid of or even undermine the party leadership. Weakening, getting rid of and undermining the party leadership will only lead to greater mistakes and invite serious disasters"[7]. This prophetic and important assertion was proven accurate by a series of catastrophic events such as the fall of the CPSU and the collapse of the Soviet Union a decade later.

With the progression of history, since the 18th CPC National Congress, the CPC has gained a more profound understanding regarding preserving its own historical awareness. Xi Jinping pointed out that "a people's history is the foundation on which it can settle and pursue its cause"[8] and "the victorious achievements of the new democratic revolution must not be lost, the achievements of the socialist revolution and construction must not be denied, and the direction of reform and opening up, and socialist modernisation must not be shaken. This is the qualification for the party and the people to settle and pursue their cause and move forward through thick and thin in today's world"[9].

He clearly pointed out that, "the historical period post reform and opening up should not be used to negate the period before reform and opening up, nor should the period before reform and opening up be used to negate the period post reform and opening up"[10], believing that if nihilistic remarks denying the party's history were allowed to flourish, they would inevitably upset the hearts and minds of the party and people, and endanger the party's leadership and the security of socialist state power. The party has consequently further intensified its efforts to preserve its own history and oppose historical nihilism. The special document on ideology issued by the Party Central Committee every year takes into account the new situation, listing the latest manifestations and claims of historical nihilism, and putting forward clear requirements and practical measures to counteract them. It has made "slandering and vilifying the party and state leaders" and "distorting the history of the party and military"[11] a violation of political discipline and requires that no media should facilitate the distortion of the party and state history and other erroneous statements, and that those who create rumours and trouble should be investigated and punished according to law. This further firms up the historical roots of the party's governance.

(III) FIRMLY GRASPING THE LEADERSHIP OF IDEOLOGICAL WORK

The most fundamental requirement for consolidating the common ideological basis of the communist party's governance is to master the leadership of ideological work, including the right to manage everything and verbal influence. Xi Jinping profoundly pointed out that, "the leadership, management and discourse of ideological work must be grasped firmly and must not be bypassed at any time or else an irreversible historical mistake will be made". This is a profound summary of the lessons learned from the communist party's leadership of ideological work.

The party's scientific theories must be used to arm the party and educate the people. This is the most fundamental requirement for bringing about the communist party's ideological leadership. The scientific theories of the communist party constitute the central expression of its political assertions, and belief in and identification with, communist party theory means acceptance of, and obedience to, the leadership of the communist party in ideological terms. Ideological obedience is the most fundamental type of obedience. Belief in and acceptance of communist party theory cannot be something that enters people's minds naturally and spontaneously but must be instilled through external "impartation", namely, through the necessary study and education. Jia Yi, a Chinese thinker of the Western Han Dynasty, said "Teaching is the essence of government. The Way is the essence of teaching. If there is the Way, then there is teaching. If there is teaching, then there will be politics. If there is politics, then the people will be persuaded. If the people are persuaded, then the country will be enriched." This profoundly points out the relationship between the Way, teaching and politics, with the Way being the basis of teaching and teaching the basis of politics. Once there is the Way then there must be corresponding teaching, and only then can the desired effect of politics and the "persuasion of the people" be achieved. This fully illustrates the important role of education of the people in the political life of the state. The wisdom of the ancients on governance is worth learning from, and the present generation should do even better than the ancients. Through various means, the party's scientific theories and the core socialist values advocated by the party should be "imparted" into the minds and hearts of the people, and turned into the basic principles, values and conscious actions of the entire party, so that the party's theories can truly become the ruling ideology, and unite and coalesce the whole society under the banner of the party's theories and cause. In the China of the new era, it is necessary to persistently arm the party, educate the people and guide work with Xi Jinping Thought on Socialism with Chinese Characteristics for a New Era, to strengthen people's confidence in the path, theory, system and culture of socialism with Chinese characteristics, and their confidence in obeying the party and following it.

It is necessary to be bold and adept in the ideological struggle and resolutely resist and oppose the corrosion and encroachment of various erroneous trends of thought. The party's leadership of ideology has been achieved in the struggle against erroneous trends of thought, and it has been consolidated and developed especially in the struggle against capitalist ideology. This struggle is not a question of whether socialist countries and the communist party want it or not but is determined by the basic orientation of capitalism to infiltrate and subvert socialism in every possible way and is not subject to the will of man. Against a background of material and technological conditions where capitalism has been strong and socialism weak for a long time, the communist party of a socialist country will be left with nothing if it gives up its ideological superiority and weapons of struggle, and must not harbour any naive ideas. The collapse of the CPSU, the disintegration of the Soviet Union and the political turmoil in China in 1989 were all caused by the competition between capitalism and socialism for the hearts and minds of the people. Since the end of the Cold War, Western hostile forces have always regarded China's development and growth as a threat to Western values and institutional models, and have been constantly carrying out ideological infiltration of China, vigorously promoting so-called "universal values", with the ultimate aim of overthrowing the leadership of the CPC and the Chinese socialist system. If this rhetoric is allowed to flourish, it will inevitably muddle up the hearts and minds of the party and the people, and even endanger the leadership of the party and the security of state power. In this regard, the CPC requires the entire party to enhance its situational awareness, enhance its proactiveness, take the initiative and fight proactively; if the party does not go out and occupy this position, then someone else will. In the process of carrying out this struggle, due to the complexity of issues in the field of ideology, there are issues of political tendencies, ideological understanding, as well as academic issues, which should be scientifically analysed, accurately grasped, differentiated between, and properly handled. With regard to academic issues, it is necessary to promote democracy, discuss matters on an equal footing and convince people with reasoning, so that research is not restricted and publicity is disciplined. With regard to issues of ideological understanding, it is necessary to strengthen positive publicity and education, and guide them in a targeted manner. With regard to major political principles and issues of right and wrong, it is necessary to be clear and firm, and not specious or ambiguous, let alone silent and voiceless. Of course, if socialism is to gain an advantage over capitalism and eliminate the ideological threat, it is ultimately necessary for it to develop itself materially and technologically, ideologically and materially, with the weapon of criticism and the criticism of the weapon; both are indispensable.

The principle of the party controlling the media must be upheld without wavering. Newspapers, journals, radio stations and news websites are important vehicles of ideology and keeping these tools of public opinion firmly in its hands is an important means for the communist party to achieve ideological leadership. Mao Zedong pointed out that, "Whenever a government is to be overthrown, public opinion must first be formed, and ideological work must first be done. This is true of the revolutionary class, and it is also true of the counter-revolutionary class"[12]. The seizure of power by the CPSU was directly linked to the acquisition of the instruments of public opinion, and Lenin said that the revolutionary uprising began with the seizure of post offices and telegraph offices. The loss of power by the CPSU was also directly linked to the loss of control over the instruments of public opinion. From the 1980s, many newspapers in the Soviet Union declared themselves "autonomous", taking the opportunity to free themselves from the shackles of the CPSU and the authorities. Some dissidents gradually took control of the main newspapers and other instruments of public opinion. All kinds of statements and articles attacking and abusing the CPSU and the socialist system were published, preparing public opinion for the overthrow of the CPSU and the Soviet Union. The CPC has always upheld the principle of party control of the media, and the principle of politicians running newspapers, magazines and websites, insisting that the media be the mouthpiece of the party. When errors in the political direction of individual media outlets are discovered, they are dealt with promptly and firmly, always ensuring that the tools of public opinion are firmly in the hands of the party. With the emergence and popularity of new media such as the internet, the party's principle of media control faces new challenges. The internet has connected the world as one entity, facilitating people's lives but also providing opportunities for various erroneous trends and arguments to become popular. The anti-communist and anti-China forces in the West advocate that "socialist countries will begin their journey into the embrace of the West by using the internet", in a bid to use the internet to "bring down China". The internet has become the main battleground in the struggle for public opinion. In this regard, Xi Jinping seriously pointed out, "If our party cannot overcome the hurdle of the internet and emerging media, it may not be able to overcome the hurdle of long-term governance." On the basis of advances in information technology, the party and the government have been focusing on the implementation of network content construction projects, strengthening management, and punishing illegal and criminal acts on the internet, and the confusing situation of internet thinking and management has been effectively resolved for a period of time.

It is necessary to attach great importance to the ideological work of schools, especially universities. Schools, especially universities, are an important venue for the production and dissemination of ideology and are inevitably a gathering place for various ideological trends, making the ideological situation complex. Many of the major incidents affecting political and ideological security within and outside China have started in universities and have gradually spread to all levels of society. In 1989, the political turmoil started with the student wave in universities. Young students represent the future, and the socialist cause will ultimately be in their hands. It is therefore necessary to firmly exercise the leadership of the communist party in the ideological work of schools and universities, which is a serious struggle for hearts and minds, for the future and for the next generation. It is necessary to uphold the direction of socialist schooling, the correct political direction of nurturing human resources, and to solve the fundamental issue surrounding the kind of people to train, how to train them, and for whom to train them. It is also necessary to attach importance to the role of the main channel and the main position of ideological and political theory education, and to give full play to the important role of teachers of professional courses in controlling ideological discourse. It is also necessary to integrate socialist core values into the whole process of running education and educating people in universities, and to guide teachers and students to be firm believers, active disseminators and exemplary practitioners of core socialist values. Schools should be built into a base for cultivating reliable successors to the socialist cause with both integrity and talent and comprehensive development.

It is necessary to attach great importance to work regarding intellectuals and conduct it effectively. Intellectuals are an important body which bears ideology. The party's scientific theories must be interpreted and disseminated by intellectuals, and the development of culture, art, philosophy and social science cannot be achieved without the creative work of intellectuals. However, it goes without saying that under the acute and complex conditions of the struggle in the field of ideology, some intellectuals may wander in their attitudes and even treat mainstream ideology with a critical attitude. In order to consolidate the governance position of the communist party, the issue of intellectuals must be dealt with properly. To a large extent, ideological work is work pertaining to intellectuals. Since the 18th CPC National Congress, Xi Jinping has put forward a major principal requirement for the unity and guidance of intellectuals on the basis of summing up both positive and negative experiences. On the one hand, it is necessary to always uphold the major political judgment of treating intellectuals as part of the working class, fully trust them, strengthen ties with them, support them in their work and ventures, allow human resources of both integrity and talent to play a role in important positions, and relaease their talents and energy to fully exercise them. On the other hand, we must strengthen political leadership and political absorption, and guide the majority of intellectuals to be firm in their ideals and beliefs, to be of one mind and one heart with the party, and to contribute to promoting national development and realising the Chinese dream. On the other hand, it is necessary to strengthen political leadership and political inclusion, guide the majority of intellectuals to be firm in their ideals and beliefs, to be united with the party, and to contribute to national development and the realisation of the Chinese dream. In terms of guidance, intellectuals from different fields and with different influences should be treated differently. For example, we should encourage experts and celebrities in the "red zone" and give full play to their positive role in guiding public opinion; for intellectuals in the "grey zone", we should fully respect them, listen to their opinions and suggestions, and have general knowledge of them, as well as prevent them from morphing into dissidents through thorough ideological and political work. For some in the "black zone" distribution points (mainly from occasional negative comments on the internet and within society), we should be brave enough to step in and push for changes, and for some individuals who break the law, it is necessary to be brave enough to take action and control them according to the law, and never let them go unchecked.

It is necessary to establish a sound institutional mechanism for leading ideological work. Ideological work is of a pragmatic nature, often "it is of primary importance to say it, secondary importance to do it, and when busy it does not get done". But once a problem occurs, it is a big problem, often unmanageable, even to the extent of endangering the political security of the party and the state. How to put ideological work into practice, do it right and do it well and effectively, is a matter of whether the party's leadership of ideological work can really be achieved. Since the 18th CPC National Congress, Xi Jinping has creatively put forward the requirement of implementing a system of responsibility for ideological work based on a summary of both positive and negative experiences within and outside China, pointing out a new path for solving the serious problems of ideological work. The general office of the CPC Central Committee issued the *Measures for the Implementation of Responsibility System for Party Committees' Ideological Work (Party Groups)* to make institutional provisions for ideological work in the form of party regulations. This is the first time this has been done in the history of socialism in the world and in the history of the party. This system requires party organisations at all levels to assume the main responsibility, that is, political responsibility and leadership, in terms of ideological awareness, responsibility and methodological measures, for strengthening the analysis and research, coordination and guidance, and promotion and implementation of ideological work. Publicity and ideology departments are to assume direct responsibility for strengthening the construction and management of their positions and take full responsibility for guarding the country; every department and front has the responsibility to actively participate. They are not to be sloppy in implementing tasks, slack in managing positions or ambiguous in accountability. Through the implementation of the responsibility system for ideological work and comprehensive measures, the once passive situation was reversed, and the party's leadership of ideological work has been strengthened.

As times develop and practice advances, the achievement and consolidation of leadership in ideological work is a historic issue to which the communist party needs to constantly provide new answers. In the great practice of long-term governance, especially in the great process of advancing governance since the 18th CPC National Congress, the Chinese communists have enriched the treasury of Marxist ideological theory with new ideas, new initiatives and new experiences, further consolidating the party's governance position and displaying the valuable spiritual ethos of the Chinese communists in the new era who dare to take charge, dare to take new paths, rise to difficulties and bravely explore.

10

THE PILLARS OF GOVERNANCE

BUILDING A STRONG ARMY AND A CONSOLIDATED NATIONAL DEFENCE COMMENSURATE WITH THE COUNTRY'S STATUS

Building a strong army is necessary for any ruling party to resist or carry out aggression externally and to consolidate power internally, and it is also a problem that any ruled class, invaded nation and its political party must face in order to seize power and fight for independence. The practice of proletarian parties from their birth onwards has shown that without a people's army, the people have nothing. The possession of a strong army and a consolidated national defence is the primary condition for the proletarian party to seize power and remain in governance in the long-term.

(I) THE PEOPLE'S ARMY IS THE COUNTRY'S GREAT WALL OF STEEL

The building of a strong revolutionary army is at the heart of Marxist military theory and a proletarian party cannot seize power and move on to the road of governance without a strong army of its own. Marx pointed out in his article *The Civil War in France*, that "In order to defend Paris, one cannot but arm its working class, organise them into a fighting military force, and temper their ranks in the war. But arming Paris was tantamount to arming the revolution. The victory of Paris over the Prussian invaders was tantamount to the victory of the French workers over the French capitalists and their state parasites"[1]. It was thanks to the "French National Self-Defence Army", made up of 300,000 Parisians, that the people of Paris won the armed uprising and founded the Paris Commune, which became the first prototype of proletarian power. The practice of the Paris Commune and the establishment of the revolutionary armies were considered by Marx to be a strong proof of the theory of communism. Lenin inherited and developed the ideas of Marx and Engels on arming the working class. He believed that the establishment of armed workers and peasants, and the armed seizure of power was an essential condition for the success of the Russian Revolution, and that "the Red Army was more important than anything else". In July 1905, Lenin published his article *Revolutionary Army and the Revolutionary Government*, emphasising that military work should be at the forefront of all work and stating that, "the revolutionary army is necessary because only by violence can the great historical problems be solved, and in modern struggles the organisation of violence means the organisation of the military"[2]. In 1916 Lenin published his article *The Military Programme of the Proletarian Revolution*, stating, "We say: to arm the proletariat in order to defeat, dispossess and disarm the bourgeoisie - this is the only viable strategy of the revolutionary class, a strategy prepared, laid down and taught by the whole objective development of capitalist militarism"[3]. These ideas of Lenin provided the guidelines for subsequent armed uprisings and military construction in Russia. It was only with a strong revolutionary army that the October Revolution was won. Without the Soviet Red Army, it would not have been possible to create the first socialist state in the world, Soviet Russia, and it would not have been possible to rapidly form a world socialist camp to counter the capitalist camp led by the US after the second world war. The rapid establishment of socialist states in Poland, Hungary, East Germany, Albania, Czechoslovakia, Bulgaria, Romania, Yugoslavia and North Korea after the second world war was also the result of the importance attached by the communist and workers' parties of these countries to building up their armed forces and the strength of their revolutionary armies, which fought for a long time with their blood. Of particular importance was the direct contribution of the Soviet Red Army to the defeat of the invaders and the important role it played in liberating these countries.

Any political party has to rely on its army to seize power as well as to consolidate it. Xi Jinping profoundly pointed out that it will never be possible for any country to be truly strong without strong military power to back it up[4]. Looking at the history of communist party governance, China offers the most valuable experience on which to draw. As a result of having such a strong army, the PLA has delivered a competent performance both internally and externally since the communist party came to power in China. On the external front, at the outset of the founding of new China, the PLA triumphantly fought the War of Resistance Against the US and Assistance to Korea. Thereafter, in the self-defence counter-attack on the Sino-Indian border in 1962, the self-defence counter-attack on Zhenbao Island in 1969, the self-defence counter-attack on the Xisha Islands in 1974 and the self-defence counter-attack against Vietnam in 1979, the PLA victoriously defended China's territorial integrity and the dignity of the motherland. Within China, the PLA has played a functional role in cracking down on separatist forces such as those proposing "the independence of Taiwan", "the independence of Tibet" and "the independence of Xinjiang", decisively quelling the Tibetan rebellion in 1959 and the political turmoil in 1989. Since 2008, the PLA has completed 31 overseas escort missions to the Gulf of Aden, safeguarding national stability and overseas interests. China has become one of the most secure countries in the world.

(II) THE NEED TO UPHOLD ABSOLUTE LEADERSHIP OF THE PARTY OVER THE ARMY

Upholding the absolute leadership of the party over the army is a major ideology of Marx and Engels' theory on the leadership of the army by a proletarian party. In March 1850, Marx and Engels profoundly pointed out in the *Address of the Central Committee to the Communist League*: "In order to resolutely and vigorously oppose this party which has been betraying the workers from the first hour of victory, the workers should be armed and organised. The entire proletariat must be armed at once with rifles, horse guns, artillery and ammunition ...... to form an independent corps under their own elected commanders or be formed into detachments of the proletarian household troops. Arms and ammunition shall not be handed over under any pretext and any attempt to disarm the workers shall be met with an armed response if necessary"[5]. This statement profoundly reveals the intrinsic relationship between building revolutionary arms, mastering the people's army and defending proletarian power.

This Marxist principle of military construction is the distinctive feature of the military theory of the proletarian party and the basic criterion for dealing with the relationship between the party and the army, which is fundamentally different from the "nationalisation of the army" advocated by the bourgeois party. The proletarian party achieved its governance position as a result of the party's leadership of the "iron army" and the people's long and bloody struggle, and the proletarian party's consolidation of its governance position is likewise inseparable from the defence and support of the army. Any communist party that abandons the party's leadership of the army will end up losing its governance position and burying the "red rivers and mountains" that were won with the lives and blood of countless revolutionary martyrs. Under the leadership of Lenin and the Bolshevik

Party, Soviet Russia created the Soviet Red Army and depending on this army won the October Revolution and established the world's first socialist state. This was followed by the successful patriotic war, which defeated fascist Germany and developed into the world's leading military power after the second world war. But in the 1980s, when CPSU leader Mikhail Gorbachev introduced "new thinking", it created ideological chaos within the army so that when the Soviet Union was facing collapse, this powerful army ignored the central government's orders and accepted the collapse of the Soviet Union without firing a single shot. This was the case in the Soviet Union and in several former socialist countries in Eastern Europe where drastic changes occurred, and these communist and workers' parties likewise lost power. The lessons of the dramatic changes in the Soviet Union since the 1980s show that advocating "nationalisation of the army", "de-partyisation of the army" and "de-politicisation of the army" is fundamentally a major means for Western capitalist countries to pursue a strategy of peaceful evolution against countries ruled by proletarian parties. Its fundamental aim is to change the political system of socialist countries where a communist party is in power into a Western multiparty system by spreading the fallacy that the army is the army of the state, that it is not accountable to any party and that it does not accept the leadership and command of any party. This is something that any ruling communist party must be wary of and guard against.

At present, socialist countries such as China, Vietnam, North Korea, Cuba and Laos, where a communist party is in power, all adhere to the principle of the party's leadership of the army. In particular, the CPC has learnt a profound lesson from the history of the First United Front when, in the face of the crisis of division caused by the new rightists led by Chiang Kai-shek who were ready to betray the revolution, Chen Duxiu and the then CPC Central Committee adopted a compromising and concessionary approach towards the KMT and prevented the KMT from drifting to the right at the expense of giving up the leadership of the proletariat. As a result, when Chiang Kai-shek launched the 12 April 1927 counter-revolutionary coup, the CPC was caught unawares, and a large number of communists and revolutionary masses fell under the enemy's butcher's knife. The Chinese communists thereby realised that in the past they had "never seriously thought about the problem of arming the workers and peasants, of the need to arm them, or of creating a truly revolutionary workers' and peasants' army" and had made the serious mistake of "not conducting a military movement but a popular movement". From this they concluded that "it is from the barrel of a gun that power is gained"[6]. On the basis of the lessons learnt from the failure of the revolution, the 7 August 1927 conference established the general guidelines for agrarian revolution and armed resistance against the KMT reactionaries. From then on, the CPC took the path to armed revolution to seize power in China, marked by the launching of the Nanchang Uprising, which began the formation of the communist party's army. After becoming the ruling party in 1949, the CPC continually explored and developed the rules for upholding absolute leadership of the party over the army. First, the CPC persisted with building up the army politically, making ideological and political construction the primary task of military and national defence construction, and guiding the officers and soldiers to build up a firm foundation of faith, to unwaveringly obey the party, to follow the party and to obey the party's commands unconditionally. Second, it established and improved the system of the party's leadership of the army, implemented the CMC Chairman responsibility system, with the supreme leadership and command of the army belonging to the CPC Central Committee and the CMC, implemented the system of party committees, political committees and political organs, with the party establishing party committees, political committees and political organs in regiments and units equivalent to regiments and above, implemented the system of the division of responsibilities among senior officials under the unified collective leadership of the party committees, and implemented the building of branches in companies. Third, the CPC upheld ruling the army strictly and disciplining the entire army with iron discipline. It is precisely from a political and ideological point of view that the officers and soldiers of the entire army are of the same mind and direction as the Party Central Committee and the CMC, and that the fundamental principle and system of the party in commanding the gun is put into practice through iron discipline, so that the Chinese PLA has been under the absolute leadership of the party since the day it was established. Although there have been some individual "vermin" within the party and the military, they have stood the test in the face of the struggle against Zhang Guotao's splitting of the party and the Red Army, and the conspiracy of Lin Biao and Jiang Qing's counter-revolutionary clique to usurp the supreme leadership of the party and the state, as well as the political turmoil of 1989. The facts have proven that "the party commands the gun" is the eternal soul of the army, which is why the CPC added the word "absolute" to the Marxist proposition of the party leading the army. This is the conclusion of history.

(III) UPHOLDING THE VITALITY OF THE PEOPLE'S ARMY LIES IN ITS COMBAT EFFECTIVENESS

The army exists because of war and develops with the practice of war. Combat effectiveness is the "litmus test" of the entire value of the army's existence and development. Under the conditions of communist party governance, the criterion of combat effectiveness has become the ruling party's fundamental requirement for the armed forces. Only when an army is able to win battles can it fulfil its functions and tasks, safeguard the security of the country, protect the stability of the regime, prevent invasion by foreign enemies, and create a happy and peaceful life for the people. Only when you can fight can you stop war, only when you are prepared to fight will you not need to, and only when you have strong combat effectiveness can you deter the enemy, and reduce and prevent war. This is the dialectic of war. Such is the case with the armed forces of the US, which was founded over 200 years ago and has not had a war on its soil except when it challenged Britain to a war of independence, such is the deterrent effect of its military might. The same is true of Russia's armed forces. Although the country's power has been greatly weakened since the collapse of the Soviet Union, its military power remains and its strength cannot be underestimated, and no country dares to have designs on its territory. Conversely, if the military is not strong enough then there can be no talk of seizing power and the power it already holds can be challenged. China's greatest failure in becoming a semi-colonial and semi-feudal society after 1840 was a military failure. Numerous lessons have shown that the vitality of an army lies in its combat effectiveness, and that the most important rule of the ruling party in governing the army is to master the rule of improving its combat effectiveness.

Improving the combat effectiveness of the army and building an invincible and powerful army is a goal that any army persistently pursues. Among the communist-ruled socialist countries in the world today, China's PLA is the most powerful people's army. The most significant experience in the generation of its combat effectiveness is the importance attached to both the important role of weapons and equipment in winning or losing wars and the decisive role of people in wars - the key being the combination of men and weapons. During the war years, this revolutionary army, with its small strength and poor weaponry, relied primarily on strong political work to effectively inspire the officers and men of the army to firmly establish the fighting spirit of fighting for the poor and not being afraid of hardship, suffering, bloodshed and sacrifice. Second, it relied on the scientific guidance of warfare, and correct strategy and tactics as an important winning factor.

As early as between 1928 and 1930, Mao Zedong explored the correct path of the Chinese revolution by encircling cities from the countryside and seizing power with armed force, and put forward the "Sixteen Characters" of guidelines on guerrilla warfare: "When the enemy advances, I retreat; when the enemy encamps, I interfere; when the enemy wearies, I fight; when the enemy retreats, I pursue". This principle of warfare was further developed during the War of Resistance Against Japan and the National Liberation War. During the Liberation War, he also put forward 10 military principles. Scientific warfare guidance and the fighting spirit of the soldiers made up for the lack of weapons and equipment, thereby enabling the army to be invincible, to overcome the strong with the weak, and the many with the few, and to go from victory to victory, defeating the KMT reactionaries and the invincible Japanese invaders. At the outset of the founding of new China, the Chinese People's Volunteers once again defeated the UN forces led by the US, equipped with advanced weapons such as aircraft and artillery, with "millet and rifles" in the face of blatant provocation by the US imperialists on the Korean peninsula.

There are different standards in different times for building a people's army that is strong in combat and capable of winning battles. In today's world, with the widespread use of information technology in the military field, war theory, forms and styles have undergone profound changes; with the in-depth development of economic globalisation, the interests of socialist countries ruled by communist parties have been extended from domestic contexts to foreign countries, and the functional mission of people's armies has been expanded from simply safeguarding national security interests to safeguarding multiple aspects including the country's economic and diplomatic interests, and national security. The standard necessary for being able to win battles has also become more demanding. Since the Gulf War in the early 1990s, China's PLA under the leadership of the CPC has realised that "the essence of high-tech warfare is information-based warfare, and information-based warfare will become the basic form of warfare in the 21st century. It is necessary to clearly place the foundation of preparation for military struggle on winning local wars in the context of information technology"[7]. It proposed to study the characteristics of modern technology, especially local wars in the context of high-tech realities, formulated strategic military policies for the new period for winning local wars in the context of high-tech realities, and developed some regular understanding and approaches through extensive research on the characteristics and laws of military governance in the new period throughout the army.

The first approach has been to take the path of developing elite troops. The army has been able to reduce the number of posts, cut military expenditure, upholding an approach of doing what needs to be done but refraining from what is not important, focus on winning local wars in the context of information technology, and concentrate on preparing for military struggle. China carried out substantial disarmament in 1985, 1997, 2003 and 2012, gradually forming a situation in which defence construction and economic construction develop in a coordinated manner.

The second approach has been to persist in building the army for the way battles are fought. Deng Xiaoping proposed the general goal of building a strong, modernised and formalised revolutionary army. Then Jiang Zemin proposed the general requirement of five phases for military construction, namely, being politically compliant, militarily masterful, strictly disciplined, having an excellent work style and providing robust protection. Hu Jintao further proposed the idea of strengthening the overall construction of the army according to the principle of unification of revolutionisation, modernisation and formalisation. Then Xi Jinping proposed the goal of having a strong military, building a people's army that obeys the party's commands, can win battles and has an excellent work style, striving to basically modernise national defence and the army by 2035 and build the people's army into a world-class army by the middle of this century.

The third approach has been to deepen military reform. In response to the new trend of the acceleration of the evolution of warfare, the new nature of China's development from enlarging to strengthening, and the new requirements of the expansion of the army's mission and tasks, the party has pushed forward in-depth reform of the army's leadership system, force structure, policies and systems, forming a setup in which the military commission is in overall charge, theatre commands are in charge of battles, and the military services are in charge of construction. The change from four headquarters to 15 functional departments transformed the organs of the military commission into advisory, executive and service bodies, reorganising and dividing the seven military regions into five major theatre commands and establishing the missile force and strategic support force.

The fourth approach has been the scientific implementation of military training because training must be conducted for actual battles. In peacetime, there are fewer and fewer opportunities to practice actual combat, and the effective way to enhance combat effectiveness is through training, exercises and the execution of urgent, difficult and dangerous tasks. China's PLA regularly organises military exercises and parades on the days of major festivals, and effectively carries out major tasks such as safeguarding maritime rights, anti-terrorist activities to maintain stability, international peacekeeping operations, escort duties in the Gulf of Aden, and humanitarian relief. Its troops engage in stability maintenance and emergency response exercises, and disaster relief and foreign military exchanges to continuously improve the army's level of competence for actual combat.

(IV) CORRECTLY HANDLING THE RELATIONSHIP BETWEEN MILITARY AND DEFENCE CONSTRUCTION, AND ECONOMIC CONSTRUCTION

National defence construction and economic construction are important aspects of national construction, like the "two axles of a car" and the "two wings of a bird". Properly handling the relationship between national defence construction and economic construction is a fundamental prerequisite for building a strong national defence and providing a strong security guarantee for economic construction. Throughout history, the strength of a country has always been backed by a strong national defence force. If a country's military strength is not strong, its security will be threatened and there is no way to even talk about economic construction. This is the context in which "North and South Korea" and "East and West Germany" emerged after the second world war. This is also the case with the recent war in Afghanistan, the US military raid on Syria and the ongoing conflict between Russia and Ukraine. History has also repeatedly proven that building a strong national defence must be based on the country's actual capabilities and practical needs. Behind a strong military and national defence force is strong economic backing. Even in the case of the world's great powers, if the investment in national defence exceeds the country's capacity for a long time, this heavy economic burden will overwhelm the country. In the Cold War with the US, the Soviet Union continued to expand its military spending in order to compete with the US for world dominance and national defence dragged down the country's economy and caused social unrest, ultimately leading to the death of the party and the country.

Both positive and negative facts show that it is not desirable to attach no importance to national defence construction or to place it in an inappropriate position. Judging from historical experience, among the socialist countries ruled by communist parties, China has been relatively successful in handling the relationship between military and national defence construction, and economic construction. Its main experience has been that it is necessary to build a strong army and a consolidated national defence that are commensurate with socioeconomic development and with the status of the country. This strong army and consolidated national defence means coordinating the layout of economic construction and national defence construction in the context of the overall situation of the party and the state, focusing on economic construction, providing security for socioeconomic development by building the army and national defence, and developing the army and national defence simultaneously in the process of economic development. After the founding of new China, at the first meeting of the National Defence Council on 18 October 1954 Mao Zedong said that, "the task ahead is to unite, train our army and people, and gradually build a modernised revolutionary army" and "China is a big country and needs to have a strong army, navy and air force. With a coastline as long as ours, we must build a strong navy"[8]. He also added that, "We will have not only a strong army but a strong air force and a strong navy"[9]. After decades of efforts, China's military power has been greatly strengthened. After the new period of reform and opening up, in the context of giving priority to economic development and during which "the army will have to wait and be patient", the army made important contributions to defer and serve the overall situation of national modernisation. Since then, with the further development of reform and opening up, and socialist modernisation, and with the changing global and regional security situation, especially the Gulf War, the dramatic changes in the Soviet Union and Eastern Europe, the Kosovo War, the Afghan War, the Taiwan Strait Crisis, the US raid on China's embassy in Yugoslavia, the Hainan Island incident and other local wars and major incidents, and after becoming the second-largest country in the world in terms of economic output, the CPC saw that the essence and extension of China's security, the spatial and temporal domains, and China's domestic and external factors were all undergoing profound changes, and that the core of building a strong national defence meant implementing a strategy of integrated military-civilian development. This was the only way to correctly handle the relationship between economic construction and national defence construction. The CPC organically integrated military and national defence construction into the system of socioeconomic development, transformed limited social resources into two-way interactive productivity and combat effectiveness, used civilian resources in peacetime and military resources in wartime, and built an integrated national strategic system capability. From the practice of the CPC over the past 70 years of its rule, the implementation of the strategy of integrated civilian-military development has done a good job of solving the issues of the army having more soldiers in peacetime, heavy burdens, ineffective use of national defence resources and weak mobilisation capacity in wartime, and has successfully achieved the transition between peacetime and wartime.

11

EXTERNAL CONDITIONS FOR GOVERNANCE

BUILDING INTERNATIONAL RELATIONS MARKED BY MUTUAL RESPECT AND MUTUALLY BENEFICIAL COOPERATION

The external conditions of governance refer to the objective social historical conditions under which the ruling party governs and are the sum of the various factors that determine the survival and development of the ruling party and affect the functioning of its governance. It is an important basis for the governance philosophy, strategies and tactics, and measures adopted by the ruling party, which in different ways govern the ruling party's governance behaviour and affect its effectiveness in governance. Good external conditions can provide the ruling party with rich resources for governing, which is conducive to improving the ruling party's governance ability and consolidating its governance position. However, poor external conditions can consume a lot of the ruling party's energy, increase the cost of governance, be detrimental to the construction of governance ability, and even endanger its ruling position. At present, as the ruling party of China, the CPC is facing extremely profound changes in the external conditions of governance and a series of serious challenges. The international financial crisis has had far-reaching effects, uncertainties and instability in global economic growth have increased, and the imbalance in global development has intensified. Geopolitical factors have become more prominent, regional instability is on the rise, hegemonism, power politics and new interventionism are on the rise, non-traditional security and global challenges are on the rise, and there is still a long way to go to safeguard world peace and promote common development. Xi Jinping pointed out that, "to keep pace with the times, we cannot be physically in the 21st century while our heads are still stuck in the past, in the old days of colonial expansion, in the old framework of Cold-War thinking and zero-sum games"[1]. The CPC has always maintained that all countries are equal, regardless of their size, strength or level of affluence, that there should be no bullying of the small by the large or the weak by the strong, or suppression of the poor by the rich and that there can be no distinction between so-called sovereign and vassal states, and core and peripheral states. In the face of the deepening of global multipolarity, economic globalisation and the continued advancement of cultural diversification and social informatisation, mankind today is in a better position than ever before to move toward the goal of peace and development, and mutually beneficial cooperation is a realistic way to achieve this goal. Therefore, in order to create good external conditions for the CPC to govern, it is necessary to build international relationships marked by mutual respect and mutually beneficial cooperation.

(I) UPHOLDING INDEPENDENCE AND AUTONOMY

Independence and autonomy underpin the construction of international relations marked by mutual respect and mutually beneficial cooperation. If a country or nation is to uphold its independence and autonomy, it will be able to decide its own destiny and establish mutually respectful international relations with other countries. This is the minimum requirement and condition for a country or nation to stand on its own feet; if a country or nation endures aggression and oppression by foreign nations, it will not be able to independently and autonomously handle its own internal affairs, nor will it be able to establish and develop cooperative relations with other countries on an equal footing and for mutual benefit.

Independence and autonomy are the prerequisites and foundations of the proletarian party's approach to interparty and international relations. Engels pointed out that, "international alliances can only exist between states, and consequently the existence of these states, their autonomy and independence in their internal affairs, is included in the very concept of internationalism"[2]. We advocate both "Proletarians of the world, unite!" but also insist that "the international movement of the proletariat is in any case only possible within the framework of independent nations". National independence is as essential a foundation as "soil, air, light and land" for the proletariat of all nationalities to achieve a genuine international alliance in the struggle against the domination of capitalism. Without national independence, all forms of international cooperation are impossible. When Lenin spoke of the unity and solidarity of the national proletariat and its parties, he stressed that such unity did not require the elimination of diversity and the abolition of national differences. He pointed out that, "it is inevitable that all nationalities will go toward socialism but all nationalities will not go in exactly the same way" and that "each nation will have its own characteristics"[3]. Therefore, it is up to the proletariat and the political parties in each country to make a judgment together on the path a country should choose, taking into account the specific circumstances of the country, rather than following a uniform model. Independence is a historical logic derived from China's bitter experience of being invaded and oppressed for over 100 years. From the invasion by foreign capitalists in 1840, feudal China gradually become a semi-colonial and semi-feudal country. The imperialist powers forced the Qing government, the northern warlords and the KMT government to sign many unequal treaties, ceding land, making reparations, opening up ports to commerce, agreeing on tariffs and consular decisions, and also establishing factories, developing mines, setting up banks, building railways and handling shipping and air transport in China. In this way, they gradually controlled and manipulated not only China's financial and economic lifelines but also its political and military power, depriving China of its autonomy and national sovereignty. Although China maintained formal independence or some independence, in reality it had become a semi-colonial, semi-feudal society. The cruel exploitation and oppression of imperialism, feudalism and bureaucratic capitalism were like three great mountains pressing down on the Chinese people, plunging the general public into the abyss of misery. The Chinese people struggled heroically wave after wave for national liberation, national independence and democratic freedom.

Independence is the inevitable conclusion of the CPC's reliance on the strength of the party and the people to implement revolution, construction and reform in the light of Chinese realities. During the period of the new democratic revolution, the party adhered to the principle of independence and autonomy in its dealings with friendly political parties, and on the basis of lessons learned, successfully put into practice the sinicisation of Marxism, effectively solved and removed the setbacks and fetters caused to the Chinese revolution by the dogmatisation of Comintern resolutions and the Soviet experience, and explored and walked along a development path suitable for the Chinese revolution. After the founding of new China, Mao Zedong pointed out that, "the Chinese people must make their own decisions and handle their own affairs, and not allow any more interference at all from any imperialist country"[4]. In the light of the critical situation facing the Chinese people and with their fundamental interests as the point of departure, the Party Central Committee adopted the three major

698

foreign policies of "starting from scratch", "cleaning the house before inviting guests" and "unconditional support", proposed and adhered to the Five Principles of Peaceful Coexistence, and rejected the Soviet Union's proposal to establish a long-wave radio station and a joint fleet under the joint administration of China and the Soviet Union on Chinese territory and in Chinese territorial waters, thereby safeguarding China's national interests and maintaining the independent and autonomous status of new China's diplomacy. After the 3rd Plenary Session of the 11th CPC Central Committee, the CPC made significant adjustments to its domestic and foreign policies. The party shifted the focus of its work to economic construction and made the significant decision to reform and open up, and, in line with this, established a foreign policy characterised by independence and non-alignment. Deng Xiaoping pointed out that, "China's affairs should be run according to China's situation and relying on the strength of the Chinese people themselves. Independence and self-reliance have been, are and will be, our standpoints"[5]. Over the past 40 years of reform and opening up, the party has highly cherished and steadfastly safeguarded the right of the Chinese people to independence and autonomy, which they have earned through long-term struggle, and upheld the basic national policy of opening up to the outside world, always examined the development of China and the world from the perspective of the interconnectedness of the international and domestic situations, considered and formulated a development strategy for China, adhered to an independent and peaceful foreign policy, and promoted the establishment of international relations marked by mutual respect and mutually beneficial cooperation.

Independence is not only the basis of all the party's theories and practices but also the fundamental guarantee for the party and the people to continue to move from victory to victory. At all times and under all circumstances, it is necessary to firmly grasp independence as the basis for the establishment and prosperity of the party and state. The core of upholding independence is to deeply understand and effectively implement the "Three Insistences" proposed by Xi Jinping. This "upholding independence means insisting that the Chinese people make their own decisions and handle their own affairs" and "upholding independence means unswervingly following the path of socialism with Chinese characteristics, neither taking the old path of closure and rigidity nor the evil path of turning away from socialism" and "upholding independence means upholding an independent and peaceful foreign policy, and unswervingly following the path of peaceful development"[6]. General Secretary Xi Jinping's important statement on independence constitutes both a profound understanding and grasp of the Marxist concept of social development and the doctrine of the state, and also a profound summary of the party's experience in leading the people in implementing revolution, construction and reform. The most important thing in upholding independence is to unswervingly follow the path of socialism with Chinese characteristics. There is no specific development model that is universally applicable in the world, nor is there an unchanging development path. After decades of independent and painstaking struggle the CPC has finally found a way to revitalise and strengthen the party and the state, which is the road of socialism with Chinese characteristics. This path, while focusing on economic construction, also comprehensively promotes economic, political, cultural, social, ecocivilisation and all other aspects of construction, not only upholds the Four Cardinal Principles but also reform and opening up, not only constantly liberates and develops social productivity but also gradually achieves common prosperity for the people as a whole and promotes all-round human development. The most important aspect of upholding independence is upholding an independent and peaceful foreign policy and taking the path of peaceful development. The party is determined to safeguard China's national sovereignty, security and development interests, not believing in evil or afraid of ghosts, and will never yield to any external pressure. Since the outset of reform and opening up, our nation and our country have stood tall in the East with our political and theoretical courage to "follow our own path and build socialism with Chinese characteristics", and brought about historic changes in the features of the Chinese people, socialist China and the CPC. The most essential aspect of upholding independence is to develop ourselves better through opening up to the outside world. We persist in pursuing a mutually beneficial and win-win opening-up strategy, promoting strong, sustainable and balanced growth in the world economy through deepening cooperation, and sharing the dividends of economic globalisation with all countries in the world. We rely on our own strength but also try to unite the people of all nations as much as we can and make use of all the international strength we can to better develop and prosper China.

(II) FOLLOWING THE PATH OF PEACEFUL DEVELOPMENT

China's pursuit of a peaceful development path is not a matter of expediency, let alone diplomatic rhetoric but a conclusion drawn from an objective judgment of history, reality and the future, and an organic unity of cultural self-confidence and practical consciousness. China's self-confidence and consciousness in taking the path of peaceful development comes from the profound origins of Chinese civilisation, from its knowledge of the conditions for achieving China's development goals, and from its grasp of the general trend of world development. In the development of civilisation over 5,000 years, the Chinese nation has always pursued and inherited a firm philosophy of peace, harmony and concord. The concepts and traditions of peace, kindness to others and "do unto others as you would have them do unto you" have been handed down in China from generation to generation and are deeply rooted in the spirit and embodied in the actions of the Chinese people. The Chinese people were invaded and bullied by the great powers for a long time but what the Chinese people have learnt from this is not the robber-baron logic of preying on the weak but a stronger determination to maintain peace. The most valuable legacy left by the victory of the Chinese People's War of Resistance Against Japanese Aggression and the World Anti-Fascist War is that we must unwaveringly follow the path of peaceful development.

China's path of peaceful development has been gradually developed through painstaking exploration and continuous practice since the founding of new China, especially since the outset of reform and opening up. The history of more than 40 years of reform and opening up has proven that peaceful development is a strategic choice made by China based on its own national conditions, social system and cultural traditions, which is in line with the trend of the times and in line with China's fundamental interests, those of neighbouring countries and those of all countries in the world, and there is no reason to change it. Over the past few years, as China has continued to develop, some people in the world have become suspicious of China's direction, fearing that it will pose a threat if it grows stronger. This is a misunderstanding. It is not in the Chinese people's genes to invade others or to dominate the world. The Chinese people, who have experienced hardships, cherish peace and will never impose their own tragic experiences on other peoples. The Chinese people do not subscribe to the archaic logic that "a strong nation must be hegemonic" and are willing to live in harmony with all peoples of the world, develop in harmony, and seek, protect and share peace together.

China's peaceful development is an opportunity for the world. China's unswerving pursuit of the path of peaceful development will be beneficial to China and also to the world. As its national strength continues to grow, China will further play its role as a responsible power, assume more international responsibilities and obligations within its capacity, and make greater contributions to the noble cause of human peace and development. Achieving the Chinese dream of the great rejuvenation of the Chinese nation is the common aspiration of China's sons and daughters in China and abroad, and will also bring more benefits and opportunities to the people of all nations. The Chinese dream is a dream of peace and upholding peaceful development, not only committed to China's own development but also emphasising China's responsibility and contribution to the world. Achieving the Chinese dream will bring peace and not turmoil to the world; it is an opportunity not a threat and it will benefit not only the Chinese people, but also the people of the whole world. In the process of achieving the Chinese dream, China will work together with the rest of the world to promote the better accomplishment of the dreams of all peoples.

(III) RESOLUTELY SAFEGUARDING NATIONAL AND ETHNIC INTERESTS

Resolutely safeguarding national and ethnic interests is the bottom line for China to follow the path of peaceful development and advocate mutually beneficial cooperation. Xi Jinping pointed out, "We must adhere to the path of peaceful development but we must not give up our legitimate rights and we must not sacrifice our core national interests. No foreign country should expect us to trade our core interests or swallow the bitter fruit of damaging our sovereignty, security and development interests"[7]. Safeguarding national and ethnic interests constitutes the most fundamental aspiration and goal of a great nation's diplomacy. Historically, it has been a consistent goal of new China's diplomacy to build a harmonious and symbiotic international order on the basis of safeguarding national and ethnic interests, and to follow a harmonious and symbiotic path of development together with other countries.

Marxists have made many important theoretical statements and practical explorations in the defence of the interests of nations and ethnic groups. Marx once pointed out that, "whatever nations do as nations is what they do for human society, and their whole value lies simply in the fact that each nation fulfils for other nations one of the main missions (the main aspect) from which mankind has experienced its own development"[8]. After the triumph of the October Revolution in Russia, Lenin's initiative to introduce a system of concessions in the Soviet state, the loans secured at the Genoa Conference and the signing of the Treaty of Rapallo with Germany are all examples of his efforts to safeguard the interests of the state and the nation.

Since its birth as the core political force driving China toward modernisation, the ideology and practice of the CPC has always revolved around fighting for and defending China's national and ethnic interests. After the Opium Wars, the signing of a series of treaties resulting in the forfeiting of China's sovereignty and in China's humiliation, and the endless cession of land and reparations caused serious violations of, and challenges to, the interests of the Chinese nation and people. Faced with the ill-fated destiny of the "extinction of the nation" and being "divided and conquered", various political forces fought hard and struggled tragically and heroically to contend for and defend China's national and ethnic interests but all of them failed at the last hurdle due to the limitations of their own class and factors unique to each era. Since its inception, the CPC has undertaken the historical mission of fighting for and safeguarding China's national and ethnic interests, from eliminating warlordism to uniting domestic forces, to opposing imperialist aggression to fighting for national sovereignty for the survival of the nation, and then to building a strong modern socialist state whereby achieving the great rejuvenation of the Chinese nation has always been the CPC's central task. In the 70 years since the founding of new China, China's position on safeguarding national independence and sovereignty and defending national dignity has been consistent. If China dared to defend its national interests and oppose world power decades ago when it was backward both economically and culturally, and never bent its back or bowed its head under external pressure, then now that China has grown stronger, it is even less likely to succumb to any external pressure. Some people describe China's defence of reasonable and legitimate national rights and interests as "aggressive", "arrogant" and "unyielding", and advocate the "China threat" but such arguments are groundless.

In order to safeguard China's national and ethnic interests, it is necessary to always take the resolute defence of national sovereignty, security and development interests as the start and end point. Safeguarding one's territorial sovereignty, and legitimate and reasonable maritime rights and interests is a responsibility that the national government must assume. It must insist on resolving disputes by peaceful means and negotiations but also be prepared to deal with various complex situations. At the international level, we will resolutely curb the destructive activities of separatist forces such as those advocating for the independence of Taiwan, the independence of Tibet and the independence of East Turkistan, and prevent the infiltration of violent international terrorist activities into China and safeguard national sovereignty and security. It will not shy away from contradictions and problems and will properly handle differences and frictions with the countries concerned while promoting exchange and cooperation in various fields, expanding the convergence of common interests through cooperation, and maintaining relations with neighbouring countries and the overall situation of regional peace and stability. China's peaceful development will not be smooth. We do not provoke trouble but are also not afraid of trouble. On issues involving China's core interests, we must dare to draw a red line and make our bottom line clear. As the process of China's peaceful development continues to unfold, there will be more and more resources and means to safeguard China's national interests, and the position of safeguarding national interests will become more and more active. China's sovereignty, security, development interests and national dignity will never permit violation by any force, while no force can shake our belief in upholding peaceful development.

(IV) PROMOTING THE ESTABLISHMENT OF A NEW TYPE OF POLITICAL PARTY RELATIONSHIP SEEKING COMMON GROUND WHILE RESERVING DIFFERENCES, AND ENCOURAGING MUTUAL RESPECT AND LEARNING

Party politics is the basic *modus operandi* of modern politics. For a long time, the issue of how different types of political parties get along with each other has not been well resolved due to inconsistent ideologies, value orientations and policy choices, and political polarisation has also emerged in many countries as a result. In his keynote speech entitled *Working Together to Build a Better World* at the opening ceremony of the 2017 High-level Dialogue between the CPC and World Political Parties, Xi Jinping proposed that political parties of different countries should enhance mutual trust, strengthen communication and work closely together, and that a new type of political party relationship based on exploring new types of international relations should be established that seeks common ground while reserving differences, and encourages mutual respect and learning from one another. This initiative elevates the CPC's theory of interparty relations to a brand-new level in accordance with the new requirements of the new era, reflecting both the CPC's new outlook on the times, global outlook and outlook on political parties, and the CPC's profound grasp and accurate positioning of its own historical mission.

Historically, the establishment of a new type of interparty relations has been a consistent idea of the CPC in developing interparty relations with the outside world and promoting party diplomacy. In the late 1970s, the Chinese communists, mainly represented by Comrade Deng Xiaoping, made a major judgment that peace and development were the themes of the times and put forward the idea of establishing new interparty relations with various political parties. In the early 1980s, in response to the question of how to handle the relationship between the CPC and other political parties in the world, the party established the four principles of interparty relations, namely, "independence, full equality, mutual respect and non-interference in each other's internal affairs", on the basis of a profound summary of the lessons learned from both positive and negative aspects. Since then, the theoretical essence and scope of application of these four principles have continued to evolve, and they have become the basic principles that the party has long followed in conducting interparty relations. Under the guidance of these theories, the CPC has experienced a breakthrough in the development of party diplomacy, promoting relations between countries through interparty relations. To date, the CPC has established and developed interparty relations with more than 600 different political parties around the world, forming a new pattern of all-round, multi-level and broad-field party diplomacy. The new type of party relations is consistent with the spirit and logic of the four principles of interparty relations, and constitutes an enrichment and improvement of the four principles of interparty relations. It not only inherits the latter's ideological core of "mutual respect" but also focuses on mutual learning and appreciation, which embodies a spirit of openness, tolerance and mutually beneficial cooperation, based on the reality that all countries are interconnected, interdependent and interwoven, and goes beyond the bilateral scope of the CPC and other political parties to provide the "CPC's solutions" and public products for exchange and cooperation among all political parties.

The establishment of a new type of political party relationship based on seeking common ground while reserving differences, mutual respect and mutual learning provides a fundamental guideline for political party exchanges and cooperation in the new era. Seeking common ground while reserving differences means transcending differences and divergences in philosophy, ethnicity, culture, beliefs and geography, and striving to find the greatest common denominator. Mutual respect means insisting that political parties are equal regardless of their size, refraining from interfering in each other's internal affairs, respecting each other's interests and concerns, and respecting each other's way of thinking and choice of path. Mutual learning means everyone has something to learn from everyone else and through exchange complementing each other's strengths and making progress together without imposing one's will and views on others or exporting one's own systems and model, while also not demanding others copy one's practices. In this regard, seeking common ground while reserving differences is the premise, mutual respect is the key, and mutual learning and appreciation are the aim. These three complement each other and are organically unified, and working together to build a community with a shared future for mankind and building a better world are the guiding principle and guidelines for handling relations between political parties.

Xi Jinping pointed out that, "there should be dialogue between civilisations, not rejection; there should be exchange, not replacment. The history of mankind is a magnificent picture of civilisations conducting exchange, learning from each other and integrating". It should be said that political parties around the world are representatives of both a particular ideology and a certain form of civilisation. Therefore, the CPC should constantly optimise the composition of its international work, carry out in-depth exchanges with political parties of various countries, share its experience in governing the party and China, conduct exchanges and dialogue on civilisation, and enhance mutual strategic trust. To carefully build up the institutionalised platform of the high-level dialogue between the CPC and the world's political parties, it is necessary to strive to build a network of international political party exchanges and cooperation in many forms and at many levels, and together with political parties and people around the world, make new and greater contributions to promoting the building of a community with a shared future for mankind and join hands to build a better world.

12

THE SELF-CONSTRUCTION OF THE RULING PARTY

THE NEED TO BE BOLD IN SELF-REVOLUTION

The self-construction of the communist party itself is closely linked to the historical tasks it undertakes, and the development of the times and practice always present new requirements for party building. The construction of the ruling party is closely linked to the task of governing the party and the state, and so it is of great significance to uphold the Marxist worldview and methodology to guide the construction of the ruling party and to scientifically summarise the laws of building the ruling party, in order to strengthen the construction of the party's progressiveness and purity, and improve its governance ability.

(I) STRENGTHENING SELF-CONSTRUCTION IS A PROJECT TO STRENGTHEN THE FOUNDATIONS OF COMMUNIST PARTY GOVERNANCE

It is of great significance for the communist party to strengthen its own construction for the sake of governance. In order to become a party which is truly influential and has fighting strength, all political parties must undertake and constantly strengthen their own construction. By taking control of state power, the ruling party elevates the will of its class into being the will of the state and becomes the leading force in the country. Marxist parties have lofty revolutionary ideals, and from the perspective of the historical development process of world socialism, political direction is the first issue for the survival and development of the party and pertains to the future prospects of the party and the success or failure of its cause.

One of the prominent features of a Marxist party maintaining its progressiveness lies in its ability to accurately grasp national conditions, the state of the world and the party, as well as the characteristics and development trends of the times. It links the exploration of the nature of socialism and the appropriate way to construct it with the questions of the kind of party which should be built and how to build it, so that party building is in line with the requirements of the historical mission the party shoulders and always maintains the correct direction of advancement. The cause that the proletarian party is engaged in is to eradicate the system of human exploitation that has been in place for thousands of years, and the highest ideal and ultimate goal of the party is to achieve communism, which is an immensely noble yet extremely difficult and great cause.

The theory of building a ruling party is an important part of the Marxist theoretical system. Marx and Engels were the founders of the doctrine of the proletarian party and gave theoretical answers to such major issues as the nature, aims, programmes, strategies and historical missions of the proletarian party. In the course of leading the building of the Bolshevik Party in Russia, Lenin conducted theoretical and practical explorations on how to strengthen party building. With the victory of the October Revolution, the Bolshevik Party became the first ruling proletarian party in the world. The status of the ruling party put forward the tasks of managing the state, leading economic construction and consolidating power, all of which required the party to strengthen its own construction in the course of practice. Lenin pointed out that the Marxist party was the only guarantee of the victory of socialism, and that any weakening of the party could lead to the restoration of capitalism. The party in power must be good at purifying its ranks[1]. It was due to the importance and strengthening of the communist party itself that Lenin led the Russian Bolshevik Party with only a few hundred thousand members to gain victory in the October Revolution, established Soviet power, gained victory over domestic counter-revolutionary rebellion and foreign armed intervention, achieved rapid recovery and development of the post-war economy, socialist construction, the establishment of the USSR and the further consolidation of proletarian power. In the late 1980s and early 1990s, the collapse of the Soviet Union and the dramatic changes in Eastern Europe plunged world socialism to a low ebb. Although there were many reasons for the collapse of the Soviet Union, the peaceful evolution of hostile forces abroad could not but be an important factor. But the main problem should be found within the CPSU itself. Starting with Khrushchev, the leadership of the party was gradually weakened and there was serious corruption within the party. Under Mikhail Gorbachev, the so-called "new thinking" was introduced, the party was westernised, there was a lack of democracy within the party, the party building was weak, it let go of the guiding position of Marxism, was severely detached from the masses, the party culture was corrupt, and corruption was widespread, the leadership of the party was not strong enough, and the leadership of the communist party was revised out of the constitution. This was a major cause of the demise of the Soviet Union and the party.

The collapse of the Soviet Union and the dramatic changes in Eastern Europe do not mean that socialism has failed, let alone that capitalism is superior to socialism. However, the dramatic changes in the Soviet Union and Eastern Europe have taught us with painful historical facts that the communist party, as the ruling party, must strengthen its own construction, constantly improve its long-term governance ability, and always maintain its progressiveness and purity. Only then can it always be at the forefront of the times and withstand all kinds of storms. Historical experience shows that the key to the success or failure of the socialist cause and the rise or fall of a socialist country lies in the party and in building up the communist party itself.

Party building is a highly effective methodology of the CPC. The party has always attached importance to party building, and it has always been a highly effective methodology for the success of the party's cause, whether in the periods of revolution, construction or reform. An important reason why the CPC has developed into a Marxist party in long-term governance with more than 90 million members and a population of more than 1.4 billion people, and why it has been able to endure hardships and difficulties without weakening, growing stronger as it fights harder, and creating countless brilliant achievements, is that the party has always upheld the management of the party and its comprehensive and strict rule, and has always focused on strengthening its own construction.

The leadership of the CPC is the most essential feature of socialism with Chinese characteristics and the greatest advantage of the socialist system with Chinese characteristics. Overcoming the risks and challenges on the road ahead depends fundamentally on the leadership of the party.

In order for the party to play a strong leading role, it must strengthen and improve its leadership, just as Xi Jinping emphasised that, "iron must harden itself". Only when the party is strong can its cause flourish and develop, the country prosper and stabilise, and the people be happy and well.

The party has united and led the people of all China's ethnic groups to complete the new democratic revolution, which led to national independence and liberation, to complete the socialist revolution, which established the basic socialist system and made great achievements in socialist construction, and to implement the new great revolution of reform and opening up, which created, upheld and developed socialism with Chinese characteristics. However, the development of the CPC has not been smooth and uneventful. At different periods of its history, the party has suffered setbacks. During the new democratic revolution, the party suffered two major setbacks. One was the failure of the revolution, and the other was the failure of the fifth anti-surge campaign [by the KMT to encircle and annihilate the communists]. During the period of socialist revolution and construction, the party also suffered two major setbacks. One was the launching of the Great Leap Forward and the implementation of the people's communes in the countryside, and the other was the Cultural Revolution. But with a spirit of courageous self-revolution, the party has faced up to problems, corrected mistakes and constantly risen from setbacks. The history of the party shows that there are many reasons why the CPC has been able to lead the Chinese people to overcome one obstacle after another, to mature in overcoming difficulties and to move from victory to victory, but one of the most fundamental reasons is that the CPC has been able to attach great importance to, and constantly strengthen, its own construction in the light of ever-changing realities, and to constantly correct its mistakes while upholding the truth. This is the fundamental guarantee of the party's perpetual vitality and vigour.

Promoting a great social revolution with the party's great self-revolution; according to Marx, revolution is the locomotive of history and a powerful factor in social and political progress. Xi Jinping pointed out that if we are not to forget our original aspirations and are to remember our mission, we must not forget that we are communists, that we are revolutionaries, and that we must not lose our revolutionary spirit. In the new era, the party must use its self-revolution to drive the great social revolution that the party is leading the people to implement. Achieving the great rejuvenation of the Chinese nation is the greatest dream of the Chinese nation since modern times. Since its birth, the CPC has been firmly charged with the historical mission of achieving the great rejuvenation of the Chinese nation. Today, in the 21st century, we are closer to, more confident in, and more capable of achieving this than at any other time in history. The key to running China well lies with the party. Without the leadership of the CPC, national rejuvenation is bound to be an empty dream. Only by continuously carrying out a great self-revolution is it possible to uphold and develop socialism with Chinese characteristics in the new era. As a Marxist ruling party, in order to successfully implement the great social revolution of upholding and developing socialism with

Chinese characteristics in the new era, the party must be brave enough to carry out a self-revolution, dare to face problems head-on, dare to wield the knife inwardly, dare to implement through treatment to get to the root of the matter, eliminate all factors that undermine the party's advancement and purity, and all viruses that erode the healthy body of the party, and ensure that the party remains permanently vibrant with powerful fighting strength. In order to be courageous in self-revolution, we must not forget our original aspirations and we must remember our mission. Practice has proven, and will continue to prove, that the CPC is capable of leading its people in a great social revolution and also in a great self-revolution. The party has no special interests of its own except the interests of the country, the nation and the people. As long as it always maintains its revolutionary spirit, implements the great self-revolution to the utmost, and likewise leads the people to carry out the great social revolution to the utmost, the Chinese dream of the great rejuvenation of the Chinese nation will certainly be achieved and the great ideals of communism are certain to be achieved!

(II) COMPREHENSIVELY PROMOTING PARTY BUILDING WITH POLITICAL CONSTRUCTION IN COMMAND

Putting political construction in commandi; it is a fundamental requirement of a Marxist party to be political. Lenin pointed out that a class cannot maintain its rule and therefore cannot solve its productive tasks if it does not deal with problems politically and correctly. The CPC has always attached great importance to the political construction of the party. The first generation of the party's central leadership with Comrade Mao Zedong at its core clearly proposed to strengthen party building in close connection with the party's political line. Mao Zedong pointed out that the core of party buildingwas the formulation and implementation of the party's political line, and that the party relied on the correctness of its political line to achieve correct leadership. The second generation of the party's central leadership, with Comrade Deng Xiaoping at its core, proposed to build the party into a strong core to lead socialist modernisation, that the party's leadership is mainly political, ideological, and organisational leadership, and that political leadership is the core essence of the party's leadership and the most fundamental aspect of leadership, determining the correct direction of ideological and organisational leadership. Deng Xiaoping pointed out that "politics must be taught at all times", stressing that the political leadership of the party should ensure the correct political direction. The third generation of the party's central leadership with

Comrade Jiang Zemin at its core, carried out education on party spirit and ethics with the main essence being "talking about learning, politics and righteousness". Jiang Zemin pointed out that politics is the core, and only by being political is it possible to maintain the correct direction of development. The Party Central Committee, with Comrade Hu Jintao as General Secretary launched a partywide educational campaign to maintain the progressiveness of communist party members, with the study and practice of the major ideology of the Three Represents as its main content. Hu Jintao has repeatedly stressed that all party comrades, especially leading cadres at all levels, should be political, take care of the overall situation and abide by discipline. Since the 18th CPC National Congress, the Party Central Committee with Comrade Xi Jinping at its core has promoted strict party governance across the board, put political construction in the first place and strictly defined the party's political discipline and political rules. Xi Jinping pointed out that politics is the fundamental guarantee for the party to strengthen its bones and body, and is the fundamental way for the party to cultivate the courage for self-revolution, enhance its ability to purify itself and improve its political immunity through detoxification and disinfection. The report of the 19th CPC National Congress clearly propounded putting the political construction of the party in command, comprehensively promoted the party's political, ideological, organisational, work style and discipline construction, with institutional construction running throughout, intensively promoting the fight against corruption, and constantly improving the quality of party building. This constitutes a major theoretical innovation, reflecting the strong determination and responsibility of the Party Central Committee with Comrade Xi Jinping at its core to uphold the management and governance of the party, raising the party's understanding of political construction to a new level. Political attributes are the first and foremost attributes of political parties. In the party's system of construction, political construction is the fundamental aspect of party building and determines the direction and effect of party building. If political construction is not kept as the root, other aspects of construction such as ideological construction will lose their support or even their direction, making it difficult to achieve the desired results.

Ideological construction is the fundamental aspect of party building. The emphasis on ideological construction is a distinctive feature of the Marxist doctrine of party building. Marx proposed that "once theory has mastered the masses, it becomes material power". Lenin pointed out that without revolutionary theories, there would be no strong socialist party, no revolutionary movement, and only a party guided by advanced theories can accomplish the role of advanced fighters. Mao Zedong's ideology of party building put the ideological construction of the party in the first place and focused on building the party based on ideology. During the democratic revolutionary period, due to the social environment and organisational composition of the party, various non-proletarian ideas were reflected in great quantity within the party. How to use proletarian ideology to guide party building became a major issue concerning the fate of the party and the success or failure of the revolutionary cause. Mao Zedong pointed out that, "mastering ideological education is the central link in uniting the whole party in the great political struggle"[2]. The Gutian Conference held in 1929 decided to use proletarian ideology to implement the construction of the army and the party, and the Yan'an Rectification Movement of 1942 was a great practice to comprehensively promote party building, starting from ideological construction. The Seventh CPC National Congress clearly emphasised the need to put ideological education and leadership at the forefront of the party's leadership. Since the 3rd Plenary Session of the 11th CPC Central Committee, the party has advanced the great new project of party building, revived the party's ideological line of seeking truth from facts, continuously promoted theoretical innovation based on practice, and continuously raised the level of Marxist ideology and theory of the entire party. Since the 18th CPC National Congress, the party Central Committee with Comrade Xi Jinping at its core has been steadfast in comprehensively and strictly ruling the party, closely integrating the ideological construction and institutional governance of the party, making ideological construction a fundamental aspect of construction, building the foundation of ideals and beliefs of party members and cadres, replenishing the party's spiritual "calcium", and solving the issue of the "main switch" of world view, outlook on life and values, resulting in great progress and results in the ideological construction of the party.

Organisational construction guarantees that the party will always maintain its organisational strength. Marx and Engels pointed out that a working-class party is not an accidental amalgamation of individual people but an organised political group and a tightly-knit bastion of combat, and that the effectiveness of the leadership of a proletarian party depends on a democratic and tightly-knit system of party organisation. The CPC is a tightly organised system formed under the guidance of Marxism in accordance with democratic centralism as a unified whole which strives to achieve a common goal. The party attaches great importance to organisational work. Since the founding of the party, its organisation has been continuously innovated in line with the party's mission and the developments of the times, thereby adapting to the needs of the Chinese revolution, construction and reform. The party's organisation is a three-dimensional structure from the central leadership to the local level, and its ability to form a strong force relies on party members' loyalty and obedience to the party organisation. This is the concept of organisation that every party member must possess and strengthen. Xi Jinping stressed that the strength of the party comes from the organisation. The accomplishment of the party's overall leadership and all of the party's work depends on a strong organisational system. The Party Central Committee is the brain and the nerve centre, and it must definitely have the ultimate authority. The fundamental task of the party's local organisations is to ensure that the decisions and arrangements of the Party Central Committee are implemented, that orders are carried out and that prohibitions are enforced. The party focuses on establishing and improving grassroots party organisations at all levels, constantly expanding the scope of party organisations, giving full play to their role as bastions of combat and exemplary leaders, enabling the effective implementation of all the party's guidelines and policies, and powerfully ensuring the healthy development of various undertakings. This is the successful experience of the party possessing strength. In contrast with this, the CPSU ended up with a lack of strength and disorganisation in the party, and its failure was also a salutary lesson.

The construction of the party's work style determines the party's mass base and the question of style is essentially a question of the relationship between the party and the people. Lenin considered detachment from the masses to be one of the most serious and terrible dangers. Close contact with the masses is one of the fine traditions and work styles of the CPC, and this is the distinctive mark of the CPC that distinguishes it from other political parties. With its excellent work style, the party has won the support and backing of the people, and has withstood severe tests time and again. Since the outset of reform and opening up, in the face of changes in the situation and tasks, the party has raised the issue of work style to "a matter of life and death for the party" and has successively made decisions on several major issues related to strengthening the party's ties with the people, strengthening the construction of the party's governance ability, and strengthening and improving party building under the new situation, all of which emphasises the importance of close contact with the masses and strengthening the construction of the party's work style. Since the 18th CPC National Congress, the Party Central Committee with Comrade Xi Jinping at its core has firmly grasped in its hands the strengthening of the party's work style, starting with implementation of the Eight-point Regulation and the fight against the "Four Malfeasances" [of going through the motions, excess bureaucracy, self-indulgence and extravagance], grasping these with an absolutely firm grip. As a result, the party's work style has improved significantly and has led to a change in the sociopolitical climate, winning the trust of the people and enhancing the party's prestige among the masses. However, as Xi Jinping has emphasised, there is never a time to rest in the construction of work style, and it is a perpetual and ongoing process. The communist party's focus on the construction of work style must be long-term, persistent and unremitting.

Discipline is the ultimate solution for the comprehensive strict governance of the party and is another unique advantage of Marxist parties. Marx and Engels firmly emphasised the extreme importance of party discipline for the proletarian party and the cause led by the party. Lenin believed that extremely strict discipline in the party was one of the basic conditions for victory over the bourgeoisie and the consolidation of proletarian power. To deny party spirit and party discipline means serving the bourgeoisie and completely disarming the proletariat[3]. The CPC is a Marxist party organised on revolutionary ideals and iron discipline, and strengthening discipline has always been a part of the whole process of carrying out China's revolution, construction and reform throughout its history. The strengthening of discipline has always been given great importance since its birth, with the Fifth CPC National Congress first establishing a discipline inspection and supervision body, which has since changed with the adjustment of the institutional set-up but has always retained the special department responsible for examining party discipline. In the face of the destruction of the party's organisation during the Cultural Revolution and the disorganisation and indiscipline of many party members, the 3rd Plenary Session of the 11th CPC Central Committee made a point of restoring the party's body for discipline inspection. Since then, the party has continued to build discipline, providing a strong guarantee for the smooth implementation of reform and opening up, and socialist modernisation. Since the 18th CPC National Congress, the Party Central Committee with Comrade Xi Jinping at its core has continued to deepen its understanding of the laws of party management and governance, and has been persistent in correcting culture and purifying discipline with a strong sense of historical responsibility, resulting in an overwhelming momentum in the struggle against corruption and continuous consolidation. The 19th CPC National Congress incorporated the construction of discipline into the general composition of party building, enriched and refined the content of discipline in the party constitution, and promoted and achieved a major innovation in the theory of party building.

(III) STRENGTHENING THE CONSTRUCTION OF THE CADRE RANKS AND NURTURING SUCCESSORS TO THE PARTY'S CAUSE

Strengthening the construction of the ranks of cadres is an important element in the construction of the proletarian party. Engels clearly proposed that party cadres should possess a certain level of theoretical knowledge, practical experience and loyalty to the party cause. Lenin pointed out that without professional revolutionaries and competent cadres, it would always be difficult for things to advance, and some orders and resolutions would be nothing but dirty scraps of paper[4]. For a proletarian party to lead the cause of revolution and construction to victory, it must not only have a correct political and ideological line but also a large number of outstanding cadres who are adapted to the needs of the party's development.

Cadres are the backbone of the cause of the party and the state. The ranks of cadres of the ruling Marxist party are the makers and implementers of the party's programme, line, guidelines and policy, and the organisers and practitioners of governance. Mao Zedong pointed out that, "after the political line has been determined, the cadres are the deciding factor"[5]. Party cadres are directly responsible for leading and organising the implementation of the party's line, guidelines and policies on all fronts, and constitute the link between the party and the masses, a bridge to propagate, mobilise, organise and lead the masses in their struggle for the party's cause. Without the ranks of strong cadres, the party will not be able to successfully lead the people to achieve the party's various tasks. The CPC has always attached great importance to the construction of its ranks of cadres and has focused on training and nurturing millions of successors to the revolutionary cause of the proletariat. One very important reason why the CPC has always maintained strong creativity, cohesion and fighting strength, become the mainstay of the development of the cause of the revolution, construction and reform, united and led the people to overcome all kinds of difficulties and obstacles, and achieved victory after victory, is that it attaches great importance to the cultivation of ranks of cadres capable of taking on weighty responsibilities.

In order for the party to unite and lead the Chinese people to achieve the struggle goals of the Two Centenaries and achieve the Chinese dream of the great rejuvenation of the Chinese nation, it is necessary to create ranks of loyal, incorrupt and responsible, high-quality cadres. History and reality have shown that the ability of a political party or a country to continuously produce outstanding leaders determines to a large extent the rise and fall of that party or country. Youth is the hope and future of the country. Socialism with Chinese characteristics is a future-oriented cause that requires generations of aspiring young people to continue to strive for it. Xi Jinping pointed out that the training and selection of outstanding young cadres is a project of vital and lasting importance that concerns the fate of the party, of China, the nation and the well-being of the people. The grassroots organisation of the party is the organisational foundation of the party's governance. If the foundation is not firm, the ground itself will be shaken. The party's grassroots organisations are rooted in the people and serve them directly. They are the window through which the people get to know and understand the party, and also an important channel through which the party understands the wishes of the people and listens to their voice. The party's line, guidelines and policy can only be implemented among the people through the party's grassroots organisations. It is necessary to fully and deeply understand and grasp the importance of strengthening the construction of grassroots party organisations, unswervingly implement the leadership of the party in all aspects of the grassroots, and constantly enhance the political and ideological leadership, mass organisation and social appeal of grassroots party organisations. It is necessary to improve the ability of grassroots cadres to develop the economy, reform and innovate, act in accordance with the law, resolve conflicts and lead the masses, and make grassroots party organisations a bastion of combat for propagating the party's position, implementing its decisions, leading grassroots governance and uniting and mobilising the masses.

(IV) STRENGTHENING CONSTRUCTION OF THE SUPERVISORY SYSTEM

Strengthening supervision is an important element in the communist party's management and governance of the party and the country. When summarising the experience of the Paris Commune, Marx and Engels proposed that the right to supervise and remove state officials is the key to ensuring the sovereignty of the people and preventing state organs and public officials from changing from "social servants" into "social masters"[6]. Lenin led the CPR to establish a special body for internal supervision of the ruling proletarian party, creating a more complete system of internal party supervision. The CPC has always attached importance to strengthening the construction of a monitoring system and has accumulated fruitful theoretical results and practical experience in its long-term practice of leading revolution, construction and reform, and has also established a series of rules and regulations.

Communist parties are subject to supervision. Power without supervision inevitably leads to corruption, and absolute power leads to absolute corruption. Corruption, as a concomitant of private ownership, is fundamentally incompatible with the nature and purpose of the communist party. The proletarian party is a new type of political party, and the power that the party has gained by leading the people is for the purposes of serving them. If the problem of supervision is not solved and corruption arises, the proletarian party and government will also degenerate. Engels pointed out that when a party was built in the midst of a bourgeois encirclement, the bourgeoisie was bound to try desperately to influence the communist party with its own ideology and way of life. With the development of the proletarian revolutionary cause and the growth of the party's ranks, a large number of small producers and other people of non-proletarian origin would enter the party, and some of them wanted to influence and transform the party with petty-bourgeois ideology, eroding the party's body and corrupting its ethos. The corrupt social atmosphere and the vulgarity of some other degenerate classes would also appear within the party. It can be argued that until the communist party's supreme programme is achieved, corruption will exist as long as there is an exploiting class and its ideology in the world. The status of a ruling Marxist party exposes the party to various tests. Under conditions of governance, when mistakes are made, they have the greatest impact and cost, and are the most difficult to redress. It is therefore essential to restrain and regulate the operation of power through effective supervision to ensure that supervision extends to wherever power is exercised. Only in this way can the state power established by the communist party in unity with the people be constantly consolidated and the sovereignty of the people be guaranteed, and the power conferred by the people always be used for the benefit of the people.

The party's internal supervision is the primary aspect of supervision. During the various periods of its long history of revolution, construction and reform, the CPC has constantly strengthened its supervision and formed a system of monitoring with Chinese characteristics. This system includes intraparty supervision, supervision of the NPC, democratic supervision, judicial supervision, audit supervision, social supervision, supervision of public opinion, and so on. These forms of supervision have played an important role in the course of historical development and under practical conditions. However, because the CPC is the ruling party, this determines that intraparty supervision is the most basic and primary among the various forms of supervision of the party and the state. Practice shows that if intraparty supervision is lacking, other supervision is also bound to fail. Only when the party's self-supervision is strong, and the party gives full play to its leadership role can it give full play to the role of other forms of supervision and form a supervisory synergy. The task of the party's intraparty supervision is to ensure that the party's constitution, regulations and discipline are effectively implemented throughout the party, to maintain the unity of the party, to focus on solving the problems of weakened party leadership, lack of party building, ineffective comprehensive strict party governance, apathy towards the concept of the party, disorganisation, lax discipline, lax party management and governance, in order to ensure that the party's organisation fully performs its functions and plays a central role, to ensure that all party members play a pioneering role, to ensure that the party's leading cadres are loyal, incorrupt and responsible. Democratic supervision by party members is a basic form of intraparty supervision which is the source of life that keeps the party's body healthy.

Supervision must be carried out in accordance with rules and regulations, and the law. All modern states have to address the issue of the rule of law, and a socialist state governed by a communist party is no exception. The rule of law is an essential requirement and important guarantee for upholding and developing socialism with Chinese characteristics and an inevitable requirement for modernising the national system of governance and governance ability. In comprehensively promoting the rule of law, the CPC emphasises the need to strengthen the institutionalisation, standardisation and proceduralisation of state governance, and to govern the country on the basis of the constitution and the law. As for the construction of the CPC itself, it is also necessary to manage and govern the party on the basis of the party constitution, discipline and regulations. In terms of the relationship between the ruling party and the laws of the country, the party leads the people in formulating laws through legal procedures and the party must operate within the confines of the law. As a party organisation and a party member, one must not only abide by party discipline but also abide by the law in an exemplary manner.

Strengthening the construction of the supervisory system leads to the formation of a supervisory synergy. To strengthen the constraints on, and supervision of, the operation of power, a scientific and effective supervisory system for the operation of power must be formed, and the supervisory synergy must be enhanced. The party has continued to explore and refine its intraparty supervision in practice. Since the 18th CPC National Congress, the Party Central Committee with Comrade Xi Jinping at its core has together comprehensively advanced the institutional reform of party building, promoted reform of the party's system of disciplinary inspection, reform of the national supervisory system, and reform of the system of discipline inspection and supervision, forming a complete supervisory system that unifies the party's discipline inspection and state supervisory systems. Both intraparty supervision and state supervision are thereby strengthened. Through the establishment of the NSC, supervisory and monitoring powers are exercised on behalf of the party and the state, performing the two duties of discipline inspection and supervision, and achieving full coverage of supervision of all public officials with public powers. This strengthens the supervision of party inspections and is a top-down supervisory system designed to achieve full coverage of inspections during one term of the party congress through regular and special inspections, giving full play to the role of the sharp sword of inspection. With regard to implementing full coverage of discipline inspection and supervision in party and government organs, and units in enterprises and institutions, in-station supervision is an integral part of the party's discipline inspection and specialised supervision of state supervision with the authority to "dispatch" and the advantage of being "stationed". It extends the antenna of supervision to the fore, fully giving play to the role of "probing" and "advance guard", thereby enabling the party and state to form a unified power-monitoring structure with full coverage of monitoring, stationing and supervision.

EPILOGUE

This is the final research result of 2015MZD059, a major project of the Marxist Theory Research & Construction Project and the National Social Science Foundation, entitled *Research on the Communist Party's Governance Law*.

Since the official launch of the project in October 2015, under the leadership of Qu Qingshan, the chief expert and former director of the Party History Research Office of the CPC Central Committee and Vice President (at full ministerial level) of the Institute of Party History and Literature of the CPC Central Committee in charge of daily work, the subject group has focused on the topic of studying the communist party's governance law. Taking the new frontier of understanding the communist party's governance law, namely Xi Jinping Thought on Socialism with Chinese Characteristics for a New Era, and the spirit of the series of major speeches by General Secretary Xi Jinping as important directions for research, it has composed a series of thematic reports and research articles, and published its research outcomes in stages, including *New Frontiers in Understanding Communist Party Governance Law* and *New Frontiers in Understanding Communist Party Governance Law (Part 2)*, which has been fully affirmed and highly evaluated by leading comrades of the central government and widely praised by social science theoretical circles, providing inspirational reference for governance and education.

The final research results of this project are guided by Marxism-Leninism and Mao Zedong Thought, Deng Xiaoping Theory, the major ideology of the Three Represents, the Scientific Outlook on Development and Xi Jinping Thought on Socialism with Chinese Characteristics for a New Era, and adhere to the principles of integrating theory and practice, history and reality, and the unity of history and logic. A multi-dimensional study of the communist party's governance law has been conducted and valuable research results have been obtained.

The comrades who participated in the research culminating in the final research results of this project come mainly from the Institute of Party History and Literature of the CPC Central Committee and the National Defence University. They undertook the task of researching this topic in addition to their own work. The specific division of labour was as follows:

General introduction: Wang Quanchun and Zhang Guo;

Part I: Fan Xiaochun;

Part II: Mu Zhaoyong, Chen Yajie, Xing Heming and Li Jian'an;

Part III: Liu Ronggang, Wen Shifang, Sun Di and Zhang Xiaofei;

Part IV: Huang Yibing and Yan Maoxu;

Conclusion: Basic Issues of Communist Party Governance Law: Qu Qingshan (vi, viii), Huang Yibing (i, iv, vii, xi), Wang Xiangkun (ii, iii, x), Qi Biao (v, ix) and Shan Wei (xii).

Lead expert, Qu Qingshan, provided guidance on designing and writing the project framework, and consolidated and finalised all the research results. Qi Biao, the expert who presided over the general work, assisted the chief expert in many specific tasks and undertook the first draft of most of the manuscript. Wang Quanchun, Mu Zhaoyong, Liu Ronggang and Huang Yibing made revisions to their assigned parts. Shan Wei and Dong Ying undertook the liaison work and part of the editorial work.

During the research process, the Bureau of Theory of the Publicity Department of the CPC Central Committee, the Office of the Marxist Theoretical Research and Construction Project, and the National Planning Office for Philosophy and Social Sciences gave specific guidance and assistance. The People's Publishing House gave strong support. We would like to express our sincere thanks to them all!

Due to the wide range of topics covered in the study and the limited time available, the final results may have many shortcomings, and we look forward to future revisions and improvements. Your valuable comments are welcome.

The Research Group on Communist Party Governance Law, CPC Central Committee Party History and Documentation Research Institute, March 2019

NOTES

1. THE INITIAL MARXIST REVELATION OF THE LAWS OF PROLETARIAN PARTIES IN POWER

1. *Complete Works of Lenin* Vol. 6, People's Publishing House, 2013 edition, p121
2. Norio Okazawa, *Political Parties*, translated by Geng Xiaoman. Economic Daily Publishing House, 1991 edition, p4
3. *Collected Works of Marx and Engels* Vol. 5, People's Publishing House, 2009 edition, pp743-744
4. *Selected Works of Marx and Engels* Vol. 3, People's Publishing House, 2012 edition, pp8, 6
5. *Collected Works of Marx and Engels* Vol. 7, People's Publishing House 2009 Edition, p278
6. *Selected Works of Marx and Engels* Vol. 1, People's Publishing House, 2012 edition, p180
7. *Selected Works of Marx and Engels* Vol. 3, People's Publishing House, 2012 edition, p779
8. *Selected Works of Mao Zedong* Vol. 4, People's Publishing House, 1991 edition, p1470
9. *Selected Works of Marx and Engels* Vol. 1, People's Publishing House, 2012 edition, pp861-862
10. L.S. Stavrianos: *Global History - The World After 1500*, translated by Wu Xiangying and Liang Chimin, Shanghai Academy of Social Sciences Press, 1999 edition, pp363-364
11. *Complete Works of Marx and Engels* Vol. 47, People's Publishing House, 2004 edition, p63
12. *Selected Works of Marx and Engels* Vol. 3, People's Publishing House, 2012 edition, p768
13. H. E. Sigerist: *Working for Humanity - A Narrative of Marx's Life*, translated by Luo Zhanglong, China Social Sciences Press, 1981, p30
14. *Selected Works of Marx and Engels* Vol. 4, People's Publishing House, 2012 edition, p203
15. *Selected Works of Marx and Engels* Vol. 1, People's Publishing House, 2012 edition, p413
16. *Complete Works of Marx and Engels* Vol. 10, People's Publishing House, 1998 edition, p744
17. *Complete Works of Marx and Engels* Vol. 10, People's Publishing House, 1998 edition, pp744-746
18. *Collected Works of Marx and Engels* Vol. 10, People's Publishing House, 2009 edition, p423
19. *Selected Works of Marx and Engels* Vol. 4, People's Publishing House, 2012 edition, p207
20. *Selected Works of Marx and Engels* Vol. 4, People's Publishing House, 2012 edition, p207
21. *Selected Works of Marx and Engels* Vol. 1, People's Publishing House, 2012 edition, p413
22. *Selected Works of Marx and Engels* Vol. 3, People's Publishing House, 2012 edition, p355
23. *Selected Works of Marx and Engels* Vol. 3, People's Publishing House, 2012 edition, p350
24. *Selected Works of Marx and Engels* Vol. 1, People's Publishing House, 2012 edition, pp413, 435
25. *Selected Works of Marx and Engels* Vol. 1, People's Publishing House, 2012 edition, pp421-422
26. *Selected Works of Marx and Engels* Vol. 1, People's Publishing House, 2012 edition, p413
27. *Selected Works of Marx and Engels* Vol. 1, People's Publishing House, 2012 edition, p413
28. *Selected Works of Marx and Engels* Vol. 1, People's Publishing House, 2012 edition, p435
29. *Selected Works of Lenin* Vol. 2, People's Publishing House, 2012 edition, p305
30. *Selected Works of Marx and Engels*, Vol. 1, People's Publishing House, 2012 edition, pp554, 558
31. *Selected Works of Marx and Engels* Vol. 1, People's Publishing House, 2012 edition, p557
32. *Selected Works of Marx and Engels* Vol. 1, People's Publishing House, 2012 edition, p532
33. *Selected Works of Marx and Engels* Vol. 1, People's Publishing House, 2012 edition, p769
34. *Selected Works of Marx and Engels* Vol. 1, People's Publishing House, 2012 edition, p541
35. *Complete Works of Marx and Engels* Vol. 7, People's Publishing House, 1959 edition, p514
36. *Selected Works of Marx and Engels* Vol. 3, People's Publishing House, 2012 edition, pp6, 10
37. *Selected Works of Marx and Engels* Vol. 3, People's Publishing House, 2012 edition, p171

38. *Selected Works of Marx and Engels* Vol. 3, People's Publishing House, 2012 edition, p11
39. Bakunin: *National System and Anarchy*, translated by Ma Xiangcong and others, Commercial Press, 1982, p35
40. Bakunin: *God and Country*, translated by Piao Ying, East China Normal University Press, 2005 edition, p4
41. Bakunin: *National System and Anarchy*, translated by Ma Xiangcong and others, Commercial Press, 1982 edition, pp192, 193
42. Zhang Wenhuan, *Several Issues in the Study of the First International History (Continued)*, Contemporary World and Socialism, Issue no. 1, 1983
43. *Selected Works of Marx and Engels* Vol. 3, People's Publishing House, 2012 edition, p95
44. *Complete Works of Marx and Engels* Vol. 10, People's Publishing House, 2009 edition, p367
45. *Selected Works of Marx and Engels* Vol. 3, People's Publishing House, 2012 edition, pp367-368
46. Zhang Wenhuan: *Several Issues in the Study of the First International History (Continued)*, Contemporary World and Socialism, Issue no. 1, 1983
47. *Complete Works of Marx and Engels* Vol. 25, People's Publishing House, 2001 edition, p170
48. *Selected Works of Marx and Engels* Vol. 3, People's Publishing House, 2012 edition, p173
49. *Selected Works of Marx and Engels* Vol. 3, People's Publishing House, 2012 edition, p40
50. *Selected Works of Marx and Engels* Vol. 3, People's Publishing House, 2012 edition, p373
51. *Selected Works of Marx and Engels* Vol. 3, People's Publishing House, 2012 edition, pp98-99
52. *Selected Works of Marx and Engels* Vol. 3, People's Publishing House, 2012 edition, p98
53. *Selected Works of Marx and Engels* Vol. 3, People's Publishing House, 2012 edition, p102
54. *Selected Works of Marx and Engels* Vol. 3, People's Publishing House, 2012 edition, p98
55. *Collected Works of Marx & Engels* Vol. 3, People's Publishing House, 2009 edition, p1006
56. *Selected Works of Marx and Engels* Vol. 3, People's Publishing House, 2012 edition, p98
57. *Selected Works of Marx and Engels* Vol. 3, People's Publishing House, 2012 edition, p277
58. *Selected Works of Marx and Engels* Vol. 4, People's Publishing House, 2012 edition, p500
59. *Selected Works of Marx and Engels* Vol. 3, People's Publishing House, 2012 edition, pp276, 277
60. *Selected Works of Lenin* Vol. 2, People's Publishing House, 2012 edition, p417
61. *Selected Works of Marx and Engels* Vol. 3, People's Publishing House, 2012 edition, p40
62. *Selected Works of Marx and Engels* Vol. 4, People's Publishing House, 2012 edition, p388
63. *Selected Works of Marx and Engels* Vol. 4, People's Publishing House, 2012 edition, p395
64. *Complete Works of Marx and Engels* Vol. 36, People's Publishing House, 1975 edition, p425
65. *Selected Works of Marx and Engels* Vol. 4, People's Publishing House, 2012 Edition, p588
66. *Selected Works of Marx and Engels* Vol. 4, People's Publishing House, 2012 edition, p281
67. *Complete Works of Marx and Engels* Vol. 38, People's Publishing House, 1972, pp72-73
68. *Complete Works of Marx and Engels* Vol. 34, People's Publishing House, 1972, p90
69. *Complete Works of Marx and Engels* Vol. 39, People's Publishing House, 1974 edition, p185
70. *Selected Works of Marx and Engels* Vol. 10, People's Publishing House, 2009 edition, p481
71. *Selected Works of Marx and Engels* Vol. 1, People's Publishing House, 2012 edition, p11
72. *Complete Works of Marx and Engels* Vol. 47, People's Publishing House, 2004 edition, p64

2. THE SOVIET COMMUNIST PARTY'S INITIAL EXPLORATION OF THE LAWS OF COMMUNIST GOVERNANCE UNDER LENIN

1. See Nosov, editor-in-chief: *A Brief History of the Soviet Union* Vol. 1, translated by the Department of Foreign Languages of Wuhan University, SDX Joint Publishing Company, 1977, pp351, 398
2. *Complete Works of Lenin* Vol. 6, People's Publishing House, 1986 edition, p76
3. *Selected Works of Lenin* Vol. 1, People's Publishing House, 2012 edition, p143
4. *Selected Works of Lenin* Vol. 1, People's Publishing House, 2012 edition, p312
5. *The Complete Works of Lenin* Vol. 14, People's Publishing House, 1988 edition, p122
6. *Selected Works of Lenin* Vol. 1, People's Publishing House, 2012 edition, pp273-275

7. *The Complete Works of Lenin* Vol. 13, People's Publishing House, 1987 edition, p210
8. *Selected Works of Lenin* Vol. 1, People's Publishing House, 2012 edition, p526
9. *The Complete Works of Lenin* Vol. 24, People's Publishing House, 1990 edition, p38
10. *Selected Works of Lenin* Vol. 1, People's Publishing House, 2012 edition, p473
11. Complete Works of Lenin Vol. 14, People's Publishing House, 1988 edition, p121
12. *Complete Works of Lenin* Vol. 11, People's Publishing House, 1987 edition, pp154-155
13. *Complete Works of Lenin* Vol. 9, People's Publishing House, 1987 edition, p257
14. In March 1918, the 7th National Congress of the Russian Social Democratic Labour Party changed its name to the Communist Party of Russia following a proposal by Lenin. In December 1925, the 14th National Congress of the Communist Party of Russia changed its name to the Communist Party of the Soviet Union. In October 1952, the 19th National Congress of the Communist Party of the USSR adopted the Resolution on the *Change of the Party's Name*, which stated that the dual name of the Party, "Communist" and "Bolshevik", came about as a result of the historical struggle with the Mensheviks. Its purpose was to distinguish itself from Menshevism, and it had by then lost its meaning. The party therefore decided to change its name from the All-Union Communist Party to the Communist Party of the USSR.
15. *Complete Works of Lenin* Vol. 16, People's Publishing House, 1988 edition, p116
16. *Complete Works of Lenin* Vol. 36, People's Publishing House, 1985 edition, p125
17. Nosov, editor-in-chief: *A Brief History of the Soviet Union* Vol. 1, Translated by the Department of Foreign Languages of Wuhan University, Life/Reading/New Knowledge, Sanlian Bookstore, 1977 edition, pp439, 446
18. Carl Kautsky: *Imperialism*, translated by historical collections, SDX Joint Publishing Company, 1964, p37
19. *Selected Works of Lenin* Vol. 2, People's Publishing House, 2012 edition, p704
20. Zhou Shangwen and others: *History of the Rise and Fall of the Soviet Union*, Shanghai People's Publishing House, 2002 edition, p8
21. *Selected Works of Lenin* Vol. 2, People's Publishing House, 2012 edition, p722
22. Nosov, editor-in-chief: *A Brief History of the Soviet Union* Vol. 1, Translated by the Department of Foreign Languages of Wuhan University, SDX Joint Publishing Company, 1977 edition, p490
23. Editor-in-Chief Sun Chengmu: *Compendium of the General History of Russia* Vol. 2, People's Publishing House, 1986 edition, p418
24. *The Complete Works of Lenin* Vol. 29, People's Publishing House, 1985 edition, p12
25. *The Complete Works of Lenin* Vol. 39, People's Publishing House, 1986 edition, p50
26. *Selected Works of Lenin* Vol. 3, People's Publishing House, 2012 edition, p85
27. *Selected Works of Lenin* Vol. 3, People's Publishing House, 2012 edition, p77
28. *The Complete Works of Lenin* Vol. 32, People's Publishing House, 1985 edition, p45
29. *Selected Works of Lenin* Vol. 3, People's Publishing House, 2012 edition, pp336, 337
30. *Complete Works of Lenin* Vol. 33, People's Publishing House, 1985 edition, p6
31. *Complete Works of Lenin* Vol. 34, People's Publishing House, 1985 edition, p7
32. *Complete Works of Lenin* Vol. 36, People's Publishing House, 1985 edition, p45
33. *Complete Works of Lenin* Vol. 33, People's Publishing House, 1985 edition, p6
34. *Selected Works of Lenin* Vol. 3, People's Publishing House, 1995 edition, p685
35. *Complete Works of Lenin* Vol. 34, People's Publishing House, 1985 edition, p286
36. *Compilation of Resolutions of the Congress of the CPSU, the Congress and the Central Plenary*, Vol. 2, translated by the Compilation Bureau of Marx, Engels, Lenin and Stalin of the CPC Central Committee, People's Publishing House, 1964 edition, p173
37. See Zhou Shangwen and others: *History of the Rise and Fall of the Soviet Union*, Shanghai People's Publishing House, 2002 edition, p62
38. Nikolai Ryazanovsky and Mark Steinberg: *History of Russia*, 7th edition, translated by Yang Ye and Qing Wenhui, Shanghai People's Publishing House, 2007 edition, p467
39. *Complete Works of Lenin* Vol. 42, People's Publishing House, 1987 edition, p176
40. *Complete Works of Lenin* Vol. 43, People's Publishing House, 1987 edition, p278
41. *Selected Works of Lenin* Vol. 4, People's Publishing House, 2012 Edition, p294
42. *Selected Works of Lenin* Vol. 3, People's Publishing House, 2012 edition, p476

43. *Selected Works of Lenin* Vol. 4, People's Publishing House, 2012 Edition, p13

44. *Selected Works of Lenin* Vol. 4, People's Publishing House, 2012 edition, p307

45. *The Complete Works of Lenin* Vol. 34, People's Publishing House, 1985 edition, pp135-136

46. The Chinese Academy of Social Sciences Institute of Foreign Literature and other editors: *"RAPP" Materials Collection* (Part 1), China Social Sciences Publishing House, 1981 edition, p3

47. *Complete Works of Lenin* Vol. 34, People's Publishing House, 1985 edition, pp8-9

48. *Complete Works of Lenin* Vol. 41, People's Publishing House, 1986 edition, p14

49. *Complete Works of Lenin* Vol. 38, People's Publishing House, 1986 edition, p311

50. *Selected Works of Lenin* Vol. 4, People's Publishing House, 2012 edition, p22

51. *Complete Works of Lenin* Vol. 37, People's Publishing House, 1986 edition, p215

52. *Complete Works of Lenin* Vol. 37, People's Publishing House, 1986 edition, p24

53. *Complete Works of Lenin* Vol. 41, People's Publishing House, 1986 edition, p92

54. *Complete Works of Lenin* Vol. 41, People's Publishing House, 1986 edition, p78

55. *Complete Works of Lenin* Vol. 38, People's Publishing House, 1986 edition, p354

56. *Selected Works of Lenin* Vol. 4, People's Publishing House, 2012 edition, pp18, 19

57. *Collected Works of Lenin* Vol. 35, People's Publishing House, 1985 edition, p168

58. *Collected Works of Lenin* Vol. 35, People's Publishing House, 1985 edition, p219

59. *Complete Works of Lenin* Vol. 34, People's Publishing House, 1985 edition, p466

60. *Complete Works of Lenin* Vol. 33, People's Publishing House, 1985 edition, p208

61. *Complete Works of Lenin* Vol. 39, People's Publishing House, 1986 edition, pp71, 128

62. *Complete Works of Lenin* Vol. 38, People's Publishing House, 1986 edition, p269

63. *Complete Works of Lenin* Vol. 39, People's Publishing House, 1986 edition, p27

64. *Selected Works of Lenin* Vol. 4, People's Publishing House, 2012 edition, pp423, 624

65. *Complete Works of Lenin* Vol. 41, People's Publishing House, 1986 edition, p55

66. *Complete Works of Lenin* Vol. 39, People's Publishing House, 1986 edition, p27

67. *Complete Works of Lenin* Vol. 42, People's Publishing House, 1987 edition, p333

68. *Selected Works of Lenin* Vol. 4, People's Publishing House, 2012 edition, p23

69. *Complete Works of Lenin* Vol. 36, People's Publishing House, 1985 edition, p60

70. *Complete Works of Lenin* Vol. 42, People's Publishing House, 1987 edition, p333

71. *Selected Works of Lenin* Vol. 3, People's Publishing House, 2012 edition, p490

72. *Selected Works of Lenin* Vol. 4, People's Publishing House, 2012 Edition, p346

73. *Selected Works of Lenin* Vol. 4, People's Publishing House, 2012 edition, p364

74. *Complete Works of Lenin* Vol. 28, People's Publishing House, 1990 edition, p172

75. *Complete Works of Lenin* Vol. 36, People's Publishing House, 1985 edition, p126

76. *Collected Works of Lenin* Vol. 35, People's Publishing House, 1985 edition, p127

77. *Complete Works of Lenin* Vol. 36, People's Publishing House, 1985 edition, p48

78. *Collected Works of Lenin* Vol. 35, People's Publishing House, 1985 edition, p416

79. *Complete Works of Lenin* Vol. 36, People's Publishing House, 1985 edition, p150

80. *Complete Works of Lenin* Vol. 34, People's Publishing House, 1985 edition, p520

81. *Complete Works of Lenin* Vol. 39, People's Publishing House, 1986 edition, p246

82. *Complete Works of Stalin* Vol. 5, People's Publishing House, 1957 edition, pp. 111-12

83. *Complete Works of Lenin* Vol. 39, People's Publishing House, 1986 edition, p. 229

84. *Selected Works of Lenin* Vol. 4, People's Publishing House, 2012 edition, page 778

85. *Selected Works of Lenin* Vol. 4, People's Publishing House 2012 edition, page 773

86. *Selected Works of Lenin* Vol. 4, People's Publishing House, 2012 edition, page 16

87. *Selected Works of Lenin* Vol. 4, People's Publishing House, 2012 edition, p797

88. *Selected Works of Lenin* Vol. 4, People's Publishing House, 2012 edition, p533

89. *Selected Works of Lenin* Vol. 4, People's Publishing House, 2012 edition, p770

90. *Complete Works of Lenin* Vol. 42, People's Publishing House, 1987 edition, page 190

91. *Selected Works of Lenin* Vol. 4, People's Publishing House, 2012 edition, page 771

92. *Compilation of Resolutions of the Congress, Soviets and Central Plenary of the CPSU* Vol. 1, translated by the Compilation Bureau of Marx, Engels, Lenin and Stalin of the CPC Central Committee, People's Publishing House, 1964 edition, p571

93. *Complete Works of Lenin* Vol. 43, People's Publishing House, 1987 edition, p64

94. *Selected Works of Lenin* Vol. 4, People's Publishing House, 2012 edition, p697

95. *Complete Works of Lenin* Vol. 41, People's Publishing House, 1986 edition, p230
96. *Complete Works of Lenin* Vol. 28, People's Publishing House, 1990 edition, p168
97. *Complete Works of Lenin* Vol. 39, People's Publishing House, 1986 edition, p299
98. *Complete Works of Lenin* Vol. 41, People's Publishing House, 1986 edition, p167
99. *Complete Works of Lenin* Vol. 30, People's Publishing House, 1985 edition, p311
100. *Complete Works of Lenin* Vol. 40, People's Publishing House, 1986 edition, p3
101. *Complete Works of Lenin* Vol. 42, People's Publishing House, 1987 edition, pp41-42
102. *Complete Works of Lenin* Vol. 43, People's Publishing House, 1987 edition, p115
103. *Compilation of Resolutions of the CPSU Congress, the Soviets and the Central Plenary* Vol. 2, translated by the Compilation Bureau of Marx, Engels, Lenin and Stalin of the Central Committee of the Communist Party of China, People's Publishing House, 1964 edition, p51
104. *Complete Works of Lenin* Vol. 42, People's Publishing House, 1987 edition, p100
105. *Selected Works of Lenin* Vol. 4, People's Publishing House, 2012 Edition, p695
106. *Selected Works of Lenin* Vol. 3, People's Publishing House, 2012 edition, p86

3. THE SOVIET COMMUNIST PARTY'S INITIAL SUMMARY OF THE LAWS OF COMMUNIST GOVERNANCE UNDER STALIN

1. *Complete Works of Stalin* Vol. 12, People's Publishing House, 1955 edition, p151
2. *Collected Works of Stalin (1934-1952)*, People's Publishing House, 1985 edition, p480
3. *Complete Works of Stalin* Vol. 13, People's Publishing House, 1956 edition, p37
4. R. R. Palmer, Joe Colton, Lloyd Kramer: *Two World Wars: The Fall of the West?*, translated by Chen Shaoheng, Zhou Xi'an and others, World Book Publishing Company, 2011 edition, p95
5. Samsonov, Editor-in-Chief: *A Brief History of the Soviet Union* Vol. 2, translated by students of the 70th and 71st classes of workers, peasants and soldiers of the Russian Department of Peking University, SDX Joint Publishing Company, 1976 edition, p348
6. R. R. Palmer, Joe Colton, Lloyd Kramer: *Two World Wars: The Fall of the West?*, translated by Chen Shaoheng, Zhou Xi'an and others, World Book Publishing Company, 2011 edition, p99
7. At present, the generally accepted total for the death toll from famine is between three and 8 million, of which the Ukraine accounts for about one third, specifically about one to three million. See Li Yan and Wang Limin: *Did Stalin Create a Famine? A Discussion on Stalin's Responsibilities in the Soviet Union's 1932-1933 Famine*, in *Russian Studies*, Issue 6, 2008
8. Samsonov, ed.: *A Brief History of the Soviet Union* Vol. 2, translated by 70th and 71st classes of Engineering, Agricultural and Military Students of the Russian Department of Peking University, SDX Joint Publishing Company, 1976 edition, pp340, 343-344 . It is said that about one million so-called "rich peasants", and about five million of their family members disappeared in the process. See also Nikolai Ryazanovsky and Mark Steinberg: *History of Russia* 7th edition, translated by Yang Ye and Qing Wenhui, Shanghai People's Publishing House, 2007 edition, pp480-481
9. *Compilation of Resolutions of the Congress, Congress and Central Plenary of the CPSU*, Vol. 4, translated by the Compilation Bureau of Marx, Engels, Lenin and Stalin of the CPC Central Committee, People's Publishing House, 1957 edition, p388
10. Zhou Shangwen and others: *History of the Rise and Fall of the Soviet Union*, Shanghai People's Publishing House, 2002 edition, p234
11. *History of the CPSU*, People's Publishing House, 1959 edition, p568
12. *Selected Works of Stalin* Vol. 2, People's Publishing House, 1979 edition, p463
13. *Selected Works of Stalin* Vol. 2, People's Publishing House, 1979 edition, pp471, 473
14. *Complete Works of Stalin* Vol. 13, People's Publishing House, 1956 edition, p37
15. *Complete Works of Stalin* Vol. 6, People's Publishing House, 1956 edition, p45

16. Samsonov, editor-in-chief: *A Brief History of the Soviet Union* Vol. 2, translated by students of 70th and 71st classes of the Russian Department of Peking University, SDX Joint Publishing Company, 1976, pp355-356

17. Military History Institute of the Ministry of National Defence: *Soviet Armed Forces*; Soviet Armed Forces translation group, Warrior Press, 1981 edition, p286

18. Samsonov, editor-in-chief: *A Brief History of the Soviet Union* Vol. 2, translated by students of the 70th and 71st classes of workers, peasants and soldiers of the Russian Department of Peking University, SDX Joint Publishing Company, 1976 edition, p383

19. *Selected Works of Stalin* Vol. 1, People's Publishing House, 1979 edition, p269

20. *Selected Works of Stalin* Vol. 2, People's Publishing House, 1979 edition, p460

21. Samsonov, editor-in-chief: *A Brief History of the Soviet Union*, translated by the students of the 70th and 71st classes of workers, peasants and soldiers of the Russian Department of Peking University, SDX Joint Publishing Company, 1976 edition, p558

22. *Complete Works of Stalin* Vol. 7, People's Publishing House, 1958 edition, p328

23. *History of the CPSU*, People's Publishing House, 1959 edition, pp516, 542

24. Aleksandrov, Galaktyanov and other editors: *Stalin's Biography*, translated by Wei Zhen, People's Publishing House, 1953, pp195, 197

25. *Selected Works of Stalin* Vol. 1, People's Publishing House, 1979 edition, pp200, 261

26. *Selected Works of Stalin* Vol. 2, People's Publishing House, 1979 edition, p468

27. *Selected Works of Stalin* Vol. 2, People's Publishing House, 1979 edition, pp615-616

28. Edited by the Ad Hoc Committee of the Central Committee of the CPSU: *A Brief Course on the History of the CPSU*, translated by the Compilation Bureau of Marx, Engels, Lenin and Stalin of the CPC Central Committee, People's Publishing House, 1975 edition, p354

29. *Selected Works of Stalin* Vol. 2, People's Publishing House, 1979 Edition, p474

30. *Complete Works of Stalin* Vol. 7, People's Publishing House, 1958 Edition, p155

31. *Selected Works of Stalin* Vol. 1, People's Publishing House, 1979 edition, p530

32. *Complete Works of Stalin* Vol. 10, People's Publishing House, 1954 Edition, p93

33. *Selected Works of Stalin* Vol. 1, People's Publishing House, 1979 edition, p414

34. *Selected Works of Stalin* Vol. 1, People's Publishing House, 1979 edition, p530

35. *Selected Works of Stalin* Vol. 2, People's Publishing House, 1979 edition, p569

36. *Selected Works of Stalin* Vol. 2, People's Publishing House, 1979 edition, p445

37. *Selected Works of Stalin* Vol. 2, People's Publishing House, 1979 edition, p579

38. *Complete Works of Stalin* Vol. 6, People's Publishing House, 1956 edition, p343

39. *Collected Works of Stalin* (1934-1952), People's Publishing House, 1985 edition, p172

40. *Selected Works of Stalin* Vol. 1, People's Publishing House, 1979 edition, pp17-18

41. *Complete Works of Stalin* Vol. 5, People's Publishing House, 1957 Edition, p79

42. *Complete Works of Stalin* Vol. 8, People's Publishing House, 1954 Edition, p200

43. *Complete Works of Stalin* Vol. 13, People's Publishing House, 1956 edition, p323

44. *Selected Works of Stalin* Vol. 2, People's Publishing House, 1979 edition, p459

45. *Selected Works of Stalin* Vol. 2, People's Publishing House, 1979 edition, p54

46. *Selected Works of Stalin* Vol. 2, People's Publishing House, 1979 edition, p7

47. *Selected Works of Stalin* Vol. 2, People's Publishing House, 1979 edition, pp58, 59

4. THE MAJOR HISTORICAL CONTRIBUTION OF THE SOVIET UNION'S COMMUNIST RULE

1. *Declaration of the Congress of the Communist and Workers' Parties of Socialist Countries held in Moscow from 14 to 16 November 1957*, People's Daily, 28 June 1960

2. *Collected Works of Marx and Engels* Vol. 4, People's Publishing House, 2009 edition, pp538, 541

3. *Selected Works of Deng Xiaoping* Vol. 3, People's Publishing House, 1993 edition, p139

4. Yu Youjun: *The Theory of the Third Leap of Socialism*, Guangdong People's Publishing House, 1995 edition, p. 198.

5. *Complete Works of Lenin* Vol. 42, People's Publishing House, 1987 edition, p246

6. Samsonov, editor-in-chief: *A Brief History of the Soviet Union* Vol. 2, translated by students of the 70th and 71st classes of Workers, Peasants and Soldiers of the Russian Department of Peking University, SDX Joint Publishing Company, 1976 edition, p389

1. CPC RULE IS THE CHOICE OF HISTORY AND THE PEOPLE

1. *Selected Works of Sun Yat-sen* Vol. 1, People's Publishing House, 2011 edition, p82
2. Zhang Yufa: *The Political Parties in the Early Years of the ROC*, Yuelu Publishing House, 2004 edition, p12
3. The *Wu Yuzhang Biography* Compilation Group of the CPC Sichuan Provincial Committee Party History Working Committee: *Collected Works of Wu Yuzhang* Vol. 2, Chongqing Publishing House, 1987 edition, p1066
4. Shi Fuliang: *The Political Line of the Centrist Faction*, Issue No. 1, *Time and Literature*, 14 March 1947
5. *Selected Works of Mao Zedong* Vol. 2, People's Publishing House, 1991 edition, p679
6. *Selected Works of Mao Zedong* Vol. 2, People's Publishing House, 1991 edition, p680
7. Zhou Xirui: *Improvement and Revolution: The Revolution of 1911 in Hubei and Hunan*, translated by Yang Shenzhi, Jiangsu People's Publishing House, 2007 edition; Yuzo Mizoguchi: *New Theory on the Revolution of 1911*, translated by Lin Shaoyang, *Opening Times*, 2008, Issue 4
8. CPC Central Committee History Research Office and Central Archives: *Selected Archives of the First National Congress of the CPC*, CPC History Publishing House, 2015 edition, p121
9. *Selected Works of Mao Zedong* Vol. 4, People's Publishing House, 1991 edition, p1480
10. *Selected Works of Mao Zedong* Vol. 4, People's Publishing House, 1991 edition, p1471
11. Compiled by the Central Committee of Literature and History of the China Democratic League: *The Historical Documents of the Chinese Democratic League (1941-1949)*, Literature and History Data Publishing House, 1983 edition, pp374, 363
12. *Selected Works of Mao Zedong* Vol. 4, People's Publishing House, 1991 edition, p1471
13. *Selected Works of Mao Zedong* Vol. 4, People's Publishing House, 1991 edition, p1516
14. Compiled by the Literature Research Office of the CPC Central Committee and the Central Archives: *Selected Works of Important Documents Since the Founding of the Party (1921-1949)* Vol. 1, Central Literature Publishing House, 2011 edition, p162
15. Compiled by the Literature Research Office of the CPC Central Committee and the Central Archives: *Selected Works of Important Documents Since the Founding of the Party (1921-1949)* Vol. 1, Central Literature Publishing House, 2011 edition, p162
16. *Selected Works of Mao Zedong* Vol. 1, People's Publishing House, 1991 edition, p48
17. *Selected Works of Zhou Enlai* Vol. 1, People's Publishing House, 1980 edition, p178
18. Central Party History Research Office of the CPC: *The History of the CPC* Vol. 1, 2011 edition of the CPC History Publishing House, p372
19. *Selected Works of Mao Zedong* Vol. 1, People's Publishing House, 1991 edition, p98
20. *Selected Works of Mao Zedong* Vol. 1, People's Publishing House, 1991 edition, p98
21. *Selected Works of Mao Zedong* Vol. 2, People's Publishing House, 1991 edition, p541
22. *Selected Works of Mao Zedong* Vol. 2, People's Publishing House, 1991 edition, p542
23. *Selected Works of Mao Zedong* Vol. 2, People's Publishing House, 1991 edition, pp543, 542
24. *Selected Works of Mao Zedong* Vol. 2, People's Publishing House, 1991 edition, pp634, 635
25. *Selected Works of Mao Zedong* Vol. 2, People's Publishing House, 1991 edition, p545
26. *Selected Works of Mao Zedong* Vol. 2, People's Publishing House, 1991 edition, p636
27. *Selected Works of Mao Zedong* Vol. 2, People's Publishing House, 1991 edition, p636
28. *Selected Works of Mao Zedong* Vol. 2, People's Publishing House, 1991 edition, p636
29. *Selected Works of Mao Zedong* Vol. 4, People's Publishing House, 1991 edition, pp1426-1427
30. *Selected Works of Mao Zedong* Vol. 1, People's Publishing House, 1991 edition, p50
31. *Selected Works of Mao Zedong* Vol. 1, People's Publishing House, 1991 edition, p77
32. *Selected Works of Mao Zedong* Vol. 1, People's Publishing House, 1991 edition, pp65-66

33. *Selected Works of Zhou Enlai* Vol. 1, People's Publishing House, 1980 edition, p161

34. *Selected Works of Mao Zedong* Vol. 3, People's Publishing House, 1991 edition, p1057

35. *Selected Works of Mao Zedong* Vol. 3, People's Publishing House, 1991 edition, p891

36. *Selected Works of Deng Xiaoping* Vol. 3, People's Publishing House, 1993 edition, p309

37. *Selected Works of Liu Shaoqi* Vol. 1, People's Publishing House, 1981 edition, p220

38. When the first historical resolution was compiled as an appendix to the third volume of Mao Zedong's Selected Works and published in 1953, the expression "Mao Zedong Thought" and "Mao Zedong Thought System" were deleted or modified, and the words "Mao Zedong Thought" were not found anywhere in the text. For more details and reasons, see *Hu Qiaomu Remembers Mao Zedong*, People's Publishing House, 1994, pp 328-329; Zhou Bing, *A Study of the Versions of the Resolution on Certain Historical Issues* in *Studies in the History of the Communist Party*, No. 3, 2012

39. *Selected Works of Mao Zedong* Vol. 3, People's Publishing House, 1991 edition, p955

40. When the first historical resolution was published in 1953, the expression: "Mao Zedong Thought" was revised in four places in the two quotations. In the first place it is changed to "Comrade Mao Zedong's line"; in the second place the word "thought" is deleted completely; in the third place it is changed to "Marxist-Leninist thought represented by Comrade Mao Zedong"; in the fourth place "in Mao Zedong Thought and under the correct leadership of the Central Committee headed by Comrade Mao Zedong" is changed to "under the correct leadership of the Central Committee headed by Comrade Mao Zedong." From *Selected Works of Mao Zedong*, Vol. 3, People's Publishing House, 1991 edition, pp98-99; Zhou Bing: *Research on the Version of 'Resolutions on Certain Historical Issues'* in *Research on the History of the CPC*, Issue no. 3, 2012

41. *Hu Qiaomu Recalls Mao Zedong*, People's Publishing House, 1994 edition, p326

42. *Collected Works of Deng Liqun* Vol. 1, Contemporary China Publishing House, 1998 edition, p596

43. Central Archives: *Selected Works of the CPC Central Committee* Vol. 15, 1991 edition, Party School Press of the CPC Central Committee, p115

44. *Selected Works of Liu Shaoqi* Vol. 1, People's Publishing House, 1981 edition, pp319, 320

45. *Selected Works of Liu Shaoqi* Vol. 1, People's Publishing House, 1981 edition, pp333, 335

46. *Selected Works of Mao Zedong* Vol. 4, People's Publishing House, 1991 edition, p1480

47. *Selected Works of Mao Zedong* Vol. 2, People's Publishing House, 1991 edition, p610

48. *Selected Works of Mao Zedong* Vol. 2, People's Publishing House, 1991 edition, p645

49. *Selected Works of Mao Zedong* Vol. 2, People's Publishing House, 1991 edition, p607

50. *Selected Works of Zhou Enlai* Vol. 1, People's Publishing House, 1980 edition, pp178-179

51. Xi Jinping: *Speech at the Symposium to Commemorate the 120th Anniversary of Comrade Mao Zedong's Birth*, People's Publishing House, 2013 edition, p5

52. *Selected Works of Marx and Engels* Vol. 1, People's Publishing House, 1972 edition, p262

53. *Selected Works of Mao Zedong* Vol. 3, People's Publishing House, 1991 edition, pp1094-1095

2. LAYING THE FOUNDATIONS OF THE CPC'S RULES OF NATIONAL GOVERNANCE

1. *Selected Works of Liu Shaoqi* Vol. 1, People's Publishing House, 1981 edition, p434

2. Compiled by the Literature Research Office of the Central Committee of the CPC and the Central Archives: *Selected Works of Important Documents Since the Founding of the Party (1921-1949)* Vol. 26, 2011 edition of the Central Literature Publishing House, p759

3. Compiled by the Literature Research Office of the CPC Central Committee: Vol. 12 of *Selected Documents Since the Founding of the PRC*, Central Literature Publishing House, 1996 edition, pp546-547

4. Mao Zedong: *The Politics of New Democracy and the Culture of New Democracy*, in *Chinese Culture* (Vol. 1), issue no. 1, p5

5. *Selected Works of Mao Zedong* Vol. 4, People's Publishing House, 1991 edition, p1235

6. *Selected Works of Mao Zedong* Vol. 4, People's Publishing House, 1991 edition, pp1480, 1475, 1478, 1479

7. *Selected Works of Mao Zedong* Vol. 2, People's Publishing House, 1991 edition, p677

8. *Selected Works of Mao Zedong* Vol. 3, People's Publishing House, 1991 edition, p1057

9. *Selected Works of Liu Shaoqi* Vol. 1, People's Publishing House, 1981 edition, p415

10. *Collected Works of Mao Zedong*, Vol. 5, People's Publishing House, 1996 edition, p136

11. Compiled by the Literature Research Office of the CPC Central Committee and the Central Archives: *Selected Documents Since the Founding of the Party (1921-1949)* Vol. 26, 2011 edition of the Central Literature Publishing House, p760

12. *Selected Works of Mao Zedong* Vol. 1, People's Publishing House, 1991 edition, p1256

13. Compiled by the Literature Research Office of the CPC Central Committee and the Central Archives: *Selected Works of Important Documents Since the Founding of the Party (1921-1949)* Vol. 26, 2011 edition of the Central Literature Publishing House, page 758.

14. *Zhou Enlai's Report on the Drafting Process and Features of the Draft Common Program of the Chinese People's Political Consultative Conference*, September 22, 1949.

15. Compiled by the Literature Research Office of the CPC Central Committee and the Central Archives: *Selections of Important Documents Since the Founding of the Party (1921-1949)* Vol. 26, 2011 edition of the Central Literature Publishing House, page 699.

16. Compiled by the Literature Research Office of the CPC Central Committee and the Central Archives: *Selected Works of Important Documents Since the Founding of the Party (1921-1949)* Vol. 26, 2011 edition of the Central Literature Publishing House, page 761.

17. Compiled by the Literature Research Office of the CPC Central Committee and the Central Archives: *Selected Works of Important Documents Since the Founding of the Party (1921-1949)*, Vol. 26, 2011 edition of the Central Literature Publishing House, page 767.

18. Chen Renbing: *Methods of Studying the Common Programme*, Zai Long and Heping: *Reference Materials for Common Program Study*, Dalu Publishing House, 1952 edition, page 97.

19. Compiled by the Literature Research Office of the CPC Central Committee and the Central Archives: *Selected Works of Important Documents Since the Founding of the Party (1921-1949)*, Vol. 26, Central Literature Publishing House, 2011 edition, page 703.

20. The Literature Research Office of the CPC Central Committee and the Central Archives: *Selected Documents Since the Founding of the Party (1921-1949)* Vol. 26, Central Literature Publishing House, 2011 edition, p761

21. The Literature Research Office of the CPC Central Committee and the Central Archives: *Selected Documents Since the Founding of the Party (1921-1949)* Vol. 26, Central Literature Publishing House, 2011 edition, pp702-3

22. The Literature Research Office of the CPC Central Committee and the Central Archives: *Selected Documents Since the Founding of the Party (1921-1949)* Vol. 26, Central Literature Publishing House, 2011 edition, pp762-3

23. The Literature Research Office of the CPC Central Committee and the Central Archives: *Selected Documents Since the Founding of the Party (1921-1949)* Vol. 26, Central Literature Publishing House, 2011 edition, p763

24. The Literature Research Office of the CPC Central Committee and the Central Archives: *Selected Documents Since the Founding of the Party (1921-1949)* Vol. 26, Central Literature Publishing House, 2011 edition, p763

25. The Literature Research Office of the CPC Central Committee and the Central Archives: *Selected Documents Since the Founding of the Party (1921-1949)* Vol. 26, Central Literature Publishing House, 2011 edition, p767

26. *Selected Works of Mao Zedong* Vol. 4, People's Publishing House, 1991 edition, p1473

27. Paul Kennedy: *The Rise and Fall of Great Powers: Economic Changes and Military Conflicts from 1500 to 2000*, translated by Wang Zhuo et al, Qiushi Press, 1988, pp455-456

28. *Selected Works of Mao Zedong* Vol. 2, People's Publishing House, 1991 edition, p668

29. *Selected Works of Mao Zedong* Vol. 2, People's Publishing House, 1991 edition, pp708-9

30. The Literature Research Office of the CPC Central Committee and the Central Archives: *Selected Documents Since the Founding of the Party (1921-1949)* Vol. 26, Central Literature Publishing House, 2011 edition, pp766-767

31. *Selected Works of Liu Shaoqi* Vol. 1, People's Publishing House, 1981 edition, p435

32. *Collected Works of Mao Zedong* Vol. 3, People's Publishing House, 1996 edition, p146-147

33. *Collected Works of Mao Zedong* Vol. 3, People's Publishing House, 1996 edition, p207

34. *Collected Works of Mao Zedong* Vol. 3, People's Publishing House, 1996 edition, p1081

35. Compiled by the Literature Research Office of the CPC Central Committee and the Central Archives: *Selected Works of Important Documents Since the Founding of the Party (1921-1949)* Vol. 26, 2011 edition of the Central Literature Publishing House, p759

36. Compiled by the Literature Research Office of the CPC Central Committee and the Central Archives: *Selected Works of Important Documents Since the Founding of the Party (1921-1949)* Vol. 26, 2011 edition of the Central Literature Publishing House, p765

37. The Central Archives and the Literature Research Office of the CPC Central Committee: *Selected Works of the CPC Central Committee (October 1949-May 1966)* Vol. 29, People's Publishing House, 2013 edition, p305

38. Gong Yuzhi: *Notes on the Party History*, Zhejiang People's Publishing House, 2002 edition, p30

39. *Selected Works of Liu Shaoqi* Vol. 1, People's Publishing House, 1981 edition, p435

40. *Collected Works of Mao Zedong* Vol. 6, People's Publishing House, 1999 edition, p80

41. *Selected Works of Liu Shaoqi* Vol.1, People's Publishing House, 1981 edition, p435

42. Compiled by the Literature Research Office of the CPC Central Committee and the Central Archives: *Selected Works of Important Documents Since the Founding of the Party (1921-1949)* Vol. 26, 2011 edition of the Central Literature Publishing House, p732

43. Two historical references, first to the old Imperial Examination System, and then to Li Zicheng, who was the Chinese peasant rebel leader who overthrew the Ming dynasty in 1644 and ruled over northern China briefly as the emperor of the short-lived Shun dynasty before his death a year later and the invasion of the Manchus who established the Qing dynasty.

44. *Selected Works of Mao Zedong* Vol. 4, People's Publishing House, 1991 edition, p1427

45. *Selected Works of Mao Zedong* Vol. 4, People's Publishing House, 1991 edition, p1438

46. "The Sixth Meeting of the Central People's Government Committee Approves Sino-Soviet Treaties and Agreements" headline in *People's Daily*, 13 April 1950

47. Peng Dehuai: *Report on the Work of the Chinese People's Volunteers to Resist US Aggression and Aid Korea*, 12 September 1953

48. *Selected Works of Liu Shaoqi* Vol. 2, People's Publishing House, 1985 edition, p91

49. *Collected Works of Mao Zedong* Vol. 6, People's Publishing House, 1999 edition, p184

50. *Collected Works of Mao Zedong*, Vol. 7, People's Publishing House, 1999 edition, p42

51. The Central Archives and Literature Research Office of the CPC Central Committee: *Selected Works of the CPC Central Committee (October 1949-May 1966)*, Vol. 5, People's Publishing House, 2013 edition, p307

52. The Central Archives and Literature Research Office of the CPC Central Committee: *Selected Works of the CPC Central Committee (October 1949-May 1966)*, Vol. 5, People's Publishing House, 2013 edition, p308

53. The Central Archives and Literature Research Office of the CPC Central Committee: *Selected Works of the CPC Central Committee (October 1949-May 1966)*, Vol. 24, People's Publishing House, 2013 edition, p24

54. "Using a Variety of Methods to Propagate Revolutionary Doctrines in Various Places, and To Widely Disseminate Marxist-Leninist Theory", *People's Daily*, 22 October 1957

55. The Central Archives and Literature Research Office of the CPC Central Committee: *Selected Works of the CPC Central Committee (October 1949-May 1966)*, Vol. 15, 2013 edition, People's Publishing House, p149

56. The Central Archives and Literature Research Office of the CPC Central Committee: *Selected Works of the CPC Central Committee (October 1949-May 1966)*, Vol. 14, 2013 edition, People's Publishing House, p526

57. The Central Archives and Literature Research Office of the CPC Central Committee: *Selected Works of the CPC Central Committee (October 1949-May 1966)*, Vol. 18, People's Publishing House, 2013 edition, pp323-324

58. The Central Archives and Literature Research Office of the CPC Central Committee: *Selected Works of the CPC Central Committee (October 1949-May 1966)*, Vol. 24, People's Publishing House, 2013 edition, pp227-228

59. The Central Archives and Literature Research Office of the CPC Central Committee:
Selected Works of the CPC Central Committee (October 1949-May 1966), Vol. 3, People's
Publishing House, 2013 edition, p1

60. *Mao Zedong Manuscripts Since the Founding of the PRC*, Vol. 1, Central Literature
Publishing House, 1987 edition, p367

61. The Central Archives and Literature Research Office of the CPC Central Committee:
Selected Works of the CPC Central Committee (October 1949-May 1966), Vol. 6, People's
Publishing House, 2013 edition, p62

62. The Central Archives and Literature Research Office of the CPC Central Committee:
Selected Works of the CPC Central Committee (October 1949-May 1966), Vol. 7, People's
Publishing House, 2013 edition, p305

63. The Central Archives and Literature Research Office of the CPC Central Committee:
Selected Works of the CPC Central Committee (October 1949-May 1966), Vol. 11, People's
Publishing House, 2013 edition, p92

64. *Mao Zedong Manuscripts Since the Founding of the PRC* Vol. 4, Central Literature Publishing
House, 1990 edition, p46

65. The Central Archives and Literature Research Office of the CPC Central Committee:
Selected Works of the CPC Central Committee (October 1949-May 1966), Vol. 11, People's
Publishing House, 2013 edition, p399

66. The Central Archives and Literature Research Office of the CPC Central Committee:
Selected Works of the CPC Central Committee (October 1949-May 1966), Vol. 24, People's
Publishing House, 2013 edition, pp99-100

67. CPC Central Committee History Research Office: *The History of the CPC* Vol. 2, CPC
History Publishing House, 2011 edition, pp171-172

68. *Collected Works of Mao Zedong* Vol. 6, People's Publishing House, 1999 edition, p322

69. The Central Archives and Literature Research Office of the CPC Central Committee:
Selected Works of the CPC Central Committee (October 1949-May 1966) Vol. 2, People's
Publishing House, 2013 edition, p137

70. The Central Archives and Literature Research Office of the CPC Central Committee:
Selected Works of the CPC Central Committee (October 1949-May 1966) Vol. 2, People's
Publishing House, 2013 edition, pp316, 318

71. *Closely Coordinating Current Work and Resolutely Carrying Out the Anti-bureaucratistic
Struggle, People's Daily*, 13 March 1953

72. Central Literature Research Office of the CPC: *Mao Zedong Chronicles (1949-1976)* Vol. 2,
Central Literature Publishing House, 2013 edition, pp562-563

73. The Central Archives and Literature Research Office of the CPC Central Committee:
Selected Works of the CPC Central Committee (October 1949-May 1966) Vol. 2, People's
Publishing House, 2013 edition, pp316, 318

74. Central Party History Research Office of the CPC: *The History of the CPC* Vol. 2, CPC
History Publishing House, 2011 edition, pp173-174

75. *Selected Works of Deng Xiaoping* Vol. 2, People's Publishing House, 1994 edition, pp328-329

3. ESTABLISHMENT OF THE BASIC SOCIALIST SYSTEM AND THE EXPLORATION OF NEW WAYS OF GOVERNING

1. Compiled by the Literature Research Office of the CPC Central Committee: *Chronicles of
Deng Xiaoping (1975-1997)* (Part 1), Central Literature Publishing House, 2004 edition, p20

2. The Central Archives and Literature Research Office of the CPC Central Committee:
Selected Works of the CPC Central Committee (October 1949-May 1966) Vol. 24, People's
Publishing House, 2013 edition, p248

3. *Selected Works of Chen Yun* Vol. 2, People's Publishing House, 1995 edition, pp309-310

4. *Selected Works of Zhou Enlai* Vol. 2, People's Publishing House, 1984, p105

5. *Selected Works of Liu Shaoqi* Vol. 2, People's Publishing House, 1985, p177

6. In 1960, the Party Central Committee re-established six Party Central Bureaus in North

China, Northeast China, East China, Northwest China, Central South, and Southwest China to unify leadership of the work of party, government and military organisations in the provinces under its jurisdiction

7. *Collected Works of Mao Zedong* Vol. 7, People's Publishing House, 1999 edition, p34
     209

8. *Selected Works of Deng Xiaoping* Vol. 2, People's Publishing House, 1994 edition, p333

9. *Collected Works of Mao Zedong* Vol. 7, People's Publishing House, 1999 edition, p24

10. *Collected Works of Mao Zedong* Vol. 7, People's Publishing House, 1999 edition, p30

11. *Collected Works of Mao Zedong* Vol. 7, People's Publishing House, 1999 edition, pp29-30

12. Editors-in-Chief Liu Keming and Jin Hui: *Seventy Years of the Soviet Political and Economic System*, China Social Sciences Press, 1990 edition, p352

13. *Collected Works of Mao Zedong* Vol. 7, People's Publishing House, 1999 edition, p31

14. *Reference Materials on the History of the CPC* (8), People's Publishing House, 1980 edition, pp504, 503-504

15. Compiled by the Literature Research Office of the CPC Central Committee: *Selected Documents Since the Founding of the PRC* Vol. 8, Central Literature Publishing House, 1994 edition, p227

16. Compiled by the Literature Research Office of the CPC Central Committee: *Selected Documents Since the Founding of the PRC* Vol. 8, Central Literature Publishing House, 1994 edition, pp229, 230

17. *Selected Works of Deng Xiaoping* Vol. 2, People's Publishing House, 1994 edition, p333

18. Wu Lengxi: *Ten Years of Debate* (Part 1), Central Literature Publishing House, 1999 edition, p67

19. Compiled by the Literature Research Office of the CPC Central Committee: *Selected Documents Since the Founding of the PRC* Vol. 9, Central Literature Publishing House, 1994 edition, p570

20. Compiled by the Literature Research Office of the CPC Central Committee: *Selected Documents Since the Founding of the PRC* Vol. 8, Central Literature Publishing House, 1994 edition, pp229, 230, 231

21. Compiled by the Literature Research Office of the CPC Central Committee: *Selected Documents Since the Founding of the PRC* Vol. 9, Central Literature Publishing House, 1994 edition, p573

22. *Collected Works of Mao Zedong* Vol. 7, People's Publishing House, 1999 edition, p125

23. *Collected Works of Mao Zedong* Vol. 7, People's Publishing House, 1999 edition, p193

24. *Collected Works of Mao Zedong* Vol. 7, People's Publishing House, 1999 edition, p194

25. *Collected Works of Mao Zedong* Vol. 7, People's Publishing House, 1999 edition, p195

26. *Collected Works of Mao Zedong* Vol. 7, People's Publishing House, 1999 edition, p253

27. Compiled by the CPC Central Literature Research Office: *A Chronicle of Liu Shaoqi* Part 2, Central Literature Publishing House, 1996 edition, p371

28. Compiuled by the CPC Central Literature Research Office: *A Chronicle of Liu Shaoqi* Part 2, Central Literature Publishing House, 1996 edition, p372

29. Compiled by the CPC Central Literature and Documents Research Office: A *Selection of Important Literature Since the Founding of the PRC* Vol. 9, Central Literature Publishing House, 1994 edition, pp579-580, 580

30. Compiled by the CPC Central Literature and Documents Research Office: A *Selection of Important Literature Since the Founding of the PRC* Vol. 9, Central Literature Publishing House, 1994 edition, p572

31. *Collected Works of Mao Zedong* Vol. 7, People's Publishing House, 1999 edition, p215

32. *Collected Works of Mao Zedong* Vol. 7, People's Publishing House, 1999 edition, p24

33. *Collected Works of Mao Zedong* Vol. 7, People's Publishing House, 1999 edition, pp240-241

34. *Collected Works of Mao Zedong* Vol. 8, People's Publishing House, 1999 edition, p78

35. *Collected Works of Mao Zedong* Vol. 8, People's Publishing House, 1999 edition, p121

36. *Collected Works of Mao Zedong* Vol. 8, People's Publishing House, 1999 edition, p123

37. *Collected Works of Mao Zedong* Vol. 7, People's Publishing House, 1999 edition, p436

38. *Collected Works of Mao Zedong* Vol. 7, People's Publishing House, 1999 edition, p437

39. *Collected Works of Mao Zedong* Vol. 7, People's Publishing House, 1999 edition, pp439, 440

40. *Collected Works of Mao Zedong* Vol. 7, People's Publishing House, 1999 edition, p440
41. *Collected Works of Mao Zedong* Vol. 7, People's Publishing House, 1999 edition, pp435, 436
42. *Collected Works of Mao Zedong* Vol. 8, People's Publishing House, 1999 edition, p34
43. *Collected Works of Mao Zedong* Vol. 7, People's Publishing House, 1999 edition, p31
44. *Collected Works of Mao Zedong* Vol. 7, People's Publishing House, 1999 edition, p29
45. *Collected Works of Mao Zedong* Vol. 8, People's Publishing House, 1999 edition, p138
46. *Collected Works of Mao Zedong* Vol.8, People's Publishing House, 1999 edition, p135
47. *Collected Works of Mao Zedong* Vol.8, People's Publishing House, 1999 edition, p293
48. *Collected Works of Mao Zedong* Vol.8, People's Publishing House, 1999 edition, p298
49. *Collected Works of Mao Zedong* Vol.7, People's Publishing House, 1999 edition, pp208, 209
50. *Collected Works of Mao Zedong* Vol.7, People's Publishing House, 1999 edition, pp296-297
51. *Collected Works of Mao Zedong* Vol.8 People's Publishing House, 1999 edition, pp294, 295
52. *Collected Works of Mao Zedong* Vol.7, People's Publishing House, 1999 edition, p54
53. *Collected Works of Mao Zedong* Vol.7, People's Publishing House, 1999 edition, p55
54. *Collected Works of Mao Zedong* Vol.7, People's Publishing House, 1999 edition, p229
55. *Collected Works of Mao Zedong* Vol.7, People's Publishing House, 1999 edition, p230
56. *Collected Works of Mao Zedong* Vol.7, People's Publishing House, 1999 edition, p232
57. *Collected Works of Mao Zedong* Vol.7, People's Publishing House, 1999 edition, p279
58. *Collected Works of Mao Zedong* Vol.7, People's Publishing House, 1999 edition, p225
59. Xi Jinping: *Some Thoughts on Party Building in New China in 60 Years* in *Study Times* September 28, 2009.
60. *Mao Zedong Manuscripts Since the Founding of the People's Republic of China*, Vol. 8, Central Literature Publishing House, 1992 edition, page 451.
61. *Mao Zedong Manuscripts Since the Founding of the PRC* Vol. 13, Central Literature Publishing House, 1998 edition, p486
62. *Reference Materials for Teaching the CPC's History: The Period of the Cultural Revolution* Vol. 25, edited and printed by the Teaching and Research Section of Party History, Party Building and Political Work, National Defence University of the Chinese PLA, 1988, p467
63. *Collected Works of Hu Qiaomu* Vol. 2, People's Publishing House, 2012 edition, p278
64. *Mao Zedong Manuscripts Since the Founding of the PRC*, Vol. 12, Central Literature Publishing House, 1998 edition, p72
65. *Selected Works of Deng Xiaoping* Vol. 2, People's Publishing House, 1994 edition, p332
66. Zhu Qiaosen and Li Lingyu, editors: *Research on the Historical Experience of the CPC*, CPC Central Party School Press, 1997 edition, p272
67. *Selected Works of Marx and Engels* Vol. 1, People's Publishing House, 2012 edition, p421
68. *Selected Works of Lenin* Vol, 4, People's Publishing House, 1995 edition, p16
69. *Selected Works of Deng Xiaoping* Vol. 3, People's Publishing House, 1993 edition, p141
70. *Collected Works of Mao Zedong* Vol. 8, People's Publishing House, 1999 edition, p116
71. *Selected Works of Deng Xiaoping*, People's Publishing House, 1993 edition, p269
72. Compiled by the Literature Research Office of the CPC Central Committee: *Selection of Important Documents Since the Third Plenary Session* (Part 2), People's Publishing House, 1982 edition, p841
73. *Selected Works of Deng Xiaoping* Vol. 3, People's Publishing House, 1993 edition, p379
74. *Selected Works of Mao Zedong* Vol. 2, People's Publishing House, 1991 edition, p533
75. *Selected Works of Deng Xiaoping* Vol. 3, People's Publishing House, 1993 edition, pp284, 313, 286
76. *Selected Works of Deng Xiaoping*, Vol. 3, People's Publishing House, 1993 edition, page 361.
77. *Selected Works of Deng Xiaoping*, Vol. 3, People's Publishing House, 1993 edition, page 78.
78. *Selected Works of Deng Xiaoping*, Vol. 3, People's Publishing House, 1993 edition, page 373.
79. *Selected Works of Deng Xiaoping*, Vol. 3, People's Publishing House, 1993 edition, page 272.
80. Compiled by the Literature Research Office of the CPC Central Committee: *Selected Documents Since the 18th National Congress of the CPC* (Part 1), Central Literature Publishing House, 2014 edition, p112.

1. PIONEERING A NEW PATH OF GOVERNANCE IN THE MIDST OF BRINGING ORDER OUT OF CHAOS, AND REFORM AND OPENING UP

1. *Resolution on Several Historical Issues of the Party Since the Founding of the PRC, People's Daily*, 1 July 1981
2. *Chronology of Deng Xiaoping (1975-1997)*, edited by the Literature Research Office of the CPC Central Committee Vol. 1, Central Party Literature Press, 2004, p157
3. *Practice is the Only Criterion for Testing Truth, Guangming Daily*, 11 May 1978
4. *Selected Works of Deng Xiaoping* Vol. 2, People's Publishing House, 1994 edition, p119
5. *Chronology of Deng Xiaoping (1975-1997)*, edited by the Literature Research Office of the CPC Central Committee Vol. 1, Central Party Literature Press, 2004, pp379-380
6. *Selected Works of Deng Xiaoping* Vol. 2, People's Publishing House, 1994 edition, p135
7. *Selected Works of Deng Xiaoping* Vol. 2, People's Publishing House, 1994 edition, p150
8. Jiang Zemin, speech at the Conference Commemorating the 20th Anniversary of the 3rd Plenary Session of the 11th CPC Central Committee, *People's Daily*, 19 December 1998
9. *Selected Works of Zhou Enlai* Vol. 2, People's Publishing House, 1984 edition, p439
10. *Selected Works of Deng Xiaoping* Vol. 2, People's Publishing House, 1994 edition, pp231-232
11. *Selected Works of Chen Yun* Vol. 3, People's Publishing House, 1995 edition, p248
12. *Chronology of Deng Xiaoping (1975-1997)*, edited by the Literature Research Office of the CPC Central Committee Vol.1, Central Party Literature Press, 2004, p496
13. *Selected Works of Deng Xiaoping* Vol. 2, People's Publishing House, 1994 edition, pp194, 196
14. *Chronology of Deng Xiaoping (1975-1997)*, edited by the Literature Research Office of the CPC Central Committee Vol.1, Central Party Literature Press, 2004, pp631-632
15. *Selected Works of Deng Xiaoping* Vol. 2, People's Publishing House, 1994 edition, p237
16. *Chronology of Deng Xiaoping (1975-1997)*, edited by the Literature Research Office of the CPC Central Committee Vol. 2, Central Party Literature Press, 2004, p732
17. *Chronology of Deng Xiaoping (1975-1997)*, edited by the Literature Research Office of the CPC Central Committee Vol. 2, Central Party Literature Press, 2004, p816
18. *Chronology of Deng Xiaoping (1975-1997)*, edited by the Literature Research Office of the CPC Central Committee Vol. 2, Central Party Literature Press, 2004, p837
19. *Selected Important Documents Since the 12th CPC National Congress*, edited by the Literature Research Office of the CPC Central Committee Vol. 1, Central Party Literature Press, 2011 edition, pp. 11-12
20. *Selected Works of Deng Xiaoping* Vol. 2, People's Publishing House, 1994 edition, pp142, 146
21. *Selected Important Documents Since the Third Plenary Session of the CPC Central Committee* Vol. 1, edited by the Literature Research Office of the CPC Central Committee, Central Party Literature Press, 2011 edition, p144
22. Peng Zhen: *On the Political and Legal Work of New China*, Central Party Literature Press, 1992 edition, p156
23. Deng Xiaoping's *Reform of the Party and State Leadership System, People's Daily*, 18 August 1980
24. Peng Zhen, *On the Political and Legal Work of New China*, Central Party Literature Press, 1992, pp323-325
25. *Selected Works of Deng Xiaoping* Vol. 2, People's Publishing House, 1994 edition, p333
26. *Selected Works of Deng Xiaoping* Vol. 2, People's Publishing House, 1994 edition, pp164-165
27. Ye Jianying, *Speech at the Conference to Celebrate the 30th Anniversary of the Founding of the PRC, People's Daily*, 30 September 1979
28. *Selected Works of Deng Xiaoping* Vol. 2, People's Publishing House, 1994 edition, pp291, 292
29. *Selected Important Documents Since the Third Plenary Session of the CPC Central Committee* Vol. 2, edited by the Literature Research Office of the CPC Central Committee, Central Party Literature Press, 2011, pp124-174

30. Ye Jianying, *Speech at the Conference to Celebrate the 30th Anniversary of the Founding of the PRC, People's Daily*, 30 September 1979

31. *Resolution on Several Historical Issues of the Party Since the Founding of the PRC, People's Daily*, 1 July 1981

32. *Chronology of Deng Xiaoping (1975-1997)*, edited by the Literature Research Office of the CPC Central Committee Vol. 1, Central Party Literature Press, 2004, p250

33. *Chronology of Deng Xiaoping (1975-1997)*, edited by the Literature Research Office of the CPC Central Committee Vol. 1, Central Party Literature Press, 2004, p271

34. *Chronology of Deng Xiaoping (1975-1997)*, edited by the Literature Research Office of the CPC Central Committee Vol. 1, Central Party Literature Press, 2004, p277

35. *Chronology of Deng Xiaoping (1975-1997)*, edited by the Literature Research Office of the CPC Central Committee Vol. 1, Central Party Literature Press, 2004, pp380, 381, 384

36. *Selected Works of Deng Xiaoping* Vol. 2, People's Publishing House, 1994 edition, pp162-163

37. Ye Jianying, *Speech at the Conference to Celebrate the 30th Anniversary of the Founding of the PRC, People's Daily*, 30 September 1979

38. *Selected Works of Deng Xiaoping* Vol. 3, People's Publishing House, 1993 edition, pp2-3

39. *Selected Important Documents Since the 12th CPC National Congress* Vol. 1, edited by the CPC Central Committee Literature Research Office, Central Party Literature Press, 2011 edition, pp. 28, 29.

40. *Selected Important Documents Since the 12th CPC National Congress* Vol. 1, edited by the CPC Central Committee Literature Research Office, Central Party Literature Press, 2011 edition, p39

41. *Some Guidelines on the Internal Political Life of the Party, People's Daily*, 15 March 1980

42. *Selected Works of Chen Yun* Vol. 3, People's Publishing House, 1995 edition, p273

43. *Selected Important Documents Since the 12th CPC National Congress* Vol. 1, edited by the CPC Central Committee Literature Research Office, Central Party Literature Press, 2011 edition, pp333-349

44. *Selected Works of Deng Xiaoping Vol. 2*, People's Publishing House, 1994 edition, p315

45. *Selected Important Documents Since the 12th CPC National Congress* Vol.2, edited by the CPC Central Committee Literature Research Office, Central Party Literature Press, 2011 edition, pp47-71

46. *Chronology of Deng Xiaoping (1975-1997)*, edited by the Literature Research Office of the CPC Central Committee Vol. 2, Central Party Literature Press, 2004, p814

47. *Chronology of Deng Xiaoping (1975-1997)*, edited by the Literature Research Office of the CPC Central Committee Vol. 2, Central Party Literature Press, 2004, p963

48. *Selected Important Documents Since the 12th CPC National Congress* Vol. 2, edited by the CPC Central Committee Literature Research Office, Central Party Literature Press, 2011 edition, pp121-135

49. *Selected Works of Deng Xiaoping* Vol. 3, People's Publishing House, 1994 edition, p233

50. *Selected Works of Deng Xiaoping* Vol. 3, People's Publishing House, 1994 edition, p210

51. *Selected Works of Deng Xiaoping* Vol. 3, People's Publishing House, 1994 edition, p241

52. *Chronology of Deng Xiaoping (1975-1997)*, edited by the Literature Research Office of the CPC Central Committee Vol. 2, Central Party Literature Press, 2004, p866

53. *Chronology of Deng Xiaoping (1975-1997)*, edited by the Literature Research Office of the CPC Central Committee Vol. 2, Central Party Literature Press, 2004, p1077

54. *Selected Works of Deng Xiaoping* Vol. 3, People's Publishing House, 1993 edition, p56

55. *Selected Works of Deng Xiaoping* Vol. 3, People's Publishing House, 1993 edition, p96

56. *Selected Works of Deng Xiaoping* Vol. 3, People's Publishing House, 1993 edition, p105

57. *Selected Important Documents Since the Third Plenary Session of the CPC Central Committee* Vol. 2, edited by the CPC Central Committee Literature Research Office, Central Party Literature Press, 2011 edition, pp166-167

58. *Selected Important Documents Since the 12th CPC National Congress* Vol. 1, edited by the CPC Central Committee Literature Research Office, Central Party Literature Press, 2011 edition, p22

59. *Selected Works of Deng Xiaoping* Vol. 3, People's Publishing House, 1993 edition, p203

60. *Selected Important Documents Since the 13th CPC National Congress* Vol. 1, edited by the CPC Central Committee Literature Research Office, Central Party Literature Press, 2011 edition, pp8-11

61. *Selected Works of Deng Xiaoping* Vol. 3, People's Publishing House, 1993 edition, p296

62. *Selected Works of Deng Xiaoping* Vol. 3, People's Publishing House, 1993 edition, pp521, 306, 308

63. *Selected Works of Deng Xiaoping* Vol. 3, People's Publishing House, 1993 edition, pp311-312

64. *Selected Works of Deng Xiaoping* Vol. 3, People's Publishing House, 1993 edition, pp318, 320, 321

65. *Selected Works of Deng Xiaoping* Vol. 3, People's Publishing House, 1993 edition, p363

66. A reference to the Tiananmen Incident, 4 June 1989

67. *Selected Works of Deng Xiaoping* Vol. 3, People's Publishing House, 1993 edition, pp370-383

68. *Selected Important Documents since the 15th CPC National Congress* Vol. 1, edited by the CPC Central Committee Literature Research Office, Central Party Literature Press, 2011 edition, pp45, 46

69. *Selected Important Documents since the 13th CPC National Congress* Vol. 1, edited by the CPC Central Committee Literature Research Office, Central Party Literature Press, 2011 edition, pp47, 48, 7, 48

70. *Selected Important Documents since the 14th CPC National Congress* Vol 1, edited by the CPC Central Committee Literature Research Office, Central Party Literature Press, 2011 edition, pp3, 12

71. *Selected Important Documents Since the 14th CPC National Congress* Vol. 2, edited by the CPC Central Committee Literature Research Office, Central Party Literature Press, 2011 edition, p370

2. EXPANDING A NEW PATH OF GOVERNANCE IN DEVELOPING THE SOCIALIST MARKET ECONOMY

1. *Selected Works of Jiang Zemin* Vol. 1, People's Publishing House, 2006 edition, p57

2. *Selected Works of Jiang Zemin* Vol. 1, People's Publishing House, 2006 edition, p68, p69

3. *Selected Important Documents since the 13th CPC National Congress* Vol. 2, edited by the CPC Central Committee Literature Research Office, Central Party Literature Press, 2011 edition, pp166, 169, 171

4. *Compilation of the CPC Constitution (from the 1st to the 18th CPC National Congress)*, compiled by the Party Constitution Research Group of the Central Party School of the CPC, Party Building Books Publishing House, 2016 edition, pp309, 311-312

5. *Chronology of Jiang Zemin's Thought (1989 - 2008)*, edited by the CPC Central Committee Literature Research Office, Central Party Literature Press, 2010 edition, p69

6. *Chronology of Jiang Zemin's Thought (1989 - 2008)*, edited by the CPC Central Committee Literature Research Office, Central Party Literature Press, 2010 edition, pp140-141

7. *The Eventful Years: Memoirs of Chen Jinhua*, Chen Jinhua, Communist Party History Press, 2005, p247

8. *The Eventful Years: Memoirs of Chen Jinhua*, Chen Jinhua, Communist Party History Press, 2005, p207

9. *Selected Works of Jiang Zemin* Vol. 1, People's Publishing House, 2006 edition, p202

10. *Selected Works of Jiang Zemin* Vol. 1, People's Publishing House, 2006 edition, p226

11. *Selected Works of Jiang Zemin* Vol. 1, People's Publishing House, 2006 edition, pp226-227

12. *Selected Works of Jiang Zemin* Vol. 1, People's Publishing House, 2006 edition, pp460-474

13. *Chronology of Jiang Zemin's Thought (1989 - 2008)*, edited by the CPC Central Committee Literature Research Office, Central Party Literature Press, 2010 edition, p208

14. *Chronology of Jiang Zemin's Thought (1989 - 2008)*, edited by the CPC Central Committee Literature Research Office, Central Party Literature Press, 2010 edition, p153

15. *Selected Works of Jiang Zemin* Vol. 3, People's Publishing House, 2006 edition, pp120, 134

16. Jiang Zemin, *On the Socialist Market Economy*, Central Party Literature Press, 2006, p569

17. *Selected Works of Deng Xiaoping* Vol. 2, People's Publishing House, 1994 edition, p208

18. *Jiang Zemin on Strengthening and Improving Construction of the Ruling Party (Thematic Extracts)*, edited by the CPC Central Committee Literature Research Office and CPC Central Committee Policy Research Office, Central Party Literature Press and Research Press, 2004 edition, p62
19. *Selected Important Documents Since the 14th CPC National Congress*, edited by the Literature Research Office of the CPC Central Committee (Vol. 2), Central Party Literature Press, 2011 edition, pp4, 5
20. *Jiang Zemin on Strengthening and Improving Construction of the Ruling Party (Thematic Extracts)*, edited by the CPC Central Committee Literature Research Office and CPC Central Committee Policy Research Office, Central Party Literature Press and Research Press, 2004 edition, p75
21. *Selected Works of Jiang Zemin* Vol. 3, People's Publishing House, 2006 edition, pp536-537
22. *Selected Important Documents Since the 14th CPC National Congress*, edited by the Literature Research Office of the CPC Central Committee (Vol. 2), Central Party Literature Press, 2011 edition, p4
23. *Selected Works of Jiang Zemin* Vol. 1, People's Publishing House, 2006 edition, p410
24. *Selected Works of Jiang Zemin* Vol. 2, People's Publishing House, 2006 edition, pp42-43
25. *Selected Works of Jiang Zemin* Vol. 1, People's Publishing House, 2006 edition, p92
26. *On Party Building*, Jiang Zemin, Central Party Literature Press, 2001 edition, p484
27. 'Jiang Zemin on Strengthening and Improving the Construction of the Ruling Party (thematic extracts)', edited by CPC Central Committee Literature Research Office and CPC Central Committee Policy Research Office, Central Party Literature Press and Research Press, 2004 edition, p. 525.
28. *Selected Works of Jiang Zemin* Vol. 1, People's Publishing House, 2006 edition, pp235, 236
29. *Selected Works of Jiang Zemin* Vol. 1, People's Publishing House, 2006 edition, p511
30. *Selected Works of Jiang Zemin* Vol. 2, People's Publishing House, 2006 edition, pp28-29
31. *Selected Works of Jiang Zemin* Vol. 3, People's Publishing House, 2006 edition, p200
32. *Selected Works of Jiang Zemin* Vol. 3, People's Publishing House, 2006 edition, p553
33. *Jiang Zemin on Strengthening and Improving Construction of the Ruling Party (Thematic Extracts)*, edited by the CPC Central Committee Literature Research Office and CPC Central Committee Policy Research Office, Central Party Literature Press and Research Press, 2004 edition, pp181-182
34. *On Party Building*, Jiang Zemin, Central Party Literature Press, 2001 edition, p381
35. *Selected Works of Jiang Zemin* Vol. 3, People's Publishing House, 2006 edition, p2
36. *Selected Works of Jiang Zemin* Vol. 3, People's Publishing House, 2006 edition, pp128-129

3. ADHERING TO AND DEVELOPING A NEW PATH OF GOVERNANCE IN THE PROCESS OF BUILDING A MODERATELY PROSPEROUS SOCIETY IN ALL RESPECTS

1. *Selected Important Documents Since the 16th CPC National Congress*, edited by the Literature Research Office of the CPC Central Committee (Vol 1), Central Party Literature Press, 2005 edition, p14
2. *Selected Important Documents Since the 16th CPC National Congress*, edited by the Literature Research Office of the CPC Central Committee (Vol 1), Central Party Literature Press, 2005 edition, p15
3. Selected Important Documents Since the 17th CPC National Congress, edited by the Literature Research Office of the CPC Central Committee (Vol. 1), Central Party Literature Press, 2009 edition, pp15-16
4. *Selected Works of Hu Jintao* Vol. 2, People's Publishing House, 2016 edition, p65
5. 'Selected Important Documents since the 16th National Congress', edited by the Literature Research Office of the CPC Central Committee (Vol.1), Central Party Literature Press, 2005 edition, p.15.

6. *Selected Works of Hu Jintao* Vol. 2, People's Publishing House, 2016 edition, p68
7. *Selected Works of Hu Jintao* Vol. 2, People's Publishing House, 2016 edition, p367
8. *Selected Important Documents Since the 16th CPC National Congress*, edited by the Literature Research Office of the CPC Central Committee (Vol. 1), Central Party Literature Press, 2005 edition, p326
9. *Selected Important Documents Since the 16th CPC National Congress*, edited by the Literature Research Office of the CPC Central Committee (Vol. 2), Central Party Literature Press, 2006 edition, pp271-297
10. *Selected Works of Hu Jintao Vol. 2*, People's Publishing House, 2006 edition, pp273-299
11. *Selected Important Documents Since the 16th CPC National Congress*, edited by the Literature Research Office of the CPC Central Committee (Vol. 2), Central Party Literature Press, 2006 edition, pp1061-1086
12. *Selected Important Documents Since the 16th CPC National Congress*, edited by the Literature Research Office of the CPC Central Committee (Vol. 3), Central Party Literature Press, 2008 edition, pp648-672
13. *Hu Jintao: On Building a Harmonious Socialist Society*, Central Party Literature Press, 2013 edition, p95
14. *Selected Important Documents Since the 16th CPC National Congress*, edited by the Literature Research Office of the CPC Central Committee (Vol. 2), Central Party Literature Press, 2006 edition, p850
15. *Selected Works of Hu Jintao*, Vol. 2, People's Publishing House, 2016 edition, pp354-355
16. *Selected Works of Hu Jintao*, Vol. 2, People's Publishing House, 2016 edition, p650
17. *Selected Works of Hu Jintao*, Vol. 2, People's Publishing House, 2016 edition, p620
18. *Selected Works of Hu Jintao* Vol. 2, People's Publishing House, 2016 edition, pp622-626

4. THE SECOND MIRACLE CREATED BY CPC GOVERNANCE

1. *Selected Works of Deng Xiaoping* Vol. 2, People's Publishing House, 1994 edition, pp163-164
2. *Selected Works of Deng Xiaoping* Vol. 3, People's Publishing House, 1993 edition, pp10-11
3. *Statistical Monitoring Report on the Process of Building a Moderately Prosperous Society in all Respects in China (2011)*, National Bureau of Statistics, Research Institute, *www.stats.gov-.cn/ztjc/ztfx/fxbg/201112/t20111219_16151.html*
4. *Selected Important Documents Since the 18th CPC National Congress*, edited by the Literature Research Office of the CPC Central Committee (Vol. 1), Central Party Literature Press, 2014 edition, p5

1. ADVANCING NEW ISSUES OF PARTY GOVERNANCE IN THE NEW ERA

1. *Selected Important Documents Since the 16th CPC National Congress*, edited by the Literature Research Office of the CPC Central Committee (Vol. 1), Central Party Literature Press, 2005 edition, p9
2. *Xi Jinping: The Governance of China* Vol. 1, Foreign Languages Press, 2018 edition, p411
3. *Selected Articles on Important Speeches by General Secretary Xi Jinping*, Central Party Literature Press, Party Building Reading Matter Publishing House, 2016 edition, p220
4. *Xi Jinping Emphasises the Importance of Following the Past and Heralding the Future, and Continuing to Advance Toward the Goal of the Great Rejuvenation of the Chinese Nation During his Visit to "The Road to Rejuvenation" Exhibition*, People's Daily, 30 November 2012
5. *Selected Articles on Important Speeches by General Secretary Xi Jinping*, Central Party Literature Press, Party Building Reading Matter Publishing House, 2016 edition, p333
6. Hu Jintao: *Firmly March on the Path of Socialism with Chinese Characteristics and Strive to Complete the Building of a Moderately Prosperous Society in All Respects, A Tutorial Guide to*

the 18th CPC National Congress Report, People's Publishing House, 2012 edition, p13

7. Hu Jintao: *Firmly March on the Path of Socialism with Chinese Characteristics and Strive to Complete the Building of a Moderately Prosperous Society in all Respects, A Tutorial Guide to the Report of the 18th CPC National Congress*, People's Publishing House, 2012 edition, pp49-50

8. Xi Jinping: *Speech at the 1st Session of the 12th NPC, People's Daily*, 18 March 2013

9. Xi Jinping: *Speech at the 1st Session of the 12th NPC, People's Daily*, 18 March 2013

10. Xi Jinping: *Speech at the 1st Session of the 12th NPC, People's Daily*, 18 March 2013

11. *Xi Jinping Stresses that the People's Aspiration for a Better Life is the Goal of the CPC's Struggles, When Meeting with Chinese and Foreign Journalists at the Politburo Standing Committee of the 18th CPC National Congress, People's Daily*, 16 November 2012

12. *Selected Works of Mao Zedong* Vol. 3, People's Publishing House, 1991 edition, p1004

13. *Selected Works of Mao Zedong* Vol. 3, People's Publishing House, 1991 edition, p243

14. Xi Jinping: *Speech at the 1st Session of the 13th NPC, People's Daily*, 21 March 2018

15. *Extracts from Xi Jinping's Discourses on Socialist Social Construction*, Central Party Literature Press, 2017 edition, p143

16. Hu Jintao: *Firmly March on the Path of Socialism with Chinese Characteristics and Strive to Complete the Building of a Moderately Prosperous Society in all Respects, A Tutorial Guide to the Report of the 18th CPC National Congress*, People's Publishing House, 2012 edition, p14

17. Xi Jinping: *Speech at the special Democratic Life Meeting of the Standing Committee of the Hebei Provincial Party Committee*, Newsletter of the CPC Central Office, No. 11, 2013

18. *At the National Propaganda and Ideological Work Conference Xi Jinping Stresses the Importance of Grasping the Big Picture, Focusing on the Major Issues and Striving to do a Better Job of Propaganda and Ideological Work, People's Daily*, 21 August 2013.

19. Xi Jinping: *The Governance of China*, Vol. 2, Foreign Languages Press, 2017 edition, p190

2. THE 'FOUR COMPREHENSIVES'

1. Xi Jinping: *Decisively Building a Moderately Prosperous Society in all Respects to Seize the Great Victory of Socialism with Chinese Characteristics in the New Era*, and *A Tutorial Guide to the 19th CPC National Congress Report*, People's Publishing House, 2017 edition, p28

2. Xi Jinping: *Decisively Building a Moderately Prosperous Society in all Respects to Seize the Great Victory of Socialism with Chinese Characteristics in the New Era*, and *A Tutorial Guide to the of the 19th CPC National Congress Report*, People's Publishing House, 2017 edition, pp28-29

3. *Xi Jinping: The Governance of China*, Vol. 1, Foreign Languages Press, 2018 edition, p114

4. *Extracts from Xi Jinping's Discourses on Comprehensively Deepening Reform*, Central Party Literature Press, 2014, pp20, 21

5. *Extracts from Xi Jinping's Discourses on Comprehensively Deepening Reform*, Central Party Literature Press, 2014, pp37, 49; *Reform Makes China's Path Ever Wider, People's Daily*, 27 February 2015

6. *Decision of the CPC Central Committee on Several Major Issues Concerning Comprehensive Promotion of the Rule of Law, People's Daily*, 29 October 2014

7. See Xi Jinping: 'The Governance of China', Vol.2, Foreign Languages Press, 2017 edition, p. 127.

8. 'During his research trip to Jiangsu Xi Jinping emphasised actively grasping and vigorously adapting to the new normal of economic development to promote reform, opening up and modernisation to a new level', *People's Daily*, 15 December 2014.

9. *Xi Jinping Emphasised that the People's Aspiration for a Better Life is the Party's Struggle Goal When Meeting with Chinese and Foreign Journalists at the Politburo Standing Committee of the 18th CPC Central Committee, People's Daily*, 16 November 2012

10. *Excerpts from Xi Jinping's Discourses on the Comprehensive Strict Governance of the Party*, Central Party Literature Press, 2016 edition, pp147, 148

3. THE NEW CONCEPT OF DEVELOPMENT

1. *Extracts from Xi Jinping's Discourses on Socialist Economic Construction*, Central Party Literature Press, 2017 edition, p 73

2. *An In-depth Study of Comrade Xi Jinping's Important Discourses*, People's Publishing House, 2013 edition, p7

3. *Extracts from Xi Jinping's Discourses on Comprehensively Deepening Reform*, Central Party Literature Press, 2014 edition, p39

4. *Extracts from Xi Jinping's Discourses on Comprehensively Deepening Reform*, Central Party Literature Press, 2014 edition, p73

5. *Extracts from Xi Jinping's Discourses on Socialist Economic Construction*, Central Party Literature Press, 2017 edition, p73

6. Edited by Cao Li et al: *A New Concept of Governance: A Comprehensive Interpretation of the New Concept of Development*, People's Publishing House, 2016 edition, p4

7. *Xi Jinping Emphasises the Importance of Adhering to the Dialectical Materialist Worldview and Methodology to Improve the Ability to Solve the Basic Problems of China's Reform and Development During the 20th Collective Study Session of the Political Bureau of the CPC Central Committee, People's Daily*, 25 January 2015

8. *Extracts from Xi Jinping's Discourses on Socialist Economic Construction*, Central Party Literature Press, 2017 edition, p74

9. *Selected Important Documents Since the 18th CPC National Congress*, edited by the Literature Research Office of the CPC Central Committee (Vol. 2), Central Party Literature Press, 2016 edition, p245

10. *Selected Important Documents Since the 18th CPC National Congress*, edited by the Literature Research Office of the CPC Central Committee (Vol. 2), Central Party Literature Press, 2016 edition, p245

11. *Selected Works of Marx and Engels*, Vol. 1, People's Publishing House, 1995 edition, p283

12. Xi Jinping: *Decisively Building a Moderately Prosperous Society in All Respects to Seize the Great Victory of Socialism with Chinese Characteristics in the New Era, A Tutorial Guide to the 19th CPC National Congress Report*, People's Publishing House, 2017 edition, pp1-2

13. Xi Jinping: *Speech at the Conference Commemorating the 200th Anniversary of the Birth of Marx*, People's Publishing House, 2018, p23

14. For data, see CPC Leadership Group of the Ministry of Education: *Developing Modern Education of Global Standard with Chinese Characteristics - Achievements and Experiences in Educational Reform and Development since the 18th Party Congress, Seeking Truth* Vol. 16, 2017; CPC Leadership Group of the Ministry of Human Resources and Social Security: *Let the Masses of People Share the Fruits of Development Further and More Fully -Main Achievements in the Development of Labour, Employment and Social Security Since the 18th Party Congress, Seeking Truth* Vol. 14, 2017; *Sustained and Rapid Growth in People's Income and Continuous Improvement in People's Quality of Life - Accomplishments in Socioeconomic Development Since the 18th Party Congress Series no. 5*, National Bureau of Statistics website, 28 July 2017

15. Xi Jinping: *Speech at the 2nd General Congress of the 5th Plenary Session of the 18th CPC Central Committee, Seeking Truth*, Vol. 1, 2016

16. *Xi Jinping: The Governance of China* Vol. 2, Foreign Languages Press, 2017 edition, p198

17. Xi Jinping: *Speech at the 2nd General Congress of the 5th Plenary Session of the 18th CPC Central Committee, Seeking Truth*, Vol. 1, 2016

18. *Xi Jinping: The Governance of China Vol. 1*, Foreign Languages Press, 2018 edition, p189

19. Xi Jinping: *Being a County Committee Secretary Like Jiao Yulu*, Central Party Literature Press, 2015, p21

20. *Extracts from Xi Jinping's Discourses on Poverty Alleviation and Development*, Central Party Literature Press, 2015 edition, pp38-39

21. *Extracts from Xi Jinping's Discourses on Poverty Alleviation and Development*, Central Party Literature Press, 2015 edition, p39

22. *A Strategic Guide for Winning the Battle against Poverty in the New Situation - An In-depth Study and Implementation of Comrade Xi Jinping's Important Discourses on Poverty Alleviation*

and Development, People's Daily, 28 November 2016

23. *Extracts from Xi Jinping's Discourses on Poverty Alleviation and Development,* Central Party Literature Press, 2015 edition, p20

24. *Always Mindful of Developing Old Revolutionary Areas - General Secretary Xi Jinping Presides Over a Poverty Alleviation Symposium in the Old Revolutionary Areas of Shaanxi, Gansu and Ningxia, People's Daily,* 17 February 2015

25. *Xi Jinping Emphasises at the Symposium for Comrades in Charge of the Main Party Committees of Some Provinces, Autonomous Regions and Municipalities the Planning of Poverty Alleviation and Development Work in the 13th Five-Year Plan Period to Ensure that the Rural Poor are Lifted Out of Poverty by 2020, People's Daily,* 20 June 2015

26. *Xi Jinping Emphasises at the Central Conference on Poverty Alleviation and Development that the Bugle to Announce the Battle Charge Against Poverty has Already been Blown and the Whole Party and Country has Grasped the Goal and Worked Hard, People's Daily,* 29 November 2015

4. RESOLUTE IN THE FACE OF CHANGES UNPRECEDENTED IN A CENTURY, SAFEGUARDING NATIONAL INTERESTS AND NATIONAL SECURITY

1. *Xi Jinping: The Governance of China* Vol.2, Foreign Languages Press, 2017 edition, p442

2. *Extracts from Xi Jinping's Discourses on the Concept of Comprehensive National Security,* Central Party Literature Press, 2018 edition, p258

3. *Xi Jinping: Decisively Building a Moderately Prosperous Society in All Respects to Seize the Great Victory of Socialism with Chinese Characteristics in the New Era, A Tutorial Guide to the of the 19th CPC National Congress Report,* People's Publishing House, 2017 edition, p57

4. Xi Jinping: *Decisively Building a Moderately Prosperous Society in All Respects to sSeize the Great Victory of Socialism with Chinese Characteristics in the New Era, A Tutorial Guide to the 19th CPC National Congress Report,* People's Publishing House, 2017 edition, p2

5. Xi Jinping: *Decisively Building a Moderately Prosperous Society in All Respects to sSeize the Great Victory of Socialism with Chinese Characteristics in the New Era, A Tutorial Guide to the 19th CPC National Congress Report,* People's Publishing House, 2017 edition, p24

6. Xi Jinping: *Decisively Building a Moderately Prosperous Society in All Respects to sSeize the Great Victory of Socialism with Chinese Characteristics in the New Era, A Tutorial Guide to the 19th CPC National Congress Report,* People's Publishing House, 2017 edition, p24

7. Xi Jinping: *Speech at the Conference to Celebrate the 95th Anniversary of the Founding of the CPC, People's Daily,* 2 July 2016

8. *Chronology of Events Since the 18th CPC National Congress,* edited by the Party History Research Office of the CPC Central Committee, People's Publishing House and CPC Party History Press, 2017 edition, p49

9. *Xi Jinping: The Governance of China Vol.1,* Foreign Languages Press, 2018 edition, p272

10. Xi Jinping: *On Persevering in Promoting the Building of a Community with a Shared Future for Mankind,* Central Literature Publishing House, 2018 edition, pp253-256

11. Xi Jinping: *On Persevering in Promoting the Building of a Community with a Shared Future for Mankind,* Central Literature Publishing House, 2018 edition, pp414-422

12. Xi Jinping: *Decisively Building a Moderately Prosperous Society in All Respects to Seize the Great Victory of Socialism with Chinese Characteristics in the New Era, A Tutorial Guide to the 19th CPC National Congress Report,* People's Publishing House, 2017 edition, p59

13. *Xi Jinping on the Belt and Road Initiative,* Central Party Literature Press, 2018 edition, p4

14. *Xi Jinping on the Belt and Road Initiative,* Central Party Literature Press, 2018 edition, pp. 35-37.

15. Zhao Zhanhui: *China's Cumulative Trade in Goods with Countries Along the Belt and Road Exceeds US$5 trillion, and FDI exceeds US$70 billion - the Scale of Opening Up and Cooperation is Constantly Growing, People's Daily,* 17 May 2018

16. Xi Jinping: *Speech at the Symposium on Studying and Implementing the Spirit of the 5th Plenary Session of the 18th CPC Central Committee for Major Leading Cadres at the Provincial and Ministerial Levels,* People's Publishing House, 2016 edition, p39

17. *Xi Jinping's Directives on the Occasion of the first National Security Education Day for all of China, People's Daily*, 15 April 2016
18. Xi Jinping: *Speech at the Symposium on National Security Work, People's Daily*, 18 February 2017
19. Xi Jinping: *Decisively Building a Moderately Prosperous Society in All Respects to Seize the Great Victory of Socialism with Chinese Characteristics in the New Era, A Tutorial Guide to the 19th CPC National Congress Report*, People's Publishing House, 2017 edition, p48
20. *Constitution of the CPC*, People's Publishing House, 2017 edition, p7

5. COMPREHENSIVELY STRENGTHENING PARTY LEADERSHIP

1. Xi Jinping: *Speech at the Conference to Celebrate the 95th Anniversary of the Founding of the CPC, People's Daily*, 2 July 2016
2. *Selected Important Documents Since the 18th CPC National Congress*, edited by the Literature Research Office of the CPC Central Committee (Vol 1), Central Party Literature Press, 2014 edition, p772
3. *Selected Important Documents Since the 18th CPC National Congress*, edited by the Literature Research Office of the CPC Central Committee (Vol. 1), Central Party Literature Press, 2014 edition, p131
4. *Excerpts from Xi Jinping's Discourses on Comprehensive Strict Party Governance*, Central Party Literature Press, 2016 edition, p80
5. Excerpts from Xi Jinping's Discourses on Comprehensive Strict Party Governance, Central Party Literature Press, 2016 edition, p87
6. *Resolutely Winning the Just War Against Corruption - a Review of the Achievements of the Party's Anti-corruption Struggle Since the 18th CPC National Congress, People's Daily*, 18 September 2017
7. *Party Building Makes Significant Historical Achievements - an Interview with Jiang Xinzhi, Deputy Head of the CPC Organisation Department, People's Daily*, 23 September 2017
8. Xi Jinping: *Decisively Building a Moderately Prosperous Society in All Respects to Seize the Great Victory of Socialism with Chinese Characteristics in the New Era, A Tutorial Guide to the 19th CPC National Congress Report*, People's Publishing House, 2017 edition, pp17, 25
9. *Extracts from Xi Jinping's Discourses on Socialist Political Construction*, Central Party Literature Press, 2017 edition, p31
10. Xi Jinping: *Speech at the 6th Plenary Session of the 18th Central Commission for Discipline Inspection*, People's Publishing House, 2016 edition, pp23-24
11. *Communiqué of the 6th Plenary Session of the 18th CPC Central Committee, People's Daily*, 28 October 2016
12. *The Pilot Reforms of the National Supervisory System Have Been Effective - an Overview of the Pilot Reforms of the National Supervisory System, People's Daily*, 6 November 2017
13. Xi Jinping: *Decisively Building a Moderately Prosperous Society in All Respects to Seize the Great Victory of Socialism with Chinese Characteristics in the New Era, A Tutorial Guide to the 19th CPC National Congress Report*, People's Publishing House, 2017 edition, pp66-67
14. *At the Ideological Work Conference Xi Jinping Stresses the Importance of Grasping the Big Picture and Striving to do a Better Job of Propaganda and Ideological Work, People's Daily*, 21 August 2013
15. Xi Jinping: *Speech at the Symposium on Literary and Art Work, People's Daily*, 15 October 2015
16. *Worthy of the Times, Worthy of the People - an Overview of the Prosperous Development of Socialist Literature and Art Since the 18th CPC National Congress, People's Daily*, 30 November 2016
17. *Xi Jinping Emphasises Adherence to Correct Direction, Innovative Methods and Means to Improve the Power of Communication and Guidance of News and Public Opinion at Party Symposium on Press and Public Opinion Work, People's Daily*, 20 February 2016

18. Xi Jinping: *Speech at the Symposium on Philosophical and Social Science Work, People's Daily,* 19 May 2016
19. *Selected Important Discourses of Xi Jinping on National Defence and Military Construction,* PLA Publishing House, 2014, p1
20. *Xi Jinping: The Governance of China* Vol 1, Foreign Languages Press, 2018 edition, p219
21. *Xi Jinping: The Governance of China* Vol. 1, Foreign Languages Press, 2018 edition, p220
22. *Selected Important Discourses of Xi Jinping on National Defence and Military Construction (II),* PLA Publishing House, 2015 edition, pp85-126
23. *Zhang Hui and Huang Chao: Constantly Deepening the Construction of Clean Politics in the Military and Party Culture and the Anti-corruption Struggle from a New Starting Point, PLA Daily,* 20 September 2017

6. THE HISTORICAL MISSION OF THE CPC IN GOVERNING CHINA IN THE NEW ERA

1. Xi Jinping: *Decisively Building a Moderately Prosperous Society in All Respects to Seize the Great Victory of Socialism with Chinese Characteristics in the New Era* and *A Tutorial Guide to the 19th CPC National Congress Report,* People's Publishing House, 2017 edition, p11
2. *Thirty Lectures on Xi Jinping Thought on Socialism with Chinese Characteristics for a New Era,* edited by the Propaganda Department of the CPC Central Committee, Learning Press, 2018, p68
3. *Thirty Lectures on Xi Jinping Thought on Socialism with Chinese Characteristics for a New Era,* edited by the Propaganda Department of the CPC Central Committee, Learning Press, 2018, pp68-69
4. Xi Jinping: *Decisively Building a Moderately Prosperous Society in All Respects to Seize the Great Victory of Socialism with Chinese Characteristics in the New Era,* and *A Tutorial Guide to the 19th CPC National Congress Report,* People's Publishing House, 2017 edition, p15
5. Hu Jintao: *Firmly March on the Path of Socialism with Chinese Characteristics and Strive to Complete the Building of a Moderately Prosperous Society in All Respects, A Tutorial Guide to the 18th CPC National Congress Report,* People's Publishing House, 2012 edition, p14
6. *When the Politburo Standing Committee of the 19th CPC Central Committee Met with Chinese and Foreign Journalists, Xi Jinping Stressed that the New Era Should Have* a New Climate and, More Importantly, New Actions to Ensure the Lives of Chinese People Improve Year by Year, *People's Daily,* 26 October 2017
7. *Xi Jinping Delivers an Important Speech at Opening Ceremony of Seminar on Learning and Implementing the Spirit of the 19th CPC National Congress, Stressing the Importance and Urgency of Opening Up a New Context in the Cause of Socialism with Chinese Characteristics in the New Era, People's Daily,* 6 January 2018

7. XI JINPING THOUGHT ON SOCIALISM WITH CHINESE CHARACTERISTICS FOR A NEW ERA

1. *Constitution of the CPC,* People's Publishing House, 2017 edition, p3
2. *The Enlarged Meeting of the Standing Committee of the Provincial Party Committee to Study the Spirit of Xi Jinping's Major Speeches and Effectively Make Due Contribution to the Great Revival of the Chinese Nation, Zhejiang Daily,* 1 December 2012; *Closely Integrating the Spirit of General Secretary Xi Jinping's Series of Major Speeches with the Actual Situation in Shigatse and Striving to Create a New Context of Breakthrough Development and Long-Term Peace in the Region, Shigatse News* (in Mandarin), 10 December 2012; *In-depth Study of Comrade Xi Jinping's Major Discourses,* People's Publishing House, 2013; *Li Zhanshu Emphasises the Need for In-depth Study and Implementation of Xi Jinping's Series of Speeches at the Conference of the National Committee of Party Secretaries, People's Daily,* 3 September 2013; *Taking Up the Historical Mission of Effective Implementation of Ideological Work - The Symposium on Learning*

the Spirit of General Secretary Xi Jinping's Series of Speeches in Capital Theoretical Circles, People's Daily, 4 November 2013; *The CPC Central Committee Issues 'Guidelines for Establishing a Sound System for Punishing and Preventing Corruption 2013-2017', People's Daily*, 26 December 2013; *The Soul of the Chinese Dream and the Path to Its Realisation: Sorting Through Xi Jinping Thought on Governance, People's Tribune*, No. 13, 2013

3. *Activities Held Throughout China to Celebrate the 92nd Anniversary of the Founding of the Party, People's Daily*, 2 July 2013
4. Xi Jinping: *Decisively Building a Moderately Prosperous Society in All Respects to Seize the Great Victory of Socialism with Chinese Characteristics in the New Era*, and *A Tutorial Guide to the 19th CPC National Congress Report*, People's Publishing House, 2017 edition, p18
5. *Xi Jinping: The Governance of China* Vol. 2, Foreign Languages Press, 2017 edition, p68
6. Xi Jinping: *Speech at the Conference to Celebrate the 40th Anniversary of Reform and Opening Up*, People's Publishing House, 2018 edition, p12
7. Xi Jinping: *Speech at the Conference to Celebrate the 40th Anniversary of Reform and Opening Up*, People's Publishing House, 2018 edition, pp14-15
8. Xi Jinping: *Speech at the Conference to Celebrate the 40th Anniversary of Reform and Opening Up*, People's Publishing House, 2018 edition, pp21-22
9. Xi Jinping: *Speech at the Conference to Celebrate the 40th Anniversary of Reform and Opening Up*, People's Publishing House, 2018 edition, p44

8. THE THIRD MIRACLE CREATED BY CPC GOVERNANCE

1. *Extracts from Xi Jinping's Discourses on Achieving the Chinese Dream for the Great Rejuvenation of the Chinese Nation*, Central Party Literature Press, 2013 edition, p5
2. *The Belt and Road, Rooted in History and Facing the Future, People's Daily*, 10 October 2018

1. LEADERSHIP IN GOVERNANCE

1. *Selected Works of Deng Xiaoping* Vol. 2, People's Publishing House, 1994 edition, pp341-342
2. *The Complete Works of Marx and Engels* Vol. 10, People's Publishing House, 1998 edition, pp744-745
3. *Selected Works of Marx and Engels* Vol. 3, People's Publishing House, 2012 edition, p276
4. *The Complete Works of Lenin* Vol. 8, People's Publishing House, 2017 edition, p363
5. *The Collected Works of Mao Zedong* Vol. 3, People's Publishing House, 1996 edition, p22
6. *Selected Works of Deng Xiaoping* Vol. 3, People's Publishing House, 1993 edition, p277

2. THE GUIDING IDEOLOGY OF GOVERNANCE

1. *Selected Works of Marx and Engels* Vol. 2, People's Publishing House, 1995 edition, pp39-40
2. *Early Manuscripts of Mao Zedong*, edited by the Literature Research Office of the CPC Central Committee and the Hunan Provincial CPC Committee's *Early Manuscripts of Mao Zedong* Editorial Group, Hunan People's Publishing House, 2013 edition, p498
3. *Selected Important Documents Since the 15th CPC National Congress*, edited by the Literature Research Office of the CPC Central Committee, Vol. 1, People's Publishing House, 2000 edition, p1
4. Xi Jinping: *Speech at the Conference to Celebrate the 95th Anniversary of the Founding of the CPC*, People's Publishing House, 2016 edition, p8
5. 'Selected Works of Marx and Engels', Vol. 1, People's Publishing House, 2012 edition, p. 376.

    [translator's note: and https://www.marxists.org/archive/marx/works/1848/communist-manifesto/preface.htm]

6. ''Collected Works of Marx and Engels, Vol. 1, People's Publishing House, 2009 edition, p. 12.

7. Xi Jinping: *Speech at the Conference to Celebrate the 95th Anniversary of the Founding of the CPC*, People's Publishing House, 2016 edition, p9

8. *Selected Works of Deng Xiaoping* Vol. 3, People's Publishing House, 1993 edition, p291

9. See 'The Complete Works of Marx and Engels', Vol. 21, People's Publishing House, 1965 edition, p. 297.

10. *Selected Works of Deng Xiaoping* Vol. 3, People's Publishing House, 1993 edition, p375

11. *Selected Important Documents Since the 18th CPC National Congress* Vol. 1, edited by the Literature Research Office of the CPC Central Committee, Central Party Literature Press, 2014 edition, p75

3. THE PATH OF GOVERNANCE

1. *Selected Works of Marx and Engels* Vol. 1, People's Publishing House, 2012 edition, p405

2. *The Complete Works of Marx and Engels* Vol. 47, People's Publishing House, 2004 edition, p35

3. *The Complete Works of Lenin* Vol. 28, People's Publishing House, 1990 edition, p163

4. *The Complete Works of Lenin* Vol. 41, People's Publishing House, 1986 edition, pp21, 50

5. *Selected Works of Mao Zedong* Vol. 2, People's Publishing House, 1991 edition, p633

6. 'Selected Works of Marx and Engels', Vol. 4, People's Publishing House, 1995 edition, pp. 337-338.

7. Z. Brzezinski: *The Grand Failure: The Birth and Death of Communism in the 20th Century*, Chinese translation by the Foreign Military Studies Department of the Military Sciences Academy, Military Science Press, 1989, p14

8. *Selected Works of Deng Xiaoping* Vol. 3, People's Publishing House, 1993 edition, pp104, 105

4. THE FUNDAMENTAL TASK OF GOVERNANCE

1. *The Complete Works of Marx and Engels* Vol. 42, People's Publishing House, 2016 edition, p170

2. *Selected Works of Deng Xiaoping* Vol. 3, People's Publishing House, 1993 edition, p137

3. *Collected Works of Marx and Engels* Vol. 1, People's Publishing House, 2009 edition, p538

4. *The Complete Works of Lenin* Vol. 38, People's Publishing House, 2017 edition, p337

5. *The Complete Works of Lenin* Vol. 40, People's Publishing House, 2017 edition, p140

6. *Selected Works of Mao Zedong* Vol. 4, People's Publishing House, 1991 edition, p1428

7. *Selected Works of Deng Xiaoping* Vol. 2, People's Publishing House, 1994 edition, p250

8. *Selected Works of Jiang Zemin* Vol. 1, People's Publishing House, 2006 edition, p222

9. *Selected Works of Hu Jintao* Vol. 2, People's Publishing House, 2016 edition, p625

10. *Selected Important Documents Since the 18th CPC National Congress* Vol. 2, edited by the Literature Research Office of the CPC Central Committee, Central Party Literature Press, 2016 edition, p245

11. 'Selected Works of Marx and Engels', Vol. 3, People's Publishing House, 1995 edition, p. 342.

12. 'Selected Works of Marx and Engels', Vol. 4, People's Publishing House, 1995 edition, p. 733.

13. 'Selected Works of Lenin', Vol. 1, People's Publishing House, 1995 edition, p. 29.

14. *Selected Works of Mao Zedong* Vol. 2, People's Publishing House, 1991 edition, p663

15. *Selected Works of Deng Xiaoping* Vol. 2, People's Publishing House, 1994 edition, p208

16. *Selected Works of Deng Xiaoping* Vol. 3, People's Publishing House, 1993 edition, p237

17. *Selected Works of Jiang Zemin* Vol. 1, People's Publishing House, 2006 edition, p571

18. *Selected Works of Hu Jintao* Vol. 2, People's Publishing House, 2016 edition, p274

19. *Selected Works of Mao Zedong* Vol. 1, People's Publishing House, 1991 edition, p137

20. *Excerpts from Xi Jinping's Discourses on Socialist Social Construction*, edited by the Literature Research Office of the CPC Central Committee, Central Literature Publishing House, 2017 edition, p13

5. THE DRIVING FORCE OF GOVERNANCE

1. *Collected Works of Marx and Engels* Vol. 10, People's Publishing House, 2009 edition, p588
2. *The Complete Works of Lenin* Vol. 60, People's Publishing House, 1990 edition, p282
3. *Selected Works of Lenin* Vol. 4, People's Publishing House, 2012 edition, p613
4. *A Chronology of Deng Xiaoping's Thought (1975-1997)*, edited by the Literature Research Office of the CPC Central Committee, Central Party Literature Press, 1998, p77
5. *Selected Works of Deng Xiaoping* Vol. 2, People's Publishing House, 1994 edition, p150
6. *Selected Works of Deng Xiaoping* Vol. 3, People's Publishing House, 1993 edition, p370
7. *Excerpts from Xi Jinping's Discourses on Coordinating the Strategic Composition of the Four Comprehensives*, Central Literature Publishing House, 2015, p52
8. *Excerpts from Xi Jinping's Discourses on Coordinating the Strategic Composition of the Four Comprehensives*, Central Literature Publishing House, 2015, p52
9. *Excerpts from Xi Jinping's Discourses on Coordinating the Strategic Composition of the Four Comprehensives*, Central Literature Publishing House, 2015, pp54-55
10. *Political Order in a Changing Society*, Samuel P. Huntington, translated into Chinese by Wang Guanhua et al, Sanlian Bookstore, 1989, pp316-317
11. *Selected Important Documents Since the 12th CPC National Congress (Vol. 2)*, edited by the CPC Central Committee Literature Research Office, Central Party Literature Press, 1986 edition, p584
12. Jiang Zemin: *Enhancing Mutual Understanding, Strengthening Friendly Cooperation*, (1 November 1997)
13. *Excerpts from Xi Jinping's Discourses on Coordinating the Strategic Composition of the Four Comprehensives*, Central Party Literature Press, 2015, p54
14. Xi Jinping: *Deepening Reform and Opening Up for a Better Asia-Pacific - Speech at the APEC Business Leaders' Summit, People's Daily*, 8 October 2013
15. Xi Jinping: *Refining and Developing Socialism with Chinese Characteristics to Promote the Modernisation of the National System of Governance and governance Ability, People's Daily*, 18 February 2014
16. Xi Jinping: *Connectivity Spearheads Development and Partnership Enables Cooperation - Speech at the Dialogue Meeting of Host Partners on Enhancing Connectivity Partnerships, People's Daily*, 9 November 2014

6. GOVERNANCE ORGANISATION AND LEADERSHIP SYSTEMS

1. See 'Selected Important Documents since the Founding of the Party (1921-1949)', Vol. 1, Literature Research Office of the CPC Central Committee and the Central Archives, eds, Central Party Literature Press, 2011 edition, p. 141.
2. *Selected Important Documents Since the Founding of the Party (1921-1949)* Vol. 15, Literature Research Office of the CPC Central Committee and the Central Archives compilation, Central Party Literature Press, 2011 edition, p753
3. *Mao Zedong's Manuscripts Since the Founding of the PRC*, Literature Research Office of the CPC Central Committee compilation, Vol. 6, Central Party Literature Press, 1992, p543
4. Huang Li: *History of the Party Constitution*, People's Publishing House, 2013, pp80-82
5. *The Constitution of the CPC*, People's Publishing House, 2017 edition, p10
6. *The Politburo of the CPC Central Committee Held a Democratic Life Meeting to Emphasise the Firmness of the Four Consciousnesses and the Four Confidences and Resolutely Achieve the Two Safeguards, Having the Courage to Take Responsibility for the Implementation of the Decision-making and Arrangements of the CPC Central Committee with a Realistic and Pragmatic Work*

Style. General Secretary of the CPC Central Committee Xi Jinping Presided Over the Meeting and Delivered a Major Speech, People's Daily, 27 December 2018

7. Xi Jinping: *Always Adhere to and Give Full Play to the Party's Unique Strengths, Qiushi [Seeking Truth]* No. 15, 2012

8. Huang Weichen: *Twenty Years Since the Demise of the CPSU: Without the People in Your Heart, You will be Abandoned by Them, Party Life* No. 9, 2011

9. *Selected Works of Deng Xiaoping* Vol. 2, People's Publishing House, 1994 edition, p330

10. *Selected Works of Deng Xiaoping* Vol. 1, People's Publishing House, 1994 edition, p303

11. *Selected Works of Mao Zedong* Vol. 3, People's Publishing House, 1991 edition, p1057

12. *Selected Works of Deng Xiaoping* Vol. 1, People's Publishing House, 1994 edition, p347

13. *The Constitution of the CPC,* People's Publishing House, 2017 edition, p10

14. *Selected Important Documents Since the 18th CPC National Congress* Vol.1, edited by the Literature Research Office of the CPC Central Committee, Central Party Literature Press, 2014 edition, p353

15. *Selected Important Documents Since the 18th CPC National Congress Vol.1,* edited by the Literature Research Office of the CPC Central Committee, Central Party Literature Press, 2014 edition, p352

16. *Selected Works of Deng Xiaoping* Vol. 2, People's Publishing House, 1994 edition, p333

17. *Selected Important Documents Since the 18th CPC National Congress* Vol. 1, edited by the CPC Central Committee Literature Research Office, Central Party Literature Press, 2014 edition, pp352, 488

18. Song Gongde: *Promoting Construction of the Party's Regulatory System on All Fronts, People's Daily,* 27 September 2018

19. *The Collected Works of Mao Zedong* Vol.3, People's Publishing House, 1996 edition, p337

7. GOVERNANCE METHODS

1. As stated in the *Decision of the CPC Central Committee on Several Major Issues Concerning Comprehensive Promotion of the Rule of Law,* adopted at the 4th Plenary Session of the 18th CPC Central Committee

8. THE BASIS OF GOVERNANCE

1. *Collected Works of Marx and Engels* Vol. 1, People's Publishing House, 2009 edition, p287

2. *Selected Works of Marx and Engels* Vol. 4, People's Publishing House, 2012 edition, p256

3. *The Complete Works of Marx and Engels* Vol. 45, People's Publishing House, 1985 edition, p716

4. *The Complete Works of Marx and Engels* Vol. 3, People's Publishing House, 2002 edition, p40

5. *The Complete Works of Lenin* Vol. 33, People's Publishing House, 2017 edition, p57

6. *The Complete Works of Lenin* Vol. 33, People's Publishing House, 2017 edition, p16

7. Selected Works of Lenin Vol. 4, People's Publishing House, 2012 edition, p695

8. *Selected Writings of Deng Xiaoping* Vol. 1, People's Publishing House, 1994 edition, p218

9. *Selected Works of Marx and Engels* Vol. 1, People's Publishing House, 2012 edition, p411

10. *Selected Works of Marx and Engels* Vol. 1, People's Publishing House, 2012 edition, p413

11. *Selected Readings from the Works of Mao Zedong,* edited by the CPC Central Committee Literature Research Office, Central Party Literature Press, 2003, p1877

12. *Selected Works of Mao Zedong* Vol. 3, People's Publishing House, 1991 edition, pp1094-95

13. Constitution of the CPC, People's Publishing House, 2017 edition, p10

14. *Selected Readings from the Works of Mao Zedong,* Vol. 2, People's Publishing House, 1986 edition, p800

15. Huang Weichen: *Twenty Years of the CPSU: Without the People in its Heart, [the Party] will be Abandoned by Them, Party Life, No. 9, 2011*

16. Selected Works of Deng Xiaoping Vol. 2, People's Publishing House, 1994 edition, p150

17. Xi Jinping: *Speech at the Symposium on Studying and Implementing the Spirit of the 5th Plenary Session of the 18th CPC Central Committee for Major Leading Cadres at the Provincial and Ministerial Levels*, People's Publishing House, 2016 edition, p24

18. Huang Lifu: *A Study of Soviet Social Class and the Soviet Revolution*, Social Sciences Academic Press, 2006, pp163-198

19. Zhao Deyu: *An Analysis of the Causes of the Disintegration of the Soviet Union, Reform and Opening Up* No. 11, 2009

20. Li Shenming et al, commentary: *Being Vigilant in Peacetime - Historical Lessons of the CPSU's Demise*

21. Cao Guiqian: *Corruption and the Decline of Communist Parties in Eastern Europe, Contemporary World and Socialism* No. 2, 2001

22. *A Chronology of Zhou Enlai (1949-1976)*, edited by the Literature Research Office of the CPC Central Committee, Vol. 2, Central Party Literature Press, 1997, p476

23. *Selected Works of Mao Zedong* Vol. 3, People's Publishing House, 1991 edition, pp1094

24. *Constitution of the CPC*, People's Publishing House, 2017 edition, p10

9. A COMMON IDEOLOGICAL BASIS FOR GOVERNANCE

1. *Selected Works of Marx and Engels* Vol. 1, People's Publishing House, 2012 edition, p178

2. V A Lisichkin, L A Serepin: *The Third World War - Information Psychological Warfare*, translated from Russian into Chinese by Xu Changhan et al, Social Sciences Academic Press, 2003, p76

3. Jiang Zemin" *On Party Building*, Central Party Literature Press, 2001, pp87-88

4. *Selected Important Documents Since the 18th CPC National Congress (Vol. 1)*, edited by the CPC Central Committee Literature Research Office, Central Party Literature Press, 2014 edition, p113

5. *Selected Works of Deng Xiaoping* Vol. 2, People's Publishing House, 1994 edition, pp366, 289

6. *Chronology of Deng Xiaoping (1975-1997)*, edited by the Literature Research Office of the CPC Central Committee (Vol. 2), Central Party Literature Press, 2004, p725

7. *Resolution on Several Historical Issues of the Party Since the Founding of the PRC, People's Daily*, 1 July 1981

8. Xi Jinping: *Speech at the Symposium Commemorating the 120th Anniversary of the Birth of Comrade Mao Zedong, People's Daily*, 27 December 2013

9. Xi Jinping: *Speech at the Symposium Commemorating the 110th Anniversary of the Birth of Comrade Deng Xiaoping, People's Daily*, 21 August 2014

10. *Selected Important Documents Since the 18th CPC National Congress (Vol. 1)*, edited by the CPC Central Committee Literature Research Office, Central Party Literature Press, 2014 edition, p112

11. *Regulations on the CPC's Discipline and Punishment, People's Daily*, 22 October 2015

12. *Mao Zedong's Manuscripts Since the Founding of the PRC*, Vol. 10, Central Party Literature Press, 1996 edition, p194

10. THE PILLARS OF GOVERNANCE

1. *Collected Works of Marx and Engels Vol. 3*, People's Publishing House, 2009 edition, pp131-132

2. 'The Complete Works of Lenin', Vol. 10, People's Publishing House, 2017 edition, p. 319.

3. 'Selected Works of Lenin', Vol. 2, People's Publishing House, 2012 edition, p. 724.

4. See 'Reader of General Secretary Xi Jinping's Series of Important Speeches', Learning Press and People's Publishing House, 2014 edition, p. 133.

5. 'Selected Works of Marx and Engels', Vol. 1, People's Publishing House, 2012 edition, p. 560.

6. 'History of the CPC - Volume I (1921-1949)', Party History Research Office of the CPC Central, Vol.1, CPC Party History Press, 2011 edition, pp. 237, 239.

7. *Selected Works of Jiang Zemin* Vol. 3, People's Publishing House, 2006 edition, p608

8. *A Chronology of Mao Zedong (1949-1976)*, edited by the Literature Research Office of the CPC Central Committee, Vol. 2, Central Literature Publishing House, 2013, pp300, 301

9. *Selected Military Writings of Mao Zedong* Vol. 6, Military Science Press and Central Party Literature Press, 1993 edition, p4

11. EXTERNAL CONDITIONS FOR GOVERNANCE

1. 'Selected Important Documents since the Eighteenth CPC National Congress' (Vol.1), edited by the CPC Central Committee Literature Research Office, Central Party Literature Press, 2014 edition, p. 260.

2. 'Marx, Engels and Lenin on Ideology' , edited by The Institute of Marxism, Chinese Academy of Social Sciences, People's Publishing House, 2009, p. 730.

3. *The Complete Works of Lenin* Vol. 28, People's Publishing House, 2017 edition, p163

4. *Selected Works of Mao Zedong* Vol. 4, People's Publishing House, 1991 edition, pp1465

5. Selected Works of Deng Xiaoping Vol. 3, People's Publishing House, 1993 edition, p3

6. *Selected Important Documents Since the 18th CPC National Congress* (Vol.1), edited by the CPC Central Committee Literature Research Office, Central Party Literature Press, 2014 edition, pp699, 700

7. *During the Third Collective Study Session of the CPC Central Committee Politburo Xi Jinping Emphasises the Importance of Better Coordination of China's Two Overall Situations, Namely, the Domestic and International Contexts, to Strengthen the Foundation of the Road to Peaceful Development, People's Daily*, 30 January 2013

8. *Marx, Engels and Lenin* on Ideology, edited by The School of Marxism Studies, Chinese Academy of Social Sciences, People's Publishing House, 2009, p573

12. THE SELF-CONSTRUCTION OF THE RULING PARTY

1. *Lenin on Party Building*, edited by the Selected Classic Works Group of the Party School of the CPC Central Committee, Party School Press of the CPC Central Committee, 1993, p13

2. *Selected Works of Mao Zedong* Vol. 3, People's Publishing House, 1991 edition, pp1094

3. *Lenin on Party Building*, edited by the Selected Classic Works Group of the CPC Central Committee Party School, CPC Central Committee Party School Press, 1993, p283

4. Lenin on the Party Building, edited by the Selected Classic Works Group of the CPC Central Committee Party School, CPC Central Committee Party School Press, 1993, p322

5. *Selected Works of Mao Zedong* Vol. 2, People's Publishing House, 1991 edition, p526

6. *Collected Works of Marx and Engels* Vol. 3, People's Publishing House, 2009 edition, p110

ABOUT **ACA**

We hope you enjoyed this research into communist party laws of governance from before Russia's October Revolution to the present day.

ALAIN CHARLES ASIA publishes an exciting range of China-focused non-fiction. From the soaring highs and grim lows of China's tumultuous history to the vivid life stories of its major and minor players, ACA has books for anyone eager to learn more about this vast, diverse nation.

To let us know what you thought of this book, or to learn more about the diverse range of exciting Chinese fiction in translation we publish, find us online. If you're as passionate about Chinese literature as we are, then we'd love to hear your thoughts!

www.alaincharlesasia.com
@aca_pub